Logic and Databases

The Roots of Relational Theory

C. J. Date

Note for Librarians: A cataloguing record for this book is available from Library and Archives Canada at www.collectionscanada.ca/amicus/index-e.html
ISBN 1-4251-2290-6

Printed in Victoria, BC, Canada. Printed on paper with minimum 30% recycled fibre. Trafford's print shop runs on "green energy" from solar, wind and other environmentally-friendly power sources.

Offices in Canada, USA, Ireland and UK

Book sales for North America and international:
Trafford Publishing, 6E–2333 Government St.,
Victoria, BC V8T 4P4 CANADA
phone 250 383 6864 (toll-free 1 888 232 4444)
fax 250 383 6804; email to orders@trafford.com
Book sales in Europe:
Trafford Publishing (UK) Limited, 9 Park End Street, 2nd Floor
Oxford, UK OX1 1HH UNITED KINGDOM
phone +44 (0)1865 722 113 (local rate 0845 230 9601)
facsimile +44 (0)1865 722 868; info.uk@trafford.com
Order online at:
trafford.com/07-0690

10 9 8 7 6 5 4 3 2

Contents

Preface   *xi*

PART I   **BASIC LOGIC**   **1**

Chapter 1   **The Building Blocks of Logic**   **3**

What's a business rule?   4
Natural language is often ambiguous   5
Propositions   8
Predicates   10
Quantification   12
Free and bound variables   16
An extended example   17
A closer look at quantifiers   19
"Customer must place order"   25
How logic helps   28
Concluding remarks   30
Acknowledgments   30
References and bibliography   30
Appendix A: Terminology   31
Appendix B: Answers to exercises   33

Chapter 2   **Some Operators Are More Equal Than Others**   **41**

The universe of discourse   42
Identity   43
Equality   45
Logical equivalence   47
Other kinds of equivalence   54
Bi-implication   55
Concluding remarks   61
Acknowledgments   61
References and bibliography   62
Appendix A: Equality in SQL   63

PART II   **LOGIC AND DATABASE MANAGEMENT**   **65**

Chapter 3   **Constraints and Predicates**   **67**

A little background   67
Values and variables   69
The suppliers-and-parts database   70

A closer look at Example 1   70
A closer look at Examples 2-6   73
Constraints are propositions   76
Relvar and database constraints   78
A note on constraint checking   79
All checking is immediate!   80
Multiple assignment   82
Relvar predicates   84
Correctness *vs.* consistency   86
A note on database design   87
Predicates for derived relvars   88
A constraint classification scheme   89
Concluding remarks   91
Acknowledgments   92
References and bibliography   93

Chapter 4   **The Closed World Assumption   95**

Basic assumptions   96
Definitions   96
Why the CWA is preferred   100
Relvar predicates revisited   104
Putting it all together   106
Dealing with uncertainty   107
Negation and disjunction   109
Concluding remarks   113
Acknowledgments   114
References and bibliography   114
Appendix A: What about outer join?   116

Chapter 5   **Why Relational DBMSs Must Be Based on Logic   119**

Overall DBMS goals   119
Propositional calculus   121
Logical systems in general   123
Predicate calculus   127
The DBMS as a logical system   129
Desirable properties of a DBMS   129
Concluding remarks   131
Exercises   131
References and bibliography   132
Appendix A: Answers to exercises   132

Chapter 6   **Why Relational DBMS Logic Must Not Be Many-Valued**   **135**

Desirable properties of a DBMS   135
A classification scheme   137
Fragments   138
Extensions   138
Extensions and deviants   139
Additional complexities   142
Other many-valued logic   147
"Relational" three-valued logics   148
Concluding remarks   148
References and bibliography   149
Appendix A: Some useful 2VL tautologies   150

PART III   **LOGIC AND DATABASE DESIGN**   **153**

Chapter 7   **All for One, One for All**   **155**

Groundwork and assumptions   155
How many cases are there?   157
Examples of confusion   161
Functions   164
Correspondences   167
Concluding remarks   172
References and bibliography   175

Chapter 8   **Normalization from Top to Bottom**   **177**

Relvars and keys   178
Defining the problem   180
Join dependencies   183
Fifth normal form   188
Join dependencies are integrity constraints   189
Multivalued dependencies   191
Fourth normal form   199
Functional dependencies   199
Boyce/Codd normal form   201
Concluding remarks   202
Acknowledgments   203
Appendix A: The first three normal forms   203
Appendix B: A little history   207
Appendix C: Sixth normal form   209
Appendix D: Answers to exercises   210

Chapter 12

Chapter 9   **Denormalization Considered Harmful   215**

Denormalize for performance?   216
What does denormalization mean?   217
Definitions   218
Examples   219
Where do we stop?   221
What denormalization isn't   222
What denormalization isn't *bis*   225
The performance argument revisited   225
The usability argument   226
The integrity argument   228
Concluding remarks   232
References and bibliography   232

PART IV   **LOGIC AND ALGEBRA   235**

Chapter 10   **Why Is It Called Relational Algebra?   237**

Basic algebra   238
Generalizing basic algebra   242
Isomorphism   246
Boolean algebra   248
The algebra of sets   252
Matrix algebra   255
Relational algebra   256
Concluding remarks   262
Acknowledgments   269
References and bibliography   270
Appendix A: Why is it called relational calculus?   272

Chapter 11   **Semijoin and Semidifference   275**

Semijoin   276
Semidifference   277
More on semijoin   278
More on semidifference   280
References and bibliography   280
Appendix A: Answers to exercises   280

Chapter 12   **The Theory of Bags: An Investigative Tutorial   283**

Containment and inclusion   284
Union, intersection, difference, and product   285
Union plus and intersection star   288

Restriction   289
What about complement?   290
The algebra of sets   292
An algebra of bags   294
Concluding remarks   297
Acknowledgments   298
References and bibliography   298

PART IV   **LOGIC AND *THE THIRD MANIFESTO*   299**

Chapter 13   **Gödel, Russell, Codd: A Recursive Golden Crowd   303**

The Paradox of Epimenides   303
Discussion   304
Remarks on **Tutorial D**   305
A remark on *The Third Manifesto*   306
References and bibliography   308

Chapter 14   **To Be Is to Be a Value of a Variable   309**

Why we want relvars   309
Critic A's objections   311
Critic B's objections   316
Multiple assignment   324
Database values and variables   326
Concluding remarks   327
References and bibliography   327

Chapter 15   **And Now for Something Completely Computational   329**

Decidability   330
Computational completeness   330
Computational completeness implies undecidability   331
Does Codd "avoid the trap"?   332
Why we want computational completeness   334
Does it all matter?   335
References and bibliography   337
Appendix A: Computable functions   337

Chapter 16   **The Logic of View Updating   339**

Predicates and constraints   339
Database variables   341
Compensatory updates   344
The Principle of Interchangeability   346

Database inclusion and equivalence   347
Total mappings   349
Partial mappings   353
Darwen's overall objection   358
Darwen's detailed objections   359
Darwen's objections to orthogonality   367
Darwen's proposals   369
Concluding remarks   373
References and bibliography   374

Appendix   **Frequently Asked Questions   377**

Mathematics and the relational model   377
Relational algebra   381
Relvar predicates   387
Relation valued attributes   391
Keys and further normalization   397
Missing information   409
Variables, types, and constraints   412
SQL criticisms   422
References and bibliography   434

Index   439

Preface

The foundation of database management is the relational model, and the foundation of the relational model is logic. Gathering, analyzing, and organizing requirements; specifying business rules; designing the database; stating integrity constraints; formulating queries and updates; interpreting results; and, last but not least, implementing the software systems that support all of these various tasks—logic underpins all of these activities and, in the final analysis, makes them possible. Logic affects everything we do. Logic is crucial.

This book is aimed at database professionals of all kinds. It explores some of the many ways in which a knowledge of logic can help you in your database work. More specifically, it presents:

- A tutorial on logic for database practitioners

- An investigation into the role played by logic in formulating and implementing constraints

- A detailed examination of the Closed World Assumption, a crucial assumption we often rely on without realizing it

- A survey of some of the major differences between two- and many-valued logics, showing in particular why from a database perpective "two is good and many is bad"

- A discussion of database design from a logical point of view

- An investigation into the connections between logic, set theory, and relational algebra and calculus

- A rigorous logical treatment of bags as well as sets

- Certain logical aspects of *The Third Manifesto,* including a discussion of view updating in particular

and much, much more. A special feature of the book is the appendix "Frequently Asked Questions," which consists of a series of short essays dealing with a variety of issues that have arisen in the seminars I've taught over the years. Overall, my goal is to help database professionals realize the importance of logic in everything they do, and also (I hope) to make them understand that logic can be fun.

Prerequisites

As I've said, my target audience is database professionals. Thus, I assume you're somewhat familiar with both the relational model and the SQL language (though certain relational and/or SQL concepts are reviewd briefly here and there—basically wherever I felt such explanations might be helpful). A more detailed summary of the kind of background material I expect you to know appears near the beginning of Chapter 4, in the section "Basic Assumptions."

A Note on the Book's Structure

The book doesn't have to be read in sequence; most of the chapters are fairly independent of one another. (The main exception here is Chapter 1, which I do recommend you read before any of the others.) Because they're independent, many of the chapters contain references and examples—sometimes even appendixes—whose numbering is unique only within the chapter in question. For the same reason, there's also a small amount of overlap among certain of the chapters; I apologize for this fact, but I felt it was better to preserve the independence of each individual chapter as much as possible.

   Note: The book is serious but (I hope) not too solemn. In particular, there are some 27 "in jokes" and literary references hidden away here and there in the text, and I might offer a small prize for the first person to identify them all correctly. You can write to me at PO Box 1000, Healdsburg, CA 95448 (snail mail only, please).

Acknowledgments

Each chapter includes specific thanks to reviewers and other parties who helped in one way or another with the chapter in question. In addition, I'd like to thank my wife Lindy for her support throughout the production of this book and all of its predecessors, and in particular for allowing me to reproduce a piece of her artwork ("Red Planet") on the front cover.

Publishing History

A few of the chapters in this book are based on earlier published writings, as indicated below.

- *The Building Blocks of Logic* (Chapter 1): Based on "The Logic of Business Rules," *www.dbdebunk.com* (June 2004); this version published by permission of Fabian Pascal.

- *Constraints and Predicates* (Chapter 3): Based on "Constraints and Predicates: A Brief Tutorial" (in three parts), *www.dbdebunk.com* (May 2001) and *www.BRCommunity.com* (May / September / November 2001); this version published by permission of Fabian Pascal and Business Rule Solutions, Inc.

- *Why Relational DBMSs Are Based on Logic; Why Relational DBMS Logic Must Not Be Many-Valued* (Chapters 5-6): Based on David McGoveran, "Nothing from Nothing": Part 1, "What's Logic Got to Do with It?"; Part 2, "Classical Logic: Nothing Compares 2 U" (*Database Programming & Design 6,* No. 12, December 1993; *7,* No. 1, January 1994), republished in C. J. Date, *Relational Database Writings 1994-1997* (Addison-Wesley, 1998). Copyright (c) 1993-1998, Alternative Technologies. All rights reserved. This version is published by permission of David McGoveran.

- *All for One, One for All* (Chapter 7): Based on an earlier paper of the same name on *www.thethirdmanifesto.com* (June 2006) and *www.BRCommunity.com* (in several parts, 2006); this version published by permission of Hugh Darwen and Business Rule Solutions, Inc.

- *Semijoin and Semidifference* (Chapter 11): Based on an earlier paper of the same name on *www.BRCommunity.com* (June 2006); this version published by permission of Business Rule Solutions, Inc.

- *Gödel, Russell, Codd: A Recursive Golden Crowd; To Be Is to Be a Value of a Variable; And Now for Something Completely Computational* (Chapters 13-15): Based on a series of papers with the generic title "A Discussion of Certain Criticisms Concerning *The Third Manifesto*," *www.thethirdmanifesto.com* (August 2006); this version published by permission of Hugh Darwen.

C. J. Date
Healdsburg, California
2007

About the Author

C. J. Date is an independent author, lecturer, researcher, and consultant, specializing in relational database technology. He is best known for his book *An Introduction to Database Systems* (8th edition, Addison-Wesley, 2004), which has sold over three quarters of a million copies at the time of writing and is used by several hundred colleges and universities worldwide. He is also the author of many other books on database management, including most recently:

- From Morgan Kaufmann: *Temporal Data and the Relational Model* (coauthored with Hugh Darwen and Nikos A. Lorentzos, 2003)

- From Addison-Wesley: *An Introduction to Database Systems* (8th edition, 2004)

- From O'Reilly: *Database in Depth: Relational Theory for Practitioners* (2005)

- From Addison-Wesley: *Databases, Types, and the Relational Model: The Third Manifesto* (3rd edition, coauthored with Hugh Darwen, 2006)

- From O'Reilly: *The Relational Database Dictionary* (2006)

- From Apress: *Date on Database: Writings 2000-2006* (2006)

Another book, *Go Faster! The TransRelational^{tm} Approach to DBMS Implementation,* is due for publication in the near future.

Mr. Date was inducted into the Computing Industry Hall of Fame in 2004. He enjoys a reputation that is second to none for his ability to communicate complex technical subjects in a clear and understandable fashion.

Part I

BASIC LOGIC

This part of the book consists of two introductory chapters. Chapter 1 is a gentle introduction to logic for database practitioners; it explains such fundamental notions as propositions, predicates, quantification, and free and bound variables. Chapter 2 expounds on some even more fundamental notions—identity, equality, equivalence, and certain related matters.

Chapter 1

The Building Blocks of Logic

Good order is the foundation of all good things.

—Edmund Burke

This opening chapter is a tutorial on logic for database practitioners. It's adapted from a paper I wrote in 2004 [5]. (*Note:* A very much abbreviated version of that paper also appeared in 2005 as an appendix to reference [6].) Like that paper, the chapter that follows refers repeatedly to *business rules;* however, business rules are really just a hook to hang the discussion on, because I firmly believe the discussion itself is of much wider applicability. Here's the preamble to that paper:

> In order to be able to frame business rules in such a way as to avoid all ambiguity, you must be armed with an elementary knowledge of logic. The purpose of this paper is to equip you with the basics of what you need in this respect. To be more specific, it shows how certain key concepts from elementary logic can be used to simplify the task of formulating business rules whose interpretation is clear, precise, and unambiguous. The concepts in question are described and illustrated in tutorial fashion. No prior knowledge of logic is assumed.

I wrote that paper in response to a letter I received from Ron Ross in 2003 or so "soliciting opinions" (his words) on a particular business rule example. Here's the text of Ron's original letter (all formatting, italics, boldface, etc., exactly as in the original):

I'd like your opinion on a fundamental question about "rule."

Example just for illustration ...

It must be that: *each* customer places *some* order.

Predicate? Proposition? Hybrid? Other?

I stick with my opinion so far that the closest thing in formal logic is logical implication, which can be taken to be a predicate.

But the quantification does make it interesting. Just a diversion? Could you equally say:

customer *must* place order.

That sounds more like a predicate, but it may be just semantics (Of course).

Any insight would be appreciated.

(And he added the handwritten note "Soliciting opinions!" at the bottom of the page.)

——————— ♦ ♦ ♦ ♦ ♦ ———————

I responded to Ron's letter as follows:

> Thanks for your communication "soliciting opinions" ... The following isn't just an opinion, however—it's meant to be *definitive* (joke)—at least as far as it goes. Hope you find it helpful.
>
> I'll start with your natural language rule:
>
> **It must be that: *each* customer places *some* order.**
>
> You ask whether this rule is, formally, a predicate, a proposition, a hybrid of both, or something else entirely. (*Note:* "Formally" here is my addition, but I assume it's what you meant.) My short answer is: It's a proposition. My longer answer follows ...

And I went on to elaborate, considerably, on this response. What follows is a considerable elaboration on that considerable elaboration.

WHAT'S A BUSINESS RULE?

First of all, I need to be clear on what's meant—at least, what I mean—by the term *business rule*.
We've heard quite a lot about such rules over the past several years; indeed, I wrote a short book about them myself a while back [4]. Here's a loose definition (taken from the *GUIDE Business Rules Project Report,* 1995):

> A *business rule* is a statement that defines or constrains some aspect of the business.

Clearly, Ron Ross's "customer must place order" is an example of such a statement. *Note:* I must make it very clear that here and throughout this chapter I use the term *statement* in its ordinary natural language sense (barring explicit remarks to the contrary), not in the rather special sense in which it's used in programming languages.

The overall aim of the business rules approach is to automate the business as much as possible, which means that, sooner or later, the rules are going to have to be translated into executable code. Now, whether the translation process itself is automated or is done manually will depend on whether the rules are stated formally or informally.[1] If they're stated informally, they'd better be precise and unambiguous, for otherwise there can be no guarantee that the automated version correctly implements the desired semantics. Of course, if they're stated formally, they'll certainly be precise and unambiguous; but it still might be the case that they don't correctly represent the desired semantics! And it's my claim that, either way, what's needed in order to achieve the desired precision and lack of ambiguity is *a knowledge of certain key concepts from elementary logic*.

As an aside, I remark that, in my opinion, the executable code we're talking about had better be executed by the DBMS, not by some application sitting on top of the DBMS. Business rules aren't, in general, application specific! Although it never used the terminology of "business rules" as such, the relational model always had as an objective the notion that implementing such rules should be the responsibility of the DBMS, not some application programmer. But this argument is developed in some depth in reference [4], and I won't pursue it further here.

NATURAL LANGUAGE IS OFTEN AMBIGUOUS

I now claim, surely noncontroversially, that informal—i.e., natural language—formulations of business rules are often ambiguous. To bolster this claim, I first quote at length a piece by Robert Graves and Alan Hodge. (Thanks to Lauri Pietarinen of Helsinki, Finland, for drawing this splendid example to my attention. The example is included and analyzed in detail in reference [8].)

——————— ♦ ♦ ♦ ♦ ♦ ———————

From the Minutes of a Borough Council Meeting:

> Councillor Trafford took exception to the proposed notice at the entrance of South Park: "No dogs must be brought to this Park except on a lead." He pointed out that this order would not prevent an owner from releasing his pets, or pet, from a lead when once safely inside the Park.
>
> *The Chairman (Colonel Vine):* What alternative wording would you propose, Councillor?
>
> *Councillor Trafford:* "Dogs are not allowed in this Park without leads."
>
> *Councillor Hogg:* Mr. Chairman, I object. The order should be addressed to the owners, not to the dogs.
>
> *Councillor Trafford:* That is a nice point. Very well then: "Owners of dogs are not allowed in this Park unless they keep them on leads."

————————————

1. By *formally* here, I simply mean the rules in question are capable of being translated into executable code automatically (in other words, they're stated in some formal and potentially compilable language). *Informally* means they're stated in natural language.

Councillor Hogg: Mr. Chairman, I object. Strictly speaking, this would keep me as a dog-owner from leaving my dog in the back-garden at home and walking with Mrs. Hogg across the Park.

Councillor Trafford: Mr. Chairman, I suggest that our legalistic friend be asked to redraft the notice himself.

Councillor Hogg: Mr. Chairman, since Councillor Trafford finds it so difficult to improve on my original wording, I accept. "Nobody without his dog on a lead is allowed in this Park."

Councillor Trafford: Mr. Chairman, I object. Strictly speaking, this notice would prevent me, as a citizen, who owns no dog, from walking in the Park without first acquiring one.

Councillor Hogg (with some warmth): Very simply, then: "Dogs must be led in this Park."

Councillor Trafford: Mr. Chairman, I object: This reads as if it were a general injunction to the Borough to lead their dogs into the Park.

Councillor Hogg interposed a remark for which he was called to order; upon his withdrawing it, it was directed to be expunged from the Minutes.

The Chairman: Councillor Trafford, Councillor Hogg has had three tries; you have had only two ...

Councillor Trafford: "All dogs must be kept on leads in this Park."

The Chairman: I see Councillor Hogg rising quite rightly to raise another objection. May I anticipate him with another amendment: "All dogs in this Park must be kept on the lead."

This draft was put to the vote and carried unanimously, with two abstentions.

Note: I can't resist pointing out that the final draft is *still* ambiguous—it could logically be interpreted to mean that all dogs in the park must be kept on the same lead. But enough of walking dogs ... Let's move on.

To bolster my claim further (my claim, that is, that natural language formulations of business rules are often ambiguous), let's get back to Ron Ross's example:

A customer must place an order.

Note: I've taken just one of Ron's two original formulations—***customer* must *place order***—for definiteness. Also, I've rephrased Ron's original text just slightly, in order to make it sound a little less stilted. Of course, my rephrasing is not intended to change the original meaning.

Now, the person responsible for formulating this rule might have thought, not unreasonably, that it constitutes a precise definition of what it means to be a customer—in order to be a customer at all, you must place an order. Certainly the rule as stated *sounds* precise! But is it? And of course the answer is *no*. The fact is, there are several different interpretations of the rule as stated, all of them at least prima facie valid, and there's no way of knowing ahead of time which of those several interpretations is the one intended. Here are a few of those candidate interpretations:

- At least one customer places at least one order.

- There's at least one order that every customer places.

- Every customer places at least one order.

- There's exactly one order that every customer places.

- Each customer places exactly one order.

Now, if you know something about customers and orders in the real world, you might be thinking that one of these interpretations (which?) is "obviously" the one intended—but how can you be sure? Perhaps more to the point, what if the rule didn't refer to comparatively well understood concepts like customers and orders but rather to ones that might be a little less familiar or a little less clearcut? For example:

- A company must hire an employee.

- A book must have an author.

- A passenger must purchase a ticket.

- A speaker must have a glass of water.

- A winetaster must not swallow.

- Adjacent assessor's parcels must have different owners.

- The Congress shall have power to declare war.

- A frammistat must grok a widget.

Can you say, with certainty, exactly what these rules mean? (Well, obviously not, in the last case; but my point is, even things like companies, passengers, assessor's parcels, and so forth are likely to be as little understood by *somebody* as frammistats and widgets are by the rest of us.)

With the foregoing examples by way of motivation, I can now state my thesis for this chapter:

In order to be able to frame business rules in such a way as to avoid all ambiguity, you must be armed with an elementary knowledge of logic.

And it's my purpose in what follows to equip you with at least the basics of what you need in this respect. In particular—noting that Ron Ross's original letter explicitly mentioned a variety of important terms from logic (*predicate, proposition, logical implication,* and *quantification*)—I want to explain what those terms, as well as several related ones, mean. Then I'll come back and relate all of these concepts to the matter at hand: namely, "the business of business rules."

Note: The next six sections are aimed at a reader who already knows something about database technology but has had little or no exposure to logic as such. Now, almost certainly you'll already have some familiarity with the terms I'll be discussing, because we often use them—or some of them, at least—in a database context (*predicate* is an obvious example). However, we don't always mean quite the same thing as the logicians do when they use those same terms; in other words, we don't always use the terms "correctly" (but see Appendix A!). Indeed, that's one reason why I think this tutorial is needed.

PROPOSITIONS

I'll begin my introduction to logic with a simple definition:

A *proposition* in logic is a statement that's categorically either true or false.[1]

Here are some examples:

- No dogs must be brought to this park except on a lead.

- Every customer places at least one order.

- The sun is a star.

- The moon is a star.

- The sun is further away than the moon.

- George W. Bush won the U.S. presidential elections in 2000 and 2004.

Note that some of these propositions evaluate to TRUE and some to FALSE (don't fall into the common trap of thinking that propositions must always evaluate to TRUE). Note too that several of the

---

1. More precisely, it's a statement *that makes an assertion* that's unequivocally either true or false; strictly speaking, it's the assertion, not the statement as such, that's either true or false. However, I won't usually bother to stress this logical difference in this book. *Note:* Analogous remarks apply to predicates as well as propositions (see later).

foregoing examples are hardly business rules as such; but it's convenient, in the discussions of logic that follow, to use examples whose interpretation requires no prior explanation of what the referenced terms mean—I don't want to have to get into details of exactly what it is that constitutes a company, or a passenger, or an assessor's parcel (and so forth). If you'd prefer more realistic examples, then I suggest you replace the propositions I'll be using by some simple business rules from your own environment that you feel comfortable with.

———————— ◆ ◆ ◆ ◆ ◆ ————————

Given a set of propositions like those shown above, we can combine propositions from that set in a variety of ways to form further propositions, using the *connectives* NOT, OR, AND, IF ... THEN ... (or IMPLIES), and IF AND ONLY IF (or " ≡ ", or BI-IMPLIES, or IS EQUIVALENT TO, or simply IFF). For example:

- (The moon is a star) OR (the sun is a star).

- (The sun is a star) OR (the sun is a star).

- (The sun is a star) AND NOT (the moon is a star).

- IF (the sun is further away than the moon) THEN (the sun is a star).

- NOT (the sun is a star) IFF ((the moon is a star) OR (George W. Bush won the U.S. presidential elections in 2000 and 2004)).

CONNECTIVES
NOT
OR
AND
IMPLIES (IF... THEN ...)
BI-IMPLIES (IFF)

Clearly, the connectives can be regarded as *logical operators:* They take propositions as their input and return another proposition as their output. *Note:* I've used parentheses in the examples to make the scope of the connectives clear. In practice, we adopt certain precedence rules that allow us to omit many of the parentheses that might otherwise be needed. Of course, it's never wrong to include them, even when they're logically unnecessary.

A proposition that involves no connectives at all is called a *simple* proposition; a proposition that's not simple is called *compound*. The truth value, TRUE or FALSE, of a compound proposition can be determined from the truth values of the constituent simple propositions in accordance with the familiar *truth tables* shown below:

IF p THEN q

NOT		OR	t f	AND	t f	IF	t f	IFF	t f
t	f	t	t t	t	t f	t	t f	t	t f
f	t	f	t f	f	f f	f	t t	f	f t

Note: For space reasons I've abbreviated TRUE and FALSE to just *t* and *f,* respectively, and IF ... THEN ... to just IF. The table for IF is meant to be interpreted as follows: If proposition *p* has the truth value shown at the left and proposition *q* has the truth value shown at the top, then the proposition IF *p* THEN *q* has truth values as shown in the body of the table.

Let's revisit a couple of examples from the set of compound propositions shown earlier:

■   (The moon is a star) OR (the sun is a star).

Here we have two simple propositions connected by OR. Since one of the constituent simple propositions (the second) evaluates to TRUE, the overall proposition evaluates to TRUE also, regardless of the value of the other.

■   IF (the sun is further away than the moon) THEN (the sun is a star).

This compound proposition is of the form IF p THEN q. Both constituent simple propositions evaluate to TRUE; the truth table for IF shows us that the overall proposition therefore evaluates to TRUE also.

By the way, a point arises here that sometimes causes confusion. In the real world, of course, it obviously doesn't follow, just because it's further away than the moon, that the sun is a star. In logic, however, we simply *define* IF p THEN q to be true if q is true, regardless of whether p is true; in fact, if p is false, we define IF p THEN q to be true, regardless of the truth value of q. You can interpret this state of affairs as saying, in effect, that if you'll believe a falsehood (p), then you'll believe anything (q). *Note:* If this discussion leaves a slightly unpleasant taste in your mouth, you're not alone. But writers and thinkers better than I have struggled with the problem of trying to justify the rule that IF p THEN q is true if p is false and q is true—see, e.g., the book by McCawley [7] discussed briefly in Appendix A. The issue isn't worth fighting over for the purposes of this chapter.

As an exercise, try stating the truth values of all of the compound propositions shown earlier. *Note:* Answers to this exercise and others in this chapter are given in Appendix B.

One last point: The five connectives NOT, OR, AND, IF, and IFF aren't all primitive (as you might already know). For example, the proposition IF p THEN q is logically equivalent to the proposition (NOT p) OR q; as already explained, therefore, it evaluates to FALSE if and only if p evaluates to TRUE and q evaluates to FALSE. In fact, all possible logical connectives involving exactly one proposition or exactly two propositions can be expressed in terms of suitable combinations of NOT and either OR or AND. (*Exercise:* Check this claim.) Perhaps even more remarkably, all such connectives can in fact be expressed in terms of just one primitive. Can you find it?

PREDICATES

Consider now the following statements:

■   No x's must be brought to this park except on a lead.

■   Every x places at least one y.

■ x is a star.

■ x is further away than the moon.

- *x* is further away than *y*.

- *x* won the *y* election in the year *z*.

[handwritten note: Propositions are categorically True or False. the truth value of a predicate depends on variable bindings.]

Clearly, these statements aren't propositions, because they aren't categorically either true or false. And the reason they aren't categorically either true or false is that they involve *parameters* (also known as *placeholders* or *free variables*). For example, the statement

x is a star

involves the parameter *x,* and we obviously can't say it's either true or false unless and until we're told what it is that *x* stands for (at which point we're no longer dealing with the given statement anyway but a different one instead—as the paragraph immediately following explains).

Now, we can substitute *arguments* for the parameters and thereby obtain propositions from the statements. For example, if we substitute the argument *the sun* for the parameter *x* in the statement just shown, we obtain

the sun is a star

[handwritten note: Substitude predicate parameters with arguments to get Propositions.]

And this statement is indeed a proposition—it clearly is "categorically either true or false" (in fact, of course, it's true). But the original statement as such—

x is a star

—is (to say it again) not itself a proposition. Rather, it's a *predicate*. Here's the definition:

A *predicate* in logic is a truth valued function.

In other words, a predicate is a function that, when invoked, returns a truth value.[1] Like all functions, it has a set of parameters; when it's invoked, arguments are substituted for the parameters; substituting arguments for the parameters effectively converts the predicate into a proposition; and we say the arguments *satisfy* the predicate if and only if that proposition is true. For example, the argument *the sun* satisfies the predicate "*x* is a star," while the argument *the moon* does not.

Let's look at another example:

x is further away than *y*

[handwritten note: arguments replace parameters. arguments satisfy a predicate if the resulting proposition is true.]

This predicate involves two parameters, *x* and *y*. Substituting arguments *the sun* for *x* and *the moon* for *y* yields a true proposition; substituting arguments *the moon* for *x* and *the sun* for *y* yields a false one.

---

1. Logicians speak not of *invoking* a predicate but rather of *instantiating* it. In fact, for reasons that need not concern us just now, their concept of instantiation is slightly more general than that of the familiar notion of function invocation.

Parameters make predicates interesting, because they
define the value.

Observe, incidentally, that a proposition can be regarded as a degenerate predicate. To be precise, a proposition is a predicate for which the corresponding set of parameters is empty (and the function thus always returns the same result, either TRUE or FALSE, every time it's invoked). In other words, all propositions are predicates, but most predicates aren't propositions.

——————— ♦ ♦ ♦ ♦ ♦ ———————

A predicate with exactly *N* parameters is an *N-place* predicate. For example, the statement "*x* won the *y* election in the year *z*" is a 3-place predicate. A proposition is a 0-place predicate. *Note:* An *N*-place predicate is also called an *N-adic* predicate. If *N* = 1, the predicate is said to be *monadic;* if *N* = 2, it's said to be *dyadic.*

Given a set of predicates, we can combine predicates from that set in a variety of ways to form further predicates, using the logical connectives already discussed—NOT, OR, AND, etc. (In other words, those connectives are logical operators that operate on predicates in general, not just on the special predicates that happen to be propositions.) A predicate that involves no connectives is called *simple;* a predicate that isn't simple is called *compound*. Here's a trivial example of a compound predicate:

x is a star OR *x* is further away than *y*   *compound and dyadic*

This predicate is also *dyadic:* not because it involves two simple predicates, but because it involves two parameters.

——————— ♦ ♦ ♦ ♦ ♦ ———————

One last point to close this section—a matter of terminology. The study of predicates and their connectives, together with the logical inferences that can be made using those predicates and connectives, is called *predicate logic* (also known as predicate calculus; the terms are used interchangeably). The well known relational calculus is an applied form of predicate calculus, tailored specifically for operating on relations. And since the relational calculus (or its logical equivalent, relational algebra) is an essential component of the relational model, it's often claimed, not unreasonably, that predicate logic is one of the foundations of the relational model.

QUANTIFICATION

I've shown in the previous section that one way to obtain a proposition from a predicate is to invoke or "instantiate" it with an appropriate set of arguments. But there's another way, too, and that's by means of *quantification*. Let *p*(*x*) be a monadic predicate (I show the single parameter *x* explicitly, for clarity). Then:

■   The expression

    EXISTS *x* (*p* (*x*))

is a proposition, and it means: "There exists at least one possible argument value *a* corresponding to the parameter *x* such that *p(a)* evaluates to TRUE" (in other words, the argument value *a* satisfies the predicate *p*). For example, if *p* is the predicate "*x* is a logician," then

```
EXISTS x ( x is a logician )
```

is a proposition—one that evaluates to TRUE, as it happens (take *x* to be, e.g., Bertrand Russell).

- The expression

```
FORALL x ( p ( x ) )
```

is a proposition, and it means: "All possible argument values *a* corresponding to the parameter *x* are such that *p(a)* evaluates to TRUE" (in other words, all such argument values *a* satisfy the predicate *p*). For example, if again *p* is the predicate "*x* is a logician," then

```
FORALL x ( x is a logician )
```

is a proposition—one that evaluates to FALSE, as it happens (take *x* to be, e.g., George W. Bush).

Note that it's sufficient to produce:

- A single example to show the truth of the EXISTS proposition

- A single counterexample to show the falsity[1] of the FORALL proposition

Note too in both cases that the parameter *x* must be constrained to "range over" some set of permissible values (the set of all people, in the examples). This is a point I'll come back to later, under a discussion of *sorted logic* in the section "Customer Must Place Order."

The term used in logic for the expressions EXISTS *x* and FORALL *x* in the foregoing discussion is *quantifiers* (the term derives from the verb *to quantify,* which simply means *to express as a quantity*—that is, to say how much of something there is or how many somethings there are). Quantifiers of the form EXISTS ... are said to be *existential;* quantifiers of the form FORALL ... are said to be *universal*. (And in logic texts, EXISTS is usually represented by a backward E and FORALL by an upside down A. I use the keywords EXISTS and FORALL in this chapter for typographical reasons—not to mention readability.)

By way of another example, let *q* be the dyadic predicate "*x* is taller than *y*." If we "quantify existentially over *x*," we obtain

```
EXISTS x ( x is taller than y )
```

---

1. This is the term logicians use for the quality of being false, though *falseness* or *falsehood* are perhaps more common in ordinary English discourse. It'll make another appearance in Chapter 5 of the present book.

Now, this statement is not a proposition, because it isn't categorically either true or false; in fact, it's a *monadic predicate,* with single parameter *y*. Suppose we invoke this predicate with argument Steve. We obtain:

```
EXISTS x ( x is taller than Steve )
```

And this statement *is* a proposition (and if there exists at least one person—Arnold, say—who is taller than Steve, then it evaluates to TRUE, of course). But another way to obtain a proposition from the original predicate *q* is to quantify over *both* of the parameters *x* and *y*. For example:

```
EXISTS x ( EXISTS y ( x is taller than y ) )
```

Note that this statement is indeed a proposition; it evaluates to FALSE only if everybody is the same height and TRUE otherwise (think about it!).

There are several lessons to be learned from the foregoing example:

- First of all, we see that to obtain a proposition from an *N*-adic predicate by quantification, it's necessary to quantify over *every* parameter. More generally, if we quantify over *M* parameters ($M \leq N$), then we obtain an *R*-adic predicate, where $R = N - M$.

- Let's focus on existential quantification only for the moment. Then there are apparently two different propositions we can obtain in the example by "quantifying over everything":

```
EXISTS x ( EXISTS y ( x is taller than y ) )
```

```
EXISTS y ( EXISTS x ( x is taller than y ) )
```

It should be clear, however, that these two propositions both mean the same thing: "There exist at least two persons *x* and *y* such that *x* is taller than *y*," or equivalently "It's not the case that everybody is the same height." More generally, in fact, it's easy to see that a series of like quantifiers (all existential or all universal) can be written in any sequence we like without changing the overall meaning of the predicate or proposition in question. We can therefore allow unnecessary parentheses to be dropped, as in this example:

```
EXISTS y EXISTS x ( x is taller than y )
```

By contrast, with *unlike* quantifiers, the sequence matters, in general (see the next bullet point below). *Note:* Partly because the sequence doesn't matter with like quantifiers, we sometimes adopt a shorthand according to which the foregoing example can be simplified to just:

```
EXISTS x, y ( x is taller than y )
```

In the same kind of way, FORALL *x* FORALL *y* (*p*(*x*,*y*)) can be abbreviated to just FORALL *x*, *y* (*p*(*x*,*y*)).

■   Third, we can (of course) use either EXISTS or FORALL in each of the applicable quantifier positions when "quantifying over everything." In the example, therefore, there are six distinct propositions that can be obtained by "full quantification," and I've listed them below. (Actually there are eight altogether, but two of those eight can be eliminated by virtue of the previous point.) *Note:* I've shown a precise natural language interpretation in each case. Observe that those interpretations are all different—*logically* different, I mean (of course!). Please observe too, however, that I've had to assume in connection with all of those interpretations that there do exist at least two distinct people "in the universe," as it were. I'll come back to this assumption later (in a discussion of *empty ranges* in the section "A Closer Look at Quantifiers").

```
EXISTS x ( EXISTS y ( x is taller than y ) )
```

Meaning: Somebody is taller than somebody else; TRUE, except in the unlikely event that everybody is the same height.

```
EXISTS x ( FORALL y ( x is taller than y ) )
```

Meaning: Somebody is taller than everybody (that particular somebody included!); clearly FALSE.

```
FORALL x ( EXISTS y ( x is taller than y ) )
```

Meaning: Everybody is taller than somebody; clearly FALSE.

```
EXISTS y ( FORALL x ( x is taller than y ) )
```

Meaning: Somebody is shorter than everybody (that particular somebody included); clearly FALSE. *Note:* Actually, when I say the meaning here is "Somebody is shorter than everybody," I'm going beyond the bounds of logic as such. We haven't stated explicitly what we mean by "shorter"! But of course we could (i.e., we could state explicitly, somehow, that the predicates "*x* is taller than *y*" and "*y* is shorter than *x*" are logically equivalent), and I'll assume for the remainder of this chapter that we've done so.

```
FORALL y ( EXISTS x ( x is taller than y ) )
```

Meaning: Everybody is shorter than somebody; clearly FALSE.

```
FORALL x ( FORALL y ( x is taller than y ) )
```

Meaning: Everybody is taller than everybody; clearly FALSE.

- Last (at the risk of pointing out the obvious): Even though five out of six of the foregoing propositions all evaluate to the same truth value, FALSE, it doesn't follow that they all mean the same thing, and indeed they don't; in fact, no two of them do.

FREE AND BOUND VARIABLES

It's time to introduce a little more terminology. I said earlier that another term for what I've been calling parameters is *free variables*. Quantifying over a free variable converts it into a *bound* variable. For example, consider again the following 2-place predicate:

    x is taller than y

The parameters *x* and *y* here are free variables. If we now "quantify existentially" over *x,* we obtain

    EXISTS x (x is taller than y)

Here *y* is still free, but *x* is now bound. And in the "fully quantified" form

    EXISTS x EXISTS y (x is taller than y)

x and *y* are both bound, and there are no free variables at all (the predicate has degenerated to a proposition).

Now, we already know that free variables correspond to parameters, in conventional programming terms. Bound variables, by contrast, don't have an exact counterpart in conventional programming terms at all; instead, they serve as a kind of *dummy*—they serve only to link the predicate inside the parentheses to the quantifier outside, as it were. For example, consider the predicate (actually a proposition)

    EXISTS x (x > 3)

This proposition merely asserts that there exists some integer greater than three. (I'm assuming that *x* here is constrained to "range over" the set of integers. Again, this is a point I'll come back to later, in the section "Customer Must Place Order.") *Note, therefore, that the meaning of the proposition would remain totally unchanged if the two x's were both replaced by some other variable y.* In other words, the proposition

    EXISTS y (y > 3)

is semantically identical to the one just shown. But now consider the predicate

    EXISTS x (x > 3) AND x < 0

Here there are three *x*'s, *but they don't all denote the same thing.* The first two are bound, and can be replaced by (say) *y* without changing the overall meaning; but the third is free and *cannot* be replaced with impunity. Thus, of the following two predicates, the first is equivalent to the one just shown and the second is not:

```
EXISTS y ( y > 3 ) AND x < 0
EXISTS y ( y > 3 ) AND y < 0
```

To close this section, I remark that we can now (re)define a proposition thus:

- A proposition is a predicate in which all variables are bound; equivalently, it's a predicate in which there are no free variables.

AN EXTENDED EXAMPLE

Abraham Lincoln once famously said: "You can fool some of the people some of the time, and some of the people all the time, but you cannot fool all the people all of the time."[1] Is this a precise logical statement? What does it mean? I suggest you have a go at translating it into precise logical form yourself before reading the discussion that follows. (Don't feel too bad if you find you can't do this exercise; fully absorbing all of the material we've been discussing takes time, and if it's all new to you then you might have some difficulty in applying it right away. But I do think the exercise is worth attempting—perhaps even more so if you're a novice in this area—because it'll give you some insight into what's involved in the precise formulation of business rules in particular.)

Discussion: Observe first that, logically speaking, the statement consists of three simple predicates (or are they propositions?) ANDed together, thus:

```
you can fool some of the people some of the time
AND
you can fool some of the people all the time
AND
you cannot fool all the people all of the time
```

Note that the English word *but* has mapped to the logical connective AND; the shade of meaning

---

1. Or did he? The text I show is as given in the *Chambers Dictionary of Quotations* (1996). But the *Bloomsbury Dictionary of Quotations* (1991) gives it as "You can fool some of the people all the time and all the people some of the time; but you can't fool all the people all the time." And the 3rd edition (1979) of *The Oxford Dictionary of Quotations* gives it as "You can fool all the people some of the time, and some of the people all the time, but you can not [*sic two separate words*] fool all the people all of the time"; and the 5th edition (1999) gives it as "You may fool all the people some of the time; you can even fool some of the people all the time; but you can't fool all of the people all of the time"—and adds "also attributed to Phineas Barnum."

conveyed by English *but* can't be represented in elementary predicate logic. However, this fact is unimportant for the purposes of this chapter (luckily for us). Anyway, let's agree to use *fool(x,y)* to stand for the predicate:

```
you can fool person x at time y
```

Now let's take the three simple propositions—yes, they are propositions, because each of them is indeed categorically either true or false—one by one. First, then: "You can fool some of the people some of the time." This one's easy:

```
EXISTS x EXISTS y ( fool ( x, y ) )
```

Meaning: There exists a person *x* and a time *y* such that you can fool person *x* at time *y;* presumably TRUE.

Next: "You can fool some of the people all the time." This one's not so clear. There are two possibilities. The first is:

```
FORALL y EXISTS x ( fool ( x, y ) )
```

Meaning: For all times *y* there exists a person *x* such that you can fool that person *x* at time *y;* probably TRUE. Alternatively:

```
EXISTS x FORALL y ( fool ( x, y ) )
```

Meaning: There exists a person *x* such that for all times *y* you can fool person *x* at time *y;* probably FALSE.

Note the logical difference between these two interpretations! The first says there's always somebody you can fool, but it might be different persons at different times; the second says there's some particular person you can always fool. Of course, we can figure out what Lincoln probably meant by appealing to things he obviously knew but didn't say (for example, the truism that nobody lives forever), but the fact remains that, considered purely from the point of view of logic as such, his second proposition is ambiguous. Now, Lincoln was a politician, and we all know that politicians thrive on ambiguity—but we surely don't want our *business rules* to be ambiguous!

The third proposition is "You cannot fool all the people all of the time." This one's even trickier.[1] Does it mean there exists at least one person and at least one time such that you can't fool that person at that time?—

---

1. It's tricky because of the negation. A common problem with negation is that there can be confusion as to just what it is that's being negated. For example, consider the statement *All that glitters is not gold* (this example illustrates a very common error). Presumably the intended meaning is *Not all that glitters is gold* (NOT FORALL x (gold(x))), but what it actually says is *Nothing that glitters is gold* (FORALL x (NOT gold(x)))—where x ranges over "all that glitters" in both cases.

```
    EXISTS x EXISTS y ( NOT ( fool ( x, y ) ) )
```

(Probably TRUE.) Or does it mean there exists at least one time when you can't fool anybody at all?—

```
    EXISTS y FORALL x ( NOT ( fool ( x, y ) ) )
```

(Probably FALSE.) Or does it mean at all times there exists some person you can't fool at that time?—

```
    FORALL y EXISTS x ( NOT ( fool ( x, y ) ) )
```

(Probably TRUE.) I do assume that Honest Abe didn't mean there's some particular person you can never fool—but he *might* have meant that:

```
    EXISTS x FORALL y ( NOT ( fool ( x, y ) ) )
```

(Probably FALSE.)

I haven't finished with this example—I'll come back to it in the next section.

A CLOSER LOOK AT QUANTIFIERS

By now I hope you agree, even if you didn't before, that natural language statements are often ambiguous. I also hope you're reasonably comfortable with the use of EXISTS and FORALL in the formulation of logical statements that don't suffer from the same drawback. However, there are a few more things I want to say about the general issue of quantification.

We Don't Need Both Quantifiers

First of all, you might have already realized that we don't actually need both EXISTS and FORALL. The reason is that any statement that can be expressed in terms of EXISTS can always be expressed in terms of FORALL instead, and vice versa. By way of example, consider again the predicate

```
    EXISTS x ( x is taller than Steve )
```

("Somebody is taller than Steve"). Another way to say the exact same thing is

```
    NOT ( FORALL x ( NOT ( x is taller than Steve ) ) )
```

("It is not the case that nobody is taller than Steve"). More generally, in fact, the statement

```
    EXISTS x ( p ( x ) )
```

is logically equivalent to the statement

```
    NOT ( FORALL x ( NOT ( p ( x ) ) ) )
```

(where the predicate *p* might legitimately involve other parameters in addition to *x*). Likewise, the statement

```
FORALL x ( p ( x ) )
```

is logically equivalent to the statement

```
NOT ( EXISTS x ( NOT ( p ( x ) ) ) )
```

(where, again, the predicate *p* might legitimately involve other parameters in addition to *x*).

It follows from the foregoing that a programming language—or a business rules language, or a database language, or any other formal language you might care to think of—need not explicitly support both EXISTS and FORALL. But it's very desirable to support both in practice. The reason is that some problems are "more naturally" formulated in terms of EXISTS, while others are "more naturally" formulated in terms of FORALL instead. For example, as you probably know, SQL supports EXISTS but not FORALL; as a consequence, certain queries are quite awkward to formulate in SQL. By way of example, consider the familiar suppliers-and-parts database and the query "Get suppliers who supply all parts." This query can be expressed in logic quite simply as follows:

```
s WHERE FORALL p EXISTS sp ( s.S# = sp.S# AND sp.P# = p.P# )
```

("Get suppliers *s* such that, for all parts *p*, there exists a shipment *sp* linking that supplier *s* to that part *p*"; the variables *s*, *p*, and *sp* are to be understood as ranging over the current set of suppliers, the current set of parts, and the current set of shipments, respectively). In SQL, by contrast, the query has to look something like this:

```
SELECT DISTINCT s.*
FROM    S AS s
WHERE   NOT EXISTS
      ( SELECT DISTINCT p.*
        FROM    P AS p
        WHERE   NOT EXISTS
              ( SELECT DISTINCT sp.*
                FROM    SP AS sp
                WHERE   s.S# = sp.S#
                AND     sp.P# = p.P# ) )
```

("Get suppliers *s* such that there does not exist a part *p* such that there does not exist a shipment *sp* linking that supplier *s* to that part *p*"). Well, single negation is bad enough (many people have difficulty with it); double negation, as in this SQL query, is much worse!

By way of another example, consider again the statement "You cannot fool all the people all of the time." Yet another candidate formulation is:

```
NOT ( FORALL x FORALL y ( fool ( x, y ) ) )
```

("It is not the case that for all times *y* and for all persons *x*, you can fool person *x* at time *y*.") *Exercise:* Is this formulation equivalent to any of those given at the end of the previous section—and if so, which?

Empty Ranges

Consider again the fact that the statements

```
EXISTS x ( p ( x ) )
```

and

```
NOT ( FORALL x ( NOT ( p ( x ) ) ) )
```

are logically equivalent. As I've explained several times in this chapter already, the bound variable *x* in each of these statements must "range over" some set of permissible values. Suppose now that the set in question is empty (it might, for example, be the set of people over fifty feet tall). Then:

- The quantifier EXISTS *x* clearly evaluates to FALSE (because no such *x* exists).

- The statement EXISTS *x* ($p(x)$)—"There exists an *x* that makes $p(x)$ evaluate to TRUE"—thus evaluates to FALSE as well, regardless of what $p(x)$ happens to be. For example, the statement "There exists a person over fifty feet tall who works for IBM" evaluates to FALSE (unsurprisingly).

- It follows that the negation NOT EXISTS *x* ($p(x)$), which is equivalent to the statement FORALL *x* (NOT ($p(x)$), evaluates to TRUE—again, regardless of what $p(x)$ happens to be. For example, the statement "All persons over fifty feet tall don't work for IBM"—or, more idiomatically, "No person over fifty feet tall works for IBM"—evaluates to TRUE (again unsurprisingly).

- But if the predicate $p(x)$ is arbitrary, then so is the predicate NOT ($p(x)$). And so we have the following possibly surprising result:

  The statement FORALL *x* (...) evaluates to TRUE if there are no *x*'s, *regardless of what appears inside the parentheses.*

  For example, the statement "All persons over fifty feet tall *do* work for IBM" also evaluates to TRUE!—because, to say it again, there are no persons over fifty feet tall.

One implication of the foregoing state of affairs for business rules in particular is that a business rule of the form FORALL *x* (...) is automatically satisfied whenever there happen not to be any *x*'s. For example, the rule "All citizens with taxable income in excess of one billion dollars must pay supertax" is automatically satisfied if no citizen has such a large taxable income.

Another implication is that certain queries will produce a result that you might not have expected (if you didn't know logic, that is). For example, the following query—

```
s WHERE FORALL p
       ( IF p.COLOR = 'Purple'
         THEN EXISTS sp ( s.S# = sp.S# AND sp.P# = p.P# ) )
```

("Get suppliers who supply all purple parts")—will return all suppliers if there are no purple parts. *Exercise:* Show an SQL formulation of this query.

Defining EXISTS and FORALL

As you might have realized, EXISTS and FORALL can be defined as an *iterated OR* and an *iterated AND,* respectively. I'll deal with EXISTS first. Let $p(x)$ be a predicate with a parameter x and let x range over the set $s = \{x1,x2,...,xn\}$. Then

```
EXISTS x ( p ( x ) )
```

is a predicate, and it's defined to be equivalent to—and hence shorthand for—the predicate

```
FALSE OR p ( x1 ) OR p ( x2 ) OR ... OR p ( xn )
```

Observe in particular that this expression evaluates to FALSE if *s* is empty (as we already know). By way of example, let $p(x)$ be "*x* has a moon" and let *s* be the set {Mercury, Venus, Earth, Mars}. Then the predicate EXISTS x ($p(x)$) becomes "EXISTS x (x has a moon)," and it's shorthand for

```
FALSE OR ( Mercury has a moon ) OR ( Venus has a moon )
       OR ( Earth has a moon )   OR ( Mars has a moon )
```

which evaluates to TRUE because (e.g.) "Mars has a moon" is true.
    Similarly,

```
FORALL x ( p ( x ) )
```

is a predicate, and it's defined to be equivalent to—and hence shorthand for—the predicate

```
TRUE AND p ( x1 ) AND p ( x2 ) AND ... AND p ( xn )
```

And this expression evaluates to TRUE if *s* is empty (again, as we already know). By way of example, let $p(x)$ and *s* be as in the EXISTS example above. Then the predicate FORALL x ($p(x)$) becomes "FORALL x (x has a moon)," and it's shorthand for

```
TRUE AND ( Mercury has a moon ) AND ( Venus has a moon )
       AND ( Earth has a moon )   AND ( Mars has a moon )
```

which evaluates to FALSE because (e.g.) "Venus has a moon" is false.
    As an aside, let me remark that—as the foregoing examples clearly demonstrate—defining

EXISTS and FORALL as iterated OR and AND, respectively, means that every predicate that involves quantification is logically equivalent to one that doesn't. Thus, you might be wondering, not without justification, what this business of quantification is really all about ... Why all the fuss? The answer is as follows: We can define EXISTS and FORALL as iterated OR and AND *only because the sets we have to deal with are—thankfully—always finite* (because we're operating in the context of computers and computers in turn are finite, of course). In pure predicate logic, where there's no such restriction, those definitions aren't valid.

Perhaps I should add that, even though we're always dealing with finite sets and EXISTS and FORALL are thus merely shorthand, they're extremely *useful* shorthand! For my part, I certainly wouldn't want to have to formulate business rules (or queries, or whatever) purely in terms of OR and AND, without being able to use the quantifiers.[1]

Prenex Normal Form

Consider this example:

        EXISTS x ($x > 3$) AND EXISTS y ($y < 0$)

("There exists an integer x such that x is greater than three and there exists an integer y such that y is less than zero"; I'm assuming here that x and y range over the set of all integers). Now, it should be clear that this predicate (which in fact happens to be a proposition) is logically equivalent to the following one:

        EXISTS x EXISTS y ($x > 3$ AND $y < 0$)

("There exists an integer x such that there exists an integer y such that x is greater than three and y is less than zero"). Without going into details, in fact, it should be fairly obvious that *any* predicate is logically equivalent to one in which all of the quantifiers appear at the beginning. A predicate satisfying this condition is said to be in *prenex normal form*. Prenex normal form is not inherently more or less correct than any other form, but with a little practice it does tend to become the most "natural" formulation—i.e., the easiest to write—in many practical cases.

Exercise: Convert the following predicates to prenex normal form:

- FORALL x ($x > 3$) AND FORALL y ($y < 0$)

- FORALL x ($x > 3$) AND FORALL x ($x < 0$)

- NOT (FORALL x ($x > 3$))

- FORALL x ($x > 3$) AND EXISTS y ($y < 0$)

_____

1. Or something equivalent to the quantifiers, perhaps I should add. (I have in mind here the relational algebra, which includes no direct support for the quantifiers but does provide equivalent functionality.)

- `IF FORALL x ( x > 3 ) THEN EXISTS y ( y < 0 )`

Other Kinds of Quantifiers

One last point on quantification: While it's probably true that EXISTS and FORALL are the most important quantifiers in practice, they aren't the only ones possible. There's no a priori reason, for example, why we shouldn't allow quantifiers of the form

> *there exist at least three x's such that*

or

> *a majority of x's are such that*

or

> *an odd number of x's are such that*

(and so on). One fairly important special case is *there exists exactly one x such that*. I'll use the keyword UNIQUE for this one. Here are some examples:

- `UNIQUE x ( x is taller than Arnold )`

Meaning: Exactly one person is taller than Arnold; probably FALSE.

- `UNIQUE x ( x has social security number y )`

Meaning: Exactly one person has social security number *y* (*y* is a parameter, of course); we can't assign a truth value to this example because it's not a proposition.

- `FORALL y UNIQUE x ( x has social security number y )`

Meaning: Everybody has a unique social security number (I'm assuming here that *y* ranges over the set of all social security numbers actually assigned, not all possible ones). *Exercise:* Does this predicate (which is in fact a proposition, of course) evaluate to TRUE?

As another exercise, what does the following one mean?

- `FORALL x UNIQUE y ( x has social security number y )`

"CUSTOMER MUST PLACE ORDER"

Now let's get back to Ron Ross's letter. Ron offers two candidate natural language formulations for a certain business rule:

- Customer must place order.

- It must be that: Each customer places some order.

Now, I assume these two formulations are meant to be equivalent, in the sense that they're essentially just two ways of saying the same thing (in effect, they both define what it means to *be* a customer—you must place at least one order in order to be recognized as a customer at all). On that assumption (i.e., that we're really talking about just one rule here, not two), there are at least two ways to state that rule using the notation of logic:

```
1.    FORALL c ( EXISTS o ( places ( c, o ) ) )


2.    FORALL x
        ( IF cust ( x )
            THEN EXISTS y ( order ( y ) AND places ( x, y ) ) )
```

Both of these statements are indeed propositions (neither contains any free variables). I'll refer to them as *Proposition 1* and *Proposition 2*, respectively. And what we might call the preamble to the second of the natural language formulations—*It must be that*—simply means the proposition in question (whichever one we choose) is required to evaluate to TRUE.

As an aside, I remark that it would be preferable for that preamble to say, not *It must be that*, but rather *It is the case that*. The word *must* muddies the water a little, because it smacks of something called "modal logic," which has to do with the notion of statements being either *necessarily* true or *possibly* true. Modal logic is beyond the scope of this chapter. Furthermore, it could be argued that a statement of the form "It must be that *p*," where *p* is a proposition, is actually a proposition about a proposition, and I don't think we want to get into that kind of complexity here, either. By contrast, the statement "It is the case that *p*" is just longhand for "*p*"; the preamble "It is the case that"—which is logically redundant, of course—is introduced purely for cosmetic reasons. (To be more specific, it gives us a standard way of expressing the *negation* in natural language of an arbitrary proposition; if *p* is a proposition, then we can express *p* as "It is the case that *p*" and the negation of *p*, NOT(*p*), as "It is not the case that *p*.")

Back to the example. Here again is *Proposition 1:*

```
FORALL c ( EXISTS o ( places ( c, o ) ) )
```

Here—as indeed I've done in all of my examples in this chapter prior to this point—I'm using what's sometimes called *sorted logic,* in which the variables (*c* and *o* in the example) are considered to be *sorted,* or what in the IT community we would more usually call *typed.*[1] (The term *sorted* here has nothing to do with sorting in the usual computing sense; it just means that each variable is of some "sort" or type.) In other words, we can imagine we've been given definitions along the following lines:

```
RANGE OF c IS CUSTOMER      /* i.e., c is of type CUSTOMER */
RANGE OF o IS ORDER         /* i.e., o is of type ORDER    */
```

(The syntax here is based on a language called Data Sublanguage ALPHA, which Codd proposed back in 1971 as a concrete language for relational systems [1]. It was one of the very first such languages—if not *the* first—to be defined, and it was firmly based on sorted logic.) Alternatively, and possibly preferably, we might specify the ranges explicitly inside the quantifiers themselves, thus:

```
FORALL c ∈ CUSTOMER ( EXISTS o ∈ ORDER ( places ( c, o ) ) )
```

(The symbol "ϵ" can be read as "belongs to" or "[is] in." Quantifiers like the ones just shown that include an explicit range specification are said to be *range coupled.*) Either way, *Proposition 1* simply says:

For all customers c, there exists at least one order o such that c places o.

The expression *places(c,o)* is an invocation of a dyadic predicate called *places* that returns TRUE if "*c* places *o*" is true and FALSE otherwise. *Note:* Of course, there's no suggestion here that "the system understands" the *places* predicate; it's just something we introduce, a kind of *deus ex machina* if you like, that we simply *define,* by fiat, to have the indicated meaning.[2]

Now let's turn to *Proposition 2:*

```
FORALL x
  ( IF cust ( x )
       THEN EXISTS y ( order ( y ) AND places ( x, y ) ) )
```

Here I'm using a more conventional *unsorted* logic (unsorted logic is the kind that logicians more usually assume, but it's slightly more cumbersome for our purposes, as will soon be apparent). In other words, instead of assuming we have some arbitrary number of distinct "sorts" (or, better, types), we assume there's just one "sort," called *the universe of discourse,* that contains everything we might ever

---

1. In particular, free variables, or in other words parameters, are typed in sorted logic. Let p be a predicate and let x be a parameter to p of type T. Whenever p is invoked (or "instantiated"), then, the argument substituted for x must also be of type T.

2. Though—at the risk of confusing you—if the database currently contains a relation corresponding to that predicate, and if the tuple $<c,o>$ appears in that relation, the system does at least know that *places(c,o)* evaluates to TRUE, even though it doesn't know what that predicate *places* "means." For further discussion of the connection between relations and predicates, I strongly recommend reference [2], by Hugh Darwen.

be interested in (customers, orders, elephants, bicycles, Mozart symphonies, redwood trees—you name it). So we need to introduce two more predicates: *cust(x)*, which returns TRUE if and only if *x* is a customer, and *order(y)*, which returns TRUE if and only if *y* is an order. Thus, *Proposition 2* says:

> For all objects *x,* if *x* is a customer, then there exists at least one object *y* such that *y* is an order and *x* places *y*.

Now, in Ron Ross's letter, he says: "I stick with my opinion so far that the closest thing [to an expression of the original rule] in formal logic is [a] logical implication, which can be taken to be a predicate." Well, it's clearly the case that *Proposition 2* does *include* a logical implication (IF ... THEN ...); however, it *is not* a logical implication—the initial quantifier ("for all objects *x*") is crucial. In other words, there's an important logical difference between the statements

    FORALL x (IF p (x) THEN q (x))

and

    IF p (x) THEN q (x)

I agree that it might be useful, intuitively, to think of the business rule as if it involved the implication only ("If *x* is a customer then *x* places an order"). However, if you do want to think that way, it does mean you're thinking—at least partly, albeit implicitly—in terms of unsorted logic; and I respectfully suggest that sorted logic would be a better basis. Why? Because *Proposition 2* (based on unsorted logic) is longer and more complicated than *Proposition 1* (based on sorted logic). What's more, the natural language interpretation of *Proposition 2* is longer and more complicated than the natural language interpretation of *Proposition 1*. Here are those two interpretations again, just to remind you:

- *Proposition 1:* For all customers *c,* there exists at least one order *o* such that *c* places *o*.

- *Proposition 2:* For all objects *x,* if *x* is a customer, then there exists at least one object *y* such that *y* is an order and *x* places *y*.

What about Ron's suggestion that logical implication "can be taken to be a predicate"? Well, there seems to be some confusion here. Let's analyze the situation:

- Some implications are propositions: for example, "IF 5 < 2 THEN Al Gore was elected U.S. president in the year 2000." By the way, this proposition is true—not necessarily for political reasons, but because 5 < 2 is false.

- Some implications are more general predicates: for example, "IF *m* < *n* THEN *x* was elected U.S. president in the year 2000." Of course, we can't assign a truth value to this latter implication without first assigning values to *m, n,* and possibly *x* as well.[1]

Thus, we might say, as Ron more or less did say, that an implication is a predicate, but that observation doesn't mean what I think he might think it means. To summarize some points from earlier in this chapter:

- All propositions are predicates; some predicates aren't propositions. To be precise, a predicate is a proposition if and only if it involves no free variables.

- A variable is free if and only if it's not bound by some quantifier.

- All implications are predicates; some implications are propositions.

So the answer to Ron's original question ("Predicate? Proposition? Hybrid? Other?") is: The rule is a proposition (and therefore it's a predicate too). As for the rest of the question, I trust it's now clear that it makes no sense. In particular, there's no such thing as a "hybrid" proposition/predicate.

HOW LOGIC HELPS

Ron says in his letter that "The quantification does make it interesting," and ask whether it's "just a diversion." I hope it's obvious from everything I've said prior to this point that the quantification is not just a diversion! The point is, logic *forces* us to make the quantifiers explicit, even when they're merely implicit in the natural language formulation. There are many, many ways of stating the original rule in natural language; for example, we might equally well say, as Ron suggests, **customer** *must* **place order** (though I don't know why he thinks this particular formulation "sounds more like a predicate").[2] And, typically, some—probably most—of those ways will be ambiguous, as I tried to show in the section "Natural Language Is Often Ambiguous" and in my discussion of the Abraham Lincoln quote, earlier.

Now, Ron's approach to addressing the problem of ambiguity is, I believe, to insist that certain

---

1. There's a point here that might strike you as a little odd. Suppose *m* and *n* have the values 5 and 2, respectively; then the overall expression evaluates to TRUE, regardless of the value of *x*. More generally, in fact, an implication of the form IF FALSE THEN $p(x)$ is true, no matter what *p* and *x* stand for. Yet the implication is still not a proposition, because $p(x)$ isn't a proposition (in general). So, while a proposition is a statement that's categorically either true or false, not all statements that are categorically either true or false are propositions. See the discussion of tautologies and contradictions in Chapter 2.

2. At this point in my original draft of this chapter, I said I also didn't know what he meant by "it may be just semantics"; but then Fabian Pascal told me that people often use the word *semantics* to mean, in effect, *syntax!* Thus, "it may be just semantics" might mean "it may be just a matter of the somewhat arbitrary nature of the words we choose to express what we're trying to say"—in other words, it might mean we're dealing with a psychological difference, not a logical one. Apologies to Ron if I'm wrong here, but Fabian's explanation did clear up a mystery for me that I'd been puzzling about, off and on, for several years.

words (e.g., *shall, must*) always be used in certain limited ways and always have certain fixed, prescribed meanings [9]. It seems to me, however, that such an approach will always be liable to error and is probably doomed to failure; we simply *can't* just edict that such commonly used words have such prescribed meanings and hope that the universe of pertinent people will never use them in any other way. I might point to the somewhat parallel case of "table" in the relational world ... I believe SQL is the mess it is, in part (but only in part!), because we refused in the early days to face up to a slightly unpalatable fact: namely, that it would have been *much* better to use the precise but unfamiliar term *relation* instead of the fuzzy term *table*. As it was, we made the wrong decision; and the rest, as they say, is history.

Here's how logic helps. As discussed earlier (in the section "Natural Language Is Often Ambiguous"), the rule designer might say simply:

A customer must place an order.

Moreover, he or she might think, not too unreasonably, that this assertion *defines* a customer (i.e., in order to be a customer at all, you must place an order). In other words, the designer might think the assertion in question constitutes a precise definition of the concept *customer*. But the person trained in logic says "Aha!—there are several different logical expressions that could correspond to this assertion" (equivalently, "There are several different interpretations of this assertion, all of which are at least prima facie valid, and I have no idea which one is intended"). For example (you might like to compare the precise interpretations that follow with the more intuitive ones given in the earlier section "Natural Language Is Often Ambiguous"):

- FORALL c EXISTS o (*places* (c,o))

  Meaning: Every customer places at least one order (this is *Proposition 1*, and presumably what was intended).

- EXISTS c EXISTS o (*places* (c,o))

  Meaning: At least one customer places at least one order.

- EXISTS o FORALL c (*places* (c,o))

  Meaning: There's at least one order that every customer places.

- FORALL c UNIQUE o (*places* (c,o))

  Meaning: Each customer places exactly one order.

- UNIQUE o FORALL c (*places* (c,o))

  Meaning: There's exactly one order that every customer places.

The logician, then, has to ask the rule designer which of the foregoing interpretations—if any (the list isn't exhaustive)—is the one intended. How much better it would be if the rule designer were trained in logic and expressed the rule in logic in the first place!

Yes, I know the counterarguments, but I don't agree with them.

CONCLUDING REMARKS

My original response to Ron Ross stopped here. But one reviewer (Hugh Darwen) said: "Counterarguments to what? Surely not to the assertion that it would be better if the rule designer were trained in logic? If so, I'd like to be told them, and perhaps some other readers would feel the same." Well, yes, I did mean counterarguments to that assertion—and it's difficult for me to do justice to them, since as I've just said I don't agree with them. In essence, however, they boil down to a claim that logic is simply too difficult for most people to deal with.

Now, that claim might be true in general (logic is a big subject). But you don't need to understand the whole of logic for the purpose at hand; in fact, I doubt whether you need much more than the material covered in this chapter. And the benefits are so huge! Surely it's worth investing a little effort up front in becoming familiar with that material in order to avoid the problems associated with ambiguous business rules. Ambiguity in business rules leads to implementation delays at best or implementation errors at worst (possibly both). And such delays and errors certainly have costs associated with them, costs that are likely to outweigh those initial learning costs many times over. In other words, framing business rules properly is a serious matter, and it requires a certain level of technical competence.

ACKNOWLEDGMENTS

I'd like to thank Hugh Darwen and Fabian Pascal for their comments on earlier drafts of this chapter, and Ron Ross for asking the question that led to the writing of it in the first place.

REFERENCES AND BIBLIOGRAPHY

1. E. F. Codd: "A Data Base Sublanguage Founded on the Relational Calculus," Proc. 1971 ACM SIGFIDET Workshop on Data Description, Access and Control, San Diego, Calif. (November 1971).

2. Hugh Darwen: "What a Database *Really* Is: Predicates and Propositions," in C. J. Date, Hugh Darwen, and David McGoveran, *Relational Database Writings 1994-1997*. Reading, Mass.: Addison-Wesley (1998).

3. C. J. Date: "Relational Calculus as an Aid to Effective Query Formulation," in C. J. Date and Hugh Darwen, *Relational Database Writings 1989-1991*. Reading, Mass.: Addison-Wesley (1992).

4. C. J. Date: *WHAT Not HOW: The Business Rules Approach to Application Development*. Reading, Mass.: Addison-Wesley (2000).

5.   C. J. Date: "The Logic of Business Rules," *www.dbdebunk.com* (June 2004).

6.   C. J. Date: *Database in Depth: Relational Theory for Practitioners.* Sebastopol, Calif.: O'Reilly Media Inc. (2006).

7.   James D. McCawley: *Everything that Linguists Have Always Wanted to Know about Logic (but were ashamed to ask).* Chicago, Ill.: University of Chicago Press (1981).

8.   Ernest Nagel: "Symbolic Notation, Haddocks' Eyes, and the Dog-Walking Ordinance," in James Newman (ed.), *The World of Mathematics, Vol. 3.* Mineola, N.Y.: Dover Publications (2000).

9.   Ronald G. Ross: *Principles of the Business Rule Approach.* Boston, Mass.: Addison-Wesley (2003).

APPENDIX A: TERMINOLOGY

In the body of this chapter (at the end of the section "Natural Language Is Often Ambiguous"), I said we often use various logical terms in database contexts, but we don't always use them "correctly." As a matter of fact, however, logicians don't always agree on the use of terms, either ... The discussion that follows is based on some things I discovered in studying a number of logic books—ten of them, to be precise—from my own personal library.

Consider the predicate LOVES (x,y), the semantics of which I take to be obvious. The first point to note is that most of the books I consulted would actually express this example more simply as just:

```
LOVES x y
```

(See, e.g., the extract from reference [7], later.) However, I prefer the syntax LOVES (x,y) as being more familiar to readers who are used to conventional programming languages.

The next point is that almost none of the books I consulted would call LOVES (x,y) a predicate anyway (though some of them would); rather, most would consider LOVES alone to be the predicate, and would typically use the term *sentence* for an expression like LOVES (x,y). (*Note:* I deliberately use the term *expression* here for what I called a statement in the body of the chapter, for reasons that should become clear in just a moment.) Furthermore, those who use *sentence* in this way typically go on to divide such sentences into two categories, *open* and *closed;* a closed sentence is a proposition, an open one is one that's not closed,[1] and the term *sentence,* unqualified, means a closed one. Furthermore, at least one writer uses *predicate letter* for *predicate, formula* for (open) *sentence,* and *statement* for (closed) *sentence* or *proposition.* And at least one uses *predicate symbol* for *predicate.*

---

1. The logicians in question thus appear not to regard a closed sentence as a degenerate open one. Or perhaps they're just not careful enough over their definitions ... though such behavior would be conduct most unbecoming, in the circumstances.

The book that made the most sense to me in this connection was the one by McCawley [7]. McCawley's term for expressions such as LOVES (x,y) is *propositional functions*. Fully instantiating such a function (i.e., substituting arguments for all parameters) yields a *proposition*. A propositional function is, precisely, a function of its *free variables* (i.e., parameters). And a proposition is also a (degenerate) propositional function. As you'll observe, most of this is in very close agreement with what I said in the body of the chapter, the sole exception being the use of the term *propositional function* in place of *predicate*. Here's McCawley's actual text (uppercase, italics, punctuation all as in the original):

> Such notions as "being a man" are generally dealt with in logic in the form of PROPOSITIONAL FUNCTIONS such as "x is a man." A simple propositional function consists of one or more VARIABLES (here, the x) and a PREDICATE (here, *man*). Let us assume that the *is* and the *a* of "x is a man" are simply meaningless syllables that are forced on us by quirks of English grammar and accordingly shift to a notation in which only the predicate and the variables appear: "man x". A propositional function is something that yields a proposition when specific entities are substituted for the variables. For example, if you substitute *Socrates* for x in "man x", you get "man Socrates", which expresses the proposition that Socrates is a man.

And he goes on to talk about propositional functions involving two or more variables and "complex" propositional functions involving simple ones, connectives, and quantifiers.
Now let me extend my example. Consider the expression

```
LOVES ( x, y ) AND EXISTS x ( LOVES ( x, Juliet ) )
```

As just indicated, McCawley would say this expression is a *complex* propositional function: It contains three occurrences of the symbol x and one of the symbol y (it also contains one occurrence of the symbol Juliet, which McCawley calls a *constant*, though I'd prefer to call it a *literal*). Several writers would then say that the first occurrence of x and the sole occurrence of y are *free* in the overall expression, while the other two occurrences of x are *bound* in the overall expression.[1] Those same writers would then typically go on to say that:

1.   A variable x is free within the expression X if and only if there is at least one free occurrence of x in X.

2.   A variable x is bound within the expression X if and only if there is at least one bound occurrence of x in X.

Note, therefore, that the very same variable can apparently be both free and bound in the very same expression!—a fact that suggests to me that the term "variable" is being used here in a rather strange sense. For my part, I would prefer to say (in the example) that there are *two different x's*—i.e.,

---

1. Some writers appear to regard the occurrence of x within the quantifier EXISTS x as neither bound nor free, but I don't think the point is very important—I mean, I think it's just a matter of convention as to whether we regard such occurrences as free, bound, or neither.

two different variables with the same name—rather than just one variable. A systematic renaming for the bound occurrences makes this point clear:

```
LOVES ( x, y ) AND EXISTS z ( LOVES ( z, Juliet ) )
```

Note: This renaming is of course legitimate—I mean, it doesn't change the meaning of the overall expression—because bound occurrences are only dummies anyway, in a sense.

As an aside, I note that, like almost all of the authors I consulted, McCawley uses *argument* to mean *parameter* (!). As for *argument* in the sense in which I used that term in the body of the chapter, writers use a variety of terms: *constant, entity, object, referent, designator* ... but, apparently, never the (to me much more obvious) term *value* (?). *Note:* McCawley also makes use of *range coupled quantifiers,* but calls them "restricted quantifiers." Unfortunately, he also uses "domain" for "range"—though this latter usage is common to many of the logic texts I consulted. (The terms are used differently in mathematics.)

APPENDIX B: ANSWERS TO EXERCISES

Several inline exercises were embedded in the body of this chapter. This appendix repeats (or paraphrases, in some cases) the text of those exercises and offers some answers.

Exercise: State the truth values of the following propositions:

- (The moon is a star) OR (the sun is a star): TRUE.

- (The sun is a star) OR (the sun is a star): TRUE.

- (The sun is a star) AND NOT (the moon is a star): TRUE.

- IF (the sun is further away than the moon) THEN (the sun is a star): TRUE.

- NOT (the sun is a star) IFF ((the moon is a star) OR (George W. Bush won the U.S. presidential elections in 2000 and 2004)): This one evaluates to TRUE if and only if "George W. Bush won the U.S. presidential elections in 2000 and 2004" evaluates to FALSE.

Exercise: Show that all possible logical connectives involving just one or two propositions can be expressed in terms of suitable combinations of NOT and either OR or AND.

Answer: First of all, there are exactly four connectives involving just one proposition, because the input to such a connective can take precisely two values, and each of those two can map to either of two possible outputs (as the following table indicates):

```
input | outputs
------+--------
  t   | t f t f
  f   | t f f t
```

The *outputs* column here shows the four possible outputs vertically; reading from left to right, the first connective maps both TRUE and FALSE to TRUE, the second maps them both to FALSE, the third leaves them unchanged (that's the *identity* connective), and the fourth interchanges them (that's NOT).

Likewise, there are exactly 16 connectives involving two propositions, because the inputs to such a connective in combination can take precisely four values, and each of those four can, again, map to either of two possible outputs:

```
    | t f
----+-----
  t | a b
  f | c d
```

Here the left column and the top row together show the possible combinations of input values, and each of the result values *a, b, c, d* can be either TRUE or FALSE. For example, if *a* is TRUE and *b, c, d* are all FALSE, then the connective is AND.

I now show how each of these operators can be expressed in terms of a suitable combination of NOT and either OR or AND. First of all, it's easy to see that we don't need both OR and AND, because (e.g.)

```
p AND q  ≡  NOT(NOT(p) OR NOT(q))
```

Because of this fact, I can freely use both OR and AND in what follows.

Now consider the connectives involving a single proposition *p*. Let *c(p)* be the connective under consideration. Then the possibilities are as follows:

```
c(p)  ≡  p OR NOT(p)    /* always TRUE  */
c(p)  ≡  p AND NOT(p)   /* always FALSE */
c(p)  ≡  p              /* identity     */
c(p)  ≡  NOT(p)         /* NOT          */
```

Now consider the connectives involving two propositions *p* and *q*. Let *c(p,q)* be the connective under consideration. Then the possibilities are as follows:

$$c\,(p,q) \quad\equiv\quad p \text{ OR NOT}(p) \text{ OR } q \text{ OR NOT}(q)$$
$$c\,(p,q) \quad\equiv\quad p \text{ AND NOT}(p) \text{ AND } q \text{ AND NOT}(q)$$
$$c\,(p,q) \quad\equiv\quad p$$
$$c\,(p,q) \quad\equiv\quad \text{NOT}(p)$$
$$c\,(p,q) \quad\equiv\quad q$$
$$c\,(p,q) \quad\equiv\quad \text{NOT}(q)$$
$$c\,(p,q) \quad\equiv\quad p \text{ OR } q$$
$$c\,(p,q) \quad\equiv\quad p \text{ AND } q$$
$$c\,(p,q) \quad\equiv\quad p \text{ OR NOT}(q)$$
$$c\,(p,q) \quad\equiv\quad p \text{ AND NOT}(q)$$
$$c\,(p,q) \quad\equiv\quad \text{NOT}(p) \text{ OR } q$$
$$c\,(p,q) \quad\equiv\quad \text{NOT}(p) \text{ AND } q$$
$$c\,(p,q) \quad\equiv\quad \text{NOT}(p) \text{ OR NOT}(q)$$
$$c\,(p,q) \quad\equiv\quad \text{NOT}(p) \text{ AND NOT}(q)$$
$$c\,(p,q) \quad\equiv\quad (\text{NOT}(p) \text{ OR } q) \text{ AND } (\text{NOT}(q) \text{ OR } p)$$
$$c\,(p,q) \quad\equiv\quad (\text{NOT}(p) \text{ AND } q) \text{ OR } (\text{NOT}(q) \text{ AND } p)$$

As a subsidiary exercise, and in order to convince yourself that the foregoing definitions do indeed cover all of the possibilities, you might like to construct the corresponding truth tables.

Exercise: All connectives involving either one or two propositions can be expressed in terms of just one primitive. Can you find it?

Answer: Actually there are two such primitives, NOR and NAND, often denoted by a down arrow, " ↓ " (the *Peirce arrow*) and a vertical bar, " | " (the *Sheffer stroke*), respectively. Here are the truth tables:

NOR	t	f		NAND	t	f
t	f	f		t	f	t
f	f	t		f	t	t

As these tables suggest, $p \downarrow q$ ("*p* NOR *q*") is equivalent to NOT (*p* OR *q*) and $p\,|\,q$ ("*p* NAND *q*") is equivalent to NOT (*p* AND *q*). In what follows, I'll concentrate on NOR (I'll leave NAND to you). Observe that this connective can be thought of as "neither nor" ("neither the first operand nor the second is true"). I now show how to define NOT, OR, and AND in terms of this operator:

$$\text{NOT}(p) \quad\equiv\quad p \downarrow p$$
$$p \text{ OR } q \quad\equiv\quad (p \downarrow q) \downarrow (p \downarrow q)$$
$$p \text{ AND } q \quad\equiv\quad (p \downarrow p) \downarrow (q \downarrow q)$$

For example, let's take a closer look at the "*p* AND *q*" case:

p	q	p↓p	q↓q	(p↓p) ↓ (q↓q)
t	t	f	f	t
t	f	f	t	f
f	t	t	f	f
f	f	t	t	f

This truth table shows that the expression $(p \downarrow p) \downarrow (q \downarrow q)$ is equivalent to p AND q, because its first, second, and final columns are identical to the pertinent columns in the truth table for AND (deliberately drawn a little differently here):

p	q	p AND q
t	t	t
t	f	f
f	t	f
f	f	f

Since I've already shown how all of the other connectives can be expressed in terms of NOT, OR, and AND, the overall conclusion follows.

Exercise: Here is another candidate formulation for the statement "You cannot fool all the people all of the time":

```
NOT ( FORALL x FORALL y ( fool ( x, y ) ) )
```

Is this formulation equivalent to any of those given at the end of the section "An Extended Example"—and if so, which?

Answer: We start with the equivalence:

```
FORALL x ( p ( x ) )  ≡  NOT ( EXISTS x ( NOT ( p ( x ) ) ) )
```

Negating both sides, we have:

```
NOT ( FORALL x ( p ( x ) ) )  ≡  EXISTS x ( NOT ( p ( x ) )
```

Hence:

```
NOT ( FORALL x FORALL y ( fool ( x, y ) ) )
```

```
≡   EXISTS x ( NOT ( FORALL y ( fool ( x, y ) ) ) )
```

```
≡   EXISTS x ( EXISTS y ( NOT ( fool ( x, y ) ) ) )
```

And this formulation is identical to the first of the four given in the body of the chapter.

Exercise: Show an SQL formulation for the query "Get suppliers who supply all purple parts."

Answer:

```
SELECT DISTINCT s.*
FROM    S AS s
WHERE   NOT EXISTS
        ( SELECT DISTINCT p.*
          FROM    P AS p
          WHERE   p.COLOR = 'Purple'
          AND     NOT EXISTS
                  ( SELECT DISTINCT sp.*
                    FROM    SP AS sp
                    WHERE   s.S# = sp.S#
                    AND     sp.P# = p.P# ) )
```

("Get suppliers *s* such that there does not exist a purple part *p* such that there does not exist a shipment *sp* linking that supplier *s* to that part *p*").

Note: It's a little tangential to the main theme of this chapter, but you might be interested to know that some while back I wrote another paper [3] to show how a knowledge of elementary logic can help in constructing complicated SQL queries like the one just shown. In other words, as I suggested near the beginning of the chapter, the uses of logic in the database context are certainly not limited just to the matter of stating business rules precisely.

Exercise: Convert the following predicates to prenex normal form.

- FORALL x (x > 3) AND FORALL y (y < 0)

   Prenex normal form equivalent:

   FORALL x FORALL y (x > 3 AND y < 0)

- FORALL x (x > 3) AND FORALL x (x < 0)

   Prenex normal form equivalent:

   FORALL x FORALL y (x > 3 AND y < 0)

Note that the following is *not* a correct answer:

```
FORALL x FORALL x ( x > 3 AND x < 0 )
```

The reason is that this formulation collapses the two *x*'s into one; it's monadic, not dyadic. In other words, converting a given predicate to prenex normal form will sometimes require a systematic renaming of bound variables, in order to avoid certain naming clashes that would otherwise occur.[1]

- ```
  NOT ( FORALL x ( x > 3 ) )
  ```

Prenex normal form equivalent:

```
EXISTS x ( NOT ( x > 3 ) )
```

- ```
  FORALL x ( x > 3 ) AND EXISTS y ( y < 0 )
  ```

Prenex normal form equivalent:

```
FORALL x EXISTS y ( x > 3 AND y < 0 )
```

Or:

```
EXISTS y FORALL x ( x > 3 AND y < 0 )
```

In the body of the chapter, I said that the sequence matters with unlike quantifiers (in general). But it doesn't matter in the case at hand, because the predicates following the quantifiers, $x > 3$ and $y < 0$, are completely unrelated to each other.

- ```
  IF FORALL x ( x > 3 ) THEN EXISTS y ( y < 0 )
  ```

Prenex normal form equivalent:

```
EXISTS x EXISTS y ( NOT ( x > 3 ) OR ( y > 0 ) )
```

———————— ◆ ◆ ◆ ◆ ◆ ————————

Exercise: Does the predicate (actually a proposition) "Everybody has a unique social security number" evaluate to TRUE?

————————————

1. That incorrect answer does suggest another question, though: What would an expression of the form FORALL *x* FORALL *x* ($p(x)$) mean? Or an expression of the form EXISTS *x* EXISTS *x* ($p(x)$)?
```

Answer: The logic formulation given in the body of the chapter was:

```
FORALL y UNIQUE x ( x has social security number y )
```

(where *y* ranges over the set of all social security numbers actually assigned, not all possible ones). This proposition is supposed to be true (at least in the USA) but is probably not: Some people have no social security number at all, while others have ones that aren't unique.

Exercise: What does the following statement mean?

```
FORALL x UNIQUE y ( x has social security number y )
```

Answer: This statement differs from the one in the previous exercise only in that FORALL *y* UNIQUE *x* has become FORALL *x* UNIQUE *y*. We might interpret it to mean "Every social security number has a unique person," or, more idiomatically, "Everybody has a unique social security number." In other words, it has the same meaning as the one in the previous exercise! The reason they're the same is that, *very* loosely speaking, *person* and *social security number* are both keys for the entities under discussion; in other words, there's a one-to-one relationship between them (at least, there's supposed to be).

I'll close this appendix (and this chapter) with one more exercise for you to think about. In the section "Predicates" in the body of the chapter, I said that if we substituted the argument *the sun* for the parameter *x* in the statement "*x* is a star," we would obtain a true proposition. What if we were to substitute *Marilyn Monroe* instead? *Hint:* Refer to the footnote in the section "Customer Must Place Order" regarding sorted logic and typed parameters.

Chapter 2

Some Operators Are

More Equal than Others

Two things are identical
if one can be substituted for the other without affecting the truth.
—Gottfried Wilhem von Leibniz

This chapter represents an attempt—for my own benefit as much as anyone's, perhaps I should add—to clarify some issues on which I've observed a certain degree of confusion, or at least lack of agreement, in the literature. And when I say literature, I don't just mean the computing literature; the issues I'm talking about have to do with certain fundamental concepts in logic, and the logic texts I've consulted themselves appear to display no consensus on the matter. I refer to the logical differences that exist among and between the following logical concepts:

- Identity

- Equality

- Equivalence

- Bi-implication

The confusions I'm talking about are compounded by the fact that, even if we limit our attention to the field of logic alone, some at least of these terms have more than one meaning. Indeed, I'm not even sure that a universally accepted "correct" usage exists in all cases. For that reason, I feel within my rights to use the terms as I see fit, just so long as (a) I spell out what I mean by them as carefully as I can, and (b) if nothing else, my definitions do conform to the spirit, at least, of the various definitions to be found in the literature.

Perhaps I should add that I'm not a logician, nor have I ever received any formal training in logic; thus, it's entirely possible that there are some egregious errors (even howlers) in what follows. If so, I apologize. *Caveat lector.*

THE UNIVERSE OF DISCOURSE

The concepts I wish to discuss—identity and the rest—all arise in connection with propositional logic[1] (and hence in connection with predicate logic also, since predicate logic is a generalization of propositional logic). A proposition in logic is an assertion, or declarative sentence, that's unequivocally either true or false. Here are some examples:

- The sun is a star.

- The moon is a star.

- Neptune is a planet.

- Mars has exactly two moons.

- George W. Bush won the U.S. presidential elections in 2000 and 2004.

If p is a proposition, it has a truth value. For the purposes of this chapter, if p is true, I'll denote its truth value by TRUE; if it's false, I'll denote its truth value by FALSE. In computing terms, we might say we have a data type called BOOLEAN that contains just these two truth values, and the literal representations of those values are TRUE and FALSE, respectively. We might also say, more simply but less accurately, that the legal values of type BOOLEAN just are TRUE and FALSE; strictly speaking, however, TRUE and FALSE aren't values as such—rather, they're literals, or symbols, that denote certain values, just as, e.g., the numeral 3 isn't a number as such but rather a literal, or symbol (more colloquially, a digit or numeral), that denotes a certain number.

To pursue the computing analogy a little further, we might also say we have a data type called PROPOSITION that contains all possible propositions. Moreover, if we adopt the convention that the literals TRUE and FALSE denote valid (albeit degenerate) propositions, then we might say that type BOOLEAN is a proper subtype of the supertype PROPOSITION [8]. *Note:* Types in computer languages are always finite, but there's no reason for the purposes of the present chapter to assume that the set of all possible propositions is finite, and I won't.

By the way, the term *valid* appears in the foregoing paragraph. *Valid* is one of those words that has a very special and precise meaning in logic; I think it's important to say, therefore, that I'll be using the term throughout this chapter in its ordinary English sense, not in the special sense of logic.

To pursue the computing analogy still further, we can of course permit variables of type BOOLEAN (truth valued variables) and variables of type PROPOSITION (proposition valued, or

---

1. Also known by various other names, including in particular *propositional calculus*. And propositions per se are sometimes called *statements* (not to be confused with statements in the programming language sense); thus, the terms *statement logic* and *statement calculus* are also sometimes used. Propositions are also referred to as *formulas*—sometimes, more specifically, as *closed* formulas. Some writers call them simply *sentences*. And so on.

propositional, variables).[1] And like all types, these types will have certain operators associated with them: namely, the operators that can be applied to values and variables of the type in question, including in particular the well known connectives NOT, OR, and AND. (I'll assume you're familiar with these operators; I'll be using them in examples in later sections. I'll also assume they follow certain obvious precedence rules, in order to cut down on the number of parentheses that might otherwise be needed.)

IDENTITY

The notion of identity, in the sense in which I propose to apply it, has some claim to being the most fundamental logical notion of all. It can be defined thus:

> Two objects are identical if and only if they're the very same object.

(I remark as an aside that the term *object* is to be understood throughout this chapter in its ordinary English sense, not in the special sense in which it's used in so called object oriented systems.)
  Following reference [13], we can also think of identity in terms of the following dyadic predicate:[2]

> *Identity:* Object x is one and the same thing as object y.

This predicate, which I'll denote by the expression $ID(x,y)$, satisfies the following important properties:

- *Reflexivity:* For all x, $ID(x,x)$ is true (everything is identical to itself).

- *Symmetry:* For all x and y, if $ID(x,y)$ is true, then $ID(y,x)$ is true (if x is identical to y, then y is identical to x).

- *Transitivity:* For all x, y, and z, if $ID(x,y)$ and $ID(y,z)$ are both true, then $ID(x,z)$ is true (if x is identical to y and y is identical to z, then x is identical to z).

- *Substitutability:* For all x and y and all predicates $P(x)$, if $ID(x,y)$ and $P(x)$ are both true, then $P(y)$ is true (if x is identical to y and P is true of x, then P is true of y).

------

1. Some writers use the term *propositional variables* to refer to what I would greatly prefer to call free variables—i.e., the variables that represent the parameters to a propositional function (also known as a predicate).

2. I'll have more to say about predicates later; for now, I'll just say that (as mentioned in a previous footnote) a predicate is basically just a propositional, or proposition valued, function. But I think I should at least draw your attention to the fact that I'm supposed to be talking about propositional logic at the moment, and predicates are part of predicate logic, not propositional logic. I'll come back to this point later too.

Of course, by my use of phrases such as "for all x" in the foregoing, I've tacitly introduced the idea that there can be, and surely will be, additional types over and above the two we already have (namely, BOOLEAN and PROPOSITION). In fact, variables such as x in the example can be of any type whatsoever. *Note:* Most logic texts pay little or no attention to the notion of types; in effect, they simply assume that everything is of the same type. As reference [3] puts it, however, "it is [sometimes] useful to divide [the set of all values] into sorts or types. The usual occasion for this is when there are various kinds of [values] for which ... predicates are not uniformly meaningful. A language with N individual types is said to be N-sorted." So what the logician calls a *sort* is the same thing as—i.e., is identical to (?)—what programming languages would call a *type*.

Before going any further, I should explain that the term *identity* does have another important meaning, even in logic. To be specific, an identity in this second sense is a special case of what's called a *tautology*. I won't be using the term in this latter sense in this chapter, but I will at least explain it (in the section "Equivalence," later).

Back to the meaning I do want to use. As I've indicated, the expression $ID(x,y)$ can be read as "Object x is one and the same thing as object y," or more simply as "x is identical to y," or just "x and y are the same thing." So in the case of type BOOLEAN in particular, where there are just two distinct "things," TRUE and FALSE, we can say that:

- TRUE is identical to TRUE.

- FALSE is identical to FALSE.

- TRUE and FALSE are not identical to each other.

What about type PROPOSITION, though? For example, consider these two propositions:

- Neptune is a planet.

- Mars has exactly two moons.

Clearly, these propositions aren't identical; equally clearly, however, they do both have the same truth value, TRUE, and so we can at least say they're *equivalent*. I'll discuss equivalence (of propositions in particular) in the next section but one. Before then, however, I have to deal with another possible confusion factor ... The fact is, the identity predicate, which I've shown as $ID(x,y)$, is more usually written thus in practice:

$x = y$

The symbol "$=$" (read as "equals," of course) is variously referred to as *the identity sign,* or *the identity symbol,* or *the equals sign,* or *the equals symbol,* or simply *equality*. So now we need to discuss this new term; in particular, we need to decide whether there's a logical difference between identity and equality.

EQUALITY

I'll begin this section by setting a stake in the ground and saying that as far as I'm concerned, identity and equality are indeed the same thing (in other words, they're identical, in exactly the sense in which I've already defined that term).[1] In reference [7], I defined them as follows:

> **equality** A truth valued operator; two values are equal if and only if they're the very same value. For example, the integer 3 is equal to the integer 3 and not to the integer 4, nor to any other integer (nor to anything else, either). More precisely, let *T* be a type; then the equality operator "=" for values of type *T* is defined as follows. Let *v1* and *v2* be two such values, and let *Op* be an operator with a parameter *x* of type *T*. Then *v1* and *v2* are equal (i.e., *v1* = *v2* evaluates to TRUE) if and only if, for all such operators *Op,* two successful invocations of *Op* that are identical in all respects except that the argument corresponding to *x* is *v1* in one invocation and *v2* in the other are indistinguishable in their effect. *Note:* The equality operator (which is—in fact, must be—defined for every type) is also known as identity.

> **identity** 1. *(General)* That which distinguishes a given entity from all others. 2. *(Operator)* Equality.

Note: I also gave definitions in reference [7] for three more meanings of the term *identity,* two of which I'll get to toward the end of the next section (the other is irrelevant for the purposes of this chapter).

In the case of type BOOLEAN, then, we can say that TRUE = TRUE, FALSE = FALSE, and TRUE ≠ FALSE (I assume my use of the symbol "≠" here is legitimate). But the trouble is, we use the symbol "=" to mean other things as well—other things, that is, in addition to identity as such. (This observation is certainly true in computing; it's also true in mathematics; whether it's true in logic depends to some extent on context and, apparently, on the logic text in question.) By way of illustration, consider the following equation:

$$x + 4 = 2x - 1$$

The symbol *x* here is meant to denote some number, and it's easy to see by solving the equation that the number in question is five. But the expressions on the two sides of the "=" symbol are self-evidently not identical; that is, the "=" symbol here does *not* denote identity. Rather, it's *the values denoted by* the expressions on the two sides of the "=" symbol that are identical. In order to make sense of the equation, therefore, we have to imagine another operator—perhaps a metalinguistic operator—which I'll call **value_of** (with the obvious semantics) that's applied implicitly to the two expressions, thus:

---

1. I think the Leibniz quote that appears as an epigraph to this chapter supports my position here. So too does *The Principle of Identity of Indiscernibles:* If there's no way whatsoever of distinguishing between two objects, then there aren't two objects but only one. As an aside, I remark that of course there's a logical difference between indiscernibility and interchangeability; two objects might be interchangeable and yet discernibly distinct (think of two pennies, for example).

value_of ($x + 4$) = *value_of* ($2x - 1$)

Now the symbol "=" can indeed be understood as identity. In fact, a case could be made that the use of "=" in the original equation represents a kind of punning (or overloading, perhaps); clearly, the expressions $x+4$ and $2x-1$ aren't *syntactically* identical, but they might be said to be *semantically* identical, in the sense that the things they denote—their denotations—are identical.

Now, at least one of the logic texts I consulted in writing this chapter, reference [13], defines an equation as (in effect) *an instantiation of the identity predicate*. So, e.g., $2 = 3$ is apparently an equation! Well, yes, it is; not all instantiations of a given predicate are true ones, in general. By contrast, the instantiation $3 = 3$ is a true equation. So is $2+1 = 3$, though in this case we clearly have to understand the identity as semantic in nature rather than syntactic.

That same reference [13], almost alone out of the many logic texts I consulted, uses the notion of a *designator* as a way of getting at what I'm here referring to as a syntactic *vs.* semantic distinction. A designator is a noun phrase that can be used within a proposition (or, more generally, a predicate) and uniquely designates some object—where, of course, the object in question can be as concrete or as abstract as we please, and different designators can designate the same object.[1] Examples include:

3 • Selma, Alabama • $2+1$ • the 1968 Democratic National Convention • you • me • Beethoven's Fifth Symphony • the successor of 2 • Neptune • the sun • TRUE

In particular, such designators can appear in equations. Thus, for example, the following is a legitimate equation, and indeed a true instantiation of the identity predicate:

Mozart = the composer of *Eine kleine Nachtmusik*

Let's get back to type BOOLEAN. In computing, at least, if not in logic, we might certainly write things like

    IF X = TRUE ...

or

    ... WHERE (Y AND Z) = FALSE

(where X, Y, and Z are, typically, variables of type BOOLEAN). And, of course, we all know what such expressions mean; the things being compared are the truth values denoted by the specified expressions, not the expressions themselves. In other words, we're appealing to the fact that the operator I earlier called *value_of* is implicitly applied to each of the expressions before the comparison is evaluated. And some logic texts, at least, make this fact explicit; they introduce an operator, which I'll call **truth_value_of**, and require that operator to be invoked explicitly when needed. I defined that

---

1. Or even no object at all, possibly; consider, for example, the designator *the moons of Mercury*.

operator thus in reference [7]:

> **truth value of** In logic, an operator (in symbols, "/.../") that, given a [truth valued] expression, returns the truth value of that expression. For example, let the symbols x and y denote integers. Then the expression $/x > y/$ returns TRUE if the integer denoted by x is greater than that denoted by y and FALSE otherwise.

Using this operator, the two examples shown earlier become:

```
IF /X/ = /TRUE/ ...
```

and

```
... WHERE ( /Y/ AND /Z/ ) = /FALSE/
```

Note that /TRUE/ and /FALSE/ yield TRUE and FALSE, respectively.

To sum up: Equality means identity. An expression of the form $x = y$ is almost always shorthand for one of the form *value_of(x) = value_of(y)*. And while such shorthands are usually acceptable (in fact, they're generally preferable to the longhand versions), I would argue that they're acceptable only so long as we do at least understand that they *are* just shorthand. However, there's one case in particular—namely, the case in which the expressions x and y denote truth values specifically—where I would argue that the foregoing shorthand should *not* be used ... which brings me to the next section.

LOGICAL EQUIVALENCE

What does it mean for two objects to be equivalent? There are many possible answers to this question; that is, the term *equivalence* has many different meanings. But I'll start with a very fundamental one—namely, the meaning it has in logic. Throughout this section, therefore, the term *equivalence,* unqualified, should be understood to mean logical equivalence specifically.

The notion of logical equivalence, also known as *truth functional* equivalence (also, for some reason, as *material* equivalence), is essentially very straightforward: Two expressions—more precisely, two propositions—p and q are logically equivalent (in symbols, $p \equiv q$, where "$\equiv$" is read as "is logically equivalent to") if and only if they have the same truth value. In other words, $p \equiv q$ if and only if $/p/ = /q/$.

I now proceed to give a series of examples, with discussion, to illustrate and elaborate on the foregoing notion. I've numbered the examples for purposes of subsequent reference; I've also included parentheses, sometimes redundantly, for clarity.

My first two examples are straightforward:

1.   (2 < 5) ≡ (7 > 3)

The propositions on either side of the " ≡ " symbol here are clearly both true, and the equivalence is thus valid.

2.   (2 > 5) ≡ (7 < 3)

This time the propositions on either side of the " ≡ " symbol are both false, so again the equivalence is valid.

3.   (Neptune is a planet) ≡ (Mars has exactly two moons)

This example is different in kind from Examples 1 and 2. Certainly the propositions on either side of the " ≡ " symbol are both true, and so the equivalence is valid once again; however, the fact that they *are* both true is just a matter of happenstance, in a sense. In Examples 1 and 2, the various propositions involved were *absolutely* true or false (as applicable)—there was no room for debate on the matter. But such is not the case in Example 3. For example, suppose we were to replace Neptune by Pluto in the first proposition; the equivalence would then no longer be valid. But it would have been valid in 2005! Or would it? Does the fact that Pluto was officially declared, in 2006, not to be a planet mean the equivalence wasn't valid in 2005 after all—in fact, never was valid? Even if so, there was a time when we at least thought it was valid, wasn't there? What's going on here?

As another illustration of the same point, suppose somebody discovers that Mars actually has three moons; again, then, Example 3 would no longer (?) be valid.

Examples like these strongly suggest that we have to take into account the logical difference between (a) our thinking, or believing, something is true or false and (b) its actually being true or false. In order to distinguish between these two different concepts, logicians make use of the notion of *possible worlds*.[1] In Examples 1 and 2, they would say there's simply no possible world in which the propositions on the two sides of the " ≡ " symbol could have different truth values. By contrast, in Example 3, the fact (?) that Neptune is a planet and the fact (?) that Mars has exactly two moons are propositions that happen to be true in our world right now, but could be false in some other possible world.

In order to distinguish formally between statements that just happen to be valid in some possible world and ones that are absolutely valid in all possible worlds, we introduce two metalinguistic symbols, " ⊢ " ("it is the case that") and " ⊨ " ("it is necessarily the case that"). The symbols are metalinguistic because they effectively allow us to make logical statements about logical statements.[2] They're known as *single turnstile* and *double turnstile*, respectively. "It is the case that" (single turnstile) means the statement following the symbol is true, but might be false in a different world. "It is necessarily the case that" (double turnstile) means the statement following the symbol is true in all possible worlds. Thus, we

---

1. This notion cries out for a characterization more precise than any I'm prepared to give here; for the purposes of this chapter, I'm just going to assume it makes good intuitive sense.

2. You might note the possibility of some kind of infinite regress here (as in, e.g., "it is the case that it is the case that ... that *p*"). I categorically refuse to be drawn into a detailed discussion of this possibility.

can rewrite Examples 1-3 as follows:

1. $\models$ (2 < 5) ≡ (7 > 3)

2. $\models$ (2 > 5) ≡ (7 < 3)

3. $\vdash$ (Neptune is a planet) ≡ (Mars has exactly two moons)

Note: Other readings of " $\vdash$ " encountered in the literature include *it is true that; it is deducible that; it is provable that;* and *it is a theorem that.* Analogously, other readings of " $\models$ " encountered in the literature include *it is universally true that; it is valid that; it is true in all possible worlds (or all states of affairs) that;* and *it is a tautology that.*

A statement of the form $p \equiv q$, where p and q are propositions, is itself a proposition; like propositions in general, therefore, it might be false. Thus, for the example, the following statement is an equivalence, formally speaking, but it isn't a valid one:

4.   (2 > 5) ≡ (7 > 3)

However, it's surely reasonable to adopt the convention that a statement of the form $p \equiv q$ means it is in fact the case that p and q are equivalent (i.e., they do have the same truth value), unless the context demands otherwise—just as, in mathematics, we adopt the convention that the equation $x = y$ means it is in fact the case that x and y are equal, unless the context demands otherwise. I'll adopt this convention myself throughout what follows.

Is the following a valid equivalence?—

5.   (p AND q) ≡ NOT (NOT (p) OR NOT (q))

Well, the symbols p and q in this example are meant to denote arbitrary propositions, and the statement overall is clearly valid (indeed, it's absolutely so—i.e., it's valid in all possible worlds). In fact, of course, it's one of De Morgan's Laws. But is it a proposition? I said a few moments ago that equivalences are propositions; but Example 5 surely can't be a proposition, because it involves variables (propositional variables, to be precise)—namely, p and q. Now, I did say earlier, in the section "The Universe of Discourse," that propositional variables were permitted. But when I said that, I was wearing my computing hat! Logic as such (propositional logic, at any rate) doesn't normally countenance any notion of variables at all. In fact, precisely because it does involve variables, Example 5 looks (to me, at least) more like a propositional function, or predicate, than it does a simple proposition. So is Example 5 an example of an equivalence at all? Do we have to conclude that I was wrong when I said an equivalence was a proposition, and that some equivalences aren't propositions after all?

Before I try to answer these questions, let me point out something else as well. (You might have already realized this for yourself, but I want to spell it out anyway.) Example 5 applies, clearly, to *all possible* propositions *p* and *q*. So shouldn't the statement include some kind of quantification? Shouldn't we be saying, rather, something like the following—

FORALL *p*, *q* ((*p* AND *q*) ≡ NOT (NOT (*p*) OR NOT (*q*)))

—where *p* and *q* are now bound variables that range over the set of all possible propositions (in other words, variables that denote arbitrary values of type PROPOSITION)? Note, incidentally, that introducing explicit quantifiers in this manner would at least have the effect of converting what was previously a predicate, with two parameters, into a simple proposition, with none. (I remark in passing that a proposition can in fact be *defined* as a predicate for which the set of parameters is empty.)

Well, yes, maybe we should introduce some quantifiers—but we can't, because we're supposed to be in the realm of propositional logic, and quantifiers, like variables, aren't part of that logic. So again it's not entirely clear, at least to me, just what's going on here.

Now, logicians might have a perfectly good explanation for all of this, and they might well be smiling (or worse) at my ignorance, or naïveté, in trying to make some sense of their specialty. But it does seem to me that there's a puzzle here that needs to be explained, or explained away. Unfortunately, I'm not at all sure I'm the person best equipped to do it; but I mean to try! I want to offer a hypothesis that, while it might not be accurate, does at least make sense to me. To be specific, it seems to me that part at least of the solution to the puzzle lies in the history of how the field of logic has developed over time. Let me elaborate.

As I've said, propositional logic doesn't really have either a concept of variables or a concept of quantification. But it does need to appeal to such notions, at least implicitly; so what does it do? Well, consider the following paraphrase[1] from a typical logic text (reference [26], page 61):

If *p* and *q* are propositions, then ... each of NOT *p*, *p* AND *q*, *p* OR *q*, and *p* ≡ *q* is a proposition.

It seems to me that phrases such as "if *p* and *q* are propositions" means exactly the same thing as "for all possible propositions *p* and *q*"—thereby introducing, tacitly, both:

- The notion that there's such a thing as a propositional variable (*p* and *q* being examples), and

- The notion of quantification ("if *p* and *q* are propositions" being, as I've already said, just another way of saying "for all propositions *p* and *q*").

In other words, it seems to me that logic texts, in talking about propositional logic, *want* to make use of both variables and quantification. But they lack the formal apparatus to do so, because propositional logic was developed before predicate logic (and it was only with predicate logic that the necessary formal apparatus was introduced). So what do they do? *Answer:* They resort to what (it seems to me) is a kind of arm waving; they use informal language along the lines of "if *p* and *q* are

---

1. The paraphrase in question involves a systematic change in notation and terminology but retains the sense of the original.

propositions," which allows them to describe what they want without having to introduce, explicitly, concepts that aren't themselves part of propositional logic as formally defined.

As further evidence to support my hypothesis here, I'd like to offer some further quotes (or paraphrases, rather) from reference [26]:

- *Page 67:* Suppose there is given a nonempty set of simple propositions [*i.e., propositions involving no connectives*] ... Further propositions can be formed using, repeatedly, and in all possible ways, the various connectives ... With each simple proposition there is associated exactly one truth value, TRUE or FALSE ... Which of TRUE and FALSE is associated with a given simple proposition is irrelevant—truth values may be assigned as the occasion demands.

  I interpret these remarks as saying among other things that "the given simple propositions" act as propositional variables, denoting either TRUE or FALSE "as the occasion demands."

- *Page 67 (cont.):* A **truth function** is a function on V^n into V where $V = \{TRUE,FALSE\}$ and $n \geq 1$. That is, a truth function is a function of n arguments where each argument can assume either TRUE or FALSE as a value and each function [invocation yields a value that] is either TRUE or FALSE.

  Surely a "truth function" is just a predicate for which all of the parameters are of type BOOLEAN? So propositional logic does admit certain predicates after all? *Note:* Reference [26] isn't alone in using *arguments* for what I would much prefer to call *parameters;* most of the logic texts I consulted seem to do the same thing.

- *Page 69:* Each truth function ... determines a proposition ... and each proposition may be considered as a truth function ... We shall feel free to regard a proposition as a truth function. In such an event, the prime components [*i.e., the constituent simple propositions*] will be considered as variables which can assume the values TRUE and FALSE.

  Here variables are mentioned explicitly, and they're clearly variables of type **PROPOSITION** specifically. As for equating propositions and truth functions, it seems to me that (as previously discussed) those "propositions" are really predicates.

- *Page 69 (cont.):* A proposition whose value is TRUE, for all possible assignments of truth values to its prime components, is a **tautology** ... We shall often write $\models a$ for "*a* is a tautology."

  And here the quantification ("for all") is mentioned explicitly, too.

  Here's what I conclude from these quotes and the accompanying discussion:

- At least when they're discussing the ideas of propositional logic informally, logicians do indulge in implicit appeals to the notions of (propositional) variables, and (propositional) functions or predicates, and (universal) quantification.

■   Statements like Example 5 (repeated here for convenience)—

(*p* AND *q*) ≡ NOT (NOT (*p*) OR NOT (*q*))

—most certainly do appear, both with and without the double turnstile, in logic texts, and they're referred to both as equivalences and, more specifically, as tautologies.

■   When the double turnstile does appear, it seems reasonable to understand it as implying the necessary quantifiers.

As we've seen, a proposition—or, more generally, a predicate—that's necessarily true, regardless of the truth values of any constituent simple propositions involved, is called a tautology. (I'll follow convention in continuing to refer to those constituents as propositions, even though I've been trying to make the case that in some respects they look more like predicates.) In particular, a statement of the form

⊨   *p* ≡ *q*

asserts that the equivalence *p* ≡ *q* is a tautology. And a tautology of this particular form (i.e., one that's an equivalence) is, perhaps a little unfortunately, sometimes called an *identity* ... Don't get the idea, though, that all tautologies are identities in this sense. For example, here's one that isn't:

⊨   *p* OR NOT (*p*)

But tautologies that are identities in this sense do turn out to be particularly important, for reasons that are beyond the scope of this chapter. (In database contexts, they're important for what's sometimes called "query rewrite"—i.e., the transformation, by either the system or the user, of one expression into another, typically for performance purposes.)

I note in passing that in computing, at least, a boolean expression of the form *exp1* = *exp2* (where *exp1* and *exp2* are expressions of the same type) that's guaranteed to evaluate to TRUE regardless of the values of any variables involved is also called an identity; an example might be the boolean expression $x(y+z) = xy+xz$. And at least one of the logic texts I consulted would, in effect, allow the logical equivalence *p* ≡ *q* to be written as *p* = *q*. As I've already said, however, I don't think we should write "=" for "≡"; I think it only confuses matters further.

I'd also like to note in passing, though it's not directly relevant to the main theme of this chapter, that tautologies in general play a role in logic analogous, somewhat, to the role played by theorems in mathematics. In logic, however, tautologies and theorems aren't necessarily the same thing (i.e., they're not identical!), though we do usually try to set up our logical systems in such a way that they *are* the same. To repeat, a tautology is something that's necessarily true; a theorem, by contrast, is something that can be deduced from given axioms according to given rules of inference. If and only if the logical system is *complete,* then all tautologies are theorems; if and only if it's *sound,* then all theorems are tautologies.

What about this example?—

6. $\vdash$ (x + 4 = 2x - 1) $\equiv$ TRUE

This statement asserts that the equation on the left of the "$\equiv$" symbol is valid; in fact, it's easy to see that it's logically equivalent [*sic*] to this simpler one:

$\vdash$ (x + 4 = 2x - 1) $\equiv$ (x = 5)

It's also equivalent to this still simpler one:

$\vdash$ (x = 5) $\equiv$ TRUE

Let's focus on this last one specifically. Clearly, this example is merely an assertion on somebody's part that the symbol x denotes, or designates, the value five. Such an assertion might be either true or false, in general, but let's assume for the sake of the present discussion that it's true. One point to note immediately, then, that x here isn't a variable!—though it would usually be called a variable in ordinary high school algebra.[1] First, it's not a variable in the sense of logic, because it's not truth valued; second, it's not a variable in the sense of computing, either, because a variable in computing is something whose value varies over time, and in the case at hand the value of x doesn't vary at all. It follows that all three versions of the example are propositions, not predicates, even though they might look like predicates at first glance.

I'd like to raise another issue here, though. Precisely because the example does at least appear to involve a variable, you might be thinking that, once again, we need some quantification ... What of this possibility? Well, here's what would happen if we introduced a FORALL into the last example:

FORALL x ((x = 5) $\equiv$ TRUE)

This statement is at least well formed (i.e., it's syntactically acceptable). But it doesn't say the same thing as before!—and in fact it's probably not even true, which is why I omitted the turnstile. (It would be true if and only if there were just one value that x was allowed to assume and that value was five.)

So much for FORALL; what about "the other" quantifier? Here's what would happen if we introduced an EXISTS instead of a FORALL:

EXISTS x ((x = 5) $\equiv$ TRUE)

Again this statement doesn't say the same thing as before (though unlike that previous example, at least it's probably true).

Now, I must admit that with this example (or series of examples, rather), I feel on even less

---

1. Sometimes, with a slightly better rationale, it would be called an unknown.

secure ground than I did with Example 5. But if my analysis is wrong, I've not been able to find anything in the numerous texts I've consulted to suggest as much; what's more, I'd very much appreciate a comprehensible (emphasis on comprehensible) explanation as to how and why it's wrong, if it is.

OTHER KINDS OF EQUIVALENCE

The previous section discussed just one kind of equivalence: namely, logical equivalence. But many other kinds of equivalence can also be defined. By way of example, let s be the (infinite) set $\{0,1,2,3,...\}$ of all nonnegative integers; then we might define elements x and y of this set to be equivalent if and only if they yield the same remainder on division by seven. According to this definition, 8 and 43 are equivalent; so are 12 and 19; and so are an infinite number of other pairs of elements of s.

Observe now that this definition of equivalence has the effect of partitioning the set s into exactly seven disjoint subsets: $s0$ (the set of all nonnegative integers exactly divisible by seven), $s1$ (the set of all nonnegative integers that yield a remainder of one on division by seven), ..., and $s6$ (the set of all nonnegative integers that yield a remainder of six on division by seven). Each of these sets $s0, s1, ..., s6$ is said to be an *equivalence class* (under the stated definition of equivalence). Further, we can now say that two elements of s are equivalent (again, under the stated definition of equivalence) if and only if they belong to the same equivalence class.

Here are some more examples:

- Let s be the set of states in the USA; define two states to be equivalent if and only if their names start with the same letter. (How many equivalence classes are there here?)

- Let s be the set of all employees in some company; define two employees to be equivalent if and only if they work in the same department. (I'm assuming here that every employee works in exactly one department.)

- Let s be the set of all predicates; define two elements of s to be equivalent if and only if they both take exactly N parameters ($N = 0, 1, 2, ...$).

- Let $x, y, ...$ denote real numbers, and let s be the set of all valid numeric expressions involving $x, y, ...$ and the usual numeric operators and literals; define two such expressions to be equivalent if and only if they necessarily denote the same number.

And so on. Now, we can continue to use the symbol " $\equiv$ " to denote equivalence in such cases, just so long as we're clear on how to interpret it in the context at hand. For instance, in the context of the last of the foregoing examples, we might reasonably write:

$$(x^2 - y^2) \equiv (x - y)(x + y)$$

Here the symbol " $\equiv$ " is clearly to be understood to mean "denotes the same number as." (I note in passing that many people would use the symbol " $=$ " here rather than the symbol " $\equiv$ ", but we've already been through that discussion.)

The foregoing general notion of equivalence and the associated notion of an equivalence class play absolutely fundamental roles in mathematics. For that reason, even though it's a little tangential to my main aims in this chapter, it seems worthwhile to try and pin those notions down precisely—and that's what the following definitions (paraphrased slightly from reference [7]) are meant to do.

We start with the concept of an *equivalence relation:*

equivalence relation An equivalence relation is a binary relation that's reflexive, symmetric, and transitive.

Explanation: Loosely, a binary relation *r* is reflexive if and only if, for all *x,* the tuple $<x,x>$ appears in *r;* it's symmetric if and only if, for all *x* and *y,* if the tuple $<x,y>$ appears in *r,* then so does the tuple $<y,x>$; and it's transitive if and only if, for all *x, y,* and *z,* if the tuples $<x,y>$ and $<y,z>$ both appear in *r,* then so does the tuple $<x,z>$. By way of example, let binary relation *r* be defined as follows: Tuple $<x,y>$ appears in *r* if and only if *x* and *y* are both U.S. state names and they start with the same letter. Then it's easy to see that *r* is (a) reflexive (e.g., the tuple $<$Ohio,Ohio$>$ appears in *r*); (b) symmetric (e.g., the tuples $<$Ohio,Oregon$>$ and $<$Oregon,Ohio$>$ both appear in *r*); and (c) transitive (e.g., the tuples $<$Ohio,Oregon$>$, $<$Oregon,Oklahoma$>$, and $<$Ohio,Oklahoma$>$ all appear in *r*).

Now we can define the term *equivalence class:*

equivalence class Let *r* be an equivalence relation, and let *x* be a value such that the tuple $<x,y>$ appears in *r* for some *y.* Given that value *x,* then, the set of all such values *y* is an equivalence class with respect to *r*—namely, that specific equivalence class that corresponds to the given value *x.*

To continue with the U.S. states example, let *x* be Ohio. Then the equivalence class that corresponds to *x* is the set containing just Ohio, Oregon, and Oklahoma (these three being the only states whose names start with O). Observe that every state belongs to just one such equivalence class, and the equivalence classes are therefore pairwise disjoint.

Finally, we can define *equivalence* in the general sense:

equivalence Let *x* and *y* be elements of some set, and let that set be partitioned into a set of equivalence classes in accordance with some equivalence relation. Then *x* and *y* are equivalent (in symbols, $x \equiv y$) if and only if they're members of the same equivalence class.

To conclude this section, here's a question for you to ponder: How does the notion of logical equivalence as defined in the previous section relate to the foregoing more general notion?

BI-IMPLICATION

Finally we come to *bi-implication*. In order to discuss this operator, I first need to say something about implication as such (*logical* implication, that is, also known as *truth functional* implication and, for some reason, as *material* implication). You're probably familiar with this operator—it's one of the usual logical connectives, with truth table as follows (where I've abbreviated TRUE and FALSE as *t* and *f,* respectively):[1]

$$
\begin{array}{cc|c}
p & q & p \Rightarrow q \\
\hline
t & t & t \\
t & f & f \\
f & t & t \\
f & f & t \\
\end{array}
$$

As the truth table indicates, I'll be using the symbol "$\Rightarrow$" ("implies") to denote this operator, at least for the purposes of the present chapter. Note too that, again as the truth table indicates, the implication $p \Rightarrow q$ is logically equivalent to the expression NOT(p) OR q. In fact, we have a tautology:

$$\vdash \quad (p \Rightarrow q) \equiv (\text{NOT} (p) \text{ OR } q)$$

I also need to say a little more about the metalinguistic operator "$\vdash$". Earlier I said that a statement of the form "$\vdash q$" was simply an assertion to the effect that the proposition q was true. More generally, a statement of the form

$$p \vdash q$$

is an assertion to the effect that the proposition q can be deduced, or proved, from the proposition p (or, more generally, the set of propositions p); in particular, therefore, if p is true, it follows that q is true. If there is no p, it just means that q is a theorem—it's not necessary to make any additional assumptions, or rely on any additional premises, in order to show that q is true.

So what's the difference between $p \vdash q$ and $p \Rightarrow q$? They both seem to say that q follows from p. But in fact there *is* a difference; "$\Rightarrow$" is simply an operator within the logic we're talking about (i.e., conventional two-valued propositional logic, which I'll abbreviate as 2VL from this point forward), whereas "$\vdash$" is an operator that allows us to make statements *about* that logic. A statement of the form $p \Rightarrow q$ can be true in one "world" and false in another; for example, the statement

$$(\text{Neptune is a planet}) \Rightarrow (\text{Mars has exactly two moons})$$

is true in the world as we know it, but would cease to be true if somebody discovers that Mars actually has three moons. By contrast, a statement of the form $p \vdash q$ is an assertion to the effect that the logic we're talking about allows us to infer q from p. For example, the statement

$$(\text{Neptune is a planet}) \text{ AND } (\text{Mars has exactly two moons})$$
$$\vdash (\text{Mars has exactly two moons})$$

is certainly a valid statement about 2VL (i.e., we can certainly infer the proposition on the right from the

---

1. I remark in passing that the symbols p and q in truth tables like this one really denote variables once again!

one on the left), as you can see by checking the definition of the AND connective.

Like implication as such, bi-implication is also one of the usual connectives. As the name suggests, the bi-implication $p \Leftrightarrow q$ is defined as $p \Rightarrow q$ AND $q \Rightarrow p$. Here's the truth table:

```
p q  |  p ⟺ q
-----+--------
t t  |    t
t f  |    f
f t  |    f
f f  |    t
```

As you can see, the expression $p \Leftrightarrow q$ yields TRUE if and only if p and q have the same truth value. In other words, the expression $p \Leftrightarrow q$ is logically equivalent—I choose my words carefully—to the expression $p \equiv q$! So are there two distinct operators here, or is there only one? What's going on?

Now, there does seem to be some mystery in this area, and I'm not sure I'm capable of clearing it up, at least not fully. But I'll try. I'll begin by summarizing, using their own words, what a couple of my favorite logic texts have to say on the matter.

First, from reference [1] (I've used my own symbols in what follows, for implication and bi-implication in particular, but haven't otherwise changed the text as quoted):

> Two statements are called (logically) *equivalent* if they take the same truth values in all possible cases ... Two statements ... are *truth-functionally equivalent* if they have the same truth value under all truth valuations ... For example, ... the statements $a \Rightarrow b$ and NOT $b \Rightarrow$ NOT a ... are equivalent.
>
> We write $p \equiv q$ to indicate that the statements p and q are equivalent. We may think of $\equiv$ as a kind of equality between statements, since if $p \equiv q$, then ... $/p/ = /q/$ ...
>
> In connection with $\equiv$, we can define a new logical operator " $\Leftrightarrow$ " called *bi-implication* (or *equivalence* [*sic!*]) as follows ... [*The appropriate truth table appears here.*] Thus $p \Leftrightarrow q$ has value TRUE exactly when p and q have the same truth value. It follows ... that $p \equiv q$ holds when and only when the statement $p \Leftrightarrow q$ is valid.

As you can see, therefore, reference [1] follows the path I've followed myself in this chapter: It begins by defining logical equivalence, then it defines bi-implication, and then it shows they're equivalent. (By the way, note the remark to the effect that "$\equiv$" is a kind of equality! Reference [11] is another logic text that adopts this position; in fact, it states explicitly that "the symbol for equality used in logic" is the symbol it uses for—apparently—both logical equivalence and bi-implication.)

Now I turn to reference [26] (again I've used my own symbols but haven't otherwise changed the material as quoted):

> The words "if and only if" are used to obtain from two sentences a **biconditional** sentence. We regard the biconditional

>   *p* if and only if *q*

as having the same meaning as

>   If *p*, then *q*, and if *q*, then *p* ...

[*The appropriate truth table appears a couple of pages later. A few pages later again, the text continues:*]

>   Let us now agree to call formula *a* **equivalent to** formula *b*, symbolized *a* ≡ *b*, iff [*i.e., if and only if*] they are equal as truth functions ... Equivalence of formulas can be characterized in terms of the concept of a valid formula, according to the following theorem.

>   THEOREM 2.2. ⊨ *a* ⇔ *b* iff *a* ≡ *b*.

As you can see, reference [26] follows the inverse of the path followed by reference [1]: It begins by defining bi-implication (though it uses the term *biconditional*), then it defines logical equivalence, and then it shows they're equivalent. (By the way, note the use of the symbol *iff* to mean "if and only if." Some logic texts use that very symbol as a symbol for either logical equivalence or bi-implication or both.)

To repeat the question, then: Are "≡" and "⇔" truly distinct operators? They seem to be one and the same. So what's going on? Well, some hint toward an answer to this question might be gained by considering three-valued logic (3VL). Now, I need to explain immediately that, in a sense, there's no such thing as "the" 3VL [6]—there are many logically distinct 3VLs, which differ on (among other things) the definitions of the connectives OR and AND. For definiteness, I'll base my discussion on the specific 3VL underlying SQL,[1] in which the truth tables for NOT, OR, and AND look like this (using *u* to represent "the third truth value," sometimes called UNKNOWN):

```
NOT |              OR | t u f          AND| t u f
----+----          ---+------          ---+------
 t  | f             t | t t t           t | t u f
 u  | u             u | t u u           u | u u f
 f  | t             f | t u f           f | f f f
```

Note: As these examples suggest, it's convenient to represent 3VL truth tables in a style a little different from that usually used with 2VL, which is the style I've been using throughout this chapter prior to this point. (By contrast, Chapter 1 used the style just illustrated.)

What about the equivalence and bi-implication connectives? Let's consider equivalence first. Recall that equivalence (logical equivalence, that is) is supposed to mean *equality of truth values* (*p* ≡ *q*

---

1. More correctly, the 3VL that *allegedly* underlies SQL. The fact is, as reference [18] points out, neither SQL's 3VL nor Codd's (which SQL's 3VL is supposed to be based on) is fully defined; indeed, that very fact is part of the problem with those logics. See also reference [6].

if and only if /*p*/ = /*q*/). So the truth table for equivalence is clearly as follows:

```
AND| t u f
---+------
 t | t f f
 u | f t f
 f | f f t
```

Turning to bi-implication: Well, first we need to consider implication as such ... and immediately we run into a problem. We could follow what is perhaps the best known of the "standard" 3VLs, the one due to Lukasiewicz, and define implication thus:

```
=▸| t u f
--+------
t | t u f
u | t t u
f | t t t
```

Now we can define bi-implication accordingly (*p* ◂=▸ *q* if and only if *p* =▸ *q* AND *q* =▸ *p*):

```
◂=▸| t u f
---+------
 t | t u f
 u | u t u
 f | f u t
```

With this definition, the 3VL versions of the operators equivalence and bi-implication are clearly not the same; so maybe there's a good logical reason for regarding them as distinct in general, even though they happen to coincide in 2VL.

Or perhaps we got the 3VL definition of "=▸" wrong? Let's see what happens if we follow 2VL and define *p* =▸ *q* as NOT(*p*) OR *q:*

```
=▸| t u f
--+------
t | t u f
u | t u u
f | t t t
```

(Note that this version of implication is indeed different from the previous version; to be specific, the definitions differ just on the case *u* =▸ *u*.) Now bi-implication (*p* =▸ *q* AND *q* =▸ *p*):

```
◄=►| t  u  f
---+---------
 t | t  u  f
 u | u  u  u
 f | f  u  t
```

Not only is this version of bi-implication different from the previous version *and* different from the 3VL version of equivalence, it doesn't even satisfy the (surely required) property that p ◄=► p is true for all $p!$—that is, p ◄=► p isn't a tautology. *Note:* Although it's not the main purpose of this chapter, perhaps you can see how discussions of this same general nature can be used to demonstrate why 3VL is a disastrously bad basis on which to construct a database system ... but I digress; see reference [6] if you want to see this line of argument pursued further.

I noted earlier that some writers use the symbol *iff* ("if and only if") as a symbol for either bi-implication or logical equivalence or both. For the record, however, I'd just like to note that at least one logician regards such a use of that symbol as inappropriate. Here's an excerpt from reference [17] (once again I've used my own symbols but haven't otherwise changed the material as quoted):

> I maintain that *a if and only if b* is exactly what the words suggest it is: the conjunction of *a if b* and *a only if b* ... [Consider the example:]
>
> My pulse goes above 100 if and only if I do heavy exercise.
>
> [It] follows ... that the expression *if and only if* is ASYMMETRIC, that is, that *a if and only if b* is not interchangeable with *b if and only if a* ... Note the result of interchanging *a* and *b* in [the foregoing example]:
>
> I do heavy exercise if and only if my pulse goes above 100.
>
> [The] temporal and/or causal relations between the two clauses are the reverse of what they were in [the original example] ... [The original example] treats the exercise as the cause of the rise in your pulse, while [the reversed form] makes it sound as if a prior change in your pulse is the reason for which you do heavy exercise (perhaps because of the mistaken belief that doing heavy exercise will lower your pulse).
>
> I thus take it as unfortunate that logicians have generally identified the expression *if and only if* with a putative logical connective (most frequently written with the symbol ≡) which is symmetric both syntactically ... and semantically ... While these properties [of symmetry] are in fact possessed by the formula that is most often offered as a "definition" of $a \equiv b$, namely, $a \Rightarrow b$ AND $b \Rightarrow a$, it is highly questionable that those properties carry over to the English expression *if and only if* (or its counterparts in other languages, e.g., German *wenn und nur wenn*), with which it is generally equated.

Note: I include the foregoing extract for what it's worth, but I feel compelled to add that—speaking purely for myself here!—I don't think it's worth very much. After all, an exactly analogous argument could be made in connection with the logician's use of the connective AND. Consider this example:

I voted for a change in leadership and I was seriously disappointed.

Surely few would claim this sentence is interchangeable with the following one:

I was seriously disappointed and I voted for a change in leadership.

In other words, it seems to me that we have an example here in which *a and b* "is not interchangeable with" *b and a*. But nobody should be surprised at this state of affairs. Indeed, anyone who has ever studied either simple logic or elementary set theory will have learned very early on that the connectives AND and OR—also IMPLIES ("⇒"), BI-IMPLIES or IF AND ONLY IF ("◄⇒"), and so on—just aren't the same thing as their natural language counterparts; instead, they're what might be called *truth functional distillates* of those natural language counterparts. And the reason is that, of course, the connectives are required to have meanings that don't depend on context but, rather, are context free. So I have to say that I don't find the arguments of reference [17] in this connection very persuasive.

CONCLUDING REMARKS

This chapter wasn't easy to write. While I'm a great fan of logic, I'm somewhat less of a fan of logicians … of their writings, at any rate. Perhaps the fault is mine, but it does seem to me that logic texts are often not as clear as they might be. For example, if I'm right that one reason for defining equivalence and bi-implication as distinct operators is that they truly are distinct in 3VL (or, more generally, NVL for all $N > 2$), it would have been helpful if the texts could have said as much—but they didn't. Which is partly why I felt it would be a good idea to write the chapter in the first place, of course.

ACKNOWLEDGMENTS

I'd like to thank Hugh Darwen for helpful comments on an earlier draft of this chapter. In fact, Hugh raised an interesting question: What does it mean for two *predicates* to be equal? Or equivalent? For example, the predicates "$a < b$" and "$x < y$" are clearly not identical, but they do "mean the same thing"; what's more, their extensions are equal, both consisting as they do of all possible true instantiations—e.g., $1 < 2$, $2 < 3$, $1 < 3$, and so forth—of the corresponding predicate. Can we say the intensions are equal as well? These are issues that deserve careful discussion—probably in a follow-on paper.

REFERENCES AND BIBLIOGRAPHY

1.   John L. Bell, David DeVidi, and Graham Solomon: *Logical Options: An Introduction to Classical and Alternative Logics*. Orchard Park, N.Y.: Broadview Press (2001).

2.   George Boolos: *Logic, Logic, and Logic*. Cambridge, Mass.: Harvard University Press (1998).

3.   Rudolf Carnap: *Introduction to Symbolic Logic and its Applications*. New York, N.Y.: Dover Publications (1958).

4.   J. N. Crossley et al: *What Is Mathematical Logic?* Mineola, N.Y.: Dover Publications (1990).

5.   John Daintith and John O. E. Clark: *The Facts on File Dictionary of Mathematics*. New York, N.Y.: Market House Books Ltd. (1999).

6.   C. J. Date: "Why Three- and Four-Valued Logic Don't Work," in *Date on Database: Writings 2000-2006*. Berkeley, Calif.: Apress (2006).

7.   C. J. Date: *The Relational Database Dictionary* (2nd edition). Sebastopol, Calif.: O'Reilly Media Inc. (to appear). *Note:* Some but not all of the definitions from this reference that are quoted in the present chapter also appear in the first edition, which was published in 2006.

8.   C. J. Date and Hugh Darwen: *Databases, Types, and the Relational Model: The Third Manifesto* (3rd edition). Boston, Mass.: Addison-Wesley (2006).

9.   Howard DeLong: *A Profile of Mathematical Logic*. Mineola, N.Y.: Dover Publications (2004).

10.   P. T. Geach: *Logic Matters*. Oxford, U.K.: Blackwell (1972).

11.   Peter M. D. Gray: *Logic, Algebra and Databases*. Chichester, England: Ellis Horwood Ltd. (1984).

12.   Samuel Guttenplan: *The Languages of Logic*. Oxford, U.K.: Blackwell (1986).

13.   Wilfrid Hodges: *Logic*. London, England: Penguin Books (1977).

14.   G. T. Kneebone: *Mathematical Logic and the Foundations of Mathematics*. Mineola, N.Y.: Dover Publications (2001).

15.   Moshé Machover: *Set Theory, Logic, and their Limitations*. Cambridge, U.K.: Cambridge University Press (1996).

16.   Zohar Manna and Richard Waldinger: *The Logical Basis for Computer Programming. Volume 1: Deductive Reasoning*. Reading, Mass.: Addison-Wesley (1985). *Volume 2: Deductive Systems*. Reading, Mass.: Addison-Wesley (1990).

17.   James D. McCawley: *Everything that Linguists Have Always Wanted to Know about Logic (but were ashamed to ask)*. Chicago, Ill.: University of Chicago Press (1981).

18.   David McGoveran: "Nothing from Nothing" (in four parts), in C. J. Date, Hugh Darwen, and David McGoveran, *Relational Database Writings 1994-1997*. Reading, Mass.: Addison-Wesley (1998).

19.   Sybil P. Parker (ed.): *The McGraw-Hill Dictionary of Mathematics*. New York, N.Y.: McGraw-Hill (1994).

20.   Howard Pospesel: *Predicate Logic: Introduction to Logic*. Englewood Cliffs, N.J.: Prentice-Hall (1976).

21.   Steve Reeves and Michael Clarke: *Logic for Computer Science*. Reading, Mass.: Addison-Wesley (1990).

22.   Raymond Reiter: "Towards a Logical Reconstruction of Relational Database Theory," in Michael L. Brodie, John Mylopoulos, and Joachim W. Schmidt (eds.), *On Conceptual Modelling: Perspectives from Artificial Intelligence, Databases, and Programming Languages*. New York, N.Y.: Springer-Verlag (1984).

23.   Nicholas Rescher: *Many-Valued Logic*. New York, N.Y.: McGraw-Hill (1969).

24.   Tom Richards: *Clausal Form Logic: An Introduction to the Logic of Computer Reasoning*. Reading, Mass.: Addison-Wesley (1989).

25.   Raymond M. Smullyan: *First-Order Logic*. Mineola, N.Y.: Dover Publications (1995).

26.   Robert R. Stoll: *Sets, Logic, and Axiomatic Theories*. San Francisco, Calif.: W. H. Freeman and Company (1961).

27.   Patrick Suppes: *Introduction to Logic*. Princeton, N.J.: Van Nostrand (1957).

28.   Paul Teller: *A Modern Formal Logic Primer. Volume I: Sentence Logic; Volume II: Predicate Logic and Metatheory*. Englewood Cliffs, N.J.: Prentice-Hall (1989).

APPENDIX A: EQUALITY IN SQL

In the body of this chapter, I said that equality has some claim to being the most fundamental logical notion of all. (Actually I made this remark in connection with *identity,* but I went on to say that equality and identity were the same thing—two values are equal if and only if they're the very same value.) I also said that the equality operator ("=") must be defined for every type. In this appendix, I simply want to note for the record some of SQL's numerous shortcomings in this regard.

- For the standard types CHAR and VARCHAR, it's possible—in fact, common—for " = " to give TRUE even when the comparands are clearly distinct (in particular, when they're of different lengths).[1]

- For numeric types, it's common (again) for " = " to give TRUE even when the comparands are clearly distinct, owing to SQL's support for implicit data type conversions (also known as coercions).

- As a direct consequence of the previous two points, it's also possible for two rows to "compare equal" even when they're clearly distinct. (Hence, the same would be true of tables also, except that SQL doesn't support equality comparisons between tables anyway—see below.)

- For the standard type XML (and the vendor-provided types BLOB and CLOB, in certain products), " = " isn't defined at all.

- For user defined types, " = " can be defined only when " < " is defined as well, and for some types " < " makes no sense; and even when " = " *is* defined, the semantics are arbitrary, in the sense that they're left to the type definer.

- For tables, " = " is simply not defined (in fact, no table comparison operators are defined at all).

- Last, it's quite common for " = " not to give TRUE even if the comparands are indistinguishable; in particular, this situation arises if both comparands are null.

---

1. It's really beyond the purview of this chapter (even of this appendix), but I can't resist pointing out that, as a direct consequence of this state of affairs, we can have two values x and y such that, in SQL, $x = y$ gives TRUE while x LIKE y gives FALSE!

Part II

LOGIC AND DATABASE MANAGEMENT

This part of the book consists of four chapters on the application (and applicability) of logic to database management in general:

3.   Constraints and Predicates

4.   The Closed World Assumption

5.   Why Relational DBMSs Are Based on Logic

6.   Why Relational DBMS Logic Must Not Be Many-Valued

Chapter 3 explains the fundamental role played by logic in the matter of data integrity, and why data integrity in turn is so important. Chapter 4 discusses the Closed World Assumption, which is adopted almost universally in the database context but seldom explicitly articulated; in particular, the chapter considers some important implications of that assumption, not all of which are immediately obvious. Finally, Chapters 5 and 6 explain in more general terms (a) why it's so important for database systems to be based on logic in general and (b) why it's so important for that logic to be conventional two-valued logic in particular.

Chapter 3

C o n s t r a i n t s   a n d   P r e d i c a t e s

Knowledge without integrity is dangerous and dreadful.

—Samuel Johnson

I first wrote a paper with a message and title very similar to those of the present chapter several years ago [7]. I wrote that paper out of a strong sense of frustration with the *status quo.* I believed then, and continue to believe now, that integrity constraints (constraints for short) and predicates are intertwined concepts that are absolutely fundamental to database management—and yet they seem to be widely underappreciated, if not completely misunderstood, in the database community at large. As we all know, the emphasis, at least in the commercial environment, seems always to be on *performance, performance, performance;* other objectives, such as ease of use, data independence, and in particular data integrity, all seem to be sacrificed to, or at best to take a back seat to, this overriding goal. But what's the point of a system that runs very fast if you can't be sure the information you're getting from it is correct? Frankly, I don't care how fast the system runs if I don't feel I can trust it to give me the right answers to my queries.

What follows is a major revision of that earlier paper. It differs from the earlier paper in several ways, of which the most important is that it does a much better job of explaining the fundamental concepts. (At least, I think it does, and I say this primarily because in the interim I've refined and improved my own understanding of those concepts considerably.) It assumes you have some familiarity with conventional two-valued logic, at least to the extent covered in reference [9], though I'll review a few pertinent concepts briefly as and when it seems appropriate to do so.

A LITTLE BACKGROUND

The notion of an integrity constraint is easy enough to understand at an intuitive level—basically it's just a truth valued expression (also known as a boolean, conditional, or logical expression) that's required to evaluate to TRUE. Here are a few simple examples, all expressed in natural language and all based on the well known suppliers-and-parts database (see the section after next for a definition of that database):

1. Every supplier status value is in the range 1 to 100 inclusive.

2. Every supplier in London has status 20.

3. If there are any parts at all, at least one of them is blue.

4. No two distinct suppliers have the same supplier number.

5. Every shipment involves an existing supplier.

6.   No supplier with status less than 20 supplies any part in a quantity greater than 500.

And so on.

Now, these examples are all fairly straightforward, and I'm sure you didn't have any difficulty understanding any of them. If history is anything to go by, however, pinning matters down more precisely turns out to be a little trickier than you might think. In support of this claim, I could cite among other things the numerous attempts, most of them not very successful, to come up with a sensible *taxonomy* or *classification scheme* for constraints. I've made several such attempts myself!—see, e.g., references [3], [6], and especially [11]. *Note:* This last reference, to spell it out, is *Databases, Types, and the Relational Model: The Third Manifesto,* a book by Hugh Darwen and myself. I'll refer to it from this point forward as the *Manifesto* book, or just the *Manifesto* for short.

Just for the record, here's a list of other writers who have tried to come up with constraint classification schemes over the years:

- Ted Codd [1]

- Ralph Kimball [14]

- Ron Ross [17]

- Mike Stonebraker [18] (the earliest attempt I know of)

- Jeff Ullman and Jennifer Widom [19]

In addition, I simply can't resist mentioning reference [15], which is a guide to the 1999 version of the SQL standard. That reference (a book) has a chapter titled "Constraints, Assertions, and Referential Integrity." What would you think of a book on biology that had a chapter titled "Birds, Feathered Bipeds, and Sparrows"? The parallel is exact. (In fairness, I should say that the SQL standard itself is partly to blame here, inasmuch as it uses the keyword CONSTRAINT in connection with some constraints and the keyword ASSERTION in connection with others. While most constraints can be expressed using either the CONSTRAINT style or the ASSERTION style, some are required to use the CONSTRAINT style and some the ASSERTION style. I have no idea why this is.)

Now I'd like to offer some evidence to support my contention that a fair number of database professionals—including in particular authors of database textbooks—don't seem to understand or appreciate the fundamental nature and importance of integrity and integrity constraints. A quick and admittedly not very scientific survey of a whole shelf load of database textbooks—37 in all, to be exact, including essentially *all* of the best known ones (in their latest editions, too)—reveals the following:[1]

---

1. It wouldn't have been appropriate to include any of my own books in this survey, and I didn't. I also didn't include reference [16], since I reviewed and commented on that book in draft form (and also wrote a foreword for it), and might therefore be accused of bias. Let me just note without further comment that that book, unlike most of the others, does include a chapter on integrity.

- Only one book had an entire chapter devoted to the topic of integrity (and even there I had severe reservations about the treatment). *Note:* At first glance it looked as if there were three others that had a whole chapter on the subject too, but closer examination revealed that one of those books was using the term to refer to normalization, while the other two were using it to refer not to integrity at all in its usual sense but rather to locking and concurrency control issues. *Caveat lector!*

- Most of the books examined didn't even mention integrity in a chapter title at all, and those that did tended to bundle it with other topics in what seems to me a very haphazard fashion ("Integrity, Views, Security, and Catalogs" is a typical example).

- I couldn't find a good explanation or definition of the concept, let alone the kind of emphasis I think the concept deserves, in any of the books at all.

With all of the foregoing in mind, I offer what follows as an aid to clarification and precise thinking (I hope!) in this potentially confusing area.

VALUES AND VARIABLES

Let me begin by observing that, logically speaking, a database is a *variable*—a large and complicated variable, probably, but a variable nonetheless. Certainly it's something that has different values at different times, and that's more or less the definition of a variable. Thus, the operation of "updating the database" causes the current value of the variable that's the database in question to be replaced by another value. And, of course, the values I'm talking about here, before and after the update, are *database values,* and the variable is a *database variable.* In other words, the crucial distinction between values and variables that I've discussed in general terms on many other occasions and in many other places (see the *Manifesto* book in particular) applies to databases in particular. *Note:* These ideas are discussed in more detail in Chapter 16 of the present book.

Likewise, the relations in a given database are also variables: They too have different values at different times. In fact, in the *Manifesto,* Hugh Darwen and I explicitly introduced the term *relation variable,* distinguishing it from the term *relation value* (relation values are the kinds of values that relation variables are permitted to have). Historically, of course, we've used the same term, *relation* (or, in SQL contexts, *table*), for both concepts—but this usage has demonstrably led to a lot of confusion, and so we decided in the *Manifesto* that we really did need two different terms. For simplicity, however, we also decided to allow those terms to be abbreviated whenever it seemed safe to do so: relation variable to *relvar,* and relation value to just *relation* (exactly as we conventionally allow, e.g., the term *integer value* to be abbreviated to just *integer*).

In the same kind of way, it would make good logical sense to talk explicitly of database values and database variables (probably allowing those terms to be abbreviated to *databases* and *dbvars,* respectively); a database variable could then be thought of, loosely, as a container for a collection of relation variables,[1] and a database value would be the value of a database variable at some particular time. Slightly against my better judgment, however, in this chapter I've decided to stick to the simple and familiar term *database* for both concepts. But I'll definitely reserve the term *relation* to mean a relation value specifically, and I'll use the term *relvar* whenever I mean a relation variable specifically.

THE SUPPLIERS-AND-PARTS DATABASE

With that preamble out of the way, let's get down to business. As usual, I'll base my examples on the suppliers-and-parts database, so let me first give a definition for that database. *Note:* That definition—which should, I hope, be more or less self-explanatory—is expressed in a slightly simplified form of **Tutorial D,** which is the language Hugh Darwen and I use as a basis for examples in the *Manifesto* book and elsewhere. For simplicity, I've omitted the underlying type (or domain) definitions, showing only the three relvar definitions—but I'm going to assume, where it makes any difference, that types INTEGER (integers) and CHAR (character strings of arbitrary length) are built in or system defined types, while types S#, NAME, P#, COLOR, WEIGHT, and QTY are user defined types.

```
VAR S BASE RELATION
    { S# S#, SNAME NAME, STATUS INTEGER, CITY CHAR }
      KEY { S# } ;

VAR P BASE RELATION
    { P# P#, PNAME NAME, COLOR COLOR, WEIGHT WEIGHT, CITY CHAR }
      KEY { P# } ;

VAR SP BASE RELATION
     { S# S#, P# P#, QTY QTY }
       KEY { S#, P# }
       FOREIGN KEY { S# } REFERENCES S
       FOREIGN KEY { P# } REFERENCES P ;
```

Fig. 3.1 (opposite) shows a set of sample values. Observe that those sample values (of course deliberately) do satisfy all of the integrity constraints 1-6 mentioned in the section "A Little Background."

A CLOSER LOOK AT EXAMPLE 1

Now we can start to consider integrity constraints as such. Essentially, an integrity constraint is a constraint on the values some given variable or combination of variables is permitted to assume. Thus, the very fact that a given variable is defined to be of a given type represents an a priori constraint on the

---

1. And, in accordance with *The Information Principle,* no other kinds of variables (see, e.g., reference [8]).

variable in question—the values that can be assumed by that variable obviously have to be values of that type. And it follows immediately (indeed, it's just a special case) that the very fact that each attribute of a given relvar is defined to be of some given type represents an a priori constraint on the relvar in question. For example, relvar S (suppliers) is constrained to contain values that are relations in which every S# value is a supplier number (a value of type S#), every SNAME value is a name (a value of type NAME), and so on.

S

S#	SNAME	STATUS	CITY
S1	Smith	20	London
S2	Jones	10	Paris
S3	Blake	30	Paris
S4	Clark	20	London
S5	Adams	30	Athens

P

P#	PNAME	COLOR	WEIGHT	CITY
P1	Nut	Red	12.0	London
P2	Bolt	Green	17.0	Paris
P3	Screw	Blue	17.0	Oslo
P4	Screw	Red	14.0	London
P5	Cam	Blue	12.0	Paris
P6	Cog	Red	19.0	London

SP

S#	P#	QTY
S1	P1	300
S1	P2	200
S1	P3	400
S1	P4	200
S1	P5	100
S1	P6	100
S2	P1	300
S2	P2	400
S3	P2	200
S4	P2	200
S4	P4	300
S4	P5	400

Fig. 3.1: The suppliers-and-parts database—sample values

However, these a priori constraints are certainly not the only ones possible; in fact, none of the examples given in the section "A Little Background" is an a priori constraint in the foregoing sense. Let's take a closer look at the first of those examples:

1.   Every supplier status value is in the range 1 to 100 inclusive.

Here's an alternative way of saying the same thing:

If *s* is a supplier, then *s* has a status value in the range 1 to 100 inclusive.

My reasons for giving this alternative formulation should become clear in a few moments.

Now, these natural language formulations are obviously quite informal. A more formal and precise formulation might look something like this:

```
FORALL s# ∈ S#, sn ∈ NAME, st ∈ INTEGER, sc ∈ CHAR
  ( IF { S# s#, SNAME sn, STATUS st, CITY sc } ∈ S
    THEN st ≥ 1 AND st ≤ 100 )
```

Before I try to explain this formulation in detail, let me say that (for reasons that are beyond the scope of this chapter) the syntax I'll be using in my formal examples isn't exactly **Tutorial D** syntax as such. But it's close to a relational calculus version of that syntax, and in particular it makes use of the truth valued operators—the technical term is *quantifiers*—FORALL and EXISTS. To review briefly (see Chapter 1 for more explanation):

- The expression FORALL $x \in X$ ($p(x)$) evaluates to TRUE if and only if the truth valued expression $p(x)$ evaluates to TRUE for all values of x in the set X (called the *range* of x).

- The expression EXISTS $x \in X$ ($p(x)$) evaluates to TRUE if and only if the truth valued expression $p(x)$ evaluates to TRUE for at least one value of x in the range X.

The x in FORALL x ... and EXISTS x ... is what's called a bound variable;[1] I'll have more to say about bound variables later. FORALL and EXISTS are known formally as the universal quantifier and the existential quantifier, respectively. Also, the symbol "ϵ" denotes the truth valued operator *is an element of;* it can alternatively be read as *belongs to,* or simply *in* (it does resemble SQL's IN operator, somewhat).

Aside: Two small points here. First, I said in Chapter 1 that the term *quantifier* applied, not to FORALL and EXISTS as such, but rather to expressions of the form FORALL x and EXISTS x. In fact, both interpretations can be found in the literature; different writers use the term in different ways. Second, I also said in Chapter 1 that quantifiers that included an explicit range specification (as in, e.g., FORALL $x \in X$) are "range coupled." All of the quantifiers shown in examples in this chapter will be range coupled in this sense. *End of aside.*

Back to the first example. It follows from all of the above that the formal version of that example can be read as follows (in rather stilted English):

For all supplier numbers *s#* and all names *sn* and all integers *st* and all character strings *sc,* if a tuple with S# *s#* and SNAME *sn* and STATUS *st* and CITY *sc* appears in the suppliers relvar, then *st* is greater than or equal to 1 and less than or equal to 100.

Perhaps you can see now why I gave that alternative natural language formulation when I originally began to discuss this example. The fact is, that alternative natural language formulation, the formal and precise formulation, and the stilted English counterpart of that precise formulation all have a certain overall "shape," as it were, that looks something like this:

---

1. More accurately, a bound variable reference.

If a certain tuple appears in a certain relvar, **then** *that tuple satisfies a certain condition.*

This shape, or pattern, is an example of what's known in logic as an *implication* (sometimes, more specifically, a *logical* or *material* implication). In general, an implication in logic takes the form

```
IF p THEN q
```

where *p* and *q* are truth valued expressions, called the *antecedent* and the *consequent,* respectively. Note that the overall implication is itself a truth valued expression in turn; it evaluates to FALSE if *p* is TRUE and *q* is FALSE, and to TRUE otherwise (in other words, IF *p* THEN *q* is logically equivalent to (NOT *p*) OR *q*).

By the way, note how the foregoing shape *implies* the FORALL quantification—"*if* a certain tuple appears" means, implicitly, "*for all* tuples that do appear."

Suppose, then, that some constraint does in fact have the foregoing shape (I don't mean to suggest that all constraints have exactly that shape, just that many do). Then it's specifically the condition that appears in the consequent that most people would regard, informally, as the integrity constraint per se. In SQL, for example, the constraint under discussion ("If *s* is a supplier, then *s* has a status value in the range 1 to 100 inclusive") would typically be expressed as follows:[1]

```
CHECK ( STATUS BETWEEN 1 AND 100 )
```

This expression would appear as part of the definition of relvar S, or what SQL would call "base table" S. And it does strongly suggest that what SQL somewhat inappropriately calls the "search condition"—i.e., the expression in parentheses—is the whole of the constraint (after all, it does say that's what's to be checked, doesn't it?).

However, while the foregoing perception (that the condition in the consequent is whole of the constraint) might perhaps be unobjectionable in informal contexts, and possibly even desirable for ergonomic reasons, it shouldn't be allowed to obscure the fact that there's really a lot more going on. That is, the SQL expression shown above must be understood as shorthand for something like the more explicit, and more complete, formal expression shown earlier.

As an aside, I note that SQL doesn't actually include any direct support for logical implication (i.e., for truth valued expressions of the form IF *p* THEN *q*) anyway—a fact that might go some way toward explaining why the SQL formulation of the constraint takes the form it does.

A CLOSER LOOK AT EXAMPLES 2-6

Let's take a look at the rest of the examples from the section "A Little Background." I'll show a precise formulation in each case and offer some commentary where I think it's needed, but I'll leave the "stilted English" and SQL formulations to you. Please understand that I make no claim that the precise

---

1. Are you sure?—I mean, are you sure that SQL's BETWEEN operator includes its specified bounds? For instance, in the example, should those bounds be 0 and 101, not 1 and 100?

formulations shown are unique, or even that they're as simple as possible; I claim only that they're correct. Each example illustrates at least one new point.

2.   Every supplier in London has status 20:

```
FORALL s# ε S#, sn ε NAME, st ε INTEGER, sc ε CHAR
  ( IF { S# s#, SNAME sn, STATUS st, CITY sc } ε S
    THEN ( IF sc = 'London' THEN st = 20 ) )
```

In this example, the consequent of the implication is itself another implication. Since an implication is a truth valued expression, it can appear wherever such an expression can appear; in particular, it can appear as the antecedent or consequent in another implication.

3.   If there are any parts at all, at least one of them is blue:

```
IF EXISTS p# ε P#, pn ε NAME, pl ε COLOR, pw ε WEIGHT, pc ε CHAR
  ( { P# p#, PNAME pn, COLOR pl, WEIGHT pw, CITY pc } ε P ) THEN
    EXISTS p# ε P#, pn ε NAME, pl ε COLOR, pw ε WEIGHT, pc ε CHAR
  ( { P# p#, PNAME pn, COLOR pl, WEIGHT pw, CITY pc } ε P ) AND
                        pl = COLOR('Blue')
```

The expression COLOR('Blue') in the last line here is a COLOR literal. Note that we can't just say "at least one part is blue"—we do have to worry about the case where there aren't any parts at all. I remark in passing that SQL tries to "help" with the formulation of this kind of constraint but predictably enough makes a hash of things ... To be specific, if the clause CHECK(*q*) is specified as part of the definition of base table *BT*, but *BT* happens to be empty, then SQL regards the constraint as satisfied *no matter what form the truth valued expression q takes* (even if it takes the form "*BT* must not be empty"!—or even the form "*BT* must have cardinality −5," or the form "1 = 0," come to that).

Incidentally, it might not be obvious, but Example 3 can in fact be made to conform to the same general shape as the first two examples, thus:

```
FORALL p# ε P#, pn ε NAME, pl ε COLOR, pw ε WEIGHT, pc ε CHAR
  ( IF { P# p#, PNAME pn, COLOR pl, WEIGHT pw, CITY pc } ε P THEN
      EXISTS q# ε P#, qn ε NAME, ql ε COLOR, qw ε WEIGHT, qc ε CHAR
    ( { P# q#, PNAME qn, COLOR ql, WEIGHT qw, CITY qc } ε P AND
                        ql = COLOR('Blue') )
```

4.   No two distinct suppliers have the same supplier number:

```
FORALL x# ε S#, xn ε NAME, xt ε INTEGER, xc ε CHAR,
        y# ε S#, yn ε NAME, yt ε INTEGER, yc ε CHAR
  ( IF { S# x#, SNAME xn, STATUS xt, CITY xc } ε S AND
        { S# y#, SNAME yn, STATUS yt, CITY yc } ε S
    THEN ( IF x# = y# THEN xn = yn AND xt = yt AND xc = yc ) )
```

This expression is just a formal statement of the fact that {S#} is a key for suppliers;[1] thus, key constraints are just a special case of constraints in general. The **Tutorial D** syntax KEY {S#} might be regarded as shorthand for the more longwinded expression. *Note:* In practice, of course, our list of constraints ought also to include (a) an analogous one for parts, saying that no two distinct parts have the same part number, and (b) an analogous one for shipments, saying that no two distinct shipments have the same supplier number and the same part number, but I've omitted these constraints for simplicity.

By the way, observe that this example takes the overall shape

If certain tuples (plural) appear in a certain relvar, **then** *those tuples satisfy a certain condition.*

Compare Examples 1-3, which all take the shape discussed in the previous section (as does Example 5, as we'll see in a moment). By contrast, Example 6 takes the overall shape

If certain tuples (plural) appear in certain relvars (also plural), **then** *those tuples satisfy a certain condition.*

The first two shapes can be regarded as special cases of this more general one.

5.   Every shipment involves an existing supplier:

```
FORALL s# ∈ S#, p# ∈ P#, q ∈ QTY
  ( IF { S# s#, P# p#, QTY q } ∈ SP
    THEN EXISTS sn ∈ NAME, st ∈ INTEGER, sc ∈ CHAR
      ( { S# s#, SNAME sn, STATUS st, CITY sc } ∈ S ) )
```

This expression is a formal statement of the fact that {S#} is a foreign key for shipments, matching the key {S#} for suppliers; thus, foreign key constraints too are just a special case of constraints in general. *Note:* In practice, of course, our list of constraints ought really to include one to say that every shipment involves an existing part as well, but again I've omitted that constraint for simplicity.

Incidentally, this example is the first we've seen to involve two distinct relvars (SP and S, in the example)—all the previous examples involved just one. It's convenient, sometimes, to refer to a constraint that involves just one relvar as a *single-relvar constraint* and a constraint that involves two or more relvars as a *multi-relvar constraint*. Certainly this distinction mirrors the way we tend to think about constraints in practice; while it might be useful from a pragmatic point of view, however, it's not very important from a theoretical one, and I won't bother with it much in the remainder of this chapter. *Note:* In various earlier writings, I've used the term *relvar constraint* to mean a single-relvar constraint and the term *database constraint* to mean a multi-relvar constraint. These latter terms are now deprecated, however, for reasons that will become apparent in the section "Relvar and Database

---

1. More precisely, it's a formal statement of the fact that {S#} is a *superkey* for suppliers. A superkey is a superset—not necessarily a proper superset, of course—of a key; thus, all keys are superkeys, but some superkeys are not keys. But this issue is tangential to the main discussion, and I won't pursue it any further here.

Constraints," later.

6. No supplier with status less than 20 supplies any part in a quantity greater than 500:

```
FORALL s# ∈ S#, sn ∈ NAME, st ∈ INTEGER, sc ∈ CHAR,
       p# ∈ P#, q ∈ QTY
  ( IF { S# s#, SNAME sn, STATUS st, CITY sc } ∈ S AND
       { S# s#, P# p#, QTY q } ∈ SP
    THEN st ≥ 20 OR q ≤ QTY(500) )
```

Like the previous example, this one too involves two distinct relvars (S and SP again, of course), but it's certainly not a foreign key constraint. Not all multi-relvar constraints are foreign key constraints. (Come to that, not all foreign key constraints are multi-relvar constraints, either—though designs in which they're not are usually contraindicated.)

CONSTRAINTS ARE PROPOSITIONS

Consider once again the precise formulation of Example 1 ("Every supplier status value is in the range 1 to 100 inclusive"):

```
FORALL s# ∈ S#, sn ∈ NAME, st ∈ INTEGER, sc ∈ CHAR
  ( IF { S# s#, SNAME sn, STATUS st, CITY sc } ∈ S
    THEN st ≥ 1 AND st ≤ 100 )
```

As I pointed out in the previous section, this constraint involves just a single relvar; in fact, it involves just one variable of any kind—namely, the suppliers relvar S. Let me immediately qualify this remark! In fact, of course, the constraint does involve certain "bound" variables as well—namely, *s#, sn, st,* and *sc.* However, bound variables aren't variables in the usual programming sense; rather, bound variables are variables in the sense of logic. You can think of a bound variable as a kind of dummy variable, in a sense. For consider:

- If we replace all appearances within the formal expression shown above of, e.g., the symbol *st* by any other symbol, say *xyz,* the constraint remains logically unchanged.

- By contrast, the same is certainly not true if we replace all appearances of, e.g., the symbol S—which denotes a "nondummy" variable, of course—by, say, the symbol SP.

From this point forward, I'll take the term *variable* to mean a variable in the usual programming sense specifically, not a variable in the sense of logic (barring explicit statements to the contrary).

To say it again, then, the formal expression of the constraint involves a variable, S. Thus, although that expression is indeed truth valued, we can't say what its value is—i.e., we can't say what truth value it yields—until we substitute a value for that variable. (Indeed, different substitutions will yield different truth values, in general.) What value do we substitute? Why, whatever value happens to be the current value of the variable in question (of course!). Thus, if the current value of relvar S happens to be as shown here—

S#	SNAME	STATUS	CITY
S1	Smith	20	London
S2	Jones	10	Paris

—then, at the time it's evaluated, the constraint is effectively replaced by this expression:

```
FORALL s# ∈ S#, sn ∈ NAME, st ∈ INTEGER, sc ∈ CHAR
( IF { S# s#,          SNAME sn,                STATUS st, CITY sc } =
     { S# S#('S1'), SNAME NAME('Smith'), STATUS 20, CITY 'London' }
  OR { S# s#,          SNAME sn,                STATUS st, CITY sc } =
     { S# S#('S2'), SNAME NAME('Jones'), STATUS 10, CITY 'Paris'  }
  THEN st ≥ 1 AND st ≤ 100 )
```

And this expression clearly evaluates to TRUE, as required.

A variable reference such as S in the formal statement of the foregoing constraint is acting as what's called a *designator*. A designator in logic is an expression—in natural language, it's a noun phrase—that can be used within a proposition and uniquely designates some object. (I remind you that a proposition in logic is something that evaluates to TRUE or FALSE, unequivocally.) In the example, the variable reference S designates the relation that happens to be the value of the relvar S at the time the constraint is checked.

Remarks analogous to the foregoing apply to constraints involving two, three, four, ..., or any number of relvars; in all cases, when we need to evaluate the expression—in other words, when we need to check the constraint—we substitute, for each relvar reference in the constraint as stated, the current value of the relvar so designated, and we wind up with an expression that evaluates to either TRUE or FALSE (and in fact is required to evaluate to TRUE).

The net of the foregoing discussion is this: *Constraints are propositions.*[1] They're formulated in terms of certain variables—certain relation variables, in fact, and no other kinds—but those variables act merely as designators, and they're effectively replaced by the current values of the designated relvars whenever the constraint is to be checked.

---

1. I'm on record elsewhere as saying that constraints are *predicates*. I could still defend that earlier position if I really had to, but I now believe the position I'm articulating here is logically preferable.

RELVAR AND DATABASE CONSTRAINTS

A relvar can be subject to any number of constraints. Let *R* be a relvar. Then *the relvar constraint* (sometimes the *total* relvar constraint, for emphasis) for *R* is the logical AND, or conjunction, of (a) all of the individual constraints that apply to (i.e., mention) relvar *R* and (b) TRUE.[1] Please don't get confused here!—each individual constraint is indeed a constraint in its own right, but *the* relvar constraint is the conjunction of all of those individual ones (and TRUE). For example, if we assume for simplicity that Examples 1-6 are the only constraints that apply to the suppliers-and-parts database (apart from a priori ones), then the relvar constraint for suppliers is the conjunction of Numbers 1, 2, 4, 5, and 6, and the relvar constraint for shipments is the conjunction of Numbers 5 and 6 (again, and TRUE in both cases; I won't keep saying this). Note, incidentally, that these two relvar constraints "overlap," in a sense, in that they have certain constituent constraints in common.

   Note: I might be accused here of moving the goalposts a little. I mentioned earlier in this chapter (in the section "A Closer Look at Examples 2-6") that I used to use the term *relvar constraint* to mean a single-relvar constraint. Accordingly, I also used to use the term "*the* relvar constraint for relvar *R*" to mean the conjunction of all *single-relvar* constraints that applied to *R*. Now I'm using the term to mean the conjunction of *all* constraints, single- and multi-relvar, that apply to *R*. My apologies to anyone who might find this shift in terminology confusing.

   Let *R* be a relvar, and let *RC* be the total relvar constraint for *R*. Clearly, then, *R* must never be allowed to have a value that, when it's substituted for *R* in *RC* (and when any other necessary similar substitutions have also been made in *RC*), causes *RC* to evaluate to FALSE. Thus, I can now introduce **The Golden Rule** (or the first version of that rule, at any rate):

   No update operation must ever assign to any relvar a value that causes its total relvar constraint to evaluate to FALSE.

   Now let *D* be a database, and let *D* contain relvars *R1, R2, ...Rn* (only). Let the relvar constraints for those relvars be *RC1, RC2, ..., RCn,* respectively. Then *the database constraint* (sometimes the *total* database constraint, for emphasis) for *D—DC,* say—is the conjunction of all of those relvar constraints and TRUE:

       DC = RC1 AND RC2 AND ... AND RCn AND TRUE

   As an aside, let me remind you that (as we've seen) two distinct relvar constraints *RCi* and *RCj* (*i* ≠ *j*) might have certain constituent constraints in common. It follows that the very same constraint might appear many times over in the database constraint *DC*. From a logical point of view, of course, there's no harm in this state of affairs, because if *p* is a proposition, then *p* AND *p* is logically equivalent to just *p*—though naturally I would hope that the system would be smart enough to evaluate any such repeated constraint once only, not many times over.

   Here then is the extended (more general, and final) version of **The Golden Rule:**

---

1. The reason for including TRUE in the conjunction is to ensure that, in the unlikely case of a relvar *R* that has no constraints explicitly defined for it at all, *R* is at least subject to the "default constraint" TRUE.

> *No update operation must ever assign to any database a value that causes its database constraint to evaluate to FALSE.*

Of course, a database constraint will evaluate to FALSE if and only if at least one of its constituent relvar constraints does so too. And a relvar constraint will evaluate to FALSE if and only if at least one of its individual constituent constraints does so too.

A NOTE ON CONSTRAINT CHECKING

I'll have more to say about **The Golden Rule** in the next section. First, however, I want to consider the question of what everything I've said so far implies for the practical issue of actually checking constraints. Once again, let's return to Example 1 ("Every supplier status value is in the range 1 to 100 inclusive"):

```
FORALL s# ε S#, sn ε NAME, st ε INTEGER, sc ε CHAR
  ( IF { S# s#, SNAME sn, STATUS st, CITY sc } ε S
     THEN st ≥ 1 AND st ≤ 100 )
```

As I pointed out earlier, this constraint is effectively saying that if a certain tuple appears in relvar S, then that tuple has to satisfy a certain condition (status in the range 1 to 100, in the case at hand). Apparently, therefore, if we try to insert a new supplier tuple with status (say) 200, the sequence of events has to be:

1.   Insert the new tuple.

2.   Check the constraint.

3.   Undo the update (because the check fails).

But this is absurd! Clearly, we would like to catch the error before the INSERT is done in the first place. So what the implementation needs to do, insofar as possible, is use the formal expression of the constraint to *infer* the appropriate check(s) to be performed on tuples that are presented for insertion before that insertion is actually performed.

I don't want to get into details of what's involved in that inference process here. However, I think you can at least see that if the overall database constraint includes a constituent constraint of the form

```
IF { S# s#, SNAME sn, STATUS st, CITY sc } ε S THEN ...
```

—i.e., if the antecedent is of the form "some tuple appears in S"—then the consequent is essentially a constraint on tuples that are presented for insertion into relvar S, and that constraint, at least, can be checked before the insertion is actually done. (Just to remind you, the antecedent is the portion between the IF and the THEN, and the consequent is the portion after the THEN.)

ALL CHECKING IS IMMEDIATE!

Here again is **The Golden Rule:**

No update operation must ever assign to any database a value that causes its database constraint to evaluate to FALSE.

Now, I didn't point it out explicitly before, but you might have realized that this rule as stated implies that *all constraint checking is immediate.* Why? Because it talks in terms of *update operations*—in other words, INSERT, DELETE, and UPDATE operations, loosely speaking—and not in terms of transactions (see below). In effect, therefore, **The Golden Rule** requires integrity constraints to be satisfied *at statement boundaries,*[1] and there's no notion of "deferred" or COMMIT-time integrity checking at all.

In order to explain the foregoing properly, I first need to say a little more about transactions. Of course, transactions are a big topic in their own right, even if we limit our attention (as I want to do here) to their integrity aspects specifically, so what follows is only the briefest of brief sketches. Reference [13]—highly recommended, by the way—is the standard reference if you want to learn more.

First of all, then, I do assume you're familiar with the basic transaction concept: in particular, with the so called ACID properties of transactions. ACID is an acronym for *atomicity - consistency - isolation - durability. Atomicity* means transactions are "all or nothing." *Consistency* means they transform a consistent state of the database into another consistent state, without necessarily preserving consistency at all intermediate points. *Isolation* means that any given transaction's updates are concealed from all other transactions, until the given transaction commits. *Durability* means that once a transaction commits, its updates survive in the database, even if there's a subsequent system crash.

To get back to **The Golden Rule:** As you'll surely realize, the idea that all checking must be immediate, not deferred, is a very unorthodox one. After all, the SQL standard certainly includes support for deferred checking, and there's at least one commercial product—namely, IBM's DB2 for VSE, originally called SQL/DS—that implements such a capability.[2] Moreover, one of the arguments in favor of the transaction concept has always been that transactions are supposed to be (among other things) *a unit of integrity:* As I put it a few moments ago, they're supposed to "transform a consistent state of the database into another consistent state, without necessarily preserving consistency at all intermediate points." So do I contradict myself? Very well, I contradict myself. To be specific, I no longer believe in transactions as a unit of integrity; instead, I now think *statements* have to be that unit.

So why have I changed my mind? I have at least five reasons, but easily the biggest is as

---

1. I realize that I need to be more precise here, but making matters more precise depends to some extent on the particular language we're dealing with. For present purposes, suffice it to say that constraints must be satisfied at the end of each and every statement that contains no other statement nested syntactically inside itself. Or (somewhat loosely): *Constraints must be satisfied at semicolons.*

2. In fact, DB2 for VSE used to allow checking to be deferred past COMMIT time (which even the SQL standard doesn't allow). I don't know whether it still does.

follows.[1] As I've written elsewhere, a database can be regarded as *a collection of propositions,* assumed by convention to be ones that evaluate to TRUE. And if that collection is ever allowed to include any inconsistencies, *then all bets are off!* You can never trust the answers you get from an inconsistent database; in fact, you can get absolutely any answer whatsoever from such a database. (Indeed, it's easy to prove that you can get absolutely any answer you like—or don't like—from such a database. See the final section in this chapter.) While proper concurrency control, or in other words the isolation or "I" property of transactions, can mean that no more than one transaction ever sees any particular inconsistency, the fact remains nonetheless that that particular transaction does see the inconsistency and can thus produce wrong answers. Indeed, it's precisely because inconsistencies can't be tolerated, not even if they're never visible to more than one transaction at a time, that we need the constraints to be enforced in the first place—and that's why integrity is such a fundamental feature of a database system.

Now, I think this first argument is strong enough to stand on its own, but I'll give the other four arguments as well, for purposes of reference if nothing else. Second, then, I don't agree that any given inconsistency can be seen by only one transaction, anyway; that is, I don't believe in the isolation property. Part of the problem here is that the word *isolation* doesn't quite mean the same thing in the world of transactions as it does in ordinary English—in particular, it doesn't mean that transactions can't communicate with one another. For if transaction *T1* produces some result, in the database or elsewhere, that's subsequently read by transaction *T2,* then *T1* and *T2* aren't truly isolated from each other (and this remark applies regardless of whether *T1* and *T2* run concurrently or otherwise). In particular, therefore, if (a) *T1* sees an inconsistent state of the database and therefore produces an incorrect result, and (b) that result is then seen by *T2,* then (c) the inconsistency seen by *T1* has effectively been propagated to *T2.* In other words, it can't be guaranteed that a given inconsistency, if permitted, will be seen by just one transaction, anyway.

Third, we surely don't want every program (or other "code unit") to have to cater for the possibility that the database might be inconsistent when it's invoked. There's a severe loss of orthogonality if a program that assumes consistency can't be used safely while constraint checking is deferred. In other words, I want to be able to design code units independently of whether they're to be executed as a transaction as such or just as part of a transaction. (In fact, I'd like support for nested transactions, but that's a topic for another day.)

Fourth, *The Principle of Interchangeability* (of base relvars and views—see, e.g., reference [8]) implies that the very same constraint might be a single-relvar constraint with one design for the database and a multi-relvar constraint with another.[2] For example, consider these two views of the suppliers relvar, LS and NLS ("London suppliers" and "non London suppliers," respectively):

```
VAR LS  VIRTUAL ( S WHERE CITY = 'London' ) ;

VAR NLS VIRTUAL ( S WHERE CITY ≠ 'London' ) ;
```

---

1. The remainder of this section consists of a lightly edited version of text from reference [8].

2. Base (or real) relvars are the *Manifesto*'s counterparts to what SQL would call base tables; likewise, virtual relvars are the *Manifesto*'s counterparts to what SQL would call views. In what follows, I'll use the terms *virtual relvar* and *view* interchangeably.

These views satisfy the constraint that no supplier number appears in both. However, there's no need to state that constraint explicitly, because it's implied by the single-relvar constraint that {S#} is a key for relvar S (along with the fact that every supplier has exactly one city, which actually is also implied by the fact that {S#} is a key for S). But suppose we made LS and NLS base relvars and defined their union as a view called S. Then the constraint would have to be stated explicitly:

```
FORALL x# ϵ S#, xn ϵ NAME, xt ϵ INTEGER, xc ϵ CHAR,
       y# ϵ S#, yn ϵ NAME, yt ϵ INTEGER, yc ϵ CHAR
  ( IF { S# x#, SNAME xn, STATUS xt, CITY xc } ϵ LS AND
       { S# y#, SNAME yn, STATUS yt, CITY yc } ϵ NLS
    THEN x# ≠ y# )
```

So what was previously a single-relvar constraint has become a multi-relvar constraint instead. Thus, if we agree that single-relvar constraints must be checked immediately, we must surely agree that multi-relvar constraints must be checked immediately as well.

Fifth and last, *semantic optimization* requires the database to be consistent at all times, not just at transaction boundaries. Now, I really don't want to get into details of semantic optimization here; suffice it to say that it's a technique for using integrity constraints to simplify queries (in order to improve performance, of course). Clearly, if some constraint is violated at some time, then any simplification based on that constraint won't be valid at that time, and query results based on that simplification will be wrong at that time (in general).

MULTIPLE ASSIGNMENT

At this point, you might object that some integrity checking simply has to be deferred, doesn't it? As a trivial example, consider the constraint "Supplier S1 and part P1 are in the same city." If supplier S1 moves, say from London to Paris, then part P1 must move from London to Paris as well. The conventional solution to this problem is to wrap the two updates up into a single transaction, like this:

```
BEGIN TRANSACTION ;
    UPDATE S WHERE S# = S#('S1') ( CITY := 'Paris' ) ;
    UPDATE P WHERE P# = P#('P1') ( CITY := 'Paris' ) ;
COMMIT ;
```

In this conventional solution, the constraint is defined to be DEFERRED, and the checking is done at COMMIT—and the database is inconsistent between the two UPDATE operations. Note in particular that if the transaction performing the UPDATEs were to ask the question "Are supplier S1 and part P1 in the same city?" between the two UPDATE operations, it would get the answer *no*.

Before I can explain the *Manifesto* solution to this kind of problem, I need to remind you that INSERT, DELETE, and UPDATE are just shorthand for certain relational assignment operations (see, e.g., reference [8]). For example, the UPDATE to relvar S in the foregoing transaction is really just shorthand for the following assignment statement:

```
S := WITH ( S WHERE S# = S#('S1') ) AS T1,
          ( EXTEND T1 ADD ( 'Paris' AS NCITY ) ) AS T2,
          ( T2 { ALL BUT CITY } ) AS T3,
          ( T3 RENAME ( NCITY AS CITY ) ) AS T4 :
     ( S MINUS T1 ) UNION T4 ;
```

Now back to the *Manifesto*. The *Manifesto* solves the kind of problem under discussion by introducing a *multiple* assignment operator [12], which lets us carry out several assignments as a single operation (i.e., as part of a single statement), without any integrity checking being done until all of the assignments in question have been executed. For example:

```
UPDATE S WHERE S# = S#('S1') ( CITY := 'Paris' ) ,
UPDATE P WHERE P# = P#('P1') ( CITY := 'Paris' ) ;
```

This "double UPDATE" is logically equivalent to a certain "double assignment" of the form:

```
S := ... , P := ... ;
```

Note the comma separator, which means the two UPDATEs—equivalently, the two individual assignments—are both part of the same statement. Of course, I don't mean to suggest that the problem under consideration can be solved simply by a tiny change in syntax! Rather, the point is that we do need to be able to bundle up the two UPDATEs into a single statement somehow, and so we need some syntax to specify that bundling. So we use a comma for that purpose, and no integrity checking is done "until we get to the semicolon." Note in particular that there's now no way for the transaction[1] to see an inconsistent state of the database between the two UPDATEs, because the notion of "between the two UPDATEs" is one that now has no meaning.

Given the availability of the multiple assignment operator, there's now no need for deferred checking—i.e., checking that's deferred to end of transaction—in the traditional sense at all. *Note:* There's much more that could and should be said about multiple assignment in general, but a detailed discussion would be out of place here. See reference [12] for further details.

---

1. Of course, we do still need the transaction concept for other purposes (in particular, we need it as the unit of recovery and the unit of concurrency), even if we reject it as a unit of integrity. I mention this point because I've been criticized in the past for wanting to eliminate transactions altogether. As a matter of fact, I do think it might be possible to eliminate transactions altogether, at least as far as the user is concerned, but that's not the point at issue here. In any case, regardless of whether transactions as such are necessary, the techniques used to implement them in today's DBMSs (e.g., locking) would still be needed to implement multiple assignment.

RELVAR PREDICATES

As we've seen, each relvar has a relvar constraint and the database overall has a database constraint. Now, I hope it's obvious that these constraints are "understood by the system": They're stated formally (they're part of the database definition, in fact), and of course they're enforced by the system, too. Now I want to go on and show that each relvar has a *relvar predicate* as well, and the database overall has a *database predicate* as well. Unlike the corresponding constraints, however, these predicates are necessarily somewhat informal; they can be thought of, loosely, as *what the data means to the user.* (By contrast, the constraints can be thought of, again loosely, as *what the data means to the system.* They can also be thought of as the system's approximation to the predicates.) Let's take a closer look. Until further notice, I'll concentrate on relvars specifically.

As just indicated, the relvar predicate for a given relvar is basically what that relvar means to the user. In the case of the suppliers relvar S, for example, the relvar predicate might look something like this:

The supplier with the specified supplier number (S#) is under contract, has the specified name (SNAME) and the specified status (STATUS) and is located in the specified city (CITY). Moreover, the status value is in the range 1 to 100 inclusive, and must be 20 if the city is London. Also, no two distinct suppliers have the same supplier number.

For the sake of the discussion that follows, however, I'm going to replace this predicate by the following simpler one:

Supplier S# is named SNAME, has status STATUS, and is located in CITY.

After all, the relvar predicate is, as already stated, only informal, so we're at liberty to make it as simple or as complex as we please (within reason, of course).

Now, note that the foregoing statement is indeed a predicate (i.e., a truth valued function)—it has four parameters, S#, SNAME, STATUS, and CITY, corresponding to the four attributes of the relvar, and when arguments of the appropriate types are substituted for those parameters, it yields a proposition (i.e., something that evaluates categorically to either TRUE or FALSE).

Each tuple appearing in relvar S at any given time can now be regarded as denoting a certain proposition, obtained by instantiating the foregoing relvar predicate. As already indicated, the instantiation involves substituting arguments of the appropriate type for the parameters of the relvar predicate. For example, if we substitute the S# value S1, the NAME value Smith, the INTEGER value 20, and the CHAR value London for the relevant parameters, we obtain the proposition:

Supplier S1 is named Smith, has status 20, and is located in London.

Likewise, if we substitute the S# value S2, the NAME value Jones, the INTEGER value 10, and the CHAR value Paris, we obtain:

Supplier S2 is named Jones, has status 10, and is located in Paris.

And so on.

To repeat, tuples of the relvar correspond to instantiations of the relvar predicate. And—very important!—those particular instantiations (in other words, those particular propositions) are ones that are understood by convention to be ones that evaluate to TRUE. For example, if the tuple

```
{ S# S#('S1'), SNAME NAME('Smith'), STATUS 20, CITY 'London' }
```

does indeed appear in relvar S at some given time, then we're to understand that "it's a true fact that" there does exist at that time a supplier with supplier number S1, named Smith, with status 20, and located in London.[1] More generally, we can say that:

```
IF ( s ε S ) THEN PS ( s )
```

("If *s* appears in S, then *PS(s)* is true.") Here:

- *s* is a supplier tuple—i.e., a tuple of the form

  ```
  { S# s#, SNAME sn, STATUS st, CITY sc }
  ```

  (where *s#* is a value of type S#, *sn* is a value of type NAME, *st* is a value of type INTEGER, and *sc* is a value of type CITY).

- *PS* is the relvar predicate for suppliers.

- *PS(s)* is the proposition obtained by instantiating *PS* with the argument values S# *s#*, SNAME *sn*, STATUS *st*, and CITY *sc*.

However, we go a step further with relvar predicates than we do with relvar constraints. To be specific, we adopt the *Closed World Assumption* [10], which says among other things that if an otherwise valid tuple does not appear in the relvar at some given time, then the proposition corresponding to that tuple is understood by convention to evaluate to FALSE at that time. For example, if the tuple

```
{ S# S#('S6'), SNAME NAME('Lopez'), STATUS 30, CITY 'Madrid' }
```

fails to appear in relvar S at some given time, then we're to understand that *it's not the case that* there exists at that time a supplier with supplier number S6, named Lopez, with status 30, and located in Madrid. More generally:

```
IF NOT ( s ε S ) THEN NOT ( PS ( s ) )
```

Putting the foregoing together, we have simply:

---

1. Yes, I know facts are true by definition and "true fact" is a pleonasm, but—like Edward Abbey—I like the emphasis.

$$s \in S \equiv PS (s)$$

In words: A given tuple appears in a given relvar at a given time if and only if that tuple causes the predicate for that relvar to evaluate to TRUE at that time. (As explained in Chapters 1 and 2, the symbol " $\equiv$ " can be read as "if and only if" or "is equivalent to.") It follows that a given relvar contains *all* and *only* the tuples that correspond to true instantiations of that relvar's predicate at the time in question.

Note: I've said that users have to understand the relvar predicates. Of course, they have to understand the relvar constraints too; but the system has to understand—indeed, *can* understand—only the constraints, not the predicates. (Though it's at least true that if tuple *t* appears in relvar *R* at some given time, then the system does "understand" that $PR(t)$, where PR is the relvar predicate for *R,* is true at the time in question.)

CORRECTNESS *vs.* CONSISTENCY

To repeat, relvar predicates and the propositions obtained by instantiating such predicates aren't, and in fact can't be, "understood by the system." There's no way, for example, that the system can know what it means for a "supplier" to "be located" somewhere, or what it means for a "supplier" to "have a status" (etc.). All such issues are matters of *interpretation;* they're matters that make sense to the user but not to the system. For example, if the supplier number S1 and the city name London happen to appear together in the same tuple, then the user can interpret that fact to mean that supplier S1 is located in London,[1] but (to repeat) there's no way the system can do anything analogous.

What's more, even if the system could know what it means for a supplier to be located somewhere, it still couldn't know a priori whether what the user tells it is true! If the user asserts to the system—typically by executing a corresponding INSERT operation—that supplier S1 is located in London, there's no way for the system to know whether that assertion is true. All the system can do is make sure that the user's assertion doesn't lead to any constraint violations (i.e., it doesn't cause any constraint to evaluate to FALSE). Assuming it doesn't, then the system must accept the user's assertion *and treat it as true from that point forward* (or, rather, until the user tells the system—typically by executing a corresponding DELETE operation—that it isn't true any more).

By the way, the foregoing paragraph shows clearly why the Closed World Assumption doesn't apply to constraints. To be specific, a tuple might satisfy the constraint for a given relvar and yet validly not appear in that relvar, because it doesn't correspond to a true proposition in the real world.

We can summarize all of the above by saying that, informally, the predicate for a given relvar is *the intended interpretation* for that relvar. As such, it's important to the user, but not to the system (at least, it's not important to the system so far as the present discussion is concerned). We can also say,

---

1. Or that supplier S1 *used to be* located in London, or that supplier S1 *has an office* in London, or that supplier S1 *doesn't* have an office in London, or any of an infinite number of other possible interpretations (corresponding, of course, to an infinite number of possible relvar predicates). *Note:* Actually, the interpretation "Supplier S1 doesn't have an office in London" would be very unlikely in practice. Chapter 4 explains why this is so, but you might like to think about the issue for yourself before you get to that chapter.

again informally, that the predicate for a given relvar is the *criterion for acceptability of updates* on the relvar in question—i.e., it dictates, at least in principle, whether a requested INSERT or DELETE or UPDATE operation on that relvar can be allowed to succeed. Ideally, therefore, the system would know and understand the predicate for every relvar, so that it could deal correctly with all possible attempts to update the database. Unfortunately, however, we've already seen that this goal is unachievable; that is, the system can't know the predicate for any given relvar, in general. *But it does know a good approximation:* It knows the corresponding constraint—and that's what it will enforce. (Thus, the pragmatic "criterion for acceptability of updates," as opposed to the ideal one, is the constraint, not the predicate.) Another way of saying the same thing is as follows:

> *The system can't enforce truth, only consistency.*

That is, the system can't guarantee that the database contains only true propositions—all it can do is guarantee that it doesn't contain anything that causes any integrity constraint to be violated (i.e. it doesn't contain any inconsistencies). Sadly, truth and consistency aren't the same thing! Indeed, we can observe that:

- If the database contains only true propositions, then it's consistent, but the converse isn't necessarily so.

- If the database is inconsistent, then it contains at least one "false fact," but the converse isn't necessarily so.

More succinctly: *Correct* implies *consistent* (but not the other way around), and *inconsistent* implies *incorrect* (but not the other way around). *Note:* By *correct* here, I mean the database is correct if and only if it fully reflects the true state of affairs in the real world.

A NOTE ON DATABASE DESIGN

I've said that relvar predicates are important to the user. Why? Well, because (as previously stated) those relvar predicates represent the intended interpretation for the corresponding relvars. The point is this: Clearly, each relvar is supposed to represent some aspect of the real world—in other words, each relvar is supposed to have a *meaning*—and users need to know those meanings (i.e., those intended interpretations) if they're to be able to use the database effectively and efficiently. That's all.

There's another point to be made here, though. The fact is, all this business of relvar predicates is very closely related to the business of (logical) *database design*. Indeed, at a certain level of abstraction—and ignoring the fact that, in practice, the process is highly iterative, as we all know—we can characterize the database design process as consisting of the following two steps:

1. Pin down the relvar predicates as carefully as possible (albeit informally, of course).

2. Map the output from the first step into a set of formal relvars and corresponding constraints.

Which brings me to a small piece of unfinished business. I've discussed relvar predicates at some length. What about the overall database? Well, as I'm sure you've guessed, the predicate for the overall database—which represents the intended interpretation for that database—is simply the conjunction (i.e., the logical AND) of the relvar predicates for all of the relvars in that database.

PREDICATES FOR DERIVED RELVARS

There's another important point that I've been ducking so far but I now need to spell out, as follows: Basically, everything I've been saying applies to *all relvars,* not just to base ones. In particular, it applies to views. Thus, views too are subject to constraints and have predicates. For example, suppose we define a view—let's call it SST—by projecting the suppliers relvar over attributes S#, SNAME, and STATUS (thereby effectively removing attribute CITY). Then the predicate for view SST looks something like this:

> *There exists some city CITY such that supplier S# is named SNAME, has status STATUS, and is located in CITY.*

Observe that, as required, this predicate does have three parameters, not four, corresponding to the three attributes of relvar SST (CITY is now no longer a parameter but a bound variable instead, thanks to the fact that it's quantified by the phrase "there exists some city"). Another, perhaps clearer, way of making the same point is to observe that the predicate as stated is logically equivalent to this one:

> *Supplier S# is named SNAME, has status STATUS, and is located in some city.*

This version of the predicate very clearly has just three parameters.

What about constraints on this view? Well, here once again are the six examples from the beginning of this chapter:

1.   Every supplier status value is in the range 1 to 100 inclusive.

2.   Every supplier in London has status 20.

3.   If there are any parts at all, at least one of them is blue.

4.   No two distinct suppliers have the same supplier number.

5.   Every shipment involves an existing supplier.

6.   No supplier with status less than 20 supplies any part in a quantity greater than 500.

Of these six, Number 3 is clearly irrelevant as far as view SST is concerned, since it has to do with parts, not suppliers. As for the rest, each of them does also apply to view SST, but in a slightly modified form. Here, for example, is the modified form of Number 5:

```
FORALL s# ε S#, p# ε P#, q ε QTY
  ( IF { S# s#, P# p#, QTY q } ε SP
    THEN EXISTS sn ε NAME, st ε INTEGER
       ( { S# s#, SNAME sn, STATUS st } ε SST ) )
```

The changes are in the third and fourth lines: All references to CITY have been dropped, and the reference to S has been replaced by a reference to SST. Note that we can regard this constraint for SST as being derived from the corresponding constraint for S, much as relvar SST itself is derived from relvar S. Note too that (to use SQL terminology) this constraint for SST is effectively a foreign key constraint from a base table to a view!

Analogous remarks apply directly to Numbers 1, 2, 4, and 6. Number 2 is slightly tricky, though. Here it is:

```
FORALL s# ε S#, sn ε NAME, st ε INTEGER
  ( IF { S# s#, SNAME sn, STATUS st } ε SST THEN
    EXISTS sc ε CHAR ( { S# s#, SNAME sn, STATUS st, CITY sc } ε S
                     AND ( IF sc = 'London' THEN st = 20 ) )
```

Again, however, we can regard this constraint as being derived from the corresponding constraint for S.

A CONSTRAINT CLASSIFICATION SCHEME

Near the beginning of this chapter, I mentioned that several people have tried to come up with a taxonomy or classification scheme for constraints. In this section I'd like to sketch the scheme I use myself. That scheme classifies constraints into multi-relvar, single-relvar, attribute, and type constraints. In outline:

- A *multi-relvar* constraint (previously called a *database* constraint) is a constraint on the values two or more given relvars are permitted to assume in combination.

- A *single-relvar* constraint (previously called just a *relvar* constraint, unqualified) is a constraint on the values a given relvar is permitted to assume.

- An *attribute* constraint is a constraint on the values a given attribute is permitted to assume.

- A *type* constraint is, precisely, a definition of the set of values that constitute a given type.

Now, I haven't really discussed type constraints at all in this chapter so far. Such constraints are conceptually very simple, however. For example, we might have a type constraint for type POINT (meaning points in two-dimensional space) that says, in effect, that something is a valid point if and only if it can be represented by a pair of numeric values x and y such that x and y are both in the range (say) -100.0 to $+100.0$. Note that this type constraint is, as required, nothing more nor less than a definition of the set of values that constitute the type in question.

Type constraints are checked as part of the execution of the applicable *selector*—where a selector is an operator that lets us "select," or specify, an arbitrary value of the type in question. For example, here are a couple of examples of selector invocations for type POINT:[1]

```
POINT ( 5.0, 2.5 )
/* selects the point with x = 5.0, y = 2.5 */

POINT ( XXX, YYY )
/* selects the point with x = XXX, y = YYY, where */
/* XXX and YYY are variables of type NUMERIC, say */
```

And here's an example of an invalid one (i.e., a POINT selector invocation that will fail):

```
POINT ( 0.0, 1000.0 )
/* error: y value out of range */
```

As you can see, selectors—or, more precisely, selector *invocations*—are a generalization of the familiar concept of a literal; that is, all literals are selector invocations, but not all selector invocations are literals. (In fact, a selector invocation is a literal if and only if its operands are all literals in turn.)

Second, *attribute constraints* are basically what I called a priori constraints near the beginning of this chapter; in other words, an attribute constraint is basically just a statement to the effect that a specified attribute of a specified relvar is of a specified type. For example, consider the following relvar definition once again:

```
VAR S BASE RELATION
  { S# S#, SNAME NAME, STATUS INTEGER, CITY CHAR }
    KEY { S# } ;
```

In this relvar:

- Values of attribute S# are constrained to be of type S#.

- Values of attribute SNAME are constrained to be of type NAME.

- Values of attribute STATUS are constrained to be of type INTEGER.

- Values of attribute CITY are constrained to be of type CHAR.

Finally, single- and multi-relvar constraints are what I've been concentrating on throughout the bulk of this chapter. I remind you, though, that the distinction between these two kinds of constraints

---

1. Actually we've already seen some examples of selector invocations earlier in this chapter; for example, the expression COLOR('Blue') is an invocation of a selector for type COLOR. *Note:* I said previously that COLOR('Blue') was a COLOR *literal*. In fact it is, as will quickly become clear.

isn't very important from a theoretical point of view (though it might be useful from a pragmatic one). In particular, relvar and database constraints are both checked "immediately," as we already know. (Of course, the same is effectively true for type and attribute constraints as well.)

Incidentally, note that *transition* constraints are subsumed by the foregoing scheme. A transition constraint is a constraint on the legal transitions that a given variable—in particular, a given relvar or a given database—can make from one value to another (for example, a person's marital status can legitimately change from never married to married but not from married to never married). Provided we have a way to refer within a single expression to both the value of the variable in question before any given update and the value of that variable after that update, then we have the means to formulate any required transition constraint. Here's an example ("No supplier's status must ever decrease"):

```
FORALL x# ε S#, xn ε NAME, xt ε INTEGER, xc ε CHAR,
       y# ε S#, yn ε NAME, yt ε INTEGER, yc ε CHAR
  ( IF { S# x#, SNAME xn, STATUS xt, CITY xc } ε S' AND
       { S# y#, SNAME yn, STATUS yt, CITY yc } ε S  AND x# = y#
     THEN xt ≤ yt )
```

Explanation: I'm appealing to a convention according to which a primed relvar name such as S' is understood to refer to the corresponding relvar as it was prior to the update under consideration. The constraint in the example can thus be understood as follows (loosely): If (a) a tuple for supplier $x\#$ appears in the relation that's the value of relvar S before the update and a tuple for supplier $y\#$ appears in the relation that's the value afterwards, and if (b) $x\#$ and $y\#$ are in fact the same supplier, then (c) the status xt of that supplier before the update mustn't be greater than the status yt of that supplier afterwards.

CONCLUDING REMARKS

I'd like to close this chapter by offering a slightly more formal perspective on some of what I've been saying. I said in the section "All Checking Is Immediate!" that a database is a collection of true propositions. In fact, a database, together with the operators that apply to the propositions in that database, is *a logical system*. And when I say "logical system" here, I mean a formal system—like euclidean geometry, for example—that has *axioms* ("given truths") and *rules of inference* by which we can prove *theorems* ("derived truths") from those axioms or given truths. Indeed, it was Ted Codd's very great insight, when he invented the relational model back in 1969, that a database isn't really just a collection of data (despite the name); rather, it's a collection of facts, or what the logicians call true propositions. Those propositions—the given ones, which is to say the ones represented in the base relvars—are the axioms of the logical system under discussion. And the inference rules are essentially the rules by which new propositions are derived from the given ones; in other words, they're the rules that tell us how to apply the operators of the relational algebra. Thus, when the system evaluates some relational expression (in particular, when it responds to some query), it's really deriving new truths from given ones; in effect, it's proving a theorem!

Once we understand the foregoing, we can see that the whole apparatus of formal logic becomes available for use in attacking "the database problem." In other words, questions such as the following—

- What should the database look like to the user?

- What should the query language look like?

- How should results be presented to the user?

- How can we best implement queries (or, more generally, evaluate database expressions)?

- How do we design the database in the first place?

—(not to mention the question I've concentrated on in this chapter, how to formulate integrity constraints) all become, in effect, questions in logic that are susceptible to logical treatment and can be given logical answers.

Of course, it goes without saying that the relational model supports the foregoing perception of what databases are all about very directly—which is why, in my opinion, the relational model is rock solid, and "right," and will endure. It's also why, again in my opinion, other "data models" are simply not in the same ballpark as the relational model ... Indeed, I seriously question whether those other "models" deserve to be called models at all, in the same sense that the relational model can be called a model.[1] Certainly most of them are ad hoc to a degree, instead of being firmly grounded, as the relational model is, in set theory and formal logic.

Finally, given that a database together with its operators is indeed a logical system, I'd like to come back to the primary topic of this chapter and reemphasize the absolutely vital importance of constraints. If the database is in violation of some constraint, then the logical system we're talking about is inconsistent. And, as I claimed earlier, we can get absolutely any answer at all from an inconsistent system. Let me conclude by demonstrating this fact. Suppose the system in question is such that it implies the truth of both p and NOT p (there's the inconsistency), where p is some proposition. Now let q be some arbitrary proposition. Then:

- From the truth of p, we can infer the truth of p OR q.

- From the truth of p OR q and the truth of NOT p, we can infer the truth of q.

But q was arbitrary! It follows that any proposition whatsoever can be shown to be TRUE in an inconsistent system.

ACKNOWLEDGMENTS

I'd like to thank Hugh Darwen, Fabian Pascal, and Ron Ross for helpful reviews of earlier drafts of this chapter.

---

1. In this connection, I'd like to refer you to two other papers of my own [4-5], and another by Hugh Darwen [2]. This last in particular is an excellent and highly readable tutorial on the notion that "database plus operators = a logical system."

REFERENCES AND BIBLIOGRAPHY

1. E. F. Codd: *The Relational Model for Database Management Version 2*. Reading, Mass.: Addison-Wesley (1990).

2. Hugh Darwen: "What a Database *Really* Is: Predicates and Propositions," in C. J. Date, Hugh Darwen, and David McGoveran, *Relational Database Writings 1994-1997*. Reading, Mass.: Addison-Wesley (1998).

3. C. J. Date: "A Matter of Integrity" (in three parts), in *Relational Database Writings 1991-1994*. Reading, Mass.: Addison-Wesley (1995).

4. C. J. Date: "Object Identifiers *vs*. Relational Keys," in C. J. Date, Hugh Darwen, and David McGoveran, *Relational Database Writings 1994-1997*. Reading, Mass.: Addison-Wesley (1998).

5. C. J. Date: "Why 'The Object Model' Is Not a Data Model," in C. J. Date, Hugh Darwen, and David McGoveran, *Relational Database Writings 1994-1997*. Reading, Mass.: Addison-Wesley (1998).

6. C. J. Date: "Integrity Revisited," in C. J. Date, Hugh Darwen, and David McGoveran, *Relational Database Writings 1994-1997*. Reading, Mass.: Addison-Wesley (1998).

7. C. J. Date: "Constraints and Predicates: A Brief Tutorial" (in three parts), *www.dbdebunk.com* (May 2001); *www.BRCommunity.com* (May-November 2001).

8. C. J. Date: *Database in Depth: Relational Theory for Practitioners*. Sebastopol, Calif.: O'Reilly Media, Inc. (2005).

9. C. J. Date: "The Building Blocks of Logic" (Chapter 1 in this book).

10. C. J. Date: "The Closed World Assumption" (Chapter 4 in this book).

11. C. J. Date and Hugh Darwen: *Databases, Types, and the Relational Model: The Third Manifesto* (3rd edition). Boston, Mass.: Addison-Wesley (2006).

12. C. J. Date and Hugh Darwen: "Multiple Assignment," in *Date on Database: Writings 2000-2006*. Berkeley, Calif.: Apress (2006).

13. Jim Gray and Andreas Reuter: *Transaction Processing: Concepts and Techniques*. San Francisco, Calif.: Morgan Kaufmann (1993).

14. Ralph Kimball: "There Are No Guarantees," *Intelligent Enterprise 3,* No. 11 (August 1st, 2000); "Enforcing the Rules," *Intelligent Enterprise 3,* No. 12 (August 18th, 2000).

15. Jim Melton and Alan R. Simon: *SQL:1999—Understanding Relational Language Components*. San Francisco, Calif.: Morgan Kaufmann (2002).

16. Fabian Pascal: *Practical Issues in Database Management*. Boston, Mass.: Addison-Wesley (2000).

17. Ronald G. Ross: *The Business Rule Book: Classifying, Defining, and Modeling Rules* (2nd edition). Houston, Texas: Business Rule Solutions LLC (1997).

18. Michael Stonebraker: "Implementation of Integrity Constraints and Views by Query Modification," Proc. 1975 ACM SIGMOD International Conference on Management of Data, San Jose, Calif. (May 14th-16th, 1975).

19. Jeffrey D. Ullman and Jennifer Widom: *A First Course in Database Systems*. Upper Saddle River, N.J.: Prentice Hall (1997).

Chapter 4

The Closed World Assumption

As we know, there are known knowns. There are things we know we know.
We also know there are known unknowns.
That is to say, we know there are some things we do not know.
But there are also unknown unknowns, the ones we don't know we don't know.

—D*n*ld R*mpf*d

Never assume anything.

—Anon.

Anyone who poses queries to a database or data warehouse is crucially dependent on what's called the Closed World Assumption. As the word *assumption* tends to suggest, however, that dependence is usually implicit—the assumption as such is rarely spelled out explicitly. So my aim in this chapter is (in effect) to make that assumption explicit; I want to explain what the Closed World Assumption is, and in particular I want to show why it's almost universally preferred over its rival, the Open World Assumption.

Note: In October 2006 I participated in a workshop in Edinburgh, Scotland, with the title "The Closed World of Databases Meets the Open World of the Semantic Web" (http://wiki.esi.ac.uk), and it was my participation in that workshop that spurred me to write this chapter. Here's a quote from the workshop announcement:

> [The] database community traditionally operates under the closed world assumption ... while the semantic web community [operates under] an open world assumption ...

I didn't believe this claim when I first read it, and I still don't. To be more specific, I don't believe people in the "semantic web community" do actually use the Open World Assumption; they might think they do, but if they do, then I don't think they can mean the same thing by the term as I do. By contrast, we in the database community certainly do use the Closed World Assumption; however, I should immediately add that we're often sloppy in specifying just what world it is that's closed. Part of my aim in this chapter is to shed some light on this latter issue also.

With regard to that workshop announcement, incidentally, I have to say too that I do detect a certain bias in the wording ... As we all know, the terms *closed* and *open* carry a certain amount of semantic baggage with them, along the lines of closed = bad, open = good (think of closed *vs.* open minds, for example). If you want to claim that closed is better, therefore, you tend to find yourself having to adopt a somewhat defensive position. So another aim of this chapter is to show that, in this context at least, closed is good, not bad. *Note:* Given the truth of the foregoing, it might be nice to come up with some better terminology—in particular, with a more positive sounding replacement for "closed world." But I'm not going to attempt any such thing here.

BASIC ASSUMPTIONS

The second of the two epigraphs to this chapter is *Never assume anything.* (Old joke: "Assume" makes an ass of u and me.) But of course I do have to assume something about the current state of your knowledge; however, at least I'll tell you what it is that I'm going to assume! To be specific, I'm going to assume you're familiar with the relational model in general and all of the following in particular:

- **Tutorial D,** which is a language (based on relational algebra) used by Hugh Darwen and myself as a basis for examples in our book on *The Third Manifesto* [12]—though in fact I think the language is pretty much self-explanatory anyway, at least to the extent I need to use it in this chapter

- The important notion of *logical difference* [9], which I'll be appealing to several times in what follows

- The fact that there's a logical difference between relation values (relations for short) and relation variables (relvars for short) in particular

- The fact that keys and the left and right sides of functional dependencies are all *sets* of attributes (for which reason I always show them enclosed in braces "{" and "}")

- The fact that every relvar has an associated *predicate* (the "relvar predicate"), which is the intended interpretation or meaning for the relvar in question

- The fact that every tuple appearing in a given relvar at a given time represents a certain *proposition,* that proposition being an instantiation of the relvar predicate for the relvar in question that (by convention) is understood to be true at the time in question

The foregoing points are all explained in numerous places; see, for example, my book *Database in Depth: Relational Theory for Practitioners* [7], or Chapter 3 in the present book.

DEFINITIONS

The Closed World Assumption (hereinafter abbreviated CWA) is due to Reiter [17,18].[1] Basically what it says is this: Everything stated or implied by the database is true; everything else is false. For example, suppose we're given the usual suppliers-and-parts database, with sample values as shown in Fig. 4.1 on the opposite page. Suppose further that the relvar predicates are as follows:

---

1. Though it's closely related to the idea of *negation as failure,* which was proposed by Clark (in a different context but at roughly the same time) in reference [1].

- Suppliers: *Supplier S# is under contract, is named SNAME, has status STATUS, and is located in city CITY.*

- Parts: *Part P# is used in the enterprise, is named PNAME, has color COLOR and weight WEIGHT, and is stored in city CITY.*

- Shipments: *Supplier S# supplies (i.e., is shipping) QTY of part P#.*

From Fig. 4.1, then, we can see that (e.g.) the following is a true proposition at this time:

Supplier S1 is under contract, is named Smith, has status 20, and is located in city London.

We can also see that (e.g.) the following is a false proposition at this time:

Supplier S6 is under contract, is named Lopez, has status 30, and is located in city Madrid.

S

S#	SNAME	STATUS	CITY
S1	Smith	20	London
S2	Jones	10	Paris
S3	Blake	30	Paris
S4	Clark	20	London
S5	Adams	30	Athens

P

P#	PNAME	COLOR	WEIGHT	CITY
P1	Nut	Red	12.0	London
P2	Bolt	Green	17.0	Paris
P3	Screw	Blue	17.0	Oslo
P4	Screw	Red	14.0	London
P5	Cam	Blue	12.0	Paris
P6	Cog	Red	19.0	London

SP

S#	P#	QTY
S1	P1	300
S1	P2	200
S1	P3	400
S1	P4	200
S1	P5	100
S1	P6	100
S2	P1	300
S2	P2	400
S3	P2	200
S4	P2	200
S4	P4	300
S4	P5	400

Fig. 4.1: The suppliers-and-parts database—sample values

By the way, note clearly that the CWA says that everything stated *or implied* by the database is true. Thus, for example, we can see from Fig. 4.1 that *Supplier S1 is under contract and has some name and some status and is located somewhere* is a true proposition, one that's implied by what the database says about supplier S1 but isn't stated, as such, explicitly. Here are some more examples of propositions that are implied but not stated explicitly by the sample values in Fig. 4.1 (and that we can therefore assume to be true):

- *Supplier S1 is under contract.*

- *Supplier S1 is located somewhere.*

- *Supplier S1 is in London and supplies part P1.*

And here are some propositions that we can assume to be false, because they're neither stated explicitly nor implied by the sample values in Fig. 4.1:

- *Supplier S6 is under contract.*

- *Supplier S6 is located somewhere.*

- *Supplier S1 is located in Paris.*

With respect to these latter examples, by the way, another way to say the same thing is that we can assume the following propositions are true, because their *negation* is neither stated explicitly nor implied (by the sample values in Fig. 4.1, that is):

- *Supplier S6 isn't under contract*—or (perhaps better) *It's not the case that supplier S6 is under contract.*

- *It's not the case that supplier S6 is located somewhere.*

- *It's not the case that supplier S1 is located in Paris.*

Aside: There's something else I should say in connection with these examples. For definiteness, let me focus on the very first of the ones I said we could assume were true: *Supplier S1 is under contract.* In effect, I was claiming that the proposition *Supplier S1 is under contract* is implied by the proposition *Supplier S1 is under contract, is named Smith, has status 20, and is located in city London.* If you're familiar with reference [13], however, you might feel there's some discrepancy here. This latter reference goes to great lengths to point out that a proposition such as *Supplier S1 is under contract* is **not** implied by a proposition such as *Supplier S1 is under contract during some interval of time.* But there's a logical difference between the two examples. The first is of the form "(*p1* AND *p2* AND *p3* AND *p4*) implies (*p1*)"—an implication that's clearly valid. The second is of the form "(*p1* during some interval) implies (*p1*)"—an implication that clearly isn't valid. Hence, no discrepancy. *End of aside.*

Here now is a more precise definition of the CWA, taken from reference [8]:

Closed World Assumption, The The assumption that (a) if a given tuple appears in a given relvar at a given time, then the proposition represented by that tuple is true at that time, and (b) if a given tuple could appear in that relvar at that time but doesn't, then the proposition represented by that tuple is false at that time. At any given time, in other words, the relvar contains all and only those tuples that correspond to true propositions—that is, invocations, or instantiations, of the relvar predicate that evaluate to TRUE—at that time. *Note:* The foregoing definition is phrased in terms of a relvar specifically. However, a precisely analogous definition applies to relations also.

Observe that the emphasis in this definition is on what the database states explicitly (thanks to the repeated references to relvars specifically); however, the last two sentences take care of implicit information also.

Other, more formal definitions and discussions of the CWA can be found in references [14], [19], and elsewhere. Though perhaps I should caution you that *more formal* doesn't necessarily mean *more accurate* ... For example, consider the following quote from reference [19]:

> The CWA lets us "deduce" facts of the form $\neg p(a1,...,ak)$ whenever the usual form of deduction does not yield $p(a1,...,ak)$.

This sentence can't actually mean what it says—which is, to paraphrase, that whenever a query fails to yield a result that includes a tuple representing some proposition *p,* then we're allowed to deduce that *p* is false. For example, the query P WHERE CITY = 'Oslo' certainly fails to yield a result that includes a tuple representing the fact that supplier S1 is under contract; so apparently we're allowed to deduce the fact that supplier S1 is *not* under contract (!).

Note: The quotation marks around *deduce* in the foregoing extract from reference [19] reflect the fact that the deductions that the CWA does let us carry out are different in kind from those that the relational calculus and the relational algebra let us carry out. As reference [19] puts it:

> [The] CWA acts as a "metarule," which talks about the deductions themselves [*where by* deductions *the author means the ones the relational calculus or the relational algebra lets us carry out*].

I'll close this section with a definition, also from reference [8], of the *Open* World Assumption (hereinafter abbreviated OWA):

> **Open World Assumption, The** The assumption—usually rejected in favor of the Closed World Assumption, q.v.—that (a) if a given tuple appears in a given relvar at a given time, then the proposition represented by that tuple is true at that time, and (b) if a given tuple could appear in that relvar at that time but doesn't, then the proposition represented by that tuple might or might not be true at that time.

Note: This definition makes no mention of implicit information, but that omission was merely an oversight on my part and needs to be rectified.[1] For the purposes of this chapter, therefore, please

---

1. I can't resist pointing out, at the risk of seriously confusing you (or myself), that if we applied the CWA to this definition of the OWA, we'd be forced to the conclusion that the OWA *doesn't* apply to implicit information.

assume—there's that word again!—that such rectification has been performed.

WHY THE CWA IS PREFERRED

Now I want to explain why, from a practical point of view as well as a theoretical one, the CWA is to be preferred over the OWA. As a basis for examples, I'll use a reduced version of the suppliers relvar with just two attributes, S# and CITY (but I'll continue to refer to it as relvar S). Here's the **Tutorial D** definition:

```
VAR S BASE RELATION { S# S#, CITY CHAR } KEY { S# } ;
```

And here's the predicate: *Supplier S# is under contract and is located in city CITY.* A sample value—a relation, of course—for this simplified suppliers relvar is shown in Fig. 4.2 (and I'll assume this particular value throughout the remainder of this chapter, barring explicit statements to the contrary).

S	S#	CITY
	S1	London
	S2	Paris
	S3	Paris
	S4	London
	S5	Athens

Fig. 4.2: Simplified suppliers relvar—sample value

I now propose to consider the query *Is supplier S1 in London?* Three points arise immediately. The first is that this is an extremely simple query—indeed, it's close to being the simplest possible query we might consider asking of a relvar like relvar S. Nonetheless, it's perfectly adequate to illustrate the points I want to make, and I'll stay with it until further notice.

The second point is that the query is expressed in natural language, of course, and (as is so often the case with natural language statements) it's somewhat imprecise and/or incomplete, if not downright ambiguous. In fact, there are at least two possible interpretations that whoever stated the query in the first place might have had in mind:

1.   *Is it the case that supplier S1 is under contract and in London?*

2.   *Is it the case that, if supplier S1 is under contract, then that supplier is in London?*

Observe that there's certainly a logical difference between these two interpretations. To be specific, if there were no tuple for supplier S1 in relvar S, then we would expect the answer *no* under the first interpretation but the answer *yes* under the second. (I'm appealing here to the conventional definition of the logical implication connective, according to which the expression IF *p* THEN *q* is defined to be equivalent to (NOT p) OR q and thus returns FALSE if p is true and q is false, TRUE otherwise.   Now, we might argue over whether *yes* is a *sensible* answer, under the second interpretation of the query, if there's no tuple for supplier S1 in relvar S, but I don't want to get into that debate here—it isn't really relevant to the main thesis of this chapter.   You can find a discussion of the issue in any good book on logic.)

From this point forward, I'll abbreviate the two candidate interpretations as follows:

1.   *Is supplier S1 under contract and in London?*

2.   *If supplier S1 is under contract, is that supplier in London?*

Also, I'll assume until further notice that the first of these two interpretations is the one intended.

The third point arising is that (as in effect I've already pointed out) the query is a yes/no query—i.e., it expects the answer *yes* or *no*.   Of course, it was a deliberate decision on my part to use such a query as a basis for my discussions, because yes/no queries illustrate some of the issues I want to examine in a very direct way.   One problem caused by that decision, however, is that SQL doesn't properly support such queries[1]—so I couldn't show my examples in SQL, even if I wanted to.   But relational algebra does properly support such queries, and so does **Tutorial D**.   Here then is a **Tutorial D** formulation of the sample query (*Is supplier S1 under contract and in London?*):

```
( S WHERE S# = S#('S1') AND CITY = 'London' ) { }
```

Explanation: The expression in parentheses (S WHERE ... 'London') yields either (a) a nonempty relation (actually containing just one tuple) if supplier S1 is represented in relvar S as being under contract and in London, or (b) an empty relation otherwise.   Call this intermediate result r.   Then the expression $r\{\}$ denotes the projection of r over no attributes at all.   Since it's over no attributes, the result of that projection is necessarily either TABLE_DEE or TABLE_DUM—TABLE_DEE if r is nonempty, TABLE_DUM otherwise.   And as reference [12] shows, these two possible result relations denote *yes* and *no,* respectively, and the overall expression thus does indeed represent the query we want it to.   *Note:*   In case you're not familiar with the important relations TABLE_DEE and TABLE_DUM, I should explain that (a) TABLE_DEE is the unique relation with no attributes and exactly one tuple (necessarily the empty tuple), and (b) TABLE_DUM is the unique relation with no attributes and no tuples at all.   They are the only relations—the only possible relations—of degree zero [3].

Well ... let's take a closer look at the conclusions of the foregoing paragraph.   Those conclusions, paraphrased, are that (a) the overall expression gives TABLE_DEE if supplier S1 is represented in relvar S as being under contract and in London, or TABLE_DUM otherwise, and hence that (b) that expression does indeed represent the query *Is supplier S1 under contract and in London?*   To spell the matter out:

- If the result is TABLE_DEE (*yes*), it means supplier S1 is under contract and in London.

---

1. It doesn't support such queries because it doesn't support tables with no columns (or, as I would prefer to say, relations with no attributes).   See reference [3] for further discussion.

- If the result is TABLE_DUM (*no*), it means *it's not the case that* supplier S1 is under contract and in London—which means in turn that supplier S1 either isn't under contract or isn't in London. (More precisely, given the semantics of the situation, it means either that supplier S1 isn't under contract or that supplier S1 is under contract but isn't in London.)

Note very carefully, however, that the foregoing interpretation (i.e., of what the **Tutorial D** expression means) *relies implicitly on the CWA*—and to be completely accurate in spelling out that interpretation, I ought really to have said as much. What would happen if we were operating under the OWA instead?

Well, under the OWA, if the result is TABLE_DEE, it would still mean that supplier S1 is under contract and in London. But what if it's TABLE_DUM? Apparently, we would have to understand a result of TABLE_DUM as meaning *it's unknown whether* supplier S1 is under contract and in London. What are the implications? One important one is as follows:

- First, we do need to be clear that the proposition *Supplier S1 is under contract and in London* actually is either true or false (for otherwise it wouldn't be a proposition, by definition).

- Let me refer to that proposition as *p*. Then a result of TABLE_DUM doesn't mean that *p* evaluates to some "third truth value" called UNKNOWN; it simply means we don't know which of TRUE and FALSE it does evaluate to. (In other words, a result of TABLE_DUM means *we don't have enough information* to conclude either that *p* is true or that it's false.)

- Observe now that there's a huge logical difference between (a) *our not knowing* whether some proposition *p* is true or false and (b) that proposition *p* actually *being* either true or false. Indeed, an attempt to pretend otherwise—i.e., an attempt to pretend that our not knowing whether *p* is true or false is the same kind of thing, logically speaking, as *p* actually being either true or false—is a huge logical mistake! And it's precisely that mistake that leads us into the quagmire of three-valued logic, and nulls, and the whole mess of "missing information" as currently "supported" by the language SQL.

As a matter of fact, I hope a warning flag was raised in your brain the moment I first mentioned the term "unknown"—especially when I raised the possibility of our not knowing whether some proposition is true or false being regarded as the same kind of thing as that proposition actually being either true or false. That way madness lies! The fact is, as I've argued many, many times and in many, many places, the whole notion of three-valued logic (3VL) is simply incompatible with the relational model. (I remark as an aside that reference [11] documents some of my most recent thinking on this topic. In particular, it gives *formal* reasons to support my contention that 3VL basically "just doesn't work"—meaning, more precisely, that it doesn't solve the problem it was originally intended to solve. Of course, the problem in question is, as already indicated, the hoary old one of "missing information.")

To recap, then: We've seen that, under the OWA, if the result of some yes/no query is TABLE_DUM, then that result has to be interpreted as meaning *we don't know* something; in other words—very loosely, and modulo the foregoing discussion—TABLE_DUM has to mean *unknown*. But if TABLE_DUM means *unknown,* then we longer have a relation that means good old plain *no!* And yet we're surely entitled, even under the OWA, to expect to get plain *no* as the right answer to certain queries. An example is provided by the alternative interpretation of our original natural language query:

If supplier S1 is under contract, is that supplier in London?

Let's consider this latter query more closely. First of all, observe that relvar S satisfies the functional dependency (FD) {S#} → {CITY}. (In fact, {S#} is the sole key for that relvar, and there are always FDs "out of keys" to everything else in the pertinent relvar; see, e.g., reference [6].) As a consequence of this FD, the answer to the query should definitely be *no* if relvar S shows supplier S1 as under contract but in some city other than London (the relvar can't show supplier S1 as being in London and in some other city simultaneously, thanks to the FD).[1] Here then is a **Tutorial D** expression that's guaranteed to evaluate to TABLE_DUM if (and only if) relvar S shows supplier S1 as under contract but in some city other than London:

```
WITH ( S WHERE S# = S#('S1') AND CITY ≠ 'London' ) AS T1 ,
     T1 { } AS T2 :
TABLE_DEE MINUS T2
```

Explanation: Relation T1 is nonempty (containing just the supplier tuple for supplier S1) if and only if relvar S shows supplier S1 as under contract and in some city other than London. Thus, relation T2 is TABLE_DEE if relvar S shows supplier S1 as under contract and not in London, TABLE_DUM otherwise; and then the expression TABLE_DEE MINUS T2 returns TABLE_DEE or TABLE_DUM according as T2 is TABLE_DUM or TABLE_DEE (in other words, it returns the complement [8] of T2, in effect replacing TABLE_DUM by TABLE_DEE and TABLE_DEE by TABLE_DUM). Thus, if the final result is TABLE_DUM, it means that relvar S shows supplier S1 as under contract and not in London—precisely the situation in which, I previously claimed, the right answer should be *no*. To repeat, therefore, there are situations, even under the OWA, in which we must be allowed to obtain *no* as the right answer to certain queries; hence, there are situations, even under the OWA, in which TABLE_DUM must mean *no*.

From examples like the foregoing, I conclude that we must reject the suggestion that if we accept the OWA, then TABLE_DUM no longer means *no*. I conclude further that there's no relation that means *unknown:* TABLE_DEE means *yes* and TABLE_DUM means *no,* and there's no "third relation with no attributes"—no "brother to TABLE_DEE and TABLE_DUM," as it were—that might be considered to represent "the third truth value" (if I might be permitted to speak as if there were such a thing, just for the moment). And I conclude still further that the OWA and the relational model are fundamentally at odds with one another.

Actually, I don't need to appeal to the alternative interpretation of the original query—*If supplier S1 is under contract, is that supplier in London?*—in order to show that, even under the OWA, a result of TABLE_DUM sometimes has to mean *no*. Let's go back to the first interpretation: *Is supplier S1 under contract and in London?* Here again is the **Tutorial D** formulation:

```
( S WHERE S# = S#('S1') AND CITY = 'London' ) { }
```

---

1. In effect, I'm performing a simple *semantic optimization* here. See reference [6] for further discussion of such matters.

Suppose once again that we're operating under the OWA. Then, to repeat, we apparently have that:

- If the result is TABLE_DEE (*yes*), it means supplier S1 is under contract and in London.

- If the result is TABLE_DUM (*unknown*), it means we don't know whether supplier S1 is under contract and in London.

Abstracting a little, this latter possibility means that a certain three-valued logic expression of the form *p* AND *q*, where *p* and *q* are propositions, evaluates to UNKNOWN. (To spell them out, proposition *p* is S# = S#('S1'), and proposition *q* is CITY = 'London'.) Now, according to both Codd [2] and SQL [15], if the 3VL expression *p* AND *q* evaluates to UNKNOWN, it means that either (a) *p* and *q* both evaluate to UNKNOWN or (b) one evaluates to UNKNOWN and the other evaluates to TRUE. In the case at hand, however, there's no way that one of the propositions can be true and the other unknown, because:

- If there's a tuple for supplier S1 in relvar S, then *Supplier S1 is under contract* is true and *Supplier S1 is in London* is either true or false (depending on whether the CITY value in that tuple is London or something else).

- So there can't be a tuple for supplier S1 in relvar S; hence both propositions are unknown, and the proposition *Supplier S1 is under contract* in particular is unknown.

The net of this argument is: If the query result is TABLE_DUM, there can't be a tuple in relvar S for supplier S1—meaning, to repeat, that *we don't know whether* supplier S1 is under contract.

But now suppose supplier S1 is under contract but is in some city other than London. In this case, relvar S will contain a tuple saying supplier S1 is under contract; yet the **Tutorial D** expression shown previously—

```
( S WHERE S# = S#('S1') AND CITY = 'London' ) { }
```

—will yield the result TABLE_DUM, which (according to the analysis of the previous paragraph) the OWA tells us has to mean *we don't know* whether supplier S1 is under contract. But we *do* know! So the OWA has given us the wrong answer.

RELVAR PREDICATES REVISITED

As we've seen, yes/no queries do indeed deliver yes/no answers, under the CWA. Contrary to popular opinion, however, this fact doesn't prevent us from getting "don't know" answers under the CWA!—it's simply a matter of what question the yes/no answer is an answer to. In order to explain this point, I need to step back a bit and say a little more about the business of relvar predicates.

When I introduced the reduced version of the suppliers relvar S near the beginning of the previous section, I said the predicate was *Supplier S# is under contract and is located in city CITY*. But it isn't—not really. To see why not, consider what happens if the user tries to introduce a tuple into the relvar, perhaps like this:[1]

```
INSERT TUPLE { S# S#('S6'), CITY 'Madrid' } INTO S ;
```

In effect, the user is asserting to the system that there's a new supplier, S6, with city Madrid. Now, the system obviously has no way of telling whether that assertion is true—all it can (and does) do is check that the requested insertion, if performed, won't cause any integrity constraints to be violated. If it won't, then the system accepts the tuple, *and interprets it as representing a "true fact" from this point forward.*

We see, therefore, that tuples in relvar S don't necessarily represent actual states of affairs in the real world; rather, they represent *what the user tells the system* about the real world, or in other words the user's *knowledge* of the real world. Thus, the predicate for relvar S isn't really just *Supplier S# is under contract and is located in city CITY;* rather, it's **We know that** *supplier S# is under contract and is located in city CITY.* And the effect of a successful INSERT operation is to make the system aware of something the user already knows. Thus, the database doesn't contain "the real world" (of course not); what it contains is, rather, *the system's knowledge of* the real world. And the system's knowledge in turn is derived from the user's knowledge (of course!—there's no magic here).

By the way, even the terms *know* and *knowledge* might be a little strong in contexts such as those under discussion (the terms *believe* and *beliefs* might be better)—but I'll stay with *know* and *knowledge* for the purposes of this chapter.

So when we pose a query, by definition that query can't be a query about the real world; instead, it is—it has to be—a query about the system's knowledge of the real world. For example, the query I discussed in the previous section (*Is supplier S1 under contract and in London?*) really means *According to the system's knowledge, is supplier S1 under contract and in London?* Or equivalently: *Do we know that supplier S1 is under contract and in London?* Or equivalently again: *Does the database say that supplier S1 is under contract and in London?* In practice, of course, we almost never talk in such precise terms; we usually elide all those qualifiers ("according to the system's knowledge," "do we know that," "does the database say that," and so on). But even if we do elide them, we certainly need to understand that, conceptually, they're there—for otherwise we'll be really confused. (Though perhaps I should add that such confusions aren't exactly unknown in practice.)

It follows from the foregoing discussion that the **Tutorial D** expression—

```
( S WHERE S# = S#('S1') AND CITY = 'London' ) { }
```

—doesn't really represent the query *Is supplier S1 under contract and in London?* (despite the fact that earlier in this chapter I said it did). Rather, it represents the query *Do we know that supplier S1 is under contract and in London?* And so it follows further that:

- If the result is TABLE_DEE (*yes*), it means we do know that supplier S1 is under contract and in London.

---

1. I note for the record that (for reasons that aren't important here) this example isn't expressed in pure **Tutorial D**.

■ If the result is TABLE_DUM (*no*), it means *we don't know whether* supplier S1 is under contract and in London. And that's a "don't know" answer if ever you saw one.

PUTTING IT ALL TOGETHER

Consider once again the question of whether supplier S1 is in London (for simplicity, let's ignore the part about the supplier being under contract). From the discussion so far, then, it should be clear that:

■ If a tuple for supplier S1 appears in relvar S and the CITY value in that tuple is London, it means yes, we know supplier S1 is in London.

■ If a tuple for supplier S1 appears in relvar S but the CITY value in that tuple is something other than London, it means no, we know supplier S1 isn't in London.

■ And if no tuple for supplier S1 appears in relvar S at all, it means we don't know whether supplier S1 is in London.

Even under the CWA, therefore—and, praise be, without having to delve into three-valued logic—we can formulate queries that return a true/false/don't know answer. Here's a possible formulation for the particular case in hand:

```
( EXTEND ( S WHERE S# = S#('S') AND CITY = 'London' ) { }
    ADD ( 'true  ' AS RESULT ) ) { RESULT }
UNION
( EXTEND ( S WHERE S# = S#('S') AND CITY ≠ 'London' ) { }
    ADD ( 'false ' AS RESULT ) ) { RESULT }
UNION
( EXTEND ( RELATION { TUPLE { S# S#('S1') } } MINUS S { S# } ) { }
    ADD ( 'unknown' AS RESULT ) ) { RESULT }
```

As you can see, this expression takes the form *a* UNION *b* UNION *c* (where each of *a, b,* and *c* is a relation of degree one), and it should be clear that exactly one of *a, b,* and *c* evaluates to a relation containing just one tuple and the other two evaluate to a relation containing no tuples at all. The overall result is thus a one-attribute, one-tuple relation; the single attribute, RESULT, is of type CHAR, and the single tuple contains the appropriate RESULT value. And the trick—though it isn't really a trick at all—is that the RESULT value is a character string, not a truth value. Thus, there's no need to get into the 3VL quagmire in order to formulate queries that can yield "true," "false," or "unknown" answers, if that's what the user wants.

By the way, we can even formulate such queries in SQL, even though as noted earlier SQL doesn't really support yes/no queries properly. By way of example, here's an SQL analog of the foregoing **Tutorial D** expression:

```
SELECT DISTINCT 'true    ' AS RESULT
FROM ( SELECT DISTINCT S.*
       FROM    S
       WHERE   S# = S#('S1')
       AND     CITY = 'London' ) AS POINTLESS1
UNION
SELECT DISTINCT 'false   ' AS RESULT
FROM ( SELECT DISTINCT S.*
       FROM    S
       WHERE   S# = S#('S1')
       AND     CITY <> 'London' ) AS POINTLESS2
UNION
SELECT DISTINCT 'unknown' AS RESULT
FROM ( VALUES ( S#('S1') AS S# )
       EXCEPT
       SELECT DISTINCT S.S#
       FROM    S ) AS POINTLESS3
```

DEALING WITH UNCERTAINTY

In my opinion, the arguments I've presented so far certainly show that the CWA makes the system easier to understand and work with. The standard counterargument, however, is that "the real world" isn't as cut and dried as I've been pretending (or assuming?) it is; in the real world, information can be uncertain—i.e., partly but not totally unknown—or even totally unknown, and the CWA is incapable of dealing with such situations. In this section, I'd like to address this counterargument.

As you should expect from the section before last, it's the relvar predicate notion—in particular, the fact that the database contains not reality as such but, rather, the system's knowledge of reality—that's the key to the problem. In fact, I've already shown in that earlier section how unknown information (i.e., information that's totally unknown) can be represented under the CWA; however, there's more that can usefully be said on that topic. Suppose, for example, that we don't know whether there's a supplier S7 located in Athens. Then the tuple with supplier number S7 and city Athens *doesn't satisfy the predicate for relvar S*—which is, to spell it out one more time, *We know that supplier S# is under contract and is located in city CITY*—and so the tuple can't be (and mustn't be) inserted into the relvar. As Wittgenstein famously said [20]:

> *Was sich überhaupt sagen lässt, lässt sich klar sagen; und wovon man nicht reden kann, darüber muss man schweigen.* (What can be said at all can be said clearly; and whereof one cannot speak, thereof one must be silent.)

In the example, we can't "speak of" supplier S7 being in Athens, and so indeed we mustn't speak of it.

But suppose now that we do know that supplier S7 exists, but we don't know the corresponding city. Well ... note first (and importantly) that there's still no city *x* such that the tuple with supplier number S7 and city *x* satisfies the predicate for relvar S.[1] So there's still no tuple for supplier S7 that we can legitimately insert into relvar S. If, despite this fact, we do want to record the fact that we know that supplier S7 exists, then there are at least two things we can do—two approaches, that is, which I'll refer to here as the Darwen approach and the McGoveran approach, respectively, since they're described in publications by Hugh Darwen [5] and David McGoveran [16], respectively:

- In the Darwen approach, we retain relvar S unchanged, with its predicate *We know that supplier S# is under contract and is located in city CITY,* and we introduce a second relvar—we might call it CITY_UNKNOWN—with just one attribute, S#, and predicate *We know supplier S# is under contract but we don't know the corresponding city.* See Fig. 4.3.

S	S#	CITY
	S1	London
	S2	Paris
	S3	Paris
	S4	London
	S5	Athens

CITY_UNKNOWN	S#
	S7

Fig. 4.3: S7 is under contract but we don't know the city—Darwen's approach

- The McGoveran approach also involves two relvars—one (which I'll continue to call S) with a single attribute, S#, and predicate *We know that supplier S# is under contract,* and the other (which I'll call SC) with attributes S# and CITY and predicate *We know that supplier S# is located in city CITY.* There's a foreign key constraint from SC to S. See Fig. 4.4.

S	S#
	S1
	S2
	S3
	S4
	S5
	S7

SC	S#	CITY
	S1	London
	S2	Paris
	S3	Paris
	S4	London
	S5	Athens

Fig. 4.4: S7 is under contract but we don't know the city—McGoveran's approach

---

1. No, not even if "*x* is null"—even assuming we can make any sense of this construction, which SQL so signally fails to do [11].

I'll have a little more to say regarding the foregoing techniques for representing "unknown information" in Appendix A. For a more detailed discussion, I refer you to references [5] and [16].

So much for "unknown" information (by which I mean information that's *totally* unknown, like the city for supplier S7 in the example just discussed). But what about information that's *partly* unknown? For example, we might know with "50 percent certainty"—i.e., we might be "50 percent sure"—that supplier S1 is in London. More generally, we might be "*x* percent sure" that supplier S# is in city CITY. Well, that's a predicate (a predicate with three parameters, in fact) ... and here's a corresponding relvar, with three attributes:

```
VAR S BASE RELATION { S# S#, CITY CHAR, X NUMBER }
       KEY { S#, CITY } ;
```

Incidentally, it's interesting to see that this design—note the key constraint KEY {S#,CITY}—would allow us to say, for example, that we're 50 percent sure that supplier S1 is in London *and* 50 percent sure that supplier S1 is in Paris, thereby providing a mechanism for representing certain kinds of disjunctive information ("We're 100 percent sure that supplier S1 is in either London or Paris, with an equal likelihood of either"). It would also allow us to say, for example, that we're zero percent sure that supplier S2 is in Athens, thereby providing a mechanism for representing certain kinds of negative information as well ("We're completely unsure that supplier S2 is in Athens").[1] See the section immediately following for further discussion.

NEGATION AND DISJUNCTION

I don't want to leave you with the impression that the CWA is perfect; *au contraire,* it's well known that it can get into difficulties over negative information and disjunctive information. Let's take a closer look. I'll start with negation.

Consider the predicate *Supplier S# isn't located in city CITY.* (For simplicity I'll ignore the part about the supplier being under contract; I'll also ignore the fact that the predicate ought more properly to begin with the qualifier *We know that.* What's more, I'll make analogous simplifications throughout the remainder of this chapter, barring explicit statements to the contrary.) Let there be a relvar, NS, corresponding to this predicate, and let that relvar contain just one tuple for supplier S2, with city Athens. Then we can certainly conclude that supplier S2 isn't in Athens. But since there isn't a tuple in relvar NS for supplier S2 with city (let's say) Madrid, the CWA allows us—in fact, forces us—to conclude that *It's not the case that supplier S2 isn't in Madrid,* or in other words that supplier S2 *is* in Madrid. At the same time, the CWA also forces us to conclude that supplier S2 is in (say) London, and

---

1. Note carefully, however, that this proposition isn't equivalent to the proposition *We're completely sure that supplier S2 isn't in Athens.* As I've had occasion to remark elsewhere, negation can often be tricky.

Berlin, and Rome, and ... (and so on).

The obvious, and highly unsatisfactory, implication of the foregoing state of affairs is that if there are N cities in total, relvar NS will have to contain $N - 1$ tuples for each and every known supplier!—one for each and every city the supplier in question is *not* located in. (I'm assuming here, as I've done throughout this chapter so far, that each supplier is located in just one city.) The sad, albeit well known, conclusion is that the relational model and the CWA in combination are simply not well suited to representing this particular kind of negative information. Though I do have to ask: How often in practice do we really want to represent such negative information, anyway?[1]

I turn now to disjunction. Consider the predicate *Supplier S# is located in either city CITYA or city CITYB*—which I'll take to be the simplified form of *We know that supplier S# is located in exactly one city, and that city is either CITYA or CITYB, but in general we don't know which.* Let there be a relvar, DS (with attributes S#, CITYA, and CITYB), corresponding to this predicate. Moreover, suppose for the sake of the example that we do know that supplier S3 is in either London or Paris, but we don't know which; suppose, therefore, that relvar DS includes a tuple for supplier S3 with CITYA and CITYB equal to London and Paris, respectively ("Supplier S3 is in either London or Paris").

So far, so good. However, now consider this question: Does relvar DS additionally include a tuple for supplier S3 with CITYA and CITYB equal to Paris and London, respectively ("Supplier S3 is in either Paris or London")?

- If the answer is *no,* the CWA forces us to conclude that supplier S3 is *not* in either Paris or London, and we have an obvious contradiction on our hands. *Note:* I'm deliberately ignoring here the fact that if relvar DS is supposed to satisfy the key constraint KEY{S#}, then the answer to the question must be *no* (the relvar wouldn't be allowed to include two distinct tuples for the same supplier); I'm concerned with the predicate (i.e., with what the relvar *means*), not with integrity constraints as such. Predicates take precedence over constraints.[2]

- So the answer must be *yes.* But then we obviously have a bad design, inasmuch as it permits—in fact, requires—some redundancy (except in the very special case in which the relvar happens to be empty).

---

1. One correspondent suggested that the answer to this question is: Very frequently. For example, it might be very important to represent customers who haven't yet been contacted (in connection with a new product, for example). But that's easy: We simply define a single-attribute relvar with predicate *Customer CUST# hasn't yet been contacted,* thereby (in a sense) turning negative information into positive.

2. What I mean by this remark is that, in principle, we can't even define the constraints for a given relvar—at least, not legitimately—until we know the predicate for that relvar [7]. Note too in the case at hand that the constraint KEY{S#} would imply that we'd have to make an arbitrary decision: We could have either of the tuples in the relvar but not both, and it would be arbitrary as to which one we chose.

Now, we can fix these problems by tightening up the predicate, thus: *Supplier S# is located in either city CITYA or city CITYB, and CITYA ≤ CITYB* (where " ≤ " refers to alphabetic ordering). With this revised predicate, (a) relvar DS can't include the additional tuple (the one with CITYA and CITYB equal to Paris and London, respectively), and (b) that omission can't be interpreted to mean that supplier S3 is in neither Paris nor London. But I'd be the first to admit that this fix is little more than a trick. What's more, it doesn't even solve all of the problems, anyway! Consider the question: Does relvar DS additionally include a tuple for supplier S3 with CITYA and CITYB both equal to London ("Supplier S3 is in either London or London")?

- The answer can't be *yes,* because such a tuple would assert definitively that supplier S3 is in London, thereby contradicting our original assumption—reflected in the tuple for supplier S3 with CITYA and CITYB equal to London and Paris, respectively—that supplier S3 is in either London or Paris, but we don't know which.

- But if the answer is *no,* the CWA forces us to conclude that supplier S3 is *not* in London, and again we have a contradiction on our hands. *Note:* Again I'm ignoring the fact that if relvar DS is supposed to satisfy the key constraint KEY{S#}, then the answer to the question must be *no;* again I'm interested in the predicate, not integrity constraints.

I don't think there's an obvious simple fix to the original predicate that can overcome this problem. We might consider revising the predicate thus: *Supplier S# is located in either city CITYA or city CITYB, and CITYA < CITYB* (i.e., replacing " ≤ " by " < ", thereby prohibiting the appearance of tuples with CITYA equal to CITYB). But the problem with this fix is that we now have no way of representing a supplier whose city we definitely do know!

We can, however, fix the problem by performing more drastic surgery, as it were, on our design. Before explaining what I mean by this remark, let me extend the example to make it a little more general. The discussion so far is sufficient to illustrate the problem but is, of course, very unrealistic; it's not likely that we would know of every supplier that the supplier in question is in exactly one of just two possible cities. Instead—let's agree for the sake of the example, at least—it's more likely that we would know of a given supplier that the supplier in question is in exactly one out of a set of *N* possible cities, where the value of *N* varies from one supplier to another. (In particular, $N = 1$ would correspond to a supplier whose city is definitely known.) For such a situation, a design with a *relation valued attribute* is more appropriate [10]:

```
VAR DS BASE RELATION { S#, CITIES RELATION { CITY CHAR } }
       KEY { S# } ;
```

A sample value, showing that supplier S1 is in either London, Paris, or Athens and supplier S3 is in either London or Paris, is given in Fig. 4.5 overleaf.

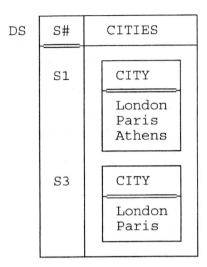

Fig. 4.5: Suppliers with a relation valued CITIES attribute—sample value

Now, we do need to be a little careful over the predicate for relvar DS (in fact, a similar remark always applies when relation valued attributes are involved). We can't just say the predicate is *Supplier S# is located in exactly one of the cities in CITIES.* (*Question:* Why not? *Answer:* Because of the CWA, of course, as a moment's reflection should be sufficient to show.) Rather, we have to say something like *Supplier S# is located in exactly one of the cities in CITIES and not in any city not in CITIES.* Thus, for example, a relation identical to that shown in Fig. 4.3 except that the supplier number in the "S3" tuple is S1 instead of S3 couldn't be a possible DS value, because it would lead to a contradiction: One tuple would say, in effect, that supplier S1 might be in Athens but the other would say that's not possible.

Observe that the foregoing design does indeed get over the CWA problem with disjunction. What's more, suppose we change the example as follows: Suppose it's possible for a given supplier to be in *any number of* a specified set of cities (for example, supplier S1 might in both London and Paris). Relvar DS can handle this situation, too, so long as we change the predicate appropriately: *Supplier S# is located in some of the cities in CITIES and not in any city not in CITIES.* In fact, this design could even handle suppliers who are in no cities at all, if we allow the CITIES value for such suppliers to be an empty relation: negative information again, of a kind.[1]

I'll close this discussion with a question for you to ponder. Consider the following **Tutorial D** expression:

---

1. I remark in passing that this state of affairs is closely related to a point I've made elsewhere (see, e.g., reference [6]): namely, that relation valued attributes provide a better basis—a *much* better basis—than nulls do for dealing with "missing information"! In particular, the operation of outer join as usually understood (see Appendix A) would be completely unnecessary if the system were to support relation valued attributes properly.

```
DS UNGROUP ( CITIES )
```

Given DS as shown in Fig. 4.5, this expression produces the "ungrouped" relation shown in Fig. 4.6.

S#	CITY
S1	London
S1	Paris
S1	Athens
S3	London
S3	Paris

Fig. 4.6: Ungrouping the relation in Fig. 4.5 on CITIES

The question for you is: Could we use an ungrouped version of relvar DS (instead of the previous version, with its relation valued attribute CITIES) to get around the CWA problems with disjunction? If not, why not?

CONCLUDING REMARKS

As I suggested near the beginning of this chapter, arguments along the lines of those I've been presenting make me extremely skeptical of claims to the effect that "the semantic web community operates under an open world assumption." In fact, I think such claims can make sense only if the "semantic web community" attaches some interpretation to the term "open world assumption" very different from the one I've been discussing. However, I'll have to leave an explanation of any such different interpretation to someone more knowledgeable than I am with respect to the semantic web (my own perhaps rather superficial search of the literature wasn't much help).

I also said near the beginning of the chapter that, while we in the database community certainly do use the Closed World Assumption, we're often rather sloppy in specifying just what world it is that's closed. As I've tried to show, that world is typically not "the real world" as such but, rather, our knowledge of that real world. Thus, the exclusion of a given tuple will typically mean we don't know the truth value of the corresponding proposition—that sounds more like the OWA—*except* in the important special case when the proposition corresponding to the excluded tuple is actually in contradiction to that corresponding to some included tuple, in which case we do know the pertinent truth value: namely, FALSE.[1]

---

1. I'm being sloppy again ... What I mean here by "the proposition corresponding to a given tuple" isn't actually the proposition corresponding to that tuple, which is of the form "We know that *p* is true" for some proposition *p*. Rather, it's that proposition *p* (i.e., it's what's left when the "We know that" portion is removed).

There's one more point I'd like to make. The fact is, I've been making yet another assumption throughout this chapter (!): I've been assuming that either every relvar in the database is subject to the CWA or every relvar in the database is subject to the OWA. But is this assumption necessary? Codd didn't think so. In reference [2]—where he talks about closed and open world *interpretations,* rather than the closed and open world assumptions—he says this:

> Although the closed world interpretation is usually the one adopted for commercial databases, there is a case for permitting some [relvars] ... to have the open world interpretation, while others ... have the closed world interpretation.

It seems to me, however, that allowing a mixture of interpretations in this way is likely to lead to serious difficulties in making sense of query results. Perhaps more study is required.

ACKNOWLEDGMENTS

I'd like to thank Peter Robson, whose request for a presentation on the subject of this chapter at the Edinburgh workshop mentioned earlier forced me to get my thoughts on that subject organized into some kind of order. I'd also like to thank Hugh Darwen for helpful comments on earlier drafts.

REFERENCES AND BIBLIOGRAPHY

1.   K. L. Clark: "Negation as Failure," in Hervé Gallaire and Jack Minker (eds.), *Logic and Data Bases.* New York, N.Y.: Plenum Press (1978).

2.   E. F. Codd: "Extending the Database Relational Model to Capture More Meaning," *ACM TODS 4,* No. 4 (December 1979).

3.   Hugh Darwen: "The Nullologist in Relationland," in C. J. Date and Hugh Darwen, *Relational Database Writings 1989-1991.* Reading, Mass.: Addison-Wesley (1992).

4.   Hugh Darwen: "Outer Join with No Nulls and Fewer Tears," in C. J. Date and Hugh Darwen, *Relational Database Writings 1989-1991.* Reading, Mass.: Addison-Wesley (1992).

5.   Hugh Darwen: "How to Handle Missing Information Without Using Nulls" (presentation slides), *www.thethirdmanifesto.com* (May 9th, 2003).

6.   C. J. Date: *An Introduction to Database Systems* (8th edition). Boston, Mass.: Addison-Wesley (2004).

7.   C. J. Date: *Database in Depth: Relational Theory for Practitioners.* Sebastopol, Calif.: O'Reilly Media, Inc. (2005).

8.   C. J. Date: *The Relational Database Dictionary.* Sebastopol, Calif.: O'Reilly Media Inc. (2006).

9. C. J. Date: "On the Notion of Logical Difference," in *Date on Database: Writings 2000-2006*. Berkeley, Calif.: Apress (2006).

10. C. J. Date: "What First Normal Form Really Means," in *Date on Database: Writings 2000-2006*. Berkeley, Calif.: Apress (2006).

11. C. J. Date: "Why Three- and Four-Valued Logic Don't Work," in *Date on Database: Writings 2000-2006*. Berkeley, Calif.: Apress (2006).

12. C. J. Date and Hugh Darwen: *Databases, Types, and the Relational Model: The Third Manifesto* (3rd edition). Boston, Mass.: Addison-Wesley (2006).

13. C. J. Date, Hugh Darwen, and Nikos A. Lorentzos: *Temporal Data and the Relational Model*. San Francisco, Calif.: Morgan Kaufmann (2003).

14. Hervé Gallaire, Jack Minker, and Jean-Marie Nicolas: "Logic and Databases: A Deductive Approach," *ACM Comp. Surv. 16,* No. 2 (June 1984).

15. International Organization for Standardization (ISO): *Database Language SQL,* Document ISO/IEC 9075:2003 (2003).

16. David McGoveran: "Nothing from Nothing" (in four parts), in C. J. Date, Hugh Darwen, and David McGoveran, *Relational Database Writings 1994-1997*. Reading, Mass.: Addison-Wesley (1998).

17. Raymond Reiter: "On Closed World Data Bases," in Hervé Gallaire and Jack Minker (eds.), *Logic and Data Bases*. New York, N.Y.: Plenum Press (1978).

18. Raymond Reiter: "Towards a Logical Reconstruction of Relational Database Theory," in Michael L. Brodie, John Mylopoulos, and Joachim W. Schmidt (eds.), *On Conceptual Modelling: Perspectives from Artificial Intelligence, Databases, and Programming Languages*. New York, N.Y.: Springer-Verlag (1984).

19. Jeffrey D. Ullman: *Principles of Database and Knowledge-Base Systems: Volume I*. Rockville, Md.: Computer Science Press (1988).

20. Ludwig J. J. Wittgenstein: Preface to *Tractatus Logico-Philosophicus* (translated by Frank Ramsey, 1921).

APPENDIX A: WHAT ABOUT OUTER JOIN?

In the body of this chapter I briefly discussed the Darwen and McGoveran approaches to "missing information." It might have occurred to you, however, in connection with both of those approaches that there's a possible problem—namely, what happens if we want to bring known and unknown information together in the result of some query? Let me briefly consider this issue. For definiteness, I'll limit the discussion to the Darwen approach, but essentially similar considerations apply to the McGoveran approach also.

Consider Fig. 4.7 (a repeat of Fig. 4.3) and the query "Get all suppliers under contract and corresponding cities." The problem is, of course, that supplier S7 has no known "corresponding city." A user familiar with SQL might therefore be tempted to formulate this query in terms of *outer join*—e.g., as follows:

```
SELECT S#, CITY
FROM    S NATURAL LEFT OUTER JOIN CITY_UNKNOWN
```

The result is shown in Fig. 4.8.

Fig. 4.7: Supplier S7's city is unknown—Darwen's approach (same as Fig. 4.3)

Fig. 4.8: SQL outer join of S and CITY_UNKNOWN from Fig. 4.7

As you can see, the result "contains a null" in the CITY column for supplier S7;[1] thus, you might conclude that all of the machinations I went through in the body of the chapter to demonstrate that we can still get "don't know" answers without resorting to nulls and three-valued logic were pretty pointless, because we still need nulls in certain query results.

But, of course, we *don't* need nulls and three-valued logic (not for the foregoing reason and not for any other reason, either). As with the example in the section "Putting It All Together" in the body of the chapter, what we can do is use character strings to represent either the name of the city, when the city is known, or the fact that no such name is known when it isn't. Here's a **Tutorial D** expression that does exactly that (I'll leave the SQL analog as an exercise for you):

```
UNION { EXTEND CITY_UNKNOWN ADD ('Unknown' AS CITY_INFO ) ) ,
          S RENAME ( CITY AS CITY_INFO ) }
```

The result is shown in Fig. 4.9.

S#	CITY_INFO
S1	London
S2	Paris
S3	Paris
S4	London
S5	Athens
S7	Unknown

Fig. 4.9: Using character strings to represent city information

Finally, let me point out that we could easily (if desired) add a "respectable" form of outer join to the relational algebra that would simplify the formulation of queries like the one just shown. Reference [4] includes some suggestions in this regard.

---

1. I apologize for the wording here; as I've written elsewhere, to talk about anything "containing a null" actually makes no logical sense. Indeed, one of the problems with nulls is precisely that you can't talk about them sensibly! As I've written elsewhere [11], the entire topic is a perfect illustration of *The Principle of Incoherence* (sometimes referred to, a trifle unkindly, as *The Incoherent Principle*)—*viz.,* it's hard to criticize something coherently if what you're trying to criticize is itself not very coherent in the first place.

Chapter 5

Why Relational DBMSs

Must Be Based on Logic

Relation elation
Edgar F. Codd
Invented a model
For large data banks
And if you think object
Orientation
Is somehow superior—
Well, thanks, but no thanks.

—Anon.: *Where Bugs Go*

Like reference [1]—which should preferably be read first—this chapter can be seen as a tutorial on logic for database practitioners.   Unlike reference [1], however, which concerned itself mostly just with logic as such, the present chapter explicitly addresses the topic from a database point of view. It's adapted, with permission, from Part 1 of a four-part paper by David McGoveran with the overall title "Nothing from Nothing," which originally appeared in *Database Programming & Design 6,* No. 12 (December 1993) and was republished in my book *Relational Database Writings 1994-1997* (Addison-Wesley, 1998).   One broad aim of that four-part paper was to show why many-valued logics were unsuitable as a basis on which to build a DBMS.   In order to achieve that aim, however, it first had to show why classical two-valued logic *was* suitable—indeed, required—as such a basis, and that's what the first part of the paper did. With a certain amount of editing and pruning, therefore, I believe that first part can serve as a good standalone tutorial on the crucial relationship between DBMSs and logic in general.

Note: Since this chapter was originally written by David McGoveran, the first person singular in what follows refers to David specifically; the first person plural refers to both of us. I should add that David is currently working on a book of his own, and the material of this chapter will doubtless appear in that book also, though in a very different form.

OVERALL DBMS GOALS

The overall purpose of a database management system (DBMS) is to provide shared, reusable, and efficient services for the definition, capture, organization, and manipulation of data. The DBMS should carry out these tasks in such a manner as to ensure the integrity of the data, regardless of user actions or system failures. But there's another goal too, one that drives much of what differentiates relational DBMSs from other kinds:

Changes to the data should not require changes to applications, and vice versa.

If this goal—i.e, the goal of *data independence,* as it's usually called—is realized, it has the effect of reducing both (a) the amount of code that must be written for a given application in the first place and (b) the amount of maintenance that must be done on that code subsequently. Curiously, however, the goal is often forgotten, although it has had a strong impact on the features needed in a relational DBMS.

Data independence implies that applications must be independent of physical data organization and access methods. If this goal is to be achieved, the user's data access language must be *declarative* (sometimes called "nonprocedural"); for otherwise a change to physical data organization or access methods, such as might be required as the database grows or is tuned for performance, will require a compensating change in applications. What's more, much of the data access code found in prerelational applications involves sorting and searching data, typically using numerous control loops. If this code can be moved out of individual applications and somehow shared by all, obvious gains can be obtained with respect to application coding and maintenance (with respect to performance optimization also).

Considerations such as the foregoing imply that we should try to minimize the number of distinct data access routines, at least as seen by applications. In other words, we need a special user language (the "data sublanguage" or "query language") that employs the smallest number of operations. At odds with the "smallest number of operations" goal, however, is the requirement that the language be capable of expressing every possible request for the pertinent application set (including ad hoc queries in particular). Also at odds with that same goal is the fact that the most efficient method of access does depend, somewhat, on physical data organization. So the question becomes: How can we map the comparatively small number of data access routines available in the user language to the possibly many such routines existing under the covers, each tailored to some particular physical data organization and some particular kind of data? And, as is well known, the answer is: By automatic data access code optimization.

Automatic optimization in this sense requires knowledge of the physical organization of the data—and if the database is changing rapidly, that knowledge must be up to the minute. So where in the overall system is that information available? Where should the shared data access code be maintained, and where should that optimization take place? The obvious answer to all of these questions is: in the DBMS.

But this line of argument leads to a fundamental problem. To be specific, how exactly can the optimizer (the code within the DBMS that performs the optimization we're talking about) be able to do its job? The techniques used by conventional language compilers for optimization of conventional procedural code are comparatively straightforward; in particular, they don't usually alter the algorithm as coded by the application developer. As a consequence, they aren't appropriate for the task at hand. What we need is a different kind of optimization, one that substitutes equivalent but more efficient algorithms—i.e., data access methods—for the user's data access routines. One important implication of this difference is that the DBMS optimizer must be able to identify algorithm equivalences; in particular, it must have provably correct rules by which it can determine such equivalences. Also, of course, it must be able to evaluate the relative cost of the algorithms available to it.

Considerations such as the foregoing lead to one inevitable conclusion: *The DBMS must be a formal logical system.*[1] In order to see what's possible in this regard, we need to take a brief look at the components and properties of formal logical systems in general.

PROPOSITIONAL CALCULUS

On the principle that "It is downright sinful to teach the abstract before the concrete" [5], I'll start with a brief overview of conventional two-valued propositional calculus (also known as propositional logic),[2] though in fact I hope you already know something about this topic. First of all, then, a *proposition* in propositional logic is something that's either true or false, unequivocally; for example, "The sun is a star" and "The sun is a planet" are both propositions (the first of which is true and the second false, of course). Propositional logic has the following four components:

- A *vocabulary*—namely, *t* and *f,* denoting the truth values TRUE and FALSE, respectively; a collection of symbols *p, q, r,* ... denoting variables whose values are propositions and hence, in effect, truth values; certain grouping indicators (parentheses, braces, and so on); and certain logical operators or *connectives* (NOT, OR, AND, and so on).

- A set of *formation rules*—i.e., rules for governing the formulation of syntactically correct truth valued expressions or *well formed formulas* (hereinafter *wffs,* pronounced "wiffs").

- A set of *axioms*—i.e., an initially given set of wffs, each of which is guaranteed, or at least assumed, to be true.

- A set of *rules of inference*—i.e., rules by which a new wff can be derived from existing wffs. I'll give examples of such rules in the subsection after the one immediately following.

Connectives

The connectives of propositional logic can be (and usually are) defined by means of *truth tables.* A truth table is a tabular structure that shows truth value(s) for the output from the connective in question given truth value(s) for its input(s).[3] For example, here are truth tables for NOT, OR, and AND:

---

1. Chapter 3 makes essentially the same claim for the database as such, and the present chapter makes the same claim, later, for database languages like **Tutorial D** [3]. There's no contradiction here, however; that is, the claims aren't mutually exclusive.

2. Throughout this chapter I'll take the term *logic,* unqualified, to refer to two-valued logic specifically, unless the context demands otherwise; from this point forward, therefore, I won't bother to spell out the qualifier *two-valued,* except occasionally for emphasis. Many-valued logics (i.e., *N*-valued logics for some *N* > 2) are discussed in the next chapter.

3. Truth tables can also be used to define inference rules (see later).

```
NOT|            OR | t f        AND| t f
———+———          ———+———        ———+———
 t | f           t | t t         t | t f
 f | t           f | t f         f | f f
```

Two other important connectives in propositional logic are IMPLIES and BI-IMPLIES (known formally as *material implication* and *material equivalence,* respectively, or just implication and equivalence for short), with truth tables as follows:

```
IMPLIES| t f      BI-IMPLIES| t f
————————+———      ——————————+———
   t    | t f         t     | t f
   f    | t t         f     | f t
```

The table for IMPLIES (the only one of those shown that's not symmetric) is meant to be read as follows: Let wffs *p* and *q* have truth values as indicated at the left and the top of the table, respectively; then the wff *p* IMPLIES *q* has truth values as indicated in the body of the table. In fact, as you can easily check for yourself, *p* IMPLIES *q* in fact has the same truth table as, and is therefore logically equivalent to, (NOT *p*) OR *q*.

In the same kind of way, *p* BI-IMPLIES *q* has the same truth table as, and is therefore logically equivalent to, (*p* IMPLIES *q*) AND (*q* IMPLIES *p*). *Note:* I use the name BI-IMPLIES in place of the more usual EQUIV, or EQUIVALENCE, for reasons of readability and intuitive understanding.

In general, a set of connectives is said to be *independent* if no connective in the set is such that its truth table can be expressed in terms of those for others in the set. It follows that, e.g., the set consisting of NOT, OR, and IMPLIES is not independent in this sense, since as we've already seen IMPLIES can be defined in terms of NOT and OR. As a matter of fact, the set consisting of NOT, OR, and AND also fails the test of independence (see the "Exercises" section later in this chapter).

Rules of Inference

To repeat, a rule of inference is a rule by which a new wff can be derived from existing ones. Moreover, if the given wffs are true, then the new one is true also and is called a *theorem.* A sequence of wffs, each of which either is an axiom or can be inferred from earlier wffs in the sequence by means of some rule of inference, is called a *proof;* to be specific, it's a proof of the final wff in the sequence. For example, suppose we're given the following wffs as axioms:

- I have no money.

- If I have no money, then I'll have to wash dishes.

Then we can infer, or deduce, that:

- I'll have to wash dishes.

This example illustrates the inference rule called *modus ponens,* which says that if we're given both *p* and *p* IMPLIES *q,* then we can infer *q.* In particular, if the first two of these wffs are true (let's assume they are, in the example), then the third is true as well; so "I'll have to wash dishes" is a theorem, and our example in fact illustrates the notion of proof as well.

Another important inference rule is the rule of *substitution,* which says that equivalent wffs can be substituted for one another. For example, given the wffs *p* IMPLIES *q* and *q* BI-IMPLIES *r,* we can infer (by substituting *r* for *q,* which is legitimate because they're equivalent) the wff *p* IMPLIES *r.*

LOGICAL SYSTEMS IN GENERAL

Now let's take a look at formal logical systems in general. In general, such a system consists of the same four kinds of objects as propositional logic does in particular: vocabulary, formation rules, axioms, and rules of inference. Note carefully, however, that:

- The vocabulary isn't necessarily the same as that of propositional logic. In particular, (a) it might include variables whose values aren't propositions, and (b) it might include different connectives. (It might also include different truth values, but for the purposes of the present chapter I'm assuming it doesn't.)

- The inference rules aren't necessarily the same as (or don't necessarily include) those of propositional logic, either.

However, the other notions introduced in connection with propositional logic (truth tables, proofs, theorems, and so forth) are still applicable. *Note:* It's important to understand that the definition of a logical system is meant to be applied in a purely mechanical fashion—that is, the process of determining whether a given object belongs to the vocabulary, or a given expression is a wff, or a given wff is an axiom, can't be based on (say) human intuition or the outcome of some random event. Determining whether or not a rule of inference has been properly applied is also meant to be a purely mechanical process.

Each possible choice for the objects that go to make up a logical system results in a different system.[1] It's true that certain logical systems can be shown to be equivalent to one another, but only in trivial ways (usually involving mere differences of notation—e.g., using Greek letters in place of English ones for symbols—or relabeling some axioms as theorems and vice versa). Not all logical systems are equally powerful.

---

1. Note that this observation is true of the axioms in particular. It follows that if sets *s1* and *s2* both consist of just the four components that go to make up (say) propositional logic, but *s1* contains one set of axioms and *s2* another, then *s1* and *s2* define two distinct propositional logics. Of course, all such logics bear a strong family resemblance to one another, as it were, so no real harm is done if we talk—as indeed we normally do—in terms of "the" propositional logic, as if there were just one such.

Relational Languages

A relational language such as **Tutorial D** [3] can be regarded, at least partially, as a formal logical system as just defined, except that the wffs in such a language can (and usually do) include references to variables that aren't themselves truth valued but, rather, have values that imply the truth or falsity of the wffs in question. For example, the expression $X > 2$ is a valid wff in **Tutorial D,** and of course it evaluates to TRUE if and only if the current value of the numeric variable X is greater than two. Apart from this point, however, such a language is in fact basically just a concrete realization of propositional logic as previously defined. For example, the components of **Tutorial D** can be regarded from this point of view as follows:

Vocabulary:

- *Variables:* Any truth valued expression (e.g., $X > 2$)
- *Grouping indicators:* ( ) { }
- *Truth values:* TRUE FALSE
- *Connectives:* NOT OR AND (etc.)

Formation Rules:

- Rules for formulating syntactically correct relational expressions (and hence syntactically correct retrieval and update statements)

Axioms:

- No explicit axioms, though each tuple in the database can be regarded as representing an axiom

Rule of Inference:

- *Substitution:* Equivalent expressions can be substituted for one another

Interpretation

Let *s* be some set of wffs in some logical system. Then a specific set of assignments of truth values to the variables mentioned in *s* is called an *interpretation* of *s*. For example, let *s* contain the wffs *p* AND *q* and *p* OR *q* (only); then assigning, say, FALSE to *p* and TRUE to *q* constitutes one possible interpretation of *s*. By way of illustration, *p* and *q* might stand for the propositions "London is the capital of France" and "Canberra is the capital of Australia," respectively—in which case the two wffs in *s*, *p* AND *q* and *p* OR *q*, would indeed evaluate to FALSE and TRUE, respectively.

    Note: As I mentioned in the previous subsection, wffs in some systems—including in particular the one that underlies relational languages such as **Tutorial D**—can include references to variables that aren't themselves truth valued but whose values imply the truth or falsity of the wffs in question. Any interpretation of such wffs will then have to include the values assigned to the (non truth valued) variables in question.

    An important illustration of the notion of interpretation is provided by the relations in a relational database.[1] Any such relation corresponds to a certain *predicate*—see later for an explanation of this term—in which each parameter corresponds to an attribute of the relation in question. For example, consider the suppliers relation S from the familiar suppliers-and-parts database. That relation has four attributes: supplier number (S#), supplier name (SNAME), status (STATUS), and city (CITY). The corresponding predicate is: "There exists a supplier under contract with S# w and SNAME x and STATUS y and CITY z" (where w, x, y, and z are parameters). A given supplier tuple, say the tuple < S1,Smith,20,London > (I adopt this simplified notation for tuples for readability), represents an "instantiation" of that predicate with particular arguments substituted for w, x, y, and z. And if substituting particular arguments for w, x, y, and z produces a tuple that does actually appear in the relation, the wff resulting from those substitutions is considered to evaluate to TRUE; otherwise, it's considered to evaluate to FALSE.

A logical system is said to be *correct* (or *sound*) if and only it has the property that every interpretation that makes all of its axioms true also makes all of its theorems true.

Truth Functional Completeness

The truth tables defining the connectives in a given logical system allow the truth value of a given wff to be determined in a purely mechanical manner from the truth values of the components of that wff. A logical system that satisfies this property is said to be *truth functional*. (Logical systems do exist that don't satisfy this property, but they're beyond the scope of the present discussion.) Further, a logical system is said to be *truth functionally complete* if and only if, given a set of connectives defined by truth tables, every possible truth table can be expressed in terms of the given ones—i.e., if and only if all possible connectives can be defined in terms of the given ones. Truth functional completeness is an extremely important property; a logical system that didn't satisfy it would be quite difficult to use (it would be like a system of arithmetic that had no support for certain operations, say the operation of addition).

Tautologies and Related Matters

Within a given logical system, a *tautology* is a wff that always evaluates to TRUE. For example, the wff p OR (NOT p) is a tautology in propositional logic: It always evaluates to TRUE, regardless of the value of p. Contrariwise, a *contradiction* is a wff that always evaluates to FALSE. For example, the wff p AND (NOT p) is a contradiction in propositional logic because it always evaluates to FALSE, again regardless of the value of p. Note that, by definition, the axioms of any given logical system are tautologies under the intended interpretation (see the subsection "Practical Application," immediately following this one). Moreover:

- If a logical system is correct (see the subsection before last) and every wff that's a theorem is also a tautology—i.e., if everything provable is true—then the system is *consistent;* otherwise, it's *inconsistent. Note:* These terms have meanings in logic that are related to, but not quite the same

---

1. The original version of this chapter was written before the term *relvar* was introduced, and its use of the term *relations* sometimes refers to what we would now call relvars.

as, their usual meanings in natural language (*inconsistent* in particular is usually understood to mean contradictory, in ordinary discourse). Logicians refer to the "ordinary discourse" meanings as *negation* consistency and inconsistency, respectively (*negation consistent* in particular meaning it's impossible for a wff and its negation both to be true).

- Conversely, if a logical system is correct and every wff that's a tautology is also a theorem—i.e., if everything true is provable—then the system is *deductively complete*. Moreover, a system is deductively complete *in a strong sense* if no wff not derivable from the axioms can be added to the axioms without making the system inconsistent. (In fact, it can be shown that adding a new independent axiom to a system that's both consistent and deductively complete in a strong sense has the effect of making that system inconsistent.)

Finally, a system is *decidable* if and only if there exists an algorithm by which it can be determined whether an arbitrary wff is a theorem. Propositional calculus is decidable. It's also deductively complete and negation consistent.

Practical Application

Most logical systems are meant to be used for some practical purpose. Let's agree to say that our understanding of the subject matter of that practical purpose—it might be accounting, for example—is an *informal theory* of the subject in question; such a theory will typically consist of some informal collection of rules, requirements, descriptions, etc. The scope of whatever such theory we happen to be dealing with is called *the universe of discourse* (for the theory in question).

The practical application of a logical system is realized by assigning meaning to the elements of the vocabulary. From that intended meaning, it should be possible to assign an obvious truth value to each truth valued variable—in other words, to specify a certain interpretation, called the *intended* interpretation. For example, in an accounting database, the intended interpretation of the attribute ACCOUNT# would be the set of permissible account numbers for the actual business; we wouldn't want users to substitute, say, a product number for ACCOUNT# (note that such a substitution would necessarily fail to satisfy the predicate the ACCOUNTS relation is supposed to correspond to).

For any such practical application, we try to set up the system in such a way that it has the properties of *correctness, deductive completeness,* and *expressive completeness,* where:

- *Correctness* (to repeat) means that every interpretation that makes all of the axioms true also makes all of the theorems true (i.e., all theorems are tautologies).

- *Deductive completeness* (also to repeat) means that every "true fact" that's expressible in the system is provable (i.e., all tautologies are theorems).

- *Expressive completeness* means that every statement of the informal theory is expressible in the system.

The first two of these objectives taken together mean that we intend, under any interpretation that makes the axioms true, for the set of true expressions to be identical to the set of provable expressions. The third objective means we haven't overlooked anything.

PREDICATE CALCULUS

As previously noted, propositional calculus is deductively complete, negation consistent, and decidable; unfortunately, however, it's expressively weak. In particular, propositional calculus is not generally capable of recognizing whether two propositions do or don't share a common subject. As a consequence, certain valid deductions can only be performed outside of the intended interpretation. For example, the Greek Stoics recognized the problem with the following (invalid) argument, called *The Nobody:*

- *Premise:* If someone is here, then he's not in Rhodes.

- *Premise:* Someone is here.

- *Conclusion:* Therefore, it's not the case that someone is in Rhodes!

This line of reasoning would, of course, be valid if we replaced the word *someone* by the name of an individual, say Ted. As it is, however, the word *someone* is ambiguous: It refers to a specific individual for part of the time and to some nonspecific individual for the rest of the time. Propositional calculus can't resolve this problem because it has no way of representing the concept of propositions that share a common subject. By contrast, *predicate* calculus does help with this kind of reasoning.

Predicate calculus—technically, *first order* predicate calculus, but the reason for and significance of that "first order" qualifier is beyond the scope of this chapter—is an extension of propositional calculus; in particular, its wffs, unlike those of propositional calculus, can be predicates. A predicate is *a truth valued function.* Like all functions, it has a set of zero or more *parameters,*[1] and it's that fact that constitutes the most fundamental difference between predicate calculus and propositional calculus. In the case of *The Nobody,* for example, it's easy to see that the three occurrences of the word *someone* don't all correspond to the same parameter, and the fallacy in the argument is thereby exposed. (Note that the parameters of predicate calculus are certainly not limited to being truth valued; rather, they can take their values from any domain we like—for example, the domain of natural numbers.)

I remark as an aside that the term *extension* is being used in the foregoing paragraph in a slightly technical sense. To be specific, when we say that predicate calculus is an extension of propositional calculus, what we mean is that if all of the additional concepts that predicate calculus introduces were to be deleted, what would remain would be, precisely, the familiar propositional calculus. (The next chapter [4] has more to say on the subject of extensions in this technical sense.)

To repeat, a predicate is a truth valued function, involving zero or more parameters. It can be thought of as an assertion to the effect that its parameters taken in combination possess a certain property. Any given parameter is interpreted by assigning it a value (an *argument*) from a domain of

---

1. Also known as *free variables.* There's a parallel here with the way algebra introduces variables to extend arithmetic, though the term *variable* doesn't mean quite the same thing in the two cases. *Note:* Some logicians refer to the parameters of predicate logic as *predicate variables,* but this term unfortunately (and incorrectly) suggests that the variables in question have predicates as their values.

possible values. (In fact, we've already touched on this notion of parameters and corresponding arguments in our discussion in the previous section—in the subsection titled "Interpretation"—of the predicates that correspond to database relations.) Note that, in any given interpretation, all occurrences of the same parameter must be assigned the same argument value. For example, in the compound predicate "*x* is red AND *x* is angry," it's not permissible to replace the first *x* by Jules and the second by Jim. *Note:* A predicate with zero parameters is just a proposition—it evaluates to either TRUE or FALSE, unequivocally.

Predicate calculus also introduces the notion of *quantifiers*. Let *P* be a predicate with sole parameter *x* (the explanations that follow are easily generalized to the case of a predicate with two or more parameters). Then the expressions EXISTS *x* (*P(x)*) and FORALL *x* (*P(x)*) are both wffs—in fact, predicates—in turn:

- EXISTS *x* (*P(x)*) is an *existentially quantified* wff; EXISTS *x* is an existential quantifier, and *x* is a *quantified variable,* also known as a *bound* variable. In effect, the wff represents a claim that there exists at least argument value *v* that can be assigned to the variable *x* that will satisfy the predicate *P*. Overall, the wff EXISTS *x* (*P(x)*) can be thought of—but only informally!—as the propositional connective OR iterated over (a) *P(v)* for all values *v* in the domain of *x* and (b) the truth value FALSE.

- FORALL *x* (*P(x)*) is a *universally* quantified wff; FORALL *x* is a universal quantifier, and *x* is (again) a quantified or bound variable. In effect, the wff represents a claim that all argument values *v* that can be assigned to the variable *x* will satisfy the predicate *P*. Overall, the wff FORALL *x* (*P(x)*) can be thought of—but again only informally—as the propositional connective AND iterated over (a) *P(v)* for all values *v* in the domain of *x* and (b) the truth value TRUE.

The reason for those "but only informally" qualifications in the foregoing explanations is this: Predicate calculus, again unlike propositional calculus, is capable of handling infinite domains (e.g., the domain of natural numbers). Clearly, any attempt to formulate an "iterated OR" algorithm for EXISTS over an infinite domain must fail, since the evaluation might never terminate (it might never find the one argument that makes the predicate true); likewise, any attempt to formulate an "iterated AND" algorithm for FORALL over an infinite domain must also fail, since again the evaluation might never terminate (it might never find the one argument that makes the predicate false). It's important to understand, therefore, that in general the predicate calculus quantifiers EXISTS and FORALL are actually not just iterated propositional OR and AND, respectively—they can validly be thought of in this way only when the number of possible values the quantified variables can take is guaranteed to be finite.

Predicate calculus is deductively complete and consistent, but it's not decidable (i.e., there's no algorithm for determining whether an arbitrary wff is a theorem). But if a restricted version of predicate calculus is constructed in which (a) the number of free and bound variables permitted in any given expression is finite and (b) the domains for those variables are also finite, then that restricted (in other words, finite) version is decidable after all. Note that, technically speaking, imposing these restrictions changes the intended meaning of the quantifiers and reduces certain rules of inference to the corresponding rules for propositional calculus. Thus, although the relational model is usually said to be based on predicate calculus, in practice any implementation of that model will be more like the finite version described here; i.e., at any given point in time, any real database will have a finite number of relations, attributes, domains, permitted values, and so on.

THE DBMS AS A LOGICAL SYSTEM

Let me now try to relate everything I've been saying to database management in particular. When we design a relational database, we specify a set of predicates (the defining predicates for relations), which we call *relation predicates*.[1] A given tuple can appear in a given relation only if it satisfies the applicable relation predicate. Each tuple actually appearing in one of these relations represents a true instantiation of the applicable relation predicate. The total set of such true instantiations can be understood as the axioms of the system; together, they effectively constitute the intended interpretation of the system.

I remark in passing that the well known discipline of normalization can be thought of as a means of helping to ensure that relation predicates don't in fact consist of several independent such predicates in combination (it's a means of eliminating redundancies of a certain specific kind). In other words, normalization helps to ensure—though of course it doesn't guarantee—the independence of the axiom set.

By establishing a set of database domains (also called *types* [3]), we effectively constrain the universe of discourse (domains, along with various integrity constraints, serve to implement the relation predicates). When we insert a tuple into the database, we're effectively claiming that substituting values from that tuple for the applicable parameters in the applicable relation predicate results in a "true fact" (i.e., a true proposition). We can regard each such tuple as a premise from which conclusions can be drawn using the formal axioms and rules of inference of the system. If a tuple could legitimately appear in a given relation but doesn't in fact appear, we regard the proposition corresponding to that tuple as false [2].

When we write a query, we're attempting, in effect, to write a wff (i.e., a predicate in its own right). Of course, the system will verify that what we've written is indeed a wff—i.e., that it's syntactically correct. The optimizer can then be understood as applying various rules of inference, axioms, and theorems to produce a set of equivalent wffs, each of which uses only operations that have a physical access method associated with them. Each tuple returned by the DBMS represents a collection of argument values that, on proper substitution into the predicate, result in propositions that evaluate to TRUE in the logical system. The set of all such returned tuples is a provable theorem of the system. The important point to remember is this: Whenever we execute a series of statements in a transaction or application, or issue a sequence of decision support queries, or embed a subquery in a query, or decompose a query into a set of subqueries, we're using the axioms and rules of inference of the logical system to prove theorems!

DESIRABLE PROPERTIES OF A DBMS

From everything I've said in this chapter prior to this point, it should be clear that certain properties are desirable of a DBMS. To be specific, the DBMS should be *a logical system* (or an implementation of such a system), and that logical system should be *familiar, uniformly interpretable, truth functional, truth*

---

1. Or *relvar* predicates [3].

functionally complete, expressively complete, deductively complete, consistent, and (ideally) *decidable.* These objectives can be explained intuitively as follows:

- *Familiar:* The common understanding of the truth values, connectives, rules of inference, and accepted tautologies should apply. In other word, users shouldn't have to learn an unfamiliar or counterintuitive logical system, one that contains surprising theorems and tautologies or invalidates commonly understood rules of inference (and thereby leads to the likelihood of user error).

- *Uniformly interpretable:* The intended interpretation of every symbol, truth value, and query should be unambiguous, irrespective of the state of the database.

- *Truth functional:* It should be possible for the evaluation of a query (i.e., a wff) to proceed mechanically from evaluation of its components. As a consequence, it should be possible to formulate and understand queries of arbitrary complexity on the basis of an understanding of the connectives alone.

- *Truth functionally complete:* The connectives in the query language should suffice to express every connective definable by means of some truth table. In other words, for every possible fact in the universe of discourse, there should be a truth valued expression that determines whether that fact is represented in or can be derived from the database.

- *Expressively complete:* All queries that are meaningful in the context of the application should be expressible. All relevant facts about the application environment should be representable in the database.

- *Deductively complete:* Every fact represented by the database, either implicitly or explicitly, should be obtainable via some query.

- *Consistent:* The result of every query should represent facts that can be inferred from the database.

- *Decidable:* Although not strictly required, a decidable and consistent system would have the advantage that a query could be checked via an algorithm to see whether it's (a) a tautology (in which case every tuple would satisfy the query), or (b) a contradiction (in which case no tuples would satisfy the query), or (c) neither.

Conventional two-valued propositional or (finite) predicate logic meets these objectives admirably. By contrast, I'll argue in the next chapter [4] that many-valued logics don't do so, and in fact *can't* do so.

CONCLUDING REMARKS

My aim in this chapter has been to make the relationship between formal logic and DBMSs a little clearer (especially for database practitioners) than it sometimes seems to be. I've stated the goals that make it advantageous to use a logical system as the basis for database management, and I've presented the desirable properties of that logical system in database terms. At the very least, I would hope that database professionals should be able to use these logical concepts in evaluating the strengths and weaknesses of a given DBMS. While errors of implementation are sometimes to blame, the causes of performance, integrity, and maintenance problems very often lie in much more serious design flaws—flaws that involve a failure to capitalize on the logical foundation of relational theory. With a little practice, the concepts discussed in this chapter should prove useful in identifying such database and application design problems. You can start by insisting that DBMS vendors meet the logical objectives outlined in this chapter ... We should all be doing everything in our power to get the vendors to step up to their responsibility in this regard.

EXERCISES

1. Using the truth tables for NOT, OR, AND, and IMPLIES, give the truth tables for the following wffs:

   a. NOT (p AND (NOT p))

   b. NOT (p AND q)

   c. (NOT p) OR (NOT q)

   d. (NOT q) IMPLIES (NOT p)

2. Show that the truth table for (NOT p) OR q is the same as that for p IMPLIES q.

3. Show that NOT, OR, and AND aren't independent.

4. Show that the following wff is a tautology:

   ((NOT p) AND (p OR q)) IMPLIES q

5. Show that the following wff is a contradiction:

   (p IMPLIES q) IMPLIES (NOT ((NOT q) IMPLIES (NOT q)))

REFERENCES AND BIBLIOGRAPHY

1. C. J. Date: "The Building Blocks of Logic" (Chapter 1 in this book).

2. C. J. Date: "The Closed World Assumption" (Chapter 4 in this book).

3. C. J. Date and Hugh Darwen: *Databases, Types, and the Relational Model: The Third Manifesto* (3rd edition). Boston, Mass.: Addison-Wesley (2006).

4. David McGoveran and C. J. Date: "Why Relational DBMS Logic Must Not be Many-Valued" (Chapter 6 in this book).

5. Z. A. Melzak: *Companion to Concrete Mathematics. Volume 1, Mathematical Techniques and Various Applications,* Wiley (1973); *Volume 2, Mathematical Ideas, Modeling & Applications* (Wiley 1976); quoted in *Concrete Mathematics: A Foundation for Computer Science,* by Ronald L. Graham, Donald E. Knuth, and Oren Patashnik (2nd edition). Reading, Mass.: Addison-Wesley (1989).

APPENDIX A: ANSWERS TO EXERCISES

1a. Give the truth table for the wff NOT (p AND (NOT p)).

Answer: Since p AND (NOT p) is a contradiction, it should be obvious by inspection that the overall expression is a tautology. Be that as it may, here's the truth table (deliberately drawn a little differently from the tables in the body of the chapter):

p	NOT p	p AND (NOT p)	NOT (p AND (NOT p))
t	f	f	t
f	t	f	t

Since the final column contains t in every position, NOT (p AND (NOT p)) is a tautology.

1b. Give the truth table for the wff NOT (p AND q).

Answer:

p	q	p AND q	NOT (p AND q)
t	t	t	f
t	f	f	t
f	t	f	t
f	f	f	t

1c. Give the truth table for the wff (NOT p) OR (NOT q).

Answer:

p	q	NOT p	NOT q	(NOT p) OR (NOT q)
t	t	f	f	f
t	f	f	t	t
f	t	t	f	t
f	f	t	t	t

Observe that Answers 1b and 1c together show that NOT(p AND q) BI-IMPLIES ((NOT p) OR (NOT q)).

1d. Give the truth table for the wff (NOT q) IMPLIES (NOT p).

Answer:

p	q	NOT p	NOT q	(NOT q) IMPLIES (NOT p)
t	t	f	f	t
t	f	f	t	f
f	t	t	f	t
f	f	t	t	t

———— ♦♦♦♦♦ ————

2.   Show that the truth table for (NOT p) OR q is the same as that for p IMPLIES q.

Answer: Here is the combined truth table for (NOT p) OR q and p IMPLIES q:

p	q	NOT p	(NOT p) OR q	p IMPLIES q
t	t	f	t	t
t	f	f	f	f
f	t	t	t	t
f	f	t	t	t

Since the two final columns are identical, the desired result follows.

———— ♦♦♦♦♦ ————

3.   Show that NOT, OR, and AND aren't independent.

Answer: This fact follows from either of the following facts (basically De Morgan's Laws):

- The expressions (*p* OR *q*) and NOT((NOT *p*) AND (NOT *q*)) have the same truth table. Thus, OR can be defined in terms of NOT and AND.

- The expressions (*p* AND *q*) and NOT((NOT *p*) OR (NOT *q*)) have the same truth table. Thus, AND can be defined in terms of NOT and OR.

It follows that either OR or AND could be discarded with no loss of truth functional completeness.

4.   Show that the following wff is a tautology:

```
((NOT p) AND (p OR q)) IMPLIES q
```

Answer: Denote the given expression ((NOT *p*) AND (*p* OR *q*)) IMPLIES *q* by *w*. Then the truth table is:

p	*q*	NOT *p*	*p* OR *q*	(NOT *p*) AND (*p* OR *q*)	*w*
t	t	f	t	f	t
t	f	f	t	f	t
f	t	t	t	t	t
f	f	t	f	f	t

Since the final column contains *t* in every position, *w* is a tautology.

5.   Show that the following wff is a contradiction:

```
(p IMPLIES q) IMPLIES (NOT ((NOT q) IMPLIES (NOT q)))
```

Answer: Trick question! Let *p* and *q* be false and true, respectively; then *p* IMPLIES *q* is false. Since FALSE implies anything, the overall expression is true in this case, and is thus not a contradiction.

Chapter 6

Why Relational DBMS Logic

Must Not Be Many-Valued

I have nothing to say
and I am saying it and that is
poetry.

—John Cage: *Lecture on Nothing*

This chapter is a sequel to the previous one [14], and I assume you're at least broadly familiar with the material discussed therein. That previous chapter showed why relational DBMSs must be based on formal logic; the present chapter shows why that logic must not be many-valued (i.e., *N*-valued for some $N > 2$) but must be two-valued specifically. It's adapted, with permission, from Part 2 of a four-part paper by David McGoveran with the overall title "Nothing from Nothing," which originally appeared in *Database Programming & Design 7,* No. 1 (January 1994) and was republished in my book *Relational Database Writings 1994-1997* (Addison-Wesley, 1998).

Note: Since this chapter was originally written by David McGoveran, the first person singular in what follows refers to David specifically; the first person plural refers to both of us. I should add that David is currently working on a book of his own, and the material of this chapter will doubtless appear in that book also, though in a very different form.

DESIRABLE PROPERTIES OF A DBMS

In reference [14], I established the following as a set of objectives for a DBMS. First of all, the DBMS should be a logical system (or an implementation of a logical system). Second, that logical system should display all of the following properties:

- *Familiar:* The common understanding of the truth values, connectives, rules of inference, and accepted tautologies should apply. In other word, users shouldn't have to learn an unfamiliar or counterintuitive logical system, one that contains surprising theorems and tautologies or invalidates commonly understood rules of inference (and thereby leads to the likelihood of user error).

- *Uniformly interpretable:* The intended interpretation of every symbol, truth value, and query should be unambiguous, irrespective of the state of the database.

- *Truth functional:* It should be possible for the evaluation of a query (i.e., a well formed formula, or wff) to proceed mechanically from evaluation of its components. As a consequence, it should be possible to formulate and understand queries of arbitrary complexity on the basis of an understanding of the connectives alone.

- *Truth functionally complete:* The connectives in the query language should suffice to express every connective definable by means of a truth table. In other words, for every possible fact in the universe of discourse, there should be a truth valued expression that determines whether that fact is represented in or can be derived from the database.

- *Expressively complete:* All queries that are meaningful in the context of the application should be expressible. All relevant facts about the application environment should be representable in the database.

- *Deductively complete:* Every fact represented by the database, either implicitly or explicitly, should be obtainable via some query.

- *Consistent:* The result of every query should represent facts that can be inferred from the database.

- *Decidable:* Although not strictly required, a decidable and consistent system would have the advantage that a query could be checked via an algorithm to see whether it's (a) a tautology (in which case every tuple would satisfy the query), or (b) a contradiction (in which case no tuples would satisfy the query), or (c) neither.

Now, I claimed in this chapter's predecessor [14] that conventional two-valued logic does display all of these desirable properties. By contrast, I contend in the present chapter that no many-valued logic can possibly do so.[1] This conclusion is significant because it's frequently suggested that some many-valued logic or other is suitable as a basis for dealing with the problem of "missing information" in databases. Codd in particular was an advocate of this position; he first mentioned the idea in reference [1] and subsequently spelled it out in some detail (though not enough!) in references [2-5]. As is well known, SQL embraces such a position also, though SQL's implementation of an already flawed idea manages to introduce additional flaws of its own. *Note:* The specific many-valued logics advocated by Codd and SQL are widely discussed, and criticized, in the literature. But the discussion that follows is more general: While it does show that Codd's and (worse) SQL's three-valued logic are both ill defined—as a result of which I find myself unable to give formal arguments against any specific formal flaws they might possess!—most of the discussion applies to the problems, both formal and informal, that arise in attempts to use *any* many-valued logic for database work.

In what follows, I limit my attention to many-valued propositional logics specifically. This simplification is legitimate for at least three reasons:

---

1. This claim sparked off a certain amount of controversy when it first appeared; reference [11] in particular was very critical. Reference [9] consists of a set of detailed responses to the criticisms of reference [11].

- First, any many-valued predicate logic can be understood as a generalization of a corresponding many-valued propositional logic. Hence, certain problems with the propositional logic version carry over to the predicate logic version.

- Second, as pointed out (though not much stressed) in reference [14], real databases are finite. At worst, therefore, only a very limited version of predicate calculus need be considered, one with a finite number of finite domains. In other words, real DBMSs support only (a) a finite number of types (or domains), (b) a finite number of possible values for each of those types or domains, and (c) well formed formulas (wffs) of some finite maximum length. As a result, the number of propositions that can be expressed in the context of a real database is necessarily finite (as everyone knows who has ever written a query that the DBMS found too big to parse).

- Third, the formal investigation of many-valued predicate logic is immature anyway (there are comparatively few such investigations in the literature).

A CLASSIFICATION SCHEME

First I need to explain to what extent many-valued logics in general resemble one another and to what extent they differ. For example, consider the case of three-valued logics specifically. Most such logics (not all) adopt the same definitions for the connectives NOT, OR, and AND; however, they typically differ with respect to (a) the definitions for other connectives, (b) which connectives they take as primitive, and (c) which rules of inference apply.

Many-valued logics can be classified into three kinds, and this classification scheme allows us to take a divide and conquer approach in our investigation. It's based on the following *reduction procedure:*

Reduce the set of truth values that can be assigned to components of wffs to just conventional TRUE and FALSE, and compare the resulting logical system with conventional two-valued propositional logic (hereinafter abbreviated 2VL).

The three classes, slightly nonstandard (and here defined only informally), are as follows:

1. *Fragments:* A many-valued logic is a *fragment* if and only if it reduces under the foregoing procedure to some fragment (i.e., some proper subset) of 2VL; that is, some 2VL connectives or rules of inference are missing or some 2VL theorems or tautologies no longer hold, or both, in the reduced version.

2. *Extensions:* A many-valued logic is an *extension* if and only if it reduces to full 2VL (not some proper subset) under the foregoing procedure.

3. *Deviants:* A many-valued logic is a *deviant* if and only if it's neither a fragment nor an extension. A number of well known (and frequently referenced) many-valued logics fall into this category. Such logics are entirely different from conventional 2VL; as a consequence, they certainly fail to satisfy the familiarity objective from the previous section. What's more, such logics either fail to be truth functionally complete or have semantics that are hard to understand, as we'll see later in

this chapter.

Note: It's important to understand that the foregoing classification scheme is exhaustive—all many-valued logics fall into one or other of the three classes. I now proceed to examine each class in turn.

FRAGMENTS

To repeat, a many-valued logic is a fragment if and only if it degenerates under the reduction procedure to a fragment of 2VL, meaning that some 2VL connectives or rules of inference are missing or some 2VL theorems or tautologies no longer hold. It follows that, in general, a fragment will require users to understand which portions of 2VL no longer apply. This fact means that fragments necessarily violate the familiarity objective.

What's more, it's easy to see that a fragment must also necessarily violate the objective of truth functional completeness. One particular connective that a many-valued logic must support if it's to be truth functionally complete is what's called *the Slupecki T-function*.[1] The Slupecki T-function is a one-place connective that maps every truth value to a specific truth value that's neither true-like nor false-like (that is, to UNKNOWN, if the logic is three-valued; I'll have more to say later regarding UNKNOWN and the notion of "true-like" and "false-like" truth values in general). Note that this connective obviously can't be defined in terms of the classical 2VL connectives, since those 2VL connectives never produce any result other than TRUE or FALSE; indeed, that's one reason why a many-valued logic can't be truth functionally complete without it. But if a logic includes it, then by definition that logic can't be a fragment.

What's more, a meaningful interpretation of the T-function for database use is hard to imagine. So the very fact that (as we've just seen) a many-valued logic has to support that function in order to be truth functionally complete should be sufficient to serve as quite strong prima facie evidence that it's unreasonable to expect a many-valued logic to be useful for database work. That is, the fact that the T-function must be included for truth functional completeness, and the importance of certain tautologies implied by it, together mean that the logical system clearly violates the familiarity objective.

EXTENSIONS

The familiarity objective requires among other things that the truth tables for the connectives of a many-valued logic degenerate to those for 2VL under the reduction procedure. For example, here are the truth tables for NOT, OR, and AND as usually defined for three-valued logic (3VL) specifically:

---

1. T for *tertium* (Latin for third).

```
NOT|            OR | t u f      AND| t u f
---+            ---+            ---+
 t | f           t | t t t       t | t u f
 u | u           u | t u u       f | u u f
 f | t           f | t u f       f | f f f
```

Here *t*, *f*, and *u* stand for TRUE, FALSE, and UNKNOWN, respectively, where UNKNOWN is "the third truth value" and is usually regarded as occupying some kind of halfway position between TRUE and FALSE. Clearly, if we delete the rows and columns corresponding to *u* (UNKNOWN), we're left with the conventional 2VL truth tables. Equally clearly, such a property is highly desirable in a logic, if that logic is to be used by a DBMS. However, a many-valued logic can reduce to 2VL if and only if it's not truth functionally complete! Indeed, this fact is easy to see:

- By definition, every connective in a truth functionally complete logical system must be expressible either directly (as a primitive operator) or indirectly (by combining primitive connectives appropriately).

- In particular, the T-function from the previous section must be so expressible.

- But the T-function obviously can't be expressed in terms of 2VL connectives.

So if the logic is truth functionally complete it isn't an extension (it doesn't degenerate to 2VL under the reduction procedure), and if it's an extension it isn't truth functionally complete (it can't possibly support the T-function). It follows that an extension must violate either the familiarity objective or the truth functional completeness objective.

EXTENSIONS AND DEVIANTS

The familiarity objective is actually harder to satisfy than the discussions so far might suggest. The reason is that extensions and deviants both violate the objective of uniform interpretability. Few many-valued logics preserve those tautologies and rules of inference that users most commonly rely upon to reason about queries (see Appendix A).[1] There are two important implications:

- First, any tautology that's not preserved must never be used, not even implicitly, when working with a database using such a logic. (A trivial example is *p* OR NOT(*p*), which is a tautology in 2VL but not in 3VL.) Thus, extensions and deviant logics are less intuitive than 2VL, and, for practical purposes at least, are thus less deductively powerful as well.

---

1. Of course, users might not realize how much they depend on those tautologies and rules!

■ Second, the permissible rules of inference (used both by the user and the optimizer) must be sensitive to both (a) whether or not the database permits nulls and (b) whether or not it actually contains nulls.[1]

Let me elaborate on this latter point. There are two possibilities. If the system prohibits nulls, conventional 2VL can be used and the many-valued logic need never be learned. But if it permits nulls, then the many-valued logic rules of inference must be used from the beginning. The meanings of query results are then definite just so long as nulls don't actually appear in the database, and the uniform interpretability objective can be preserved. But if nulls actually appear, all queries become indefinite in meaning—even if the nulls appear in tables not accessed in the query under consideration![2] (I exclude here the rather bizarre possibility that the tables containing the nulls have no relationship whatsoever to the tables being accessed.) One null, anywhere in the database, changes the meaning of all related tables and thereby violates the uniform interpretability objective. Why? Because we can no longer think of the accessed tables as if they simply contained rows representing facts about the universe of discourse; instead, each row now represents a fact that has some relationship to information that's missing for some reason. By way of example, consider the familiar suppliers-and-parts database, with sample values as shown in Fig. 6.1 opposite.

Now, if the database prohibits nulls, then the results of all queries will have a definite and fairly intuitive meaning. But if rows like the one shown in Fig. 6.1 for part P2 in table P are permitted, the very meaning of both "parts" and "suppliers" changes! (To be more precise, the corresponding predicates change.) "Parts" are no longer things that are definitely located in a known city. And since "suppliers" are defined as supplying parts, by extension they're no longer suppliers of parts that are definitely located in a known city. Thus, even querying the suppliers table S—which contains no nulls—results in a fundamentally different kind of answer when the parts table P is permitted to contain nulls!

Now consider the difference between merely permitting rows with nulls and such a row actually appearing. As we've just seen, merely permitting such a row changes the meanings of the tables; in addition, however, such a row actually appearing changes the meaning of query results—even when the row in question is explicitly avoided, as it were. For example, suppose we want to see only suppliers "not affected" (?) by rows in table P with a null city. To retrieve those suppliers, we must first presume

---

1. By the term *null,* I mean a placeholder for an argument—not an argument as such (in other words, not a value)—that, typically, forces the applicable predicate to evaluate to neither TRUE nor FALSE. (SQL's NULL construct is a particularly bad implementation of such a placeholder.) Note that nulls are distinct from the UNKNOWN truth value; moreover, they can be of various kinds ("not applicable," "applicable but unknown," and so on).

2. I use the SQL terminology of tables, rows, and columns in this chapter (in place of the relational model terminology of relations, tuples, and attributes) because SQL does "support" many-valued logic and the relational model doesn't.

S

S#	SNAME	STATUS	CITY
S1	Smith	20	London
S2	Jones	10	Paris

SP

S#	P#	QTY
S1	P1	300
S1	P2	200
S2	P2	400

P

P#	PNAME	COLOR	WEIGHT	CITY
P1	Nut	Red	12.0	London
P2	Bolt	Green	17.0	*-null-*

Fig. 6.1: The suppliers-and-parts database—sample values

the existence of a relationship to rows in table P with a null city; we must then use that relationship to exclude those suppliers that *are* so "affected." In SQL, in other words, we must write a query along the following lines:

```
SELECT DISTINCT S.*
FROM    S
EXCEPT
SELECT DISTINCT S.*
FROM    S, SP, P
WHERE   S.S# = SP.S#
AND     SP.P# = P.P#
AND     P.CITY IS NULL
```

If there are no rows in table P with a null city, then this query gives suppliers who supply (if anything at all) parts that are definitely located in a known city. But if there *are* rows in table P "with a null city," then it gives suppliers who definitely don't supply those parts that are indefinitely located! Strange as it might seem, when rows with nulls actually appear in the database, the results of "null avoiding" queries are, in a sense, more definite regarding the indefinite!

Now, the reader might object that I've chosen a particular interpretation of null to illustrate these problems. However, I invite consideration of other interpretations as an exercise. No matter what the interpretation, the net effect is that if many-valued logic is in use, then database designers, developers, and users must all learn a whole new way of thinking. The practical costs of this state of affairs are hard to assess; certainly they do violence to the goals we set out to satisfy with a relational DBMS.

What about the objective of truth functional completeness? Sometimes we can make a many-valued logic truth functionally complete by adding a new axiom or a new connective (e.g., the Slupecki T-function discussed earlier). But adding a new axiom or new connective always has at least one of three undesirable consequences:

- It leads to theorems that have no counterpart in 2VL;

- Or it makes the system inconsistent;

- Or it makes the system truth functionally incomplete.

In fact, so long as the system fails to contain certain types of undesirable theorems (namely, ones having no 2VL counterpart, which would violate the familiarity objective), we can say, based on work by the logician Rose (see reference [15], page 166), that at least one of two consequences must result: Either the new axiom makes the system inconsistent, or the new axiom is a tautology of 2VL (i.e., it's something we intuitively thought was already true but actually wasn't). To elaborate briefly:

- The first of these alternatives (inconsistency) is clearly undesirable—it means that every wff becomes a tautology, even ones that would otherwise be contradictions. In an inconsistent system, you can prove anything! Suppose an SQL SELECT were issued against a database managed by a DBMS based on such a system. Regardless of the predicate in the WHERE clause, that predicate would be treated as TRUE for every row examined and would therefore never restrict the result set (i.e., every query would return all rows!).

- As for the second alternative (the new axiom is a 2VL tautology): In this case, the system can't be an extension of 2VL (since an extension requires adding a many-valued logic tautology and results in an inconsistent system). Thus, it's either a fragment or a deviant and is subject to the problems discussed earlier for such many-valued logics.

ADDITIONAL COMPLEXITIES

Suppose we're willing to give up on the truth functional completeness objective, under the assumption that the theorems that therefore can't be expressed (owing to the omission of certain connectives) are somehow "obscure." Perhaps we're even willing to give up, partly, on the familiarity objective, under the assumption that learning new tautologies and rules of inference isn't too burdensome a task. Even so, a many-valued logic introduces further undesirable complexities, having to do with (among other things) the number of connectives, the number of meaning assignments for connectives, meanings of query results, arbitrariness in the number of truth values, loss of deductive power, and unusual or nonintuitive semantics. I'll discuss each of these issues in turn.

Number of connectives: The number of connectives in a logic depends exponentially on the number N of permissible truth values and therefore grows rapidly with N. As is well known, in 2VL there are four one-place and 16 two-place connectives. Here are the truth tables for all 16 of these latter:

```
    | t f          | t f          | t f          | t f
----+----      ----+----      ----+----      ----+----
 t  | t t       t  | t f       t  | f t       t  | f f
 f  | t t       f  | t t       f  | t t       f  | t t


    | t f          | t f          | t f          | t f
----+----      ----+----      ----+----      ----+----
 t  | t t       t  | t f       t  | f t       t  | f f
 f  | t f       f  | t f       f  | t f       f  | t f


    | t f          | t f          | t f          | t f
----+----      ----+----      ----+----      ----+----
 t  | t t       t  | t f       t  | f t       t  | f f
 f  | f t       f  | f t       f  | f t       f  | f t


    | t f          | t f          | t f          | t f
----+----      ----+----      ----+----      ----+----
 t  | t t       t  | t f       t  | f t       t  | f f
 f  | f f       f  | f f       f  | f f       f  | f f
```

For a three-valued logic, however, the corresponding numbers are 27 one-place connectives and 19,683 two-place connectives, respectively!—see reference [15], page 63. More generally, the following table shows the number of one- and two-place connectives for N-valued logics for arbitrary $N > 1$:

truth values	1-place connectives	2-place connectives
2	4	16
3	27	19,683
4	256	4,294,967,296
. . .	. . .	. . . . . .
N	N^2	$N^{(N^2)}$

Of course, even in the 2VL case we don't normally need to remember or use all of the connectives explicitly, because just a few suffice to express all the others (indeed, this fact gets at the very essence of truth functional completeness). Likewise, not all possible connectives in a many-valued logic need be memorized if the primitive set is truth functionally complete.

Aside: Actually that primitive set can be very small; in fact, a single two-place connective suffices. In a system with N truth values, if the truth values are represented by the natural numbers from 1 to N (1 being "the most false" and N "the most true"), the connective in question, here denoted $\ominus$, can be defined thus: $p \ominus q = (\max(p,q) \bmod N) + 1$ (see reference [15], page 65). Of course, knowing that one connective suffices isn't the same as knowing how any given connective can be expressed in terms of it! *End of aside.*

Back to the main argument: If the system isn't truth functionally complete, however, both users and the optimizer must be prepared to use and understand all 27 one-place and 19,683 two-place connectives (in the three-valued case) individually! Such complexity is surely beyond the grasp of most users; not only would they find it frustrating, but they would almost certainly make mistakes, using the wrong connective for a desired result.[1] This same complexity also applies, with possibly even more force, to the design of the optimizer and the amount of code required to implement it.

Note: Contrary to Codd's position on the foregoing issue as articulated in reference [6], the number of distinct logical connectives in a truth functionally complete logic isn't analogous to the infinite number of distinct arithmetic functions that can be defined in ordinary arithmetic. Instead, it's analogous to the number of distinct operations (e.g., addition and multiplication) that are needed to *define* that infinite number of arithmetic functions. For arithmetic, that number is very small.

Number of meaning assignments: In addition to huge increases in the number of connectives, the number of distinct *meaning assignments* for those connectives increases as well. In a many-valued logic system, any truth value can be treated as *true-like* ("designated"), *false-like* ("antidesignated"), or neither ("undesignated"). These distinctions are necessary for identifying tautologies and contradictions in many-valued logics [15]. For example, in a three-valued logic, there are three distinct one-place connectives, any of which could reasonably be called NOT (all three map TRUE to FALSE and FALSE to TRUE, of course, but they differ in their treatment of UNKNOWN, mapping it to TRUE, FALSE, and UNKNOWN, respectively). But if UNKNOWN can be either designated, antidesignated, or undesignated, those three possibilities become *nine!* The nine possibilities are indicated below ("+" = designated, "-" = antidesignated):

p	NOT p
$+t$	f
u	u
$-f$	t

p	NOT p
$+t$	f
$+u$	u
$-f$	t

p	NOT p
$+t$	f
$-u$	u
$-f$	t

p	NOT p
$+t$	f
u	f
$-f$	t

p	NOT p
$+t$	f
$+u$	f
$-f$	t

p	NOT p
$+t$	f
$-u$	f
$-f$	t

p	NOT p
$+t$	f
u	t
$-f$	t

p	NOT p
$+t$	f
$+u$	t
$-f$	t

p	NOT p
$+t$	f
$-u$	t
$-f$	t

---

1. Even in simple 2VL, people sometimes make mistakes over OR and AND. As a simple example, the formal analog of the natural language query "Get suppliers in London and Paris" involves OR, not AND.

Such complexity clearly violates one of the motivations for using a logical system in the first place. Surely no user wants to work with such a DBMS.

Meanings of query results: If the users and designers of a database don't agree on the meanings of query results, confusion is inevitable; furthermore, that confusion will eventually lead to a loss of data integrity (users will eventually update the database in ways that violate the intended, but unenforceable, interpretation). In order to assign truth values to propositions (which is, of course, part of the process of defining the intended interpretation), the designer of the database must have a consistent understanding of what each truth value means (our uniform interpretability objective). That meaning must be (a) understandable to users and (b) consistent with the connectives and rules of inference. Although the meanings of individual truth values might seem reasonable—as (it might be argued) they do in the case of Codd's 3VL extensions to the relational model as described in reference [2]—those meanings can have nonintuitive consequences and can lead to incorrect results. *Note:* In reference [6], Codd categorizes such results as either "mildly" incorrect (meaning a wff has evaluated to UNKNOWN when it should have been either TRUE or FALSE) or "severely" incorrect (meaning a wff has evaluated to TRUE or FALSE when it should have been UNKNOWN). But either way, the fact that the DBMS is capable of giving incorrect results means "Don't trust the DBMS!" It's like saying of a certain calculator that 1 plus 1 sometimes equals 2 and sometimes doesn't, so check it yourself (in which case, why use the calculator in the first place?).[1]

Arbitrary number of truth values: A many-valued logic can have any number of truth values (that is, the number of distinct truth values needed can't be definitively established). As soon as we permit ourselves the liberty of introducing "a third truth value" UNKNOWN as some kind of intermediate value between TRUE and FALSE in some 3VL, there's no obvious reason to stop at three; in fact, there are immediately apparent reasons not to. As a matter of fact, Codd actually advocates a four-valued logic in order to deal with both "unknown" and "inapplicable" missing values [3-6]. But what if we need to insert a row with a missing value into a table, but we don't know whether that missing value is "unknown" or "inapplicable"? Clearly, we need yet another kind of "missing value" and a fifth truth value. Where does this process end?

Note: In reference [6], Codd responded to this criticism by saying, in effect, that "inapplicable" is a catchall and therefore terminates the process. This response is incorrect. The system needs a mechanical procedure by which it can determine which wffs evaluate to the truth value corresponding to the "value inapplicable" null and which to the truth value corresponding to the "value unknown" null.

---

1. *Chris Date adds:* I'd like to repeat (or paraphrase, rather) here what I had to say on this particular issue in reference [6], since I feel quite strongly about it. It seems to me that this whole business of severe *vs.* mild errors is nothing more than a rearguard attempt to shore up an already suspect position. After all, if we were talking about integers instead of truth values, what would we think of a system that occasionally produced the answer 2 when the correct answer was 1 or 3? And in what sense could this be any more acceptable than one that occasionally produced 1 or 3 when the correct answer was 2? ... Suppose the DBMS says it doesn't know whether Country X is developing a nuclear weapon, whereas in fact Country X is not doing so; and suppose Country Y therefore decides to bomb Country X "back to the Stone Age," just in case. The error here can hardly be said to be mild. (This example is not to my taste; I choose it deliberately for its shock value.)

Note that the very fact that "value inapplicable" is to be distinguished from "value unknown" implies the need for such a procedure.

Loss of deductive power: Please understand that I'm not saying (at any rate, not if properties such as completeness are unimportant) that it's impossible to extend a 2VL system to handle an arbitrary number of truth values. But as the number of truth values increases, the number of tautologies generally decreases; and since tautologies are essential tools of deduction, this decrease means a practical loss in deductive power, if not a formal one. And let's not forget the implications for the optimizer—which is, of course, the DBMS component that not only offers performance improvements but also enables data independence! Among other things, an optimizer that uses many-valued logic is less likely to recognize when wffs are semantically equivalent, and less likely to be able to simplify complex wffs via rules of inference and tautologies, than one that uses standard 2VL.

What makes matters worse is the particular tautologies that tend to be lost [15]. I've already mentioned the case of p OR NOT(p), which is a tautology in 2VL but not in 3VL. Two more simple examples are p IMPLIES p and p BI-IMPLIES $p,$ both of which are (again) tautologies in 2VL but not in some 3VLs [9]. As another example, the wff

$$(\ p \ \text{IMPLIES} \ p \ ) \ \text{BI-IMPLIES} \ (\ (\ \text{NOT} \ p \ ) \ \text{OR} \ p \ )$$

isn't a tautology in some many-valued logics, though intuitively it should be.

The impact of this loss in deductive power is serious. Some optimizers effectively just give up when faced with many-valued logic and make no expression transformations whatsoever. Others make invalid ones—i.e., ones that would be valid in 2VL but aren't valid in many-valued logic. (Some optimizers even fail to use an index if the indexed columns can contain nulls, regardless of whether they actually do or not!) And the reduction in deductive power implied by such failures makes it much more difficult for users to reason toward a desired answer using a sequence of queries. The poorer the optimizer in this regard, the more the user must "optimize by hand," as it were, carefully selecting the exact manner in which a query should be expressed (two wffs might seem to be equivalent but actually be so only for specific arguments). And this fact means not only that users must understand the logical system very well indeed, but also that they must be willing to give up some data independence.

Unusual semantics: Although perhaps interesting from a formal perspective, the many-valued logics proposed by Codd (and related proposals by Vassiliou, Lipski, Biskup, and others) leave much to be desired from the perspective of understandable semantics. In Codd's scheme (as elaborated by Grahne [11]), a table that contains one or more SQL-style nulls can be seen as shorthand for a set of tables, one such for each combination of legally substitutable values for the nulls in the original table. In order to construct understandable queries in such a system, the user must somehow keep in mind the combinatorial explosion of all of the possible substitutions. Such semantics make the systems highly nonintuitive and error prone. In an informal survey of some 30 database designers and administrators, all of the parties concerned expressed amazement at this interpretation and felt it was unacceptable.

OTHER MANY-VALUED LOGICS

Most of the many-valued logics discussed in the literature are variations on systems developed by Lukasiewicz, Post, and Kleene. In particular, variations on the systems of Lukasiewicz are sometimes said to be the basis for SQL's 3VL. While this claim can't possibly be correct,[1] it's worth taking a moment to examine the properties of such systems.

- First of all, such systems aren't truth functionally complete (so the system would be unable to verify certain facts using the available operators).

- They're also not natural extensions of 2VL; certain tautologies of 2VL cease to be true in the Lukasiewicz systems, and, conversely, certain tautologies of the Lukasiewicz systems have no counterpart in 2VL. (In other words, they're deviants, to use our terminology. They were originally intended to treat contingent—especially future contingent—propositions as being "temporarily unknown." For example, the truth value of "It will rain tomorrow" would initially be UNKNOWN, but would eventually be determined to be either TRUE or FALSE. In other words, the Lukasiewicz UNKNOWN is a temporary placeholder for a standard truth value.)

The foregoing properties are sufficient to eliminate Lukasiewicz systems from further consideration. They aren't suitable candidates for use as the logical system of a DBMS.

Certain other many-valued logics are truth functionally complete (they're all consistent by definition if at least one truth value is undesignated), but have semantics that are clearly inappropriate for a DBMS. Here are a few examples:

- In the systems of Post, truth valuations apply only to sets of propositions (i.e., sets of rows), not to individual propositions per se.

- Kleene had in mind the truth valuations of propositions involving mathematical functions that were undefined for certain arguments.

- Bochvar created a system with a set of "internal" truth tables and a set of "external" truth tables, treating UNKNOWN as "undecidable" or "meaningless." This scheme resembles SQL in the sense that SQL effectively returns FALSE (the external system) to the user when the answer is UNKNOWN (the internal system), but differs from SQL in other respects.

---

1. Lukasiewicz takes IMPLIES and NOT as primitives, deriving OR and AND from them. In particular, his version of IMPLIES defines p IMPLIES p to give TRUE, not UNKNOWN, if p is UNKNOWN. By contrast, if we follow 2VL and define p IMPLIES q as (NOT p) OR p, then p IMPLIES p gives UNKNOWN if p is UNKNOWN. In fact, Lukasiewicz's IMPLIES can't be derived from NOT, OR, and AND. The reason is that NOT, OR, and AND as usually defined for 3VL each yield UNKNOWN if their inputs include UNKNOWN (and therefore so do all possible combinations of these operators), whereas Lukasiewicz's IMPLIES does not. Since SQL doesn't even define IMPLIES, claims that it's based on Lukasiewicz's system must ipso facto be incorrect.

"RELATIONAL" THREE-VALUED LOGIC

The arguments I've presented so far are generic—they apply to many-valued logics in general—and the problems I've raised can't be fixed (indeed, logicians don't perceive them as "problems" that *need* to be fixed!). Now I want to consider, albeit briefly, the specific three- and four-valued logics proposed by Codd and the three-valued logic implemented in SQL. Although it's my thesis that *no* many-valued logic is suitable for the needs of a DBMS, I feel compelled to point out a few specific problems that apply to these pragmatically important cases.

- As noted earlier, my discussion of the problems associated with the use of many-valued logic was forced to be general, because both Codd's and SQL's 3VL aren't completely defined (rules of inference, axioms, and primitive connectives are all unspecified). In particular, as explained in the previous section, they're definitely not Lukasiewicz systems; they're also not one of the systems defined by Post or Kleene or Bochvar. What, exactly, *are* the definitions of these systems?

- To repeat, the rules of inference are unspecified. Now, we can assume in the case of SQL that (since subqueries are supported) a limited rule of substitution is supposed to hold; but what about other standard rules such as *modus ponens* (if *p* IMPLIES *q* and *p*, then *q*)? Note that in a many-valued logic there are many forms of this rule (two such if the logic is three-valued); if *modus ponens* is supposed to hold, therefore, it's clearly important to say which one is intended. Similar remarks apply to other rules of inference, such as *modus tollens* and De Morgan's Laws.

- Although many-valued logics are mostly based on an extension to propositional logic, the relational model is supposedly based on *predicate* logic. Certainly SQL "supports" the existential quantifier EXISTS, and the universal quantifier FORALL can be simulated (though both get into trouble over nulls and related matters [8]). Unfortunately, however, there's no discussion in the literature of how a many-valued predicate logic is supposed to work in conjunction with the relational model. For example, how the system should treat the quantifiers and what rules of inference should apply are both left largely to the imagination. However, we do know that the relational model and SQL both treat EXISTS as a finite iteration of OR; in practice, therefore (and assuming that nulls aren't permitted), the logical system is at best the finite version of predicate calculus as discussed, briefly, in reference [14]. *Note:* It would be good if this logical system were the intended one, since such a system does at least have the desirable property of being both complete and decidable.

CONCLUDING REMARKS

The criticisms of many-valued logics in this chapter have simple, practical consequences. Based on those criticisms, I recommend (in the DBMS context specifically) strict adherence to the following guidelines:

- Avoid nulls and many-valued logic.

- Don't use SQL operations like outer join and outer union that generate nulls.

- Until you can implement these first two actions, review the meanings of queries and query results carefully. The more complex the query, the more important this review process becomes.

- Lobby vendors to drop support for nulls and many-valued logic from their products.

- Ask vendors to make full use of predicate calculus in their optimizers.

- Demand that DBMS vendors place high priority on the goals and objectives outlined in reference [14]. To this end, they must recommend against the use of many-valued logic in their products and must oppose it in the SQL standard.

- Demand that, until vendors can comply with these guidelines, they supply a configuration option to disable the use of nulls and many-valued logic at the system level.

To summarize (a trifle glibly), the key conclusion readers should draw from the discussions of this chapter is that "nothing can be gained from nothing"; nothing compares to 2VL. In fact, a great deal of knowledge, power, usability, performance, and maintainability is at risk if many-valued logic is used in a DBMS. Apply Occam's Razor: Eliminate all the nothing from your databases.

Of course, you might object at this point (not unreasonably) that we do have to do *something* in order to handle "missing information" in our databases; so what can we do, if we're not allowed to use nulls and many-valued logic? My aim in the present chapter hasn't been to provide a good answer to this question; rather, my aim has merely been to show that nulls and many-valued logic are a disastrously bad one. But various "good" solutions have been proposed in the literature, and I suggest you seek them out and evaluate them for yourself. I've offered one proposal myself (see reference [13]). Reference [7] is also recommended for your consideration.

REFERENCES AND BIBLIOGRAPHY

1.   E. F. Codd: "A Data Base Sublanguage Founded on the Relational Calculus," Proc. 1971 ACM SIGFIDET Workshop on Data Description, Access and Control, San Diego, Calif. (November 1971).

2.   E. F. Codd: "Extending the Database Relational Model to Capture More Meaning," *ACM TODS 4,* No. 4 (December 1979).

3.   E. F. Codd: "Missing Information (Applicable and Inapplicable) in Relational Databases," *ACM SIGMOD Record 15,* No. 4 (December 1986).

4.   E. F. Codd: *The Relational Model for Database Management Version 2.* Reading, Mass.: Addison-Wesley (1990).

5.   E. F. Codd: *The 25th Anniversary of the Creation of the Relational Model for Database*

Management (published by the consulting company Codd & Date Inc. in 1994). *Note:* That company is no longer in existence, and this reference might thus be no longer available.

6. E. F. Codd and C. J. Date: "Much Ado About Nothing," in C. J. Date, *Relational Database Writings 1991-1994*. Reading, Mass.: Addison-Wesley (1995).

7. Hugh Darwen: "How to Handle Missing Information Without Using Nulls" (presentation slides), *www.thethirdmanifesto.com* (May 9th, 2003).

8. C. J. Date: "EXISTS Is Not "Exists"! (Some Logical Flaws in SQL)," in *Relational Database Writings 1985-1989*. Reading, Mass.: Addison-Wesley (1990).

9. C. J. Date: "Why Three- and Four-Valued Logic Don't Work," in *Date on Database: Writings 2000-2006*. Berkeley, Calif.: Apress (2006).

10. C. J. Date, Hugh Darwen, and David McGoveran: "Nothing to Do with the Case" and "Up to a Point, Lord Copper," in *Relational Database Writings 1994-1997* (Addison-Wesley 1998).

11. G. Grahne: *The Problem of Incomplete Information in Relational Databases*. New York, N.Y.: Springer-Verlag (1991).

12. Tom Johnston: "MVL: Case Open," *Database Programming & Design 8,* No. 2 (February 1995); "The Case for MVL," *Database Programming & Design 8,* No. 3 (March 1995); "More to the Point," *Database Programming & Design 8,* No. 11 (November 1995).

13. David McGoveran: "Nothing from Nothing" (Parts 3 and 4), in C. J. Date, Hugh Darwen, and David McGoveran, *Relational Database Writings 1994-1997*. Reading, Mass.: Addison-Wesley (1998).

14. David McGoveran and C. J. Date: "Why Relational DBMSs Are Based on Logic" (Chapter 5 in this book).

15. Nicholas Rescher: *Many-Valued Logic*. New York, N.Y.: McGraw-Hill (1969).

16. Patrick Suppes: *Introduction to Logic*. Princeton, N.J.: Van Nostrand (1957).

APPENDIX A: SOME USEFUL 2VL TAUTOLOGIES

This appendix simply lists some useful tautologies (and, in effect, rules of inference) in 2VL. It's adapted from a list given in reference [16], page 34. In the interest of succinctness, (a) I've used symbols instead of keywords to represent the connectives, and (b) I've assumed certain syntactic precedence rules, as follows:

- "¬" means NOT (highest precedence).

- "|" and "&" mean OR and AND, respectively (medium precedence).

- "→" and "↔" mean IMPLIES and BI-IMPLIES, respectively (lowest precedence).

Tautological Implications

- Law of Detachment $\qquad\qquad\qquad\qquad p\ \&\ (p \rightarrow q)\ \rightarrow\ q$

- *Modus Ponens* $\qquad\qquad\qquad\qquad\qquad p\ \&\ (p \rightarrow q)\ \rightarrow\ q$

- *Modus Tollens* $\qquad\qquad\qquad\qquad\qquad \neg q\ \&\ (p \rightarrow q)\ \rightarrow\ \neg p$

- Law of Simplification $\qquad\qquad\qquad\qquad p\ \&\ q \rightarrow p$

- Law of Adjunction $\qquad\qquad\qquad\qquad\quad p\ \&\ q \rightarrow p\ \&\ q$

- Law of Hypothetical Syllogism $\qquad\qquad (p \rightarrow q)\ \&\ (q \rightarrow r)\ \rightarrow\ (p \rightarrow r)$

- Law of Exportation $\qquad\qquad\qquad\quad (p\ \&\ q \rightarrow r)\ \rightarrow\ (p \rightarrow (q \rightarrow r))$

- Law of Importation $\qquad\qquad\qquad\quad (p \rightarrow (q \rightarrow r))\ \rightarrow\ (p\ \&\ q \rightarrow r)$

- Law of Absurdity $\qquad\qquad\qquad\qquad (p \rightarrow q\ \&\ \neg q)\ \rightarrow\ \neg p$

- Law of Addition $\qquad\qquad\qquad\qquad\quad p \rightarrow p\ |\ q$

Tautological Equivalences

- Law of Double Negation $\qquad\qquad\qquad p \leftrightarrow \neg\neg p$

- Law of Contraposition $\qquad\qquad\qquad (p \rightarrow q) \leftrightarrow (\neg q \rightarrow \neg p)$

- De Morgan's Laws $\qquad\qquad\qquad\quad \neg(p\ |\ q) \leftrightarrow (\neg p\ \&\ \neg q)$
  $\qquad\qquad\qquad\qquad\qquad\qquad\ \neg(p\ \&\ q) \leftrightarrow (\neg p\ |\ \neg q)$

- Commutative Laws $\qquad\qquad\qquad\quad p\ \&\ q \leftrightarrow q\ \&\ p$
  $\qquad\qquad\qquad\qquad\qquad\qquad\ p\ |\ q \leftrightarrow q\ |\ p$

- Law of Equivalence for Implication and Disjunction $\quad (p \rightarrow q) \leftrightarrow (\neg p\ |\ q)$

- Law of Negation for Implication $\qquad\ \neg(p \rightarrow q) \leftrightarrow p\ \&\ \neg q$

- Laws for Biconditional Sentences $\quad (p \leftrightarrow q) \leftrightarrow (p \rightarrow q)\ \&\ (q \rightarrow p)$
  $\qquad\qquad\qquad\qquad\qquad\qquad\ (p \leftrightarrow q) \leftrightarrow (p\ \&\ q)\ |\ (\neg p\ \&\ \neg q)$

Two Further Tautologies

- Law of the Excluded Middle

  $p \mid \neg p$

- Law of Contradiction

  $\neg (p \ \& \ \neg p)$

Part III

LOGIC AND DATABASE DESIGN

This part of the book consists of three chapters. Chapter 7 tries to make some logical sense of terms like *many-to-one relationship*—terms that, as we all know, are widely used in connection with database design and yet don't seem to have a universally agreed definition. Chapter 8 offers a fresh perspective on the familiar subject of normalization (which is, of course, highly relevant to logical database design). Finally, Chapter 9 offers some arguments in favor of not denormalizing: logical arguments, that is, though it does also briefly examine the performance arguments as well.

Chapter 7

All for One, One for All

Mathematically, there is a correspondence between mappings and relationships.
—James Martin and James J. Odell

It might just be me, but I'm never quite certain what people mean when they use expressions like *one-to-one relationship, many-to-one mapping,* and so forth. For example, consider this quote from reference [5]:

> There is a one-to-one ... relationship between flight segments and aircraft. A particular flight segment on a given day uses one and only one aircraft.

Well, clearly a particular flight segment on a given day does use one and only one aircraft. Surely, however, a particular aircraft can be used on one, two, ... or any reasonable number of flight segments on a given day—possibly even none at all? So isn't the relationship not one-to-one but, rather, many-to-one ("Many flight segments on a given day use a given aircraft"), where "many" includes the zero case? Or is it perhaps one-to-many ("A given aircraft is used on many flight segments on a given day"), where again "many" includes the zero case?

This chapter is an attempt to clarify such matters and inject a little rigor into the terminology. Let me immediately admit, therefore, that it might well be regarded as having an awful lot to say about not very much ... As I've indicated, its aim is to pin down the exact nature of one-to-one, many-to-one, one-to-many, and many-to-many relationships, and in particular to come up with precise definitions for these concepts. It might thus be dismissed by some readers as mere pedantry. It might also be accused of making very heavy weather over what are essentially very simple concepts. But a survey of the literature certainly betrays confusion and lack of systematic thinking in this area, and (as I've had occasion to remark elsewhere) in the field of computing in general, and in the field of database management in particular, clarity, accuracy, and precision are surely paramount; without them we're surely lost. So you be the judge.

Note: I need to warn you that some of the definitions in what follows are inevitably a little complicated, or at least might appear so on a first reading. *Caveat lector.*

GROUNDWORK AND ASSUMPTIONS

I'll begin by laying a little groundwork and spelling out some assumptions:

- I assume you have an intuitive understanding of what's meant by the term *relationship*. Please note that I'm not using that term in any loaded kind of way; in particular, I'm not giving it any specifically relational interpretation, in the sense of the relational model, nor am I using it in any specific "entity/relationship modeling" kind of sense (if there can be said to be any such sense).

■   Mention of the term *entity* reminds me: It's possible, and I think highly desirable, to discuss this subject without using that fuzzy term at all. As you'll quickly find, therefore, my definitions (of *relationship* and the like) are all phrased in terms of the mathematical concept of a *set*. That term itself can be defined as follows:

set A collection of objects, or elements, with the property that given an arbitrary object *x,* it can be determined whether or not *x* appears in that collection. Sets have no ordering to their elements, nor do they contain any duplicate elements.

In particular, observe that the mathematical term (and the term I'll be using) for the objects that are members of sets is *elements*. *Note:* Many of the definitions in this chapter, including the foregoing definition of the term *set* in particular, are based on ones given in reference [2], as are many of the examples also (at least the more mathematical ones).

■   For simplicity, I assume all relationships are binary. All of the ideas to be discussed extend to ternary, quaternary, etc., relationships in a straightforward manner.

■   For definiteness, I assume all relationships are directed. As a consequence, if there's a relationship from *A* to *B,* there's an inverse relationship (also directed, of course) from *B* to *A* as well. *Note:* It would be possible to talk of relationships as bidirectional and thus avoid the need to introduce the notion of inverse relationships, but I think clarity would suffer.

■   From this point forward I'll take "many" to include the zero case throughout (i.e., "many" means zero or more), barring explicit statements to the contrary.

Here then is a generic definition of the term *relationship:*

relationship Let *A* and *B* be sets, not necessarily distinct. Then a relationship from *A* to *B* is a rule pairing elements of *A* with elements of *B*. (Equivalently, we might just say the relationship is that pairing itself.)

Note: Since I'm taking relationships to be directed, I do think it makes better sense to think of a relationship as being *from* one set *A to* another set *B* than it does to think of it being *between* those two sets. Also, as already indicated, I'll distinguish the relationship in question from its inverse, which is a relationship from set *B* to set *A*.

By way of illustration, let *A* be the set of letters of the alphabet {A,B,...,Z} and let *B* be the set of digits {0,1,...,9}. Then the following pairing, spelled out in detail on telephone handsets,[1] is a well known example of a relationship from *A* to *B:*

---

1. Actually handsets vary; in the U.S. in particular, some omit the letters Q and Z. My example is based on the handset sitting on my desk at the time of writing.

nil	0	JKL	5
nil	1	MNO	6
ABC	2	PQRS	7
DEF	3	TUV	8
GHI	4	WXYZ	9

There's also an inverse relationship from *B* to *A* (in which, as you can see, it happens that certain elements of *B*—namely, 0 and 1—are actually paired with no elements of *A* at all).

HOW MANY CASES ARE THERE?

Given the notion of a relationship as I've defined it, along with the notion that any given relationship has an inverse relationship, how many distinct kinds of relationships—or combinations thereof, rather—can reasonably exist involving two sets *A* and *B?* Well, using lowercase *a* and *b* to refer to arbitrary elements of *A* and *B*, respectively, it should be clear that:

- For a given *a* there could be at most one *b;* exactly one *b;* at least one *b;* or many *b*'s (i.e., M *b*'s for some M ≥ 0).

- In each of the foregoing cases, for a given *b* there could be at most one *a;* exactly one *a;* at least one *a;* or many *a*'s (i.e., M *a*'s for some M ≥ 0).

On the face of it, therefore, there are 16 possible combinations. Fig. 7.1 presents a summary of the 16 cases in the form of a matrix; Fig. 7.2 (overleaf) shows them pictorially, as they might be represented in, e.g., a UML diagram—though I should say in the interest of accuracy that the notation in Fig. 7.2 is not exactly that of UML, though it's close (see reference [1]).

b has → *a* has ↓	at most one *a*	exactly one *a*	at least one *a*	M *a*'s (M ≥ 0)
at most one *b*	Case 1.1	Case 1.2	Case 1.3	Case 1.4
exactly one *b*	Case 2.1	Case 2.2	Case 2.3	Case 2.4
at least one *b*	Case 3.1	Case 3.2	Case 3.3	Case 3.4
M *b*'s (M ≥ 0)	Case 4.1	Case 4.2	Case 4.3	Case 4.4

Fig. 7.1: The 16 cases in matrix form

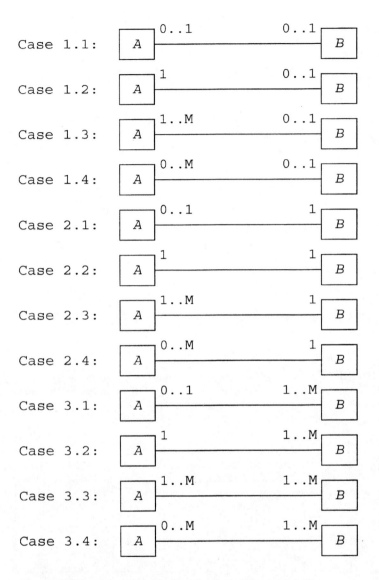

Fig. 7.2: The 16 cases in pictorial form (Part 1 of 2)

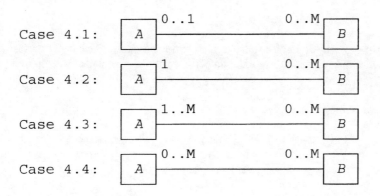

Fig. 7.2: The 16 cases in pictorial form (Part 2 of 2)

Let's consider a realistic—well, fairly realistic—example of each of the 16 cases. *Note:* You might want to make a copy of either Fig. 7.1 or Fig. 7.2 and use it as an aid to memory as you read through the remainder of this chapter.

1.1   *Each a has at most one b, each b has at most one a.*

Example: At a given time, a given man has at most one wife and a given woman has at most one husband (assuming no polygamy); however, some men have no wife and some women have no husband.

1.2   *Each a has at most one b, each b has exactly one a.*

Example: In a certain company at a given time, each employee manages at most one department and each department has exactly one manager (i.e., employee who manages the department); however, some employees aren't managers. *Note:* I'd like to point out in passing that this case occurs ubiquitously in connection with type inheritance as described in, e.g., reference [4]. For example, let *A* and *B* be types RECTANGLE and SQUARE, respectively, and let SQUARE be a subtype of supertype RECTANGLE. Then the supertype/subtype relationship is such that a given rectangle "has" a corresponding square if and only if the rectangle in question is in fact that square, and a given square "has" a corresponding rectangle that's precisely the rectangle that the square in question happens to be. (Of course, every square is a rectangle, but many rectangles aren't squares.) In this example, the relationship from RECTANGLE to SQUARE and the inverse relationship from SQUARE to RECTANGLE are both *identity* (i.e., "is the same rectangle as," or simply "is equal to")—see Chapter 2.

1.3   *Each a has at most one b, each b has at least one a.*

Example: In a certain company at a given time, each employee has at most one department (but some employees have no department at all) and each department has at least one employee.

1.4   *Each a has at most one b, each b has many a's.*

Example: In a certain company at a given time, each employee has at most one department (but some employees have no department at all) and each department has any number of employees (possibly none at all).

2.1   *Each a has exactly one b, each b has at most one a.*

Example: This is just Case 1.2 with *A* and *B* interchanged. Hence, an example is: In a certain company at a given time, each department has exactly one manager (i.e., employee who manages the department), and each employee manages at most one department.

2.2   *Each a has exactly one b, each b has exactly one a.*

Example: In a certain shipping company, a given shipment has exactly one corresponding invoice and a given invoice has exactly one corresponding shipment.

2.3   *Each a has exactly one b, each b has at least one a.*

Example: In a certain company at a given time, each employee has exactly one department and each department has at least one employee.

2.4   *Each a has exactly one b, each b has many a's.*

Example: In a certain company at a given time, each employee has exactly one department and each department has any number of employees (possibly none at all). As another example, every person has exactly one biological mother, and every woman is the biological mother of zero or more children.

3.1   *Each a has at least one b, each b has at most one a.*

Example: This is Case 1.3 with *A* and *B* interchanged; see that case for an example.

3.2   *Each a has at least one b, each b has exactly one a.*

Example: This is Case 2.3 with *A* and *B* interchanged; see that case for an example.

3.3   *Each a has at least one b, each b has at least one a.*

Example: Every book has at least one author, every author (that is, every *book* author) is by definition author of at least one book.

3.4   *Each a has at least one b, each b has many a's.*

    Example: Every sporting event has at least one winner (possibly more than one if ties are allowed), every competitor is the winner of zero or more such events.

4.1   *Each a has many b's, each b has at most one a.*

    Example: This is Case 1.4 with *A* and *B* interchanged; see that case for an example.

4.2   *Each a has many b's, each b has exactly one a.*

    Example: This is Case 2.4 with *A* and *B* interchanged; see that case for an example.

4.3   *Each a has many b's, each b has at least one a.*

    Example: This is Case 3.4 with *A* and *B* interchanged; see that case for an example.

4.4   *Each a has many b's, each b has many a's.*

    Example: In the well known suppliers-and-parts database, each supplier is located in the same city as zero or more parts and each part is located in the same city as zero or more suppliers.

So there aren't really 16 distinct cases after all but only 10. Notice, by the way, that several of the examples correspond to business policies or business rules (see, e.g., Cases 1.4 and 2.3). Others might be merely fortuitous (see, e.g., Case 4.4), but can be interesting nevertheless—some user might certainly want to "exploit the relationship," as common parlance has it, in order to determine which parts are located in the same city as a given supplier, for example.

Now, I opened this section by asking: How many distinct kinds of relationships can reasonably exist involving two sets *A* and *B?* Of course, the emphasis here is on *reasonably.* It would obviously be possible to classify the various "many" cases further (at most two, exactly two, at least two, at most three, and so on). To quote reference [8]: "For example, a meeting must have at least two people, and tango contests must have an even number of participants." However, such further classification doesn't seem particularly rewarding (it adds a lot of complexity, and the law of diminishing returns comes into play very quickly), and I won't consider such possibilities any further in this chapter.

EXAMPLES OF CONFUSION

Now let's take a look at some actual quotes from the literature that demonstrate, at least arguably, a certain amount of confusion in this area. The first is a longer extract from reference [5] (the quote at the beginning of this chapter was taken from this extract, as you can see).

For example, consider the following relationship descriptions:

- There is a one-to-one equipment-use relationship between flight segments and aircraft. A particular flight segment on a given day uses one and only one aircraft.

- There is a one-to-one departure relationship between flight segments and airports, and another one-to-one arrival relationship between flight segments and airports. Each flight segment has exactly one departure airport and one arrival airport.

- There is a one-to-many publication relationship between publishers and books. Each publisher can publish many books, and each book can be published by only one publisher.

- There is a many-to-many authoring relationship between papers and people. Each paper can be authored by one or more people, and each person can author one or more papers.

Let's analyze each of these examples in turn. I'll repeat the examples to make the analysis easier to follow.

- There is a one-to-one equipment-use relationship between flight segments and aircraft. A particular flight segment on a given day uses one and only one aircraft.

As noted earlier, the true situation here is as follows: Each flight segment ("on a given day") has exactly one aircraft; each aircraft has many flight segments (possibly none at all)—again, on a given day. Thus, we're dealing here with an example of Case 2.4 (or Case 4.2, if we look at the example in the inverse direction).

- There is a one-to-one departure relationship between flight segments and airports, and another one-to-one arrival relationship between flight segments and airports. Each flight segment has exactly one departure airport and one arrival airport.

Actually, each flight segment has exactly one departure airport, but each airport has many flight segments departing from it (where, I presume, "many" does *not* include the zero case); so I think we're dealing here with Case 2.3 (or Case 3.2). Similarly for arrivals.

- There is a one-to-many publication relationship between publishers and books. Each publisher can publish many books, and each book can be published by only one publisher.

Accurate analysis of this example depends on exactly what's meant by the term *book*. For example, most people would surely say that *Pride and Prejudice* is a book, but it's been published by many distinct publishers (even simultaneously; in fact it's available from several distinct publishers right now, at the time of writing). And some books are published jointly by two or more publishers, anyway; I have in my own professional library at least one book published jointly by the ACM Press and Addison-Wesley. So I would say the situation is that each publisher has many books and each book has many publishers, where neither of those "many"s includes the zero case: Case 3.3.

- There is a many-to-many authoring relationship between papers and people. Each paper can be authored by one or more people, and each person can author one or more papers.

  Actually, each paper has at least one author, while each person is an author for zero or more papers: Case 3.4 (or Case 4.3).

Note: Just to show that I don't mean to pick unfairly on one particular publication or one particular writer as a target for criticism, here are a couple more examples that demonstrate confusions similar to those just discussed:

- From reference [6]: "*One-to-one relationship* ... A typical example might be ... that one and only one FACTORY manufactures the particular PRODUCT." Well, surely—unless, as is very unlikely, a given factory produces just one product—FACTORY to PRODUCT here is one-to-many, not one-to-one? *Note:* I take the liberty of using the term *one-to-many* here even though I still haven't defined it precisely. I'll do so eventually, I promise.

- From reference [7]: "[A] one-to-one mapping ... means that *at every instance [sic] in time, each value of A has one and only one value of B associated with it.* There is a one-to-one mapping between EMPLOYEE NAME and SALARY." But surely—unless, as is very unlikely, no two employees have the same salary—EMPLOYEE NAME to SALARY here is many-to-one, not one-to-one?

To return for a moment to the examples from reference [5], I do think part of the confusion is due to the writer's use of the word *between*—as in "a one-to-many ... relationship *between* publishers and books," for example (my italics). As I said earlier, I think relationships (at least, directed relationships) are better regarded as being *from* one set to another, not *between* two sets. Thus, it might be plausible to suggest that (for example) the relationship from A to B is one-to-one while the inverse relationship from B to A, is many-to-one (i.e., Case 2.4, possibly); but I think it's hard to come up with a clear and unambiguous characterization of "the relationship *between*" A and B in such a situation.

Incidentally, I said earlier that a survey of the literature also displays some lack of systematic thinking in this area. One example of that lack of systematic thinking occurs in connection with this issue of whether "many" includes the zero case. Consider Fig. 7.2 once again; for definiteness, consider Case 1.4 from that figure (repeated here for convenience):

Case 1.4:
```
              0..M              0..1
   +---+ _____ +---+
   | A |                              | B |
   +---+                              +---+
```

The line between the two boxes here represents both the relationship from A to B and the inverse relationship from B to A, and the annotation on that line represents what are often called the *cardinality constraints* on those relationships. To be precise, the specification 0..1 indicates that for one a there can be from zero to one (i.e., at most one) b; the specification 0..M indicates that for one b there can be any number of a's, from zero to some undefined upper bound M. The other specifications in Fig. 7.2 have analogous interpretations.

Incidentally, I feel obliged to mention in passing that the UML term for the concept under discussion is not cardinality but *multiplicity*. As reference [1] puts it, "multiplicity" is "a specification of the range of allowable cardinality values—the size—that a set may assume." Well, I've complained before about our field's cavalier way with terms, but this has to be a fairly grotesque example ... The fact is, *multiplicity* simply doesn't mean what UML wants it to mean (and I say this in full knowledge of Humpty Dumpty's pronouncements on such matters). *Chambers Twentieth Century Dictionary* defines the term thus:

> **multiplicity** the state of being manifold: a great number

(*Manifold* here just means "many in number.") Thus, we might reasonably say that, e.g., "UML suffers from a multiplicity of terms—far more terms than it has concepts" (to pick an example at random). However, we can't reasonably say that, e.g., "the multiplicity of the set $\{a,b,c\}$ is three." (The *cardinality* of that set is three, of course.) *Note:* For an extended discussion of UML's troubles over terms and concepts, see reference [3].

Anyway, to get back to cardinality constraints as such: The terms *mandatory* and *optional* are often used in an attempt to get at the question of whether or not "many" includes the zero case. But there doesn't seem to be any consensus on exactly what these terms mean. Consider the following quotes:

- From reference [8]: "The zero indicates that each object *may* not map to any object. The one indicates that each object *must* map to at least one object. Because of the *may* and *must* aspects of these two minimum constraints, they [*sic*] are sometimes referred to respectively as *optional* or *mandatory* mappings."

- From reference [9]: "*Optional:* The existence of either entity in the relationship is not dependent on the relationship ... *Mandatory:* The existence of both entities is dependent upon the relationship."

Do you think these definitions display "systematic thinking"? (I don't.) Do you think they're clear? (Surely not.) Do you think they're saying the same thing? (Very hard to say.)

Well, enough of this griping. One concept I think can help us arrive at more precise definitions in this area is the concept of a function. Let's take a closer look.

FUNCTIONS

Functions are ubiquitous in computing contexts, and I'm sure you have at least an intuitive understanding of what a function is. Like many other terms in computing that have their origins in mathematics, however, the term *function* has unfortunately had its meaning muddied and diluted somewhat over the years, to our loss. Here I'd like to get back to the original mathematical definition, because as I've already said I think it can be quite helpful in clarifying the relationship concept. Here is such a definition:

> **function** Let *A* and *B* be sets, not necessarily distinct. Then a function *f* is a rule that pairs each element of *A* (the *domain* of *f*) with exactly one element of *B* (the *codomain* of *f*); equivalently, we might just say *f* is that pairing itself. The unique element *b* of *B* corresponding to element *a* of *A*

is the *image* of *a* (under *f*), and the set of all such images is the *range* of *f*. Note that the range is a subset, often a proper subset, of the codomain.

The telephone example quoted earlier in this chapter illustrates this definition: The function is a rule that pairs letters with integers (equivalently, it's the specified pairing as such); the domain is the set of letters A-Z, the codomain is the set of integers 0-9, and the range is the set of integers 2-9 (a proper subset of the codomain). Under that function, the image of (for example) the letter H is the integer 4.

As another example, let *f* be the rule that pairs nonnegative integers *x* with their squares x^2. Then *f* is a function with domain and codomain both the set of all nonnegative integers and range that proper subset of the codomain (of the domain too, in fact) that consists only of perfect squares. *Note:* From this point forward I'll tend to favor examples like this one (i.e., ones with a slightly mathematical flavor) because their semantics are, or should be, crystal clear—we don't have to get into arguments about what exactly is meant by less well defined concepts such as *department* or *book* or *flight segment* (etc.).

By the way, there are two further terms that mean exactly the same thing in mathematics as *function:* namely, *mapping* and *transformation* (abbreviated *map* and *transform,* respectively). Again, however, you should be aware that the meanings of these terms have become somewhat muddied and diluted in computing contexts, to our loss, and you can certainly find conflicting definitions in the literature. Again, *caveat lector.*

So what does the notion of a function have to do with that of a relationship? Well, if *f* is a function with domain *A,* codomain *B,* and range *C* (where *C* is a subset of *B*), it should be clear that:

- Function *f* defines a relationship from *A* to *B* according to which, for each element *a* in *A,* there exists exactly one element *b* in *B* (the image of *a* under *f*).

- Likewise, function *f* defines a relationship from *A* to *C* according to which, for each element *a* in *A,* there exists exactly one element *c* in *C* (the image of *a* under *f*).

- Function *f* also defines, at least implicitly, an inverse relationship from *B* to *A* according to which, for each element *b* in *B,* there exist M elements *a* in *A* such that *b* is the image of *a* under *f* (M ≥ 0). *Note:* In general, of course, that inverse relationship won't be a function; in fact, it'll be a function if and only if M = 1 for all elements *b* in *B.*

- Likewise, function *f* also defines, at least implicitly, an inverse relationship from *C* to *A* according to which, for each element *c* in *C,* there exist M elements *a* in *A* such that *c* is the image of *a* under *f* (M > 0). *Note:* Again that inverse relationship will be a function if and only if M = 1 for all elements *c* in *C.*

These facts give some hint as to how the notion of a function can help in pinning down the meaning of terms such as *many-to-one relationship* more precisely, as I'll now try to show.

By definition, any given function *f* has the property that an arbitrary number M (M > 0) of elements *a* from its domain *A* can map to a given element *c* in its range *C.* For that reason, we can and do say that the relationship from *A* to *C* is *many-to-one* ("many" here *not* including the zero case, please note). Furthermore, we often describe that relationship (for emphasis) more specifically as many-to-one *onto,* since by definition there's no element *c* in *C* that isn't the image of something in *A.* As for the relationship from *A* to the codomain *B,* we describe that relationship as many-to-one *into,* since in general there are some elements *b* of *B* that aren't the image of anything at all in *A*. *Note:* Many-to-one onto is a special case of many-to-one into, of course. Also, I should make it clear that in the case of many-to-one into (though not many-to-one onto), the qualifier *many-to-one* is being used in a slightly sloppy sense. See the section "Correspondences" (subsection "Many-to-One Correspondence"), following the present section.

Here are a couple of examples:

1. The telephone example (where *A* is the set of letters A-Z, *B* is the set of integers 0-9, and *C* is the set of integers 2-9) provides an example of a many-to-one into relationship from *A* to *B*—and, of course, a many-to-one onto relationship from *A* to *C*.

2. Likewise, the function that maps nonnegative integers *x* to their squares x^2 (where *A* and *B* are both the set of all nonnegative integers and *C* is the set of all perfect squares) also provides an example of a many-to-one into relationship from *A* to *B* and a many-to-one onto relationship from *A* to *C*.

More terminology: A many-to-one onto relationship is also known as a *surjective* function (or mapping), or just a *surjection* for short. For the record, here's the definition:

> **surjection** Let *f* be a function with domain *A* and codomain *B*. Then *f* is a surjection (also known as a *many-to-one onto relationship*) if and only if each element *b* in *B* is the image of at least one element *a* in *A*—in other words, if and only if the range is equal to the codomain.

Note: The range of a function is supposed to be a subset of the codomain. But since by definition every set is a subset of itself, having the range and the codomain be equal, which is what happens with a surjection, doesn't count as a violation of this requirement on functions in general.

Now let's consider the squares example again, where the domain *A* and range *C* are the set of all nonnegative integers and the set of all perfect squares, respectively, and *f* is the function that maps nonnegative integers *x* to their squares x^2. This particular function satisfies the property—as most functions do not—that if *a1* and *a2* are distinct elements in *A*, then their images *c1* and *c2* are distinct elements in *C*; in other words, each element in *C* is the image of exactly one element in *A*. In such a case, we can and do say that the relationship from *A* to *B* is *one-to-one*, or one-to-one *onto* to be more precise. As for the relationship from *A* to the codomain *B*, we describe that relationship as one-to-one *into*, since in general there are some elements *b* of *B* that aren't the image of anything at all in *A*. *Note:* One-to-one onto is a special case of one-to-one into, of course, and one-to-one in general is a special case of many-to-one. Also, I should make it clear that in the case of one-to-one into (though not one-to-one onto), the qualifier *one-to-one* is being used in a slightly sloppy sense. See the section "Correspondences" (subsection "One-to-One Correspondence"), following the present section.

Yet more terminology: A one-to-one onto relationship is also known as a *bijective* function (or mapping), or just a *bijection* for short; a one-to-one into relationship is also known as an *injective* function (or mapping), or just an *injection* for short. For completeness, here are the definitions:

> **bijection** Let *f* be a function with domain *A* and codomain *B*. Then *f* is a bijection (also known as a *one-to-one onto relationship*) if and only if each element *b* in *B* is the image of exactly one element *a* in *A*.

injection Let *f* be a function with domain *A* and codomain *B*. Then *f* is an injection (also known as a *one-to-one into relationship*) if and only if each element *b* in *B* is the image of at most one element *a* in *A*.

Note in particular that a function is a bijection if and only if it's both an injection and a surjection. Equivalently, a bijection is a function (from domain *A* to codomain *B*) for which the inverse relationship (from *B* to *A*) is a function—in fact a bijection—too. Here's a simple example: Let *A* and *B* both be the set of all integers, and let *f* be the function that maps integers *x* to their successors $x+1$. Then *f* is a bijection from *A* to itself (and so the inverse function, which maps integers *x* to their predecessors $x-1$, is a bijection from *A* to itself as well).

Note further that a bijection can be regarded as a *nonloss* mapping in the sense that, given an arbitrary element *a* in the domain, we can always get back to that element *a* from its image *b* in the codomain by using the inverse mapping, which is a bijection also. *Note:* Bijections are sometimes also referred to as *isomorphic* mappings, though this terminology is deprecated (see the section "Closing Remarks").

Let me now relate the terms I've defined in this section to the cases identified in the section "How Many Cases Are There?" (where possible). It should be clear without too much discussion that:

- Case 2.1 is an injection, or one-to-one into relationship, from *A* to *B* (and Case 1.2 is an injection from *B* to *A*).

- Case 2.2 is a bijection, or one-to-one onto relationship, from *A* to *B* (and also from *B* to *A*).

- Case 2.3 is a surjection, or many-to-one onto relationship, from *A* to *B* (and Case 3.2 is a surjection from *B* to *A*).

- Case 2.4 is a function from *A* to *B* that isn't an injection, bijection, or surjection (and Case 4.2 is a function from *B* to *A* that isn't an injection, bijection, or surjection).

So now we've dealt with four of the ten distinct cases, or seven of the 16 cases overall. What about the others? Obviously the notion of function can only take us so far; in order to deal with the other cases properly, we need some more concepts, and more definitions.

CORRESPONDENCES

The mathematical notion of a correspondence is more general than that of a function—in fact, it can be seen as a formalization of the intuitive notion of a directed binary relationship (some but not all such relationships being functions, as we've seen). As you'd probably expect, correspondences come in four flavors: one-to-one, many-to-one, one-to-many, and many-to-many (though many-to-one and one-to-many are really just the same thing looked at from two different points of view, again as you'd probably expect). I'll treat each case in a subsection of its own.

One-to-One Correspondence

Here's a precise definition:

> **one-to-one correspondence** Let A and B be sets, not necessarily distinct. Then a one-to-one correspondence from A to B is a rule that pairs each element of A with exactly one element of B and each element of B with exactly one element of A. Equivalently, we might just say the one-to-one correspondence is that pairing itself.

By way of example, let A be the set of all integers. Then the pairing of elements x with their successors $x+1$ is a one-to-one correspondence from A to itself, and so is the pairing of elements x with their predecessors $x-1$.

Now, I hope it's obvious that (as the example suggests) a one-to-one correspondence is nothing more nor less than a bijection as previously defined. The trouble is, the term *one-to-one correspondence* is often used, loosely, to mean something slightly different from a bijection as such. To be specific, it's often used to mean one or other of the following (note the various subtle differences here):

1.   A pairing such that each element of A corresponds to at most one element of B (while each element of B corresponds to exactly one element of A)

2.   A pairing such that (while each element of A corresponds to exactly one element of B) each element of B corresponds to at most one element of A

3.   A pairing such that each element of A corresponds to at most one element of B and each element of B corresponds to at most one element of A

I'll refer (for the moment) to these three interpretations of the term *one-to-one correspondence* as *Type 1, Type 2,* and *Type 3,* respectively, and I'll refer to the strict (bijective) interpretation as *Type 0.* Let me now relate the four interpretations to the cases identified in the section "How Many Cases Are There?" (where possible). In fact, it should be clear that:

■   Case 2.2 (previously identified, correctly, as a bijection, or one-to-one onto relationship, from A to B and also from B to A) can also be identified as a *Type 0* one-to-one correspondence from A to B (and also from B to A).

■   Case 1.2 (previously identified, correctly, as an injection, or one-to-one into relationship, from B to A) can also be identified as a *Type 1* one-to-one correspondence from A to B.

■   Case 2.1 (previously identified, correctly, as an injection, or one-to-one into relationship, from A to B) can also be identified as a *Type 2* one-to-one correspondence from A to B.

■   Case 1.1 can be identified as a *Type 3* one-to-one correspondence from A to B (and also from B to A).

Note: Given that (as I've said) the *Type 1, Type 2,* and *Type 3* interpretations are loose, you can now see why I said earlier (in the section "Functions") that in the case of a one-to-one into relationship in particular, the qualifier *one-to-one* was being used in a slightly sloppy sense.

Many-to-One Correspondence

Again I'll start with a definition:

> **many-to-one correspondence** Let *A* and *B* be sets, not necessarily distinct. Then a many-to-one correspondence from *A* to *B* is a rule that pairs each element of *A* with exactly one element of *B* and each element of *B* with at least one element of *A*. Equivalently, we might just say the many-to-one correspondence is that pairing itself.

By way of example, let *A* and *B* be the set of all integers and the set of all nonnegative integers, respectively. Then the pairing of integers *x* with their absolute values $|x|$ is a many-to-one correspondence from *A* to *B*.

Now, I hope it's obvious that a many-to-one correspondence is nothing more nor less than a surjection as previously defined. The trouble is, the term *many-to-one correspondence* is often used, loosely, to mean something slightly different from a surjection as such. To be specific, it's often used to mean one or other of the following:

1. A pairing such that each element of *A* corresponds to at most one element of *B* (while each element of *B* corresponds to at least one element of *A*)

2. A pairing such that (while each element of *A* corresponds to exactly one element of *B*) each element of *B* corresponds to any number of elements of *A* (possibly none at all)

3. A pairing such that each element of *A* corresponds to at most one element of *B* and each element of *B* corresponds to any number of elements of *A* (possibly none at all)

I'll refer for the moment to these three interpretations of the term *many-to-one correspondence* as *Type 1, Type 2,* and *Type 3,* respectively, and I'll refer to the strict (surjective) interpretation as *Type 0.* Let me now relate the four interpretations to the cases identified in the section "How Many Cases Are There?" (where possible). Again it should be clear that:

- Case 2.3 (previously identified, correctly, as a surjection, or many-to-one onto relationship, from *A* to *B*) can also be identified as a *Type 0* many-to-one correspondence from *A* to *B*.

- Case 1.3 can be identified as a *Type 1* many-to-one correspondence from *A* to *B*.

- Case 2.4 (previously identified, correctly, as a function that's not an injection, bijection, or surjection) can also be identified as a *Type 2* many-to-one correspondence from *A* to *B*.

- Case 1.4 can be identified as a *Type 3* many-to-one correspondence from *A* to *B*.

    Note: Given that (as I've said) the *Type 1, Type 2,* and *Type 3* interpretations are loose, you can now see why I said earlier (in the section "Functions") that in the case of a many-to-one into relationship in particular, the qualifier *many-to-one* was being used in a slightly sloppy sense.

One-to-Many Correspondence

Again I'll start with a definition:

> **one-to-many correspondence** Let A and B be sets, not necessarily distinct. Then a one-to-many correspondence from A to B is a rule that pairs each element of A with at least one element of B and each element of B with exactly one element of A. Equivalently, we might just say the one-to-many correspondence is that pairing itself.

By way of example, let A and B be the set of all nonnegative numbers and the set of all numbers, respectively. Then the pairing of integers x with their square roots $\pm\sqrt{x}$ is a one-to-many correspondence from A to B.

The trouble is, the term *one-to-many correspondence* is often used, loosely, to mean something slightly different from the concept as just precisely defined. To be specific, it's often used to mean one or other of the following:

1.   A pairing such that each element of A corresponds to any number of elements of B, possibly none at all (while each element of B corresponds to exactly one element of A)

2.   A pairing such that (while each element of A corresponds to at least one element of B) each element of B corresponds to at most one element of A

3.   A pairing such that each element of A corresponds to any number of elements of B, possibly none at all, and each element of B corresponds to at most one element of A

I'll refer for the moment to these three interpretations of the term *one-to-many correspondence* as *Type 1, Type 2,* and *Type 3,* respectively, and I'll refer to the strict interpretation as *Type 0.* Let me now relate the four interpretations to the cases identified in the section "How Many Cases Are There?" (where possible). Once again it should be clear that:

■   Case 3.2 (previously identified, correctly, as a surjection, or many-to-one onto relationship, from B to A) can also be identified as a *Type 0* one-to-many correspondence from A to B.

■   Case 4.2 (previously identified, correctly, as a function from B to A that isn't an injection, bijection, or surjection) can also be identified as a *Type 1* one-to-many correspondence from A to B.

■   Case 3.1 can be identified as a *Type 2* one-to-many correspondence from A to B.

■   Case 4.1 can be identified as a *Type 3* one-to-many correspondence from A to B.

Many-to-Many Correspondence

Again I'll start with a definition:

> **many-to-many correspondence** Let *A* and *B* be sets, not necessarily distinct. Then a many-to-many correspondence from *A* to *B* is a rule that pairs each element of *A* with at least one element of *B* and each element of *B* with at least one element of *A*. Equivalently, we might just say the many-to-many correspondence is that pairing itself.

By way of example, let *A* be the set of all positive integers. Consider the pairing of positive integers *x* and *y* defined as follows: Positive integers *x* and *y* are paired if and only if they have the same number of digits in conventional decimal notation. Then that pairing is a many-to-many correspondence from *A* to itself.

The trouble is, the term *many-to-many correspondence* is often used, loosely, to mean something slightly different from the concept as just precisely defined. To be specific, it's often used to mean one or other of the following:

1. A pairing such that each element of *A* corresponds to any number of elements of *B*, possibly none at all (while each element of *B* corresponds to at least one element of *A*)

2. A pairing such that (while each element of *A* corresponds to at least one element of *B*) each element of *B* corresponds to any number of elements of *A* (possibly none at all)

3. A pairing such that each element of *A* corresponds to any number of elements of *B* (possibly none at all) and each element of *B* corresponds to any number of elements of *A* (possibly none at all)

I'll refer to these three interpretations of the term *many-to-many correspondence* as *Type 1*, *Type 2*, and *Type 3*, respectively, and I'll refer to the strict interpretation as *Type 0*. Let me now relate the four interpretations to the cases identified in the section "How Many Cases Are There?" (where possible). Yet again it should be clear that:

- Case 3.3 can be identified as a *Type 0* many-to-many correspondence from *A* to *B* (and also from *B* to *A*).

- Case 4.3 can be identified as a *Type 1* many-to-many correspondence from *A* to *B*.

- Case 3.4 can be identified as a *Type 2* many-to-many correspondence from *A* to *B*.

- Case 4.4 can be identified as a *Type 3* many-to-many correspondence from *A* to *B* (and also from *B* to *A*).

Summary

All 16 cases have now been covered. Fig. 7.3, an edited form of Fig. 7.1, summarizes the situation at this point. *Note:* I've used several self-explanatory abbreviations in that figure (for example, M:1 for many-to-one). Also, some of the entries in the matrix could be stated in more than one way; in such cases, I've chosen the form of text that I personally find most helpful (for example, I prefer "1:1 onto" to "1:1 *Type 0*"). The notation $A \rightarrow B$ means "from A to B"; the notation $A \leftrightarrow B$ means "from A to B and also from B to A."

	b has → at most one *a*	exactly one *a*	at least one *a*	M a's (M ≥ 0)
a has ↓				
at most one *b*	1:1 *Type 3* $A \leftrightarrow B$	1:1 into *Type 1* $A \rightarrow B$	M:1 *Type 1* $A \rightarrow B$	M:1 *Type 3* $A \rightarrow B$
exactly one *b*	1:1 into *Type 2* $A \rightarrow B$	1:1 onto *Type 0* $A \leftrightarrow B$	M:1 onto *Type 0* $A \rightarrow B$	M:1 *Type 2* $A \rightarrow B$
at least one *b*	1:M *Type 2* $A \rightarrow B$	1:M into *Type 0* $A \rightarrow B$	M:M *Type 0* $A \leftrightarrow B$	M:M *Type 2* $A \rightarrow B$
M *b*'s (M ≥ 0)	1:M *Type 3* $A \rightarrow B$	1:M *Type 1* $A \rightarrow B$	M:M *Type 1* $A \rightarrow B$	M:M *Type 3* $A \leftrightarrow B$

Fig. 7.3: The 16 cases summarized

CONCLUDING REMARKS

I'd like to close with a series of recommendations. I'll start with a couple of small ones. First, I said earlier that it makes more sense to think of a relationship as being from one set to another than it does to think of it being between those sets; I even described the use of "between" as a source of some of the confusions we observe in this area. However, there are a couple of cases where "between" is acceptable, and possibly even the better term: namely, Cases 2.2 and 3.3—where, just to remind you, Case 2.2 is the strict one-to-one case and Case 3.3 is the strict many-to-many case. And an argument could be made (I don't think I'd subscribe to it, but it's hardly an earth-shattering issue) that "between" is also acceptable in Cases 1.1 and 4.4. In all other cases, however, I would definitely recommend staying with "from" and "to" and avoiding "between."

Second, I noted earlier that a bijection is sometimes said to be an isomorphic mapping—but I also said that term was deprecated. The reason it's deprecated is that, mathematically speaking, an isomorphism is more than just a bijection (loosely, it's a bijection plus operators). Here's the definition:

isomorphism Let A and B be sets, not necessarily distinct, and let f be a bijective mapping from A to B. Let OpA be an operator that takes elements of A as its operands and yields an element of A as its result. Then f is an isomorphism if and only if, for all such operators OpA, there exists an analogous operator OpB that takes elements of B as its operands and yields an element of B as its result such that, whenever OpA applied to $a1, a2, \ldots, an$ yields a, then OpB applied to $b1$, $b2, \ldots, bn$ yields b, where $b1, b2, \ldots, bn$, and b are the images of $a1, a2, \ldots, an$, and a, respectively, under f.

In other words, a bijective mapping is an isomorphism if and only if it preserves the algebraic structure of the domain A in the codomain B (see Chapter 10 for further discussion). Of course, if a given bijective mapping f is an isomorphism, then its inverse is an isomorphism as well.

Now I turn to a more serious recommendation. I've shown in this chapter that the situation regarding relationships in general is quite complex—more complex than it's usually given credit for. In fact, I think it's sufficiently complex that our usual reliance in this area on somewhat simplified terminology is a trifle dangerous, or at least misleading. Instead of relying on such simplified (or oversimplified) terminology, therefore, I think we should strive, as suggested earlier, for a better set of terms—terms that are clearer, more accurate, and more precise than the ones we usually use. To be more specific:

- I don't think we should refer to the various different cases by reference numbers ("Case 3.2" and the like), because such reference numbers always need some kind of guide or key by which they can be interpreted. Of course, I used such reference numbers in the body of the chapter, but that was because I was trying to imposing a systematic structure on the subject matter for purposes of analysis. I'd be very surprised if you didn't have difficulty in remembering which case was which, especially if you didn't keep a copy of Fig. 7.1 or Fig. 7.2 by you as a key.

- I don't think we should use labels like *optional* and *mandatory,* because their meanings are essentially arbitrary (even if we can agree on them, something I'm not at all sanguine about anyway). *Note:* I remark in this connection that several other similar terms can also be found in the literature: *conditional* relationships, *contingent* relationships, *complex* relationships, *singular* relationships, *exclusive* relationships, and so on (this isn't an exhaustive list). Do you think the precise meanings of these terms are all obvious? Or all universally agreed upon?

- I don't think we should use mathematical terms like *function, injection, surjection,* or *bijection,* even though those terms do at least have precise definitions. One problem is that few people are familiar with those definitions (and in any case, I think the meanings of *injection* and *surjection,* at least, are difficult to remember). Another is that—rather annoyingly!—the terms don't cover all cases. Yet another is that the term *function,* at least, is often used in a very imprecise manner (despite its having a precise definition), thus increasing the likelihood of breakdowns in communication.

- Similar remarks apply to the terms *one-to-one onto* (and *into*) and *many-to-one onto* (and *into*).

- I've pointed out that each of the terms *one-to-one correspondence, many-to-one correspondence, one-to-many correspondence,* and *many-to-many correspondence* has three loose interpretations as well as one strict one. As a consequence, I think these terms should be avoided too, except in situations where there's no possibility of misunderstanding (you might like to meditate on whether any such situations exist). I certainly wouldn't use terms like "*Type 2* one-to-many correspondence" at all! Like the terms "Case 3.2" (etc.), I used those terms in the body of the chapter only because I was trying to imposing a systematic structure on the subject matter for purposes of analysis, and I'd be very surprised if you didn't have difficulty in remembering exactly what they all meant.

So what terms do I think we should use? Well, I certainly think we should use terms that are *absolutely explicit*—thereby saying things like "zero or one to one or more," if that's what we really mean, instead of using an approximation like "one-to-many" and hoping that our audience knows that "one" here includes the zero case and "many" doesn't. So here are the terms I would recommend. Note that they can all be immediately derived from the annotation in Fig. 7.2. Note too that I do have to use the terminology of "Case 3.2" (etc.) in this list!—but, I hope, for the very last time.

- Case 1.1: at most one to at most one

- Case 1.2: exactly one to at most one

- Case 1.3: one or more to at most one

- Case 1.4: zero or more to at most one

- Case 2.1: at most one to exactly one

- Case 2.2: exactly one to exactly one

- Case 2.3: one or more to exactly one

- Case 2.4: zero or more to exactly one

- Case 3.1: at most one to one or more

- Case 3.2: exactly one to one or more

- Case 3.3: one or more to one or more

- Case 3.4: zero or more to one or more

- Case 4.1: at most one to zero or more

- Case 4.2: exactly one to zero or more

- Case 4.3: one or more to zero or more

- Case 4.4: zero or more to zero or more

Let me admit immediately that the foregoing terms are still not as transparently clear as I could wish them to be. In the case of "zero or one to one or more," for example, it has to be clearly understood that the "zero or one" means that each *b* has at most one *a* and not the other way around, and the "one or more" means each *a* has at least one *b* and not the other way around. So perhaps I'm still in the market for some better terms ... but until such terms come along, I think the foregoing ones should serve. *Note:* In this connection, Hugh Darwen has suggested the following numeric substitutions for the phrases "at most one" (etc.):[1]

at most one	1^-
exactly one	1
one or more	1^+
zero or more	0^+

Using these replacements, "at most one to zero or more" (for example) becomes "1^- to 0^+" (or, perhaps better, just "$1^-:0^+$"). This notation is at least more succinct and avoids the use of English words; but I still don't think it's perfect.

I'll leave you with some questions to ponder. In this chapter, I've offered precise definitions of (among other things) the terms *function, one-to-one correspondence, many-to-one correspondence, one-to-many correspondence,* and *many-to-many correspondence.* Here now is a precise definition of a *binary relation* (in the mathematical sense of that term):

> **binary relation** Let *A* and *C* be sets, not necessarily distinct. Then a binary relation *r* is a rule that pairs each element of *A* (the *domain* of *r*) with at least one element of *C* (the *range* of *r*); equivalently, we might just say *r* is that pairing itself.

So what exactly do you think the relationship is between relationships as I've defined them in this chapter and the mathematical concept of a binary relation? And what do you think the relationship is between relationships and relations as defined in the relational model? And why do you think the relational model is so called?

REFERENCES AND BIBLIOGRAPHY

1. Grady Booch, James Rumbaugh, and Ivar Jacobson, *The Unified Modeling Language User Guide.* Reading, Mass.: Addison-Wesley (1999).

2. C. J. Date: *The Relational Database Dictionary.* Sebastopol, Calif.: O'Reilly Media Inc. (2006).

3. C. J. Date: "Basic Concepts in UML: A Request for Clarification," in *Date on Database:*

---

1. In passing, let me acknowledge Hugh's careful review of an earlier draft of this chapter.

Writings 2000-2006. Berkeley, Calif.: Apress (2006).

4.   C. J. Date and Hugh Darwen: *Databases, Types, and the Relational Model: The Third Manifesto* (3rd edition). Boston, Mass.: Addison-Wesley (2006).

5.   Mary E. S. Loomis: *Object Databases: The Essentials*. Reading, Mass.: Addison-Wesley (1995).

6.   Michael M. Gorman: *Database Management Systems: Understanding and Applying the Technology*. Wellesley, Mass.: QED Information Sciences (1991).

7.   James Martin: *Computer Data-Base Organization* (2nd edition). Englewood Cliffs, N.J.: Prentice-Hall (1977).

8.   James Martin and James J. Odell: *Object-Oriented Methods: A Foundation* (2nd edition). Englewood Cliffs, N.J.: Prentice-Hall (1997).

9.   Toby J. Torey and James P. Fry: *Design of Database Structures*. Englewood Cliffs, N.J.: Prentice-Hall (1982).

Chapter 8

Normalization

from Top to Bottom

You too may be a big hero
Once you've learned to count backwards to zero.

—Tom Lehrer

Normalization has been part of the database designer's stock-in-trade for many years. However, there's plenty of room for improvement in the level of understanding in this area, at least if the existing literature is anything to go by. This chapter is an attempt to address this problem. What I want to do is explain the ideas of normalization in a way that, while not necessarily very rigorous, is at least fairly precise, and accurate, and (perhaps most significant) novel—by which I mean I'll be "starting from the other end," as it were. (I'll explain what I mean by this remark in the section "Defining the Problem," later.) My goal is to give database designers and other database professionals a deeper understanding of one of the most important tools of their trade.

Now, the database literature is chock-a-block with tutorials on normalization. But this one is different. To be specific, although it is basically a tutorial, it's aimed specifically at readers who already have a working knowledge of the subject matter. In other words, I assume you already have a reasonable familiarity with normalization concepts and can therefore see where some of the discussions are heading. In particular, I assume you know there was a historical progression from first normal form (1NF) to second (2NF) and third (3NF), and then on to Boyce/Codd normal form (BCNF), fourth normal form (4NF), and fifth normal form (5NF). However, that progression was simply the way the subject developed historically; there's no particular reaon why a presentation of the ideas has to recapitulate that history, and the one that follows doesn't. Indeed, I think there are fresh insights, and perhaps a better overall appreciation of the formalisms involved, to be gained by taking a look at the subject from an alternative and—as I said before—novel perspective.

By the way, you can see from the foregoing paragraph that the labels "fourth" and "fifth" in 4NF and 5NF aren't exactly the most appropriate!—by rights, those normal forms should have been called fifth and sixth, respectively, and BCNF should have been called fourth. (As a matter of fact, BCNF actually was called fourth at one time, as Appendix B explains.) I should mention too that a sixth—or seventh?—normal form (6NF) also exists; however, it's only tangentially relevant to my aims in this chapter, and I won't discuss it further here, except very briefly in Appendix C.

Two more preliminary remarks: First, as I'm sure you know, the various normal forms are all defined in terms of various kinds of "dependencies"—to be specific, functional dependencies (FDs), multivalued dependencies (MVDs), and join dependencies (JDs). However, I think it's worth stressing the fact up front that, of these, it's really FDs and JDs that are the important ones; MVDs are just a kind of halfway house between the other two. I think it's even fair to say that if JDs had been defined first, then we might never have bothered to define MVDs, as a special case of JDs in general, at all. Bear this point in mind as you read through the material that follows.

My second point follows from the previous one. Again, you probably know that BCNF, 4NF, and 5NF are, respectively, *the* normal form with respect to FDs, *the* normal form with respect to MVDs, and *the* normal form with respect to JDs. Since I've already said that MVDs as such aren't all that important, it follows that 4NF as such isn't all that important either; BCNF and 5NF are the really important ones. Again, please bear this point in mind as you read through the rest of the chapter.

RELVARS AND KEYS

I'll begin with a quick review of some of the most basic concepts of all. First, relational databases contain relation variables or *relvars*. A relvar is a variable whose permitted values are relation values (relations for short). For example, we might have an employees relvar EMP2[1] that looks like this (in outline):

```
EMP2 { EMP#, SS#, SALARY, DEPT#, BUDGET }
     KEY { EMP# }
     KEY { SS# }
```

Explanation: EMP# (employee number), SS# (social security number), SALARY (employee salary), DEPT# (department number), and BUDGET (department budget) are the *attributes* of relvar EMP2. (Strictly speaking, each attribute definition should include a specification of the corresponding type, but types are unimportant for the purposes of this chapter.) The set of all of those attributes is the *heading* of the relvar, and its *keys*—strictly, *candidate* keys, but I'll abbreviate this term to just keys throughout this chapter—are {EMP#} and {SS#}. A sample value for relvar EMP2 is shown in Fig. 8.1. *Note:* Attribute values—e.g., social security number *s1*, salary 50K—are shown in that figure in symbolic form, for simplicity.

EMP2

EMP#	SS#	SALARY	DEPT#	BUDGET
e1	*s1*	50K	*d1*	800K
e2	*s2*	45K	*d1*	800K
e3	*s3*	50K	*d1*	800K
e4	*s4*	60K	*d2*	900K
e5	*s5*	50K	*d2*	900K
e6	*s6*	60K	*d3*	800K

Fig. 8.1: Relvar EMP2 (sample value)

---

1. "EMP2" because we'll see in Appendix A that the relvar is in second normal form and not in third.

Just for the record, I'll also give a precise definition of the term *key,* even though I'm quite sure you're familiar with the concept. Let *K* be a subset of the heading of relvar *R* (in other words, *K* is a set of attributes of *R*). Then *K* is a key for *R* if and only if it possesses both of the following properties:

- *Uniqueness:* No value of *R* ever contains two distinct tuples with the same value for *K*.

- *Irreducibility:* No proper subset of *K* has the uniqueness property.

Points arising from this definition:

- Every relvar has at least one key (why?). *Note:* Questions and exercises like this one are scattered throughout the chapter. Answers to most of them can be found in Appendix D.

- To repeat, the keys for relvar EMP2 are {EMP#} and {SS#}. Note the braces, by the way: Keys are always sets of attributes, not attributes per se, even if the set in question contains just a single attribute. To stress this point, I always show the relevant attribute name(s) enclosed in braces, as in the examples at hand.

- In practice, if there's more than one key, we usually choose one and call it the *primary* key. From a formal point of view, however (for normalization purposes in particular), it's candidate keys, not primary keys, that are important, and so I ignore primary keys, as such, throughout this chapter. For the same reason, I also abandon my usual convention of using double underlining in figures like Fig. 8.1 to mark attributes that are part of the primary key. Of course, if there's only one candidate key, you can think of it as "primary" if you like—it won't do any serious harm—but it won't have escaped your notice that I deliberately chose an example of a relvar, EMP2, with two distinct keys.

Another concept that will turn out to be very important in what follows is that of a superkey. A *superkey* is a superset of a key; equivalently, a subset of the heading of relvar *R* is a superkey for *R* if and only if it possesses the uniqueness property but not necessarily the irreducibility property. In the case of relvar EMP2, for example, every subset of the heading that contains either EMP# or SS# or both is a superkey. Here are some examples:

```
{ EMP# }                    { SS# }
{ EMP#, SALARY }            { SS#, SALARY }
{ EMP#, BUDGET }            { SS#, BUDGET }
{ EMP#, SS#, DEPT# }        { SS#, SALARY, EMP# }
```

Note that, by definition, every key is a superkey, but most superkeys aren't keys. Note too that the heading in particular is always a superkey. *Exercise:* How many superkeys does relvar EMP2 have? I'll close this section by defining two more useful terms:

- A *key attribute* for relvar *R* is an attribute of *R* that's part of at least one key for *R*.

- A *subkey* is a subset of a key; equivalently, a subset X of the heading of relvar R is a subkey for R if and only if there exists some key K for R such that K is a superset of X. For example, here are all of the subkeys for EMP2:

```
{ EMP# }
{ SS# }
{ }
```

Note that, by definition, the empty set is always a subkey.

DEFINING THE PROBLEM

Now, I'm sure you realized right away (in fact, I effectively said as much, in a footnote) that relvar EMP2 in the previous section wasn't fully normalized.[1] As a consequence, it suffers from a variety of problems, of which the most fundamental—most if not all of the others stem from this basic one—is *redundancy:* Certain information (to be specific, the fact that certain departments have certain budgets) is represented in the relvar several times.

Of course, the problems caused by such redundancy are well known, and I'm not going to expound on them in this chapter. More important, the solution to those problems is well known too: We decompose the relvar into two smaller ones EX and EY as suggested by Fig. 8.2. The redundancy is thereby eliminated, and the problems caused by it therefore go away too.

EX

EMP#	SS#	SALARY	DEPT#
e1	s1	50K	d1
e2	s2	45K	d1
e3	s3	50K	d1
e4	s4	60K	d2
e5	s5	50K	d2
e6	s6	60K	d3

EY

DEPT#	BUDGET
d1	800K
d2	900K
d3	800K

Fig. 8.2: Nonloss decomposition of relvar EMP2 (sample values)

Informally, we can say the original design as illustrated in Fig. 8.1 is bad because it bundles together two kinds of information, one having to do with employees as such and one with departments. (A little more formally, we can say it's bad because it muddles and mixes two distinct *predicates,* one for employees and one for departments. See Chapter 3 for a detailed discussion of relvar predicates.) One consequence of this bundling is that if we were to delete an EMP2 tuple, *we would delete too much;* since

---

1. I'll give a precise definition for this term—i.e., *fully normalized*—in the section "Fifth Normal Form," later.

relvar EMP2 contains information about both employees and departments, "deleting an employee" would cause department information to be deleted as well. Clearly, the solution to this problem is to *unbundle*—place employee information in one relvar and department information in another, as illustrated in Fig. 8.2. Thus, an informal way to characterize the decomposition process is as a process of unbundling: *Place logically distinct information in distinct relvars.*

> *Aside:* There's another good reason to unbundle, too, which is that an unbundled design allows us to represent certain kinds of information that a bundled one doesn't. For example, the design illustrated in Fig. 8.2 allows us to represent departments that currently have no employees, whereas the design illustrated in Fig. 8.1 doesn't. Like the notion of 6NF touched on earlier, however, this benefit, though important, is only tangentially relevant to the aims of this chapter, and I won't discuss it any further here. (As a matter of fact there are several other advantages to unbundling in general, but I don't plan to discuss any of them any further in this chapter. A short list of such advantages can be found in my book *Database in Depth: Relational Theory for Practitioners,* O'Reilly Media Inc., 2005.) *End of aside.*

Now let's get a little more precise. Formally, the decomposition process is a process of *taking projections* (relvars EX and EY in Fig. 8.2 are both projections of relvar EMP2—EX over attributes EMP#, SS#, SALARY, and DEPT#, and EY over attributes DEPT# and BUDGET). In other words, the decomposition operator is the well known *project* operator of relational algebra. Furthermore, the recomposition operator is *join:* When we join those projections back together again (over their common attribute DEPT#), we reconstruct the original relvar. In other words, the decomposition process is *nonloss,* also called *lossless.*

> *Note:* I'm being a little sloppy here. Strictly speaking, project and join, and indeed all of the operators of the relational algebra, apply to relations, not relvars. Thus, when I say that, e.g., relvar EY is the projection of relvar EMP2 over DEPT# and BUDGET, what I really mean is that, at all times, the relation that's the current value of relvar EY is the projection over attributes DEPT# and BUDGET of the relation that's the current value of relvar EMP2. (More precisely, it's the projection over attributes DEPT# and BUDGET of the relation that *would have been* the current value of relvar EMP2 if we hadn't replaced that relvar by relvars EX and EY in the first place.) I hope this slight sloppiness on my part—which I plan to continue to indulge in throughout the rest of this chapter—won't confuse you.

By the way, I hope it's obvious why we want the process to be nonloss: If it wasn't, we wouldn't be able to reconstruct the original relvar, and so we'd lose information in the decomposition. For example, suppose we were to decompose relvar EMP2 into its projections EZ and EY as suggested by Fig. 8.3 overleaf (where EY is the same as before—see Fig. 8.2—but EZ differs from EX in that it has a BUDGET attribute instead of a DEPT# attribute). In that decomposition, we would lose information as to which employee is in which department, and the decomposition would therefore be *lossy.* To be specific, joining the projections together again over their common attribute BUDGET wouldn't reconstruct the original EMP2.

Let me elaborate briefly on this last point. When we say that a certain ("lossy") decomposition loses information, what we really mean is that when we perform the corresponding recomposition, *certain additional tuples appear in the result* (see Fig. 8.4, which shows the join of the projections from Fig. 8.3; I've marked the additional tuples with an asterisk). In other words, we get all of the original tuples—we can never get anything less than all of the original tuples, of course—but we also get what might be called "spurious" tuples as well. Since we have no way in general of knowing which tuples are spurious and which "genuine," we have indeed lost information.

EZ

EMP#	SS#	SALARY	BUDGET
e1	s1	50K	800K
e2	s2	45K	800K
e3	s3	50K	800K
e4	s4	60K	900K
e5	s5	50K	900K
e6	s6	60K	800K

EY

DEPT#	BUDGET
d1	800K
d2	900K
d3	800K

Fig. 8.3: Lossy decomposition of relvar EMP2 (sample values)

EMP#	SS#	SALARY	DEPT#	BUDGET	
e1	s1	50K	d1	800K	
e1	s1	50K	d3	800K	(*)
e2	s2	45K	d1	800K	
e2	s2	45K	d3	800K	(*)
e3	s3	50K	d1	800K	
e3	s3	50K	d3	800K	(*)
e4	s4	60K	d2	900K	
e5	s5	50K	d2	900K	
e6	s6	60K	d3	800K	
e6	s6	60K	d1	800K	(*)

Fig. 8.4: Join of projections EZ and EY from Fig. 8.3

So far, then, we've learned—actually I'm sure you knew all this already, but I had to go through it in order to lay some groundwork for what's to come—that (a) decomposition via projection is the solution to the redundancy problem, but (b) not all such decompositions are valid, because they aren't all nonloss. Clearly, then, what we need to do is as follows:

- We need to pin down exactly the conditions under which a nonloss decomposition is possible.

- When it is possible, we need to pin down exactly what that decomposition is.

And the structure of this chapter—to be specific, the "alternative and novel" perspective mentioned near the beginning—is motivated by these observations. Usually, the topic of normalization is presented simply as a kind of *fait accompli,* with a set of definitions ("Relvar *R* is in *N*th normal form if and only if it possesses certain properties") and an accompanying set of rules ("If relvar *R* isn't in *N*th normal form then decompose it into projections that are")—but it isn't always clear where those definitions and rules come from, or why they are the way they are, or how to apply them, even when they're accompanied by illustrative examples. In this chapter, by contrast, I want to start at the other end, as it were; in particular, I want to try and explain the motivation behind those definitions and rules (or some of that motivation, at any rate).

> *Aside:* What I've just suggested, in effect, is that pinning down the conditions under which a nonloss decomposition is possible represents a novel perspective on the topic—but actually that suggestion isn't valid at all. On the contrary, pinning down those conditions is exactly what the researchers in this field have always tried to do. Codd himself gave us a magnificent start on the problem in his very first paper on the relational model, "Derivability, Redundancy, and Consistency of Relations Stored in Large Data Banks" (IBM Research Report RJ599, August 19th, 1969). And subsequent important work was done by many people, including Heath, Codd again, Boyce, Rissanen, and especially Fagin (see Appendix B). So when I say the perspective is novel, it isn't really; but nor is it the way we usually think about the issue, at least in the commercial IT world. *End of aside.*

Let's get back to the main thread of the discussion. Actually there's another aspect to nonloss decomposition—one that's often overlooked in discussions of this subject—and that's as follows: *We want all of the projections to be needed in the recomposition process.* For example, if we were to decompose relvar EMP2 into its projections EX and EY, as in Fig. 8.2, *as well as* its projection EW on EMP# and SS#, then that decomposition would clearly be nonloss (if we were to join EX, EY, and EW together, we would certainly get back to EMP2). Yet projection EW would be redundant in that decomposition—we wouldn't need it in the recomposition process, and in fact we could discard it entirely without loss. In what follows, therefore, I'll assume, where it makes any difference, that none of the projections produced in the decomposition process is in fact redundant in the foregoing sense.

JOIN DEPENDENCIES

To paraphrase a remark from the previous section, one of the questions we need to address is: When is a nonloss decomposition possible? And the answer is: When the relvar in question is less than fully normalized (i.e., when it isn't in 5NF).[1] Let me elaborate.

I'll begin with a definition. Let *R* be a relvar. Then a *join dependency* (JD) is an expression of the form

---

1. At least, this is part of the answer, and it's the part that's important for the purposes of this paper: If a relvar is less than fully normalized, then we generally do want to decompose it. Note, however, that it will often be possible (and perhaps even desirable) to decompose a relvar that *is* fully normalized. For example, let relvar EMP have attributes EMP#, SALARY, and DEPT#, with the obvious semantics; then EMP is in 5NF, but it can certainly be nonloss decomposed into its (5NF) projections on {EMP#,SALARY} and {EMP#,DEPT#}. The point is, however, that this decomposition doesn't help in any way with the goal of reducing redundancy, which is what this paper is supposed to be all about.

☼ { A, B, C, ... }

("star *A, B, C, ...*"), where each of *A, B, C,* ... is a subset of the heading of *R*. Moreover, relvar *R* *satisfies* the JD ☼{*A,B,C,...*}—equivalently, that JD *holds* in *R*—if and only if *R* is equal to the join of its projections on *A, B, C,* ... (in other words, if and only if *R* can be nonloss decomposed into those projections). Points arising:

- If the JD is in fact satisfied by *R*, then the set theory union of *A, B, C,* ... must be equal to the heading of *R* (i.e., every attribute of *R* must be mentioned in at least one of *A, B, C, ...*), for otherwise *R* couldn't possibly be equal to the join of the corresponding projections.

- The definition relies on the fact that join is both (a) commutative, which means that for all *R1* and *R2, R1* JOIN *R2 = R2* JOIN *R1*, and (b) associative, which means that for all *R1, R2,* and *R3, R1* JOIN (*R2* JOIN *R3*) = (*R1* JOIN *R2*) JOIN *R3*. As a consequence, we can join a given set of relvars in any order and always get the same result, loosely speaking, which means in turn that we can speak unambiguously of *the* join of any given set of relvars.

- Following on from the previous point: In particular, it's convenient to allow the phrase "any given set of relvars" to include the special case of a singleton set (i.e., a set of cardinality one), which we can do by defining the join of just one relvar *R* to be identically equal to *R*.[1] Thus, any relvar *R* certainly satisfies the join dependency ☼{*H*}, where *H* is the heading of *R*.

- It follows from the previous point that one legally valid "nonloss decomposition" of relvar *R* is the projection of *R* on all of its attributes, or in other words just *R* itself: the *identity projection* of *R*. Of course, if *R* suffers from redundancy problems, this particular decomposition won't solve them!—but it's still useful to regard it as a valid decomposition, at least formally, because it can have the effect among other things of simplifying some of the definitions.

By way of example, consider relvar EMP2 once again, with its attributes EMP#, SS#, SALARY, DEPT#, and BUDGET. For simplicity, let's agree to use the letters E, S, Y, D, and B to stand for the sets {EMP#}, {SS#}, {SALARY}, {DEPT#}, and {BUDGET}, respectively. Let's further agree to use concatenations of these letters to stand for the corresponding set theory unions; e.g., ESY stands for the set of attributes {EMP#,SS#,SALARY}. (I'll use this same kind of shorthand throughout the rest of this chapter.) Here then are some of the many JDs that are satisfied by relvar EMP2:

☼ { ESYD, DB }

☼ { ESYD, EB }

---

1. In fact, it's desirable to allow that phrase to include the case of the empty set as well. However, this possibility, and the reason why it's desirable, are beyond the scope of this chapter.

☉ { ESY, ESD, ESB }

☉ { EY, SD, DB, ES }

☉ { ES, EYD, SDB }

☉ { ESYDB }

The first of these—☉{ESYD,DB}—is interpreted as follows: Relvar EMP2 is equal to the join of its projections on ESYD (= {EMP#,SS#,SALARY,DEPT#}) and DB (= {DEPT#,BUDGET}), and can therefore be nonloss decomposed into those projections (as indeed we already know, since this was the decomposition illustrated in Fig. 8.2). I'll leave the meanings of the other five for you to figure out. Observe in particular that the corresponding decompositions are indeed nonloss in every case. *Note:* I don't mean to suggest that all of those decompositions are sensible ones (some are, some aren't); all I'm trying to do is show some possible ones. In fact, of course, the rationale behind the rules that drive the normalization process has a lot to do with this question of which decompositions are sensible ones. But it's not my intent in this chapter to discuss those rules as such; in fact, I assume you're already familiar with them, though I might come back and deal with them in some future writing.

Well ... perhaps I should say just a little more about the question as to which decompositions are sensible ones. First, let's call the decomposition corresponding to the first JD in the foregoing list Decomposition 1. Now consider the second JD in the list, ☉{ESYD,EB}, which states that relvar EMP2 is equal to the join of its projections on ESYD (= {EMP#,SS#,SALARY,DEPT#}) and EB (= {EMP#,BUDGET}), and can therefore be nonloss decomposed into those projections. Let's call the decomposition corresponding to this JD Decomposition 2. Note that the projections in Decomposition 2 are both in 5NF; yet this decomposition isn't a very sensible one. Here are two important reasons why not:

- I pointed out earlier that one advantage of Decomposition 1 was that it let us represent departments that currently have no employees. Decomposition 2 doesn't.

- In Decomposition 1, certain updates can be made to either of the two projections without regard for the other, but the same is not true for Decomposition 2. For example, suppose employee *e1* moves from department *d1* to department *d2;* in Decomposition 1, then, all we need do is replace the tuple in projection EX for *e1* and *d1* by one for *e1* and *d2* instead (refer to Fig. 8.2). In Decomposition 2, by contrast, we would have to perform this same replacement *and* we would have to replace the tuple in the other projection for *e1* (with budget 800K) by one for *e1* with budget 900K.

As the foregoing discussion suggests, the projections in Decomposition 2 suffer from a certain unpleasant interdependence, as it were, while the same is not true for Decomposition 1. More precisely, a certain integrity constraint—namely, the constraint that every department has exactly one budget—is a comparatively simple single-relvar constraint in Decomposition 1 but a more complicated multi-relvar constraint in Decomposition 2 (see Chapter 3; see also the next section but one in the present chapter, "Join Dependencies Are Integrity Constraints"). Such considerations thus provide some guidelines for help in choosing "sensible" decompositions.[1]

——————— ♦ ♦ ♦ ♦ ♦ ———————

There's one more important point arising from the join dependency definition. In that definition, I said the JD ✩{$A,B,C,...$} was an expression. Well, so it is; formally, in fact, it's a truth valued expression, or in other words a *proposition*. Note, therefore, that—like all propositions in logic—it can evaluate to either TRUE or FALSE (i.e., it can be either satisfied or not). For example, we've already seen that relvar EMP2 satisfies the JD ✩{ESYD,DB} but not the JD ✩{ESYB,DB}. *It's a very common error to assume that a JD isn't a JD unless it's satisfied.* But if such was the case, then we'd have no way—no simple way, at any rate—of saying that (for example) a certain relvar failed to satisfy a certain JD, because by that definition such a JD wouldn't even be a JD in the first place!

——————— ♦ ♦ ♦ ♦ ♦ ———————

Certain JDs are necessarily satisfied by every relvar. To be specific, every relvar necessarily satisfies (a) certain *trivial* JDs and (b) certain JDs that are *implied by superkeys*. I'll elaborate on each case in turn.

First, let relvar R satisfy the JD ✩{$A,B,C,...$}; then that JD is *trivial* if and only if at least one of A, B, C, ... is the entire heading of R and thus corresponds to the identity projection of R. (I'll have more to say about this definition in the aside immediately following this paragraph.) For example, relvar EMP2 certainly satisfies any JD in which ESYDB is one of the specified sets of attributes, including

   ✩ { ESYDB, ESD, ESB }

   ✩ { ESYDB, E, S, Y, D, B }

   ✩ { ESYDB, ESYD, SB }

   ✩ { ESYDB }

and many others. And these examples should be sufficient to show why such JDs are trivial: They're just not very interesting, pragmatically speaking, nor are they very useful, because they correspond to trivial decompositions—i.e., decompositions in which at least one of the projections is identical to the original relvar. As a result, they don't help at all with the redundancy problem that nonloss decomposition is supposed to address.

> *Aside:* Strictly speaking, the foregoing definition of what it means for a JD to be trivial is only a *logical consequence* of the original formal definition. That definition can be stated as follows. Let H be a set of attributes and let J be a JD in which every specified set of attributes is some subset of H; then J is trivial if and only if every relation with heading H satisfies it. (Similar

———————

1. Those guidelines go by the formal name of *dependency preservation*. Dependency preservation in general is a topic beyond the scope of this chapter, but I'll have a little more to say about it in Appendix B.

remarks apply to my definition of other kinds of trivial dependencies later in this chapter, but I won't bother to spell them out, letting this one aside do duty for all.) *End of aside.*

Second, assume again that relvar *R* satisfies the JD ✩$\{A,B,C,...\}$; then that JD is *implied by superkeys* if and only if each of *A, B, C,* ... is a superkey for *R*. (Again I'll have more to say about this definition in the aside immediately following this paragraph.) For example, relvar EMP2 certainly satisfies many such JDs, including

✩ { ES, EY, ED, EB }

✩ { SE, SY, ED, SB }

✩ { ESY, ESDB }

✩ { ESYDB }

and many others. (You should take the time to convince yourself that relvar EMP2 does indeed satisfy all of these JDs, if it's not immediately obvious.) JDs that are implied by superkeys, like trivial JDs, aren't all that interesting for present purposes, because the corresponding decompositions don't "buy us anything," so to speak (why not?); certainly they don't help with the redundancy problem.

Aside: Strictly speaking, the foregoing definition of what it means for a JD that's satisfied by some relvar *R* to be implied by superkeys is only a logical consequence of the original formal definition. That definition can be stated as follows. The JD ✩$\{A,B,C,...\}$ is implied by superkeys if and only if both of the following conditions are satisfied:

1.   Each of *A, B, C,* ... is a superkey for *R* (as previously stated).

2.   The keys of *R* can be ordered in such a way that for each such key, there exists at least one of *A, B, C,* ... that includes both that key and its successor with respect to that ordering.

(Observe that all of the examples in the previous paragraph did indeed satisfy both of these conditions.) However, it's easy to see that if JD *j* (a) satisfies Condition 1 *and* (b) is satisfied by relvar *R*, then (c) it must satisfy Condition 2 as well. *Proof:* Suppose not. Call keys *Kx* and *Kz* of *R connected* if and only if there exists both (a) a sequence of keys *Ky1, Ky2, ..., Kym* of *R* ($m \geq 0$) and (b) a subset *SK1, SK2, ..., SKn* of the superkeys mentioned in *j* ($n \geq 1$) such that keys *Kx* and *Ky1* are both included in some *SKi* ($1 \leq i \leq n$), keys *Ky1* and *Ky2* are both included in some *SKi* ($1 \leq i \leq n$), ..., and keys *Kym* and *Kz* are both included in some *SKi* ($1 \leq i \leq n$). Then if *j* fails to satisfy Condition 2, there must exist some pair of distinct keys *Kx* and *Kz* that aren't connected. As a consequence, *R* can't be equal to the join of its projections on *A, B, C,* ..., thereby violating our assumption that *R* satisfies *j:* Contradiction! The desired result follows. *End of aside.*

FIFTH NORMAL FORM

To summarize so far: Every relvar necessarily satisfies certain JDs that are either trivial or implied by superkeys; we can never get rid of those JDs. It's if the relvar satisfies any additional JDs that we have redundancy and the problems that redundancy causes. For example, we know from earlier discussions that relvar EMP2 can be nonloss decomposed into its projections on ESYD and DB; in other words, we know it satisfies the JD

$$\Join \ \{ \ \texttt{ESYD, DB} \ \}$$

(which is neither trivial nor implied by superkeys, as you can easily see). We also know that relvar EMP2 suffers from redundancy. So let's agree to say that a relvar is *fully normalized* if and only if the only JDs it satisfies are ones that are either trivial or implied by superkeys; then we can say that the problem with relvar EMP2 is precisely that it's less than fully normalized (i.e., it's that fact that causes the redundancy).

Let me immediately add that, as I'm sure you realize, what I'm here calling "fully normalized" is what's called in the literature either *fifth normal form* (5NF) or *projection-join normal form* (PJ/NF). This latter name reflects the fact that, so long as we limit ourselves to projection as the decomposition operator and join as the recomposition operator, then PJ/NF is *the* normal form. Why? Because it follows immediately from the definition (i.e., of PJ/NF) that *there's nowhere else to go;* there simply is no "higher" normal form—PJ/NF is *the final normal form* with respect to projection and join.[1] So the name PJ/NF really does make good logical sense; in this chapter, however, I'll bow to convention and stay with the name 5NF from this point forward.

Now, it can be proved—i.e., it's a theorem—that any relvar that's less than fully normalized must satisfy a JD in which each specified set of attributes corresponds to a projection that *is* fully normalized. In other words, 5NF is always achievable. In the case of relvar EMP2, for example, the join dependency

$$\Join \ \{ \ \texttt{ESYD, DB} \ \}$$

is one such JD (the projections corresponding to ESYD and DB are both in 5NF). Given a relvar that's less than fully normalized, therefore, the goal is to find such a JD and to use it as a basis for decomposing the relvar into fully normalized projections.

On the face of it, therefore, it looks as if we're now faced with another problem: How do we find the desired JD? In practice, however, we don't have to find it—we already know it (for otherwise we wouldn't know the relvar was less than fully normalized in the first place!). In the case of EMP2, for example, it's the very fact that we know it satisfies the JD $\Join\{$ESYD,DB$\}$ that tells us it's not in 5NF; so we can use that JD to decompose it into the corresponding projections (on ESYD and DB), as we did in

---

1. This statement doesn't mean we can't define any other normal forms; it just means such normal forms either won't be based on projection and join or won't reduce redundancy any further, or both. It also doesn't mean that a 5NF (or PJ/NF) relvar can't be nonloss decomposed any further; it just means that any projections resulting from such a decomposition will themselves still be in 5NF (or PJ/NF).

Fig. 8.2. See the section immediately following for further discussion.

By the way, you might object at this point, if you haven't already done so, that it's surely the fact that relvar EMP2 satisfies the *functional* dependency {DEPT#} → {BUDGET} that tells us the relvar isn't in 5NF (or even BCNF, as a matter of fact). Well, that's true, of course—but it's really just another way of saying what I did say, namely, that it's the fact that it satisfies the JD ☼ {ESYD,DB} that tells us it's not in 5NF. In other words, the two statements are logically equivalent, as I'll show in the section "Functional Dependencies," later.

Note: There is a small (?) issue here, though: It might be the case that relvar *R* satisfies several distinct JDs, all having the property that every specified set of attributes corresponds to a 5NF projection. So which of those JDs do we use as a basis for decomposition? The answer is as follows (but observe that it amounts to no more than a rule of thumb): Use whichever leads to the smallest number of projections. And if two or more lead to the same smallest number, then it's arbitrary (?) as to which you choose.[1]

JOIN DEPENDENCIES ARE INTEGRITY CONSTRAINTS

Clearly, to say that relvar *R* satisfies a certain JD is to say there's a certain integrity constraint that applies to *R*. For example, to say that relvar EMP2 satisfies the JD ☼ {ESYD,DB} is to say, precisely, that if the tuples $<e,s,y,d>$ and $<d,b>$ appear in the projections of EMP2 on ESYD and DB, respectively, then the tuple $<e,s,y,d,b>$ appears in EMP2.[2] In **Tutorial D** (a language I've used as the basis for examples in many of my writings), we might express that constraint thus:

```
CONSTRAINT EMP2_JD_X
    EMP2 = EMP2 { EMP#, SS#, SALARY, DEPT# } JOIN
           EMP2 { DEPT#, BUDGET } ;
```

As you can see, this formulation simply states that EMP2 is equal to the join of its projections on {EMP#,SS#,SALARY,DEPT#} and {DEPT#,BUDGET}, and thus reflects the JD very directly. Incidentally, note the reliance on a relational comparison in this constraint (the comparands to the "=" operator are relational expressions and evaluate at run time to certain relation values).

Now, every integrity constraint derives, ultimately, from some natural language *business rule*. In the case at hand, that rule might look like this:

---

1. An oversimplification (as noted in the previous section, the notion of dependency preservation can help with the choice). Nevertheless, it's still the case that there can be some arbitrariness involved—which is one reason why, as I've written elsewhere, normalization per se is no panacea; there are many design issues that it simply doesn't address. On the other hand, as I've also written elsewhere, it does at least represent a small piece of science in an endeavor, database design, that's mostly not very scientific at all.

2. Of course, the converse—that if the tuple $<e,s,y,d,b>$ appears in EMP2, then the tuples $<e,s,y,d>$ and $<d,b>$ appear in the projections of EMP2 on ESYD and DB, respectively—is *obviously* true (right?). *Note:* The informal notation I'm using here for tuples is meant to be self-explanatory. I'll continue to use it throughout the rest of this chapter.

Every employee has exactly one employee number, exactly one social security number, exactly one salary, and exactly one department, and every department has exactly one department number and exactly one budget.

(The fact that employee numbers and social security numbers are unique to a given employee and the fact that department numbers are unique to a given department are also business rules, of course, in our EMP2 example.) And it's the business rules that come first, in a sense; I mean, business rules need to be, and presumably are, articulated at a very early stage in the overall design process. Once those rules are pinned down, we can get on with the process of designing the corresponding relvars—and when those rules correspond to join dependencies, we can use them to ensure that those relvars are all fully normalized.

Let's consider a slightly more complex example. Suppose we're asked to design a database representing agents, products, and regions, and we're given the following business rule:

> If agent *a* sells product *p,* and product *p* is sold in region *r,* and region *r* is in agent *a*'s territory, then agent *a* sells product *p* in region *r*.

For simplicity, let's assume this is the only business rule that's relevant (apart from the obvious one that every agent, every region, and every product has a unique identifier).

Now, the first thing we might try is to bundle agents, products, and regions into a single relvar SELLS, with attributes A (agent), P (product), and R (region), such that tuple $<a,p,r>$ appears in relvar SELLS if and only if agent *a* sells product *p* in region *r*. With this design, the given business rule translates into a constraint looking like this:

> If the tuples $<a,p>$, $<p,r>$, and $<r,a>$ appear in the projections of SELLS on AP (= {A,P}), PR (= {P,R}), and RA (= {R,A}), respectively—equivalently, if SALES includes the tuples $<a,p,x>$, $<y,p,r>$, and $<a,z,r>$ for some *x, y, z*—then the tuple $<a,p,r>$ appears in SELLS.

I suggest you check this constraint against the sample value shown in Fig. 8.5. Here's the constraint formulated in **Tutorial D:**

```
CONSTRAINT SELLS_JD_X
  SELLS = JOIN { SELLS { A, P }, SELLS { P, R }, SELLS { R, A } } ;
```

In other words, we clearly have a join dependency on our hands!—relvar SELLS satisfies the JD

```
☼ { AP, PR, RA }
```

Furthermore, this JD is obviously not trivial, nor is it implied by the sole superkey of SELLS (which is in fact a key; it's just the combination of all three attributes). Relvar SELLS is thus not fully normalized—it suffers from redundancy problems, as Fig. 8.5 shows—and so we decompose it into its 5NF projections LX, LY, and LZ on AP, PR, and RA, respectively (see Fig. 8.6).

SELLS

A	P	R
a1	p1	r2
a1	p2	r1
a2	p1	r1
a1	p1	r1

Fig. 8.5: Relvar SELLS (sample value)

LX

A	P
a1	p1
a1	p2
a2	p1

LY

P	R
p1	r2
p2	r1
p1	r1

LZ

R	A
r2	a1
r1	a1
r1	a2

Fig. 8.6: Nonloss decomposition of relvar SELLS (sample values)

As an exercise, confirm that the relation in Fig. 8.5 is equal to the join of all three (and not of any two) of its projections as shown in Fig. 8.6. Confirm also that there's redundancy in Fig. 8.5 but not in Fig. 8.6.

MULTIVALUED DEPENDENCIES

An obvious difference between the SELLS example discussed in the previous section and our earlier EMP2 example is that we had to decompose SELLS into three projections, whereas we were able to decompose EMP2 into just two. It's convenient to introduce another term: I'll define a JD to be *N-ary* if it specifies exactly N sets of attributes, meaning the relvar in question can be nonloss decomposed into exactly the N corresponding projections. Thus, relvar SELLS satisfies a ternary JD (and no binary ones),[1] while relvar EMP2 does satisfy a binary one.

In practice, it's very unusual to find a relvar that satisfies an *N*-ary JD for some $N > 2$ but doesn't satisfy any binary ones. (In over 25 years of personal experience I've only ever encountered a

_____

1. Is it obvious that SELLS satisfies no binary JDs?

handful of genuine examples—though I have to admit it's been quite a while since I looked at any real world database designs in depth.) It therefore seems worthwhile to take a closer look at the particular case $N = 2$; maybe there's something special about it? And indeed there is. To be a little more specific (but speaking *very* loosely, please note!), it turns out that if *R1* is a relvar that satisfies a binary JD and *R2* is one that doesn't, then *R1* enjoys an attractive informal characterization that *R2* doesn't; in other words, relvars like *R1* are intuitively easier to understand. Let's take a closer look.

Again I'll begin with a definition. Let R be a relvar. Then a *multivalued dependency* (MVD) is an expression of the form

$$A \twoheadrightarrow B$$

("*A* double arrow *B*," or "*A* multidetermines *B*," or "*B* is multidependent on *A*"), where each of *A* and *B* is a subset of the heading of *R*. Moreover, let *C* be a subset of the heading of *R* such that the set theory union of *A, B,* and *C* is equal to that heading; also, let *AB* denote the set theory union of *A* and *B,* and similarly for *AC*. Then relvar *R satisfies* the MVDs $A \twoheadrightarrow B$ and $A \twoheadrightarrow C$—equivalently, those MVDs *hold* in *R*—if and only if *R* satisfies the binary JD $\Join \{AB, AC\}$. Points arising:

- Noting that the definition is symmetric in *B* and *C,* we can see that MVDs always come in pairs. For this reason, we often write such pairs as a single expression, as here (note the vertical bar separator):

$$A \twoheadrightarrow B \mid C$$

- It's immediate from the definition that *R* can be nonloss decomposed into its projections on *AB* and *AC* if and only if it satisfies the MVDs $A \twoheadrightarrow B \mid C$.

- It's also immediate—well, almost immediate—from the definition that if *R* (a) satisfies the MVDs $A \twoheadrightarrow B \mid C$ and (b) contains the tuples $<a, b1, c1>$ and $<a, b2, c2>$, then (c) it also contains the tuples $<a, b1, c2>$ and $<a, b2, c1>$. In other words, there's a kind of "cartesian product" quality to such a relvar: For each *a* that appears in the relvar at all, every *b* that applies to that *a* appears in combination with every *c* that applies to that *a*. I'll illustrate this point in a few moments.

- Like JDs in general, MVDs are in fact propositions, and can thus evaluate to either TRUE or FALSE. For example, we know that relvar EMP2 satisfies the MVDs $D \twoheadrightarrow ESY \mid B$ but not the MVDs $B \twoheadrightarrow ESY \mid D$. *It's a very common error to assume that an MVD isn't an MVD unless it's satisfied.* But if such was the case, then we'd have no simple way of saying that (for example) a certain relvar failed to satisfy a certain MVD, because by that definition such an MVD wouldn't be an MVD in the first place.

To repeat, our usual relvar EMP2, with its binary JD $\Join \{ESYD, DB\}$, satisfies the MVDs

$$D \twoheadrightarrow ESY \mid B$$

and can therefore be nonloss decomposed into its projections on ESYD and DB, as we already know. However, relvar EMP2 isn't very suitable as a basis for making some of the points I want to make in what follows, so let me introduce another example. (EMP2 isn't very suitable because the MVD D $\rightarrow\!\!\!\rightarrow$ B in fact degenerates to the functional dependency D $\rightarrow$ B, as we'll see in the section "Functional Dependencies," later.)

Suppose we're given a relvar PROPS—see Fig. 8.7 overleaf for a sample value—with attributes P (person), HH (hobbies), and SS (skills), representing the fact that certain persons have a certain set of hobbies and a certain set of skills. *Note:* As you can see from the figure, attributes HH and SS are relation valued. Contrary to popular belief, relation valued attributes do not in and of themselves constitute a violation of any particular level of normalization. In particular, such relvars are certainly in first normal form. I've discussed this issue in detail in "What First Normal Form Really Means," in my book *Date on Database: Writings 2000-2006* (Apress, 2006), and I refer you to that book if you need further explanation.

Now, if we eliminate those relation valued attributes from relvar PROPS—which we can do in **Tutorial D** by means of the expression

```
PROPS UNGROUP ( HH, SS )
```

—we obtain the result (I'll call it PUG) shown in Fig. 8.8.

From the way we derived it, it should be obvious that relvar PUG satisfies the following constraint: If the tuple $<p,hh,ss>$ appears in PROPS, then the tuple $<p,h,s>$ appears in PUG for all h in hh and all s in ss (this is where the "cartesian product" property shows up). Or equivalently: If the tuples $<p,h>$ and $<p,s>$ appear in the projections of PUG on PH (= {P,H}) and PS (= {P,S}), respectively, then the tuple $<p,h,s>$ appears in PUG. In **Tutorial D:**

```
CONSTRAINT PUG_JD_X
    PUG = PUG { P, H } JOIN PUG { P, S } ;
```

In other words, we have a JD on our hands once again—relvar PUG satisfies the binary JD

$$\Leftstar \{ PH, PS \}$$

Given that the sole key for PUG is the combination of all three attributes (obviously enough), we can also see that this JD:

- Isn't trivial (neither PH nor PS is equal to the heading of PUG)

- Isn't implied by superkeys (neither PH nor PS is a superkey for PUG)

PROPS

P	HH	SS
Richard	H gardening chess	S mathematics public speaking
Mary	H chess	S mathematics music dancing

Fig. 8.7: Relvar PROPS (sample value)

PUG

P	H	S
Richard	gardening	mathematics
Richard	gardening	public speaking
Richard	chess	mathematics
Richard	chess	public speaking
Mary	chess	mathematics
Mary	chess	music
Mary	chess	dancing

Fig. 8.8: Relvar PUG (sample value)

PUG is thus not fully normalized (and indeed it suffers from certain redundancy problems—see Fig. 8.8); so we decompose it as shown in Fig. 8.9. Both of the relvars illustrated in Fig. 8.9 are "all key" (just as PUG was, in fact). *Exercise:* Confirm that the relation in Fig. 8.8 is equal to the join of those in Fig. 8.9. Confirm also that there's redundancy in Fig. 8.8 but not in Fig. 8.9.

PX

P	H
Richard	gardening
Richard	chess
Mary	chess

PY

P	S
Richard	mathematics
Richard	public speaking
Mary	mathematics
Mary	music
Mary	dancing

Fig. 8.9: Nonloss decomposition of relvar PUG (sample values)

Now let's analyze this example from an intuitive point of view. Relvar PUG satisfies the JD ☼{PH,PS} and therefore, by definition, the MVDs

P ➙➙ H | S

Let's concentrate on the MVD P ➙➙ H (the analysis for P ➙➙ S is similar, of course). Intuitively, what this MVD means is that, although a given person doesn't have just one specific corresponding hobby (in general), that person nevertheless does have a well defined *set* of corresponding hobbies.[1] By "well defined" here I mean, more precisely, that for a given person p and a given skill s, the set of hobbies $\{h\}$ matching the pair (p,s) in PUG depends on the person p alone—it makes no difference which particular skill s we choose. Taking p = Richard, for example, we see that the matching set of hobbies is {gardening, chess}, and this observation is valid regardless of which of Richard's skills we want to talk about. In other words:

For any given person, the set of hobbies and the set of skills are completely independent of each other.

The foregoing analysis enables us to formulate a different (though of course equivalent) definition of MVDs, as follows: Let A, B, and C be subsets of the heading of relvar R, such that the set theory union of A, B, and C is equal to that heading. Then R satisfies the MVD A ➙➙ B if and only if, in every legal value of R, the set of B values matching a given AC value depends only on the A value and is independent of the C value. *Note:* As usual, I'm using the expression AC to denote the set theory union of A and C.

In my opinion, the foregoing characterization makes MVDs intuitively much easier to understand—more user friendly, if you like—than the more general N-ary JDs discussed earlier. What that characterization means, loosely but very simply, is that whenever we encounter a business rule of the form "a given A has a set of B's and a set of C's, and those B's and C's have nothing to do with each other," *we need to do some unbundling*—we need to put the A's with their B's in one relvar and the A's

---

1. Could that set be empty?

with their *C*'s in another.

I hope you agree, therefore, that binary JDs are reasonably easy to understand. By contrast, an *N*-ary JD for $N > 2$ isn't nearly as easy to characterize from an intuitive point of view. Consider again this business rule from the previous section:

> If agent *a* sells product *p*, and product *p* is sold in region *r*, and region *r* is in agent *a*'s territory, then agent *a* sells product *p* in region *r*.

The best I can do by way of informal characterization for rules like this one is to point out their *cyclic nature* ("if *a* is logically connected to *p* and *p* is logically connected to *r* and *r* is logically connected to *a*, then *a* and *p* and *r* must all be *directly* logically connected"). Thus, the particular rule under discussion says that, if, e.g., (a) Smith sells monkey wrenches, and (b) monkey wrenches are sold in Manhattan, and (c) Manhattan is in Smith's territory, then (d) Smith sells monkey wrenches in Manhattan. Note very carefully that (a), (b), and (c) together normally would not imply (d); that is, it would normally be an error to infer (d) knowing only (a), (b), and (c). But the fact that there's a join dependency—which is, recall, really an integrity constraint—tells us that, in this particular case, the inference is valid after all.

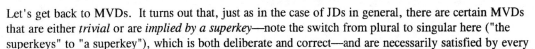

Let's get back to MVDs. It turns out that, just as in the case of JDs in general, there are certain MVDs that are either *trivial* or are *implied by a superkey*—note the switch from plural to singular here ("the superkeys" to "a superkey"), which is both deliberate and correct—and are necessarily satisfied by every relvar:

- The MVD $A \twoheadrightarrow B$ is *trivial* if and only if (a) the set theory union of *A* and *B* is equal to the heading of the relvar in question[1] or (b) *B* is a subset of *A*. *Note:* Possibility (a) here is basically just the definition of "trivial JD" as it applies when the JD in question happens to be binary. As for possibility (b), if *B* is a subset of *A*, then it's surely obvious that the set of *B* values matching a given *AC* value depends only on the *A* value—after all, that "set of *B* values" is *part of* that *A* value, and is thus clearly independent of the *C* value.

- The MVD $A \twoheadrightarrow B$ is *implied by a superkey* if and only if *A* is a superkey for the relvar in question. *Note:* If *A* is a superkey, then it's obvious that the set of *B* values matching a given *AC* value depends only on the *A* value, because there's only one tuple containing that *A* value, and therefore only one corresponding *B* value (and one corresponding *C* value). Observe, therefore, that if *A* is a superkey for relvar *R*, then the MVD $A \twoheadrightarrow B$ holds for every subset *B* of the heading of *R*.

One last point to close this section: It's a sad fact that MVDs (not to mention JDs in general!) are

---

1. If relvar *R* satisfies the MVDs $A \twoheadrightarrow B \mid C$ and the set theory union of *A* and *B* is equal to the heading of *R*, and if *B* and *C* are disjoint, then *C* must be the empty set. What does the corresponding nonloss decomposition look like in this case?

widely misunderstood in the database community at large; indeed, they're often "defined" incorrectly in the literature. Here's a typical example:

> **(Warning! Incorrect!)** Relvar *R* satisfies the MVD *A* ⤜→ *B* if and only if for each *A* value there's a corresponding set of *B* values.

But this "definition" implies that the MVD *A* ⤜→ *B* holds for *every* pair *A* and *B* of subsets of the heading of *R! Caveat lector.*

◆ ◆ ◆ ◆ ◆

There are a couple of additional points I want to make regarding MVDs. I began this whole section by defining MVDs in terms of, specifically, binary JDs, and I used that definition as a basis for building up to the following intuitive rule:

> Whenever we encounter a business rule of the form "a given *A* has a set of *B*'s and a set of *C*'s, and those *B*'s and *C*'s have nothing to do with each other," we need to put the *A*'s with their *B*'s in one relvar and the *A*'s with their *C*'s in another.

And I gave as an example the business rule "a given person has a set of hobbies and a set of skills."

However, the thought might have occurred to you that a given *A* could have a set of *B*'s, a set of *C*'s, and a set of *D*'s ... or, more generally, any number of sets of properties, each of which is quite independent of all the others. For example, a given person could have a set of hobbies, a set of skills, and a set of children. Thus, we could imagine an extended form PUGX of relvar PUG, with attributes P (person), H (hobby), S (skill), and C (child)—and it's intuitively obvious that PUGX will satisfy the ternary JD

☆ { PH, PS, PC }

(i.e., it can be nonloss decomposed into its projections on {P,H}, {P,S}, and {P,C}). So couldn't we say that relvar PUGX satisfies a kind of triple (instead of a pair) of MVDs, which we might write as P ⤜→ H|S|C? And doesn't this example undermine my previous definition of MVDs in terms of binary JDs specifically?

Well, no, it doesn't. First, let me make it very clear that the expression "P ⤜→ H|S|C" is actually meaningless; in particular, it doesn't correspond in any way to the definition of an MVD, as you can easily confirm for yourself. Second, while it's true that relvar PUGX does satisfy a ternary JD, *it also satisfies a binary JD,* or in other words a *pair* of MVDs:

P ⤜→ H | SC

So we can break it down into its projections on {P,H} and {P,S,C}. And then, of course, the second of those projections in turn satisfies another pair of MVDs—

P ⤜→ S | C

—and can be broken down in turn. *Note:* Of course, it's also true that PUGX satisfies the MVDs P $\twoheadrightarrow$ HS|C and P $\twoheadrightarrow$ S|CH, but the final set of binary relvars is the same no matter which MVDs we start with.

The net of this discussion is this: Certain ternary JDs (or, more generally, certain *N*-ary JDs for *N* > 2) are really just, in effect, "nests" of binary JDs; such JDs can be completely understood in terms of MVDs. However, other ternary or higher degree JDs can't be understood in this way—the JD $\Join$ {AP,PR,RA} satisfied by relvar SELLS in the section "Join Dependencies Are Integrity Constraints" is a case in point—and these latter JDs are, in a sense, the interesting ones.

I turn now to the second of my "additional points." Consider once again the following intuitive rule:

Whenever we encounter a business rule of the form "a given *A* has a set of *B*'s and a set of *C*'s, and those *B*'s and *C*'s have nothing to do with each other," we need to put the *A*'s with their *B*'s in one relvar and the *A*'s with their *C*'s in another.

The point I want to make now is that, in principle at any rate, the "given *A*" might not exist!—or might not be explicitly referenced, at least. Here's a simple example: Suppose we're given a relvar UG representing, specifically, *my* hobbies and skills. See Fig. 8.10 for a sample value.

UG

H	S
hiking	losing things
music	losing things
reading	losing things
hiking	spending money
music	spending money
reading	spending money

Fig. 8.10: Relvar UG (sample value)

Now, I hope it's obvious that relvar UG is just the cartesian product of its projections on {H} and {S} (in other words, this example illustrates what I previously referred to as "a kind of cartesian product quality" in its extreme form). So the relvar clearly satisfies the following join dependency:

$$\Join \ \{ \ H, \ S \ \}$$

(Cartesian product is, of course, just a degenerate form of join.) Equivalently, the relvar satisfies the following MVDs:

$$\{ \ \} \ \twoheadrightarrow H \ | \ S$$

Note carefully that these MVDs are neither trivial nor implied by a superkey, and relvar UG is thus not in fourth normal form (see the section immediately following) and should accordingly be replaced by its two unary projections.

FOURTH NORMAL FORM

We've seen that every relvar necessarily satisfies certain MVDs that are either trivial or implied by a superkey; we can never get rid of those MVDs. It's if the relvar satisfies any additional MVDs that we have redundancy and the problems that redundancy causes. For example, we know that relvar PUG from the previous section satisfies the MVDs

$$P \twoheadrightarrow H \mid S$$

(which are neither trivial nor implied by a superkey), and we also know that relvar PUG suffers from redundancy problems. So we can define another normal form: Relvar R is in *fourth normal form* (4NF) if and only if the only MVDs it satisfies are either trivial or implied by a superkey. And now we can say that the problem with relvar PUG is precisely that it's not in 4NF (that's what causes the redundancy). And so we decompose it in accordance with the corresponding MVDs (which is to say, in accordance with the equivalent binary JD). The projections are in 4NF, and in fact 5NF as well.

It follows immediately from the definitions that if R is in 5NF, it's certainly in 4NF. It follows further that 4NF is always achievable. And it follows still further that, just as 5NF is *the* normal form when we take JDs in general into account, so 4NF is *the* normal form if we limit our attention to JDs that are in fact MVDs (as it were).

FUNCTIONAL DEPENDENCIES

We've seen that, loosely speaking, to say that the MVDs

$$A \twoheadrightarrow B \mid C$$

are satisfied by some relvar R is to say that any given A value has an associated set of B values and an associated set of C values, and those B and C values have nothing to do with each other. A very important special case of this state of affairs occurs when, for every A value, one of those two sets is guaranteed to be a singleton set (i.e., a set of cardinality one). To fix our ideas, let's assume the set in question is the set of B values; that is, let's assume that the set of B values matching any given A value is always of cardinality one. Then the MVD of B on A degenerates to a *functional* dependency (FD) of B on A.[1] And, just as it turned out to be intuitively worthwhile to examine MVDs as a special case of JDs in general, it turns out to be intuitively worthwhile to examine FDs as a special case of MVDs in general.

---

1. Once again I'm simplifying matters slightly; it would be more accurate to say, not that the MVD "degenerates to" an FD, but rather that the FD is a logical consequence of the MVD. Note in particular that (as we'll see) the definition of the FD $A \rightarrow B$ relies on the notion of cardinality, while that of the MVD $A \twoheadrightarrow B$ does not.

To be specific, it turns out that if *mvd1* is an MVD that is in fact an FD and *mvd2* is one that isn't, then *mvd1* enjoys an attractive informal characterization that *mvd2* doesn't; in other words, FDs are intuitively easier to understand. Let's take a closer look.

First, here's the formal definition: Let *R* be a relvar. Then a *functional dependency* (FD) is an expression of the form

$$A \rightarrow B$$

("*A* arrow *B*," or "*A* functionally determines *B*," or "*B* is functionally dependent on *A*"), where each of *A* and *B* is a subset of the heading of *R*. Moreover, relvar *R* *satisfies* the FD $A \rightarrow B$—equivalently, that FD *holds* in *R*—if and only if, in every legal value of *R*, whenever two tuples of *R* agree on their *A* value, they also agree on their *B* value. Points arising:

- If *R* satisfies the FD $A \rightarrow B$, then each *A* value in *R* has associated with it exactly one *B* value in *R*; loosely, for one *A* value there's one *B* value (this is the attractive informal characterization alluded to above).

- Every FD is an MVD; that is, if $A \rightarrow B$, then certainly $A \rightarrow\!\!\!\rightarrow B$ (but, of course, most MVDs aren't FDs). In other words, FDs are a special case of MVDs, just as MVDs are a special case of JDs; equivalently, MVDs are a generalization of FDs, just as JDs are a generalization of MVDs.

- Another way of stating the previous point is this: If *R* satisfies the FD $A \rightarrow B$, then *R* satisfies the JD

$$\star \ \{ \ AB, \ AC \ \}$$

(where *C* is the set containing all of the attributes of *R* not contained in either *A* or *B*); in other words, *R* can be nonloss decomposed into its projections on *AB* and *AC*. By way of example, consider relvar EMP2 once again. That relvar satisfies the FD

$$D \rightarrow B$$

It follows that (as we already know) it can be nonloss decomposed into its projections over (a) ESYD (= all attributes except BUDGET) and (b) DB (= attributes DEPT# and BUDGET).

- As we also already know (but the fact is worth spelling out explicitly), the converse of the previous point is *not* true. That is, the fact that *R* satisfies the JD

$$\star \ \{ \ AB, \ AC \ \}$$

does *not* imply that *R* satisfies the FD $A \rightarrow B$; rather, it implies only that *R* satisfies the weaker constraint $A \rightarrow\!\!\!\rightarrow B$ (and hence $A \rightarrow\!\!\!\rightarrow C$ as well).

- Something I personally find very helpful to remember is this: If relvar *R* satisfies the FD $A \rightarrow B$, then certainly it satisfies the FD $A^+ \rightarrow B^-$, where (a) A^+ is any superset of *A* (provided, of course, that every attribute mentioned in that superset is an attribute of *R*) and (b) B^- is any subset of *B*. In other words, we can always add attributes to the left side and/or subtract attributes from the right side of any valid FD, and what results is a valid FD also.

■　　Finally, like JDs and MVDs in general, FDs are in fact propositions and can thus evaluate to either TRUE or FALSE. For example, we know that relvar EMP2 satisfies the FD D → B but not the FD B → D. *It's a very common error to assume that an FD isn't an FD unless it's satisfied.* But if such was the case, then we'd have no simple way of saying that (for example) a certain relvar failed to satisfy a certain FD, because by that definition such an FD wouldn't be an FD in the first place.

By now you're probably expecting the next point ... It turns out that there are certain FDs that are either *trivial* or are *implied by a superkey* and are necessarily satisfied by every relvar:

■　　The FD *A* → *B* is *trivial* if and only if *B* is a subset of *A*. *Note:* This definition is basically just the definition of "trivial MVD," part (b), as it applies when the MVD in question happens to be an FD.

■　　The FD *A* → *B* is *implied by a superkey* if and only if *A* is a superkey for the relvar in question. Note in particular, therefore (*important!*), that if *A* is a superkey for relvar *R*, then the FD *A* → *B* holds, where *B* is an arbitrary subset of the heading of *R*.

I don't intend to say much more about FDs as such here because they're "the easy case"—by which I mean I'm sure you knew all this material already, though you might not have seen it presented in this form before.

BOYCE/CODD NORMAL FORM

We've seen that every relvar necessarily satisfies certain FDs that are either trivial or implied by a superkey; we can never get rid of those FDs. It's if the relvar satisfies any additional FDs that we have redundancy and the problems that redundancy causes. For example, we know that relvar EMP2 satisfies the FD

```
D → B
```

(which is neither trivial nor implied by a superkey), and we also know that relvar EMP2 suffers from redundancy problems. So we can define another normal form: Relvar *R* is in *Boyce/Codd normal form* (BCNF)[1] if and only if the only FDs it satisfies are either trivial or implied by a superkey. And now we

---

1. See Appendix B for an explanation of the name.

can say that the problem with relvar EMP2 is precisely that it's not in BCNF (that's what causes the redundancy) ... and so we decompose it in accordance with the corresponding FD (which is to say, in accordance with the equivalent binary JD). The projections are in BCNF, and in fact 4NF and 5NF as well.

It's worth observing—because the definition is intuitively easier to understand—that BCNF can equivalently be defined as follows: Relvar R is in BCNF if and only if the only nontrivial FDs it satisfies are of the form $A \rightarrow B$ for some superkey A and some subset B of the heading of R. In other words (loosely): The only FDs are "arrows out of superkeys."

Note: It follows immediately from the definitions that if R is in 4NF, it's certainly in BCNF. It follows further that BCNF is always achievable. And it follows still further that, just as 5NF is *the* normal form when we take JDs in general into account and 4NF is *the* normal form if we limit our attention to JDs that are in fact MVDs, so BCNF is *the* normal form if we limit our attention to MVDs that are in fact FDs (as it were).

CONCLUDING REMARKS

This brings me to the end of my discussion of 5NF (or PJ/NF), 4NF, and BCNF. But what about the first three normal forms (1NF, 2NF, 3NF)? Well, the truth is, those three aren't really very interesting, except from a historical point of view (they were, of course, the original point of departure for investigation into the whole field of normal forms). I therefore don't plan to discuss them in detail; however, a brief discussion appears in Appendix A, and a few historical notes can be found in Appendix B.

Overall, my goal in this chapter has been to present a tutorial on the "familiar" (?) ideas of normalization from a somewhat different point of view: Instead of starting with 1NF and gradually refining it all the way to 5NF, I started with an arbitrary relvar and considered what properties it would have to satisfy in order to be "fully normalized," or in other words to be in 5NF—namely, it would have to satisfy no nontrivial JDs other than those implied by superkeys. Then I showed that binary JDs in particular were, not just a special case (that's obvious), but an important special case, of JDs in general: A relvar that satisfies a given binary JD can equivalently be said to satisfy a certain pair of MVDs, and a relvar is in 4NF if and only if it satisfies no nontrivial MVDs other than those implied by superkeys. And then I showed that FDs in particular were an important special case of MVDs in general: The MVD $A \twoheadrightarrow B$ is in fact an FD if and only if for every A value the corresponding set of B values has cardinality one, and a relvar is in BCNF if and only if it satisfies no nontrivial FDs other than those implied by superkeys.

One point I didn't stress in the body of the chapter but I'd like to mention now is the following: Be aware that people often use the term JD to mean, very specifically, a JD that isn't an MVD, and the term MVD similarly to mean an MVD that isn't an FD. This manner of speaking can be acceptable, and indeed useful, in informal contexts. From a formal point of view, however, there are only JDs; some JDs are in fact MVDs, and some MVDs are in fact FDs (speaking a little loosely in both cases). In a similar manner, people often use the term BCNF to mean "BCNF and not 4NF," and 4NF to mean "4NF and not 5NF." Again, this manner of speaking can be acceptable and useful in informal contexts. From a formal point of view, however (and ignoring the first three normal forms again, for simplicity), there's only BCNF; some BCNF relvars are in fact in 4NF, and some 4NF relvars are in fact in 5NF.

Let me finish by saying that I've tried to be reasonably precise in this chapter—as far as it goes!—but I certainly haven't tried to be exhaustive: There are plenty of additional topics having to do with normalization that I've deliberately omitted. Here are some of them:

- I've assumed that none of the projections produced in the decomposition process is redundant in the corresponding recomposition process. What are the implications, if any, of this assumption?

- Do we really have to know, explicitly, all of the JDs satisfied by a given relvar *R* in order to determine whether *R* is fully normalized?

- 5NF is always achievable (and therefore 4NF, BCNF, and even 3NF and 2NF are always achievable too); but what are the costs? Is there a penalty involved in full normalization? *Note:* Please understand that I'm expressly not talking here about performance issues; in a properly architected system, there would be no performance penalty whatsoever for full normalization. See the next chapter ("Denormalization Considered Harmful") for further discussion of this point.

- How can the rules that drive the normalization process best be stated in order to be of truly practical use?

- What are some of the design problems that normalization fails to address? What can we do about such problems?

- A number of myths and misconceptions have grown up over the years regarding normalization. For example, is it true, or is it just a myth, that binary relvars are always in 5NF?

- Is 5NF *really* "the end of the road"? (Well, no, it isn't; I mentioned near the beginning of this chapter that it's possible to define a "sixth" normal form, at least—see Appendix C. So what exactly does *it's possible* mean here?)

Watch this space for future developments!

ACKNOWLEDGMENTS

I'd like to thank Ron Fagin and Hugh Darwen for numerous helpful comments on earlier drafts of this chapter. Of course, any errors remaining are my own responsibility.

APPENDIX A: THE FIRST THREE NORMAL FORMS

For completeness, this appendix briefly discusses the first three normal forms, even though as noted in the body of the chapter they're interesting, mostly, only from a historical point of view. Two remarks right away:

- I'll be making even less of an attempt at rigor in this appendix than I did in the body of the chapter; in fact, the treatment is deliberately quite informal.

■   The distinctions between the first three normal forms (and between those three and BCNF) are different in kind from those between BCNF, 4NF, and 5NF. The distinction between BCNF and 4NF relies on a generalization of the notion of FD (namely, MVDs); likewise, the distinction between 4NF and 5NF relies on a generalization of the notion of MVD (namely, JDs). But the only kind of dependency that's relevant to normal forms "lower than 4NF" (as it were) is, specifically, the FD. Where the distinctions lie is in what's permitted on the left side, and what on the right, in any such FD—as we'll see.

I'd also like to remind you of the term *subkey*. A subkey is a subset of a key. In the case of the "all key" relvar PUG, for example, with its attributes P, H, and S (see Fig. 8.8 in the body of the chapter for a sample value), the following are all subkeys:

```
{ P, H, S }          { P }
{ P, H }             { H }
{ H, S }             { S }
{ S, P }             { }
```

In fact, of course, for any relvar like PUG that's all key, every subset of the heading is a subkey.

Third Normal Form

To recap, Boyce/Codd normal form can be defined as follows:

■   Relvar R is in BCNF if and only if, for every nontrivial FD $A \rightarrow B$ it satisfies, A is a superkey.

Third normal form (3NF) differs from BCNF only in that it additionally allows the relvar to satisfy nontrivial FDs of the form $A \rightarrow B$ where A isn't a superkey, just so long as B is a subkey. In other words:

■   Relvar R is in 3NF if and only if, for every nontrivial FD $A \rightarrow B$ that holds in R, either A is a superkey (as for BCNF) or B is a subkey.

Note immediately that B here can't be empty, for otherwise $A \rightarrow B$ would be trivial (because the empty set is a subset of every set A, even if A is empty too). Note too that every BCNF relvar is necessarily in 3NF. Here then is an example of a relvar that's in 3NF but not BCNF:

```
EMP3 { EMP#, SS#, PROJ#, HOURS }
     KEY { EMP#, PROJ# }
     KEY { SS#, PROJ# }
```

Explanation: EMP# (employee number) and SS# (social security number) are as in relvar EMP2 in the body of the chapter; PROJ# identifies a project, and HOURS is the number of hours spent per week by the specified employee on the specified project. In addition to those FDs that are either trivial or implied by a superkey, therefore, relvar EMP3 satisfies the FDs

```
{ EMP# } → { SS# }
{ SS# } → { EMP# }
```

These FDs are neither trivial nor implied by a superkey, and so relvar EMP3 isn't in BCNF. However, it is in 3NF, because in each of these two FDs, although the left side isn't a superkey, the right side is a subkey (and the relvar doesn't satisfy any additional nontrivial FDs). Note, moreover, that relvar EMP3 does suffer from redundancy problems—check the sample value in Fig. 8.11 for an illustration of this point—and should therefore be nonloss decomposed. I won't bother to go into details, since I know you can easily figure them out for yourself (and similar remarks apply to later examples in this appendix also).

EMP3

EMP#	SS#	PROJ#	HOURS
e1	s1	j1	25
e1	s1	j2	10
e1	s1	j3	5
e2	s2	j1	10
e2	s2	j2	10
e2	s2	j3	20

Fig. 8.11: Relvar EMP3 (sample value)

Second Normal Form

Moving down to the next lower level: Second normal form (2NF) differs from 3NF only in that it additionally allows the relvar to satisfy nontrivial FDs of the form $A \rightarrow B$, just so long as A isn't a subkey. In other words:

- Relvar R is in 2NF if and only if, for every nontrivial FD $A \rightarrow B$ that holds in R, (a) A is a superkey (as for BCNF) or (b) A is not a subkey or (c) B is a subkey (as for 3NF).

Note that every 3NF relvar is necessarily in 2NF. In particular, our original EMP2 relvar—

```
EMP2 { EMP#, SS#, SALARY, DEPT#, BUDGET }
     KEY { EMP# }
     KEY { SS# }
```

—is in 2NF but not 3NF, because (in addition to those FDs that are either trivial or implied by a superkey) it satisfies the FD

```
{ DEPT# } → { BUDGET }
```

This FD is neither trivial nor implied by a superkey, and so relvar EMP2 isn't in BCNF. Nor is it in 3NF, because {DEPT#} isn't a subkey. However, the relvar is in 2NF, precisely because {DEPT#} isn't a subkey either (and the relvar doesn't satisfy any additional nontrivial FDs, other than ones that are logical consequences of those already mentioned). And we already know the relvar suffers from redundancy problems (check the sample value in Fig. 8.1 in the body of the chapter) and needs to be nonloss decomposed.

First Normal Form

Finally to the lowest level of all, first normal form (1NF): 1NF differs from 2NF only in that it additionally allows the relvar to satisfy nontrivial FDs of the form $A \to B$ where A is a subkey. In other words:

- Relvar R is in 1NF if and only if, for every nontrivial FD $A \to B$ that holds in R, (a) A is a superkey (as for BCNF) or (b) A is not a subkey (as for 2NF) or (c) B is a subkey (as for 3NF) or (d) A is a subkey.

But this definition can obviously be simplified! In fact, we can ignore conditions (a) and (c), because conditions (b) and (d) together basically just say that every nontrivial FD that holds in R is of the form $A \to B$ where A either is or is not a subkey—which clearly covers all possible FDs that might hold in R! So the definition overall reduces to simply:

- Every relvar is in 1NF.

In particular, every 2NF relvar is in 1NF. Here's an example of a relvar—EMP1, a revised version of EMP3—that's "only" in 1NF (i.e., it's not in 2NF, and hence not in 3NF, etc., either):

```
EMP1 { EMP#, SS#, PROJ#, SALARY, HOURS }
     KEY { EMP#, PROJ# }
     KEY { SS#, PROJ# }
```

This relvar satisfies the FD

```
{ EMP# } → { SALARY }
```

So it's not in 2NF, because {EMP#} is a subkey. But, of course, it certainly is in 1NF—and of course it suffers from various redundancy problems, as you can easily confirm, and needs to be nonloss decomposed.

Let me close this appendix by repeating for the record that every relvar is in at least 1NF; there's no such thing as a relvar that's not in 1NF. I've discussed this issue in depth elsewhere—actually in "What First Normal Form Really Means," in my book *Date on Database: Writings 2000-2006* (Apress, 2006)—and I don't propose to discuss it any further here.

APPENDIX B: A LITTLE HISTORY

Historically, the normal forms were developed in the sequence 1NF, 2NF, 3NF, BCNF, 4NF, 5NF. For interest, this appendix provides a brief summary of that historical development; it includes references to a few of the principal papers, with some indication of the contribution in each case.

As noted in the body of the chapter, Codd himself first addressed the problem of normalization in his very first paper on the relational model:

■   E. F. Codd: "Derivability, Redundancy, and Consistency of Relations Stored in Large Data Banks," IBM Research Report RJ599 (August 19th, 1969).

Here's a quote from this paper: "Suppose we are given two binary relations, which have some [attribute] in common. Under what circumstances can we [join] these relations to form a ternary relation which preserves all of the information in the given relations?"[1] Codd uses this question as a basis for laying the groundwork for the theory of FDs and the concept of nonloss decomposition. In fact, he gives an example that shows he was aware, back in 1969, of the fact that some relations can't be nonloss decomposed into two projections but can be nonloss decomposed into three!—in other words, there exist relations that don't satisfy any binary JD but do satisfy some *N*-ary JD for some $N > 2$. That example was apparently overlooked by most of the paper's original readers; at any rate, it seemed to come as a surprise to the research community when that same fact was rediscovered several years later (in 1977, to be precise). Indeed, it was that rediscovery that led to Fagin's work on the "final" normal form, 5NF (see below).

Codd continued his investigations in:

■   E. F. Codd: "Further Normalization of the Data Base Relational Model," in R. Rustin (ed.), *Data Base Systems,* Courant Computer Science Symposia Series 6 (Prentice-Hall, 1972).

This is the paper that first formally defined the concept of FD and the normal forms 2NF and 3NF. *Note:* Codd's definitions of these concepts are rather different from those given in this chapter, owing partly to improvements that have been made in terminology since the early 1970s. The definitions are, however, equivalent (or, at least, so I believe).

The next paper I want to mention is:

■   I. J. Heath: "Unacceptable File Operations in a Relational Database," Proc. 1971 ACM SIGFIDET Workshop on Data Description, Access, and Control, San Diego, Calif. (November 1971).

In this paper, Heath gives a definition of what he calls 3NF but is in fact BCNF. He also proves

---

1. See the section "Defining the Problem" in the body of the chapter for an explanation of what it might mean for a join not to preserve "all of the information in the given relations." Note too that Codd frames the question in terms of relations, not relvars—but that's because the earliest relational papers (Codd's in particular) failed, in effect, to distinguish adequately between these two concepts.

the following theorem (though not in these terms): Let *A, B,* and *C* be subsets of the heading of relvar *R* such that the set theory union *ABC* is equal to that heading; then, if—*if,* please note, not *if and only if*—*R* satisfies the FD *A* → *B,* it also satisfies the JD ✿{*AB,AC*} (i.e., it can be nonloss decomposed into its projections on *AB* and *AC*). *Note:* The apparent anomaly that Heath's paper talks about "3NF" before Codd's own paper on the subject was published is explained by the fact that Codd's paper was originally circulated in 1971 as an IBM Research Report.
My next reference is:

- R. F. Boyce: "Fourth Normal Form and its Associated Decomposition Algorithm," IBM Technical Disclosure Bulletin 16, No. 1 (June 1973)

In this paper, Boyce independently defines what he calls 4NF (now called BCNF). A related paper is:

- E. F. Codd: "Recent Investigations Into Relational Data Base Systems," Proc. 1974 IFIP Congress, Stockholm, Sweden (August 1974) and elsewhere.

Among other things, this paper was the first to present BCNF (here confusingly called "an improved 3NF") to a wide audience. *Note:* The name "BCNF" derives from the fact that it was Codd who helped Boyce refine his definition of what he had previously called 4NF.
My next reference is:

- Jorma Rissanen: "Independent Components of Relations," *ACM TODS 2,* No. 4 (December 1977).

This is the paper that introduced the idea of *dependency preservation*. Let relvar *R* have attributes *A, B,* and *C,* and let *R* satisfy the FDs *A* → *B* and *B* → *C;* then the paper suggests that *R* should be decomposed into its projections on {*A,B*} and {*B,C*}, not into its projections on {*A,B*} and {*A,C*} (the first two projections are said to be *independent*). Rissanen shows that projections *R1* and *R2* of relvar *R* are independent in the foregoing sense if and only if both the following are true:

- Every FD satisfied by *R* is a logical consequence of those satisfied by *R1* and *R2*.

- The common attributes of *R1* and *R2* form a key for at least one of the pair.

My last two references are both by Fagin:

- Ronald Fagin: "Multivalued Dependencies and a New Normal Form for Relational Databases," *ACM TODS 2,* No. 3 (September 1977)

In this paper, Fagin defines MVDs and 4NF, and proves the following stronger version of Heath's theorem: Let *A, B,* and *C* be subsets of the heading of relvar *R* such that the set theory union *ABC* is equal to that heading; then, if *and only if R* satisfies the MVDs *A* →→ *B | C,* it also satisfies the JD ✿{*AB,AC*}.

- Ronald Fagin: "Normal Forms and Relational Database Operators," Proc. 1979 ACM SIGMOD Int. Conf. on Management of Data, Boston, Mass. (May/June 1979)

This beautiful paper is the definitive work on what might be called classical normalization theory. Among other things, it defines 5NF (though it calls it PJ/NF). It also points out, albeit not in these words, the following attractive parallelism among the definitions of BCNF, 4NF, and 5NF:

- A relvar R is in BCNF if and only if every nontrivial FD satisfied by R is implied by the superkeys of R.

- A relvar R is in 4NF if and only if every nontrivial MVD satisfied by R is implied by the superkeys of R.

- A relvar R is in 5NF if and only if every nontrivial JD satisfied by R is implied by the superkeys of R.

Note: For BCNF and 4NF (but not 5NF), the phrase *implied by the superkeys* can be strengthened to *implied by some superkey* (this fact is shown by Fagin in his 1979 paper). In all three cases, moreover, the term *superkeys* can be strengthened to just *keys*.

APPENDIX C: SIXTH NORMAL FORM

I pointed out in the body of the chapter that the fact that 5NF is "the final normal form" doesn't mean we can't define any other normal forms—it just means such normal forms either (a) won't be based on projection and join or (b) won't reduce redundancy any further (or both). Sixth normal form, 6NF, is an important illustration of the first of these two possibilities. To be specific, it turns out to be possible, and desirable, to define:

- Generalized versions of the projection and join operators, and hence

- A generalized form of join dependency, and hence

- A new normal form, 6NF.

These developments are particularly important in connection with support for temporal data, and they're discussed in detail in the book *Temporal Data and the Relational Model* by Hugh Darwen, Nikos Lorentzos, and myself (Morgan Kaufmann, 2003). However, all I want to do here is give a definition of 6NF that works for "regular" (that is, nontemporal) relvars and "regular" JDs. Here it is:

- Relvar R is in 6NF if and only if it satisfies no nontrivial JDs at all.

Observe in particular that a regular relvar is certainly in 6NF if it consists of a single key K plus at most one attribute that's not part of K.

Note: A 6NF relvar is sometimes said to be **irreducible,** because it can't be nonloss decomposed via projection at all. Any 6NF relvar is necessarily in 5NF. Note too that just because relvar *R* is in 6NF, it doesn't automatically follow that relvar *R* is well designed! E.g., with reference to the JD examples in the section "Join Dependencies," the projection of EMP2 over EMP# and BUDGET is in 6NF, but it certainly isn't well designed. (This example is thus yet another illustration of the fact that normalization as such is no panacea.)

APPENDIX D: ANSWERS TO EXERCISES

Several inline exercises were embedded in the body of this chapter. This appendix repeats or paraphrases the text of those exercises and offers some answers.

——————— ♦ ♦ ♦ ♦ ♦ ———————

Exercise: Every relvar has at least one key; why?

Answer: No relation ever includes any duplicate tuples. Therefore, the heading of any given relvar is certainly a superkey (i.e., it certainly possesses the uniqueness property). Hence either the heading is a key, or there exists some proper subset of the heading that's a key.

——————— ♦ ♦ ♦ ♦ ♦ ———————

Exercise: Relvar EMP2 looks like this:

```
EMP2 { EMP#, SS#, SALARY, DEPT#, BUDGET }
      KEY { EMP# }
      KEY { SS# }
```

How many superkeys does it have?

Answer: Let *SK* be such a superkey. Then *SK* is a subset of the heading of EMP2 that contains EMP#, SS#, or both, together with any number (possibly none at all) of the other three attributes. Therefore, since a set of cardinality three has exactly eight distinct subsets, relvar EMP2 has exactly 24 distinct superkeys—eight containing EMP# and not SS#, eight containing SS# and not EMP#, and eight containing both.

——————— ♦ ♦ ♦ ♦ ♦ ———————

Exercise: JDs that are implied by superkeys aren't very interesting for normalization purposes, because the corresponding decompositions don't "buy us anything," so to speak. Why not?

Answer: By way of example, consider relvar EMP2 and the JD

```
✩ { ED, SY, ES, SB }
```

which is certainly satisfied by EMP2 and is indeed implied by superkeys. Just to remind you, the keys in this example are E (= {EMP#}) and S (= {SS#}). Suppose, therefore, that we perform the indicated nonloss decomposition of EMP2 into projections as follows:

> *pED* = projection on ED
> *pSY* = projection on SY
> *pES* = projection on ES
> *pSB* = projection on SB

Note that each of these projections has the same cardinality as EMP2 does. Now consider what happens when we join the projections back together again. For simplicity, let's start with *pES* (which includes both keys of EMP2), and join it to *pED*. The join is clearly one-to-one (over EMP#), and the effect is simply to extend each tuple of *pES* with the corresponding DEPT# value. Next, let's join this result to *pSY* (over SS#); again the join is one-to-one, and the effect is to extend each tuple with the corresponding SALARY value. Finally, we join this result to *pSB* (over SS# again); yet again the join is one-to-one, and the effect is to extend each tuple with the corresponding BUDGET value. The overall result is equal to EMP2, of course.

As this example shows, a JD that's implied by superkeys corresponds to a nonloss decomposition with the property that the corresponding recomposition can be done by a sequence of one-to-one joins. In other words, any redundancies present in the original relvar must necessarily still be present in the decomposition, and no redundancies are or can be eliminated by the decomposition.

Exercise: Relvar EMP2 satisfies the JD ☼{ESYD,DB}. Check that this JD is neither trivial nor implied by superkeys.

Answer: The JD is nontrivial because neither ESYD nor DB is the heading of EMP2. And it isn't implied by superkeys because it isn't the case that ESYD and DB are both superkeys for EMP2.

Exercise: Confirm that the relation in Fig. 8.5 is equal to the join of all three (and not of any two) of its projections as shown in Fig. 8.6. Confirm also that there's redundancy in Fig. 8.5 but not in Fig. 8.6.

Answer: Let's agree to refer to the relation shown in Fig. 8.5 as SELLS and the three projections of that relation shown in Fig. 8.6 as LX, LY, and LZ (as the figures suggest). If we join LX and LY (over P), we obtain a relation containing the following tuples:

```
<a1,p1,r2>
<a1,p1,r1>
<a1,p2,r1>
<a2,p1,r2>  (*)
<a2,p1,r1>
```

This relation is identical to SELLS except that it includes one additional or "spurious" tuple (marked above with an asterisk). If we now join this relation and LZ (over R and A), however, that spurious tuple is eliminated, because there isn't any $<r2,a2>$ tuple in LZ, and so the final result is equal to the original SELLS. In other words, that original relation is equal to the join of all three of its binary projections. Furthermore, the net result is the same whatever pair of projections we choose for the first join, though the intermediate result is different in each case, and so the original relation isn't equal to the join of any two of its binary projections.

SELLS displays some redundancy inasmuch as the fact that *a1* sells *p1,* the fact that *p1* is sold in *r1,* and the fact that *r1* is in *a1*'s territory, are all represented twice. LX, LY, and LZ do not display such redundancy.

Exercise: With the same naming conventions as in the previous exercise, SELLS satisfies the constraint that if tuples $<a,p>$, $<p,r>$, and $<r,a>$ appear in LX, LY, and LZ, respectively, then tuple $<a,p,r>$ appears in SELLS. Check this constraint against Fig. 8.5.

Answer: The answer to the previous exercise effectively answers this one too.

Exercise: Is it obvious that relvar SELLS satisfies no binary JDs?

Answer: Well, no, it isn't 100 percent obvious, and it isn't even 100 percent true. For example, relvar SELLS obviously does satisfy any (trivial) binary JD in which one of the specified sets of attributes contains all three attributes—for example:

☼ { APR, A }

But does it satisfy any nontrivial binary JDs? Suppose it does; to be specific, suppose it satisfies the JD

☼ { X, Y }

where X and Y are both proper subsets of the heading (they must be proper subsets, for otherwise the JD would be trivial), and the set theory union of X and Y is equal to that heading. Then:

- We know from the previous two exercises that X and Y can't both contain exactly two attributes.

- We know that X and Y can't both contain fewer than two attributes, for then their set theory union couldn't possibly be equal to the heading.

So one of X and Y (X, say) must contain two attributes and the other (Y) just one. Moreover, if X contains (say) attributes A and P, then Y must contain just attribute R (for otherwise their set theory union wouldn't be equal to the heading). But the join of two relations with no common attributes degenerates to the corresponding cartesian product, and relvar SELLS is certainly not equal to the cartesian product of its projections on AP and R.

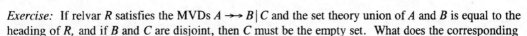

Exercise: Confirm that the relation in Fig. 8.8 is equal to the join of those in Fig. 8.9. Confirm also that there's redundancy in Fig. 8.8 but not in Fig. 8.9.

No answer provided.

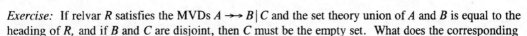

Exercise: Loosely speaking, the MVD P $\twoheadrightarrow$ H (satisfied by relvar PUG) means that a given person has a set of hobbies that's independent of that person's skills. Can that set be empty?

Answer: Consider Fig. 8.9 once again. Suppose Richard has no hobbies. Then there won't be any tuples for Richard in relvar PX, and so there won't be any such tuples in the join of relvars PX and PY, either. Thus, the design illustrated in Fig. 8.8 is incapable of representing a person who has no hobbies. By contrast, the design illustrated in Fig. 8.9 is capable of representing such a person, and so is the design illustrated in Fig. 8.7 (with its relation valued hobbies attribute). So the answer to the question is: The set can't be empty with the design shown in Fig. 8.8, but it can be with the design shown in either Fig. 8.7 or Fig. 8.9.

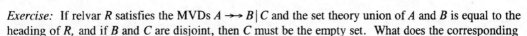

Exercise: If relvar *R* satisfies the MVDs $A \twoheadrightarrow B\,|\,C$ and the set theory union of *A* and *B* is equal to the heading of *R,* and if *B* and *C* are disjoint, then *C* must be the empty set. What does the corresponding nonloss decomposition look like in this case?

Answer: By definition, the MVDs $A \twoheadrightarrow B\,|\,C$ together are equivalent to the JD $\Leftrightarrow\{AB,AC\}$. In the case at hand, however, *AB* is equal to the entire heading of *R* and *AC* degenerates to just *A;* the JD thus becomes $\Leftrightarrow\{H,A\}$, where *H* is the heading,[1] and the associated decomposition consists of the identity projection of *R* together with the projection of *R* over *A*—which is certainly nonloss, for what it's worth.

---

1. *A remark on notation:* Elsewhere in this book (as you might have noticed), headings are denoted {*H*} instead of just *H*. In the present chapter, by contrast, I find it more convenient—not only in this exercise and answer—to use just *H*.

Chapter 9

Denormalization

Considered Harmful

Denormalize? No, normalize!
Let no JDs evade your eyes!

—Anon.: *Where Bugs Go*

In an early paper, Ted Codd stated that one of his objectives in defining the relational model was "to introduce a theoretical foundation ... into database management, a field sadly lacking in solid principles and guidelines" [1]. In order to meet that worthy objective, he found it necessary to introduce a number of new terms, and in particular to give those terms very precise meanings. In other words, it was and still is necessary to be very careful over the way terminology is used. Sloppy usage usually implies, and certainly encourages, sloppy thinking.

Regular readers of my writings will know that sloppy terminology is one of my pet peeves. For example, consider the phrase, often encountered in SQL contexts, "tables and views." The problem with this phrase is that it clearly suggests that a view, whatever else it might be, is not a table; but the whole point about a view in the relational model is precisely that it is a table—or rather, as I would prefer to say, a *relvar*.

Before I go any further, I need to elaborate on that term *relvar*. It's short for *relation variable*. As I've explained in many places (see, e.g. reference [5]), the "tables" in a relational database are indeed relation variables; that is, they're variables whose permitted values are relation values. In the familiar suppliers-and-parts database, for example, updating the suppliers "table" (e.g., inserting another supplier) causes one value of that "table" to be replaced by another such value—and anything that's updatable is a variable by definition. For further discussion, see reference [12], where the term *relvar* was first introduced.

Back to the matter of sloppy terminology. There are, regrettably, many more examples I could give to illustrate my thesis in this connection; in fact, as you might already know, a little while back I published the first few installments of an occasional series devoted solely to this topic [8]. The first installment was called "On the Notion of Logical Difference"—a reference to Wittgenstein's dictum "All logical differences are big differences," which you might recognize as the informing principle for *The Third Manifesto,* by Hugh Darwen and myself [12]. The overall purpose of that series is to serve as a plea for precision in a discipline in which (it seems to me) precision is crucial ... Without it, we're surely lost.

Be that as it may, in the present chapter I want to examine one particular area in which lack of such precision seems ubiquitous: namely, that of denormalization. *Note:* Some of this material originally appeared in reference [6], but significant portions are new. And I'm not aware of any other publication that pulls together all of the pertinent arguments in the way I've tried to do in what follows.

DENORMALIZE FOR PERFORMANCE?

Ever since SQL products first started coming into production use, the notion that we must "denormalize for performance" has been widely promulgated. The following quote from reference [15] is quite typical: "[The] major drawback to normalization ... is poor system performance." The supporting argument goes something like this:

1.   Full normalization means lots of logically separate base relvars ("base tables" if you prefer).

2.   Lots of logically separate base relvars means lots of physically separate stored files.

3.   Lots of physically separate stored files means lots of I/O.

For example, consider the suppliers-and-parts database again, with definition as follows (in outline):

```
S  { S#, SNAME, STATUS, CITY }
   KEY { S# }

P  { P#, PNAME, COLOR, WEIGHT, CITY }
   KEY { P# }

SP { S#, P#, QTY }
   KEY { S#, P# }
```

Here now is a **Tutorial D** formulation[1] of the query "Get supplier details for suppliers who supply red parts":

```
S MATCHING ( SP MATCHING ( P WHERE COLOR = 'Red' ) )
```

Or if you prefer SQL:

```
SELECT DISTINCT S.*
FROM   P, SP, S
WHERE  P.COLOR = 'Red'
AND    P.P# = SP.P#
AND    SP.S# = S.S#
```

Either way, this query clearly involves two joins—first, red parts to shipments, say, and then the result of that join to suppliers (speaking very loosely). And those two joins will require lots of I/O and

---

1. **Tutorial D** is the language used for examples in reference [12] and elsewhere.

will therefore perform badly, since the three relvars map to three physically separate stored files (at least, so people who argue this way assume).

Now, the foregoing argument is strictly invalid, of course, because the relational model nowhere stipulates that base relvars have to map one for one to stored files. In the case of suppliers and parts, for example, there's no logical reason why we couldn't physically store the join of the three relvars—possibly redundantly—as one single stored file on the disk, which would clearly reduce the amount of I/O significantly for the query under consideration. The point is irrelevant for present purposes, however, because:

- First, this area is one in which the DBMS vendors have seriously let us down; most SQL products do indeed map base relvars one for one to stored files, pretty much. Even the exceptions to this general pattern fail to provide as much data independence as we might like, or as much as relational systems are theoretically capable of delivering. As a practical matter, therefore, the argument sketched at the beginning of the present section in favor of denormalization is valid (as far as it goes) for most SQL products today.

- Second, even if base relvars didn't map one for one to stored files, denormalization might still be desirable at the stored file level.[1] Indeed, a major reason why mappings that aren't one for one would be desirable is precisely that they would permit denormalization to be done at the physical level without it having to show through to—and thereby corrupt—the logical level.

So let's assume for the sake of discussion that denormalization does sometimes have to be done, at some level or other. But what is denormalization?

WHAT DOES DENORMALIZATION MEAN?

Before we can sensibly discuss denormalization, we obviously need to know what it is. As it turns out, there's considerable confusion in the community over this very point. Some while ago I had occasion to read a paper by Sam Hamdan titled "Denormalization and SQL-DBMS" [13]. Hamdan first argues *against* denormalization:

> I think the normalization principles should be treated as *commandments* ... unless you're faced with performance problems that money, hardware scalability, current SQL technology, network optimization, parallelization, or other performance techniques can't resolve [*slightly reworded, italics added*].

I couldn't agree more with this position of Hamdan's. Indeed, I'm on record as saying very much the same thing myself; in a paper I wrote some time ago on the use of SQL in practice [3], I recommended using denormalization as a performance tactic "only if all else fails." (Of course, this

---

1. More precisely, some physical counterpart to denormalization might be desirable. Like normalization, denormalization really applies to relvars, not stored files; it's a logical concept, not a physical one. In this chapter, however, I'll use the unqualified term *denormalization* from time to time as a convenient shorthand for its physical counterpart.

advice was intended to apply specifically to those products for which the mapping from base relvars to stored files was indeed one for one. As I've already said, however, this category includes most of the mainstream SQL products on the market today.) Unfortunately, however, Hamdan's paper tends to suggest that the author doesn't really know what denormalization is; after the opening position statement quoted above, it goes on to give some eight separate examples of "denormalizing for performance," and all but one of those examples have absolutely nothing to do with denormalization per se! (I'll discuss some of those examples later in this chapter, in the section "What Denormalization Isn't.")

In Hamdan's defense, however, I must say it does seem to be quite difficult to find a precise definition for the term *denormalization* in the literature. In fact, the concept wasn't even mentioned in most of the books I consulted when I first read Hamdan's paper (my own included, I hasten to add, though I've taken steps to remedy the omission since that time). Now, it might be argued that no such definition is needed, given that (a) denormalization, whatever else it might be, is surely the opposite of normalization, and (b) normalization in turn certainly is precisely defined. For the record, however, I'll give some idea as to what a precise definition of denormalization might look like in the next section.

Before tackling that task, though, let me make it clear that I have no particular quarrel with the specific design tactics Hamdan recommends in his paper; indeed, I suggested several of those same tactics myself in a paper I first wrote as far back as 1982 [2]. To repeat, my quarrel is only with the fact that he refers to those recommendations as denormalization tactics specifically.

DEFINITIONS

I assume you're familiar with the basic idea of normalization (more precisely, *further* normalization). Just to review briefly, if R is a relvar, then *normalizing R* means

- Replacing R by a set of projections $R1, R2, ..., Rn$ (say),[1] such that

- For all possible values r of relvar R, if the corresponding values $r1, r2, ..., rn$ of projections $R1, R2, ..., Rn$ (respectively) are joined back together again, then the result of that join is guaranteed to be equal to r.

Note: The latter part of this definition is required in order to guarantee that the decomposition in part a. is *nonloss;* in other words, the normalization process must be *reversible,* implying that no information is lost during that process. And we ought really to impose the additional requirement that $r1, r2, ..., rn$ are all needed in the join, in order to guarantee that the decomposition in part a. avoids certain redundancies that might otherwise occur. For simplicity, however, let's agree to ignore this additional requirement from the purposes of the present chapter.

As is well known, the overall objective of normalization is to reduce redundancy, by decomposing the original relvar R in such a way that each of the resulting projections $R1, R2, ..., Rn$ is at the highest possible level of normalization. That highest level is *fifth normal form* (5NF), also known as

---

1. I'm speaking a trifle loosely here; operations like projection really apply to relation values, not to relation variables. But I think my general meaning is clear.

projection/join normal form (PJ/NF).[1] However, since many readers will probably be more familiar with Boyce/Codd normal form (BCNF), we can pretend for present purposes that our target is merely BCNF, not 5NF; the distinction isn't important here.

> *Aside:* Tutorials on BCNF can be found in many places; see, e.g., reference [4]. Note too that I choose to talk in terms of BCNF rather than third normal form or 3NF. That's because comparatively few relvars—very few in practice, I'm quite sure—are in 3NF and not BCNF; in fact, I strongly suspect that most people, when they talk about "third" normal form, really mean Boyce/Codd normal form anyway. However, if the point bothers you, feel free to replace all references in what follows to BCNF by references to 3NF instead; it won't make any substantive difference to the argument. *End of aside.*

Now I can give a definition of denormalization. Let *R1, R2, ..., Rn* be a set of relvars. Then *denormalizing* those relvars means:

- Replacing them by their join *R* (say), such that

- For all possible values *r1, r2, ..., rn* of *R1, R2, ..., Rn* (respectively), projecting the corresponding value *r* of *R* over the attributes of *Ri* is guaranteed to yield *ri* again (*i* = 1, 2, ..., *n*).

The overall objective is to *increase* redundancy, by ensuring that *R* is at a lower level of normalization than the relvars *R1, R2, ..., Rn*. (More precisely, the objective is to reduce the number of joins that need to be done at run time by, in effect, doing some of those joins ahead of time, as part of the database design.) *Note:* If *R1, R2, ..., Rn* were in fact obtained by performing a nonloss decomposition of *R* in the first place—in other words, if the denormalization is really undoing an earlier normalization—then the requirement that projecting *r* over the attributes of *Ri* must yield *ri* (*i* = 1, 2, ..., *n*) will be satisfied automatically.

EXAMPLES

Suppose we're given a relvar EMP, with attributes EMP#, SALARY, DEPT#, and DEPTMGR#, where:

- The attributes have the obvious meanings.

- {EMP#} is the sole candidate key (and hence in fact the primary key—but I don't want to get side-tracked here into a discussion of candidate *vs.* primary keys). *Note:* From this point forward I'll abbreviate the term *candidate key* to just *key,* for simplicity.

---

1. Actually it's possible to define a still higher level of normalization called sixth normal form (see, e.g. reference [5]), but the point isn't important for the purposes of the present chapter.

- The functional dependency {DEPT#} → {DEPTMGR#} holds (that is, each department has just one employee as a manager).

- The functional dependency {DEPTMGR#} → {DEPT#} does *not* hold (that is, the same employee can manage several departments at once).

A sample EMP value—that is, a sample relation—is shown in Fig. 9.1. Note that EMP is in 2NF but not in BCNF (because of the functional dependency {DEPT#} → {DEPTMGR#}).

EMP

EMP#	SALARY	DEPT#	DEPTMGR#
E1	50K	D1	E5
E2	45K	D1	E5
E3	55K	D2	E3
E4	72K	D2	E3
E5	96K	D3	E5

Fig. 9.1: Sample EMP relation value

We can break this relvar down—that is, we can normalize it—as indicated in Fig. 9.2; the two projections ESD and DD are both in BCNF, and their join over {DEPT#} is equal to EMP. And, of course, we can denormalize relvars ESD and DD by replacing them by EMP again. *Note:* It's relevant to remark that many people would probably describe this latter process as one of "denormalizing ESD" (alone)—presumably on the grounds that EMP can be thought of as an extended version of ESD (it's "ESD plus one more attribute," and it has the same number of tuples as ESD). By contrast, I'm trying to make it clear that, logically speaking, denormalization is a process that applies to a set of relvars, not to a single relvar considered in isolation.

ESD

EMP#	SALARY	DEPT#
E1	50K	D1
E2	45K	D1
E3	55K	D2
E4	72K	D2
E5	96K	D3

DD

DEPT#	DEPTMGR#
D1	E5
D2	E3
D3	E5

Fig. 9.2: Normalizing EMP

By the way, it's important to understand that not all decompositions of a given relvar into BCNF projections are valid normalizations. Consider, for example, the decomposition of EMP into ESM and DD shown in Fig. 9.3 (DD is the same as before, but ESM differs from ESD in that it has a DEPTMGR# attribute instead of a DEPT# attribute). ESM and DD are certainly both BCNF projections of EMP; however, the result of joining those projections together, EMP' say (see Fig. 9.4), is clearly not equal to the original EMP. In other words, the decomposition in Fig. 9.3 is not nonloss (some writers would say it's *lossy*).

ESM

EMP#	SALARY	DEPTMGR#
E1	50K	E5
E2	45K	E5
E3	55K	E3
E4	72K	E3
E5	96K	E5

DD

DEPT#	DEPTMGR#
D1	E5
D2	E3
D3	E5

Fig. 9.3: Another decomposition of EMP into BCNF projections

EMP'

EMP#	SALARY	DEPT#	DEPTMGR#
E1	50K	D1	E5
E1	50K	D3	E5
E2	45K	D1	E5
E2	45K	D3	E5
E3	55K	D2	E3
E4	72K	D2	E3
E5	96K	D1	E5
E5	96K	D3	E5

Fig. 9.4: The join of projections ESM and DD (contrast Fig. 9.1)

WHERE DO WE STOP?

Before going any further, I want to stress the point that once we make the decision to denormalize, we've embarked on a very slippery slope. The question is: Where do we stop? The situation is different with normalization, where there are clear logical reasons for continuing the process until we reach the highest possible normal form. Do we then conclude that with denormalization we should proceed until we reach the lowest possible normal form? Obviously not; yet there are no logical criteria for deciding exactly where the process should stop. In choosing to denormalize, in other words, we've backed off from a position that does at least have some solid science and logical theory behind it, and replaced it by one that's purely pragmatic in nature, and necessarily subjective.

WHAT DENORMALIZATION ISN'T

To repeat: Denormalization means increasing redundancy. But it doesn't follow that increasing redundancy means denormalization! This is one of the traps Hamdan falls into in his paper; his design tactics do sometimes increase redundancy, but they're not—with, as noted earlier, just one exception—applications of denormalization per se. More generally, in fact, if "*p* implies *q*" is true, it doesn't follow that "*q* implies *p*" is true. To argue otherwise is a well known example of faulty reasoning: so well known, in fact, that it enjoys a special name, *The Fallacy of False Conversion* (thanks to David McGoveran for this information).

Let's examine some of the suggestions from Hamdan's paper. In one example, we're given the self-explanatory relvars ITEM and SALES as follows:

```
ITEM { ITEM#, NAME }
     KEY { ITEM# }

SALES { STORE#, ITEM#, QTY }
     KEY { STORE#, ITEM# }
     FOREIGN KEY { ITEM# } REFERENCES ITEM
```

For performance reasons, Hamdan suggests adding a TOTAL_QTY attribute to the ITEM relvar, whose value for any given item is the total sales of that item taken over all stores:

```
ITEM { ITEM#, NAME, TOTAL_QTY }
     KEY { ITEM# }
```

Now, it's certainly true that this design includes some redundancy, but the fact remains that both relvars are still in BCNF; in particular, {TOTAL_QTY} in relvar ITEM is functionally dependent on the key {ITEM#}. In other words, there's no denormalization, as such, in this example.

Note: In contrast to Hamdan's first example, consider the following relvar (the semantics are meant to be obvious):

```
ITEM { ITEM#, PRICE, QTY, TOTAL_COST }
     KEY { ITEM# }
```

This relvar is in 2NF but not BCNF, because it satisfies the functional dependency

```
{ PRICE, QTY } → { TOTAL_COST }
```

It might thus be regarded as the result of denormalizing the following pair of relvars:

```
ITEM_X { ITEM#, PRICE, QTY }
      KEY { ITEM# }

ITEM_Y { ITEM#, TOTAL_COST }
      KEY { ITEM# }
```

Relvars ITEM_X and ITEM_Y are both in BCNF. As this example clearly demonstrates, therefore, BCNF might be necessary for a good design, but it's certainly not sufficient!—the two-relvar design is almost certainly not a good one, precisely because it does still involve some redundancy (TOTAL_COST is redundant because it can be computed from PRICE and QTY). To spell the point out: Just because a design is fully normalized, it doesn't follow that it's redundancy free. *Note:* I've addressed the general question of redundancy and normalization (among other things) in reference [9].

Back to Hamdan's paper. Another example in that paper involves an "internal array within a tuple":

```
EMP { EMP#, JAN_PAY, FEB_PAY, ..., DEC_PAY }
      KEY { EMP# }
```

Now, Hamdan doesn't say as much explicitly, but this "tuple oriented" design is presumably meant to be contrasted with—and, for performance (?) reasons, possibly preferred to—the following "attribute oriented" analog:

```
EMP { EMP#, MONTH, PAY }
    KEY { EMP#, MONTH }
```

But both designs are in BCNF. Again, there's no denormalization here. (Which isn't to say the "tuple oriented" design is a good one. In fact, the example serves to illustrate the point once again that BCNF might be necessary for a good design, but it's certainly not sufficient. In other words, there's much more to database design than just normalization; normalization can be regarded as one small piece of science in a field—database design—that is, sadly, not very scientific at all, for the most part. We need more science! But now I'm beginning to stray from the main topic of this chapter ... Let's get back to the matter at hand.)

Yet another example in Hamdan's paper involves splitting a RESELLERS relvar "horizontally" into two separate relvars, ACTIVE_RESELLERS and INACTIVE_RESELLERS. In other words, the original relvar is decomposed via restriction, not projection, and is reconstructed from the two restrictions via union, not join. So we're clearly not talking here about normalization in the classical sense at all (recall that classical normalization is really projection/join normalization specifically). A fortiori, therefore, we're not talking about classical denormalization either. *Note:* As I've explained elsewhere [4], we might possibly define a new kind of normalization based on restriction and union instead of projection and join; and if we did, well, then I suppose we'd have a new kind of denormalization on our hands also. But I'm pretty sure that such considerations weren't what Hamdan had in mind with his RESELLERS example.

One final example from Hamdan's paper. This one starts with STORE and EMP relvars as follows:

```
STORE { STORE#, REGION#, STATE_CODE, ... }
      KEY { STORE#, REGION#, STATE_CODE }

EMP { EMP#, STORE#, REGION#, STATE_CODE, ... }
    KEY { EMP# }
    FOREIGN KEY { STORE#, REGION#, STATE_CODE } REFERENCES STORE
```

Here the suggestion is to introduce a surrogate identifier for stores, say STORE_CODE, thereby modifying the design as follows:

```
STORE { STORE_CODE, STORE#, REGION#, STATE_CODE, ... }
      KEY { STORE_CODE }
      KEY { STORE#, REGION#, STATE_CODE }

EMP { EMP#, STORE_CODE, ... }
    KEY { EMP# }
    FOREIGN KEY { STORE_CODE } REFERENCES STORE
```

But this redesign not only involves no denormalization and no increase in redundancy, it actually reduces redundancy!—because the association of a given STORE# with a given REGION# and a given STATE_CODE now appears just once, instead of once for every employee of the store in question.

In closing this section, I'd like to make it very clear that the foregoing discussions are in no way intended as an attack on Hamdan or his paper. Indeed, the following quote from that paper should make it clear that the two of us are really on the same page on the bigger issues:

> [We should] stop criticizing the relational model and make a clear distinction between what's SQL and what's relational ... The two are totally different.

I couldn't agree more with this position, nor with the implication that the only reason we have to worry about such matters as denormalizing at the logical level is because of a failure on the part of today's SQL products to provide as much physical data independence as we would like (or, as I put it previously, as much as relational products are theoretically capable of delivering). To say it one more time: In an ideal system, we would never have to denormalize at all at the logical level![1]

---

1. In particular this remark would apply to any system implemented using the facilities described in reference [11]. Indeed, not only would full normalization involve no performance penalty in such a system, but anything less than full normalization *would* involve some penalty!—possibly, though not necessarily, a performance penalty in particular. Further details are beyond the scope of this chapter.

WHAT DENORMALIZATION ISN'T *bis*

I don't want to give the impression that my sole objective in all of the foregoing has been to criticize Sam Hamdan specifically. So let me now quote from a different source, namely, an interview with Richard Finkelstein [14], which shows that Hamdan isn't the only one with misconceptions regarding the true nature of denormalization. Identifying the errors in what follows is left as an exercise for the reader!

> *Finkelstein:* The problems ... largely result from normalizing data across multiple [relvars] ... Many queries, however, are much easier to understand if the data is denormalized ...

> *Interviewer:* Doesn't denormalization potentially lower data integrity and reduce flexibility in supporting unanticipated queries?

> *Finkelstein:* Normalization, and its emphasis on elimination of redundant storage, is purely a transaction processing issue. When users view data, they see it in a redundant form. In order to transform data into a form that is useful to users, it must be denormalized by means of a join, which is essentially a way of dynamically denormalizing data for greater ease of use ... The problem is that users can't tolerate the time and cost of joins. To address the problem, companies replicate data in an ever increasing number of decision support databases, which represent denormalized views of the data.

THE PERFORMANCE ARGUMENT REVISITED

Let's get back to denormalization per se. Regardless of whether we're talking about

- "Proper" denormalization, which is done at the physical level only, or

- The kind of denormalization we have to do in most of today's SQL DBMSs, which affects the logical level as well,

the point isn't widely enough appreciated that when people say "denormalize for performance," they're really referring to the performance *of specific applications*. Any given physical design is almost certainly good for some applications but bad for others (in terms of its performance characteristics, that is). Let me illustrate. To simplify the discussion, let's assume that each stored file consists of a physically contiguous collection of stored records, one for each tuple currently appearing in the relvar the stored file represents. Then:

- Suppose that (as suggested in the section "Denormalize for Performance?") the join of the suppliers, shipments, and parts relvars is physically represented as one single stored file. Then I presume we could agree that the query "Get supplier details for suppliers who supply red parts" will perform well against this physical structure.

- However, the query "Get supplier details for London suppliers" will perform worse against this structure than it would against the structure in which the three relvars map to three physically separate stored files! Why? Because in the latter design, all supplier stored records will be physically contiguous, whereas in the former design they'll effectively be spread over a wider area, and will therefore require more I/O.

Analogous remarks apply to any other query that accesses suppliers only (e.g., "Get all suppliers not in Paris")—or indeed any query that accesses parts only, or shipments only, instead of performing some kind of join.

Observe, incidentally, that the applications just discussed are all retrieval applications specifically (that is, they're all queries). I mention this point deliberately, because it's widely believed that since it increases redundancy, denormalization is "good for retrieval but bad for update" (where good and bad are measured in terms of performance specifically). As the examples show, denormalization can be bad for retrieval too (again, with respect to performance specifically). *Note:* It might be nice if the system allowed the data to be stored both ways simultaneously and the optimizer were smart enough to know which version to use for which queries. However, I'm not aware of any commercial product or prototype that actually behaves in such an "intelligent" manner.

The point is worth mentioning too that denormalization—again because it increases redundancy—will probably lead to larger stored records, and this fact in turn can lead to more I/O, not less. For example, a 4K page can hold two 2K stored records but only one 3K stored record; hence, a denormalization that increases redundancy by 50 percent could increase I/O by 100 percent. (I'm speaking pretty loosely here, of course.)

THE USABILITY ARGUMENT

So much for the effect of denormalization on performance. Now I want to point out that there's a usability argument against denormalization too, *even for retrieval operations;* that is, denormalization can actually make certain queries more difficult to express. (The fact that there's a usability argument against denormalization for update operations is well known, of course.) By way of an example, suppose we denormalize parts and shipments to produce a relvar PSQ, with sample value as indicated in Fig. 9.5. Observe that PSQ is not even in 2NF—its sole key is {P#,S#}, and it satisfies the following functional dependencies among others:

PSQ

P#	PNAME	COLOR	WEIGHT	CITY	S#	QTY
P1	Nut	Red	12.0	London	S1	300
P1	Nut	Red	12.0	London	S2	300
P2	Bolt	Green	17.0	Paris	S1	200
P6	Cog	Red	19.0	London	S1	100

Fig. 9.5: Denormalizing parts and shipments

```
{ P# } → { PNAME }
{ P# } → { COLOR }
{ P# } → { WEIGHT }
{ P# } → { CITY }
```

Now consider the query "For each part color, get the average weight." Given the relation value shown in Fig. 9.5, the desired result is:

COLOR	AVGWT
Red	200
Green	200

Note in particular that the average for red parts is 200, not 233.33... (there are only two red parts, not three).

Now, given the original fully normalized design, a suitable **Tutorial D** formulation is straightforward:

```
SUMMARIZE P BY { COLOR } ADD ( AVG ( WEIGHT ) AS AVGWT )
```

Or if you prefer SQL:

```
SELECT DISTINCT P.COLOR, AVG ( P.WEIGHT ) AS AVGWT
FROM    P
GROUP   BY P.COLOR
```

Given the denormalized design of Fig. 9.5, however, the query is a little trickier to formulate—not to mention the fact that the formulation in question relies on the strong and generally invalid assumption that every part does have at least one shipment. Here it is in **Tutorial D:**

```
SUMMARIZE PSQ { P#, COLOR, WEIGHT } BY { COLOR }
                        ADD ( AVG ( WEIGHT ) AS AVGWT )
```

Or in SQL:[1]

```
SELECT DISTINCT TEMP.COLOR, AVG ( TEMP.WEIGHT ) AS AVGWT
FROM ( SELECT DISTINCT PSQ.P#, PSQ.COLOR, PSQ.WEIGHT
       FROM    PSQ ) AS TEMP
GROUP   BY P.COLOR
```

---

1. Does your favorite SQL product in fact support this formulation, with its nested subquery in the FROM clause?

What's more, these formulations are likely to perform worse, too (worse than the previous versions, that is), given the state of today's implementations. *Note:* It's worth pointing out also that the following SQL expressions, which might look at least superficially as if they're valid formulations of the query, are in fact incorrect (why, exactly, in each case?).

```
SELECT  DISTINCT PSQ.COLOR, AVG ( PSQ.WEIGHT ) AS AVGWT
FROM    PSQ
GROUP   BY PSQ.COLOR

SELECT  DISTINCT PSQ.P#, PSQ.COLOR, AVG ( PSQ.WEIGHT ) AS AVGWT
FROM    PSQ
GROUP   BY PSQ.P#, PSQ.COLOR
```

If you study these formulations carefully, you'll surely agree that in this particular example, at least, denormalization has made the query formulation process considerably harder.

To summarize: We've already seen that the common perception that denormalization is good for retrieval but bad for update is incorrect, even if we limit our attention to performance considerations only; now we see it's incorrect from the point of view of usability too. (Of course, I'm assuming here that we're talking about the kind of denormalization that shows through to the logical level; I don't mean the kind of denormalization we ought to be able to do, which would affect the physical level only.)

THE INTEGRITY ARGUMENT

It's well known that denormalized designs suffer from what for historical reasons are usually called "update anomalies." Consider relvar PSQ again:

```
PSQ { P#, PNAME, COLOR, WEIGHT, CITY, S#, QTY }
    KEY { S#, P# }
```

Now suppose there are no shipments for some part, say part P7. Then relvar PSQ cannot contain a tuple for part P7. Why not? Well, by definition, any such tuple would have to represent a true proposition of the form:

Part P7 has name n, color col, weight wt, city c, and is supplied by supplier s in quantity q

(where *n, col, wt, c, s,* and *q* are valid PNAME, COLOR, WEIGHT, CITY, S#, and QTY values, respectively). And if no supplier *s* supplies part P7, *there simply is no such true proposition,* and hence no such tuple.[1]

---

1. In case you might be wondering: No, nulls don't solve the problem. Indeed, the very argument just presented could and probably should be expanded into one demonstrating that nulls are ipso facto nonsense—but I certainly don't want to get into that argument here.

It follows from the foregoing that relvar PSQ is subject to both an INSERT anomaly and a DELETE anomaly:

- *INSERT:* As we've already seen, if part P7 has no shipments, then we can't insert a tuple for part P7 into the relvar.

- *DELETE:* Given the sample value for the relvar shown in Fig. 9.5, if supplier S1 ceases to supply part P6 and we therefore delete the tuple for S1 and P6, we lose the information that part P6 exists. (Part P6 becomes a part, like part P7, with no shipments.)

In fact it suffers from an UPDATE anomaly too: It might be possible to update it in such a way that a given part is shown as having (for example) one color in one tuple and a different color in another. For simplicity, however, I'll concentrate on the INSERT and DELETE anomalies in what follows.

In order to be able to represent parts in the database that have no shipments, we clearly need another relvar, P say, looking perhaps as shown in Fig. 9.6. *Note:* I'm assuming that relvar P contains only tuples for parts for which there are no shipments, for otherwise relvars PSQ and P would overlap considerably (i.e., there would be a lot more redundancy); in fact, this latter design would consitute a violation of *The Principle of Orthogonal Design*. See reference [9] for an extended discussion of this principle.

P

P#	PNAME	COLOR	WEIGHT	CITY
P6	Cog	Red	19.0	London
P7	Bolt	Blue	12.0	London

Fig. 9.6: Relvar P (sample value)

This two-relvar design is subject to a number of integrity constraints, of course. Here are some of the most important of them:

- {P#} is the sole key for relvar P.

- {P#,S#} is the sole key for relvar PSQ.

- The functional dependencies mentioned in the previous section—

```
{ P# } → { PNAME }
{ P# } → { COLOR }
{ P# } → { WEIGHT }
{ P# } → { CITY }
```

—all hold in relvar PSQ.

- No part number appears in both relvars. Formally:

```
CONSTRAINT P_PSQ_DISJOINT
    IS_EMPTY ( P { P# } JOIN PSQ { P# } ) ;
```

Note: I assume, reasonably enough (?), that these constraints are all defined to, and enforced by, the DBMS.

Now let's consider what's involved in inserting and deleting information with this design. Here first are pseudocode algorithms for INSERT:

```
/* INSERT (1 of 2) :                                      */

/* part p has name n, color col, weight wt, city c, and is */
/* supplied by supplier s in quantity q : insert this info */

if relvar P includes a tuple t with t.P# = p
   then if t.PNAME = n and
           t.COLOR = col and
           t.WEIGHT = wt and
           t.CITY = c
           then delete tuple t from relvar P ;
           else signal error /* part mismatch */ ;
        end if ;
end if ;

insert tuple (p,n,col,wt,c,s,q) into relvar PSQ ;
/* might fail on integrity constraint violation : if it */
/* does, delete (if any) on relvar P should be undone    */

/* INSERT (2 of 2) :                                      */

/* part p has name n, color col, weight wt, and city c : */
/* insert this info                                       */

if relvar PSQ includes a tuple t with t.P# = p
   then if t.PNAME = n and
           t.COLOR = col and
           t.WEIGHT = wt and
           t.CITY = c
           then signal error /* part already exists */ ;
           else signal error /* part mismatch */ ;
        end if ;
   else insert tuple (p,n,col,wt,c) into relvar P ;
   /* might fail on integrity constraint violation */
end if ;
```

And here are algorithms for DELETE:

```
/* DELETE (1 of 2):                                              */

/* supplier s no longer supplies part p : perform updates  */
/* to reflect this fact                                      */

if relvar PSQ includes a tuple t with t.S# = s and t.P# = p
   then begin ;
           delete t from relvar PSQ ;
           if relvar PSQ includes a tuple u with u.P# = p
              then ;
              else insert tuple
                    ( p, t.PNAME, t.COLOR, t.WEIGHT, t.CITY )
                             into relvar P ;
           end if ;
         end ;
    else signal error /* shipment does not exist */ ;
end if ;


/* DELETE (2 of 2) :                                             */

/* part p no longer exists : perform updates to reflect */
/* this fact                                                    */

if relvar P   includes a tuple t with t.P# = p
or relvar PSQ includes a tuple u with u.P# = p
   then begin ;
           delete (P   where P# = p) ;
           delete (PSQ where P# = p) ;
         end ;
    else signal error /* part does not exist */ ;
end if ;
```

The message is clear: We all know that "individually denormalized" relvars like PSQ suffer from update anomalies, and those anomalies cause update problems. But *realistic* denormalized designs (like the one that includes relvar P as well as the "individually denormalized" relvar PSQ) suffer from update problems too—arguably even more serious ones; certainly updates in general are considerably more complicated with such designs than they are with their fully normalized counterparts. *Note:* Of course, the updates in question must in fact be done, in order to conform with the specified integrity constraints.[1] As I've argued elsewhere, in many places (see, e.g., reference [10]), keeping the database in a state of integrity is, or should be, the overriding concern in a database system. I don't care how fast your system runs if I can't trust the answers it gives me.

There's yet another important point to be made in connection with integrity constraints: Contrary to popular belief, even if the database is read only, *it's still necessary to state the constraints*. Why? Because those constraints effectively define, at least in part, the meaning of the data. As a consequence, stating those constraints is a precise way of conveying that meaning to the user (as well as to the system, which might be able to use those constraints in its process of optimization—to say it again, even if the database is read only). And keeping the database in a fully normalized form—in other words, not denormalizing—provides a very simple way of stating certain important constraints. To be specific, full normalization implies that the only functional, multivalued, and join dependencies that hold in the relvars in question are those implied by keys; hence it's sufficient just to declare those keys to state those dependencies—and those dependencies are, precisely, the "important constraints" in question. What's more, it's sufficient to enforce the uniqueness of those keys (which is easy, of course) in order to *enforce* those "important constraints."

CONCLUDING REMARKS

As I've written elsewhere [7], normalization is certainly no panacea—but it's vastly preferable to the alternative! I believe very strongly that, almost always, anything less than full normalization is strongly contraindicated. A fully normalized design can be regarded as a "good" representation of the real world—one that's intuitively easy to understand and is a good base for future growth. Note too that good top down design methodologies tend to generate fully normalized designs; why do you think this is?

REFERENCES AND BIBLIOGRAPHY

1.   E. F. Codd: "Recent Investigations into Relational Data Base Systems," Proc. IFIP Congress, Stockholm, Sweden (1974), and elsewhere.

2.   C. J. Date: "A Practical Guide to Database Design," IBM Technical Report TR 03.220 (December 1982). Republished in expanded and revised form under the title "A Practical Approach to Database Design," *Relational Database: Selected Writings*. Reading, Mass.: Addison-Wesley (1986).

3.   C. J. Date: "SQL Dos and Don'ts," in *Relational Database Writings 1985-1989*. Reading, Mass.: Addison-Wesley (1990).

---

1. In other words, denormalization isn't just bad for update—it's *very* bad for update. As a consequence, any retrieval performance gains that derive from denormalization might well be nullified by the increased cost of maintaining integrity (depending, of course, on the retrieval/update ratio).

4.   C. J. Date: *An Introduction to Database Systems* (8th edition). Boston, Mass.: Addison-Wesley (2004).

5.   C. J. Date: *Database in Depth: Relational Theory for Practitioners*. Sebastopol, Calif.: O'Reilly Media, Inc. (2005).

6.   C. J. Date: "The Normal Is So ... Interesting" (in two parts), in *Relational Database Writings 1998-2001*. Privately published (2006).

7.   C. J. Date: "Normalization Is No Panacea," in *Relational Database Writings 1998-2001*. Privately published (2006).

8.   C. J. Date: "On the Notion of Logical Difference," "On the Logical Difference Between Model and Implementation," and "On the Logical Differences Between Types, Values, and Variables," in *Date on Database: Writings 2000-2006*. Berkeley, Calif.: Apress (2006).

9.   C. J. Date: "Data Redundancy and Database Design" and "Data Redundancy and Database Design: Further Thoughts Number One," in *Date on Database: Writings 2000-2006*. Berkeley, Calif.: Apress (2006).

10. C. J. Date: "Constraints and Predicates" (Chapter 3 in this book).

11. C. J. Date: *Go Faster! The TransRelational^{tm} Approach to DBMS Implementation* (to appear). See also Appendix A of reference [4], which contains an introductory description of some of the material in this book.

12. C. J. Date and Hugh Darwen: *Databases, Types, and the Relational Model: The Third Manifesto* (3rd edition). Boston, Mass.: Addison-Wesley (2006).

13. Sam Hamdan: "Denormalization and SQL-DBMS," *SQL Forum 4*, No. 1 (January/February, 1995).

14. Richard Finkelstein: Interview, *Data Base Newsletter 22*, No. 5 (September/October, 1994).

15. William H. Inmon: "Denormalize for Efficiency," *Computerworld* (March 16th, 1987).

Part IV

LOGIC AND ALGEBRA

The disciplines of logic and algebra are tightly interrelated; relational algebra in particular is well known to be equivalent in a certain sense to relational calculus, which is a form of predicate logic. The first chapter in this part of the book examines the twin questions of what exactly it means to be an algebra in general and what exactly it is that constitutes the relational algebra in particular. The next chapter briefly discusses two extremely useful but little known relational algebra operators, called semijoin and semidifference. The third chapter considers the question of whether it's possible to define an algebra of bags as opposed to sets—a question of some practical significance, since in general SQL's tables contain bags, not sets, of rows.

Chapter 10

Why Is It Called

Relational Algebra?

O O O O that Garbled Abel Rag—
It's so elegant
So intelligent

—Anon.: *Where Bugs Go*

For no very good reason I've always quietly enjoyed the fact that the French counterpart to "It's all Greek to me" is *C'est de l'algèbre pour moi.* Recently, however, I came to realize that algebra itself might be *de l'algèbre pour moi;* I mean, I came to realize that I didn't have anything like as clear an understanding as I ought to of what algebra really is—a confession embarrassing enough for someone who used to be a mathematician, and especially embarrassing for someone who has spent a large part of his career using, teaching, and writing about relational algebra in particular.

What brought me to this distressing realization was the difficulty I had in trying to come up with good definitions for algebra in general and relational algebra in particular in my recent book *The Relational Database Dictionary* [11]. Here for the record are the definitions I did finally settle on:

algebra 1. Generically, a formal system consisting of a set of objects and a set of operators that together satisfy certain laws and properties (certainly closure, probably commutativity and associativity, and so on). The word algebra itself derives from Arabic *al-jebr,* meaning a resetting (of something broken) or a combination. 2. Relational algebra specifically (if the context demands).

relational algebra An open-ended collection of read-only operators on relations, each of which takes one or more relations as operands and produces a relation as a result. Exactly which operators are included is somewhat arbitrary, but the collection is required to be at least as powerful as relational calculus, in the sense that every relational calculus expression is semantically equivalent to some relational algebra expression. Also, the operators are generic, in the sense that they apply to all possible relations (loosely speaking).

Actually I don't think these definitions are too bad, at least as far as they go—a point I'll come back to in the final section of this chapter, "Concluding Remarks"—but there's a lot more that could usefully be said. From a database perspective in particular, there are some obvious questions that it would be nice to be able to answer definitively:

- In what sense exactly is relational algebra an algebra?

237

- In fact, is it an algebra at all?

- What's more, aren't there several different relational algebras, anyway? Is there any such thing as "the" relational algebra?

Questions like these have arisen from time to time on the seminars I've taught over the years, and I'm sorry to say I don't think I've ever answered them satisfactorily. So I thought it would be a good idea to investigate the matter, with a view to finally answering those questions once and for all. Hence the present chapter.

The plan of the chapter is as follows. Following these introductory remarks, the next two sections sketch the basic concepts of conventional high school algebra and explain what's involved in extending those concepts to construct what's called (sometimes, at least) an *abstract* algebra. Then, after a brief digression on the topic of isomorphism, the next three sections examine in some detail (a) boolean algebra, (b) the algebra of sets, and (c) matrix algebra, respectively. Finally, there's a lengthy section on the topic of relational algebra specifically, followed by a "Concluding Remarks" section containing what, to be honest, is something of a miscellany—in other words, topics I don't want to lose but don't fit well into any of the preceding sections.

I'll close these preliminary remarks with a few caveats. First, you might be forgiven for thinking that, especially given its title, the chapter takes an awfully long time in getting to the point. Well, I'm afraid that's true, in a way; but I also think it's necessary to build up carefully to that point and not to skimp on the development. At the same time, of course, it's only fair to warn you of this state of affairs.

Second, I'd like to make it clear that the chapter is meant for the "interested amateur," not for people with a detailed knowledge of mathematics. In other words, I do assume you know something about databases and the relational model, but I don't assume you're a mathematician; thus, my definitions, explanations, and examples are designed to make sense to database readers, and they might not always be as pure as a mathematician might like.

My final caveat is this: I'm categorically not an algebra expert; thus, what follows is just my own distillation and understanding of material from numerous textbooks and other sources, and it could be wildly wrong. But I hope it isn't, and I don't believe it is.

BASIC ALGEBRA

Algebra had its origins in what might be called *a theory of equations:* a theory that led to, among other things, a vastly improved understanding of the concept of *number* (in particular, to an understanding that there are many more kinds of numbers than just the simple counting numbers). It began as a fairly straightforward generalization of ordinary arithmetic—what we now call, loosely, high school algebra—and that's probably the way most people still think of it (if they think of it at all, that is). The generalization in question consists in using symbols, usually letters, in place of numbers, as in the following equation:

$$5x - 1 = x + 11$$

The symbols (x in the example) denote *variables* or *unknowns*. Since they stand for numbers, however, they can be operated upon just like numbers: They can be added, multiplied, and so on. In particular, equations like the one in the example can be *solved* by repeatedly applying certain important rules for transforming such equations. There are two principal kinds of transformations:

- *Transposition:* Moving a term from one side of the equation to the other and changing its sign

- *Cancelation:* Canceling terms that appear on both sides of the equation

I won't bother to illustrate these rules, since they're familiar to everyone; however, let me at least explain where they come from. In fact, they both derive from a famous text by the ninth century Persian mathematician al-Khwarizmi, titled *al-Kitab al-mukhtasar fi hisab al-jabr wa'l-muqabalah,* which translates to "a handbook of the science of calculation by transposition and cancelation." As stated in the definition quoted earlier from reference [11], the very word *algebra* derives from *al-jebr* (or *al-jabr*—sources differ on the spelling, as indeed they do on that of the author's name and the title, and on the precise translation of that title into English, of his book); *transposition* is a slightly more formal rendering than *resetting.* As an aside, it's interesting to note that we owe our word *algorithm* to the same source—to be specific, it's a corruption of the author's name.[1] The word *algorism,* defined by *Chambers Twentieth Century Dictionary* as "the Arabic system of numeration," comes from the same source as well.

Now, I said earlier that symbols such as x in the example stand for numbers and can therefore be operated upon just like numbers: They can be added, multiplied, and so on. In fact, algebraic notation provides a convenient way of specifying just what it is that we *can* do with numbers, as follows. Let a, b, and c be arbitrary numbers (not necessarily distinct). As usual, we define two numbers to be equal if and only if they're the very same number; otherwise they're unequal. (I remark in passing that an analogous *axiom of equality* applies to all of the algebras to be discussed in this chapter; I won't bother to spell it out every time but will let this one statement do duty for all. See Chapter 2 for further discussion.) Then, using infix "+" and infix "*" to denote addition and multiplication, respectively, we can state the rules—or *axioms,* or *laws* as they're more usually called—governing those operations, thus:

- **Commutative laws:**

      a + b = b + a
      a * b = b * a

- **Associative laws:**

      a + (b + c) = (a + b) + c
      a * (b * c) = (a * b) * c

---

1. Reference [18] gives the author's full name as Abu Ja'far Muhammad ibn Musa al-Khwarizmi, translating it as "Father of Ja'far, Mohammed, son of Musa, the Khwarizmian" (although again sources differ, and not just on the spelling), and explaining that Khwarizm was a state in what is now Uzbekistan. The word *algorithm* derives from another book by al-Khwarizmi, on Indian numerals, which survives only in Latin translation and opens with the words "Dixit Algorithmi" (i.e., "According to al-Khwarizmi").

- **Identity laws:**

```
a + 0 = a
a * 1 = a
```

- **Inverse laws:**

```
a + ( -a )  = 0
a * ( 1/a ) = 1 except for a = 0
```

- **Distributive law:**

```
a * ( b + c ) = ( a * b ) + ( a * c )
```

Explanation: Let's ignore multiplication for the moment and concentrate on addition. Observe first of all that the sum $a+b$ of any two numbers a and b is a number in turn; that is, the set of numbers is *closed* under the operation of addition.[1] Then:

- The commutative law says it makes no difference, when applying the operator "+" to two numbers, which of those numbers we take as the first operand and which the second.

- The associative law says that, given either of the expressions $a+(b+c)$ and $(a+b)+c$, we can drop the parentheses without ambiguity, thereby simplifying the expression to just $a+b+c$. It follows that we can express a sequence of additions of any length without having to use parentheses, as in, e.g., $a+b+c+d+e$ (and so on). Also, from the commutative and associative laws taken together, it follows that the order in which the individual additions in such a sequence are performed makes no difference to the overall result.

- The identity law says there exists a special number, zero ("0"), with the property that adding it to any number a just yields a. That special number is *the identity with respect to addition,* or *the additive identity.* *Note:* Please note that I'll be using the term *identity* in the foregoing sense (or in a sense analogous to the foregoing sense) throughout this chapter. In particular, I won't be using it as I did in Chapter 2 as a synonym for equality or logical equivalence.

- The inverse law says that, given any number a, there exists an *inverse* number, denoted $-a$, with the property that the sum of the given number and its inverse is zero. More precisely, $-a$ is the

---

1. As I'm sure you know, closure in general is important for many reasons—not least because it allows us to write nested expressions.

inverse *with respect to addition,* or *the additive inverse,* of a.[1] Observe that if $-a$ is the inverse of a, then a is the inverse of $-a$; in other words, a and $-a$ are inverses of each other. Also, zero is its own inverse (i.e., $-0 = 0$). Observe too that the inverse law implies that subtraction is possible as well as addition; the expression $a-b$, denoting the subtraction of b from a, is an abbreviation for $a+(-b)$.

Turning now to multiplication: First, the product $a*b$ of two numbers a and b is a number in turn; that is, the set of numbers is closed under the operation of multiplication as well as under the operation of addition. Moreover:

- The commutative law says it makes no difference, when applying the operator "*" to two numbers, which of those numbers we take as the first operand and which the second.

- The associative law says that, given either of the expressions $a*(b*c)$ and $(a*b)*c$, we can drop the parentheses without ambiguity, thereby simplifying the expression to just $a*b*c$. In fact, we can express a sequence of multiplications of any length without having to use parentheses, as in, e.g., $a*b*c*d*e$ (and so on); furthermore, thanks to the commutative and associative laws taken together, the order in which the individual multiplications in such a sequence are performed makes no difference to the overall result.

- The identity law says there exists a special number, one ("1"), with the property that multiplying any number a by it just yields a. That special number is *the identity with respect to multiplication,* or *the multiplicative identity*.

- The inverse law says, given any number a other than zero, there exists an *inverse* number, denoted $1/a$, with the property that the product of the given number and its inverse is one. More precisely, $1/a$ is the inverse *with respect to multiplication,* or *the multiplicative inverse,* of a. Observe that if $1/a$ is the inverse of a, then a is the inverse of $1/a$; in other words, a and $1/a$ are inverses of each other. Also, one is its own inverse (i.e., $1/1 = 1$). Observe too that the inverse law implies that division is possible as well as multiplication, except when the divisor is zero; the expression a/b, denoting the division of a by b, is an abbreviation for $a*(1/b)$.

Finally, the distributive law states, formally, that *multiplication distributes over addition.* Less formally, we can say that it interrelates the operations of addition and multiplication, in the sense that it allows a product of sums to be rewritten as a sum of products and vice versa.

One last point to close this section: I said earlier that symbols such as x in the equation

$$5x - 1 = x + 11$$

denote what are usually—at least in the context of high school algebra—referred to as *variables* or

---

1. The expression $-a$ can also be regarded as denoting the application of the *monadic operator* " $-$ " to the number a. Monadic " $+$ " can also be defined, of course, albeit "harmlessly" (since the expression $+a$ simply returns the value of a).

unknowns. Given my target readership, however, I think it's worth pointing out that neither of these terms means the same in high school algebra as it does in the database world. A variable in the database world (and more generally in the programming languages world) is something whose value varies over time; in the example, however, the "variable" *x* clearly has the constant value three and doesn't vary at all. And *unknown* in the database world generally has something to do with "missing information" (a term I don't much care for, by the way [11], but let that pass); in the example, however, there's clearly no information missing, in the database sense, at all.

GENERALIZING BASIC ALGEBRA

As we've seen, the laws in the previous section effectively define the addition and multiplication operators of regular arithmetic, albeit in a somewhat abstract way. (Well, they don't exactly define those operators; what they do is define certain important properties of those operators—commutativity, associativity, and so on.) But now we can stand matters on their head, as it were: By abstracting a little further—i.e., by stating the laws themselves in a slightly more general form—we can define a certain formal structure, called *an algebra* (note the indefinite article), with the property that numbers, with their conventional "+" and "*" operations, are just one possible concrete realization of that abstract formal structure: one *model,* to use the jargon.[1] But other models are possible as well, as we'll see. Thus, the effect of that further abstraction is to generalize the original notion of high school algebra, thereby making it applicable to a wider class of problems. As reference [25] puts it:

> [Algebra in general] deals not primarily with the manipulation of sums and products of numbers ... but with sums and products of elements of any sort—under the assumption that the sum and product for the elements considered satisfy the appropriate basic laws or "axioms."

Here then is the definition: An *algebra* (sometimes called an *algebraic structure*), *A,* consists of a set *S* of elements *a, b, c,* ... together with two distinct dyadic operators "+" and "*" (usually called addition and multiplication, respectively, but it must be clearly understood that they aren't necessarily the operators known by those names in conventional arithmetic), such that:

- **Closure laws:** *S* is closed under both "+" and "*"; that is, for all *a* and *b* in *S,* each of the expressions $a+b$ and $a*b$ yields an element of *S.*

- **Commutative laws:** For all *a* and *b* in *S, $a+b = b+a$* and $a*b = b*a$.

- **Associative laws:** For all *a, b,* and *c* in *S, $a+(b+c) = (a+b)+c$* and $a*(b*c) = (a*b)*c$.

---

1. I've complained elsewhere that the term *model* "is grotesquely overused—not to say misused, or abused—in the IT world, especially in the database portions of that world" [15]. I stand by this opinion in general and try hard not to misuse the term myself. In the context under discussion, however, the usage is sanctified by academic practice. See, e.g., references [28] and [29].

- **Identity laws:** There exist elements 0 and 1 in S such that for all a in S, $a+0 = a$ and $a*1 = a$.

- **Inverse laws:** For all a in S, there exist elements $-a$ and (unless $a = 0$) $1/a$ in S such that $a+(-a) = 0$ and $a*(1/a) = 1$.

- **Distributive law** (of "*" over "+"): For all a, b, and c in S, $a*(b+c) = (a*b)+(a*c)$.

Together, these rules constitute *The Laws of Algebra.*

I remark in passing that, to borrow some terminology from *The Third Manifesto* [16], (a) the elements a, b, c, ... of the set S can be thought of as values, and (b) the operators "+" and "*" are, specifically, read-only operators (they "read" their operands without changing them, and they produce a value as their result).[1] Also, I've followed convention in making heavy use of parentheses in formulating the laws; however, I've done so only to save writing (I could have written the laws out in words, albeit much more verbosely, without using parentheses at all). In other words, those parentheses don't in and of themselves denote operators of the algebra A. *Note:* That said, of course, there's nothing wrong in defining additional operators—but those operators won't be part of the algebra A as such: Either they'll merely be shorthand for some combination of existing operators, or they'll be totally new operators, over and above the operators of the algebra A as such.

- As an example of the first case, we might define an operator called "sigma(n)," which returns the value of the expression $(n/2)*(n+1)$—i.e., the sum of the first n natural numbers. This operator is self-evidently just shorthand for a certain combination of "+" and "*" operations.

- As an example of the second case, we might define an exponentiate operator ("↑") according to which $a↑b$ is equal to a raised to the power b. This operator isn't just shorthand for some combination of "+" and "*" operations, in general (consider, e.g., the case $b = ½$ in ordinary arithmetic).

Given the notion of an algebra as just defined, then, what would a model of such an algebra look like that's different from the familiar model (i.e., numbers, with their conventional "+" and "*" operators)? Well, here's a simple example. Take the set S to be the set {EVEN,ODD}—the names are meant to be suggestive—and let operators "+" and "*" be defined as follows:

---

1. One reviewer wanted me to use the term *function* here instead of "read-only operator." I agree that read-only operators are, precisely, functions in the mathematical sense; indeed, reference [11] defines them that way. The trouble is (as I've pointed out elsewhere in the present book), the term *function*—like many other terms in computing that have their origins in mathematics—has had its meaning muddied and diluted somewhat over the years, to our loss, and if I were to use it here I would run the risk of confusing some readers. I prefer the *Manifesto* term *read-only operator,* therefore (at least in this context), because, clumsy though it might be, it is at least precise.

```
EVEN + EVEN = EVEN          EVEN * EVEN = EVEN
EVEN + ODD  = ODD           EVEN * ODD  = EVEN
ODD  + EVEN = ODD           ODD  * EVEN = EVEN
ODD  + ODD  = EVEN          ODD  * ODD  = ODD
```

Then we have:

- **Closure:** For all *a* and *b* in *S*, *a*+*b* and *a*b* both yield values in *S*.

- **Commutativity:** For all *a* and *b* in *S*, *a*+*b* = *b*+*a* and *a*b* = *b*a*.

- **Associativity:** For all *a*, *b*, and *c* in *S*, *a*+(*b*+*c*) = (*a*+*b*)+*c* and *a**(*b*c*) = (*a*b*)*c. (*Exercise:* Check these claims. Does doing this exercise remind you of anything?)

- **Identities:** The identities with respect to "+" and "*" are EVEN and ODD, respectively: For all possible values *a* in *S*, *a* + EVEN = *a* and *a* * ODD = *a* (in other words, EVEN is the "0" element and ODD is the "1" element). *Note:* The fact that with conventional numbers 0 is even and 1 is odd should help you remember which is which here.

- **Inverses:** The additive inverses of EVEN and ODD are EVEN and ODD, respectively (i.e., each is its own inverse), because EVEN + EVEN and ODD + ODD both yield EVEN (recall that "0" is EVEN in this system). The multiplicative inverse of ODD is ODD (i.e., ODD is its own inverse), because ODD * ODD yields ODD (recall that "1" is ODD in this system). EVEN, being the "0" element, has no multiplicative inverse (there is no *a* in *S* such that EVEN * *a* = ODD).

- **Distributivity:** I'll leave it as another exercise for you to check that for all *a*, *b*, and *c* in *S*, *a**(*b*+*c*) = (*a*b*)+(*a*c*).

It follows that the set *S* = {EVEN,ODD}, together with the operators "+" and "*" as defined above, constitutes an algebra as previously defined.

Note: There's a possible confusion here that I'd like to clear up before going any further. As just explained, the set {EVEN,ODD} with appropriately defined "+" and "*" operators is an algebra. But didn't I open my discussion of that example by saying I was going to give a *model* of an algebra? Isn't the set {EVEN,ODD}, with its "+" and "*" operators, supposed to be a model of the algebra *A* as I defined it earlier, rather than an algebra as such? Well, in fact it's both. A model *M* of an algebra *A* is still an algebra—but it's one that's a little more concrete, as it were, than the original algebra *A*. Thus, we might reasonably say that *A* is an *abstract* algebra and *M* (in the example, the set {EVEN,ODD} with its "+" and "*" operators) is a *concrete realization,* or *interpretation,* of that abstract algebra.

Let's consider the EVEN/ODD example a little further. Suppose we change the names EVEN and ODD to *f* and *t*, respectively (after all, names are arbitrary: right?—though I note that this particular renaming is in keeping with the normal conventions in logic and computing to the effect that 0 means false and 1 means true). Suppose we also change the names (or symbols) " + " and "*" to XOR and AND, respectively. The operator definitions now look like this:

```
f XOR f = f          f AND f = f
f XOR t = t          f AND t = f
t XOR f = t          t AND f = f
t XOR t = f          t AND t = t
```

As you can see, these definitions are basically just the truth tables, written in a slightly unconventional form, for the operators exclusive OR (XOR) and conjunction (AND) of conventional two-valued logic (2VL). It follows that the set of truth values of 2VL, together with the conventional 2VL operators (or *connectives*) XOR and AND, is an algebra! What's more, we can determine the various identity and inverse elements of that algebra by mechanically mapping the identities and inverses of the EVEN/ODD algebra over into the new terminology. But it's worth spelling out the details, so I will.

First, then, the additive identity (i.e., the identity with respect to XOR) is *f,* because *f* XOR *f* yields *f* and *t* XOR *f* yields *t;* also, *f* and *t* are each their own inverses with respect to XOR, because *f* XOR *f* and *t* XOR *t* both yield *f.* The multiplicative identity (i.e., the identity with respect to AND) is *t,* because *f* AND *t* yields *f* and *t* AND *t* yields *t;* also, *t* is its own inverse with respect to AND, because *t* AND *t* yields *t* (*f,* being "the zero element," has no multiplicative inverse).

———————— ♦ ♦ ♦ ♦ ♦ ————————

I can use the EVEN/ODD example to illustrate another point. Suppose we change the names EVEN and ODD to *t* and *f,* respectively (intuitively "the wrong way round," as it were, but a legitimate change nonetheless); at the same time, suppose we change the names (or symbols) " + " and "*" to EQ and OR, respectively. Now the operator definitions look like this:

```
t EQ t = t          t OR t = t
t EQ f = f          t OR f = t
f EQ t = f          f OR t = t
f EQ f = t          f OR f = f
```

As you can see, these definitions are basically just the truth tables for the operators equivalence (EQ) and disjunction (OR) of conventional two-valued logic. So it follows that the set of truth values of 2VL, together with the 2VL operators EQ and OR, is another algebra. (It's different from the previous one because its "add" and "multiply" operators are different.) As before, we can now determine the various identity and inverse elements of that algebra by mechanically mapping the identities and inverses of the original EVEN/ODD algebra over into the new terminology. Again, however, it's worth spelling out the details, and so I will.

First, then, the additive identity (i.e., the identity with respect to EQ) is *t,* because *t* EQ *t* = *t* and *f* EQ *t* = *f;* also, *t* and *f* are each their own inverses with respect to EQ, because *t* EQ *t* = *t* and *f* EQ *f* = *t.* The multiplicative identity (i.e., the identity with respect to OR) is *f,* because *t* OR *f* = *t* and *f* OR *f* = *f;* also, *f* is its own inverse with respect to OR, because *f* OR *f* = *f* (*t,* being "the zero element," has no multiplicative inverse).

———————— ♦ ♦ ♦ ♦ ♦ ————————

At this point, you might be thinking I've missed an obvious trick with respect to the EVEN/ODD example; to be specific, why not change EVEN and ODD to *f* and *t*, respectively (in accordance with normal convention and as in the first of the two foregoing discussions), and "+" and "*" to OR and AND, respectively? (By OR and AND here, I mean the usual logical operators of those names, of course. In fact, some logic texts actually use the symbols "+" and "*" to denote OR and AND, respectively.) The definitions will now look like this:

f OR *f* = *f*			*f* AND *f* = *f*
f OR *t* = *t*			*f* AND *t* = *f*
t OR *f* = *t*			*t* AND *f* = *f*
t OR *t* = *f*			*t* AND *t* = *t*

But you see what's happened: While the definition for AND is indeed just the truth table for conjunction, *the definition for OR is not the truth table for disjunction* (because it shows *t* OR *t* as *f*, not *t*). Thus, the set of truth values of 2VL, together with the 2VL operators OR and AND as conventionally understood, is *not* an algebra—at least, not in the sense of that term as I defined it near the start of the present section (and not in any other sense I'm aware of, either).

I'll make another assertion, too (without attempting to prove it here). First, it's well known—see, e.g., Chapter 1 in the present book—that there are exactly four monadic and 16 dyadic operators in 2VL. However, no two of those operators are such that both of the following statements are true:

- The operators fit the algebraic definitions of "+" and "*".

- The operators are *expressively complete,* in the sense that the complete array of four monadic and 16 dyadic operators can all be defined in terms of them.

It follows that 2VL as conventionally understood, with its complete array of logical operators, is not an algebra as I defined that term near the start of the present section. (That is, it's not "just" an algebra; however, it does include two such algebra as proper subsets, as it were—one in which the "+" operator is XOR and the "*" operator is AND, and one in which the "+" operator is EQ and the "*" operator is OR.)

ISOMORPHISM

It's something of a digression from the main topic of this chapter, but I'd like to say a few words on the subject of isomorphism—not least because this is a term that often gets misused in the database world (I'm guilty of a few transgressions in this regard myself).

Let's go back to the two "concrete" EVEN/ODD algebras from the previous section again. Here they are, summarized:

1.   EVEN : *f*   "+" : XOR
     ODD : *t*   "*" : AND

2. EVEN : *t*   "+" : EQ
    ODD : *f*   "*" : OR

These are, as stated, different algebras: The set $S = \{f,t\}$ is the same in the two cases, but the "+" and "*" operators are different. Although the algebras aren't the same, however, they're certainly *isomorphic*. What this means, loosely, is that each can be mapped, or transformed, into the other. Of course, the mapping in the example is obvious. Here it is:

```
Algebra 1  ◄═►  Algebra 2

f          ◄═►  t
t          ◄═►  f
XOR        ◄═►  EQ
AND        ◄═►  OR
```

From this mapping, it follows that every expression in either of the algebras has an exact counterpart in the other. But what does this statement mean? I don't think it's immediately obvious. In order to explain it, in fact, it helps to introduce an explicit NOT operator in both cases, the purpose of which is to map *f* to *t* and vice versa. That operator isn't part of the algebra per se in either case (in particular, it can't be defined in terms of the available operators in either case); rather, it's a kind of "meta" operator, which I introduce purely to take care of the fact that the mapping between the algebras requires *f* and *t* to map to *t* and *f,* respectively.

Let me digress for a moment to expand on this notion of NOT being a "meta" operator. Consider Algebra 1, with its operators XOR and AND. Since *f* XOR *f* and *f* AND *f* both yield *f,* there's no expression involving only *f*'s, XORs, and ANDs that can possibly yield *t;* therefore, NOT isn't part of Algebra 1, because there's no operator that, given *f,* will yield *t.* A similar argument applies to Algebra 2 (another exercise for the reader). Incidentally, it follows directly that—this is a point I've already made in different words in the previous section—neither Algebra 1 nor Algebra 2 is the whole of 2VL (since NOT *is* part of "the whole of 2VL").

Now I can illustrate my claim that every Algebra 1 expression has an exact counterpart in Algebra 2 and vice versa. By way of example, consider the following Algebra 1 expression:

((*a* XOR *b*) AND *c*) XOR *t*

To transform such an expression into its Algebra 2 equivalent, we have to replace every *t* by *f,* every *f* by *t,* every XOR by EQ, every AND by OR, and every variable reference *x* by its negation NOT *x.* In the case at hand, these replacements yield:

(((NOT *a*) EQ (NOT *b*)) OR (NOT *c*)) EQ *f*

This isn't an Algebra 2 expression, of course, precisely because it includes those invocations of NOT. However, those invocations are really just shorthand, in a sense; for example, the invocation NOT *a* is to be understood as a "meta" level instruction to edit the expression, as it were, along the lines of "If *a* is *f,* replace it by *t;* if *a* is *t,* replace it by *f.*" After all such replacements have been performed, the resulting expression is an Algebra 2 expression, and it yields *f* precisely where the original Algebra 1 expression yields *t* and vice versa. I'll leave it as yet another exercise for you to check this claim.

Here then is a definition of isomorphism, based on one given in reference [11] but reworded somewhat here:

> **isomorphism** Let *Sx* and *Sy* be sets, not necessarily distinct, and let *m* be a bijective mapping from *Sx* to *Sy* (in other words, let *m* be such that every element of *Sy* is the image under that mapping of exactly one element of *Sx*). Let *OpX* be an operator that takes elements of *Sx* as its operands and yields an element of *Sx* as its result. Then *m* is an isomorphism if and only if, for all such operators *OpX*, there exists an analogous operator *OpY* that takes elements of *Sy* as its operands and yields an element of *Sy* as its result such that, whenever *OpX* applied to *x1, x2, ...,* *xn* yields *x*, then *OpY* applied to *y1, y2, ..., yn* yields *y*, where *y1, y2, ..., yn,* and *y* are the images of *x1, x2, ..., xn,* and *x*, respectively, under *m*. In other words, a bijective mapping is an isomorphism if and only if it preserves the algebraic structure of the set *Sx* in the set *Sy*.

Observe that if the bijective mapping *m* is an isomorphism, then its inverse is an isomorphism as well.

Now, earlier I said the term *isomorphism* is often misused in the database world. Now I can explain this remark. Actually the point is quite simple: The term is often used for what more correctly would be called just a bijective mapping, or in other words a one-to-one mapping between the elements of one set and the elements of another. But an isomorphism is more than just a mapping of elements; it's a mapping of elements *together with a mapping of operators* (as we saw in the example of mapping Algebra 1 to Algebra 2, earlier).

Let me close this section by saying that, clearly, if two algebras are isomorphic, they aren't necessarily equal (though they're certainly equivalent, in a sense). But, of course, if two algebras are equal, then they're certainly isomorphic; in fact, if they're equal, they're the same algebra.

BOOLEAN ALGEBRA

If you're reading this book, you'll certainly be familiar with the basic idea of boolean algebra. Unless you're a mathematician, however, you might not know that in mathematics, at least, the term actually has two different meanings (where the second can be regarded as a generalization of the first). The simpler one can be defined as follows: Let *S* be the set {*f,t*}. Then boolean algebra consists of the set *S*, together with one monadic operator NOT and two distinct dyadic operators OR and AND. Of course, these operators are all very familiar, and I won't bother to define them here, but I think it's worth stating the following properties explicitly:

- **Closure:** *S* is closed under NOT, OR, and AND.

- **Commutativity:** OR and AND are both commutative.

- **Associativity:** OR and AND are both associative.

- **Identities:** The identity elements for OR and AND are *f* and *t,* respectively.

- **Inverses:** For OR, *f* is its own inverse but *t* has no inverse (there is no *i* in *S* such that *t* OR *i* yields *f*); similarly, for AND, *t* is its own inverse but *f* has no inverse (there is no *i* in *S* such that *f* AND *i* yields *t*).

- **Distributivity:** Each of OR and AND distributes over the other. In other words, for all *a, b,* and *c* in *S,* we have *a* OR (*b* AND *c*) = (*a* OR *b*) AND (*a* OR *c*) and *a* AND (*b* OR *c*) = (*a* AND *b*) OR (*a* AND *c*).

I now observe that the "classical" boolean algebra as just defined doesn't conform to the definition of an abstract algebra, *A,* as given earlier in the section "Generalizing Basic Algebra"! (So is it in fact an algebra? I leave this question for you to judge.) To be specific, we can observe at least three points of difference between classical boolean algebra and the abstract algebra *A* as earlier defined:

- Boolean algebra includes a monadic operator (NOT); the algebra *A,* by contrast, requires only the usual two dyadic operators.

- The algebra *A* requires every element to have an additive inverse. In boolean algebra, by contrast, *f* has no inverse with respect to AND and *t* has no inverse with respect to OR; thus, neither AND nor OR fully fits the definition of the "+" operator. (At the same time, they both fully fit the definition of the "*" operator. See the bullet item immediately following.)

- Each of the dyadic operators of boolean algebra distributes over the other (the algebra *A,* by contrast, requires only that "*" distribute over "+"). As a consequence, which of OR and AND is "+" and which "*" in boolean algebra is arbitrary, in a sense.

  Aside: This fact—i.e., the fact that it's somewhat arbitrary as to which of OR and AND is "+" and which "*"—is closely related to *The Principle of Duality,* which I'll explain just briefly here. Let *X* be either a statement or an expression of boolean algebra, and let *X'* be obtained from *X* by replacing all occurrences of *f* by *t,* all occurrences of *t* by *f,* all occurrences of OR by AND, and all occurrences of AND by OR; *X'* is said to be the *dual* of *X.* Then *The Principle of Duality* states that *X* is a theorem if and only if [it's a statement and] its dual statement *X'* is also a theorem. Two comments: First, this principle can be regarded as a specific application of isomorphism as previously discussed. Second, the principle, or one exactly analogous, applies to the algebra of sets also. I choose not to discuss it any further in this chapter for space reasons. *End of aside.*

It follows that if we do want to regard the classical boolean algebra as an algebra per se (which we certainly do if we want to be in conformance with the literature in this area), then we need to revise or extend our definition of abstract algebra in general. Unfortunately, however, I haven't been able to find any such revised or extended definition in the numerous references I've consulted. (In particular, books with "Algebra" in their title almost never seem to come out and say exactly what they mean by "an algebra"!) So it seems the best I can do for now is just to say that, in general, "an algebra" is a formal system that conforms *somewhat* to the definition of the abstract algebra *A* as given earlier—not a very satisfactory situation, I feel bound to say, though perhaps it's not very important for the purposes of this chapter. However, I'll return to this issue (i.e., of terminology) in the section "Concluding Remarks," later.

Back to the classical boolean algebra per se. I've given a definition and stated certain fundamental properties of that algebra (closure, commutativity, and so on), but I think it's worth mentioning a variety of additional properties as well—properties, that is, that apply to boolean algebra in particular but not necessarily to other algebras:

- **Involution law:** For all a in S, NOT (NOT a) = a.

- **Idempotence laws:** For all a in S, a OR a = a and a AND a = a. (In case you might be wondering, XOR and EQ in conventional two-valued logic are examples of dyadic operators that aren't idempotent.)

- **Complementarity laws:** For all a and b in S, a OR (NOT a) = t and a AND (NOT a) = f; also, if a OR b = t and a AND b = f, then b = NOT a.

- **Absorption laws:** For all a and b in S, a OR (a AND b) = a and a AND (a OR b) = a.

- **De Morgan's laws:** For all a and b in S, NOT (a OR b) = (NOT a) AND (NOT b) and NOT (a AND b) = (NOT a) OR (NOT b).

Now I turn to the second (extended) meaning of the term *boolean algebra*. Here's a definition; it's based on one in reference [2], but I've edited it fairly heavily here.

- Let S be a set.

- Let a partial ordering operator (here denoted "≤") be defined on the elements of S. In other words, let the operator "≤" be such that, for all a, b, and c in S:

  - $a \leq b$ or $b \leq a$ (or both, or possibly neither).

  - *Reflexivity:* $a \leq a$.

  - *Transitivity:* If $a \leq b$ and $b \leq c$, then $a \leq c$.

  - *Antisymmetry:* If $a \leq b$ and $b \leq a$, then $a = b$.

- Let there exist one monadic operator and two distinct dyadic operators (here denoted prefix "¬" and infix "+" and "*", respectively) that apply to elements of S, such that:

  - The monadic operator "¬" ("complement") satisfies the closure and involution laws.

- The dyadic operators "+" ("add") and "*" ("multiply") satisfy the closure, commutative, associative, distributive, idempotence, and absorption laws. *Note:* With regard to the distributive law in particular, each of "+" and "*" distributes over the other.

- The monadic and dyadic operators together satisfy De Morgan's laws.

- Finally, let *S* include two elements 0 and 1 such that:

  - 0 is the identity for "+".

  - 1 is the identity for "*".

  - For all *a* in *S*, $0 \leq a$ and $a \leq 1$.

Then the combination of the set *S* and all of the foregoing operators is a **boolean algebra**.

Points arising from the foregoing definition:

- Not all authorities include a requirement for the ordering operator "≤" in their definition of a boolean algebra; however, I choose to follow reference [2] and include it. See the next section for further discussion.

- The classical boolean algebra as defined earlier in this section is indeed a boolean algebra in the foregoing extended sense, as I now show:

  - *S* is the set {*f*,*t*}.

  - Adopting the familiar convention that, in a sense, *f* is strictly "less than" *t* (and *t* is strictly "greater than" *f*), we can define the necessary ordering operator "≤" to be such that $f \leq f$, $f \leq t$, and $t \leq t$ (and it is not the case that $t \leq f$). This operator clearly satisfies the definition of a partial ordering operator; in particular, it's reflexive, transitive, and antisymmetric.

  - The "¬", "+", and "*" operators are NOT, OR, and AND, respectively. The closure, involution, commutative, associative, distributive, idempotence, and absorption laws (and De Morgan's laws), as applicable, are all satisfied by these operators.

  - The elements 0 and 1 are *f* and *t*, respectively.

- Propositional logic (which includes the propositional operators NOT, OR, and AND) is another boolean algebra. Here the set *S* is the set of all propositions (including the degenerate propositions *f* and *t* in particular), and $p \leq q$ is defined to be equivalent to /*p*/ ≤ /*q*/ (where /*p*/ and /*q*/ denote the truth values of propositions *p* and *q*, respectively, and /*p*/ ≤ /*q*/ is interpreted in terms of the "≤" operator as just defined for classical boolean algebra).

Here's another example, one that differs in certain important respects from previous examples. Let *S* be a set; let *P* be the corresponding *power set* (i.e., the set of all subsets of *S*); and let *A, B,* and *C* be arbitrary elements of *P* (i.e., arbitrary subsets of *S*). Define operations on elements of *P* as follows:

- "≤": Define $A \leq B$ to be *set inclusion;* i.e., define $A \leq B$ to be true if and only if *A* is a subset—not necessarily a proper subset—of *B*. Note that this operator is certainly reflexive, transitive, and antisymmetric; note further that it's entirely possible for $A \leq B$ and $B \leq A$ both to be false.

- "¬", "+", and "*": Define ¬*A* to be the *complement* of *A* (i.e., the set of all elements of *S* not included in *A*); define $A+B$ and $A*B$ to be the union of *A* and *B* and the intersection of *A* and *B,* respectively. The closure, involution, commutative, associative, distributive, idempotence, and absorption laws (and De Morgan's laws), as applicable, are all satisfied by these operators.

Finally, define 0 and 1 to be the empty set and the universal set, respectively (where by *the universal set* I mean that subset of *S* that's equal to *S,* or in other words simply *S* itself); note that these sets satisfy the requirement that, for all *A* in *S,* $0 \leq A$ and $A \leq 1$. Then the combination of the power set *P* and all of the operators just defined is a boolean algebra.

But surely the particular boolean algebra just defined is isomorphic to, or even identical to, an algebra of *sets?* Well, yes, so it is; the algebra of sets is indeed a boolean algebra! Here's a quote from reference [2]:

The present chapter [is] devoted to describing the algebra of classes (boolean algebra) and its generalizations (lattice theory).

So reference [2] actually equates boolean algebra and the algebra of sets. (Mathematicians often use *class* as a synonym for *set,* as you probably know.) So let's move on immediately to consider the algebra of sets.

THE ALGEBRA OF SETS

Once again I'll begin with a definition. Let *S* be a set, let *P* be the corresponding power set, and let *A, B,* and *C* be arbitrary elements of *P*. Then we saw in the previous section that the set *P* together with the operations of set inclusion, set complement, set union, and set intersection (all as conventionally defined) is an algebra: in fact, a boolean algebra specifically. What's more, it should be clear that there are exactly as many such algebras as there are possible sets *S;* if we start with a different set *S,* we wind up with a different algebra. But, of course, those algebras are all very similar to one another (they bear a strong family resemblance, as it were); so we can reasonably define *the* algebra of sets to be the obvious generalization of all of those individual algebras—and, in essence, that's exactly what we're doing when we talk about "the" algebra of sets. Analogous remarks apply to many other algebras also, including in particular both matrix algebra and relational algebra (see the next two sections).

So the algebra of sets is basically just a boolean algebra, in the generalized sense of that term.

But there are certain points, not all of them immediate consequences of that fact, that are worth calling out explicitly. *Note:* For consistency with the discussions in the previous section, I continue to use the symbols " ≤ ", " ¬ ", " + ", and "*" to denote set inclusion, set complement, set union, and set intersection, respectively. You might like to draw Venn diagrams to help you understand the following definitions and discussions.

- The algebra of sets is usually regarded as including a *set difference* operator (" - ") as well. However, that operator isn't a new primitive; rather, if A and B are elements of P, then the difference between A and B (in that order), $A - B$, is equal to $A*(\neg B)$ (the intersection of A and the complement of B). Note that this operator isn't commutative; that is, $A - B$ and $B - A$ aren't equal (in general).

- We can also define a *symmetric* difference operator (" | "), as follows: If A and B are elements of P, then the symmetric difference between A and B, $A | B$, is equal to $(A - B) + (B - A)$ (the union of the differences $A - B$ and $B - A$). Obviously enough, this operator *is* commutative. *Note:* There doesn't seem to be a universally accepted symbol for symmetric difference; my own symbol (" | ") is chosen merely to avoid conflict with other symbols used in this chapter—though I remark that in other contexts " | " is often pronounced OR, and symmetric difference is a kind of set theory analog of exclusive OR in logic.

- *Differences from abstract algebra as defined in the section "Generalizing Basic Algebra":*

    - The algebra of sets includes an ordering operator (" ≤ ") and a monadic complement operator (" ¬ ") in addition to the dyadic operators " + " and "*" required by abstract algebra in general.

    - As stated in the previous section, the identity with respect to union (the "0" element of P) is the empty set, and the identity with respect to intersection (the "1" element of P) is the universal set S. However, there's no inverse for union (given an arbitrary set A, there's no set I in P such that $A + I = 0$, except in the special case where A and I both themselves happen to be 0). Likewise, there's no inverse for intersection (given an arbitrary set A, there's no set I in P such that $A*I = 1$, except in the special case where A and I both themselves happen to be 1).

    - Each of union and intersection distributes over the other (by contrast, abstract algebra in general requires only that "*" distribute over " + "). In fact, which of union and intersection is " + " and which "*" is arbitrary, in a sense.

I can now explain that business of whether or not the definition of boolean algebra should include the ordering operator (" ≤ "). As we've seen, the definition given in reference [2] does include it; but it does so, it seems to me, simply in order to allow it subsequently to equate boolean algebra and set algebra. Other authorities (e.g., reference [20]) don't include that operator in their definitions; consequently, they have to introduce it separately if and when they get to the algebra of sets (and for those authorities, of course, it can't be the case that boolean algebra and the algebra of sets are isomorphic). Frankly, I think that's all there is to it!

By the way, you might be thinking there's no need to include the ordering operator explicitly anyway, because the equality operator " = " is always available and could be used to serve the purpose. (Note that " = " is indeed a partial ordering operator, as you can easily see by checking the definition.) But if the ordering operator for boolean algebra B is " = ", then we would have, for all a in the underlying set S, $0 = a$ and $a = 1$. Hence, S would contain just one element; the operators " + " and "*" thus would not (*could* not) be distinct; and so B wouldn't be a boolean algebra after all, by definition, because the definition does require those operators to be distinct.

Although it's a little repetitious, I'd like to close this section by summarizing just what it is that constitutes the algebra of sets (since that concept is so all important). The following definition is based on one in reference [29]; it's equivalent to the one I gave earlier but is deliberately stated in somewhat different form. Let A, B, C be arbitrary subsets of some set U,[1] and assume the availability of the set inclusion operator (" ≤ ") and the usual set operators union (" + "), intersection ("*"), and complement ("¬"). Then we have:

1. **Closure:** $A+B$ and $A*B$ both yield subsets of U.

2. **Commutativity:** $A+B = B+A$ and $A*B = B*A$.

3. **Associativity:** $A+(B+C) = (A+B)+C$ and $A*(B*C) = (A*B)*C$.

4. **Distributivity:** $A*(B+C) = (A*B)+(A*C)$ and $A+(B*C) = (A+B)*(A+C)$.

5. **Identities:** $A+O = A*U = A$. *Note:* Here and elsewhere in this definition I use O to denote the 0 element (i.e., the empty set).

6. $A+U = U$ and $A*O = O$.

7. **Involution:** $¬(¬A) = A$.

8. $¬O = U$ and $¬U = O$.

9. **Complementarity:** $A+(¬A) = U$ and $A*(¬A) = O$; also, if $A+B = U$ and $A*B = O$, then $B = ¬A$.

10. If $A+B = A$ for all A, then $B = O$; if $A*B = A$ for all A, then $B = U$.

11. **Idempotence:** $A+A = A*A = A$.

12. **Absorption:** $A+(A*B) = A*(A+B) = A$.

---

1. To quote reference [29]: "For the sake of uniformity, [the laws are all formulated in terms of] subsets of a universal set U. However, for some of [those laws] this is a purely artificial restriction, as an examination of the proofs will show." Of course, I'm not giving those proofs here anyway.

13. **De Morgan:** $\neg(A+B) = (\neg A)*(\neg B)$ and $\neg(A*B) = (\neg A)+(\neg B)$.

14. **Consistency:** The following three statements are all equivalent:

- $A \leq B$.

- $A*B = A$.

- $A+B = B$.

This concludes the definition. Note that the various laws aren't all independent (but it's useful to state them all explicitly nevertheless). Note too that many of the laws have well established names, but a few of them don't.

MATRIX ALGEBRA

There's one more algebra, matrix algebra, that I'd like to consider briefly before I can get to the real target of this chapter (i.e., relational algebra). I don't want to get into a lot of detail—I just want to make the following points.

As I'm sure you know, a matrix is a rectangular array of numbers; hence, given some particular matrix, we can sensibly talk about the *rows* and *columns* of that matrix. Now, one of the operators included in matrix algebra is *matrix addition*. However, not all pairs of matrices can be added together; rather, the sum $A+B$ of two matrices A and B is defined only if A and B are *conformable for addition*, meaning they have the same number of rows and the same number of columns. So we have here a radically new notion: namely, the notion that one of the dyadic algebraic operators can be applied only to certain pairs of elements (instead of arbitrary pairs of elements) from the underlying set of all such elements.

Another of the operators of matrix algebra is *matrix multiplication*. Again, however, not all pairs of matrices can be multiplied together; rather, the product $A*B$ of two matrices A and B, in that order, is defined only if A and B are *conformable for multiplication in that order*, meaning the number of columns in A is the same as the number of rows in B. So here we have another radically new notion: namely, the notion that even if the product $A*B$ is defined, the product $B*A$ might not be[1] (and even if it is, it's not the case, in general, that the two products are equal). So matrix multiplication, even when it's defined, is not in general commutative. (By contrast, matrix addition, when it's defined, is commutative, and indeed associative also.)

Yet another pertinent observation is that none of the three notions of conformability just defined (conformability for addition, conformability for multiplication in one order, conformability for

---

1. In case it's not obvious, let me spell the point out: If A has m rows and n columns and B has n rows and p columns, then we can certainly form the product $A*B$—but we can form the product $B*A$ only if $p = m$, which in general won't be the case.

multiplication in the other order) implies the other two. On the other hand, conformability for addition and conformability for multiplication in one order, taken together, do imply conformability for multiplication in the other order (why?). Thus, if *A* and *B* are two arbitrary matrices, any of the following might be the case:

- None of *A+B, A*B, B*A* is defined.

- *A+B* is defined but *A*B* and *B*A* aren't.

- *A*B* is defined but *B*A* and *A+B* aren't.

- *B*A* is defined but *A+B* and *A*B* aren't.

- *A*B* and *B*A* are defined but *A+B* isn't.

- *A+B, A*B, B*A* are all defined.

So we have here a number of departures from the general notion of an algebra as originally defined, and once again it would be nice to have a suitably extended definition of that generic term *algebra*. But we don't (at least, I'm not aware of any such); so it seems that we simply have to assert, by fiat as it were, that there is indeed such a thing as matrix algebra, and it is indeed an algebra, and it's defined in a certain way. I omit the details here; the interested reader can find them in, e.g., reference [26].

RELATIONAL ALGEBRA

My original motivation for writing this chapter was, of course, to answer those questions listed near the beginning of the chapter regarding relational algebra specifically—and at last I'm in a position to do so (or try to do so, at least).

Operators that we would certainly now regard as relational algebra operators were described by Codd in his very first papers on the relational model [4,5]; in particular, he introduced the restrict, project, and join operations in those papers, though it's interesting to note in passing that the definitions he gave for restrict and join, at least, were rather different from those usually given today. Be that as it may, he didn't actually use the term *relational algebra* (so far as I'm aware) until his 1972 paper [6], where he said this: "[We] define a collection of operations on relations, and this collection is called a relational algebra." And he went on to define that algebra as consisting of the following operations:

cartesian product
union, intersection, and difference
Θ-restriction
projection
Θ-join and natural join
division

I assume you're basically familiar with these operations, or most of them at any rate (I don't think many people can claim to be familiar with relational division!); it's not my purpose in this chapter to define all of the various relational operators I'll be touching on, unless there's some specific point I want to make that requires me to give such a definition. Detailed definitions can be found, if you need them, in references [11] and [16] and elsewhere; tutorial treatments can be found in references [9] and [10] and elsewhere.

Since Codd's 1972 definition, many additional algebras (or many additional algebraic operators, at least) have been defined, by many different writers and researchers. In particular, reference [16], by Hugh Darwen and myself, defines a language called **Tutorial D** that includes explicit support for all of the following algebraic operators:

rename	union	extend
restrict	intersection	summarize
project	difference	semijoin
join	disjoint union	semidifference
compose	divide	substitute
wrap	group	tclose
unwrap	ungroup	

This set does include, directly or indirectly, all of Codd's original operators, though there are numerous differences of detail between Codd's original definitions and ours. (There are differences of style, too; we were strongly influenced in our definitions by the algebra of Hall, Hitchcock, and Todd as reported in reference [22], which certainly differed in stylistic respects from Codd's original.)

In addition, reference [17], by Hugh Darwen, Nikos Lorentzos, and myself, defines still more operators of an algebraic nature: pack, unpack, and what we call "U_ operators" (U_project, U_union, U_join, and so on), which you can think of as generalized versions of the corresponding regular operators.

Now, one of the questions I raised near the beginning of this chapter was as follows (though I deliberately reword it here): Is there really such a thing as "the" relational algebra? In other words, aren't there really several different formal systems, all of them having some legitimate claim to being "a" relational algebra? The discussions of this section so far might be taken to suggest that the answer to this question is yes, there are indeed several different relational algebras. But are there really?

In order to address this latter question, I want to appeal to reference [16] once again. That book includes an appendix, Appendix A, with the title "A New Relational Algebra." Here are the opening sentences from that appendix:

In this appendix, we describe a new relational algebra that we call **A**. The name **A** is a doubly recursive acronym: It stands for *ALGEBRA,* which in turn stands for *A Logical Genesis Explains Basic Relational Algebra.* As this expanded name suggests, **A** has been designed in such a way as to emphasize, perhaps more clearly than previous algebras have done, its close relationship to and solid foundation in the discipline of predicate logic.

The appendix then goes on to show that all of the algebraic operators supported by the language **Tutorial D**—except for tclose, which (in the form of ◄TCLOSE►) is supported by **A** directly—can be defined in terms of just two **A** operators, ◄REMOVE► and either ◄NAND► or ◄NOR►, where:

- ◄REMOVE► is essentially projection of some relation over all of its attributes except some specified one.

- ◄NAND► and ◄NOR► are essentially "union of complements" and "intersection of complements," respectively. *Note:* In the interest of accuracy, I should explain that reference [16] doesn't actually define either ◄NAND► or ◄NOR► as a primitive **A** operator; rather, it defines **A** as including explicit ◄NOT►, ◄AND►, and ◄OR► operators. However, it then goes on to say: "We do not actually need both ◄AND► and ◄OR► ... [We] could ... collapse ◄NOT► and ◄OR► into a single operator, ◄NOR► ... [and/or] ◄AND► and ◄NOT► into a single operator, ◄NAND►." So no serious harm is done by thinking of either ◄NAND► or ◄NOR►, like ◄REMOVE►, as a primitive operator of **A**.

Moreover, reference [17] shows that the operators introduced in that reference (pack, unpack, and the various "U_ operators") are all just shorthand, too: They can all be defined in terms of operators already supported in **Tutorial D,** and hence, ultimately, in terms of operators in **A**. In a sense, therefore, I think it can be claimed that **A** is "the one true relational algebra," and all other contenders for the title are merely syntactic variations on that one (where the variations are introduced for reasons of user friendliness, of course). And if and when some operator is introduced into some algebra or some language that *isn't* definable in terms of existing operators in **A,** then **A** itself can be suitably extended. (In fact, this was more or less what happened when we decided to incorporate support for the tclose operator into **Tutorial D**—i.e., we added an operator called ◄TCLOSE► to **A**.)

— ♦ ♦ ♦ ♦ ♦ —

I also asked near the beginning of this chapter whether relational algebra was an algebra at all (and if so, in what sense). Now I can answer this question too, albeit in a somewhat weaselly way: If we agree that set algebra and matrix algebra are algebras, then we must also agree—at least, if we want to avoid being accused of inconsistency—that relational algebra is an algebra as well. Let me immediately try to justify this claim!

First, like addition and multiplication in the matrix algebra, many of the operations of relational algebra are defined only for operands that conform in certain specific ways to the requirements of the operation in question. In particular, relational theory relies heavily on the notion of *type*—observe that the algebra of sets as commonly understood includes nothing analogous to this notion—and many of the relational operations impose requirements on the types of their operands. For example:

- Relational union requires its operands to be of the same type. *Note:* The type in question is, specifically, a relation type; all values are typed in the relational model, and relations, being values [11,16], are no exception to this rule.

- The same remark applies to relational intersection and difference.

- Join and divide each require attributes of their operands with the same name to be of the same type.

And so on.

Second, let's see how relational algebra compares to the algebra of sets as defined earlier in this chapter. For the purpose of this investigation, I'll consider the operators ◄REMOVE►, ◄NOT►, ◄OR►, and ◄AND► of the algebra **A** (even though, as indicated earlier, we could actually replace ◄NOT►, ◄OR►, and ◄AND► by either ◄NAND► or ◄NOR► without loss). As previously noted, ◄REMOVE► is basically projection of some relation over all of its attributes except one; as for the other three, ◄OR► and ◄AND► are basically **A**'s union and intersection, respectively, and ◄NOT► is a relation complement operator (see further discussion below). *Note:* It would be more correct to say that ◄AND► is **A**'s join rather than its intersection, but for simplicity I'll assume until further notice that we are indeed talking about intersection and not join. Of course, join is a much more interesting (and more general, and more useful) operator than simple intersection. However, my objective here is merely to show that relational algebra, like the algebra of sets, is indeed an algebra, and it turns out to be easier for that purpose to frame the discussion in terms of intersection rather than join. I'll get to join later.

In order to facilitate comparison with the algebra of sets, in what follows I'll replace ◄NOT►, ◄OR►, and ◄AND► by "¬", "+", and "*", respectively. As for ◄REMOVE►, I'll ignore that operator until further notice.

Now, our definition of the algebra of sets began by saying: Let *A, B, C* be arbitrary subsets of some set *U*. The relational analog of this starting point has to be a little more complicated, however, because (as already suggested) relations, unlike the sets of general set theory, are typed. So:

- Let *T* be a relation type.

- Let *U* be the universal relation of type *T*—i.e., the relation containing all possible tuples of the applicable *tuple* type (see reference [11] for further explanation).

- Let *O* be the empty relation of type *T*.

- Let *A, B,* and *C* be arbitrary relations of type *T*.

- Let an inclusion operator ("≤") be defined for relations of type *T*. *Note:* In connection with this last point, I remark that inclusion is not a relational operator as such, because it yields a truth value, not a relation; however, such an operator is included implicitly in **A** and explicitly in **Tutorial D**. The discussions of this chapter strongly suggest that any would-be relational algebra should include such an operator.

Now let's examine the 14 laws of set algebra, reinterpreting and discussing them as necessary in relational terms:

1. **Closure:** $A+B$ and $A*B$ both yield relations of type T.

2. **Commutativity:** $A+B = B+A$ and $A*B = B*A$.

3. **Associativity:** $A+(B+C) = (A+B)+C$ and $A*(B*C) = (A*B)*C$.

4. **Distributivity:** $A*(B+C) = (A*B)+(A*C)$ and $A+(B*C) = (A+B)*(A+C)$.

5.   **Identities:** $A+O = A*U = A$.

6. $A+U = U$ and $A*O = O$.

7.   **Involution:** $\neg(\neg A) = A$. *Note:* This is the first reference to "$\neg$" in these relational laws, so perhaps I should say a little more about it. Basically, the complement $\neg A$ of relation A is that relation of type T that contains all possible tuples of the applicable tuple type other than those appearing in relation A. Commercial products don't usually support "$\neg$" directly; however, they do support difference ("$-$"), and $\neg A$ is clearly equal to $U-A$. In practice, it's to be hoped (for performance reasons, at least) that it will never actually be necessary for the expression $\neg A$ to be evaluated.

8. $\neg O = U$ and $\neg U = O$.

9.   **Complementarity:** $A+(\neg A) = U$ and $A*(\neg A) = O$; also, if $A+B = U$ and $A*B = O$ are both true, then $B = \neg A$.

10.   If $A+B = A$ for all A, then $B = O$; if $A*B = A$ for all A, then $B = U$.

11.   **Idempotence:** $A+A = A*A = A$.

12.   **Absorption:** $A+(A*B) = A*(A+B) = A$.

13.   **De Morgan:** $\neg(A+B) = (\neg A)*(\neg B)$ and $\neg(A*B) = (\neg A)+(\neg B)$.

14.   **Consistency:** The following three statements are all equivalent:

  ▪ $A \leq B$.

  ▪ $A*B = A$.

  ▪ $A+B = B$.

Thus far, then, it does seem reasonable to say that relational algebra is indeed an algebra, at least to the extent that set algebra and matrix algebra are algebras. But what about the ◄REMOVE► operator? Well, I said in the section "Generalizing Basic Algebra" that, given an algebra A, there's nothing wrong in defining additional operators, but those operators won't be part of the algebra A as such. Let me now add that I don't think there's any harm in thinking of them as part of that algebra A if we want to, so long as they're at least in the spirit of that algebra (as it were). In the case at hand, regarding ◄REMOVE►, we'd want to check laws 1–14 again; some of them won't apply, but where they do apply we'd certainly like them not to be violated. So let's take a look.

Notation: Let T, U, O, A, B, and C be as before. Also, let T include attributes X, Y, and Z, and let V be the relation type that results if X is removed from T. For simplicity, I'll abbreviate the expression "◄REMOVE► attribute X from relation r" to just $r\{-X\}$.

1. **Closure:** $A\{-X\}$ yields a relation of type V.

2. **Commutativity:** $(A\{-Y\})\{-X\} = (A\{-X\})\{-Y\}$.

3. **Associativity:** $((A\{-Y\})\{-Z\})\{-X\} = ((A\{-X\})\{-Y\})\{-Z\}$.

4. **Distributivity:** $(A+B)\{-X\} = (A\{-X\})+(B\{-X\})$ and $(A*B)\{-X\} = (A\{-X\})*(B\{-X\})$.

5. **Identities:** Not applicable. However, it's worth pointing out that with conventional projection (as opposed to ◄REMOVE►, which always "removes" exactly one attribute), every relation A is identically equal to A itself projected on all of its attributes.

The remaining laws 6-14 aren't applicable. So the net of this exercise is that nothing unpleasant happens—that is, no harm is done—if we choose to regard ◄REMOVE► as part of the algebra as such. (In fact, we *must* include it if we're to meet the requirement that relational algebra must be at least as powerful as relational calculus. See the section "Concluding Remarks," later.)

Now what happens if we interpret "*" (i.e., ◄AND►) as join instead of intersection, as indeed we really should? Basically, we'll need to check laws 1-14 once again; as before, some of them won't apply, but where they do apply we'd like them not to be violated. I won't bother to go through that exercise here; let me just observe that, as I'm sure you'd expect, nothing unpleasant happens, and it's thus completely reasonable to regard join as part of the algebra. However, there's one point of detail that's worth calling out explicitly.

As I showed earlier, the identity element with respect to intersection is the universal relation of the pertinent type. But join is a *generalized* intersection; in particular, it doesn't require its operands to be of the same type, and indeed they usually aren't. As a direct consequence of this fact, join has what might be called a *general* identity element: namely, TABLE_DEE [8], which is the unique relation with no attributes and exactly one tuple (necessarily the empty tuple). To elaborate: If A is a relation of type T and U is the corresponding universal relation, then it's certainly true that the join of A and U is equal to A. But the join of A and TABLE_DEE is also equal to A, and this latter equality is guaranteed to hold *no matter what the type of A happens to be*. Thus, we might reasonably say that join (i.e., ◄AND►) has both (a) a specific identity element for each specific relation type and (b) a generic identity element, TABLE_DEE, that's independent of relation type.

Analogously, the ◄OR► operator of **A** isn't just the regular relational union but is, rather, a generalized form of that operator that doesn't require its operands to be of the same type. As a consequence of this fact, ◄OR► too has a generic identity element as well as a specific identity element for each specific relation type. The specific identity element for relation type T is the empty relation O of type T; the generic identity element is TABLE_DUM [8], which is the unique relation with no attributes and no tuples. *Note:* I don't want to mislead you here, though. Real relational languages like **Tutorial D** certainly will support the generalized form of intersection (i.e., ◄AND►, or join); for reasons explained in reference [16], however, they probably won't support the generalized form of union (i.e., ◄OR►). The fact that TABLE_DUM is the generic identity element for this latter operator is thus significant mainly for theoretical reasons. By contrast, the fact that TABLE_DEE is the generic identity element for join is significant for major practical, as well as theoretical, reasons.

CONCLUDING REMARKS

This chapter has been something of a journey of discovery for me; when I set out to write it, I wasn't sure where it was going to wind up. One thing I've learned is that the term *algebra* no longer has just one inviolate meaning, if indeed it ever did. *Au contraire,* in fact: Even if it did start out with just one such meaning, that meaning has clearly been extended, and generalized, and possibly even diluted, over the years. More specifically, certain algebraic laws or axioms seem to have been weakened (even dropped, in some cases), while others have been added. One conclusion I draw is that my original definition in reference [11] wasn't too bad! Here's that definition again:

> **algebra** 1. Generically, a formal system consisting of a set of objects and a set of operators that together satisfy certain laws and properties (certainly closure, probably commutativity and associativity, and so on). The word algebra itself derives from Arabic *al-jebr,* meaning a resetting (of something broken) or a combination. 2. Relational algebra specifically (if the context demands).

With hindsight, I wish I'd talked in terms of elements rather than "objects" (*object* is such a loaded term in computing contexts). However, I was right in including, and indeed emphasizing, the role of the operators (though I should have said they were read-only operators specifically). I was also right in insisting on the closure property; every algebra I've looked at certainly requires closure, though the precise meaning of that term depends on context somewhat. And I was right in saying that commutativity and associativity "probably" apply; as we've seen, matrix multiplication in particular has neither of these properties, in general, and yet we talk of an algebra of matrices despite this fact. As for that "and so on" in my definition, the discussions in this chapter should serve to give some idea as to what that phrase might need to cover.

What's more, I think my definition in reference [11] of relational algebra specifically wasn't too bad either. Here it is:

> **relational algebra** An open-ended collection of read-only operators on relations, each of which takes one or more relations as operands and produces a relation as a result. Exactly which operators are included is somewhat arbitrary, but the collection is required to be at least as powerful as relational calculus, in the sense that every relational calculus expression is semantically equivalent to some relational algebra expression. Also, the operators are generic, in the sense that they apply to all possible relations (loosely speaking).

This definition fails to mention the all important relational inclusion operator but otherwise seems fairly satisfactory to me. The qualifier *open-ended* covers the possibility of defining additional shorthand operators (e.g., semijoin, which is equivalent to a join followed by a projection); it also covers the possibility of defining new primitive operators, as happened when we added ◄TCLOSE► to the algebra **A**. The remark to the effect that which operators are included is somewhat arbitrary addresses the point that, for example, there's no need to support either cartesian product or intersection explicitly if join is properly supported. At the same time, the remark to the effect that the operators together are required to be "at least as powerful as relational calculus" puts a lower bound on what must be supported; for example, a would-be algebra that provided no way to do projections would ipso facto not be a relational algebra.[1] Finally, the claim that the operators are generic excludes systems that—for example—need one kind of "join" to join departments and employees and a different kind of "join" to join suppliers and parts (speaking very loosely, of course); in particular, it excludes both object oriented languages and conventional programming languages, in which "joins" have to be hand coded, and indeed probably *hard* coded (i.e., tailored to specific operands) as well.

To paraphrase something I said earlier, much of the material in this chapter represents my own distillation of material from numerous textbooks and other sources. Nowhere is this remark more true than with respect to the definition I gave for "an algebra" (meaning an *abstract* algebra) in particular. Most of the definitions I found in the literature were vague in the extreme—even deliberately so, it seemed to me, in some cases (though to be fair some of the findings of this chapter might give some hint as to why those definitions have to be vague, necessarily). References [18], [21], [24], [26], and [28] came closest to giving a crisp, clear definition; even in those cases, however, I don't think the definitions could be said to be beyond criticism.

Anyway, I thought it might be interesting to document for the record some of the definitions I found. *Note:* Perhaps the label "definitions" is too strong here; some of the "definitions" that follow are no more than brief informal characterizations, and I doubt whether the authors responsible would claim they're anything else. Others are simply too technical, relying as they do on formal terms whose meaning the reader just has to know if he or she is to understand the definition in question.

- *From reference [7]:* An algebra consists of a number of mathematical entities (e.g., matrices or sets) and operations (e.g., addition or set inclusion) with formal rules for the relationships between the mathematical entities.

- *From reference [25]:* An algebraic system [is] a set of elements of any sort on which functions such as addition and multiplication operate, provided only that these operations satisfy certain basic rules.

- *From reference [27]:* An [algebra is an] abstract mathematical system consisting of a vector space together with a multiplication by which two vectors may be combined to yield a third, and some axioms relating this multiplication to vector addition and scalar multiplication. *Note:* I deliberately choose not to get into specifics here regarding what a *vector space* is.

- *From reference [30]:* [Algebra is] (1) a mathematical system that is a generalization of arithmetic, in which letters or other symbols are used to represent numbers; (2) the study of the formal relations between symbols belonging to sets on which one or more operations has [*sic*] been

---

1. Note too that the fact that the algebra is required to be at least as powerful as the calculus implies that the algebra must include analogs of the quantifiers of logic. Without going into details, let me just state for the record that—speaking very loosely indeed—relational projection is an algebraic counterpart to the existential quantifier, and relational division is an algebraic counterpart to the universal quantifier. See reference [6] for more specifics.

defined.

- *From reference [31]:* [Algebra is] the branch of mathematics dealing with group theory and coding theory which studies number systems and operations within them.

- *From reference [18]:* Algebra is the part of advanced mathematics that is not calculus. *Note:* Actually, I rather like this one! It's tongue in cheek, of course, and I should make it clear that it refers to high school algebra specifically. Later in the same book, the author goes on to define an (abstract) algebra to be "a vector space in which two vectors can not only be added but also multiplied, giving another vector as a result" (I've reworded this definition slightly). And he continues:

> This is, I agree, not a very happy usage. The word "algebra" already has a perfectly good meaning ... Why confuse the issue by sticking an indefinite article in front and using it to name this new kind of mathematical object? It's no good complaining, though. The usage is now universal. If you hear of some mathematical object spoken of as "an algebra," it is almost certainly a vector space with some way to multiply vectors added on to it.

Later, he adds:

> To make an algebra work at all [*sic!*], you may have to relax certain rules—the commutative rule in most cases ... Often you have to relax the associative rule, too ...

In other words, algebras often fail to satisfy some of the most fundamental Laws of Algebra as defined earlier in this chapter!

Let me now observe that the construct that, following some but not all of the references I consulted in writing this chapter, I have defined as "an abstract algebra" is known in mathematics, more precisely, as a *field*. Here's a definition (from reference [27]):

> **field** An algebraic system possessing two operations which have all the properties that addition and multiplication of real numbers have.

Of course, this definition does beg the question of what an algebraic system is! Be that as it may, it does seem likely (though I must make it clear that this is mere speculation on my part) that the reason the term *algebra,* or *abstract algebra,* is often used to mean a field specifically is due to the way the subject developed historically. What I mean by this speculation is that, historically speaking, the first abstract algebra to be defined was indeed a field specifically (as we effectively saw in the section "Generalizing Basic Algebra" earlier in this chapter).

By the way, *groups* and *rings* are (important) examples of algebras that have some but not all of "the properties that addition and multiplication of real numbers have." Here are loose definitions:

> **group** A set with an associative dyadic operator, "+", such that an additive identity exists and every element has an additive inverse. *Note:* The operator "+" might or might not be

commutative. If it is, the group is said to be commutative or Abelian,[1] otherwise it's said to be noncommutative.

ring An Abelian group with certain extra properties (another associative dyadic operator "*", distributivity of "*" over "+").

And just as a ring is a group with certain extra properties, so a field is a ring with certain extra properties (commutativity of "*" and so on). *Note:* Matrix algebra is an example of an algebra that doesn't even have all of the properties of groups. At least, this remark is true of matrix algebra in general; but if we limit our attention to square matrices of some fixed order—i.e., *N*-by-*N* matrices for some fixed *N*—then the resulting algebra is in fact a ring.[2]

But given all of the above, what are we to make of the following extract from reference [30]?

Many new types of algebraic structures have been defined and studied ... Today, in addition to groups and fields, mathematicians study algebraic structures called rings, semigroups, and algebras to name a few. (Here *algebra* refers to a particular type of mathematical object.)

In this chapter, I've discussed, at different levels of detail, (a) basic or high school algebra; (b) abstract algebras in general; (c) boolean algebra; (d) set algebra; (e) matrix algebra; and of course (f) relational algebra. But many, many other algebras have been defined as well ... Just for interest, here are some of them (this list is extracted from reference [31]):

alternate algebra • alternating algebra • Banach algebra • Borel Sigma algebra • Cayley algebra • Clifford algebra • commutative algebra • division algebra • exterior algebra • graded algebra • Grassmann algebra • Hecke algebra • Heyting algebra • homological algebra • Hopf algebra • Jordan algebra • Lie algebra • linear algebra • measure algebra • Robbins algebra • Schur algebra • semisimple algebra • sigma algebra • Steenrod algebra • von Neumann algebra

Obviously I have no intention of discussing, or even defining, any of the algebras in this list. But the fact that so many algebras exist does raise a question: Are there any other algebras that might be relevant to the database world?

Well, my original aim in writing this chapter was to consider relational algebra—that is, the algebra associated with relational database systems—specifically. But the vast majority of "relational"

---

1. After the Norwegian mathematician Niels Henrik Abel (pronounced *ah'bul*).

2. What's more, reference [18] says: "We can make a case that this [i.e., the family of all *N*-by-*N* matrices] is the most important of all algebras." Two comments: First, of course, we mustn't forget the operators. Second, each distinct *N* gives rise to a different algebra, strictly speaking—so once again it looks like one of those situations where we have to define *the* algebra (of square matrices, in the case at hand) to be an obvious generalization of an infinite set of individual algebras.

database systems commercially available at the time of writing aren't relational systems at all but, rather, SQL systems. So is SQL based on some algebra? If so, what does that algebra look like?

In order to study this question, the first thing we'd have to do would be to pin down the precise nature of the basic object in SQL—namely, the SQL table, which (as is well known) is very different from the basic object, the relation, of relational algebra. Here are some of the most obvious differences between SQL tables and relations [11]:

- SQL tables have a left to right ordering to their columns; relations have no left to right ordering to their attributes.

- SQL tables can contain duplicate rows (i.e., they contain bags, not sets, of rows, in general); relations never contain duplicate tuples.

- SQL tables can contain nulls; relations never do. *Note:* I apologize for the solecism here—to talk of nulls being "contained in" tables really makes no sense—but it's always hard to talk (or write) coherently about anything to do with nulls.

- SQL tables can have two or more columns with the same name; relations never have two or more attributes with the same name.

- SQL tables can effectively have columns with no name at all; relations never have any unnamed attributes.

One immediate consequence of all of these points is that SQL's *table type* notion[1] is much more complicated than its relational counterpart (i.e., the notion of *relation type*). Also, SQL has no "table inclusion" operator (as far as I know), though it does have analogs of the relational union, intersection, and difference operators.

A further immediate consequence is that SQL's underlying algebra, if it exists, is certainly not relational algebra. But is it an algebra at all? An investigation of this issue would require us to determine the effect of all of the points just enumerated (and others) on the 14 laws discussed several times earlier in this chapter. And while I was working on an early draft of the chapter, I actually set out to do such an analysis. I got as far as commutativity (law number 2) and then gave up ... and even there I didn't consider intersection, limiting my attention to union only (though the two cases are presumably similar). Some of the issues that arose in connection with the commutativity or otherwise of SQL's union operator were as follows:

- In order even to be able to talk about commutativity, we need a notion of table equality. SQL appears to have no such notion.

---

1. To the extent that such a notion can even be said to exist, that is. No such thing is defined in the SQL standard [23].

■ In any case, which SQL union are we talking about? There are three basic union "flavors" in SQL (UNION CORRESPONDING BY, UNION CORRESPONDING, and "plain" union), each of which additionally has a DISTINCT *vs.* ALL option, for a total of six possible combinations.

■ In the case of UNION CORRESPONDING, at least, the operation is definitely not commutative, in general (regardless of whether DISTINCT or ALL applies).

■ SQL performs certain *type coercions* automatically, with the (bizarre!) consequence that certain unions produce results containing rows that appear in neither operand. The full implications of this point are unclear, at least to me.

■ SQL considers certain values to be "distinct but equal" (!); an example is provided by the character strings 'AB' and 'AB ' (note the trailing space in the second of these), which are clearly distinct and yet are sometimes regarded as equal. One consequence is that, again, certain unions produce results containing rows that appear in neither operand. An even weirder consequence is the results of certain unions aren't even well defined!

■ I certainly didn't explore in detail any additional problems that the presence of nulls might give rise to in connection with the foregoing points. I'll just mention one thing. Suppose tables *A* and *B* both have just one column and one row; suppose the single row and column intersection "contains a null" in both cases; and suppose we evaluate both of the expressions *A* UNION *B* and *B* UNION *A* (not intended to be actual SQL syntax). Then both result tables also have just one column and just one row, and in both cases the single row and column intersection contains a null (despite the fact that nulls aren't equal to one another!). Yet the two result tables aren't equal, precisely because nulls aren't equal; in this case, therefore, I really don't see how we can sensibly say that *A* UNION *B* = *B* UNION *A*.

From this rather abortive attempt on my part, I conclude that trying to demonstrate that SQL is indeed founded on some algebra would be a nontrivial exercise—certainly not one that I myself would be anxious to undertake. But I do think it should be undertaken, if we're ever to be convinced that SQL is a sound basis on which to build systems (database systems and application systems). *Note:* Of course, I say this in full knowledge that many thousands of such systems have already been built, and continue to be built, at the time of writing; but the existence of such systems does not in and of itself suffice to show that SQL is founded on some algebra, or more generally that it's sound.

As a matter of fact, it could be argued that the exercise I'm suggesting has already been undertaken. In reference [19], Garcia-Molina et al. present what they call "a relational algebra on bags" [*sic*]. Here's a quote:

> Moreover, relational algebra was originally designed as if [*sic*] relations were sets. Yet relations in SQL [*sic*] are really *bags,* or *multisets* ... Thus, we shall introduce relational algebra as an algebra on bags.

In another paper of my own, however [14], I present arguments that among other things raise serious doubts as to whether the "algebra" of reference [19] deserves to be called an algebra at all. And even if it does, there are serious discrepancies between it and the way SQL actually behaves. For example:

- It simply ignores the fact that SQL tables have a left to right column ordering.

- It does admit that "the distributive law of intersection over union ... holds for sets, but not for bags," but it doesn't consider the implications of this fact for the claim that what's being described is an algebra.

And so on. So I think I have to conclude that reference [19], at least, doesn't succeed in demonstrating that SQL is truly founded on an algebra as such.

Perhaps I should add that one thing reference [19] does manage to demonstrate—though I think it was precisely the authors' intent not to demonstrate any such thing!—is that whatever foundation SQL can claim to have is much less satisfactory than relational algebra: less satisfactory, that is, for reasons of usability, implementability, optimizability ("query rewrite"), performance, and possibly others.

The foregoing conclusion is supported by the findings of reference [1], which shows among other things that "no boolean algebra structure is available for bags if it is desired that the bag operations [i.e., bag union, bag intersection, and bag difference] have their standard semantics when restricted to sets." I'd like to say a little more about those bag operations, however. *Note:* Chapter 12 goes into more detail; what follows here is only the briefest of sketches.

First let me define the operators briefly. Let *A, B,* and *C* be bags, and let *x* be a typical element, occurring exactly ax times in *A*, bx times in *B*, and cx times in *C*. Then:

- *C* is the *bag union* of *A* and *B* if and only if, for all *x* in *C*, $cx = \text{MAX}(ax, bx)$.

- *C* is the *bag intersection* of *A* and *B* if and only if, for all *x* in *C*, $cx = \text{MIN}(ax, bx)$.

- *C* is the *bag difference* between *A* and *B* (in that order) if and only if, for all *x* in *C*, $cx = \text{MAX}(ax - bx, 0)$.

Reference [1] also defines an operation it calls *bag concatenation,* which, using the same notation as above, can be defined thus:

- *C* is the *bag concatenation* of *A* and *B* if and only if, for all *x* in *C*, $cx = ax + bx$. (References [12] and [17] call this operation "union+".)

Interestingly, reference [1] also shows that this operator (i.e., bag concatenation) can't be expressed in terms of bag union, bag intersection, and bag difference.

Now, claims are often made to the effect that SQL is based on bag theory instead of set theory. For example, here's a quote from reference [3]: "SQL uses a multiset model instead of a pure set model."[1] But do such claims hold up? In particular, does SQL actually support the operations of bag theory?

Well, SQL's INTERSECT ALL and EXCEPT ALL operators do correspond, more or less, to bag intersection and bag difference, respectively. However, SQL's UNION ALL does not correspond to bag union; rather, it corresponds to bag concatenation. In fact, SQL has no direct support for bag union at all. (Perhaps I should add that if DISTINCT is specified instead of ALL, then the SQL operators reduce to something approximating their *set* counterparts. Thus, SQL really does have no direct support for bag union.) *Note:* The remarks of this paragraph apply also to the "relational algebra on bags" of reference [19], which I mentioned in the previous subsection.

————— ♦ ♦ ♦ ♦ ♦ —————

A couple of final points:

- As you might have noticed, I've said nothing at all about updating in this chapter. That's because updating operations (INSERT, DELETE, UPDATE, and more generally relational assignment), though certainly relational operations, aren't relational algebra operations as such. And that's because the operations of relational algebra, like those of any other algebra, are read-only operations specifically; update operations, by definition, aren't truly algebraic operations as such.

- A currently hot topic in the database world is XML, together with its query language XQuery. There have been attempts to define an XML algebra, too (though I feel bound to point out that, inauspiciously, those attempts began after XML itself had already been defined). Some obvious questions arise: Is there truly an XML algebra? Is XML truly founded on it? How does it compare with relational algebra? I leave these questions for other investigators to address.

ACKNOWLEDGMENTS

I'd like to thank Hugh Darwen and David Livingstone for helpful comments on earlier drafts of this chapter.

———————

1. As mentioned previously, *multiset* is just another word for *bag*. Incidentally, you might be interested to hear the "justification" offered by that same reference [3] for SQL's reliance on bags instead of sets, which is as follows: "Removing redundant duplicates was considered too expensive and too strange for programmers." Expensive? Only if costs are measured in a very unsophisticated manner *and* the implementation is very unsophisticated as well. Strange for programmers? Even if it can be shown that there's any truth to this claim (which, frankly, I doubt), I would say the alternative is *very* strange for people who know what a set is—and I venture to suggest there are far more of those than there are programmers (not to mention the point that "people who know what a set is" surely includes most programmers, anyway).

REFERENCES AND BIBLIOGRAPHY

1.   Joseph Albert: "Algebraic Properties of Bag Data Types," Proc. 17th Int. Conf. on Very Large Data Bases, Barcelona, Spain (September 1991).

2.   Garrett Birkhoff and Saunders Mac Lane: *A Survey of Modern Algebra* (revised edition). New York, N.Y.: MacMillan (1953).

3.   Joe Celko: *Joe Celko's Data and Databases: Concepts in Practice.* San Francisco, Calif.: Morgan Kaufmann (1999).

4.   E. F. Codd: "Derivability, Redundancy, and Consistency of Relations Stored in Large Data Banks," IBM Research Report RJ599 (August 19th, 1969).

5.   E. F. Codd: "A Relational Model of Data for Large Shared Data Banks," *CACM 13,* No. 6 (June 1970). Republished in *Milestones of Research—Selected Papers 1958-1982 (CACM 25th Anniversary Issue), CACM 26,* No. 1 (January 1983).

6.   E. F. Codd: "Relational Completeness of Data Base Sublanguages," in Randall Rustin (ed.): *Data Base Systems:* Courant Computer Science Symposia *6.* Englewood Cliffs, N.J.: Prentice-Hall (1972).

7.   John Daintith and John O. E. Clark: *The Facts on File Dictionary of Mathematics.* New York, N.Y.: Market House Books Ltd. (1999).

8.   Hugh Darwen: "The Nullologist in Relationland," in C. J. Date and Hugh Darwen, *Relational Database Writings 1989-1991.* Reading, Mass.: Addison-Wesley (1992).

9.   C. J. Date: *An Introduction to Database Systems* (8th edition). Boston, Mass.: Addison-Wesley (2004).

10. C. J. Date: *Database in Depth: Relational Theory for Practitioners.* Sebastopol, Calif.: O'Reilly Media, Inc. (2005).

11. C. J. Date: *The Relational Database Dictionary.* Sebastopol, Calif.: O'Reilly Media Inc. (2006).

12. C. J. Date: "What First Normal Form Really Means," in *Date on Database: Writings 2000-2006.* Berkeley, Calif.: Apress (2006).

13. C. J. Date: "Two Remarks on SQL's UNION," in *Date on Database: Writings 2000-2006.* Berkeley, Calif.: Apress (2006).

14. C. J. Date: "Double Trouble, Double Trouble," in *Date on Database: Writings 2000-2006.* Berkeley, Calif.: Apress (2006).

15. C. J. Date: "Models, Models, Everywhere, Nor Any Time to Think," in *Date on Database: Writings 2000-2006*. Berkeley, Calif.: Apress (2006).

16. C. J. Date and Hugh Darwen: *Databases, Types, and the Relational Model: The Third Manifesto* (3rd edition). Boston, Mass.: Addison-Wesley (2006).

17. C. J. Date, Hugh Darwen, and Nikos A. Lorentzos: *Temporal Data and the Relational Model*. San Francisco, Calif.: Morgan Kaufmann (2003).

18. John Derbyshire: *Unknown Quantity: A Real and Imaginary History of Algebra*. Washington, D.C.: Joseph Henry Press (2006).

19. Hector Garcia-Molina, Jeffrey D. Ullman, and Jennifer Widom: *Database System Implementation*. Upper Saddle River, N.J.: Prentice-Hall (2000).

20. R. L. Goodstein: *Boolean Algebra*. Oxford, U.K.: Pergamon Press (1963).

21. Jan Gullberg: *Mathematics: From the Birth of Numbers*. New York, N.Y.: W. W. Norton & Company (1997).

22. Patrick Hall, Peter Hitchcock, and Stephen Todd: "An Algebra of Relations for Machine Computation," Conf. Record of the 2nd ACM Symposium on Principles of Programming Languages, Palo Alto, Calif. (January 1975).

23. International Organization for Standardization (ISO): *Database Language SQL,* Document ISO/IEC 9075:2003 (2003).

24. Frank Land: *The Language of Mathematics*. London, U.K.: John Murray (1960).

25. Saunders Mac Lane and Garrett Birkhoff: *Algebra* (3rd edition). Providence, R.I.: AMS Chelsea Publishing (1999).

26. L. Mirsky: *An Introduction to Linear Algebra*. London, U.K.: Oxford University Press (1955).

27. Sybil P. Parker (ed.): *The McGraw-Hill Dictionary of Mathematics*. New York, N.Y.: McGraw-Hill (1994).

28. John Stillwell: *Yearning for the Impossible: The Surprising Truths of Mathematics*. Wellesley, MA: A K Peters Ltd. (2006).

29. Robert R. Stoll: *Sets, Logic, and Axiomatic Theories*. San Francisco, Calif.: W. H. Freeman and Company (1961).

30. John Tabak: *Algebra: Sets, Symbols, and the Laws of Thought*. New York, N.Y.: Facts on File, Inc. (2004).

31.   Eric W. Weisstein: *CRC Concise Encyclopedia of Mathematics*. Boca Raton, Fla.: CRC Press
       (1999).

APPENDIX A: WHY IS IT CALLED RELATIONAL CALCULUS?

The body of this chapter has shown that the term *algebra* isn't very precisely defined, though at least
there are certain laws—closure, for example—that do seem to apply to most (all?) algebras. In the case
of relational algebra in particular, however, we've seen that there's a kind of lower bound on the
functionality that must be included; to be specific, the relational algebra is required to be "at least as
powerful as relational calculus." But that claim in turn raises questions rather similar to those I raised
earlier in connection with relational algebra:

▪   What exactly is a calculus?

▪   In what sense exactly is relational calculus a calculus? In fact, is it a calculus at all?

▪   Is there any such thing as "the" relational calculus?

       Now, I could be wrong, but it seems to me, based on the numerous sources I consulted in writing
this chapter, that matters here are even fuzzier, in a sense, than they are in the algebraic case. Here's a
generic definition of the term *calculus* (this is the definition I gave in reference [11]):

       calculus 1. Generically, a system of formal computation (the Latin word *calculus* means a
       pebble, perhaps used in counting or some other form of reckoning). 2. Relational calculus
       specifically (if the context demands).

       Note that this definition is so general—or so vague—that it could even be argued that relational
algebra is "a calculus"! Be that as it may, it's certainly true that the calculus label is applied to several
distinct "systems of computation." What we call calculus at high school is, more properly, the
differential and integral calculus; it has to do with the differentiation and integration of functions. But
there are many others: the calculus of vectors, the calculus of variations, the calculus of residues, the
calculus of tensors, and so on. In particular, there's the *predicate* calculus (which is just another name
for predicate logic [29]). And since relational calculus is essentially just a version of predicate calculus
that's tailored for use with relations specifically, it makes at least intuitive sense to refer to it as relational
calculus specifically. Frankly, I think that's all there is to it—except perhaps to add that it's useful from
a pragmatic point of view to have a distinct term for a "system of computation with relations" that
directly and explicitly includes support for the quantifiers and other related predicate calculus

constructs.[1]

So now I think I've answered all of the questions I raised a few moments ago, except possibly the last one: Is there any such thing as "the" relational calculus? Here I believe the situation is analogous to that with respect to the relational algebra: We can call anything we like "relational calculus," just so long as it includes at least a certain minimum level of functionality—basically the level defined by Codd in reference [6]—and moreover provides that functionality in what might be called "predicate calculus style." *Note:* The reason I say "basically" in the foregoing sentence is that the calculus as originally defined in reference [6] had no counterpart to the algebraic union operator, with the result that it was strictly less powerful than the algebra. This omission was a mere oversight, however, and was subsequently fixed; thus, it's now fair to say that the relational algebra and the relational calculus are each exactly as powerful as the other, and the differences between them are, in a sense, more a matter of style than anything else.

---

1. Perhaps I should also mention that relational calculus as conventionally understood comes in two flavors anyway—tuple calculus, in which the so called range variables range over relations and thus denote tuples from those relations, and domain calculus, in which the range variables range over domains (or types) instead of relations and thus denote values from those domains.

Chapter 11

S e m i j o i n   a n d   S e m i d i f f e r e n c e

Sometimes doing things by halves
Can be a good idea

—Anon.: *Where Bugs Go*

Not too many people are familiar with the relational operators semijoin and semidifference—which is a pity, because those operators can be extremely useful in practice, as I hope to show in this short chapter. As usual, I'll use the well known suppliers-and-parts database as a basis for my examples. Fig. 11.1 shows the usual set of sample values.

S

S#	SNAME	STATUS	CITY
S1	Smith	20	London
S2	Jones	10	Paris
S3	Blake	30	Paris
S4	Clark	20	London
S5	Adams	30	Athens

SP

S#	P#	QTY
S1	P1	300
S1	P2	200
S1	P3	400
S1	P4	200
S1	P5	100
S1	P6	100
S2	P1	300
S2	P2	400
S3	P2	200
S4	P2	200
S4	P4	300
S4	P5	400

P

P#	PNAME	COLOR	WEIGHT	CITY
P1	Nut	Red	12.0	London
P2	Bolt	Green	17.0	Paris
P3	Screw	Blue	17.0	Oslo
P4	Screw	Red	14.0	London
P5	Cam	Blue	12.0	Paris
P6	Cog	Red	19.0	London

Fig. 11.1: The suppliers-and-parts database—sample values

Here's the database definition, expressed as usual in **Tutorial D**:

```
VAR S BASE RELATION
    { S# S#, SNAME NAME, STATUS INTEGER, CITY CHAR }
    KEY { S# } ;
```

```
VAR P BASE RELATION
    { P# P#, PNAME NAME, COLOR COLOR, WEIGHT WEIGHT, CITY CHAR }
      KEY { P# } ;

VAR SP BASE RELATION
    { S# S#, P# P#, QTY QTY }
      KEY { S#, P# }
      FOREIGN KEY { S# } REFERENCES S
      FOREIGN KEY { P# } REFERENCES P ;
```

Note: What follows is a considerably expanded version of material that first appeared in reference [1]. I assume you're familiar with the regular join and difference (and projection) operators of conventional relational algebra; these operators too are discussed and illustrated in reference [1].

SEMIJOIN

I'll begin with a definition. Let *r1* and *r2* be relations (not necessarily distinct, of course); then the *semijoin* of *r1* with *r2*, in that order, is the join of *r1* and *r2*, projected back on the attributes of *r1*. Note the phrasing, incidentally—we speak of "the semijoin of *r1* with *r2*," not "the semijoin of *r1* and *r2*," because the order *r1* then *r2* is significant, as should be clear from the definition.

By way of example, consider the query "Get suppliers who supply at least one part." If we form the regular join of suppliers and parts, we obtain a relation with heading as follows (attribute types omitted for simplicity):

```
{ S#, SNAME, STATUS, CITY, P#, QTY }
```

This relation contains at least one tuple for each supplier who does supply at least one part, and no tuples at all for suppliers who supply no parts at all. (Given the sample values from Fig. 11.1, it contains tuples for suppliers S1, S2, S3, and S4, but no tuple for supplier S5.) In order to obtain the desired result, therefore—i.e., a relation containing supplier information (number, name, status, and city) for suppliers who do supply at least one part—we need to project this intermediate result relation over just the attributes S#, SNAME, STATUS, and CITY. So the desired overall result is indeed found by joining S and SP and then projecting on the attributes of S: in other words, by forming the semijoin of S with SP. In **Tutorial D,** we can express this overall sequence of operations very simply, thus:

```
S SEMIJOIN SP
```

Here by contrast is the same query in SQL:

```
SELECT DISTINCT S.*
FROM   S, SP
WHERE  S.S# = SP.S#
```

Or:

```
SELECT DISTINCT S.*
FROM    S NATURAL JOIN SP
```

Not quite so straightforward, I think you'll agree. In fact, the SQL formulations effectively spell out the definition of the operation: The FROM clause (together with the WHERE clause, in the first formulation) does the join, and the SELECT clause does the projection. Given that, in practice, queries that need to do a join at all often really need to do a semijoin, it might be nice if SQL were to provide direct support for that operator, as **Tutorial D** does.

By the way, you can probably see that the query "Get suppliers who supply at least one part" can be thought of as asking for just those suppliers that *match* at least one shipment (as it were). **Tutorial D** therefore provides a more user friendly spelling for SEMIJOIN that directly reflects that perception by allowing the query to be expressed thus:

```
S MATCHING SP
```

In the rest of this chapter, I'll favor this latter style.

SEMIDIFFERENCE

If semijoin is in some ways more important than join, a similar remark applies to semidifference (also known as *semiminus*) as well, but with even more force; that is, queries that need to form a difference at all "almost always" really need to form a semidifference. Here's the definition: The *semidifference* between relations $r1$ and $r2$, in that order, is the difference between $r1$ and $r1$ MATCHING $r2$; that is, $r1$ SEMIMINUS $r2$ is equivalent to (and thus shorthand for) $r1$ MINUS ($r1$ MATCHING $r2$). As usual, $r1$ and $r2$ here aren't necessarily distinct.

By way of example, consider the query "Get suppliers who supply no parts at all" (in other words, suppliers who match no shipments at all; given the sample data of Fig. 11.1, the result contains just one tuple, for supplier S5). Note that this query is the complement, in a sense, of the one discussed in the previous section. Here's a **Tutorial D** formulation:

```
S SEMIMINUS SP
```

And here's an SQL analog:

```
SELECT DISTINCT S.*
FROM    S
EXCEPT
SELECT DISTINCT S.*
FROM    S, SP
WHERE   S.S# = SP.S#
```

Or:

```
SELECT DISTINCT S.*
FROM     S
EXCEPT
SELECT DISTINCT S.*
FROM     S NATURAL JOIN SP
```

As you can see, again the SQL formulations effectively spell out the definition of the operation.

As an aside, I remark that the DISTINCT specifications could safely have been omitted from the foregoing SQL "semidifference" formulations. However, they can't safely be omitted from the SQL "semijoin" formulations in the previous section! As I've written elsewhere [3], I think it's far too much trouble, in general, to expect the user to work out when it's safe to omit such specifications and when it isn't. For that reason, I prefer not even to think about it; instead, I always include DISTINCT specifications in my SQL queries, even when they're logically unnecessary.

> *Aside:* As an aside within an aside, as it were, let me admit that I've received a considerable amount of flak on the foregoing issue. For example, I made an essentially similar observation in reference [1], causing one reviewer to respond thus: "Those who really know SQL well will be shocked at the thought of coding SELECT DISTINCT by default." Well, maybe. In that same reference [1], I discuss the issue at some length, and if you're interested you might like to take a look at that discussion. *End of aside.*

Onward. Clearly, it would be nice if (as in the case of semijoin) SQL were to provide direct support for the operator, as **Tutorial D** does. *Note:* **Tutorial D** also provides a more user friendly spelling for SEMIMINUS that allows the foregoing query to be expressed thus:

```
S NOT MATCHING SP
```

Again, in the rest of this chapter I'll favor this latter style.

MORE ON SEMIJOIN

There are several more points that need to be made in connection with both semijoin and semidifference. I'll concentrate on semijoin in this section.

Observe first of all that while *r1* JOIN *r2* and *r2* JOIN *r1* are equivalent (that is, regular join is *commutative*), *r1* MATCHING *r2* and *r2* MATCHING *r1* are not equivalent, in general. To be specific, *r1* MATCHING *r2* yields a relation with the same attributes as *r1,* while *r2* MATCHING *r1* yields a relation with the same attributes as *r2.* Consider, for example, the logical difference between the expressions S MATCHING P and P MATCHING S:

- S MATCHING P yields suppliers who are in the same city as at least one part.

- By contrast, P MATCHING S yields parts that are in the same city as at least one supplier.

To repeat, *r1* MATCHING *r2* and *r2* MATCHING *r1* are not equivalent, in general. So the obvious question is: When exactly are they equivalent? And the answer is: When (and only when) relations *r1* and *r2* are of the same type—i.e., when (and only when) they have exactly the same attributes as each other. For example, the expressions (S{S#}) MATCHING (SP{S#}) and (SP{S#}) MATCHING (S{S#}) are equivalent.

Here are a few more obvious questions (answers are given in Appendix A):

- What happens if *r1* and *r2* aren't just of the same type but are in fact the same relation?

- Contrariwise, what happens if *r1* and *r2* have no attributes in common?

- Is there a relation that serves as an identity with respect to semijoin?

Next, as I'm sure you know, join is not only commutative, it's *associative*—i.e., *r1* JOIN (*r2* JOIN *r3*) is always equal to (*r1* JOIN *r2*) JOIN *r3*. By contrast, semijoin is not associative. For example:

- S MATCHING (SP MATCHING P) yields suppliers who supply at least one part (more precisely, suppliers who supply at least one of the parts that are supplied).

- By contrast, (S MATCHING SP) MATCHING P yields suppliers who supply at least one part and are in the same city as at least one of the parts that are supplied.

Next (*important!*), note that neither of the operators join and semijoin is a special case of the other, in general—i.e., some (in fact, most) joins aren't semijoins, and some (in fact, most) semijoins aren't joins, either. Thus, to spell the point out:

- S JOIN SP can't be expressed in terms of S, SP, and MATCHING (and nothing else).

- Likewise, S MATCHING SP can't be expressed in terms of S, SP, and JOIN (and nothing else).

However, there's a special case in which join does degenerate to semijoin—i.e., a special case in which the join is indeed a semijoin after all. To be specific, consider what happens to *r1* JOIN *r2* if every attribute of *r2* is also an attribute of *r1*. As I hope you can see, *r1* JOIN *r2* degenerates to *r1* MATCHING *r2* in this case (but only in this case). By way of example, consider the expression:

```
S JOIN ( SP { S# } )
```

Here *r1* is just suppliers and *r2* is the projection of shipments over S#; thus, every attribute of *r2* is indeed an attribute of *r1,* the result of the query is (again) suppliers who match at least one shipment, and the overall expression is clearly equivalent to S MATCHING (SP{S#}).

MORE ON SEMIDIFFERENCE

As we've seen, join and semijoin are related operators, but they're logically distinct (neither is a special case of the other). In the case of difference and semidifference, however, the operators aren't just "related"; rather, regular difference is a special case of semidifference ("all differences are semidifferences," you might say). To be specific, consider what happens to *r1* MINUS *r2* if each of *r1* and *r2* has exactly the same attributes as the other. As I hope you can see, *r1* MINUS *r2* degenerates to *r1* NOT MATCHING *r2* in this case (and only in this case). By way of example, consider the expression:

```
( S { S# } ) MINUS ( SP { S# } )
```

Here *r1* and *r2* are the projection of suppliers over S# and the projection of shipments over S#, respectively; thus, *r1* and *r2* do indeed have the same attributes, the result of the query is supplier numbers for suppliers who don't match any shipments at all, and the overall expression is clearly equivalent to (S{S#}) NOT MATCHING (SP{S#}).

It follows from the foregoing that, in a sense, semidifference is a more fundamental operation than difference (since the latter is just a special case of the former, while the converse is not true). *Exercise:* Which if any of the familiar algebraic properties (commutativity, etc.) apply to semidifference?

REFERENCES AND BIBLIOGRAPHY

1.   C. J. Date: *Database in Depth: Relational Theory for Practitioners*. Sebastopol, Calif.: O'Reilly Media Inc. (2005).

2.   C. J. Date: *The Relational Database Dictionary*. Sebastopol, Calif.: O'Reilly Media Inc. (2006).

3.   C. J. Date: "Frequently Asked Questions" (elsewhere in this book).

APPENDIX A: ANSWERS TO EXERCISES

Several inline exercises were embedded in the body of this chapter. This appendix repeats (or paraphrases, in most cases) the text of those exercises and offers some answers.

Exercise: In the expression *r1* MATCHING *r2*, what happens if *r1* and *r2* aren't just of the same type but are in fact the same relation?

Answer: The result is equal to *r1;* i.e., the expression degenerates to just *r1*.

Exercise: In the expression *r1* MATCHING *r2*, what happens if *r1* and *r2* have no attributes in common?

Answer: Again the result is equal to *r1;* i.e., the expression degenerates to just *r1*.

Exercise: Is there a relation that serves as an identity with respect to semijoin?

Answer: (a) Let relation *r* be of type *T*, and let *u* be the universal relation of type *T* [2]. Then *r* MATCHING *u* is equal to *r* for all such relations *r*. (b) More generally, *r* MATCHING TABLE_DEE is equal to *r* for all possible relations *r*. In both cases (a) and (b), however, the "identity relation" in question—*u* for (a), TABLE_DEE for (b)—is a right identity but not a left identity. For example, TABLE_DEE MATCHING *r* isn't equal to *r*, in general, though *r* MATCHING TABLE_DEE is. *Subsidiary exercise:* When *is* TABLE_DEE MATCHING *r* equal to *r?*

Exercise: Which if any of the familiar algebraic properties (commutativity, etc.) apply to semidifference?

Answer: Almost none of them applies. However, TABLE_DUM serves as a right identity—i.e., *r* NOT MATCHING TABLE_DUM is equal to *r* for all possible relations *r*.

Chapter 12

The Theory of Bags:

An Investigative Tutorial

Bags of mystery, bags of trouble
Bags just mean you're seeing double
The same thing there and over here—
How can *this be a good idea?*

—Anon.: *Where Bugs Go*

A **bag** (also known as a *multiset*) can be thought of, loosely, as "a set with duplicate elements." More precisely, a bag can be defined as an unordered collection of elements with the property that the same element can appear any number of times: for example, the collection (3,3,2,4,3,4), or equivalently the collection (2,3,3,3,4,4). The number of times a given element appears in a given bag is called, not altogether appropriately [5], the *multiplicity* of that element with respect to that bag; for example, in the bag (2,3,3,3,4,4), the multiplicities of 2, 3, and 4 are one, three, and two, respectively. Observe that a bag in which the multiplicity of every element is one is a set; in other words, all sets are bags, but most bags aren't sets.

> *Aside:* Observe that the foregoing definitions rely crucially on the assumption that there's a way to count duplicates—for otherwise, how can we say that, e.g., the multiplicity of element 4 in the example is two? Personally, I find this assumption rather suspect; indeed, I'm on record elsewhere (see, e.g., reference [3]) as claiming that it effectively means that bags must be defined in terms of sets, and hence that bag theory is really nothing more than a particular application of set theory. For the purposes of this chapter, however, I propose to overlook these possible objections. *End of aside.*

My aim in the rest of this chapter is to explore some of the formal properties of bags. In particular, I want to see if it's possible to define an algebra of bags, and if so what such an algebra might look like.

Before going any further, perhaps I should ask: Why would we want to define an algebra of bags, anyway? One general answer to this question is that such an algebra, if it could be defined, would provide a rigorous body of knowledge (theorems, etc.) that could be useful in a variety of contexts—e.g., in the design of a bag-based query language. A more specific answer is that it would provide a set of identities, or equivalences, that could be used as a basis for implementing such a language—in particular, for expression transformation ("query rewrite") and optimization purposes. There might be other answers too.

The plan of the chapter is as follows. Following these introductory remarks, the next two sections consider certain familiar operations from set theory—inclusion, union, intersection, and so on—and show

how they can be extended to deal with bags as well as sets. The next section then discusses two operations, union plus and intersection star, that apply to bags but not to sets. Then there's a section discussing the well known restriction operation, followed by one examining the question of whether we can define any kind of "bag complement" operation. Finally, there's a section reviewing the algebra of sets, an outline of an analogous algebra of bags (including a discussion of certain implications of that algebra), and a brief "Concluding Remarks" section.

CONTAINMENT AND INCLUSION

Let b and e be a bag and an element, respectively; then the boolean expression "$e \in b$" evaluates to TRUE if and only if element e appears at least once in bag b. That expression "$e \in b$" can be read as "e is contained in b," or "e appears in b," or "e is a member of b," or simply "e is in b." The operator "$\in$" is the *containment* operator.

Now let $b1$ and $b2$ be bags, and let element e appear exactly $n1$ times in $b1$ and exactly $n2$ times in $b2$ ($n1 \geq 0$, $n2 \geq 0$). Then bag $b1$ is included in bag $b2$ ("$b1 \; \|\leq\| \; b2$")[1] if and only if $n1 \leq n2$ for all such elements e. Further points arising from this definition:

- Bag $b2$ includes bag $b1$ ("$b2 \; \|\geq\| \; b1$") if and only if $b1$ is included in $b2$.

- The operator "$\|\leq\|$" is the *inclusion* operator. (Note that it is indeed "$\|\leq\|$", not "$\|\geq\|$", that's the inclusion operator as such, though in a sense the choice as to which of the two we assign that label to is a little arbitrary. The same is true in set theory, of course.)

- Bags $b1$ and $b2$ are equal ("$b1 = b2$") if and only if each is included in the other.

- Bag $b1$ is properly included in bag $b2$ ("$b1 \; \|<\| \; b2$") if and only if $b1$ is included in $b2$ and $b1 \neq b2$.

- Bag $b2$ properly includes bag $b1$ ("$b2 \; \|>\| \; b1$") if and only if $b1$ is properly included in $b2$.

If bag $b1$ is included in bag $b2$, then $b1$ is a subbag of $b2$ and $b2$ is a superbag of $b1$. If the inclusion in question is proper, then $b1$ and $b2$ are a proper subbag and a proper superbag, respectively; otherwise they're an improper subbag and an improper superbag, respectively.

Finally, let b be a bag; then the *power set* of b, $P(b)$, is the set of all subbags of b. Note that $P(b)$ is indeed a set and not just a bag.

Examples: Let $b1$ and $b2$ be the bags (3,3,4) and (2,3,3,3,4,4), respectively. Then $b1$ is a proper subbag of $b2$, $b2$ is a proper superbag of $b1$, and $P(b1)$ is the following set:

---

1. For typographical reasons, in this chapter I use the symbols $\|\geq\|$, $\|\leq\|$, $\|>\|$, and $\|<\|$ to mean, respectively, "includes," "is included in," "properly includes," and "is properly included in."

{ (), (3), (4), (3,3), (3,4), (3,3,4) }

Observe that the power set $P(b)$ of any bag b necessarily contains the empty bag, ().[1]

It's important to note that all of the concepts defined in this section so far for bags reduce to their set counterparts if the bags in question are in fact sets. In particular, it makes sense to use the same name *inclusion* for both the bag operator and the set operator—though I'll sometimes use a *bag* or *set* qualifier for emphasis—since we're only extending and generalizing the set operator, not redefining or overloading it. Analogous remarks apply to the containment operator "ϵ".

Now let s be a set of bags $\{a,b,c,...\}$; then the inclusion operator " $\|\leq\|$ " induces a *partial ordering* on s. To be specific, let a, b, and c be arbitrary elements (i.e., bags) in s. Then we have:

- $a \|\leq\| b$ or $b \|\leq\| a$ (or both, or possibly neither).

- *Reflexivity:* $a \|\leq\| a$.

- *Transitivity:* If $a \|\leq\| b$ and $b \|\leq\| c$, then $a \|\leq\| c$.

- *Antisymmetry:* If $a \|\leq\| b$ and $b \|\leq\| a$, then $a = b$.

The existence of this partial ordering is crucial to the goal of defining an algebra of bags, as we'll see later.

UNION, INTERSECTION, DIFFERENCE, AND PRODUCT

The familiar set theory operations union, intersection, difference, and product can all be generalized to apply to bags as well as sets. Again, let $b1$ and $b2$ be bags, and let element e appear exactly $n1$ times in $b1$ and exactly $n2$ times in $b2$ ($n1 \geq 0$, $n2 \geq 0$). Let Op denote one of the operations union, intersection, and difference, and let b be the bag obtained by applying Op to bags $b1$ and $b2$ (in that order, in the case of difference). Then element e appears exactly n times in b, where n is:

- $MAX(n1,n2)$ if Op is *union* (UNION)

- $MIN(n1,n2)$ if Op is *intersection* (INTERSECT)

- $MAX(n1-n2,0)$ if Op is *difference* (MINUS)

In no case does b contain any other elements.

Examples: Let $b1$ and $b2$ be the bags $(1,1,2,3,3)$ and $(2,3,3,3,4,4)$, respectively. Then the following expressions yield the indicated results:

---

1. Of course, the empty bag () and the empty set {} are identically equal to each other. For that reason, I'll feel free on occasion to use the expression "()" instead of "{}" to denote the empty set as well (but only in this chapter).

- *b1* UNION *b2* : (1,1,2,3,3,3,4,4)

- *b1* INTERSECT *b2* : (2,3,3)

- *b1* MINUS *b2* : (1,1)

- *b2* MINUS *b1* : (3,4,4)

Now let elements *e1* and *e2* appear exactly *n1* times in *b1* and exactly *n2* times in *b2,* respectively ($n1 \geq 0$, $n2 \geq 0$), and let *b* be the (cartesian) *product* of *b1* and *b2,* in that order. Then the pair $<e1,e2>$ appears exactly $n1*n2$ times in *b,* and *b* contains no other elements.

Example: Again let *b1* and *b2* be the bags (1,1,2,3,3) and (2,3,3,3,4,4), respectively, as in the union, intersection, and difference examples earlier. Then the bag *b1* TIMES *b2* contains exactly the following pairs:

$$<1,2>,<1,2>,<2,2>,<3,2>,<3,2>,$$
$$<1,3>,<1,3>,<2,3>,<3,3>,<3,3>,$$
$$<1,3>,<1,3>,<2,3>,<3,3>,<3,3>,$$
$$<1,3>,<1,3>,<2,3>,<3,3>,<3,3>,$$
$$<1,4>,<1,4>,<2,4>,<3,4>,<3,4>,$$
$$<1,4>,<1,4>,<2,4>,<3,4>,<3,4>$$

As in the case of inclusion, all of the operators defined in this section reduce to their set theory counterparts if the bags in question are in fact sets—i.e., we're only extending and generalizing the set operators, not redefining or overloading them—and so it makes sense to refer to those operators by their conventional set theory names. *Note:* Product in particular is included here purely for the record. It has little part to play in the discussions in the remainder of this chapter.

Identities

Several set theory laws concerning commutativity, associativity, and so on carry over to bags. The laws in question are sometimes described as *identities* or *equivalences;* they're also referred to more specifically as *laws of transformation*. This subsection lists some of the most important ones. I omit the proofs, since they're straightforward (usually involving nothing more than simple arithmetic on element multiplicities). *Notation:* I use *a, b, c,* ... to denote arbitrary bags. Also, for consistency with Chapter 10 I use "=" to mean "is identically equal to," though there's a strong argument that I should really be using the symbol "≡" instead (see Chapter 2).

- **Commutative laws:**

```
a. UNION b       =   b UNION a
a INTERSECT b    =   b INTERSECT a
```

■   **Associative laws:**

```
a UNION ( b UNION c )         =  ( a UNION b ) UNION c
a INTERSECT ( b INTERSECT c ) =  ( a INTERSECT b ) INTERSECT c
```

■   **Distributive laws:**

```
a UNION ( b INTERSECT c )
               =  ( a UNION b ) INTERSECT ( a UNION c )

a INTERSECT ( b UNION c )
               =  ( a INTERSECT b ) UNION ( a INTERSECT c )
```

■   **Idempotence laws:**

```
a UNION a     =  a
a INTERSECT a =  a
```

■   **Absorption laws:**

```
a UNION ( a INTERSECT b )  =  a
a INTERSECT ( a UNION b )  =  a
```

Points arising:

■   Union and intersection in particular are dyadic operations (the same is true for difference and product, of course, but the fact is irrelevant for present purposes). Since those operations are both commutative and associative, however, it's easy, and useful, to define N-adic versions of them for arbitrary $N > 0$. In particular, we can allow the case $N = 1$; the union or intersection of just one bag b is simply b.

■   In the case of union, we can even allow N to be zero; the union of no bags at all is the empty bag, (). For intersection, by contrast, N must be nonzero. *Note:* The situation is different in set theory; with sets, we can allow N to be zero for intersection as well as for union. For further explanation, see the section "What about Complement?" later.

There's one more law of transformation I want to consider here:

```
a INTERSECT b  =  a MINUS ( a MINUS b )
```

This one too is easily proved by simple arithmetic on element multiplicities. It's important because it shows that intersection isn't primitive—it can be defined in terms of difference (as indeed it can in set theory also, of course). I'll come back to this point at the end of the section immediately following.

UNION PLUS AND INTERSECTION STAR

Two further "set theory like" operations can be defined for bags. (I call them "set theory like," but they have no exact counterpart in set theory, except that intersection star does bear some resemblance to the join operation of the relational model.) I'll call them union plus and intersection star.[1] Let b be the bag obtained by applying one of these operations to bags $b1$ and $b2$, where once again element e appears exactly $n1$ times in $b1$ and exactly $n2$ times in $b2$ ($n1 \geq 0$, $n2 \geq 0$). Then element e appears exactly n times in b, where n is:

- $n1 + n2$ if Op is *union plus* (UNION+)

- $n1*n2$ if Op is *intersection star* (INTERSECT*)

In neither case does b contain any other elements.

Examples: Once again let $b1$ and $b2$ be the bags $(1,1,2,3,3)$ and $(2,3,3,3,4,4)$, respectively. Then the following expressions yield the indicated results:

- $b1$ UNION+ $b2$: $(1,1,2,2,3,3,3,3,3,4,4)$

- $b1$ INTERSECT* $b2$: $(2,3,3,3,3,3,3)$

I remark in passing that SQL supports union plus but calls it union (more precisely, "union all");[2] it doesn't support union—meaning union for bags as opposed to sets—at all. Nor does it support intersection star (at least, not directly). *Note:* I mention intersection star here just for the record; it has little part to play in the discussions in the remainder of this chapter.

Identities

It's obvious that union plus and intersection star are both commutative and associative and that each distributes over the other. It's also obvious that the idempotence and absorption laws do *not* apply. However, there's at least one additional law that merits discussion:

        a UNION b = (a MINUS b) UNION+ b

Once again the proof is trivial, and I'll omit it here. The reason this particular law is important, however, is that it shows that union isn't primitive—it can be defined in terms of difference and union

---

1. These names don't appear in the literature, but there doesn't seem to be any consensus in the literature on any other particular names either. Names that do appear in the literature include *bag sum* and *bag concatenation* (for union plus) and *bag product* (for intersection star).

2. Thus, union at least is overloaded, in SQL.

plus. Since we already know that intersection can be defined in terms of difference, it follows that the combination of union plus and difference provides all of the functionality of union and intersection. What's more, reference [1] shows that the converse isn't true; that is, (a) union plus can't be defined in terms of union, intersection, and difference, and (b) difference can't be defined in terms of union, intersection, and union plus. Among other things, therefore, a bag-based query language that supports union plus and difference will provide strictly more functionality, in a sense, than one that supports only union and intersection.

RESTRICTION

Restriction is another set theory operation that can easily and usefully be generalized to bags. Let $b1$ be a bag, and let x be a boolean expression with the property that it can be evaluated for a given element of $b1$ by examining just that element in isolation. Then the *restriction b1* WHERE x is a bag $b2$ defined as follows: Element e appears in $b2$ if and only if it appears in $b1$ and x evaluates to TRUE for e; moreover, if element e appears in $b2$ at all, then its multiplicity in $b2$ is equal to its multiplicity in $b1$.

Examples: Let $b1$ be the bag (1,2,2,2,4,4), and let e denote a typical element of $b1$. Then the following expressions yield the indicated results:

- $b1$ WHERE $e < 2$: (1)

- $b1$ WHERE $e = 2$: (2,2,2)

- $b1$ WHERE $e > 2$: (4,4)

- $b1$ WHERE $e > 4$: ()

- $b1$ WHERE NOT ($e < 2$) : (2,2,2,4,4)

Observe that, as these examples suggest, there's no way to restrict a given bag b in such a manner that some but not all appearances of a given element of b are retained in the result. (For this reason, in fact, reference [1] describes restriction as having *all-or-nothing semantics*.) As a consequence, not all subbags of a given bag b can be obtained by restriction, in general. For example, let $b = $ (1,2,2,2,4,4); then no subbag of b containing just one 4 and/or just one or two 2's can be obtained by restricting b. However, those subbags can be obtained by other means: in particular, by means of the difference operation. For example, let $c = $ (1,2,2,4); then the expression b MINUS c yields the subbag (2,4).

Aside: Once again there's no overloading here: Restriction as just defined (like union, intersection, and so forth as defined earlier) degenerates to regular set restriction if the bag being restricted is in fact a set. However, it would be possible to define further operations on bags of a restriction nature (thanks to Hugh Darwen for this observation). For example, we might define the operation $b1$ REDUCE (m) to return a bag $b2$ defined as follows: Element e appears in $b2$ only if it appears in $b1$, and its multiplicity in $b2$ is equal to MAX($n-m,0$) where n is its multiplicity in $b1$. For example, let $b1 = $ (1,2,2,2,4,4) and let $m = 1$; then $b2 = $ (2,2,4). Note, however, that this operation would necessarily be specific to bags as such—it wouldn't make much sense for sets. *End of aside.*

Identities

The following easily proved identities relate restriction to union, intersection, and difference:

- *b* WHERE (*x* OR *y*)   =   (*b* WHERE *x*) UNION (*b* WHERE *y*)

- *b* WHERE (*x* AND *y*)   =   (*b* WHERE *x*) INTERSECT (*b* WHERE *y*)

- *b* WHERE NOT (*x*)   =   *b* MINUS (*b* WHERE *x*)

- (*b* WHERE *x*) WHERE *y* = (*b* WHERE *y*) WHERE *x*

    =   *b* WHERE (*x* AND *y*)

WHAT ABOUT COMPLEMENT?

You might have noticed that I've said nothing so far about any kind of bag complement operation. The reason is as follows. In set theory, the complement of a given set is the set of all elements not appearing in the given set. But a moment's thought shows that the analogous concept for bags—"the bag of all elements not appearing in a given bag"—makes no sense; I mean, it isn't well defined (certainly it isn't *uniquely* defined). For example, suppose the only legal elements are integers in the range 1-5 inclusive, and let *b* be the bag (1,2,2,2,4,4). Then "the complement of *b*," if such a thing could be defined, would presumably contain the elements 3 and 5; but what would their multiplicities be? And mightn't it also contain one or more of the elements 1 or 2 or 4? If it does, then, again, what would their multiplicities be?

Another way to look at this issue is as follows. In set theory, we can define what's called *the universal set,* which is the set that contains all of the elements that are of interest in some given context. For example, suppose again that the only legal elements are integers in the range 1-5 inclusive; then the universal set is simply the set {1,2,3,4,5}—as indeed the assertion that "the only legal elements are integers in the range 1-5 inclusive" says, more or less explicitly. And it's the universal set notion that, in turn, allows us to define the complement of a given set: The complement of set *s* is just *u* MINUS *s,* where *u* is the universal set. But there's nothing in bag theory analogous to the universal set concept—i.e., there's no such thing as "the universal bag"—and hence there's no bag theory counterpart to the set theory expression *u* MINUS *s.*

Incidentally, the foregoing argument shows why *N* can't be zero for *N*-adic (bag) intersection. In set theory, the intersection of no sets at all is the universal set. Since there's no universal bag, however, it follows that there's no bag theory counterpart to the intersection of no sets at all—that is, the concept of "the intersection of no bags at all" isn't well defined. (Thus, there's an unpleasant asymmetry here between intersection and union. The consequences of this situation aren't immediately clear, but are probably undesirable.)

Because there's no bag complement, any set theory identity that appeals to the notion of set complement will fail to carry over to bags. To be more specific, the following identities (in which I'll use the symbols *u* and ¬*s* to denote the universal set and the complement of set *s*, respectively) apply to sets but not bags:

- **Involution law** *(for sets not bags):*

      ¬ (¬a) = a

- **Complementarity laws** *(for sets not bags):*

      a UNION (¬a)   = u
      a INTERSECT (¬a) = ()

- **De Morgan's Laws** *(for sets not bags):*

      ¬ (a UNION b)   = (¬a) INTERSECT (¬b)
      ¬ (a INTERSECT b) = (¬a) UNION (¬b)

Precisely because the foregoing identities don't hold for bags, certain further identities also fail to hold for bags, even though they do hold for sets. For example, it's easy to see that the following identity holds for sets:

      a MINUS (b UNION c) = (a MINUS b) MINUS c

But it doesn't hold for bags. For example, let *a, b,* and *c* be (1,2,2), (2), and (2), respectively. Then the left side evaluates to (1,2), but the right side evaluates to (1). *Note:* Perhaps I should point out, for what it's worth, that the identity would hold for bags if we were to replace UNION by UNION+.

I've shown that the concept of what might be called an "absolute" complement makes no sense for bags. However, it's possible to define a kind of *relative* complement—the complement, that is, of a bag *b* with respect to another bag *a*—*if and only if b is some restriction of a* (this condition is important). Here's the definition:

- Let *a* be a bag and let *b* be the restriction *a* WHERE *x* for some boolean expression *x*.

- Then the relative complement of *b* with respect to *a* is defined to be equal to *a* WHERE NOT(*x*), or equivalently to *a* MINUS *b*.

For example, let *a* be the bag (1,1,2,3,3,3,4,4,5,5,5), and let *x* be the boolean expression *e* > 2 AND *e* < 5 (where *e* denotes a typical element of *a*). Then *b* = *a* WHERE *x* = (3,3,3,4,4), and the relative complement of *b* with respect to *a* = *a* WHERE NOT(*x*) = *a* MINUS *b* = (1,1,2,5,5,5).

Note very carefully, however, that not all subbags of *a* have complements with respect to *a;* e.g., with *a* as in the foregoing example, the subbag (1,2,3,4,5) doesn't. To spell the point out, subbag *b* of *a* has a complement with respect to *a* if and only if *b* is a restriction of *a,* in which case the complement in question is also a restriction of *a* (see the remark in the previous section regarding "all-or-nothing semantics").

Identities

Adjusting notation slightly, let *u* be a bag, and let *a* and *b* be restrictions of *u;* further, let's agree to use the expression ¬*a* as shorthand for the relative complement *u* MINUS *a* if *u* is understood. Then it's easy to show that the following identities hold:

- **Involution law** *(bag theory, "¬" = relative complement):*

    ¬ (¬*a*)   =   *a*

- **Complementarity laws** *(bag theory, "¬" = relative complement):*

    a UNION (¬*a*)   =   *u*
    a INTERSECT (¬*a*)   =   ()

- **De Morgan's Laws** *(bag theory, "¬" = relative complement):*

    ¬ (*a* UNION *b*)   =   (¬*a*) INTERSECT (¬*b*)
    ¬ (*a* INTERSECT *b*)   =   (¬*a*) UNION (¬*b*)

To repeat, however, I must stress that in these identities:

- Bags *a* and *b* aren't arbitrary bags but are, specifically, restrictions of the given bag *u*.

- The expression ¬*a* doesn't denote the *absolute* complement of *a* (since no such notion exists); rather, it denotes the relative complement of *a* with respect to *u*.

THE ALGEBRA OF SETS

I've now covered as many of the basic ideas of bag theory as I mean to in the present chapter. Now I want to investigate the possibility of defining a bag algebra. In order to do so, let me first briefly summarize, as a point of departure as it were, just what it is that constitutes the algebra of *sets*. (The following text is adapted from material in Chapter 10.)

   The algebra of sets is in fact a *boolean* algebra. Let *a, b,* and *c* be arbitrary subsets of some given set *u*—equivalently, let *a, b,* and *c* be arbitrary elements of the power set $P(u)$—and let "$\|\leq\|$" denote set inclusion. Then the formal system consisting of $P(u)$, "$\|\leq\|$", and the set theory union, intersection, and difference operators is a boolean algebra because it satisfies the following 14 requirements:

1.   **Closure:** *a* UNION *b* and *a* INTERSECT *b* both yield elements of $P(u)$.

2. **Commutativity:**

   ```
   a UNION b      =   b UNION a
   a INTERSECT b  =   b INTERSECT a
   ```

3. **Associativity:**

   ```
   a UNION ( b UNION c )          =   ( a UNION b ) UNION c
   a INTERSECT ( b INTERSECT c )  =   ( a INTERSECT b ) INTERSECT c
   ```

4. **Distributivity:**

   ```
   a UNION ( b INTERSECT c )
                   =   ( a UNION b ) INTERSECT ( a UNION c )

   a INTERSECT ( b UNION c )
                   =   ( a INTERSECT b ) UNION ( a INTERSECT c )
   ```

5. **Identities:**

   ```
   a UNION o      =   a
   a INTERSECT u  =   a
   ```

   Note: Here and elsewhere in this section I use *o* to denote the empty set. Also, the term *identities* in this context refers not to the fact that the expressions on either side of the equals sign are identically equal to one another but, rather, to the fact that *o* is the identity value with respect to union and *u* is the identity value with respect to intersection. See reference [4] for further discussion.

6.
   ```
   a UNION u      =   u
   a INTERSECT o  =   o
   ```

7. **Involution:**

   ```
   ¬ ( ¬a )  =   a
   ```

   Note: Here and elsewhere in this section I use "¬" to denote the (absolute) set complement operation; that is, ¬*a* = *u* MINUS *a*.

8.
   ```
   ¬o  =  u
   ¬u  =  o
   ```

9. **Complementarity:**

    ```
    a UNION ( ¬a )   =   u
    a INTERSECT ( ¬a )   =   o
    ```

    Also, if a UNION $b = u$ and a INTERSECT $b = o$, then $b = \neg a$.

10. If a UNION $b = a$ for all a, then $b = o$; if a INTERSECT $b = a$ for all a, then $b = u$.

11. **Idempotence:**

    ```
    a UNION a       =   a
    a INTERSECT a   =   a
    ```

12. **Absorption:**

    ```
    a UNION ( a INTERSECT b )   =   a
    a INTERSECT ( a UNION b )   =   a
    ```

13. **De Morgan:**

    ```
    ¬ ( a UNION b )       =   ( ¬a ) INTERSECT ( ¬b )
    ¬ ( a INTERSECT b )   =   ( ¬a ) UNION ( ¬b )
    ```

14. **Consistency:** The following three statements are all equivalent:

    - $a \; \| \leq \| \; b.$

    - a UNION $b = b.$

    - a INTERSECT $b = a.$

This concludes the definition. Note that the various laws, or requirements, aren't all independent (but it's useful to state them all explicitly nevertheless). Note too that many of the laws have well established names, but a few of them don't.

AN ALGEBRA OF BAGS

As the previous section shows, the algebra of sets is defined in terms of the power set $P(u)$ of some given set u, together with certain operators (set inclusion in particular). So the obvious place to start, if we want to try to define an analogous algebra for bags, is with the power set $P(u)$ of some given bag u, together with certain operators (bag inclusion in particular). Given this context:

- We know from the section "Union, Intersection, Difference, and Product" that the commutativity, associativity, distributivity, idempotence, and absorption laws are satisfied.

- However, we also know from the section "What about Complement?" that the involution and complementarity laws and De Morgan's laws are *not* satisfied. (As a consequence, law number 8 isn't satisfied either.)

It's immediate, therefore, that the power set $P(u)$ of the given bag u together with the union, intersection, and inclusion operators do not form a boolean algebra, and in a way that's all that needs to be said. However, it's instructive to take a slightly closer look at those of the 14 requirements that are satisfied (in addition to the ones already mentioned, that is), and I will. The following points are keyed to the laws, or requirements, as listed in the previous section.

1. **Closure:** Both a UNION b and a INTERSECT b yield elements of $P(u)$. (Note, however, that UNION+ and INTERSECT* do *not* necessarily yield elements of $P(u)$; for example, neither u UNION+ u nor u INTERSECT* u is such an element.)

5. **Identities:** The identity with respect to UNION is the empty bag o; the identity with respect to INTERSECT is the given bag u. *Note:* Here and elsewhere in this section I use o to denote the empty bag.

6. a UNION $u = u$; a INTERSECT $o = o$.

10. If a UNION $b = a$ for all a, then $b = o$; if a INTERSECT $b = a$ for all a, then $b = u$.

14. **Consistency:** The following statements are equivalent:

   - $a \parallel \leq \parallel b$.

   - a UNION $b = b$.

   - a INTERSECT $b = a$.

Despite the somewhat negative tenor of our conclusions so far, it's still possible to define a boolean algebra for bags, but the algebra in question is strictly less powerful, in a sense, than its counterpart for sets. The key is to define it, not in terms of arbitrary elements of the power set $P(u)$ of the given bag u, but in terms of just those elements that are (bag) restrictions of u. Thus, let b be a bag. Then the *restriction set*[1] of b, $R(b)$, is the set of all restrictions of b—that is, the set of all subbags of b that can be

---

1. Not the best term, perhaps, but it's hard to come up with a better one that's equally succinct. (I should add that the term is my own invention; there doesn't seem to be a standard term for this concept in the literature.)

obtained from *b* by means of the restriction operator as defined earlier in this chapter. For example, let *b* be the bag (2,3,3,3,4,4); then *R*(*b*) is the following set:

{ (), (2), (3,3,3), (4,4), (2,3,3,3), (2,4,4), (3,3,3,4,4), (2,3,3,3,4,4) }

Note that *R*(*b*) is indeed a set and not just a bag.

It's easy to see, then, that the formal system consisting of *R*(*u*), " $\| \le \|$ ", and the bag theory union, intersection, and difference operators is a boolean algebra, because it does satisfy all 14 of the requirements as listed in the previous section. So that formal system can indeed be described as an algebra of bags, and it can be used as a basis for (e.g.) language design, "query rewrite," and so forth.

That being said, there are still some problems. First of all, the laws of that algebra, and logical consequences of those laws, apply only to bags that are restrictions of the given bag *u*. If a query language provides any means of expressing bags that aren't such restrictions, then the algebra won't apply to them. This fact suggests several possibilities, all of them undesirable to a degree:

- The query language could be subject to certain rules, syntactic or semantic or both, that might be hard to explain, remember, justify, apply, and enforce. Imagine, for example, a rule that says that the bag literal "(2,3,3,3)" is legal but the bag literal "(2,2,3,3)" isn't (because the first denotes a bag that is a restriction of the given bag *u* but the second doesn't); or a rule that says, in effect, that some union plus invocations are legal but others aren't, for essentially similar reasons. How usable would such a system be?

- The implementation might perform certain expression transformations (in the interests of query optimization) that are in fact logically incorrect, thereby producing answers that are also incorrect. (Is it possible that this criticism applies to any of today's SQL products?)

- The implementation might be unable to tell whether a given transformation is legal and so decide to avoid it (even when it would have been logically correct), thereby delivering worse performance than might (or should) have been achievable.

- In particular, the implementation might be unable to tell whether the bags it's dealing with are in fact sets, and might thus be unable to apply the optimizations that derive from the more powerful algebra of sets.[1]

Second, the very notion of "the given bag *u*" raises serious issues in any case. In the set theory context, every set we ever have to deal with is some subset of a certain universal set, *u*. And the concept of that universal set *u* is well defined and easy to understand: It's simply the set of all legal elements (sometimes called *the universe of discourse*). In the bag theory context, by contrast, every bag we ever have to deal with is, specifically, some bag restriction—not just some arbitrary subbag—of the given bag *u*. (I'm assuming here that we do want to stay in the realm to which the bag algebra applies, of course.)

---

1. In practice many SQL users do indeed, and sensibly, abide by a "no duplicates" discipline, even in today's systems, and hence suffer from exactly this problem [2].

So what exactly is that given bag *u?* Clearly it has to contain all legal elements—but once again we have to ask: with what multiplicities? Consider some specific element *e;* suppose the multiplicity of that element in *u* is *n.* Then *every bag we ever have to deal with in which e appears at all will have to contain exactly n appearances of e.* In other words, we don't just have to impose an upper limit on the number of duplicate appearances of *e* that can ever appear in any bag—we actually have to impose a lower limit as well! (A lower limit that applies if *e* actually appears, that is; it's always possible for *e* not to appear at all, of course.)

An obvious question is: What are the implications of all of the foregoing for the language SQL? Well, since SQL tables contain (in general) not sets but bags of rows, everything I've been saying about bags in general applies to those bags of rows in particular. Because those bags are indeed bags of rows as such, however, there are quite a few more specific points that can be made regarding the "algebra"—if such a thing can be said to exist—underlying SQL. I've discussed this issue in some detail elsewhere in this book, however (in Chapter 10 to be specific). Here I'd just like to make a few additional points:

- First, I remind you that SQL supports union plus but not union. I remind you further than union can't be simulated by means of the other "set theory like" operators. Whatever else might be said about it, therefore, it's certainly the case that SQL's bags have a hole in them, as it were. (Sorry about that. I couldn't resist it.)

- Second, SQL doesn't insist that all bags be restrictions of some given bag *u. Au contraire,* it allows a given row to appear within a given table an arbitrary number of times (barring integrity constraints to the contrary, of course). As a consequence, the ability of the implementation to perform "query rewrite" optimization is severely curtailed. An example illustrating some of the negative implications of this state of affairs is discussed in detail in reference [2], pages 48-52, also in reference [3].

- Third, all of the operations on bags I've been discussing in this chapter rely, obviously enough, on the ability to tell whether two elements *e1* and *e2* are equal (i.e., are really one and the same). In the SQL case, of course, those elements are rows ... and, for a variety of different reasons (some of which are documented in the appendix to reference [4]), SQL *doesn't* provide a proper mechanism for telling whether two rows are one and the same! The implications of this (to me) staggering omission on the part of SQL I'll leave as something for you to meditate on.

CONCLUDING REMARKS

In this chapter, I've investigated the question of whether the various familiar set theory operations—inclusion, union, intersection, and so on—can be cleanly extended or generalized to apply to bags. The answer is a partial yes; however, the formal system that results is not a proper boolean algebra. In addition, I've shown that, by imposing certain limits on the bags that can be treated, it is indeed possible to define a proper boolean algebra for bags after all; but it's not at all clear whether those limits would be acceptable in practice. All in all, I believe the investigations of this chapter serve only to bolster my long held belief that (as common parlance has it) "duplicates are bad news."

ACKNOWLEDGMENTS

I'd like to acknowledge my heavy debt to reference [1], by Joseph Albert, on which much of the formal material in the present chapter is based. I've been complaining about bags as opposed to sets for many years, but it was reading Albert's paper that persuaded me to try and get my thoughts on the subject into some kind of order. I'd also like to thank Hugh Darwen for helpful comments on an earlier draft.

REFERENCES AND BIBLIOGRAPHY

1.   Joseph Albert: "Algebraic Properties of Bag Data Types," Proc. 17th Int. Conf. on Very Large Data Bases, Barcelona, Spain (September 1991).

2.   C. J. Date: *Database in Depth: Relational Theory for Practitioners*. Sebastopol, Calif.: O'Reilly Media, Inc. (2005).

3.   C. J. Date: "Double Trouble, Double Trouble," in *Date on Database: Writings 2000-2006*. Berkeley, Calif.: Apress (2006).

4.   C. J. Date: "Some Operators Are More Equal than Others" (Chapter 2 in this book).

5.   C. J. Date: "All for One, One for All" (Chapter 7 in this book).

LOGIC AND *THE THIRD MANIFESTO*

The Third Manifesto (the *Manifesto* for short) is a proposal by Hugh Darwen and myself, solidly grounded in classical two-valued logic, for a foundation for data and database management systems (DBMSs). Like Codd's original papers on the relational model, it can be seen as an abstract, logical blueprint for the design of a DBMS. It consists in essence of a rigorous set of principles, stated in the form of a series of prescriptions and proscriptions, that we—i.e., Hugh and myself—require adherence to on the part of a hypothetical database programming language that we call **D**. The various prescriptions and proscriptions are described in detail in our book *Databases, Types, and the Relational Model: The Third Manifesto,* 3rd edition (Addison-Wesley, 2006), which I'll refer to in the remainder of this introduction as "the *Manifesto* book."

Now, any serious scientific endeavor is quite properly the subject of careful scrutiny and questioning, and the *Manifesto* and its language **D** are no exception in this regard. Indeed, some of the improvements we've been able to make over the years have been the direct result of criticisms we've received at various times. In other cases, we've been able to show that the criticisms were invalid for some reason; in still others, the jury is still out, in the sense that it's not yet clear whether changes are needed or not. The chapters that follow have to do with criticisms that fall at least partly into this third category. Most of the criticisms in question arose in the course of a private correspondence in late 2005 and early 2006 between Hugh and two other parties (deliberately not named here). In essence, our critics claimed that:

- **D** permits the formulation of undecidable (because paradoxical) expressions.

- **D** is required to be computationally complete.

- **D** is required to support relation variables (relvars) and relational assignment.

Let me say immediately that the second and third of these claims are certainly true (at least, they're true so long as we assume, as the *Manifesto* book explicitly does, that the language **D** is imperative in style), and the first is probably true too (at least, it doesn't hurt to assume for the purposes of these introductory remarks that it is). In each case, therefore, what's at issue isn't so much the claim itself as it is the consequences of that claim. I've addressed the three claims in Chapters 13, 14, and 15, respectively:

13.   Gödel, Russell, Codd: A Recursive Golden Crowd

14.   And Now for Something Completely Computational

15.   To Be Is to Be a Value of a Variable

Please understand that these chapters aren't necessarily the last word on the subject; they're merely my own best shot at responding to the criticisms (in particular, at bringing various relevant issues to the surface, as it were, so that they can be carefully examined). The chapters are somewhat interrelated; however, I've written them in such a way as to allow each to stand on its own—partly because I think the issues can be treated separately to some degree but also, and more importantly, because I think it makes the arguments less indigestible than might otherwise be the case. However, I have to warn you that this decision on my part does mean the chapters include a small amount of overlap.

Chapter 16 is a little different; here the debate is not so much between external critics and ourselves as it is between Hugh and myself. The *Manifesto* book includes an appendix on the subject of view updating. However, view updating is a topic on which Hugh's views and mine (pun intended) aren't totally in agreement, and that appendix contains both a set of specific proposals by myself and a set of criticisms of those proposals by Hugh. Chapter 16, then, is a further attempt on my part to explain, and perhaps improve, the logical arguments that (I believe) support my proposals.

There are a couple more preliminary remarks I need to make in this introduction. The first has to do with **Tutorial D** (which has already appeared ubiquitously in earlier parts of this book, of course) and how it relates to the language **D**. The name **D** is meant to be generic—it refers generically to any language that conforms to the principles laid down in the *Manifesto*. Thus, there could be any number of distinct languages all qualifying as a valid **D**. **Tutorial D** is intended to be one such; it's defined, more or less formally, in the *Manifesto* book itself, and it's used throughout that book and elsewhere as a basis for examples. Unfortunately, however, our critics often don't properly distinguish between **D** and **Tutorial D,** even though there's a clear logical difference between the two. As a result, it's sometimes hard to tell whether a given criticism is aimed at the *Manifesto* in general or at **Tutorial D,** considered as a specific and perhaps flawed attempt at defining a **D,** in particular—a state of affairs that can make it hard to respond properly, sometimes, to the criticism in question.

As for the second of my preliminary remarks, I'll begin with a lightly edited extract from the *Manifesto* book itself:

> We must stress that what we are *not* doing is proposing some kind of "new" or "extended" relational model. Rather, we're concerned with what might be called the "classical" version of that model; we've tried to provide as careful and accurate a description of that classical model as we possibly can. It's true that we've taken the opportunity to dot a few *i*'s and cross a few *t*'s (i.e., to perform a few minor tidying activities here and there); however, the model as we describe it departs in no essential respects from Codd's original vision as documented in [his earliest relational papers] ... The ideas of the *Manifesto* are in no way intended to supersede those of the relational model, nor do they do so; rather, they use the ideas of the relational model as a base on which to build ... We see our *Manifesto* as being very much in the spirit of Codd's original work and continuing along the path he originally laid down. We're interested in evolution, not revolution.

The reason I quote this passage here, at length, is because of a phenomenon we've observed in certain criticisms of our work: namely, a tendency to complain that something we propose conflicts with something in Codd's own writings—presumably with the implication that what we're proposing must therefore be wrong, ipso facto. We reject the existence of such conflict as adequate justification for criticism, and we reject the presumed implication. Our admiration for Codd's genius in inventing the relational model in the first place, and for the extraordinary series of papers he wrote on the subject in the years 1969-1974, is second to none. However, it doesn't follow that we agree with all of Codd's relational writings unreservedly, and indeed we don't. Thus, there are indeed aspects of the *Manifesto* where our ideas depart from Codd's—not many, I hasten to add, but some. Support for nulls is a case in point; Codd required it (albeit not in the earliest of his relational papers), but the *Manifesto* categorically rejects it.

Chapter 13

Gödel, Russell, Codd:

A Recursive Golden Crowd

A paradox? A paradox!
A most ingenious paradox!

—W. S. Gilbert

This chapter is a response to certain criticisms that have been made of (a) *The Third Manifesto*—see reference [6]—and (b) the language **Tutorial D,** which is used in reference [6] to illustrate *Third Manifesto* ideas. The criticisms in question appear in reference [1] and can be summarized thus: *The Third Manifesto* in general, and **Tutorial D** in particular, both permit the formulation of expressions that are paradoxical, and hence undecidable.

THE PARADOX OF EPIMENIDES

Consider the following example:

- Let p be the predicate "There are no true instantiations of predicate p." Assume for now that p is indeed a valid predicate (I'll examine this assumption in the next section); then in fact it's not only a predicate but a proposition, because it has no parameters.

- Let r be the relation corresponding to p (i.e., the relation whose body contains all and only those tuples that represent true instantiations of p). Since p has no parameters, r has no attributes (i.e., it's of degree zero), and so it must be either TABLE_DEE or TABLE_DUM—where, just to remind you, TABLE_DEE is the unique relation with no attributes and just one tuple (the 0-tuple), and TABLE_DUM is the unique relation with no attributes and no tuples at all [2].

- Suppose r is TABLE_DEE. Then the interpretation (of the sole tuple in r) is that p is true—in which case, by definition, there are no true instantiations of p, and r shouldn't contain any tuples after all (i.e., it should be TABLE_DUM).

- Conversely, suppose r is TABLE_DUM. Then the interpretation (of the fact that there aren't any tuples in r) is that p is false—in which case, by definition, there must be at least one (actually, exactly one) true instantiation of p, and r should therefore contain at least one (actually, exactly one) tuple after all (i.e., it should be TABLE_DEE).

Of course, you've probably realized that this example is basically just the well known Paradox of

Epimenides ("This statement is false") in relational form. As you can surely also see, the root of the problem is the self reference: Predicate *p* refers to itself.

In case you're not comfortable with arguments that rely on the special relations TABLE_DEE and TABLE_DUM, let me give another example that illustrates the same general point. This example is a greatly simplified version of one originally due to David McGoveran and documented by myself in a couple of my early *DBP&D* columns [4]. Let *r* be a relation with a single attribute, N, of type INTEGER, and let the predicate for *r* be "The cardinality of *r* is N."[1] If *r* is empty, then the cardinality of *r* is zero, so the tuple *t* = TUPLE {N 0} should appear in *r*, so *r* shouldn't be empty after all. But then if tuple *t* = TUPLE {N 0} does appear in *r*, then *r* isn't empty and its cardinality clearly isn't zero, and so tuple *t* shouldn't appear in *r* after all. Again, therefore, we seem to have some kind of paradox on our hands.

DISCUSSION

For the remainder of the chapter I revert to the example involving TABLE_DEE and TABLE_DUM. Now, I said in connection with that example that *p* was a predicate, and in fact a proposition—but is it? By definition, a proposition is a statement that's unequivocally either true or false. (More precisely, it's a statement that makes an assertion that's unequivocally either true or false.) But *p* is clearly neither true nor false—because if it's true it's false and vice versa—so perhaps I was wrong to say it was a proposition, as I did in the previous section.

More fundamentally, though, I don't think we need argue over whether *p* is a predicate, or more specifically a proposition; what we do need to do is decide whether our formal system—whatever system we happen to be talking about—treats it as such. If it does, we have a problem. Note very carefully, however, that:

- The problem isn't a problem with **Tutorial D** specifically; in fact I don't see how it could be, since I didn't appeal to **Tutorial D** at all in the example.

- Nor is it a problem with *The Third Manifesto* specifically, since I didn't appeal the *Manifesto* at all in the example, either; all I did was appeal to the well known fact that any given predicate has a corresponding relation—namely, that relation whose body contains all and only those tuples that represent true instantiations of the predicate in question. (Equivalently, the corresponding relation is that relation whose body represents the *extension* of the predicate in question.)

- Nor is it a problem with the relational model specifically, for essentially the same reason.

---

1. If we call this predicate *q*, then it can equivalently be stated in the form "There are exactly N true instantiations of predicate *q*"—a formulation that serves to highlight both the self reference as such and the parallel with the previous example.

- Nor is it a problem that arises from the fact that *The Third Manifesto* requires **Tutorial D** (indirectly) to be computationally complete. I mention this point because the *Manifesto* has been criticized on precisely these grounds: the grounds, that is, that computational completeness "creates a language with logical expressions ... that are provably not decidable" [1]. Note carefully that I'm not saying, here, that this criticism is incorrect; I'm merely pointing out that the lack of decidability in the specific example under discussion, regarding whether relation *r* contains a tuple or not, doesn't seem to have anything to do with the fact that **Tutorial D** is computationally complete.

Rather, the problem, if problem there is, seems to be with *logic*. That is, either logic admits *p* as a predicate or it doesn't. If it does, there's a problem with logic. If it doesn't, then the problem with logic goes away, and hence the problems (if any) with the relational model, *The Third Manifesto,* and **Tutorial D** all go away too, a fortiori.

Note: As I understand it, Russell's theory of types had something to do with the idea that *p* and statements like it might need to be rejected as legal predicates. Even if so, however, this state of affairs doesn't invalidate my point, which is (to repeat) that if there's a problem in this area, then it's intrinsic—it isn't the fault of either *The Third Manifesto* or **Tutorial D** as such.

REMARKS ON TUTORIAL D

Now let me concentrate on **Tutorial D** specifically for a moment. It might be thought that the following is a formulation of the Paradox of Epimenides in **Tutorial D** terms (and if it is, it might therefore be thought that there is indeed a problem with **Tutorial D** specifically):

```
VAR R BASE RELATION { } KEY { } ;

CONSTRAINT EPIMENIDES COUNT ( R ) = 0 ;
```

More specifically, it might be thought that constraint EPIMENIDES is a formal expression of predicate *p* ("There are no true instantiations of predicate *p*," or equivalently "The number of true instantiations of predicate *p* is zero"). But it isn't. The reason it isn't is that The Closed World Assumption doesn't apply to constraints. The Closed World Assumption says (speaking rather loosely) that relvar *R* should contain all and only the tuples at a given time that satisfy the predicate for *R* at that time. But **Tutorial D** isn't aware, and can't be aware, of relvar predicates; all it can be aware of is relvar constraints. And there's no requirement—nor can there be a requirement, in general—that relvar *R* contain all and only the tuples at a given time that satisfy the constraints that apply to *R* at that time. So the fact that (in the example) relvar *R* is always empty does not of itself lead to any paradox.

I switch now to another tack. Here's another attempt to formulate the Paradox of Epimenides in **Tutorial D** terms:

```
VAR R BASE RELATION { } KEY { } ;

CONSTRAINT EPIMENIDES
    IF  COUNT ( R ) = 1  THEN  COUNT ( R ) = 0  AND
    IF  COUNT ( R ) = 0  THEN  COUNT ( R ) = 1 ;
```

Constraint EPIMENIDES here is logically equivalent to the following:

If there exists a tuple in relvar *R,* then relvar *R* must be empty, and if relvar *R* is empty, then there must exist a tuple in relvar *R.*

In other words, the constraint is a contradiction. (Please note that I'm using the term *contradiction* here in its formal logical sense. A contradiction in logic is a predicate whose every possible invocation is guaranteed to yield FALSE, regardless of what arguments are substituted for its parameters.) But if a constraint is a contradiction, then there is—or at least should be—no way to introduce it into the system in the first place! To be more precise, if some user attempts to define some new constraint for some database, the first thing the system must do is check that the database in question currently satisfies it. If that check fails, the constraint must obviously be rejected; and if that constraint is a contradiction, there's no way the database can currently satisfy it.

Of course, I'm assuming here for the sake of the argument that the system is indeed able to detect the fact that the database fails to satisfy some proposed constraint. What happens if this assumption is invalid is discussed, implicitly, in reference [5]. For completeness, however, I give here a brief sketch of what should happen in a properly designed system when some user attempts to define some new integrity constraint *C:*

1.   The system evaluates *C* against the current state of the database.

2.   If the result of that evaluation is TRUE, the system accepts *C* as a legitimate constraint and enforces it from this point forward (until such time as it's dropped again).

3.   If the result of that evaluation is FALSE, the system rejects *C* as not being legitimate at this time.

4.   If the evaluation fails to terminate after some prescribed period of time, a time-out occurs and the system rejects *C*—not because it knows it's not legitimate, but because it's too complex for the system to handle.

A REMARK ON *THE THIRD MANIFESTO*

Since it's essentially rather simple, the Paradox of Epimenides as such doesn't illustrate the point, but in general the idea of "predicates referencing predicates" corresponds in relational terms to relations having relation valued attributes (RVAs). In particular, a directly self referencing predicate—i.e., a predicate *p* that includes a direct, explicit reference to *p* itself—would correspond to a relation of some type *T* that has an attribute of that same type *T*. A type like *T* here is a *recursively defined* type, or just a recursive type for short. Reference [6] has the following to say on such matters (observe that the extract quoted covers indirectly defined recursive types as well as directly defined ones). *Note:* I've modified the text slightly, but I haven't changed the meaning in any important respect. You can ignore the reference to "possreps" if you don't know what they are.

It's an open question as to whether any relation type can be defined, either directly or indirectly, in terms of itself. More precisely, let RELATION{*H*} be a relation type, and let $S(1)$, $S(2)$, ... be a sequence of sets defined as follows:

$S(1) = \{\ t : t$ is the type of some attribute in $\{H\}\ \}$

$S(i) = \{\ t : t$ is the type of some component of some possrep for some scalar type, or the type of some attribute of some relation type, in $S(i-1)\ \}$
$(i > 1)$

If there exists some n ($n > 0$) such that RELATION{*H*} is a member of $S(n)$, then that type RELATION{*H*} is recursively defined. (This definition requires a slight extension if type inheritance is supported, but this detail needn't concern us here.) Thus, the open question is whether such recursively defined types should be permitted. We don't feel obliged to legislate on this question so far as our model is concerned; for the purposes of the present book, however, we follow *The Principle of Cautious Design* [3] and assume (where it makes any difference) that such types aren't permitted.

It seems to me that the arguments of the present chapter make it desirable to strengthen the foregoing position. Specifically, I now think that recursively defined relation types should be explicitly prohibited. Points arising from this position:

- Please understand that I'm not saying that relation valued attributes (RVAs) should be prohibited. I mention this point because *The Third Manifesto* has been criticized by many people for supporting RVAs, on the basis that they take us into the realms of second (or higher) order logic. This latter claim might be true, but nobody has yet demonstrated a specific problem that's caused by that fact (by that fact alone, that is)—at least, nobody has demonstrated such a problem to us, the authors of reference [6].[1]

- The extract quoted above from reference [6] says, to repeat, that for the purposes of that book we assume that recursively defined types aren't permitted. However, **Tutorial D** as described in that same book does permit such types to be defined (possibly indirectly). Here's a simple example:

```
VAR RX BASE RELATION { A1 INTEGER, A2 SAME_TYPE_AS ( RX ) } ;
```

Here's a slightly more complex example:

---

1. The issue of RVAs and higher order logic is explored further in the appendix to this book, "Frequently Asked Questions."

```
VAR RX BASE RELATION { A1 INTEGER, A2 SAME_TYPE_AS ( RY ) } ;

VAR RY BASE RELATION { A3 INTEGER, A4 SAME_TYPE_AS ( RX ) } ;
```

So perhaps **Tutorial D** as described in reference [6] does suffer from a lack of decidability. I presume, however, that the implementation could be designed to reject any attempt to make use of this "feature" by rejecting (preferably at compile time) any attempt to define, either directly or indirectly, a type *T* in terms of itself—much as the system should reject any attempt to define a constraint that can't be shown to evaluate to TRUE at the time it's defined.

REFERENCES AND BIBLIOGRAPHY

1.   Anon.: Private correspondence with Hugh Darwen (December 2005 - January 2006).

2.   Hugh Darwen: "The Nullologist in Relationland; *or,* Nothing Really Matters," in C. J. Date and Hugh Darwen, *Relational Database Writings 1989-1991*. Reading, Mass.: Addison-Wesley (1992).

3.   C. J. Date: "The Principle of Cautious Design," in C. J. Date and Hugh Darwen, *Relational Database Writings 1989-1991*. Reading, Mass.: Addison-Wesley (1992).

4.   C. J. Date: "How We Missed the Relational Boat" and "Answers to Puzzle Corner Problems (Installments 13-17)," in *Relational Database Writings 1991-1994*. Reading, Mass.: Addison-Wesley (1995).

5.   C. J. Date: "And Now for Something Completely Computational" (Chapter 15 in this book).

6.   C. J. Date and Hugh Darwen: *Databases, Types, and the Relational Model: The Third Manifesto* (3rd edition). Boston, Mass.: Addison-Wesley (2006).

Chapter 14

To Be Is to Be

a Value of a Variable

If we want things to stay as they are, things will have to change.
—Giuseppe di Lampedusa

"Change" is scientific, "progress" is ethical;
change is indubitable, whereas progress is a matter of controversy.
—Bertrand Russell

In reference [1], two writers, referred to herein as *Critics A and B*, criticize *The Third Manifesto* for its support for relation variables and relational assignment. This chapter is a response to that criticism. Readers are expected to be familiar with the following concepts and terminology:

- A relation variable (relvar for short) is a variable whose permitted values are relation values (relations for short).

- Relational assignment is an operation by which some relation *r* is assigned to some relvar *R*.

Reference [14] explains these notions in detail, using the language **Tutorial D** as a basis for examples.

WHY WE WANT RELVARS

To repeat, the term *relvar* is short for relation variable. It was coined by Hugh Darwen and myself in reference [9], the first published version of *The Third Manifesto;* Codd's first papers on the relational model [3-4] used the term *time-varying relation* instead, but "time-varying relations" are just relvars by another name. Of course, we don't claim to be the first to recognize the logical difference between relation values and relation variables (relations and relvars for short); however, we do believe we were the first to draw wide attention to that difference. *Note:* Reference [2], which predated the first version of *The Third Manifesto* by several years, also clearly distinguished between relations and relvars (it called them tables and table variables, respectively). However, it did so only as a direct consequence of comments by myself on an earlier draft, which didn't.

We believe further that relvars and the related notion of relational assignment are essential if we're to be able to update the database. Note that variables and assignment go hand in hand (we can't have one without the other)—to be a variable is to be assignable to, to be assignable to is to be a variable. Note further that "assignable to" and "updatable" mean exactly the same thing. Hence, to object to relvars is to object to relational updating; equivalently, to object to relational updating is to object to relvars.

Perhaps a little additional explanation is needed here. Most people, if they think about relational updating at all, probably think about the conventional INSERT, DELETE, and UPDATE operators, not about relational assignment as such—especially as SQL in particular doesn't support relational assignment (though it does support INSERT, DELETE, and UPDATE, of course). But INSERT, DELETE, and UPDATE are all in the final analysis just shorthand for certain relational assignments. For example, consider the usual suppliers-and-parts database (see Fig. 14.1 for a set of sample values).

S

S#	SNAME	STATUS	CITY
S1	Smith	20	London
S2	Jones	10	Paris
S3	Blake	30	Paris
S4	Clark	20	London
S5	Adams	30	Athens

P

P#	PNAME	COLOR	WEIGHT	CITY
P1	Nut	Red	12.0	London
P2	Bolt	Green	17.0	Paris
P3	Screw	Blue	17.0	Oslo
P4	Screw	Red	14.0	London
P5	Cam	Blue	12.0	Paris
P6	Cog	Red	19.0	London

SP

S#	P#	QTY
S1	P1	300
S1	P2	200
S1	P3	400
S1	P4	200
S1	P5	100
S1	P6	100
S2	P1	300
S2	P2	400
S3	P2	200
S4	P2	200
S4	P4	300
S4	P5	400

Fig. 14.1: The suppliers-and-parts database—sample values

Given this database, the **Tutorial D** INSERT statement

```
INSERT SP RELATION
    { TUPLE { S# S#('S3'), P# P#('P1'), QTY QTY(150) },
      TUPLE { S# S#('S5'), P# P#('P1'), QTY QTY(500) } } ;
```

is basically[1] just shorthand for the relational assignment

---

1. The reason I say "basically" is that the assignment as shown implies that an attempt to insert a tuple that's already present is not an error. If we wanted an exception to be raised in such a situation, the UNION in the expansion would have to be replaced by D_UNION (see Chapter 16).

```
SP := ( SP ) UNION ( RELATION
              { TUPLE { S# S#('S3'), P# P#('P1'), QTY QTY(150) },
                TUPLE { S# S#('S5'), P# P#('P1'), QTY QTY(500) } } ) ;
```

Likewise, the **Tutorial D** DELETE statement

```
DELETE S WHERE CITY = 'Athens' ;
```

is shorthand for the relational assignment

```
S := S WHERE NOT ( CITY = 'Athens' ) ;
```

And the **Tutorial D** UPDATE statement

```
UPDATE P WHERE CITY = 'London'
              ( WEIGHT := 2 * WEIGHT, CITY := 'Oslo' ) ;
```

—a little trickier, this one—is shorthand for the relational assignment

```
P := WITH ( P WHERE CITY = 'London' ) AS T1,
          ( EXTEND T1
              ADD ( 2 * WEIGHT AS NW, 'Oslo' AS NC ) ) AS T2,
          ( T2 { ALL BUT WEIGHT, CITY } ) AS T3,
          ( T3 RENAME ( NW AS WEIGHT, NC AS CITY ) ) AS T4,
          ( P MINUS T1 ) AS T5 :
     T5 UNION T4 ;
```

It should be clear, therefore, that relational assignment is fundamentally the only relational updating operator we need. For that reason, I'll focus on relational assignment as such for the remainder of this chapter. Also, throughout the chapter from this point forward, I'll take the unqualified term *assignment* to mean relational assignment specifically. Also, as already mentioned, I'll take the unqualified term *relation* to mean a relation value specifically (except sometimes in quotes from other writers).

CRITIC A'S OBJECTIONS

Relvars and assignment are criticized in a lengthy series of messages from *Critics A and B* to Hugh Darwen [1]. The overall exchange was sparked off by a question on an issue only tangentially related to the matter at hand (for which reason I'll ignore the substance of that issue here). In his reply to the questioner, *Critic A* said this:[1]

> I and [*Critic B*] do not subscribe to relvars and think Codd did not either.

Hugh responded:

> I'm baffled by your nonsubscription to relvars ... Don't you subscribe to INSERT, DELETE, UPDATE, and relational assignment? Codd certainly did. The target operand for all of these operations is a relation variable (relvar for short).

To which *Critic A* replied:

> More precisely, we don't subscribe to explicit relvars and Codd used "time-varying relations" to avoid them ... Bearing in mind that simplicity was one of Codd's main objectives, we think he may have refrained intentionally from introducing relvars. He was obviously aware of the time dimension of databases, yet as far as we have been able to determine, he never included time-variance semantics in his formal model. Had he done so, the language of sets and mathematical relations would have been rather strained because, as Date himself points out, every object in the language has a fixed value. Since relationships within and among Codd's relations are evaluated at a point in time, this permits the use of set semantics ... While conceptually Codd's "time-varying relation" has to be something like a relvar, the "gloss" permitted Codd to stick to simple sets (which cannot change), yet still contend with updates ... It is, perhaps, significant that later, in his RM/T paper, he referred to insert-update-delete as "transition rules," not operations.

And in a subsequent email he (i.e., *Critic A*) went on to say:

> Please note that it is not claimed there are no relvars involved. The only claim is that it is not a good idea to deal with them explicitly in the data language, because it creates complexity due to problems with unfixed sets. It's hard to believe that Codd did not think about variables, and that he used the term "time-varying relation" lightly.

At this point I'd like to interject some blow-by-blow responses of my own to these various remarks of *Critic A*'s. I've repeated and numbered those remarks for purposes of reference.

1. More precisely, we don't subscribe to explicit relvars.

    This statement seems to suggest that *Critic A* does subscribe to "implicit" relvars, whatever they might be. So apparently relvars are bad only if they're explicit. I don't understand this position.

---

1. For reasons of clarity and flow I've edited most of the quotes in this chapter, sometimes drastically so.

2.   Codd used "time-varying relations" to avoid [explicit relvars].

There are two ways to interpret this remark. The first is: Codd used the *concept* of "time-varying relations" in order to avoid having to deal with the *concept* of relvars (explicit or otherwise). If this interpretation is the intended one, then I'd like to know exactly what the difference is between these two concepts; our critics claim a difference exists, but they never seem to come out and say what it is.

   The second interpretation is: Codd used the *term* "time-varying relations" in order to avoid having to use the *term* "relvars" (again, explicit or otherwise). If this interpretation is the intended one, then I simply don't believe it. I worked with Codd for many years and knew him well, and I had many discussions with him on this very point. While I don't think I can do complete justice to his position on the matter, I can at least state with some authority that there was no hidden agenda behind his use of the term "time-varying relation"; it was just the term he used, that's all, and I don't think he attached any great significance to it.

   More particularly (and contrary to both of the foregoing possible interpretations of *Critic A*'s remark), the papers (references [3] and [4]) in which Codd first used the term contain not the slightest hint that he introduced it to avoid discussing variables and/or updating. *Au contraire,* in fact: In both of those papers, he explicitly discussed the question of relational updating. To quote: "Insertions take the form of adding new elements to declared relations ... Deletions ... take the form of removing elements from declared relations." What's more (in case you might be wondering what Codd meant by the term *declared relation*), references [3] and [4] both make it clear that a declared relation is a named relation ("time-varying," of course) that:

   ▪   Is explicitly declared as such to the system,

   ▪   Is described in the system catalog,

   ▪   Can be updated (so the declared name denotes different relations—that is, different relation *values*—at different times), and

   ▪   Can be referenced in queries (and constraints, presumably).

That looks like a relvar to me, and an explicit one to boot.

3.   Bearing in mind that simplicity was one of Codd's main objectives, we think he may have refrained intentionally from introducing relvars.

I find no evidence in any of his writings that Codd ever intended any such thing; in fact, I find a great deal of evidence to the contrary—not only in the remarks just quoted regarding insertions and deletions and declared relations, but in numerous remarks elsewhere as well (e.g., in reference [5], which I'll be discussing later).

4. He was obviously aware of the time dimension of databases, yet as far as we have been able to determine, he never included time-variance semantics in his formal model.

    If "time-variance semantics" merely means that Codd's time-varying relations vary over time, there is clear evidence—not solely in the name—that he did include such semantics. In particular, he certainly included relational assignment "in his formal model," another issue I'll come back to later.

5. Had he done so, the language of sets and mathematical relations would have been rather strained because, as Date himself points out, every object in the language has a fixed value.

    I don't know what this means, nor do I know what writings of my own are being referred to here.

6. Since relationships within and among Codd's relations are evaluated at a point in time, this permits the use of set semantics.

    The phrase "set semantics" and a slight variant, "set theoretic semantics," appear repeatedly in reference [1], but I don't really know what they mean. From other remarks in reference [1] I can guess they refer to something that includes set operators such as union and intersection but excludes assignment; but then why not talk about (e.g.) "arithmetic semantics," meaning something that includes arithmetic operators such as "+" and "*" but excludes assignment? (I won't repeat these questions every time one of the unclear phrases appears, letting this one paragraph do duty for all.) Overall, I don't think this remark of *Critic A*'s means anything other than that the value of a relvar at any given point in time is a relation (whose body is a set, of course: namely, a set of tuples). If that's indeed what it means, then of course I agree, but I can't attach any special significance to it.

7. While conceptually Codd's "time-varying relation" has to be something like a relvar, the "gloss" permitted Codd to stick to simple sets (which cannot change), yet still contend with updates.

    I agree with Hugh's response on this one. To quote:

    > Well, somebody will have to explain to me what the difference is [*between a relvar and a "time-varying relation"*] ... If it walks like a duck, swims like a duck, flies like a duck, and quacks like a duck, what is it?

    See also my own earlier comments on this same issue. *Note:* I might add that I don't really understand what's meant by the term "gloss" here, either, but perhaps it's not important.

8. It is, perhaps, significant that later, in his RM/T paper, he referred to insert-update-delete as "transition rules," not operations.

    No, he didn't. What he actually said was this (and here I quote directly from the RM/T paper [6]):

All insertions into, updates of, and deletions from ... relations are constrained by the following two rules [*and he goes on to give definitions of the entity and referential integrity rules. Then he explicitly states that the relational model includes those two rules, and he refers to them generically as*] the insert-update-delete rules.

Note the explicit reference to "insertions into, updates of, and deletions from" relations! (Incidentally, the paper continues to refer to the targets of such operations as "time-varying relations.")

9. Please note that it is not claimed there are no relvars involved. The only claim is that it is not a good idea to deal with them explicitly in the data language, because it creates complexity due to problems with unfixed sets.

    To the extent that I understand these remarks (which isn't very far), they just look like arm waving to me. See my response to *Critic A*'s remark no. 1.

10. It's hard to believe that Codd did not think about variables, and that he used the term "time-varying relation" lightly.

    No, it's not. See my response to *Critic A*'s remarks nos. 2 and 4.

I've already quoted part of Hugh's response to *Critic A*'s remarks. That response continues:

I thought "relational assignment" was Codd's term, and one of his twelve rules ... Codd's accounts of assignment, insert, update, and delete on pp 87-94 of the RM/V2 book look indistinguishable from those of **Tutorial D** ...

Well, I can confirm that Codd did use the term *relational assignment* in "the RM/V2 book" [8], though it isn't actually one of his "twelve rules" [7]. (One of those rules does have to do with INSERT, DELETE, and UPDATE, but there's no rule regarding assignment as such.) But he certainly included the *concept* of assignment, and explicit syntax for that concept, much earlier than that—in the RM/T paper [6], to be specific (which appeared in 1979), and possibly earlier still.

As an aside, I'd like to add that it's not true to say that RM/V2's facilities in this area are "indistinguishable from those of **Tutorial D**." For example, the RM/V2 facilities include the idea that certain deletes can cause the introduction of nulls into the database, which **Tutorial D** certainly doesn't support. At the same time they don't include support for multiple assignment, which **Tutorial D** does support (see the section after next). What's more, the text on pages 87-94 of the RM/V2 book contains much material not directly related to the semantics of the operators as such, including many details that surely don't belong in an abstract model at all—e.g.:

■ "Whenever rows are withheld by the DBMS from insertion (to avoid duplicate rows in the result), the *duplicate row indicator* is turned on."

- "If one or more indexes exist for the target relation, the DBMS will automatically update these indexes to support the inserted rows."

And so on. It also contains several prescriptions that are in direct conflict with *The Third Manifesto*—e.g.:

- "The domain of any column of T in which the values are derived by means of a function is identified [in the catalog] as *function-derived,* because the DBMS usually cannot be more specific than that."

- "The relational model includes the *cascading option* in some of its manipulative operators."[1]

And so on. All of that being said, however, I do of course agree with Hugh that the general functionality being defined in this part of the RM/V2 book is essentially similar to that found in the analogous portions of **Tutorial D**.

To all of the above I add that as early as 1971 Codd was proposing explicit support for INSERT, DELETE, and UPDATE (albeit not for assignment as such); I refer to his paper on Data Sublanguage ALPHA [5], in which 12 examples (out of a total of 32, or nearly 40 percent) were updating examples specifically.

CRITIC B'S OBJECTIONS

After the exchanges between *Critic A* and Hugh discussed above, *Critic B* joined the debate (effectively taking over from *Critic A*, who didn't contribute any further). In his first message, *Critic B* said this among other things:

> The conflation of set theoretic language (which has only equivalence) and a computational language (which has both assignment and equivalence) results in muddy semantics, which neither Hugh nor Chris have discussed or even acknowledged. Furthermore, neither seem[s] to have applied any of the vast literature on nondecidability and incompleteness to *The Third Manifesto*.

Well, it's true that *The Third Manifesto* prescribes, and **Tutorial D** (like every other imperative language I know) supports, "both assignment and equivalence." In fact, the *Manifesto* prescribes, and **Tutorial D** supports, all three of the following:

- *Logical equivalence* ("$\equiv$"): If p and q are predicates, the equivalence $(p) \equiv (q)$—not meant to be actual **Tutorial D** syntax—is a predicate also, evaluating to TRUE if and only if p and q both evaluate to the same truth value.

---

1. *The Third Manifesto* does not prohibit "cascading options" that are specified declaratively (it doesn't prescribe them, either); however, Codd is suggesting here that they might be specified procedurally instead.

- *Value equality* ("="): Values *v1* and *v2* are equal if and only if they're the very same value.

- *Assignment* (":="), *relational or otherwise:* The assignment $V := v$ causes the specified value *v* to be assigned to the specified variable *V* (after which, the comparison $V = v$ is required to evaluate to TRUE).

I'd like to elaborate on value equality in particular, since certain subsequent remarks of *Critic B*'s suggest there might be some breakdown in communication in this area. As I've said, values *v1* and *v2* are equal if and only if they're the very same value (and I note in passing that the term *identity* might reasonably be used instead of equality for this concept, as explained in Chapter 2). It's our position, reflected in the *Manifesto,* that:

- Any given value—the integer three, for example—exists (a) for all time and (b) exactly once in the universe, as it were.

- However, any number of distinct *appearances,* or *occurrences* (or, perhaps better, *representations*), of that given value can exist simultaneously, in many different places.

And if two such "places" happen to contain appearances of the same value at the same time, then comparing those two "places" for equality will give TRUE (they'll "compare equal") at that time.[1] Here's some text from reference [10] that explains the overall situation:

> Observe that there's a logical difference between a value as such and an appearance of that value—for example, an appearance as the current value of some variable or as some attribute value within the current value of some relvar. Each such appearance consists internally of some physical representation of the value in question (and distinct appearances of the same value might have distinct physical representations). Thus, there's also a logical difference between an appearance of a value, on the one hand, and the physical representation of that appearance, on the other; there might even be a logical difference between the physical representations used for distinct appearances of the same value. All of that being said, however, it's usual to abbreviate *physical representation of an appearance of a value* to just *appearance of a value,* or (more often) just *value,* so long as there's no risk of ambiguity in doing so. Note that *appearance of a value* is a model concept, whereas *physical representation of an appearance* is an implementation concept—for example, users certainly might need to know whether two variables contain appearances of the same value, but they don't need to know whether those appearances use the same physical representation.
>
> *Example:* Let N1 and N2 be variables of type INTEGER. After the following assignments, then, N1 and N2 both contain an appearance of the integer value three. The corresponding physical representations might or might not be the same (for example, N1 might use a binary representation and N2 a packed decimal representation), but it's of no concern to the

---

1. So I suppose we could say we have here an example of yet another kind of equality, which we might call *appearance equality.* No such term is used in the *Manifesto,* however.

user either way.

```
N1  :=  3  ;
N2  :=  3  ;
```

What if anything is wrong with the foregoing state of affairs? *Note:* If (as *Critic B*'s next sentence—"neither [Hugh nor Chris seems] to have applied any of the vast literature on nondecidability and incompleteness to *The Third Manifesto*"—might suggest) the answer to this question is that it gives rise to undecidability, then I've dealt with that issue in references [11] and [12], and I won't discuss it further here. But I can't tell from the quoted extract whether the problem that *Critic B* is referring to is indeed that one.

I'd also like to know exactly what's "muddy" about the semantics of **Tutorial D**. Hugh asked the same question:

> Please justify by showing concrete examples in **Tutorial D** where our "semantics" are "muddy." Please also explain what you think it takes for semantics to be muddy. I understand indeterminacy (as found in SQL), but I believe we have none of that.

Critic B never explicitly responded to these requests, as far as I can tell, unless the following is a response:

> Your request that I explain what **Tutorial D** does wrong through examples in **Tutorial D** is absurd! You cannot give examples in any language of what that language does NOT do!

I'll come back to these particular remarks of *Critic B*'s a little later. Anyway, Hugh wrote a long response to *Critic B*'s complaint, of which the following is the substance:

> If the database language has no named relvars, how are updates expressed in it, and how are constraints expressed? And how are queries expressed? ... The answers must be accompanied by examples in some concrete syntax. This requirement is a stringent one and I might not respond to a response that does not attempt to address it. The syntax should be based, where appropriate, on relational algebra ...
>
> We have assignment so that the database can be updated. As far as the database is concerned, assignment is restricted to relational assignment only, because relation variables are the only kind allowed in the database ... A proposal to do away with relation variables needs to demonstrate two very important things: first and foremost, an alternative way of updating the database; second, the advantages of this alternative way over assignment to relvars.

Critic B returned to the fray:

> To clarify, I have NOT proposed doing away with the concept of relation variables per se ...
>
> Your question goes to the heart of the very great difference in semantics between set theoretic and computational languages ... The set theoretic analog of "updating" semantics is two sets (e.g., A and B) connected by a "set transformation" or "transition" rule ... Semantically, this is VERY different from saying that A becomes B via some update operator because—in set

theoretic language—B does not replace A and so there is no assignment of values to some variable. Instead both always exist but are merely related in a known way.

The problem created by combining set theoretic language and computational language semantics in some completely unspecified manner makes *The Third Manifesto* as flawed as the NULL problems in SQL!

Your request that I explain what **Tutorial D** does wrong through examples in **Tutorial D** is absurd! You cannot give examples in any language of what that language does NOT do!

In **Tutorial D,** I do not know how to interpret "equivalence"—sometimes you seem to want the set theoretic concept (i.e., an assertion of identity) and sometimes you seem to want the computational concept (an assertion of value equivalence). If the first is not intended, then how does **Tutorial D** support inference? And if it is, how do you square this with assignment, which is obviously at odds with the set theoretic semantics for which there is no concept of variable?

I have some blow-by-blow responses of my own to all this:

1.   To clarify, I have NOT proposed doing away with the concept of relation variables per se.

      This claim seems to be related to *Critic A*'s remark to the effect that (apparently) explicit relvars are bad but implicit ones might be OK. I still fail to understand what exactly is being proposed here, or what exactly is being objected to.

2.   Your question goes to the heart of the very great difference in semantics between set theoretic and computational languages.

      The question referred to is, I presume, the one in which Hugh asks how updates are to be done without relvars; if not, then I don't understand.

3.   The set theoretic analog of "updating" semantics is two sets (e.g., A and B) connected by a "set transformation" or "transition" rule.

      I merely note here that *Critic A* also referred to transition rules, though in fact his reference was incorrect.

4.   Semantically, this is VERY different from saying that A becomes B via some update operator because—in set theoretic language—B does not replace A and so there is no assignment of values to some variable. Instead both always exist but are merely related in a known way.

      First, *The Third Manifesto* never talks in terms of "one set becoming another"; rather, it talks in terms of a variable which has one value at one time and another at another (in particular, it talks in terms of a *relation* variable having one *relation* value at one time and another at another). Second, it also never talks in terms of one set replacing another; since all values "always exist," all sets also "always exist," a fortiori (in fact, sets *are* values). However, it does talk in terms of a variable being updated, which means the *appearance* of one value (in that variable) is replaced by an *appearance* of another. In fact, it tries very hard to be precise over such matters—over the logical difference, in particular, between a value as such and an appearance of such a value in some context, as I tried to explain a couple of pages back—and it's truly frustrating to be so roundly misunderstood. Overall, these two sentences of *Critic B*'s just look like an attempt to state fuzzily what the *Manifesto* states very precisely.

5. The problem created by combining set theoretic language and computational language semantics in some completely unspecified manner makes *The Third Manifesto* as flawed as the NULL problems in SQL!

What exactly is it in *The Third Manifesto* that's "completely unspecified"? If anything's unspecified here, I'd have to say it's the meaning of "computational language semantics"—not to mention "set theoretic semantics," a notion I've already commented on. Also, what exactly does "as flawed as the NULL problems in SQL" mean? Nulls give rise to some kind of many-valued logic, which most authorities agree causes horrible problems; but I'm not aware that the *Manifesto*'s insistence on "computational language semantics" necessitates any departure from conventional two-valued logic. At best, therefore, the reference to nulls is a red herring, and the claim that the *Manifesto* is "as flawed as the NULL problems in SQL" is an apples and oranges comparison.

Note added later: It occurs to me that the phrase "the problem created by combining set theoretic language and computational language semantics" might refer to something we categorically prohibit: namely, the possibility that a new value might be assigned to some variable during the process of evaluating some expression that involves that very same variable. We agree that allowing such a possibility could have adverse consequences (though some languages do in fact permit it). For that reason, any language that's supposed to conform to *The Third Manifesto* is required to satisfy the following prescriptions among others (and of course **Tutorial D** does satisfy these prescriptions):

- Syntactically, no assignment is an expression; more generally, no update operator invocation is an expression.

- Syntactically, therefore, no expression (no relational expression in particular) is allowed to include either an assignment or, more generally, an update operator invocation of any kind.

- By contrast, an expression (a relational expression in particular) is allowed to include a read-only operator invocation. However, such an invocation is itself fundamentally just shorthand for another expression; by definition, therefore, it includes no assignments and no update operator invocations of any kind.[1]

---

1. The code that implements a given read-only operator is always logically equivalent to a single RETURN statement, the operand to which is itself formulated as an expression. While that implementation code might in fact be written in such a way as to update certain variables that are purely local to the operator in question, such updates have no lasting effect. Thus, such an operator cannot and does not update anything in its environment; in particular, it cannot and does not update anything in the database.

It follows from all of the above that if a given relational expression *exp* includes any references to some relvar *R,* then throughout evaluation of *exp* those references all denote the same thing: namely, the relation *r* that's the value of *R* immediately before evaluation of *exp* begins.

6.   Your request that I explain what **Tutorial D** does wrong through examples in **Tutorial D** is absurd! You cannot give examples in any language of what that language does NOT do!

Well, I thought the point at issue was (see references [11-12]) that **Tutorial D** allows expressions that can't be evaluated. If so, it must be possible to give an example of such an expression. Now, I agree it might be difficult to do so—I mean, the expression might be extremely complex—but *Critic B* is saying it's impossible. So perhaps *Critic B* is referring to something else that **Tutorial D** "does wrong." In fact, I think he must be—since he goes on to suggest that there's something the language "does NOT do," and allowing expressions that can't be evaluated is something that it does do (at least according to *Critic B*).

     When the foregoing points are clarified, I'd then like to know why analogous criticisms don't apply to the hypothetical language described in Codd's original papers [3-4] or to his ALPHA language [5]. And assuming I'm right in thinking those criticisms do apply, I'd also like to see a language to which they don't.

7.   In **Tutorial D,** I don't know how to interpret "equivalence"; sometimes you seem to want the set theoretic concept (e.g., an assertion of identity) and sometimes you seem to want the computational concept (an assertion of value equivalence). If the first is not intended, then how does **Tutorial D** support inference? And if it is, how do you square this with assignment, which is obviously at odds with the set theoretic semantics for which there is no concept of variable?

I'm afraid I'm far from fully understanding these remarks. I *think* what *Critic B* here calls "assertion of identity" is what we call equality. I *think* what *Critic B* here calls "assertion of value equivalence" is what I earlier suggested (in a footnote) might be called "appearance equality." I've already tried to explain these constructs (i.e., equality and "appearance equality"), and I believe the *Manifesto* is perfectly explicit on when and where they can be used and what their semantics are. As for "[the *Manifesto*] supporting inference": I *think* what *Critic B* is referring to here is the process of determining the value of a relational expression (in particular, the process of responding to a query). If so, then I believe the *Manifesto* is perfectly explicit on what's involved in that process. What's more, I fail to see how assignment and "the concept of variable" come into the picture, since—as I tried to explain a little while back—neither has any role to play in that process.

◆ ◆ ◆ ◆ ◆

In a subsequent message, *Critic B* said this:

> My desire is not to introduce a database language with no variable names, etc., but that **Tutorial D** should cleanly separate set theoretic semantics and computer language semantics. You want a single language which has both, but I don't believe this is possible unless (for example and at least) truth value equivalence is distinct from cardinal and ordinal value equivalence.

As I said earlier, **Tutorial D** has logical equivalence (which is presumably the same as what *Critic B* here calls truth value equivalence), together with value equality,[1] together with assignment (which *Critic B* previously at least suggested was also a kind of equivalence). Now he additionally talks about "cardinal and ordinal value equivalence." I have no idea whether or not this is one of the three kinds **Tutorial D** has; I don't know whether "cardinal and ordinal value equivalence" is one kind or two; and I don't even know whether *Critic B* thinks it would be good or bad if **Tutorial D** supported it (or them). Anyway, Hugh responded:

> I have explained what we mean by "equals," in response to certain statements from you that indicated you were worried that we had two different kinds. (I didn't understand both of the two kinds, but our only kind appears to be the one you want. See RM Prescription 8.)

What Hugh here calls "our only kind" is specifically value equality, the semantics of which are precisely specified in *The Third Manifesto*'s RM Prescription 8. *Critic B* replied:

> I realize you don't understand that there are two (actually many) kinds of "equal" ... As best I can guess, your ability to think in purely set theoretic terms when talking about **Tutorial D** is mentally blocked. Let me simply say that value equivalence is not the same as identity. Value refers to a comparison of measures of a quantitative property, while identity pertains to what mathematicians often call entities ("things").

Well, I'm going to have to repeat some things I've already said (and I apologize up front for the repetition) ... but I strongly suspect from these remarks that *Critic B* hasn't taken on board exactly what *The Third Manifesto* means by the term *value*. I also suspect that what he calls "value equivalence" is what we mean when we talk of equality of distinct *appearances* of the *same* value (where we would say that—by definition—there's just one value, as such). I further suspect that this misunderstanding on his part (of our use of terms) has led him into a criticism that has no basis in fact. I also think, contrary to what *Critic B* is saying here, that our "value equivalence" (I used the term "value equality" earlier) *is* "the same as identity": Two appearances are equal ("value equal"?) if and only if they're appearances of the *identical* value. As for the notion that there are many kinds of equality: Well, it might be true (I really don't know) that many kinds can be defined, but I think the important one is the one we define in RM Prescription 8—and that's the one we appeal to, explicitly or implicitly, whenever we talk about equality as such in the context of *The Third Manifesto*.

In the same message, *Critic B* also says this:

---

1. And possibly "appearance equality," too.

I have not stated how I think updates to the database should be expressed, except that we can safely use the set theoretic representation as having both a "canonical" method and a "canonical" semantics. I object to assignment because I see it as being at odds with the set theoretic representation and importing a "before and after semantics" which is inherently procedural.

Here are my responses:

1. I have not stated how I think updates to the database should be expressed.

    Well, as I said earlier (quoting Hugh), a proposal to do away with relation variables needs to demonstrate two very important things: first and foremost, an alternative way of updating the database; second, the advantages of this alternative way over assignment to relvars. It's truly frustrating to be told over and over that our approach doesn't work—especially without being told clearly why it doesn't work, and especially when it's essentially the same as the approach supported by all imperative languages since programming languages were first invented—without at the same time being told about some alternative approach that does work.

2. We can safely use the set theoretic representation as having both a "canonical" method and a "canonical" semantics.

    The significance of these observations is unclear to me.

3. I object to assignment because I see it as being at odds with the set theoretic representation and importing a "before and after semantics" which is inherently procedural.

    Assume for the sake of the discussion that (a) it's true that set theory has no notion of assignment and that (b) it's true that updates are a requirement. (For my part I have no difficulty in accepting either of these assumptions.) Then the obvious conclusion is not that assignment is inherently flawed; rather, it's that set theory by itself is inadequate as a theoretical basis for a database programming language. However, *Critic B* asserts that assignment and set theory (or "the set theoretic representation") are actually at odds with each other—i.e., they're actually in conflict, suggesting that if we support one we can't support the other. If this is true, then so much the worse for set theory; but frankly, I don't see why it's true. *Note:* Replace "set theory" by "logic" throughout the foregoing remarks, and the resulting argument is something I would also sign on to.
    What's more, the notion of "before and after semantics" is indeed implied by assignment. More significantly, however, it's implied by—*derives from* might be a better way of putting it—the fundamental way time works in our universe! (I suppose we might say that being "inherently procedural" derives from the way time works in our universe, too, if we could agree that "procedural" just means performing one action after another, in sequence; but the problem here is that the label "procedural" is usually taken to mean "*low level* procedural" and hence is used, almost always, in a pejorative sense.) If set theory can't deal with "before and after semantics," then so much the worse for set theory. *Note:* Again, replace "set theory" by "logic" throughout the foregoing remarks and the resulting argument is something I would also sign on to.

MULTIPLE ASSIGNMENT

The Third Manifesto prescribes not just assignment per se but what it calls *multiple* assignment. Multiple assignment is an operation that allows several individual assignments all to be performed simultaneously, as it were, without any integrity checking being done until all of those individual assignments have been executed in their entirety. For example, the following "double DELETE" is, logically, a multiple assignment operation:

```
DELETE S  WHERE S# = S#('S1') ,
DELETE SP WHERE S# = S#('S1') ;
```

Note the comma separator after the first DELETE, which indicates syntactically that the end of the overall statement has not yet been reached.

In reference [1], *Critic B* raises several questions about multiple assignment. To quote:

> I am uncertain as to how you intend multiple assignment to be implemented. If there are, e.g., five individual assignments, are they processed in order as stated from top to bottom or is the order arbitrary or are they expected to be processed in parallel? Your rewrite algorithm for eliminating multiple references to the same variable raises more issues than it solves. At best, it seems to assume there are no side effects among the individual assignments, so that order does not matter. If this is the assumption, then clearly there are certain ordered sets of assignments (normally coded as transactions) that cannot be rewritten as a multiple assignment because they will produce a result different than that which was originally intended ... I like the idea of multiple assignment but not at the expense of transactions and therefore not at the expense of deferred constraint checking.

Some blow-by-blow responses:

1. I am uncertain as to how you intend multiple assignment to be implemented.

    We expect it to be implemented as specified. The semantics are specified in *The Third Manifesto* [14] and also in a standalone paper [13].

2. If there are, e.g., five individual assignments, are they processed in order as stated from top to bottom or is the order arbitrary or are they expected to be processed in parallel?

    This question is fully answered in references [13] and [14]. For the record (and simplifying slightly), the basic idea is that (a) the expressions on the right sides of the individual assignments are evaluated (in arbitrary order, because the order makes no difference) and then (b) the individual assignments to the variables on the left sides are executed in sequence as written.

3. Your rewrite algorithm for eliminating multiple references to the same variable raises more issues than it solves.

References [13] and [14] do include a "rewrite algorithm" for combining—not eliminating!—"multiple references to the same variable." If that algorithm truly does raise "more issues than it solves," it would be helpful to be given more specifics regarding those issues. Until then, it's hard to respond to this criticism.

4.   At best, it seems to assume there are no side effects among the individual assignments, so that order does not matter.

"It" here is apparently the rewrite algorithm. That algorithm certainly doesn't "assume there are no side effects among the individual assignments." *Au contraire,* in fact: The whole point of that algorithm is precisely to make sure those side effects occur instead of being lost.

5.   If this is the assumption, then clearly there are certain ordered sets of assignments (normally coded as transactions) that cannot be rewritten as a multiple assignment because they will produce a result different than that which was originally intended ...

I can't resist twitting *Critic B* slightly here on his use of the phrase "ordered sets" ... More important, however, we would like to see an example of a sequence of assignments that can't be rewritten as a multiple assignment. The obvious suggestion would be seem to be something along these lines:

```
X  :=  x ;
Y  :=  f(X)  ;
```

But the following multiple assignment will achieve what's presumably intended:

```
X  :=  x ,
Y  :=  f(x)  ;
```

6.   I like the idea of multiple assignment but not at the expense of transactions and therefore not at the expense of deferred constraint checking.

We like multiple assignment, too; in fact, we regard it as a sine qua non. Please note, however, that we haven't proposed it as a replacement for transactions. In reference [1], Hugh says the following (and I agree with these remarks):

> I believe that transactions can theoretically be dispensed with but I prefer to keep them for what I believe are strong and possibly compelling reasons of convenience. I know people who disagree with me here and would prefer to get rid of transactions altogether. I respond to them by agreeing that that might be nice but I need to see some specific language proposals to address the inconvenience that transactions currently address.

DATABASE VALUES AND VARIABLES

Despite everything I've said in this chapter so far, there's one sense in which relvars and relational assignment were and are a mistake after all, as I'll now try to explain.

We want to be able to update the database. Now, I said earlier that "updatable" and "assignable to" mean exactly the same thing; I also said that to be assignable to is to be a variable, and to be a variable is to be assignable to. Doesn't it follow from these remarks that the database is a variable? And since the notion of variables containing variables is a logical absurdity, doesn't it follow further that the database, being a variable, can't possibly contain relation variables?

The answer to both of these questions is in fact *yes:* The database is a variable, and it can't contain other variables (not relation variables and not any other kind) nested inside itself. Here's a quote from Appendix D of reference [14]:

> The first version of *The Third Manifesto* drew a distinction between database values and database variables, analogous to that between relation values and relation variables. It also introduced the term *dbvar* as shorthand for *database variable*. While we still believe this distinction to be a valid one, we found it had little direct relevance to other aspects of the *Manifesto*. We therefore decided, in the interest of familiarity, to revert to more traditional terminology.

After elaborating slightly on these remarks, Appendix D of reference [14] continues:

> Now this bad decision has come home to roost! With hindsight, it would have been much better to "bite the bullet" and adopt the more logically correct terms *database value* and *database variable* (or dbvar), despite their lack of familiarity.

And it goes on to show that (a) a database variable is really a *tuple* variable, with one (relation valued) attribute for each "relation variable" contained in that database variable; (b) relation variables are really *pseudovariables*, which allow update operations to "zap" individual components of the containing database variable.[1] As Hugh puts it in reference [1]:

> Chris and I contemplated the idea of regarding the database as a single variable [but] we were unable to devise convenient syntax for the usual kinds of ... updating that are expected (assignment of the complete database for every required update being obviously unthinkable). Or rather, the only convenient syntax we could come up with involved dividing the database up into the named "portions" that we call relation variables.

Now, I mention all this merely for completeness and to head off at the pass, as it were, certain criticisms of our position that might occur to some readers. The fact is, even though the database is really a variable and relvars are really pseudovariables, it's my belief that this state of affairs in no way invalidates any of the arguments I've been making earlier in this chapter.

---

1. See Chapter 16 for an elaboration of both of these points.

CONCLUDING REMARKS

I'd like to conclude with a couple of final observations:

1.   First and foremost, the position of *Critics A and B* with regard to relvars remains extremely unclear: They seem to think relvars are fundamentally flawed, and yet at the same time they seem to want to retain them, at least "implicitly" (?). They also fail to explain what the logical difference is between a relvar as such and a "time-varying relation."

2.   It's true that certain programming languages—specifically, the so called logic languages (e.g., Prolog) and functional languages (e.g., LISP)—do apparently manage to exist without assignment: indeed, without any notion of "persistent memory" at all. As far as I know, however, all such languages simply cheat when it comes to updating the database; in effect, they perform some kind of assignment, possibly as a side effect, even though assignment as such isn't part of the logic or functional programming style.

REFERENCES AND BIBLIOGRAPHY

1.   Anon.: Private correspondence with Hugh Darwen (December 2005 - January 2006).

2.   E. O. de Brock: "Tables, Table Variables, and Static Integrity Constraints." University of Technology, Eindhoven, Netherlands (1980).

3.   E. F. Codd: "Derivability, Redundancy, and Consistency of Relations Stored in Large Data Banks," IBM Research Report RJ599 (August 19th, 1969).

4.   E. F. Codd: "A Relational Model of Data for Large Shared Data Banks," *CACM 13,* No. 6 (June 1970). Republished in *Milestones of Research—Selected Papers 1958-1982 (CACM 25th Anniversary Issue), CACM 26,* No. 1 (January 1983).

5.   E. F. Codd: "A Data Base Sublanguage Founded on the Relational Calculus," Proc. 1971 ACM SIGFIDET Workshop on Data Description, Access and Control, San Diego, Calif. (November 1971).

6.   E. F. Codd: "Extending the Database Relational Model to Capture More Meaning," *ACM TODS 4,* No. 4 (December 1979).

7.   E. F. Codd: "Is Your DBMS Really Relational?" (*Computerworld*, October 14th, 1985); "Does Your DBMS Run By The Rules?" (*Computerworld*, October 21st, 1985).

8.   E. F. Codd: *The Relational Model for Database Management Version 2*. Reading, Mass.: Addison-Wesley (1990).

9.   Hugh Darwen and C. J. Date: *The Third Manifesto. ACM SIGMOD Record 24,* No. 1 (March 1995).

10. C. J. Date: *The Relational Database Dictionary.* Sebastopol, Calif.: O'Reilly Media Inc. (2005).

11. C. J. Date: "Gödel, Russell, Codd: A Recursive Golden Crowd" (Chapter 13 in this book).

12. C. J. Date: "And Now for Something Completely Computational" (Chapter 15 in this book).

13. C. J. Date and Hugh Darwen: "Multiple Assignment," in *Date on Database: Writings 2000-2006.* Berkeley, Calif.: Apress (2006).

14. C. J. Date and Hugh Darwen: *Databases, Types, and the Relational Model: The Third Manifesto* (3rd edition). Boston, Mass.: Addison-Wesley (2006).

Chapter 15

And Now for Something

Completely Computational

Myself when young did eagerly frequent
Doctor and Saint, and heard great Argument
About it and about; but evermore
Came out by the same Door as in I went.
　　　　　　　　—Edward Fitzgerald: *The Rubáiyát of Omar Khayyam*

The Third Manifesto, by Hugh Darwen and myself ("the *Manifesto*" for short), lays down a set of prescriptions and proscriptions regarding the design of a database programming language it calls **D** (see reference [9]). One prescription in particular—"OO Prescription 3"—reads as follows:

> **D** shall be **computationally complete**. That is, **D** may support, but shall not require, invocation from so-called host programs written in languages other than **D**. Similarly, **D** may support, but shall not require, the use of other languages for implementation of user-defined operators.

However, reference [1] argues that this prescription implies that the *Manifesto* is deeply flawed. To quote:[1]

> It's an error to make **Tutorial D** computationally complete because it creates a language with logical expressions that are provably not decidable—yet a decision procedure must exist for any logical expression to be evaluated.

Note: This quote refers to **Tutorial D,** not **D** as such, so I need to explain how **Tutorial D** relates to **D**. To begin with, the name **D** is generic—it's used in reference [9] to refer generically to any language that conforms to the principles laid down in *The Third Manifesto*. Thus, there could be any number of distinct languages all qualifying as a valid **D**. **Tutorial D** is intended to be one such; it's defined more or less formally in reference [9], and it's used throughout that book, and elsewhere, as a basis for examples. For definiteness I'll concentrate on **Tutorial D** myself (mostly) in the present chapter, since that's what reference [1] does, but the discussions and arguments actually apply to any valid **D**.

---

1. For reasons of clarity and flow I've edited most of the quotes in this chapter, sometimes drastically so.

DECIDABILITY

To say it again, reference [1] claims that **Tutorial D** suffers from a lack of decidability; more precisely, it claims that certain **Tutorial D** logical expressions aren't decidable. What does this mean?

Well, first, any given expression denotes a value; more precisely, it can be thought of as a rule for computing the value in question. Hence, a logical expression in particular can be thought of as a rule for computing a truth value. So a logical expression is an expression, formulated in some language *L,* that's supposed to denote either TRUE or FALSE.[1] Let *exp* be such an expression; to say *exp* is undecidable, then, is to say that although it's well formed—meaning it's constructed in full accordance with the syntax rules of *L* (it must be well formed, of course, for otherwise it wouldn't be an expression of the language in the first place)—there doesn't exist an algorithm that can determine in finite time whether *exp* evaluates to TRUE. By extension, the language *L* is said to be undecidable in turn if and only if there exists at least one *L* expression that's undecidable. I remark in passing that propositional calculus is decidable but predicate calculus is not.

If language *L* is decidable, then by definition there exists a general purpose algorithm (a "decision procedure") for determining in finite time whether an arbitrary *L* expression evaluates to TRUE. By contrast, if *L* is undecidable, then no such algorithm exists. What's more, if *L* is undecidable, there isn't even an algorithm for determining ahead of time, as it were, whether a given *L* expression is decidable (if there were, the system could avoid the problem, in effect, by not even attempting to evaluate expressions that are undecidable).

It follows from the foregoing that if **Tutorial D** in particular is undecidable, there'll be certain **Tutorial D** expressions, and hence certain **Tutorial D** queries (namely, ones including such expressions), that the system won't be able to deal with satisfactorily. On the face of it, then, the fact that **Tutorial D** is undecidable, if it is a fact, looks like a serious flaw.

COMPUTATIONAL COMPLETENESS

Reference [1] claims that it's specifically the fact that **Tutorial D** is computationally complete that makes it undecidable:

> If a given language incorporates predicate logic *and is computationally complete,* it's a logical consequence that some syntactically correct expressions of that language will be undecidable [*italics added*].

So what exactly does it mean for a language to be computationally complete?

Oddly enough, I was unable to find a definition of the term *computational completeness* in any of the fairly large number of computing references I examined. But many of them did include a definition of the term *computable function,* and I think it's a reasonable guess that a language is computationally complete if and only if it supports the computation of all computable functions. I'll take that as my working definition, anyway. So what's a computable function? Here are a couple of definitions from the

---

1. Naturally I limit my attention here to two-valued logic only.

literature:

- A computable function is a function that can be computed by a Turing machine in a finite number of steps [11].

- A computable function is a function that can be coded using WHILE loops [12].

COMPUTATIONAL COMPLETENESS IMPLIES UNDECIDABILITY

As I've said, reference [1] claims it's specifically the fact that **Tutorial D** is computationally complete that makes it undecidable. Here's a more complete version of the extract I quoted near the beginning of the previous section:

> The problem is simply this: If a given language incorporates predicate logic and is computationally complete, it's a logical consequence that the set of syntactically correct expressions of that language will include self referential expressions, and some of those will be undecidable. This is what Gödel showed in the process of constructing his first incompleteness theorem ... So, if **Tutorial D** is computationally complete, the set of syntactically correct **Tutorial D** expressions includes self referential, undecidable expressions. I merely apply Gödel to **Tutorial D**.

Reference [1] appeals to Gödel's second theorem, too. Here's a more complete version of the extract I quoted near the beginning of this chapter:

> It's an error to make **Tutorial D** computationally complete because it creates a language with logical expressions that are provably not decidable—yet a decision procedure must exist for any logical expression to be evaluated (see Gödel's second incompleteness theorem). Is an example in **Tutorial D** more convincing than a proven theorem? Codd carefully avoided this trap, but *The Third Manifesto* does not!

I'll come back to the question of whether Codd "avoided this trap" in the next section. First, however, let me state for the record Gödel's two incompleteness theorems. *Note:* Actually those theorems can be stated in many different forms; the versions I give here are somewhat simplified—in fact, oversimplified—but they're good enough for present purposes. Note too that for the purposes of this discussion I'm regarding the terms *expression* and *statement* as interchangeable, even though they're not usually so regarded in conventional programming language contexts.

- *Gödel's First Incompleteness Theorem:* Let S be a consistent formal system that's at least as powerful as elementary arithmetic; then S is incomplete, in the sense that there exist statements in S that are true but can't be proved in S.

- *Gödel's Second Incompleteness Theorem:* Let S be a consistent formal system that's at least as powerful as elementary arithmetic; then the consistency of S can't be proved in S.

I confess I don't directly see the relevance of the second theorem to the arguments of reference [1], but the first clearly does support those arguments. What's more, since Gödel's proof of his first theorem (a) involves the explicit construction of a self referential statement—in effect an arithmetic analog of the statement "This statement can't be proved in *S*"—and then (b) proves that precisely that statement can't be proved in *S* (and is therefore true!), it follows more specifically that the set of undecidable expressions in *S* includes certain self referential expressions. So all right: If **Tutorial D** is computationally complete, it's undecidable, in the sense that its expressions include ones that are self referential and undecidable.

DOES CODD "AVOID THE TRAP"?

So far we've seen that reference [1] claims, apparently correctly, that **Tutorial D,** being computationally complete, is undecidable. What's more, it also claims, at least implicitly, that Codd's relational algebra and relational calculus are decidable; in fact, they must be, since Codd's calculus is essentially an applied form of propositional calculus, which is decidable, and Codd's algebra is logically equivalent to his calculus.

Two asides here: First, relational calculus is usually thought of as being an applied form of predicate calculus, not propositional calculus; however, the fact that we're dealing with finite systems means that it is indeed propositional calculus that we're talking about, at least from a logical point of view. Second, Codd's original calculus was actually less expressive than his algebra (i.e., there were certain algebraic expressions that had no equivalent in the calculus), but this deficiency in the calculus was subsequently remedied. The details need not concern us further in this chapter.

As we've seen, reference [1] also claims that Codd "avoids the trap" of requiring computational completeness and thereby getting into the problem of undecidability. Now, that same reference [1] never actually comes out and states exactly how this goal—i.e., avoiding the trap—is or can be achieved, but it does imply very strongly that it's a matter of drawing a sharp dividing line between the database and computational portions of the language:

> My desire is that **Tutorial D** should cleanly separate set theoretic semantics and computer language semantics[1] ... OO Prescription 3 should be restated to say that **D**'s application sublanguage shall be computationally complete and entirely procedural and **D**'s database sublanguage shall not be computationally complete, shall be entirely nonprocedural, and shall be decidable (though I would still be concerned about how these sublanguages interact with each other) ... [*Another attempt, later:*] Separate **D** into **RD** (the relational, nonprocedural part) and **CD** (the computational, procedural part). Then OO Prescription 3 should be restated to say that **RD** shall not be computationally complete and shall not invoke any operator that cannot be implemented in **RD** ... A relational database language **RD** must be decidable. It follows that it must not be computationally complete, nor should it invoke any procedure that cannot, in principle, be implemented in **RD**.

---

1. On the issue of "set theoretic semantics and computer language semantics," see reference [8].

So do Codd's own language proposals abide by such restrictions? No, they don't! Consider the following quotes from Codd's own writings:

- *From the very first (1969) paper on the relational model* [2]: Let us denote the retrieval sublanguage by R and the host language by H ... R permits the specification for retrieval of any subset of data from the data bank ... The class of qualification expressions which can be used in a set specification is in a precisely specified ... correspondence with the class of well formed formulas of the predicate calculus ... *Any arithmetic functions needed can be defined in H and invoked in R* [italics added].

- *From the revised version of the 1969 paper that appeared in 1970 in Communications of the ACM* [3]: Let us denote the data sublanguage by R and the host language by H ... R permits the specification for retrieval of any subset of data from the data bank ... [The] class of qualification expressions which can be used in a set specification must have the descriptive power of the class of well formed formulas of an applied predicate calculus ... *Arithmetic functions may be needed in the qualification or other parts of retrieval statements. Such functions can be defined in H and invoked in R* [italics added].

And Codd's paper on what he called Data Sublanguage ALPHA [4] had this to say:

All computation of functions is defined in host language statements; all retrieval and storage operations in data sublanguage statements. A data sublanguage statement can, however, contain a use of a function defined in host statements ... An expandable library of functions which can be invoked in queries provides a means of extending the selective capability of DSL ALPHA.

The paper goes on to give several examples of the use of such functions, in both the "target list" and "qualification" portions of queries. So I would say that, in all three of these papers [2], [3], and [4], Codd didn't just fail to "avoid the trap"—apparently, he didn't even think there was a trap to avoid in the first place.

Note: Commenting on an earlier draft of the present chapter, the author of reference [1] claimed that Codd's separation of the languages *R* and *H* was sufficient to "avoid the trap." In particular, he claimed that (a) one effect of that separation was that an invocation in *R* of a function defined in *H* could be regarded as a constant so far as *R* was concerned, and (b) the trap was avoided because functions defined in *H* had no access to the variables of *R*. On reflection, I don't understand these claims. In particular, the specific functions Codd uses in examples in reference [4] most certainly do have access to "the variables of *R*"—the functions in question include analogs of the familiar aggregate operators COUNT, SUM, AVG, MAX, and MIN, all of which are of course explicitly defined to operate on relations (i.e., "the variables of *R*"). And if the point is that these functions only read their operands and don't update them, then a precisely analogous remark could be made in respect of **Tutorial D,** so presumably that isn't the point.

As an aside, I'd like to add that, for reasons it would be invidious to go into detail on here, I've never been much of a fan of the data sublanguage idea anyway[1] (which is partly why the *Manifesto*'s OO Prescription 3 reads the way it does). As I wrote in reference [7]:

> Personally, I've never been entirely convinced that factoring out data access into a separate "sublanguage" was a good idea, [although it's] been with us, in the shape of embedded SQL, for a good while now. In this connection, incidentally, it's interesting to note that with the addition in 1996 of the PSM feature ("Persistent Stored Modules") to the SQL standard, SQL has now become a computationally complete language in its own right!—meaning that a host language as such is no longer logically necessary (with SQL, that is).

In the interests of fairness and accuracy, however, I should add that SQL doesn't include any I/O capabilities, so a host language might still be needed to provide that functionality.

WHY WE WANT COMPUTATIONAL COMPLETENESS

Here again is OO Prescription 3 as originally stated:

> **D** shall be **computationally complete**. That is, **D** may support, but shall not require, invocation from so-called host programs written in languages other than **D**. Similarly, **D** may support, but shall not require, the use of other languages for implementation of user-defined operators.

Reference [1] commented on this prescription as follows:

> I don't understand the text beginning "That is"—it isn't a definition of what it would mean for a language to be computationally complete. Being invocable from, or being able to invoke, programs written in other languages does not make a language computationally complete.

I certainly agree that the text beginning "That is" isn't a definition of computational completeness; it wasn't meant to be, and some rewording might be desirable. Rather, it was meant to spell out certain consequences that follow if **D** is computationally complete—in other words, it was meant to explain why we thought computational completeness was a good idea. As Hugh wrote in his own portion of reference [1]:

> I hope the justification for our inclusion of computational completeness is clear. It is partly so that applications can be written in **D,** to avoid the problems inherent in writing them in some other language, and partly to allow implementations of user defined operators to be coded in **D**.

Later in the correspondence, in response to the criticisms I've already discussed, Hugh said this:

---

1. I mean, I prefer the idea of a single, integrated language that provides both database functionality and conventional programming language functionality—in other words, a language like **Tutorial D**.

We could perhaps have said something like this instead: **D** shall include comprehensive facilities for the implementation of database applications and user defined operators. A computationally complete language would suffice for these purposes but **D** is not required to be computationally complete; nor are applications and user defined operators required to be written in **D**.

But if we agree to back off from computational completeness, how far do we go?—i.e., where do we draw the line? How much computation can we safely support? If it's true that computational completeness just means being able to compute all computable functions, and a computable function just means a function that can be coded using WHILE loops, do we have to prohibit WHILE loops? If so, where does that leave us? *Note:* These questions are rhetorical, of course. My point, in case it isn't obvious, is that I don't think we *can* back off from computational completeness. What's more, Hugh agrees with me; his suggestion that **D** might not need to be computationally complete was never meant as more than a straw man (sorry, straw person).

But there's another issue I need to address under the rubric of why we wanted **D** to be computationally complete. Computational completeness implies among other things that relational expressions can include invocations of user defined, read-only, relation valued operators—operators whose implementation might be coded in **D** itself, perhaps using loops or other procedural constructs—and some critics seem to think that such a state of affairs is contrary to Codd's original intent that queries, etc., should all be expressed declaratively. However, we would argue that all read-only operator invocations are equally "declarative," regardless of where, how, by whom, and in what language(s) those operators are implemented (and regardless of whether they're relation valued). By way of illustration, consider the following example:

```
OPERATOR TABLE_NUM ( K INTEGER ) RETURNS RELATION { N INTEGER } ;
    ... implementation code ...
END OPERATOR ;
```

When invoked, this operator returns a relation representing the predicate "*N* is an integer in the range 1 to *K*" (the utility of such an operator is demonstrated in reference [6]). Surely, then, an invocation such as TABLE_NUM (9999) is equally "declarative" regardless of whether the implementation code (a) is written in **D** by the user doing the invoking, or (b) is written in **D** by some other user, or (c) is written by some user in some other language, or (d) is provided as part of the DBMS.

DOES IT ALL MATTER?

Reference [1] again:

> If **Tutorial D** is undecidable, sooner or later, whether by human user accident or by machine generation, an attempt will be made to evaluate an undecidable statement and the implementation will fail. You might object by pointing out that this does not happen in computationally complete languages such as Ada or Pascal or Fortran or Java. However, you would be quite wrong. It is actually quite easy to code an infinite procedural loop which no compiler can detect.

More specifically, as we've seen, reference [1] claims that a relational language must have an associated decision procedure ("a decision procedure must exist for any logical expression to be evaluated"). But is this claim correct? Predicate calculus has no decision procedure, but at least it's possible to come up with a procedure that's sound and complete. To paraphrase reference [10]:

> Given a well formed formula of predicate calculus, such a procedure will correctly return TRUE if and only if that formula evaluates to TRUE; however, if the formula evaluates to FALSE, either the procedure will return FALSE or it will run forever. (In other words, if some formula is true, it's provably true; if it's false, however, it might not be provably false.)

In practice, therefore, we can incorporate such a procedure into the system implementation. Moreover, we can incorporate a time-out mechanism into that procedure, such that if evaluation of some given expression fails to halt after some predetermined period of time, the system can terminate evaluation and return a message to the user, along the lines of *Expression too complex to evaluate.* (What it mustn't do, of course, is return either TRUE or FALSE! To do that would be to return what Codd—albeit writing in a very different context—called a "severely incorrect" result [5].)

To summarize, therefore:

- Clearly we would like a system in which all possible expressions can be evaluated in finite time.

- This objective can't be achieved if we insist on computational completeness.

- However, we are at least aware of this fact, and so we can plan for it.

- In particular, we can build code into the system that allows it to respond to certain queries by saying, in effect, "I can't answer this query because it's too complex."

In conclusion, I'd like to point out that:

- Inability to respond definitively to certain queries is a common occurrence in ordinary human discourse. We deal with such situations all the time. So having the system occasionally respond with the message *Expression too complex to evaluate* doesn't necessarily mean the system is completely useless.

- In any case, even without computational completeness, it seems likely that there will exist queries that, though answerable in finite time in principle, might take so long to answer in practice that they are effectively unanswerable after all. In other words, the undecidability problem exists, in a sense, even without computational completeness. And our pragmatic fix for that problem (implementing a time-out mechanism) is therefore presumably needed anyway.

- Finally, if computational completeness leads to a lack of decidability, then it follows that conventional programming languages are undecidable. But we've lived with this problem for many years now, and as far as I know it hasn't led to any insuperable difficulties. Why should database languages be any different in this regard?

REFERENCES AND BIBLIOGRAPHY

1.   Anon.: Private correspondence with Hugh Darwen (December 2005 - January 2006).

2.   E. F. Codd: "Derivability, Redundancy, and Consistency of Relations Stored in Large Data Banks," IBM Research Report RJ599 (August 19th, 1969).

3.   E. F. Codd: "A Relational Model of Data for Large Shared Data Banks," *CACM 13,* No. 6 (June 1970). Republished in *Milestones of Research—Selected Papers 1958-1982 (CACM 25th Anniversary Issue), CACM 26,* No. 1 (January 1983).

4.   E. F. Codd: "A Data Base Sublanguage Founded on the Relational Calculus," Proc. 1971 ACM SIGFIDET Workshop on Data Description, Access and Control, San Diego, Calif. (November 1971).

5.   E. F. Codd and C. J. Date: "Much Ado About Nothing," in C. J. Date, *Relational Database Writings 1991-1994* (Addison-Wesley, 1995).

6.   Hugh Darwen (writing as Andrew Warden): "A Constant Friend," in C. J. Date, *Relational Database Writings 1985-1989* (Addison-Wesley, 1990).

7.   C. J. Date: *The Database Relational Model: A Retrospective Review and Analysis*. Reading, Mass.: Addison-Wesley (2000).

8.   C. J. Date: "To Be Is to Be a Value of a Variable" (Chapter 14 in this book).

9.   C. J. Date and Hugh Darwen: *Databases, Types, and the Relational Model: The Third Manifesto* (3rd edition). Boston, Mass.: Addison-Wesley (2006).

10.   Zohar Manna and Richard Waldinger: *The Logical Basis for Computer Programming, Volume 2: Deductive Systems*. Reading, Mass.: Addison-Wesley (1990).

11.   Sybil P. Parker (ed.): *The McGraw-Hill Dictionary of Mathematics*. New York, N.Y.: McGraw-Hill (1994).

12.   Eric W. Weisstein: *CRC Concise Encyclopedia of Mathematics*. Boca Raton, Fla.: Chapman & Hall / CRC (1999).

APPENDIX A: COMPUTABLE FUNCTIONS

In the body of this chapter, I quoted reference [12] as defining a computable function to be one that can be coded using WHILE loops. Following this definition, that reference goes on to say:

FOR loops (which have a fixed iteration limit) are a special case of WHILE loops, so computable functions can also be coded using a combination of FOR and WHILE loops. The Ackermann function is the simplest example of a function which is computable but not primitive recursive.

Let me elaborate briefly on these remarks. First, a function is said to be *recursive* if and only if it "can be obtained [i.e., defined] by a finite number of operations, computations, or algorithms" [11]. (Note that the term "recursive" here is not being used in the usual programming language sense; in fact, it seems to mean nothing more nor less than computable, as that term was previously defined.) Second, a function is said to be *primitive recursive* if and only if it can be coded using FOR loops only [12].

Now, I don't know in what sense the Ackermann function can be said to be "the simplest example" of a function that's recursive (or at any rate computable) but not primitive recursive. For interest, however, I give the definition of that function here (and I note that this definition in particular is certainly recursive in the usual programming language sense). Here it is: Let x and y denote nonnegative integers. Then the Ackermann function $ACK(x,y)$ can be defined thus:

```
OPERATOR ACK ( X NONNEG_INT, Y NONNEG_INT ) RETURNS NONNEG_INT ;
    RETURN ( CASE
                 WHEN X = 0 THEN Y + 1
                 WHEN Y = 0 THEN ACK ( X - 1, 1 )
                 ELSE ACK ( X - 1, ACK ( X, Y - 1 ) )
             END CASE ) ;
END OPERATOR ;
```

Warning: Please don't try to execute this algorithm on a real machine, not even for fairly small x and y.

Chapter 16

The Logic of View Updating

Distance lends enchantment to the view.

—Thomas Campbell

The book *Databases, Types, and the Relational Model: The Third Manifesto* [8], by Hugh Darwen and myself, includes an appendix (reference [12]) on the subject of view updating. The following is a lightly edited extract from the introduction to that appendix:

> In the interest of full disclosure, we must explain that view updating is an area where—unusually!—the authors of this book are not yet in full agreement. Given the importance of the subject matter, however, we decided to go ahead and set our thoughts down in writing anyway, with the hope of at least getting some debate going among those who are interested in such matters. We also decided to present Date's opinions first and Darwen's, as an alternative perspective, second. For obvious reasons, we also decided, again unusually, to write in the first person singular where appropriate.

This chapter is a sequel to that appendix. In it, I want to do two things:

1. To expand on and clarify the arguments I originally advanced in that appendix in support of my view updating proposals

2. To respond to Darwen's objections to those proposals (which are also documented in that appendix)

My view updating proposals as such are also described in that appendix, and I won't bother to explain them again here. (Some of the examples in what follows rely on them, of course, but I think those examples are reasonably self-explanatory anyway.) However, those proposals are based on a series of more fundamental notions—for example, predicates and constraints—and I do want to explain those more fundamental notions briefly before I get into the substance of the chapter. Such is the purpose of the next four sections. Let me immediately add that the discussions in those sections are intended more by way of review than anything else; they're included mainly in order to make the chapter more self-contained, and they're not meant to be controversial.

PREDICATES AND CONSTRAINTS

Let *R* be a relvar (not necessarily a base relvar); then *R* has both a *relvar predicate* and a *relvar constraint*. The relvar predicate—*the predicate* for short—is the intended interpretation for *R;* it is, loosely, what *R* means to the user. The relvar constraint—*the constraint* for short—is the logical AND of all individual constraints that mention *R;* it is, loosely, what *R* means to the system, and it can be regarded as the system's approximation to the corresponding predicate. What I mean by this latter remark is that, in a perfect world, the system would reject updates on *R* that cause the predicate for *R* to be violated; but the system cannot possibly understand that predicate, in general (at least, not completely), and so the best it can do is reject updates on *R* that cause the corresponding constraint to be violated instead.

> *Aside:* Reference [8] uses the terms *base relvar* and *real relvar* interchangeably, and I'll do the same in this chapter. It also refers, sometimes, to the relvar constraint for a given relvar as the *total* constraint for that relvar, and again I'll do the same in this chapter. I should also mention that I've used the terms *external predicate* and *internal predicate* in other writings for what I'm here calling the relvar predicate and the relvar constraint, respectively; however, I now prefer these latter terms. *End of aside.*

By way of illustration, consider the familiar suppliers relvar S, with its attributes S#, STATUS, and CITY. (Usually an SNAME attribute is included as well, but I'll ignore supplier names throughout this chapter for simplicity.) The predicate for that relvar might look like this:

> *The supplier with the specified supplier number (S#) is under contract, has the specified status (STATUS), and is located in the specified city (CITY); also, the status value is in the range 1 to 100 inclusive, and must be 20 if the city is London.*

Observe that this statement is, of necessity, somewhat informal. What about the corresponding constraint? Here's a first attempt:

> *Attributes S#, STATUS, and CITY are of types S#, INTEGER, and CITY, respectively, and S# values are unique; also, STATUS is in the range 1 to 100 inclusive, and if CITY = 'London' then STATUS = 20.*

As you can see, however, this statement is still not all that formal. Here by contrast is a more formal version (involving, as you can see, three separate statements—one relvar definition and two constraint definitions):

```
VAR S BASE RELATION { S# S#, STATUS INTEGER, CITY CHAR }
     KEY { S# } ;

CONSTRAINT SC1 IS_EMPTY ( S WHERE STATUS < 1 OR STATUS > 100 ) ;

CONSTRAINT SC2 IS_EMPTY
          ( S WHERE CITY = 'London' AND STATUS ≠ 20 ) ;
```

Note: As usual, I use **Tutorial D** in this chapter as a basis for coding examples. A detailed definition of that language can be found in reference [8].

Given the foregoing definitions, and assuming for simplicity that no other constraints are in effect, we can say that *the* (total) relvar constraint for relvar S is the logical AND of the key constraint

KEY{S#} and constraints SC1 and SC2. Notice how that total constraint captures part but not all of the corresponding predicate; it's obviously desirable as a general rule that the constraint capture as much as possible of the corresponding predicate, but that "as much as possible" will always be less than 100 percent. In the case at hand, for example, aspects of the predicate such as the specified supplier "being under contract" or "being located somewhere" are, of necessity, not captured by the constraint—they're matters of *interpretation,* and (to repeat) they're understood by the user but not by the system.

Now, I've already said that in a perfect world the system would reject updates that cause the applicable predicate to be violated, but the best it can do is reject updates that cause the applicable constraint to be violated instead. In a similar manner, in a perfect world we would like view updating to be "driven" (as it were) by the applicable predicates; the best we can hope for, however, is for it to be driven by the applicable constraints instead.

DATABASE VARIABLES

Clearly, just as we can observe a logical difference between relation values and variables [8], so too we can observe a logical difference between database values and variables. Now, we don't usually bother to recognize or act on this latter distinction (at least, not explicitly); usually we just use the single term *database* to mean either a database value or a database variable, as the context demands. In this chapter, however, I do need to pay attention to this logical difference. From this point forward, therefore, I'll take care to frame my remarks in terms of database values when it really is database values that I mean, and in terms of database variables when it really is database variables that I mean. Furthermore, just as we customarily use *relation* and *relvar* as abbreviations for relation value and relation variable, respectively, from this point forward I'll use *database* and *dbvar* as abbreviations for database value and database variable, respectively.

It follows from the foregoing that when we "update a relvar," what we're really doing is updating the portion of the applicable dbvar that contains that relvar (i.e., the portion that, in a sense, "is" the relvar in question). For example, if we "insert a tuple"—I'm speaking rather loosely here—into the suppliers relvar S, what we're really doing is inserting that tuple into the suppliers portion of the suppliers-and-parts dbvar. More generally, when we execute a relational assignment of the form

    R := r

(where *R* is a relvar name and *r* is a relational expression), that reference to *R* on the left side is really acting as a *pseudovariable* [8]—the assignment overall is shorthand for one that "zaps" a specified component of the applicable dbvar. While it's convenient, informally, to think of relvars as if they truly were variables in their own right, in some contexts it's important to be more precise about what's really going on. And as you were probably expecting, the topic of the present chapter, view updating, is one such context.

Now, what exactly do we mean when we talk of "components" of some dbvar? What exactly do such components look like? In other words, just what kind of variable is a dbvar? The answer is: It's a *tuple* variable (*tuplevar* for short). As reference [11] explains, the tuplevar in question has one attribute for each relvar "in" the dbvar[1]—those attributes being the components in question—and each of those attributes is relation valued. (Also, of course, it doesn't have any other attributes.) In the case of suppliers and parts, for example, we can think of the overall dbvar as a tuplevar of the following tuple type:

```
TUPLE { S   RELATION { S# S#, STATUS INTEGER, CITY CHAR },
        P   RELATION { P# P#, COLOR COLOR, CITY CHAR },
        SP RELATION { S# S#, P# P#, QTY QTY } }
```

A couple of explanatory points here:

- As I've already said, I'm ignoring supplier names in this chapter. For simplicity, I'll ignore part names and weights as well. Thus, the version of suppliers and parts I'm using here is a little simpler than the one you'll find in many of my other writings.

- More important, when I say the dbvar (or tuplevar) has one attribute for each relvar in the dbvar and no other attributes, I'm tacitly assuming that none of the relvars in the dbvar can be derived from any of the others, because any such derived relvar could be dropped without loss; thus, all of the relvars in the dbvar are independent of one another, in a sense. I'll continue to make this simplifying assumption throughout this chapter, barring explicit statements to the contrary.

Back to suppliers and parts. Let's agree to refer to the suppliers-and-parts dbvar (or tuplevar) as SPDB. Now consider this example of an update on the shipments relvar SP (which is, of course, a relvar in that dbvar):

```
DELETE SP WHERE QTY < QTY(150) ;
```

Now, it's well known that INSERT, DELETE, and UPDATE statements are all really just shorthand for certain assignments [8]. For example, the DELETE statement just shown can be regarded as shorthand for the following assignment to the variable SPDB:

```
SPDB := TUPLE { S    S   FROM SPDB ) ,
                P    P   FROM SPDB ) ,
                SP ( SP FROM SPDB )
                         WHERE NOT ( QTY < QTY(150) ) } ;
```

Explanation: The expression on the right side here is a tuple expression; by definition, therefore,

---

1. I set the word "in" in quotation marks here because (as I've explained in reference [4] and elsewhere) the idea of one variable being contained in another in fact makes no logical sense; in other words, those "relvars" aren't really variables in their own right at all—instead, they're *components of* a variable. From this point forward, however, I'll continue to talk as if relvars were variables in their own right, and I'll continue to refer to them as being in dbvars (without the quotation marks), for simplicity.

it denotes a specific tuple. That tuple has three attributes, called S, P, and SP, respectively. The value of attribute S is specified as S FROM SPDB, which is an expression that denotes the value of the S attribute of the tuple that's the current value of SPDB; in other words, the value in question is simply the current value of the suppliers relvar S. Likewise, the value of attribute P is the current value of the parts relvar P, and the value of attribute SP is a certain restriction of the current value of the shipments relvar SP—namely, that restriction that satisfies the condition NOT(QTY < QTY(150)). Thus, the net effect of the assignment, and hence of the original DELETE, is to update the SP component of SPDB appropriately while leaving the other two components unchanged.

All of that being said, let me now add that of course it's convenient most of the time, at least informally, to talk in terms of updating relvars as such, instead of in terms of updating portions of a dbvar, and I'll continue to do so, as and when appropriate, throughout the remainder of this chapter.

I'll close this section by reminding you of two important properties of assignments—in other words, updates—in general. First, all assignments are required to abide by *The Assignment Principle,* which can be stated as follows:

- After assignment of value v to variable V, the comparison $v = V$ is required to evaluate to TRUE.

    Note that this requirement was certainly satisfied in the case of the DELETE example just discussed (which, as we saw, was really an assignment to the variable SPDB).

Second, assignments to dbvars in particular are required to abide by **The Golden Rule:**

- No dbvar is allowed to have a value that violates its own total dbvar constraint.[1]

    This one requires a little more explanation. We already know that any given relvar *R* has its own (total) relvar constraint, *RC*. Let *DB* be a dbvar, and let *DB* contain relvars *R1, R2, ..., Rn* (only). Let the constraints for those relvars be *RC1, RC2, ..., RCn,* respectively. Then *the* (total) dbvar constraint for *DB* is just the logical AND of all of those relvar constraints and TRUE:

    (RC1) AND (RC2) AND ... AND (RCn) AND TRUE

    Of course, the only way this total dbvar constraint could be violated (i.e., evaluate to FALSE) is if at least one of *RC1, RC2, ..., RCn* is violated. Thus, it's a logical consequence of **The Golden Rule** that no relvar is allowed to have a value that violates its own total relvar constraint either. This latter, weaker requirement is sometimes referred to as **The Golden Rule** as well; indeed, I'll use the term this way myself, at least implicitly, in later parts of this chapter.

---

1. In other writings I've used the term *database constraint* instead of dbvar constraint, precisely because (as previously noted) in those writings I've used the term *database* to refer to both databases and dbvars.

COMPENSATORY UPDATES

In the case of suppliers and parts, there's a foreign key constraint (also known as a referential constraint) from relvar SP to relvar S, and another from relvar SP to relvar P. For definiteness, let's focus on the one from SP to S. Consider the following update on relvar S:

```
DELETE S WHERE S# = S#('S1') ;
```

Clearly, this update has the potential to violate the foregoing referential constraint (and hence to fail). In practice, however, systems usually support certain *foreign key rules,* which can be used to get the system to perform certain *compensatory updates* in such a situation—updates, that is, that will guarantee that the overall result satisfies the referential constraint after all. In the example, the obvious compensatory update is for the system to "cascade the delete" to delete the shipments for supplier S1 as well. To request such an action on the part of the system, we can specify the appropriate rule as part of the applicable foreign key definition, perhaps as follows:

```
VAR SP BASE RELATION { ... } ...
     FOREIGN KEY { S# } REFERENCES S ON DELETE CASCADE ;
```

The effect of such a specification can best be explained in terms of multiple assignment [9]. To be specific, the DELETE statement shown previously—

```
DELETE S WHERE S# = S#('S1') ;
```

—can (and must) now be understood as shorthand for the following "double DELETE":

```
DELETE S  WHERE S# = S#('S1') ,
DELETE SP WHERE S# = S#('S1') ;
```

And this double delete in turn is shorthand for a certain multiple assignment, of course.

Here are some lessons to be learned from this example:

- Compensatory updates can be used in certain situations to avoid certain integrity violations—i.e., certain violations of **The Golden Rule**—that might otherwise occur.

- There must be a way of notifying the system, declaratively, of what compensatory updates are to be performed when. *Note:* The particular notification syntax used in the example—ON DELETE CASCADE—might unfortunately have the effect of causing the compensatory update to be performed only when an explicit DELETE and not a logically equivalent assignment is requested. However, fixing this problem is a matter of proper language design (probably; at any rate, it's beyond the purview of the present chapter).

■   Users too must be made aware of what compensatory updates are to be performed when. Of course, whatever linguistic mechanism is used to notify the system, as required by the previous bullet item, can serve this purpose as well.

■   Certain update requests on the part of the user must now be understood as shorthand for certain expanded requests: certain multiple assignments, to be specific.

Let's look at another example. Suppose we replace the suppliers relvar by two relvars, NLS and NPS; NLS ("non London suppliers") contains tuples for suppliers not in London, and NPS ("non Paris suppliers") contains tuples for suppliers not in Paris. Here are the **Tutorial D** definitions:

```
VAR NLS BASE RELATION { S# S#, STATUS INTEGER, CITY CHAR }
    KEY { S# } ; /* suppliers not in London */

VAR NPS BASE RELATION { S# S#, STATUS INTEGER, CITY CHAR }
    KEY { S# } ; /* suppliers not in Paris  */
```

Of course, this is a very bad design, but at least it's a possible one. It's bad because it leads to redundancy; to be specific, any supplier located in a city other than London or Paris must be represented in both relvars.[1] In other words, the following constraint is in effect (among others):

```
CONSTRAINT OVERLAP
    ( NLS WHERE CITY ≠ 'Paris' ) = ( NPS WHERE CITY ≠ 'London' ) ;
```

Observe that one consequence of stating the foregoing constraint explicitly is that the user, as well as the system, is now aware that the constraint in question is in force.

Consider now the following update on relvar NLS:

```
INSERT NLS RELATION
            { TUPLE { S# S#('S9'), STATUS 40, CITY 'Athens' } } ;
```

Note: I'm assuming here that no tuple for supplier S9 appears in the dbvar prior to the update (and I'll make this same assumption in examples throughout the remainder of this chapter).

On the face of it, this update will fail on a violation of **The Golden Rule:** more specifically, a violation of constraint OVERLAP. Again, however, we could imagine the system performing an appropriate compensatory update—this time, an appropriate INSERT on relvar NPS—such that the constraint isn't violated after all. Of course, we would need a way of declaring to the system, and to the user, that such compensatory updating is to be done; I omit detailed consideration of this point here,

---

1. More precisely, the design is bad because it violates *The Principle of Orthogonal Design* [5]—indeed, it violates what I called in reference [12] a strong form of that principle—precisely because suppliers in neither London nor Paris *must* be represented in both NLS and NPS. (For an explanation of why such a supplier must be represented in both relvars, see reference [5].)

since it's essentially just a language design issue. But assuming the appropriate declaration has been made, the INSERT statement shown previously—

```
INSERT NLS RELATION
          { TUPLE { S# S#('S9'), STATUS 40, CITY 'Athens' } } ;
```

—can (and must) now be understood as shorthand for the following "double INSERT":

```
INSERT NLS RELATION
          { TUPLE { S# S#('S9'), STATUS 40, CITY 'Athens' } } ,
INSERT NPS RELATION
          { TUPLE { S# S#('S9'), STATUS 40, CITY 'Athens' } } ;
```

For the remainder of this chapter, I'll assume that compensatory updates have *not* been requested, barring explicit statements to the contrary.

THE PRINCIPLE OF INTERCHANGEABILITY

As I've demonstrated elsewhere—see, e.g., references [2] and [3]—the question as to which relvars are base ones and which views is to a very large extent arbitrary. I'll use the suppliers example to explain what I mean. Clearly, one possible design for suppliers involves just a single base relvar, like this:

```
S { S#, STATUS, CITY }
```

(irrelevant details omitted for simplicity). Given this design, we could then go on to define the following projections of that base relvar as views:

```
ST { S#, STATUS }
SC { S#, CITY }
```

Alternatively, we could come up with a design in which ST and SC are base relvars, and we could then define their join S as a view. From a logical standpoint, these two designs are equally valid; certainly they both represent the same information. (I'm deliberately ignoring, for now, the fact that the design in which ST and SC are base relvars is capable of representing certain suppliers—namely, those for whom just one of the status and the city is known—that the other design can't represent. I'll come back and revisit this possibility in the section "Partial Mappings," later in the chapter.)

> *Aside:* Before going any further, I need to explain that I'm using the terms *join* and *projection* in the foregoing discussion in a slightly special sense (though I hasten to add that my usage is in full accord with convention in such matters). To be specific, when I say that, e.g., relvar ST is the projection of relvar S on attributes S# and STATUS, I mean that the relation that's the value of relvar ST at any given time is equal to the projection on S# and STATUS of the relation that's the value of relvar S at that time. Analogous remarks apply to all of my references throughout this chapter to relational operators in general (union, restriction, and so on). *End of aside.*

On the basis of examples like this one, I've claimed (in references [2], [3], and elsewhere) that there must be no arbitrary and unnecessary distinctions between base relvars and views: *The Principle of Interchangeability* (of base relvars and views). And I've claimed further that, as a logical consequence of that principle, we must be able to update views, because the updatability of a given relvar must not depend on the essentially arbitrary decision as to whether we choose to make the relvar in question a base relvar or a view.

Now, much of my analysis in reference [12]—my analysis of updating joins and projections in particular—was based on the foregoing principle. However, I now realize, partly as a result of a careful study of Darwen's criticisms in that same reference, that I didn't do an adequate job of justifying either that analysis per se or the proposals that I developed based on it. To be more specific, while I think I did at least touch on most of the relevant issues, I don't think I really said enough about them. The rest of this chapter is an attempt to remedy that omission. (And if there are any serious discrepancies between the present chapter and reference [12]—actually I don't think there are, but I'm saying this to cover myself—then the discussions in this chapter should be regarded as superseding.)

DATABASE INCLUSION AND EQUIVALENCE

As is well known (see, e.g., reference [3]), a database can be regarded as representing *a set of propositions,* assumed by convention to be true ones. Let the sets of propositions represented by databases *dbx* and *dby* be *x* and *y,* respectively. Then database *dbx* is *included in* database *dby* if and only if every proposition in *x* can be derived from those in *y* (where by *derived* I mean "derived in accordance with the normal rules of logic"). Analogously, dbvar *DBx* is *included in* dbvar *DBy* if and only if, at all times, the database that's the current value of *DBx* is included in the database that's the current value of *DBy.* And databases *dbx* and *dby* are *equivalent* if and only if each is included in the other, and dbvars *DBx* and *DBy* are *equivalent* if and only if each is included in the other.

By way of example, let dbvars *DBx* and *DBy* contain, respectively, just the suppliers relvar S and just the relvars ST and SC from the previous section. Let S be defined as the join of ST and SC, thus:

    Myx: S =d ST JOIN SC

(*Myx* here can be read as "the mapping from *DBy* to *DBx*"; in the example, we can get from *DBy* to *DBx*—i.e., we can derive *DBx* from *DBy*—by joining the relvars in *DBy.* The symbol "*=d*" means "is defined as.") Given this definition, then, I hope it's clear that *DBx* is included in *DBy:* Every proposition represented in *DBx* at any given time can certainly be derived from those represented in *DBy* at that time. *Note:* From this point forward, I'll usually omit phrases such as "at any given time" and "at that time," leaving them to be understood from context if necessary. Also, I'll talk for simplicity in terms of propositions being "in" databases or dbvars, instead of saying they're "represented by" those databases or dbvars.

Now, as the example suggests, if *DBx* is included in *DBy,* there must exist a mapping *Myx* from *DBy* to *DBx,* expressible in terms of operators of the relational algebra, according to which *DBx* is defined in terms of (i.e., derivable from) *DBy.* Note the direction here: The mapping is from *DBy* to *DBx,* not the other way around. Note too that the mapping is a function whose range is the whole of

DBx but whose domain is *some subset* of *DBy*[1]—in general, there can be propositions represented in *DBy* that have no counterpart in *DBx*. In the case at hand, either ST or SC might include tuples for suppliers not represented in the other, and therefore not represented in the join either. Indeed, the ability to represent a supplier who has some status but no city or vice versa would typically be cited as a good reason for replacing *DBx* by *DBy* in the first place. *More terminology:* If the mapping *Myx* is such that the domain is the whole of *DBy* (i.e., the subset isn't a proper subset), then *Myx* is a **total** mapping; otherwise it's a **partial** mapping.

Note: Mathematically speaking, a total mapping is just a special case of a partial mapping (i.e., some partial mappings are in fact total). Intuitively, however, we often use the term *partial mapping* to mean one that isn't total, and I'll follow that convention in this chapter.

Once again let dbvar *DBx* be included in dbvar *DBy*. By definition, then, there's a subset *DBz* of *DBy* that's equivalent to *DBx* (and if *DBz* = *DBy*, the mapping *Myx* is total, otherwise it's partial). As a consequence:

- Every query *Qx* on *DBx* has a semantically equivalent counterpart query *Qz* on *DBz* (obviously enough).

- Every update *Ux* on *DBx* has a semantically equivalent counterpart update *Uz* on *DBz* (for otherwise the property that *DBx* is included in *DBz* couldn't be maintained). *Note:* I'm assuming here that the update *Ux* actually succeeds, of course, for otherwise the "update" isn't in fact an update at all, and the question of semantic equivalence doesn't arise.

In particular, therefore, if (a) *DBz* contains base relvars only and *DBx* contains views only—views, that is, that are views of those base relvars specifically—and (b) *DBx* is the dbvar that's made available to some user *U,* then (c) that user *U* must be able to request updates on those views in *DBx,* and those updates, if successful, must map to semantically equivalent updates on the base relvars in *DBz* in terms of which those views are defined. In other words, those views must "look and feel" like base relvars to that user *U*. *Note:* From this point forward I'll use the terms *real dbvar* and *virtual dbvar* to mean, respectively, a dbvar like *DBz* that contains real (i.e., base) relvars only and one like *DBx* that contains views (i.e., virtual relvars) only. I'll also assume in such contexts that the views in the virtual dbvar are views of the base relvars in the real dbvar, barring explicit statements to the contrary.

To return to the example involving relvars S, ST, and SC: Let me now extend the example by imposing a constraint on *DBy* to the effect that projections ST{S#} and SC{S#} are equal, thus:

```
CONSTRAINT ... ST { S# } = SC { S# } ;
```

Now every supplier number appearing in either ST or SC also appears in the other, and so we can say, not only that S is the join of ST and SC, but also that ST and SC are projections of S. In addition to the total mapping *Myx*, in other words, we now have a total mapping *Mxy* in the other direction, and *DBx*

---

1. I'm using the terms *function, domain,* and *range* here in their strict mathematical sense: Given two sets, not necessarily distinct, a function is a rule pairing each element of the first set (the domain) with exactly one element of the second set (the range), such that each element of the range is the image of at least one element of the domain.

and *DBy* are each defined in terms of the other:

```
Myx: S  =d ST JOIN SC

Mxy: ST =d S { S#, STATUS }
     SC =d S { S#, CITY }
```

The two dbvars are now clearly equivalent. *Note:* Mapping *Mxy* here is necessarily total, of course (a mapping from a relvar to some of its projections must always be total), but mapping *Myx* would not be if either of ST and SC contained any tuples with no counterpart in the other (such tuples wouldn't map to anything in the join); that's why we need the constraint.

TOTAL MAPPINGS

I now proceed to examine a series of detailed examples involving, first, total mappings (in this section), and then partial mappings (in the next). *Note:* I assume for simplicity throughout the rest of the chapter that each dbvar contains just the relvars I specify and no others. This simplifying assumption has no material effect on any of the arguments I want to make, of course.

I'll start with a few further remarks on the example from the previous section, repeated here as Example 1.

Example 1:

```
DBx:                        |  DBy:
                            |
                            |
S { S#, STATUS, CITY }      |  ST { S#, STATUS }
   KEY { S# }               |     KEY { S# }
                            |
                            |  SC { S#, CITY }
                            |     KEY { S# }
                            |
                            |  CONSTRAINT ...
                            |     ST { S# } = SC { S# }
                            |
Myx: S =d ST JOIN SC        |  Mxy: ST =d S { S#, STATUS }
                            |       SC =d S { S#, CITY }
```

Note: For simplicity, I've omitted certain constraints that might be required in practice (in particular, constraints SC1 and SC2 on *DBx* and their analogs on *DBy*[1]—see the section "Predicates and

---

1. I note in passing that SC2 is a single-relvar constraint on *DBx* but its analog on *DBy* is a multi-relvar constraint. See reference [6] for further discussion—in particular, for arguments in support of the *Third Manifesto* position that such constraints must be checked immediately, regardless of whether they're formulated as single- or multi-relvar constraints.

Constraints," earlier). However, I've included the constraint on *DBy* that guarantees that mappings *Mxy* and *Myx* are both total. I'll discuss what happens if we drop that constraint in the next section, under Example 4.

If we now take *DBx* to be virtual and *DBy* real, we can come up with a set of rules for updating views that are "total joins"; I did exactly this in reference [12]. (I assume my use of the term *total join* here is self-explanatory.) Conversely, if we take *DBy* to be virtual and *DBx* real, we can come up with a set of rules for updating views whose join is total (i.e., rules for updating certain projections); again I did this in reference [12]. Though I should add that I didn't limit myself in reference [12], as Example 1 does, to cases in which the pertinent joins are one-to-one; however, the considerations that apply in the one-to-many and many-to-many cases are essentially similar to those that apply in the one-to-one case. See reference [12] for further discussion.

———————— ◆ ◆ ◆ ◆ ◆ ————————

I turn now to an example in which the mapping operators are restriction and union instead of projection and join. Relvar S is our usual suppliers relvar; relvars LS and NLS represent London suppliers and "non London" suppliers, respectively.

Example 2:

```
DBx:                        |   DBy:
                            |
S { S#, STATUS, CITY }      |   LS  { S#, STATUS, CITY }
   KEY { S# }               |       KEY { S# }
                            |       /* suppliers in London */
                            |
                            |   NLS { S#, STATUS, CITY }
                            |       KEY { S# }
                            |       /* suppliers not in London */
                            |
                            |   /* no supplier appears in both */
                            |   /* LS and NLS :                */
                            |   CONSTRAINT ... IS_EMPTY
                            |       ( LS { S# } JOIN NLS { S# } )
                            |
Myx: S =d LS UNION NLS      |   Mxy: LS  =d S WHERE CITY = 'London'
                            |        NLS =d S WHERE CITY ≠ 'London'
```

Again I've omitted certain constraints for simplicity (e.g., the constraints that CITY must be London in NLS and mustn't be London in NLS). *Note:* Actually the union in *Myx* here is a disjoint union and could be explicitly stated as such in **Tutorial D,** thus:

```
Myx: S =d LS D_UNION NLS
```

Mappings *Mxy* and *Myx* are clearly both total. Consideration of examples like this one allows us to come up with, among other things, a set of rules for updating "total unions" (i.e., unions obtained via a total mapping), at least in the case where the unions are in fact disjoint unions; again I did this in reference [12]. (We can also use such examples to come up with a set of rules for updating restrictions; I omit further discussion of this issue here, however, because the rules for updating restrictions are fairly noncontroversial, for the most part.)

Here now is a considerably modified version of Example 2 in which the union is not disjoint:

Example 3:

```
DBx:                          |   DBy:
                              |
S { S#, STATUS, CITY }        |   NLS { S#, STATUS, CITY }
   KEY { S# }                 |      KEY { S# }
                              |      /* suppliers not in London */
                              |
                              |   NPS { S#, STATUS, CITY }
                              |      KEY { S# }
                              |      /* suppliers not in Paris  */
                              |
                              |   /* suppliers in neither London */
                              |   /* nor Paris appear in both    */
                              |   /* NLS and NPS :               */
                              |   CONSTRAINT ...
                              |   ( NLS WHERE CITY ≠ 'Paris' ) =
                              |   ( NPS WHERE CITY ≠ 'London' )
                              |
Myx: S =d NLS UNION NPS        |   Mxy: NLS =d S WHERE CITY ≠ 'London'
                              |        NPS =d S WHERE CITY ≠ 'Paris'
```

I've omitted the constraints on *DBy* that CITY mustn't be London in NLS and mustn't be Paris in NPS, also the constraint that no supplier is in both Paris and London. Note that mappings *Mxy* and *Myx* are still both total (though they're a bit more complicated than those in Examples 1 and 2); in other words, *DBx* and *DBy* are still equivalent.

Now, we already know that to say that *DBx* and *DBy* are equivalent is to say, among other things, that every update *Ux* on *DBx* has a semantically equivalent counterpart *Uy* on *DBy* (and vice versa, of course). For example, suppose *Ux* is:

```
INSERT S RELATION
        { TUPLE { S# S#('S9'), STATUS 40, CITY 'Athens' } } ;
```

Clearly, the semantically equivalent counterpart *Uy* on *DBy* is the following double INSERT:

```
INSERT NLS RELATION
          { TUPLE { S# S#('S9'), STATUS 40, CITY 'Athens' } } ,
INSERT NPS RELATION
          { TUPLE { S# S#('S9'), STATUS 40, CITY 'Athens' } } ;
```

So if *DBx* is virtual and *DBy* real, the single INSERT *Ux* must map to (i.e., be implemented as) the double INSERT *Uy;* conversely, if *DBx* is real and *DBy* virtual, the double INSERT *Uy* must map to (i.e., be implemented as) the single INSERT *Ux.* Either way, what must not be allowed is the following single INSERT on *DBy:*

```
INSERT NLS RELATION
          { TUPLE { S# S#('S9'), STATUS 40, CITY 'Athens' } } ;
```

(It mustn't be allowed because there's no semantically equivalent update that can be applied to *DBx*.) So what happens if, nevertheless, that single INSERT is attempted? Clearly there are two possibilities:

- A suitable compensatory update has been requested on *DBy*. In this case, the single INSERT is really just shorthand for a certain double INSERT, and the update succeeds (and corresponds to a certain counterpart update on *DBx,* as already discussed).

- No such compensatory update has been requested on *DBy*. What happens now depends on whether *DBy* is real or virtual:

  - If it's real, the update will fail on a violation of **The Golden Rule** (to be specific, it will fail on a violation of the constraint that suppliers in neither London nor Paris are supposed to be represented in both NLS and NPS).

  - If it's virtual, the best the system can do is map the update to an INSERT on real relvar S. But then the new tuple will appear in NPS (as well as in NLS, as requested), and the update will fail on a violation of *The Assignment Principle* on dbvar *DBy*.

The conclusion is: Regardless of whether *DBy* is real or virtual, suitable compensatory updates *must* be requested for that dbvar in order to maintain equivalence between *DBx* and *DBy*. (As a matter of fact, not requesting compensatory updates would constitute a violation of *The Principle of Interchangeability,* because it would give rise to different errors in the real and virtual cases.)

Consideration of examples along the lines of those above allows us to come up with, among other things, a set of rules for updating total unions, even when the unions in question aren't disjoint unions. Once again I did this in reference [12].

One last point to close this section. I said earlier that the rules for updating restriction views weren't controversial—but maybe that's not quite true. To be specific, the analysis of Example 3 shows that *compensatory updates must be requested whenever restriction views overlap* (as it were). Now, in reference [2], I mentioned the possibility of side effects arising from certain view updates. Here's an extract from that reference:

Several of the rules and examples discussed ... refer to the possibility of side effects ... [It's] well known that side effects are usually undesirable; however, side effects might be unavoidable if [the views being updated] happen to represent overlapping [restrictions] of the same underlying relvar ... What's more, the side effects in question are (for once) desirable, not undesirable.

Now I'm explicitly disavowing that former position! In fact, my instincts were right all along: Side effects *are* undesirable, at least if they're implicit. As I believe the analysis of Example 3 shows, if side effects are visible to the user—in particular, if the user is aware of updates to distinct but overlapping restriction views—then those side effects should, in effect, be made explicit via suitable compensatory update specifications that are themselves visible to the user in turn.

PARTIAL MAPPINGS

The view updating rules I gave in reference [12]—in particular, the rules for deleting through join and inserting through union, which as we'll see later are the ones that Darwen most objects to—were obtained by detailed analysis of examples similar to Examples 1-3 in the previous section, where all mappings were total. What I failed to treat adequately, however, was the case in which the pertinent mappings were partial; in the present section, therefore, I turn my attention to that case. Before I do so, however, let me just note for the record that, based on Darwen's own proposals for inserting through union and deleting through intersection (see the section "Darwen's Proposals" later in the present chapter), it seems that Darwen and I are not in full agreement, even when the mappings are total.

As noted under Example 1 in the previous section (in which *DBx* contained just relvar S and *DBy* just relvars ST and SC), if we were to drop the constraint that ST{S#} = SC{S#}, then mapping *Myx* would no longer be total (at least, it wouldn't be guaranteed to be total). This possibility is summarized as Example 4 below.

Example 4:

```
DBx:                          |   DBy:
                              |
S { S#, STATUS, CITY }        |   ST { S#, STATUS }
   KEY { S# }                 |      KEY { S# }
                              |
                              |   SC { S#, CITY }
                              |      KEY { S# }
                              |
Myx: S =d ST JOIN SC          |   Mxy: ST ‖≥‖d S { S#, STATUS }
                              |        SC ‖≥‖d S { S#, CITY }
```

Note that we can no longer say that relvars ST and SC are projections, as such, of relvar S; the most we can say is that they *include* the corresponding projections. I've used the symbol "$\|\geq\|d$" in the mapping *Mxy* to represent this state of affairs. (Of course, that mapping is no longer completely specified; or, to state the matter more precisely, we know the range of that mapping—namely, the two projections—but we don't know the full codomain.) *Note:* The codomain of a mapping is a superset of the range. For example, in the mapping from integers to their squares, we could say the codomain is the set of all nonnegative integers and the range is that proper subset of the codomain consisting just of the perfect squares 1, 4, 9, ..., and so on. (Of course, the domain in this example is just the set of all integers, positive or negative.)

Now, because *Myx* is partial (meaning there are propositions in *DBy* that don't map to anything in *DBx*), there are certain queries and updates on *DBy* that have no exact counterpart on *DBx*—for example:

- *Query:*

```
ST  /* retrieve all and only the tuples in relvar ST */
```

This query has no counterpart on *DBx* because there can be tuples in ST that have no counterpart in S. (In particular, the expression S{S#,STATUS}, denoting the projection of relvar S on attributes S# and STATUS, is *not* equivalent to the expression ST.)

- *Update:*

```
INSERT ST RELATION { TUPLE { S# S#('S9'), STATUS 40 } }
```

This update has no counterpart on *DBx* because relvar S is incapable of representing a supplier whose status is known but whose city isn't.

So if we take *DBy* to be real and *DBx* virtual (meaning the join S is a view), we might be able to come up with a set of rules for updating joins when the joins in question are *not* obtained via a total mapping. Let's take a closer look. Consider the following update on view S:

```
DELETE S WHERE S# = S#('S1') ;
```

Assume for simplicity that a tuple for supplier S1 does exist in both relvars ST and SC and hence that such a tuple appears in view S also. Then the rule I gave in reference [12] for deleting through a join would cause the ST tuple for S1 *and* the SC tuple for S1 both to be deleted. Such behavior is clearly required if the mapping *Myx* is total; but in the case at hand, of course, it isn't (that's the whole point), and the desired effect of the update—i.e., deleting the tuple for S1 from S—could be achieved by deleting the S1 tuple from just one of ST and SC. Nevertheless, I argued in reference [12] that we should still delete from both. Here are the arguments I gave in support of this position:

- Deleting from both ST and SC at least has the advantage of symmetry. *Note:* I'll have more to say regarding the virtues of symmetry later in this chapter, when I respond to Darwen's criticisms.

- In particular, symmetry has the advantage of avoiding an arbitrary choice (regarding which of ST and SC to delete from). Note that one consequence of *not* appealing to symmetry could be that the expressions ST JOIN SC and SC JOIN ST might have different semantics—surely an undesirable state of affairs.

- Deleting from both also means we have one universal rule for deleting through join, instead of having to deal with possibly many different rules for possibly many different cases. *Note:* I don't mean to suggest that the brief characterization "delete from both" captures the essence of that universal rule—deleting from both just happens to be the degenerate form of the rule that applies in the one-to-one case. See reference [12] for further discussion.

- It's intuitively obvious that inserting a tuple into S must cause a tuple to be inserted into both ST and SC, even if the mapping *Myx* isn't total (for otherwise the new tuple wouldn't appear in the join, as required).[1] Thus, deleting from both in the case under discussion means not only that the delete rule is symmetric in itself, but also that it's symmetric with respect to the insert rule.

- Finally, we can of course avoid deleting from both, if we want to, by not deleting from S in the first place—in particular, by not giving the user delete rights over that view.

I still subscribe to the foregoing arguments, but now I want to appeal to an additional one. In the example under discussion, it would indeed be safe for the system to delete the S1 tuple from just one of ST and SC, as we've seen. However, it would be safe *only because the mapping Myx is partial;* it would definitely be unsafe, and in fact incorrect, otherwise. So the question is: Is the system aware of this fact—the fact, that is, that mapping *Myx* is partial?[2] More generally, does the system know which mappings are partial and which total?

Well, it seems to me the most the system could do to address this question is, given a particular view update, to try the effects of implementing that update in more than one way (I mean, of course, more than one way that appears at least superficially reasonable). Now, I'm pretty sure the system isn't going to do this—but if it did, then if different implementations led to different results, the mapping would clearly be partial. If they didn't, however, then of course it still wouldn't follow that the mapping was total. In principle, therefore, the system *might* sometimes know that a given mapping is partial; but I don't think it could ever know for sure that a given mapping is total. So I could be wrong, but it seems to me that, in general, the answer to the question ("Does the system know which mappings are partial and which total?") must be *no*.

If the analysis of the previous paragraph is correct, then the next question is: Which assumption is safer?—assume mappings are always partial, or assume they're always total? Let's examine this question.

Suppose the system assumes mappings are always partial. For a given update request, then, the system will have to choose the most appropriate way to respond to that request. In the case at hand, for example, the system will have to choose among the following options:

---

1. I'm assuming here, as I did in reference [12] (and as Darwen does too—see later), that inserting a tuple that already exists in the target relvar is a no op.

2. I remind you that, in the example under discussion, mapping *Myx* as declared to the system merely asserts that S is the join of ST and SC. In this particular case, therefore, the question becomes: Is the system able to determine unequivocally, from this assertion alone, that *Myx* is partial? To jump ahead of myself for a moment, it seems obvious to me that the answer to this question is *no*.

1.   Reject the DELETE entirely, on the grounds that there isn't enough information to choose any other option.

2.   Delete from just ST or just SC.

3.   Delete from both ST and SC.

Option 1 seems unsatisfactory, because the update will fail when it could have succeeded (and indeed *should* have succeeded if the mapping happened to be total). Option 2 raises the question of how the system is to decide which relvar to delete from; not only does there seem to be no good way to answer this question, but (as noted earlier) it raises the unpleasant possibility that the expressions ST JOIN SC and SC JOIN ST might have different semantics. What's more, the update will fail in this case (on a **Golden Rule** violation) if the mapping does happen to be total, when again it should have succeeded. Overall, therefore, I think the system should go for Option 3.

But, of course, Option 3 is the only sensible option if the mapping is total (in that case, indeed, it's the only one that's logically correct). I therefore conclude that it's better for the system to adopt the assumption that mappings are always total—with the implication that the view updating rules I gave in reference [12] should be followed in all cases. In other words, I think we should abide by a universal set of rules that do at least always work and do guarantee that mappings are total when they're supposed to be. If those rules do sometimes give rise to consequences that are considered unpalatable for some reason, then there are always certain pragmatic fixes, such as using the system's security subsystem to prohibit certain updates, that can be adopted to avoid those consequences.

Note: Please don't misunderstand me here. I'm not saying we *must* employ those pragmatic fixes in order for the system to work properly. A system that relies for its correct operation on the user, or the database administrator, "doing the right thing"—e.g., using the security subsystem appropriately—is obviously not acceptable. So we must always at least permit view updates, even when the mappings aren't total, and we must have a set of rules that work even in that case. That's why I advocate the position I do.

Example 5 below is a modified version of Example 3, in which I've dropped the constraint to the effect that suppliers in neither London nor Paris are represented in both NLS and NPS. *Myx* is now a partial mapping; a supplier in neither London nor Paris must be represented in at least one of NLS and NPS, but given only their union we can't tell whether it's one or both, and if it's one then which one it is. *Note:* I'll have more to say about the intuitive aspects of this example at the end of the section.

Example 5:

```
DBx:                              |  DBy:
                                  |
S { S#, STATUS, CITY }            |  NLS { S#, STATUS, CITY }
   KEY { S# }                     |     KEY { S# }
                                  |     /* suppliers not in London */
                                  |
                                  |  NPS { S#, STATUS, CITY }
                                  |     KEY { S# }
                                  |     /* suppliers not in Paris  */
                                  |
Myx: S =d NLS UNION NPS           |  Mxy: NLS ‖≤‖d S WHERE CITY ≠ 'London'
                                  |       NPS ‖≤‖d S WHERE CITY ≠ 'Paris'
```

Note: The symbol "$\|\leq\|d$" in *Mxy* is meant to suggest that relvars NLS and NPS are included in, but aren't necessarily equal to, the corresponding restrictions. (As in Example 4, in fact, the mapping isn't completely specified.)

Now let *DBx* be virtual and *DBy* real, and consider the following update on S:

```
INSERT S RELATION
        { TUPLE { S# S#('S9'), STATUS 40, CITY 'Athens' } } ;
```

The rule I gave in reference [12] for inserting through a union would cause the tuple for S9 to be inserted into both NLS and NPS. It's clear, however, that the desired effect of the update (i.e., inserting the S9 tuple into S) could be achieved by inserting it into just one of NLS and NPS. But the advantages of inserting into both are similar to those I gave under Example 4 in favor of my proposed rule for deleting through a join: Basically, it means we have one universal rule—one symmetric rule, moreover—for dealing uniformly with all cases. What's more, the option of inserting into just one of NLS and NPS is available only because the mapping *Myx* is partial. Again, therefore, I have to ask: Does the system know which mappings are partial and which total? And my answer to this question, and the conclusions I draw from that answer, are essentially the same as they were under Example 4, earlier.

To close this section, let me now confess that the foregoing example (i.e., Example 5) intuitively fails. As you might recall, I said earlier that any supplier in neither London nor Paris *must* be represented in both NLS and NPS. When I said that, however, I was making a tacit assumption about the relvar predicates; to be specific, I was assuming there was no particular reason why such a supplier should be represented in one of the relvars and not the other. (Given that assumption, in fact, permitting some supplier to be represented in just one of the relvars would constitute a violation of *The Closed World Assumption* [7].) However, examples of the same general nature as Example 5 can and certainly do arise in practice—examples, that is, in which some "entity" (apologies for this sloppy terminology) is legitimately supposed to be represented in one relvar and not another, and the system doesn't know which relvar is the right one. Let me justify this claim by briefly describing such a situation:

- Suppose that any given supplier is (a) either preferred or not and (b) either expensive or not, and suppose preferred suppliers are represented in relvar PS and expensive ones in relvar XS.

■   Suppose further that the database designer has decided, for some reason, not to introduce an attribute anywhere that might be used to indicate (a) whether a given supplier is preferred or not or (b) whether a given supplier is expensive or not. (Such a design might be open to criticism, but at least it's a possible one.)

Now suppose the user wishes to insert a new supplier tuple, say for supplier S9. Then the user knows whether that tuple is to be inserted into PS or XS or both, *but the system doesn't;* the system has no way of deciding for itself which action is appropriate, because there aren't any attributes it can use as a basis for such a decision.

DARWEN'S OVERALL OBJECTION

I turn now to Darwen's objections, as documented in reference [12], to my view updating proposals. *Note:* Darwen uses the term *database* in his objections where the term *dbvar* would sometimes be more appropriate (this observation is just a statement of fact—it's not meant as a criticism). For consistency, therefore, my responses in what follows will sometimes do the same.

Darwen begins thus:

My objection to Date's approach is simply that the rules for inserting through union and deleting through join require the system sometimes to make an arbitrary interpretation of an ambiguous request. I maintain instead that ambiguous requests should be rejected.

This paragraph represents a summary statement of Darwen's overall position, so let me begin my response by summarizing my overall reaction to it. Darwen claims that "[my] rules for inserting through union and deleting through join require the system sometimes to make an arbitrary interpretation of an ambiguous request." I don't disagree with the essence of this claim; as I've shown in this chapter already, there are indeed situations where certain view updates might be implemented in more than one way. However, I've also given my reasons (some but not all of which are just a repeat of ones given previously in reference [12]) for opting for one specific implementation in such cases. So Darwen and I don't disagree on the facts of the matter; what we do disagree on is what to do about those facts.

Before going any further, let me explain what I mean when I say I agree with "the essence of" Darwen's claim. The fact is, I have some quibbles over the exact phrasing of that claim. First, I don't much care for the adjectives *arbitrary* and *ambiguous,* which seem to me unnecessarily pejorative. I've already explained why I don't regard my rules as arbitrary. As for ambiguity, part of the point of my rules is precisely to make requests that might otherwise be thought ambiguous *un*ambiguous, meaning their effect is precisely specified. Moreover, given the discussions in earlier sections of this chapter, it's not even clear to me that the system can always know whether a given request is in fact ambiguous anyway, in the sense in which I think Darwen is using that term. In other words, I'm not sure it's even possible for the system, selectively and appropriately, to reject some updates while accepting others.

I note also that Darwen juxtaposes "inserting through union" with "deleting through join," rather than the more obvious "deleting through intersection." Of course, I realize that intersection is just a special case of join (and my rules for updating through join do degenerate to those for updating through intersection when the join in question is in fact an intersection); but I find it more apt and more convenient, sometimes, to refer to deleting through intersection specifically in what follows, even though I did discuss deleting through join in an earlier section of this chapter.

DARWEN'S DETAILED OBJECTIONS

Darwen begins his detailed criticisms as follows:

> As a basis for the discussions to follow, I now introduce some notation, of my own personal preference ... Let *R* be a relvar. Then I define the expression *R(t)* to be equivalent to the truth valued expression $t \in R$. The notation appeals to my perception of a relvar as representing a time-varying truth valued function—the extension of the relvar predicate varies over time (though the intension of course does not). Thus, the expression *R(t)* can be thought of as denoting an invocation of that function.

Comment: It's not really germane to the present discussion, but I must say I don't much care for the term *time-varying function*. Functions in mathematics, truth valued or otherwise, don't vary over time. Indeed, it was precisely the fact that we—i.e., Darwen and I—found Codd's use, in his early papers [1], of the term "time-varying *relation*" to be rather unfortunate that led us to introduce the term *relvar*. (Functions are a special case of relations in general, of course.)

Be that as it may, Darwen continues:

> I consider the simplest database imaginable that is sufficient for the purpose at hand: one consisting of just two relvars, both of degree zero ... To give my example a semblance of realism, imagine the enterprise to be a shop. At all times the shop is either open for business or closed. The shop is equipped with a burglar alarm. At all times the alarm is either set or not set. The purpose of the database is to record (a) whether or not the shop is open and (b) whether or not the alarm is set. Assume until further notice that the two [relvars] are not subject to any constraint, even though it might seem a little peculiar to allow the alarm to be set while the shop is open. Here are the **Tutorial D** definitions:

```
VAR THE_SHOP_IS_OPEN ... RELATION { } KEY { } ;

VAR THE_ALARM_IS_SET ... RELATION { } KEY { } ;
```

Either of the following statements will suffice to record the fact that the shop is open:

```
THE_SHOP_IS_OPEN := TABLE_DEE ;

INSERT THE_SHOP_IS_OPEN TABLE_DEE ;
```

Likewise, either of the following will suffice to record the fact that the alarm is not set:

```
THE_ALARM_IS_SET := TABLE_DUM ;
```

```
DELETE THE_ALARM_IS_SET ;
```

Observe now that, using my *R(t)* notation, the expression

```
THE_SHOP_IS_OPEN ( TUPLE { } )
```

is a formal assertion of the truth of the proposition "The shop is open." I will abbreviate it from this point forward to just

```
THE_SHOP_IS_OPEN ( )
```

And I will define the expression

```
THE_ALARM_IS_SET ( )
```

("The alarm is set") analogously.

Comment: I have two comments here, one minor, one less so. First the minor one: When Darwen says THE_SHOP_IS_OPEN(TUPLE{}) is a formal statement, or assertion, of the truth of the proposition "The shop is open," surely he means it's a formal statement of the truth *value* of that proposition. (Because that assertion might evaluate to FALSE, of course; and if it does, it means the shop is shut. To be specific, the assertion will evaluate to TRUE if and only if the 0-tuple TUPLE{} does in fact appear in the relvar THE_SHOP_IS_OPEN.)

My more serious comment is that Darwen's "simplest database imaginable" might in fact be too simple to illustrate the points I think he wants to make, for reasons that I hope will become clear as proceed. I note also that another design, logically equivalent to Darwen's but perhaps more intuitively obvious, would involve a single relvar SHOP with two truth valued attributes OPEN and ALARMED, with the obvious semantics. The following mappings demonstrate the equivalence of the two designs:

```
/* from THE_SHOP_IS_OPEN and THE_ALARM_IS_SET to SHOP: */

SHOP =d RELATION { TUPLE
                 { OPEN    ( THE_SHOP_IS_OPEN = TABLE_DEE ) ,
                   ALARMED ( THE_ALARM_IS_SET = TABLE_DEE ) } }
/* from SHOP to THE_SHOP_IS_OPEN and THE_ALARM_IS_SET: */

THE_SHOP_IS_OPEN =d ( SHOP WHERE OPEN ) { }
THE_ALARM_IS_SET =d ( SHOP WHERE ALARMED ) { }
```

Note that relvar SHOP always contains exactly one tuple (and it has an empty key—i.e., it satisfies the key constraint KEY{}). Interpreting the various observations that Darwen makes in what follows, based on his two-relvar design, in terms of this single-relvar design can serve, I think, to throw additional light on some of those observations.

Darwen continues:

I would also like to introduce some new notation for updating the database. In *The Third Manifesto,* we regard relational assignment as the fundamental update operator, and of course I have no problem with that position. For present purposes, however (and possibly others), I prefer to think of *expressing belief in a single "atomic" proposition* as being even more fundamental than relational assignment. To "insert a tuple" into a relvar is to express belief in the truth of the proposition represented by the appearance of that tuple in that relvar; to "delete a tuple" from a relvar is to express the corresponding disbelief (i.e., belief in the truth of the negation of that proposition). In keeping with that perception, I will use imperatives of the following deliberately verbose form—

```
IT IS [ NOT ] THE CASE THAT R ( [ t ] ) ;
```

—where the 0-tuple is implicit if *t* is omitted. So IT IS THE CASE THAT $R(t)$ is equivalent to $R := R$ UNION RELATION$\{t\}$ and also to INSERT R RELATION$\{t\}$; likewise, IT IS NOT THE CASE THAT $R(t)$ is equivalent to $R := R$ MINUS RELATION$\{t\}$ and also to some DELETE statement. Thus, for example, to record the opening of the shop for business and the simultaneous turning off of the alarm, I can write:

```
IT IS THE CASE THAT THE_SHOP_IS_OPEN ( ) ,
IT IS NOT THE CASE THAT THE_ALARM_IS_SET ( ) ;
```

(a multiple assignment).

Now let me introduce a couple of views:

```
VAR THE_SHOP_IS_OPEN_OR_THE_ALARM_IS_SET VIRTUAL
  ( THE_SHOP_IS_OPEN UNION THE_ALARM_IS_SET ) ;

VAR THE_SHOP_IS_OPEN_AND_THE_ALARM_IS_SET VIRTUAL
  ( THE_SHOP_IS_OPEN JOIN THE_ALARM_IS_SET ) ;
```

Comment: I observe at this juncture that the dbvar that contains just these two views is certainly not equivalent to the dbvar that contains just the two base relvars; more specifically, the latter dbvar isn't included in the former (there are propositions in the latter that can't be derived from those in the former). For example, the query THE_SHOP_IS_OPEN ("Retrieve the set of tuples currently appearing in relvar THE_SHOP_IS_OPEN") has no counterpart query in terms of those views. It seems to me, therefore, that anyone who attempts to update those views must be prepared for those updates to have possibly undesirable effects. For that very reason, indeed, I might be tempted to prohibit them (the updates, I mean). But I certainly wouldn't *insist* on such prohibition.

By the way, I have no objection to the idea of "expressing belief in propositions" as a basis for the design of certain update operations. Indeed, I'm on record as suggesting very much the same thing myself, in references [3] and [10].

Note: Here for the record are analogs of Darwen's two views in terms of my suggested single-relvar design:

```
VAR THE_SHOP_IS_OPEN_OR_THE_ALARM_IS_SET VIRTUAL
    ( ( EXTEND SHOP ADD ( ( OPEN OR ALARMED ) AS X ) ) { X } ) ;

VAR THE_SHOP_IS_OPEN_AND_THE_ALARM_IS_SET VIRTUAL
    ( ( EXTEND SHOP ADD ( ( OPEN AND ALARMED ) AS X ) ) { X } ) ;
```

———————— ◆ ◆ ◆ ◆ ◆ ————————

Darwen continues:

Under Date's proposals the following updates would both be legal:

```
IT IS THE CASE THAT THE_SHOP_IS_OPEN_OR_THE_ALARM_IS_SET ( ) ;

IT IS NOT THE CASE THAT THE_SHOP_IS_OPEN_AND_THE_ALARM_IS_SET ( ) ;
```

Under the semantics of UNION and JOIN, those two update statements both mean exactly what they say, and therefore they are both ambiguous—indeterminate—as far as the required effect on the database is concerned. The first can be implemented by assigning TABLE_DEE to either THE_SHOP_IS_OPEN or THE_ALARM_IS_SET, or both. Date proposes that the DBMS be required to choose the third possibility, advancing an observation regarding symmetry as justification. Similarly, the second can be implemented by assigning TABLE_DUM to either THE_SHOP_IS_OPEN or THE_ALARM_IS_SET, or both, and again Date's proposal requires the DBMS to choose the third possibility and again the observation regarding symmetry is advanced as justification. I remark that this justification could also be used to allow an expression of the form $x+y$ (or a name standing for that expression, to make the analogy with views a little closer) to be the target of an assignment: If z is the value to be assigned, just assign $z/2$ to both x and y.

Comment: I'd like to break in here to defend the notion of symmetry—a notion that Darwen appears not to have much use for, at least in the present context. First let me say that I very much agree with Polya when he says in reference [13]: "If a problem is symmetric in some ways we may derive some profit from noticing its interchangeable parts and it often pays to treat those parts which play the same role in the same fashion ... Try to treat symmetrically what is symmetrical, and do not destroy wantonly any natural symmetry." I also agree with him when he says in reference [14]: "We expect that any symmetry found in the data and condition of the problem will be mirrored by the solution ... Symmetry should result from symmetry."

Now, I seriously doubt whether Darwen would disagree with these remarks of Polya's. After all, he and I have appealed to the notion of symmetry ourselves in connection with, e.g., our rejection of the rule that certain keys be designated as "primary" and therefore treated as special in some way [8]. Even in the matter at hand, in fact (inserting through union, deleting through intersection), I observe that Darwen's preferred solution—namely, simply rejecting the update—can be regarded as an appeal to symmetry, in part.

So where exactly do we differ? I think the difference is: I want the update to succeed; Darwen wants it to fail. Having it succeed seems more useful to me!—indeed, having it succeed is logically required in some circumstances, as I've tried to argue earlier in this chapter. Given this state of affairs, I therefore appeal to symmetry, among other things (not, as Darwen's text seems to suggest, to symmetry alone), in formulating my proposals.

To return to Polya for a moment, I observe that his remarks regarding symmetry are actually a logical consequence of what he calls *The Principle of Insufficient Reason* [14]:

> *No [solution] should be favored of eligible possibilities among which there is no sufficient reason to choose.*

I would invoke this principle in rejecting Darwen's suggestion that assigning z to $x+y$ might be carried out by assigning $z/2$ to both x and y, because this solution is just one out of many possibilities, with no good ("sufficient") reason to choose it over any other. (Not to mention the fact that I see no benefit in allowing assignment to expressions such as $x+y$ anyway—especially if, as I'm quite sure would have to be the case, such assignments were allowed but assignments to $x-y$ weren't.) By contrast, I've tried to argue that there *are* sufficient reasons for choosing my rules over other possibilities for inserting through union and deleting through intersection. Of course, Darwen might appeal to *The Principle of Insufficient Reason* as justification for *his* position: namely, that inserting through union and deleting through intersection should fail (at least in "ambiguous" cases). However, I've already explained why I think those updates should succeed.

All of that being said, let me now point out that, while it's true that under my proposals the following update *requests* would both be legal—

    IT IS THE CASE THAT THE_SHOP_IS_OPEN_OR_THE_ALARM_IS_SET ( ) ;

    IT IS NOT THE CASE THAT THE_SHOP_IS_OPEN_AND_THE_ALARM_IS_SET ( ) ;

—it's also true that they'll either both fail or be no ops. To be specific, the first will fail on a violation of *The Assignment Principle* (on the *virtual* dbvar), unless "the shop is open" and "the alarm is set" are currently both true, in which case the update is a no op. Similarly, the second will fail (again on a violation of *The Assignment Principle* on the virtual dbvar), unless "the shop is open" and "the alarm is set" are currently both false, in which case the update is again a no op. *Note:* The reason they fail, in the cases where they do, is that updating either view as requested will update the other one as well, as was *not* requested.

——————— ◆ ◆ ◆ ◆ ———————

Darwen continues:

> In my opinion, both updates should be rejected. The reader who thinks that position harsh should perhaps consider what advantages database users might gain from the proposals that I am rejecting. The ability to insert through union? Well, if I, the designer of THE_SHOP_IS_OPEN and THE_ALARM_IS_SET, really want my users to be able to insert into their union, I would resort to the following artifice in the view definition:

```
VAR THE_SHOP_IS_OPEN_OR_THE_ALARM_IS_SET VIRTUAL
  ( WITH RELATION { TUPLE { STATUS 'open'   } } AS OPEN,
         RELATION { TUPLE { STATUS 'alarmed' } } AS ALARMED :
     ( THE_SHOP_IS_OPEN JOIN OPEN ) UNION
     ( THE_ALARM_IS_SET JOIN ALARMED ) ) ;
```

Here it is clear that the operands of the UNION are disjoint. Now, for example, the opening of the shop can be expressed as:

```
IT IS THE CASE THAT THE_SHOP_IS_OPEN_OR_THE_ALARM_IS_SET
                              ( TUPLE { STATUS 'open' } ) ;
```

Similarly, the turning off of the alarm can be expressed as:

```
IT IS NOT THE CASE THAT THE_SHOP_IS_OPEN_OR_THE_ALARM_IS_SET
                              ( TUPLE { STATUS 'alarmed' } ) ;
```

I assume here that the two joins and the union mentioned in the view definition would indeed be updatable, under both Date's proposal and the proper subset of that proposal that I believe I would not object to. (I use JOIN rather than EXTEND in the view definition just to float the idea that a dyadic operator invocation might be updatable even if only one of its operands is a variable.)

Comment: I'm glad to see that Darwen is not opposed to inserting through union in all cases (presumably he wants the operation to fail only in those cases he regards as ambiguous). However, his use of what he calls an "artifice" to avoid such ambiguity seems to me to come very close to adopting my own proposals (in reference [12] and elsewhere) regarding "the strong form of orthogonality"!—see the next section, also Example 2 in the section "Total Mappings," earlier.

I have no objection to the idea floated in Darwen's final (parenthesized) sentence here. I didn't consider it explicitly in reference [12] purely for space reasons.

───────── ♦ ♦ ♦ ♦ ─────────

Darwen continues:

Now let me get back to the original view definitions:

```
VAR THE_SHOP_IS_OPEN_OR_THE_ALARM_IS_SET VIRTUAL
  ( THE_SHOP_IS_OPEN UNION THE_ALARM_IS_SET ) ;
```

```
VAR THE_SHOP_IS_OPEN_AND_THE_ALARM_IS_SET VIRTUAL
  ( THE_SHOP_IS_OPEN JOIN THE_ALARM_IS_SET ) ;
```

I note in passing, incidentally, that if these two views are the only relvars ever used as targets of update operations, then under Date's approach they will always be equal in value in spite of the stark logical difference (OR *vs.* AND) in the predicates they represent.

Comment: I regard this "note in passing" as seriously unfair. Darwen wants to have his cake and eat it too! Let me explain. First, the proviso that the two views be "the only relvars ever used as targets" is of course crucial; in practice, it seems to me quite unlikely that they *would* be the only such targets—and if they aren't, then the observation is hardly very relevant. (As I pointed out earlier, the dbvar that contains just these two views is not equivalent to—it's not even included in—the dbvar that contains just the two base relvars, and we should therefore not be surprised if updates on the former sometimes have undesirable effects.)

Second, it was Darwen, not me, who imposed the condition that the two relvars (THE_SHOP_IS_OPEN and THE_ALARM_IS_SET) "are not subject to any constraint." Given the intended interpretations—i.e., the predicates—for those two relvars, however, I think they should, and probably would, be subject to some constraint. To be specific, I think the following intuitively reasonable constraint should and probably would be in effect:

    CONSTRAINT ALARMED_IFF_SHUT THE_ALARM_IS_SET ≠ THE_SHOP_IS_OPEN ;

("The alarm is set if and only if the shop is shut"). If it is, then the updates

    IT IS THE CASE THAT THE_SHOP_IS_OPEN_OR_THE_ALARM_IS_SET ( ) ;

and

    IT IS NOT THE CASE THAT THE_SHOP_IS_OPEN_AND_THE_ALARM_IS_SET ( ) ;

will both fail on a violation of **The Golden Rule** (more specifically, of the constraint ALARMED_IFF_SHUT) under my view updating proposals. (And if they don't violate **The Golden Rule,** because the constraint isn't in effect after all, then as previously discussed they'll violate *The Assignment Principle* instead, unless they're no ops.)

There's a little more I'd like to say regarding the constraint ALARMED_IFF_SHUT. First, Darwen himself says "it might seem a little peculiar to allow the alarm to be set while the shop is open" (a state of affairs that *is* allowed if there aren't any constraints). But if the constraint ALARMED_IFF_SHUT does apply, there doesn't seem to be much point in having both relvars (i.e., THE_SHOP_IS_OPEN and THE_ALARM_IS_SET) in the first place. In fact, if that constraint does apply, then the union view will always be equal to TABLE_DEE and the intersection view will always be equal to TABLE_DUM.[1] For definiteness, let's focus on the union view. Since that view is always equal to TABLE_DEE, it should surely be the case that the suggested insert should simply be a no op—but the presence of the constraint has the effect of converting that no op into an operation that fails. Of course, the status quo is preserved either way, but for different reasons in the two cases. Which means, of course, that the constraint ought really to be accompanied by an appropriate compensatory update specification!—for otherwise we'll have a violation of *The Principle of Interchangeability* on our hands once again (see the discussion of Example 3 in the section "Total Mappings," earlier).

---

1. What's the analog of that constraint with my single-relvar design? What are the implications?

My point here can be summed up as follows: If the predicates for relvars *A* and *B* don't allow the same tuple to appear in both *A* and *B* at the same time but the corresponding constraints do, then we simply haven't done a very good design job; I mean, we haven't done a very good job of capturing the intent of the predicates in the constraints, and the design isn't a very faithful model of the real world. In which case I don't think it's reasonable to complain that certain updates don't behave in the way we might think we want them to.

What's more, in the example at hand, if the two relvars are indeed not subject to any constraint, then I don't think I'd try to perform the proposed view updates anyway. As noted earlier, in fact, I think I might even use the system's security mechanism to prohibit them.

Let me immediately anticipate one of Darwen's reactions to the foregoing paragraph. The idea that if you don't like what happens when you do *X*, then you shouldn't do *X*—"If it hurts when you hit yourself over the head with a hammer, then don't hit yourself over the head with a hammer"—is sometimes called *The Groucho Principle.* My suggestion (i.e., if you don't like what happens when you do certain updates, then don't do those updates) can be seen as an appeal to that principle. And I believe Darwen would claim that if the only argument you can find in support of some position is an appeal to *The Groucho Principle,* then that position must be pretty weak.

I agree with this claim in general. But, of course, I don't believe in the case at hand that an appeal to *The Groucho Principle* is the only argument I have to support my position. Rather, I believe my position is supported by—among several other things!—(a) *The Principle of Interchangeability,* together with (b) the fact that the problem is unlikely to arise in a well designed database anyway, together with (c) the fact that even in a badly designed database, if the updates are done after all, then at least their effects are well defined. In particular, as noted earlier, my view updating rules certainly don't *require* the use of security constraints in any particular circumstance.

———— ♦ ♦ ♦ ♦ ————

Darwen continues:

> I have shown that [the foregoing] updates are indeterminate. However, I agree that if those indeterminacies can be resolved by the existence of an appropriate constraint, then the update in question might be permitted. For example, suppose the shop sensibly decides that it is not a good idea ever to set the alarm when it is open for business:

```
CONSTRAINT NOT_ALARMED_WHEN_OPEN
    IS_EMPTY ( THE_SHOP_IS_OPEN JOIN THE_ALARM_IS_SET ) ;
```

Comment: I don't like this constraint!—I mean, I don't find it intuitively reasonable (unlike my constraint ALARMED_IFF_SHUT). Note in particular that it's satisfied if the shop is shut and the alarm isn't set: intuitively not a very desirable state of affairs. Still, never mind. Darwen continues:

> But this particular constraint does not resolve the indeterminacies. For the first update [i.e., insert through union], the DBMS knows that just one of the two underlying real relvars is to be assigned TABLE_DEE, but it does not know which. For the second [i.e., delete through intersection], all three possibilities satisfy the constraint.

Comment: I agree the specified constraint doesn't resolve the indeterminacies (though, to repeat, I don't think that constraint is intuitively reasonable anyway). Under my rules, however, both updates will either fail or be no ops anyway, as previously discussed; either way, they'll have no effect.

DARWEN'S OBJECTIONS TO ORTHOGONALITY

Darwen also objects to something else I advocate: namely, *The Principle of Orthogonal Design* (or, at least, he objects to what I called in reference [12] a "strong form" of that principle). To quote:

> Date also advances, in connection with his position on insert-through-union, a certain "strong form" of *The Principle of Orthogonal Design,* observing that results such as the one I object to are avoided if that strong form of the principle is followed. (I remark that there does not seem to be a counterpart to this observation that could apply to delete-through-join, except in the special case where the join degenerates to intersection.) I do not hold with this strong form of the principle at all. I see no advantage, ever—and sometimes positive disadvantage—in choosing a design that adheres to it over one that does not, as I now explain.

Comment: Darwen says "there does not seem to be a counterpart to this observation that could apply to delete-through-join, *except in the special case where the join degenerates to intersection*" (my italics). Well, yes—exactly! I think this argument of Darwen's serves to bolster the complaint I made earlier, to the effect that he should really be talking about deleting through intersection instead of through join.

Darwen also says he sees no advantage in adhering to the strong form of *The Principle of Orthogonal Design.*[1] Well, of course, I would argue that one advantage is precisely that such adherence guarantees that the view updating rules don't have any of the effects he objects to. Please understand, however, that I don't argue that such adherence be slavish, unthinking, and unconditional; rather, I argue merely that, where such adherence is absent, appropriate care should be taken over view updating.

Darwen continues:

> Date gives the following informal definition of (a certain logical consequence of) *The Principle of Orthogonal Design:*

> Let *A* and *B* be distinct relvars. Then the constraints for *A* and *B* should not be such as to require the same tuple to appear in both.

> I cannot dispute that any violation of this principle, as far as it goes, would lead to redundancy, but I remark that it does not go very far. There are many ways in which redundancy can occur without the same tuple appearing in two relvars. For example, let relvars *A* and *B* have the same heading except that one attribute of *B* has a different name (say *Y* instead of *X*) from its

---

1. Despite the fact that (as I pointed out in the previous section) he effectively subscribed to it himself in his suggested "artifice" for permitting insert through union.

counterpart in *A*. Further, let there be a constraint in effect that requires *A* to be equal at all times to *B* RENAME (*Y* AS *X*). This case is perhaps the simplest of the many that are not covered by the principle as stated. (Date does not disagree with this observation; in fact, he and I have worked together on the more general definition of the principle.)

[Date then] goes on to show that adherence to [a certain] "strong form" of the principle will avoid the undesired effects that sometimes arise in his approach to the updating of unions and joins.

I perceive a tacit suggestion here that adherence to the strong form of orthogonality is a good database design principle to follow, especially if undesired effects of update operations are to be avoided. I disagree on two counts:

1. I disagree with the tacit suggestion, because (a) as I have already explained, even the weak form given in Date's informal definition only scratches the surface of redundancy, and (b) the strong form does not appear to address any cases of redundancy that the weak form misses and, worse, rules out many designs that do not entail redundancy at all.

2. I disagree with the idea that a database should be designed "correctly" or "appropriately" in order to ensure that operators never have undesired effects—in particular, effects that represent unsafe conclusions from the premises that are represented by invocations of update operators (under our agreed interpretation).

Comment: I respond to each of these two counts in turn.

1. With regard to point (a), it's true that *The Principle of Orthogonal Design* "only scratches the surface of redundancy"; in fact, I've discussed this very issue at some length in reference [5]. Note, however, that exactly the same criticism could be leveled at the principles of normalization. Does Darwen think that adherence to normalization is not a good design principle to follow? As for point (b):

   ▪ First, I made no claim in reference [12] (or anywhere else) that the strong form of the principle addresses "any cases of redundancy that the weak form misses." Of course not!—to claim otherwise would be a logical absurdity. *Au contraire:* I merely used that strong form as a basis for simplifying a discussion of how adherence to *The Principle of Orthogonal Design* could serve to avoid what might be regarded as certain undesirable effects of certain of the view updating rules.

   ▪ Second, regarding the suggestion that the strong form of the principle "worse, rules out many designs that do not entail redundancy at all": Well, I've already said I don't insist on adherence to that strong form; in fact, I agree there are sometimes good reasons for violating it. But such cases are precisely the cases where I would suggest being careful over inserting through unions and deleting through intersections. And (to repeat a point I've made a couple of times already) if you do perform such inserts and deletes, at least their effects are always completely predictable.

2.   Here I simply observe that updates can have undesired effects if the database is less than fully normalized, too. Does Darwen think a database should not be designed in accordance with the principles of normalization in order to ensure that operators never have undesired effects?

DARWEN'S PROPOSALS

Darwen introduces his own view updating proposals with these words:

> The question now arises, to what extent do *I* think views might be updatable? And what general principles underlie *my* position? I address the second question first.
>   I accept **The Golden Rule** without question.
>   I accept *The Assignment Principle* without question but not without comment. Of course, any update operator invocation is equivalent to some assignment (possibly multiple). What assignment it is equivalent to depends on the definition of the operator being invoked. For example, we have given what we think are reasonable, useful, and intuitive definitions for the familiar INSERT, DELETE, and UPDATE operators in terms of relational assignment. It follows that every INSERT, DELETE, or UPDATE invocation should have the same effect on its target relvar as the assignment to which it is equivalent; for if not, *The Assignment Principle* is violated. My comment is that it might be possible to subvert the intent of *The Assignment Principle* by defining perverse update operators (a possibility I actually consider in my notes on UPDATE-through-extension and UPDATE-through-JOIN).

Comment: I don't fully understand this paragraph; the second and final sentences seem to contradict each other. Some clarification is needed. Be that as it may, Darwen continues:

> As already noted, I reject the strong form of *The Principle of Orthogonal Design* ... [However, I do propose the following additional principle]:

- *The Principle of No Ambiguity:* If relation *r* is to be assigned to view *R*, then there must exist exactly one corresponding set of assignments to the real relvars on which *R* is defined such that **The Golden Rule** and *The Assignment Principle* are adhered to; otherwise, the assignment is rejected.

Comment: I interrupt here to observe that this principle clearly violates *The Principle of Interchangeability*. I think it could be argued that it violates Polya's *Principle of Insufficient Reason,* too, though this claim is perhaps more debatable. Anyway, I reject it. Indeed, I see no good reason to accept it, since I think my definitions of insert through union and delete through join are useful and yet clearly don't abide by it. Moreover, I'm not even sure the system is capable of distinguishing adequately between situations that satisfy the proposed principle and ones that don't. Anyway, back to Darwen:

> [I also propose the following additional principle]:

- *The Principle of View and Pseudovariable Equivalence:* Every permitted assignment to view *R* is also permitted, with exactly the same effect, to the expression *x* on which *R* is defined. (That expression *x,* when appearing as a target, is therefore acting as a pseudovariable.)

Note: I state [this principle] only because Date does not do so explicitly himself. We are not in disagreement here.

In [the rest of this commentary], I provide some notes on each operator of the relational algebra through which I see some reasonable opportunity for updatability. I have put these notes together with more haste than usual ... The serious student should scrutinize them carefully and perhaps with a certain amount of suspicion.

Comment: In what follows, I won't include Darwen's proposals in their entirety (for the most part) but will just quote those aspects on which I have some comments.

Projection

Darwen says:

If view *V* is defined on some projection of relvar *R1,* then deletions from *V* are permitted but insertions, in general, are not.

Comment: I agree that deletions are permitted but not that insertions aren't. My proposals in reference [12] include a careful and reasoned analysis of inserting through projection. Such inserts will sometimes fail; when they do, however, they do so not because they're categorically prohibited but because they violate either **The Golden Rule** or *The Assignment Principle.*

Later, Darwen says:

However, it has been proposed (and this proposal has been implemented in more than one product) to make a special case of projections whose attributes include a key of *R1,* simply because ... [in this case] to insert a single tuple is not arbitrary after all.

Comment: My own rules for inserting through projection include the foregoing as a special case. Be that as it may, Darwen continues:

A further thought: It might be possible to allow *V* to appear as the target of an UPDATE without the foregoing INSERT limitation (to the effect that the attributes of *V* must include a key of *R1*). For example, if *V* is defined as EMP {SALARY}, we could give everybody a 10 percent salary increase as follows:

```
UPDATE V ( SALARY := SALARY * 1.1 ) ;
```

Is it really so important for UPDATE to be shorthand for DELETE followed by INSERT? I suppose we can keep it that way with a bit of sleight of hand, by defining it as DELETE-but-remember-the-deleted-tuples, then apply the updates to the remembered tuples, then INSERT. For UPDATE through projection we would have to propagate those three steps to the underlying relvar.

Comment: I would say it *is* important for UPDATE to be shorthand for DELETE followed by INSERT; I mean, it's a little late in the day to be thinking of departing from such a long established and widely held position. Of course, this fact doesn't prevent us from defining a new update operator that behaves in the way that Darwen is suggesting here, if we want to—I just wouldn't call that operator UPDATE, that's all.

Extension

As part of his discussion of the EXTEND operator, Darwen says the following:

> UPDATE through extension is a case where *The Assignment Principle* might be seen as an annoyance. Intuitively it seems not unreasonable (and possibly desirable) to permit UPDATE invocations that affect only those attributes of *V* that are inherited from *R1*, with the additional attributes of *V* being recomputed. This treatment might be acceptable if some agreeable extension to the definition of UPDATE can be formulated such that *The Assignment Principle* is not violated under it.

Comment: I don't think it's clear that Darwen is not proposing a departure from *The Assignment Principle* here, even though I believe the foregoing text is one of the discussions he was referring to earlier when he said he would be "considering the possibility of subverting the intent of *The Assignment Principle*." Certainly I don't think the rather trivial functionality being proposed is worth jettisoning that principle for. Rather, what he's doing is suggesting another new update operator. I have no major objection to introducing such an operator, but (again) I probably wouldn't call it UPDATE.

Join

Here I quote Darwen's text in its entirety:

> If *V* is defined on some conjunction *R1* AND *R2,* then *V* is the join of *R1* and *R2* (with *R1* INTERSECT *R2* and, if the heading of *R2* is a subset of that of *R1*, *R1* MATCHING *R2* as degenerate but not special cases). Insertions into *V* are permitted; for IT IS THE CASE THAT *V(t)* is equivalent to *R1(u)* AND *R2(v)*, where *u* is the projection of *t* over the attributes of *R1* and *v* is the projection of *t* over the attributes of *R2*. (I assume that inserting a tuple that already exists in the target relvar is a no op.) However, deletions from *V* are not permitted, in general, for IT IS NOT THE CASE THAT *V(t)* can be effected by any of the following logically distinct invocations:

```
1.    IT IS NOT THE CASE THAT R1(u) ;

2.    IT IS NOT THE CASE THAT R2(v) ;

3.    IT IS NOT THE CASE THAT R1(u) ,
      IT IS NOT THE CASE THAT R2(v) ;
```

(No. 3 is a multiple assignment.) Because *R1* and *R2* are both subject to change, it is not possible to identify exactly one of these invocations to effect deletion of *t* from *V*.

   Note: I would relax the foregoing general prohibition in cases where exactly one of the choices satisfies both **The Golden Rule** and *The Assignment Principle.* I would also consider relaxing the prohibition in the specific case where the common attributes of *R1* and *R2* include a key of *R2*. Some people advocate supporting deletion (and therefore UPDATE) in such cases by propagating the operation to *R1* only. The justification for this position is that each tuple being deleted from *V* has exactly one matching tuple in *R1*, as a consequence of which *The Assignment Principle* is guaranteed to hold. In the case where the matching tuple in *R2* is matched by no other tuples in *R1*, *The Assignment Principle* also holds if that matching tuple is deleted from *R2*, but it seems reasonable to resolve the ambiguity by applying the same treatment as in the more general case. Unfortunately, this relaxation for many-to-one joins would appear to have to permit deletion from both operands in the one-to-one case where the common attributes include a key of *R1* as well as a key of *R2*. If you think this treatment of DELETE seems a bit suspect (as it does to me, at least), I remark that it does seem utterly reasonable to permit UPDATE in these cases, noting that if common attributes are affected then we would have a possible violation of *The Assignment Principle* on our hands (and again I very tentatively wonder about the possibility of extending the definition of UPDATE to avoid such violation).

   Comment: As this extract makes clear, Darwen agrees that his prohibition on deleting through join (and in particular through intersection) could be relaxed in certain circumstances, but I don't think the circumstances he considers include all pertinent cases; in other words, I believe his rules will sometimes cause an update to fail when it could *and should* succeed. I also reject the suggestion that many-to-one joins might somehow be special, and a fortiori that one-to-one joins might be "even more special" (as it were); my own rules for updating joins treat all cases uniformly. Finally, I observe that one implication of Darwen's proposals is that relvars might exist with the property that we can insert a tuple into them and then not be able to delete that tuple again: not a very desirable state of affairs, it seems to me.

Union

Again I quote Darwen's text in its entirety:

   If *V* is defined on some disjunction *R1* OR *p*, then we are talking about *R1* UNION *R2* (for other kinds of disjunction where *R1* is one of the disjuncts are not permitted). The situation is the inverse of what applies in the conjunction cases. Inserting into *V* is prohibited, because IT IS THE CASE THAT *V(t)* can be effected by any of the following logically distinct invocations:

```
1.    IT IS THE CASE THAT R1(u) ;

2.    IT IS THE CASE THAT R2(v) ;

3.    IT IS THE CASE THAT R1(u) ,
      IT IS THE CASE THAT R2(v) ;
```

(where, as it happens, $u = v = t$), or both. There is no justification for choosing exactly one of these three possibilities over the other two. However, all deletions are permitted. Deleting t from V is effected by deleting u from $R1$ and v from $R2$ (i.e., deleting t from both $R1$ and $R2$).

The prohibition on insertion might be relaxed when there is a constraint to the effect that $R1$ and $R2$ be at all times disjoint, provided that the constraint in question can be used to determine to which unique operand a given tuple, proffered for insertion, must belong. For example, the constraint NOT_ALARMED_WHEN_OPEN (see earlier) cannot be used for the purpose at hand. However, a constraint such as the following (expressed for convenience in logic notation)—

```
FORALL t ( R1(t) ⇒ t.A > 5 & R2(t) ⇒ t.A ≤ 5 )
```

—could perhaps be used. For any given tuple t the system needs only to evaluate the expression $t.A > 5$ to determine whether t is to be inserted into $R1$ or $R2$ (not both). A common shorthand for constraints such as these allows one to write something like CHECK A > 5 inside the relvar definition; use of such syntax might make it comparatively easy for the system to determine at compile time whether the constraint can be used to disambiguate inserts into unions.

Comment: As with the case of deleting through join, I believe Darwen's rules for inserting through union will sometimes cause an update to fail when it could and should succeed. In particular, I reject the idea that inserting through union should succeed only when the union is disjoint. Moreover, I observe that one implication of Darwen's proposals is that relvars might exist with the property that we can delete a tuple from them and then not be able to insert that tuple again (and I would argue again that such a state of affairs is very undesirable).

Difference and Semidifference

Darwen's notes include a discussion of the relational difference and semidifference operations. I omit that discussion here because Darwen does not discuss our disagreements over these operators (though such disagreements do exist) in his original objections to my proposals. Let me just note that my proposals include what I regard as a systematic approach to inserting and deleting through these operators also.

CONCLUDING REMARKS

In conclusion, I'd like to summarize what I regard as the principal advantages of my rules for inserting through union and deleting through intersection. The last four are repeated from reference [12].

- A and B are treated symmetrically in both A UNION B and A INTERSECT B (and more generally in A JOIN B).

- INSERT and DELETE are treated symmetrically in both A UNION B and A INTERSECT B (and more generally in A JOIN B).

- INSERT through UNION and DELETE through INTERSECT (and JOIN) can succeed where they would fail in Darwen's proposals.

- Following on from the previous two points, INSERT and DELETE are inverses of each other, insofar as makes logical sense, with respect to both UNION and INTERSECT (and JOIN). For example, inserting a tuple into *A* UNION *B* and then deleting it again is guaranteed to restore the status quo (unless the tuple in question already existed in *A* UNION *B* before the INSERT, of course). By contrast, this desirable property is not satisfied by Darwen's proposals.

- The rules satisfy *The Principle of Interchangeability,* whereas Darwen's proposals don't. (It follows that updates on views can fail under my rules, but only for reasons that exactly parallel those for which updates on base relvars can fail. Such reasons include integrity or security violations but do *not* include any such notion as "ambiguity.")

- The rules ensure that mappings that are supposed to be total are indeed so, where applicable.

- All views are potentially updatable (as is not the case under Darwen's proposals); in fact, all kinds of updates—INSERTs, DELETEs, and UPDATEs—are supported and can succeed on all kinds of views (modulo integrity or security violations).

- The rules give a predictable result in every case.

- Moreover, they give the intuitively expected and useful result in most cases (possibly not in all).

- If *The Principle of Orthogonal Design* is followed—"strong form" or otherwise—then the number of cases (it is tempting to call them pathological) in which the result might not be "expected and useful" is further reduced.

Let me close by saying that despite everything I've said in response to Darwen's objections in this chapter, I suspect that Darwen's opinions and mine are actually not all that far apart. From my perspective, I would be more than happy with a DBMS that implemented my view updating proposals as I've described them. As I said in reference [12], however, I don't claim those proposals are the last word on the subject, nor am I irrevocably opposed to making any changes to them. At the very least, I'm sure they'll need a fair amount of polishing in order to make them watertight. All I've tried to do, both here and in reference [12], is to set down my own thinking on the matter as clearly as I can; as Bertrand Russell once said (with reference to the general question of how we make progress in scientific disciplines), clarity above all has been my aim. Resolving what differences still exist between Darwen and myself on this subject remains a high priority for both of us.

REFERENCES AND BIBLIOGRAPHY

1.   E. F. Codd: "Derivability, Redundancy, and Consistency of Relations Stored in Large Data Banks," IBM Research Report RJ599 (August 19th, 1969); "A Relational Model of Data for Large Shared Data Banks," *CACM 13,* No. 6 (June 1970), republished in *Milestones of*

Research—Selected Papers 1958-1982 (CACM 25th Anniversary Issue), CACM 26, No. 1 (January 1983).

2. C. J. Date: *An Introduction to Database Systems* (8th edition). Boston. Mass.: Addison-Wesley (2004).

3. C. J. Date: *Database in Depth: Relational Theory for Practitioners.* Sebastopol, Calif.: O'Reilly Media, Inc. (2005).

4. C. J. Date: "On the Logical Differences Between Types, Values, and Variables," in *Date on Database: Writings 2000-2006.* Berkeley, Calif.: Apress (2006).

5. C. J. Date: "Data Redundancy and Database Design" and "Data Redundancy and Database Design: Further Thoughts Number One," in *Date on Database: Writings 2000-2006.* Berkeley, Calif.: Apress (2006).

6. C. J. Date: "Constraints and Predicates" (Chapter 3 in this book).

7. C. J. Date: "The Closed World Assumption" (Chapter 4 in this book).

8. C. J. Date and Hugh Darwen: *Databases, Types, and the Relational Model: The Third Manifesto* (3rd edition). Boston, Mass.: Addison-Wesley (2006).

9. C. J. Date and Hugh Darwen: "Multiple Assignment," in *Date on Database: Writings 2000-2006.* Berkeley, Calif.: Apress (2006).

10. C. J. Date, Hugh Darwen, and Nikos A. Lorentzos: *Temporal Data and the Relational Model.* San Francisco, Calif.: Morgan Kaufmann (2003).

11. Appendix D ("What Is a Database?") of reference [8].

12. Appendix E ("View Updating") of reference [8].

13. George Polya: *How to Solve It* (2nd edition). Princeton, N.J.: Princeton University Press (1971).

14. George Polya: *Mathematical Discovery: On Understanding, Learning, and Teaching Problem Solving* (combined edition). New York, N.Y.: John Wiley & Sons (1981).

Appendix

Frequently Asked Questions

*Ask an impertinent question,
and you are on the way to a pertinent answer.*

—Jacob Bronowski

This appendix consists of a collection of frequently asked questions, and some answers, on various aspects of relational data management. The questions are genuine, in the sense that they're all based on real questions I've been asked over the years, but I've edited them for style, flow, nomenclature, and so forth. I should state for the record that my answers aren't always meant to be definitive! Codd himself undertook a similar exercise several years ago; he wrote a regular column in *FDT* (the predecessor to what's now called *SIGMOD Record*), starting with the issue of June 1973 [8]. In that first installment, he wrote this:

Q: Does the fact that you are launching this column mean that you think you know everything there is to know about relations and databases?

A: Normally we shall not deal with such personal questions, but in this case we'll make an exception. Our answer is "Lord, no." We have a lot to learn in both areas ... Occasionally, we may have to say "we don't know." (Have you noticed, incidentally, how seldom other column writers say this?)

My sentiments exactly. Now read on ...

MATHEMATICS AND THE RELATIONAL MODEL

Relational advocates are always claiming that the relational model is based on mathematics. Yet I see several differences between relations as understood in mathematics and relations in the relational model. Can you comment?

It's certainly true that such differences exist. I think it's fair to say this: While Codd used the concept of a mathematical relation, together with various related concepts from set theory (e.g., operators such as union), as a basis on which to define his relational model, he deliberately didn't limit himself in his definition to those concepts as they were known at the time. Rather, what he did do was use those concepts to develop (or begin to develop) a whole new branch of mathematics in its own right—because that's what relational theory, in the database sense, is. Thus, while that theory is certainly based on relations in their original mathematical sense, it goes some way beyond classical (i.e., mathematical) relation theory. Here are some of the principal points of difference between the two:

- Database relations are typed—they emphasize, much more than mathematical relations do, the significance of the heading. (In other words, the relational model assumes, as classical relation theory does not, the existence of a supporting theory of types. See reference [41] for further discussion.)

- The heading of a database relation has no left to right ordering to its attributes; the heading of a mathematical relation does have such an ordering. (In fact, of course, the term *attribute* is never used in the database sense at all in the mathematical context.) More specifically, database relations have named attributes, while mathematical relations don't (so every attribute can be identified by its name, and we don't need to talk about, e.g., the third attribute, or the last attribute, or whatever). Those names in turn play a crucial role in the relational algebra, especially with respect to relation type inference. What's more, those attribute names are conceptually distinct from the underlying domain names. *Note: Domain* was the term Codd originally used for the type concept; myself, I very much prefer the term *type,* and these days I almost always use this latter term, except when I'm quoting from other writers.

- The emphasis in mathematics is on binary relations specifically. Database relations, by contrast, are N-ary, where N can be 0, 1, 2, 3, ... It was one of Codd's many great contributions to show that N-ary relations are interesting in their own right—i.e., they enjoy interesting formal properties that aren't apparent if they're regarded merely as "nests" or compositions of binary relations. Note the cases $N = 0$ and $N = 1$ in particular! The case $N = 0$ turns out to be crucially important for all kinds of fundamental reasons [12,18,37]. *Note:* In the interest of accuracy, I should add that Codd actually never discussed this case. The first paper I'm aware of that did is reference [11].

- *Relational algebra:* Very little work seems to have been done in mathematics on general N-ary relational operators, presumably because of the emphasis already noted on binary relations specifically. For example, reference [50] defines an operator it calls *relative product*:[1] If $r(A,B)$ and $s(B,C)$ are two binary relations, then their relative product $t(A,C)$ is the binary relation consisting of all pairs (a,c) such that, for some b, the pair (a,b) appears in r and the pair (b,c) appears in s. In database terms, this is the projection over (A,C) of the join of r and s over B. But notice how the operation is specifically defined to produce a binary relation as its result; the ternary relation that is the intermediate result—i.e., the join—is never explicitly mentioned. (Notice too how the definition relies on the fact that attributes have a left to right ordering.)

   Thus, although operators such as join (and all of the other operators of the relational algebra) are clearly applicable to mathematical relations, it's fair to say they were first defined, for the most part, in the context of relations in the database sense. Indeed, the theory of such operators (including the laws of expression transformation and the associated principles of optimization) can reasonably be regarded as part of the "new branch of mathematics" I referred to earlier, a part that arose specifically as part of the development of the relational approach to the problem of database management.

---

1. More usually called *composition*.

- *Dependency theory:* To say it again, the emphasis in mathematics is on binary relations specifically, whereas the emphasis in the relational model is on *N*-ary relations instead. And the entire field of what's now usually called dependency theory—the large body of theorems and techniques concerning such matters as keys, functional dependence, multivalued dependence, join dependence, higher normal forms, and so forth—is crucially dependent on this difference in emphasis. For example, the concept of Boyce/Codd normal form (BCNF) is really only relevant to relations of degree three or more, because almost all relations of degree less than three are necessarily in BCNF.[1] In fact, the entire field of dependency theory—like the theory of *N*-ary relational operators mentioned previously—can be regarded as another new branch of mathematics, one that was brought into being by the special requirements of a theory of data and a theory of *N*-ary relations (as opposed to a theory of binary relations merely).

- *Relation values vs. relation variables:* So far as I know, mathematics has no notion of a relation variable, in the database sense, at all—it deals with relation values only. Database theory, by contrast, is crucially dependent on relation variables, at least if we ever want to update the database (that's meant to be a joke). In fact, the dependency theory mentioned under the previous bullet item only makes sense if we are dealing with relation variables specifically—it would be pretty pointless if we had relation values only.

- *Integrity:* To generalize from the previous point, everything having to do with data integrity in any way also makes sense only if we are dealing with relation variables specifically. In particular, integrity constraints apply to relation variables specifically.

- *Views* and *view updating theory* are further aspects of database relations (or relvars, rather) that depend on integrity theory and have no counterpart in traditional mathematics, so far as I know.

What's the difference between a relation and a relationship?

Well, that depends on how you define the term *relationship!* Personally, I try to use it as little as possible, if I can help it (in particular, I was never much of a fan of "entity/relationship modeling"). The term was introduced, it seems to me, primarily by people without a mathematical background, or at least by people who prefer fuzzy concepts to precise ones. Though in fairness perhaps I should add that in Codd's famous 1970 paper on the relational model [4], we find the following:

[We] propose that users deal, not with relations which are domain-ordered, but with *relationships* which are their domain-unordered counterparts ... [Users] should interact with a relational model of the data consisting of a collection of time-varying relationships (rather than relations).

---

1. *Almost* all, please note—not quite all. Finding one that isn't is left as an exercise.

In other words, the domains (and hence attributes) of a (database) relation were originally considered by Codd to have a left to right ordering, but the relational model as such was supposed to be concerned with "relationships" instead of relations. In all of his subsequent writings, however, Codd used the term *relation* to mean what he originally called a relationship. So I suppose it's possible, though I think it's a bit of a stretch, to lay the blame for "relationships" at Codd's door.

So how do I define the term *relationship?* Well, here's what I said in reference [26]:

> **relationship** 1. A term used briefly in Codd's early papers (later discarded) to mean what we would now call either a relation or a relvar, as the context demands. 2. In E/R modeling, "an association among entities" (definition taken from the original E/R paper). 3. More generally, given two sets (not necessarily distinct), a rule pairing elements of the first set with elements of the second set; equivalently, that pairing itself. This definition can easily be extended to three, four, ..., or any number of given sets.

Note that the third of these definitions can be regarded as a very loose definition of a relation in the database sense, except for (a) its reliance on ordinality ("first" set, "second" set, and so forth) and (b) the fact that it assumes that "relationships" must have degree at least two.

The mathematical theory of relations includes some concepts—reflexivity, symmetry, and transitivity—that I never see mentioned in discussions of the relational model. Don't those concepts have any role to play in connection with database relations?

Reflexivity, symmetry, and transitivity are properties possessed by certain binary relations. To repeat some text from reference [37]:

> Loosely, a binary relation r is reflexive if and only if, for all x, the tuple $<x,x>$ appears in r;[1] it's symmetric if and only if, for all x and y, if the tuple $<x,y>$ appears in r, then so does the tuple $<y,x>$; and it's transitive if and only if, for all x, y, and z, if the tuples $<x,y>$ and $<y,z>$ both appear in r, then so does the tuple $<x,z>$.

In a database context, it's more interesting if the three properties are supposed to hold, not just for some given binary relation r, but for all possible values r of some given binary relvar R. If they are, then they're just integrity constraints on that relvar:[2]

---

1. You might reasonably ask whether "for all x" here means "for all values of the pertinent type" or "for all values of the pertinent attribute." Actually it makes no difference—if some value of the pertinent type fails to appear as a value of the pertinent attribute, we can simply ignore it for present purposes.

2. Here and elsewhere in this appendix I use the symbol "$\| \leq \|$" to denote the operation of set inclusion (or relation inclusion, to be more specific).

```
VAR R BASE RELATION { X T, Y T } KEY { X, Y } ;

CONSTRAINT REFLEXIVE
    ( EXTEND ( R { X } ) ADD ( X AS Y ) ) ‖≤‖ R ;

CONSTRAINT SYMMETRIC
    ( R RENAME ( X AS Z, Y AS X, Z AS Y ) ) = R ;

CONSTRAINT TRANSITIVE
    ( ( ( R JOIN ( R RENAME ( Y AS Z, X AS Y ) ) ) { X, Z } )
                                    RENAME ( Z AS Y ) ) ‖≤‖ R ;
```

Of course, it would be possible to define shorthands for these constraints that would enable us to define such a relvar much more simply—for example:

```
VAR R BASE RELATION { X T, Y T } KEY { X, Y }
        REFLEXIVE SYMMETRIC TRANSITIVE ;
```

Such shorthands, like the familiar KEY shorthand, might have the additional advantage that they would enable the system to implement the relvar more efficiently; in particular, they might allow the system to avoid certain obvious redundancies in the data as stored. That said, however, I'm not sure I'd support such shorthands if they really did apply to binary relvars only. Perhaps there's a way to generalize the ideas to apply to *N*-ary relvars for arbitrary *N;* perhaps more research is required.

RELATIONAL ALGEBRA

I often hear claims to the effect that relational algebra and relational calculus are logically equivalent. What exactly do such claims mean?

Essentially, relational algebra and relational calculus are both formalisms for writing relational expressions—expressions, that is, that evaluate to, or in other words denote, relations. Such expressions can be used for a variety of purposes, of which the most obvious is the formulation of queries. For example, here are algebraic and calculus formulations of the query "Get supplier numbers for suppliers who supply at least one red part":

Algebra:

```
( S { S# } ) MATCHING ( SP MATCHING ( P WHERE COLOR = 'Red' ) ) )
```

Calculus:

```
( S.S# ) WHERE EXISTS SP ( EXISTS P
        ( S.S# = SP.S# AND SP.P# = P.P# AND P.COLOR = 'Red' ) )
```

The two formalisms are logically equivalent because *every* algebraic expression has an exact counterpart in the calculus and vice versa; that is, every relation that can be defined by means of some algebraic expression can also be defined by means of some expression in the calculus and vice versa.

Given this state of affairs, the choice between the two comes down in some ways to a mere matter of personal preference. It's sometimes suggested that programmers prefer the algebra while end users prefer the calculus, though I think it's probably closer to the truth to say that the algebra is better suited to some tasks while the calculus is better suited to others. Codd himself, in the paper in which he defined the two formalisms [7], gave arguments for regarding the calculus as superior (or at least more user friendly), and he even claimed in reference [5] that the calculus was at a higher level of abstraction than the algebra. In reference [22], however, I give my own reasons for thinking those arguments don't really stand up; in other words, I stand by my position that the choice is somewhat arbitrary.

One more thing: The algebra, consisting as it does of explicit operators, is more obviously implementable than the calculus (albeit not necessarily efficiently so!); the calculus looks a little more like natural language, and its implementability is thus not so immediately apparent. Thus, by showing in reference [7] that any expression of the calculus could be mapped into a logically equivalent expression of the algebra, Codd provided a basis for implementing the calculus.

Exercise: Because the algebra and the calculus are logically equivalent, the design of a database language can reasonably be based on either. Given that this is so, which do you think SQL is based on?

——————— ◆◆◆◆◆ ———————

I thought there was such a thing as "the" relational algebra—namely, the set of operators (restrict, project, join, and so forth) originally defined by Codd. But in recent writings of yours, and elsewhere, I've seen mention of all kinds of other operators (group, ungroup, semijoin, semidifference, and many others) that are described as algebraic operators too. What's going on here? Is there or isn't there a unique true algebra?

I've addressed this question in some detail elsewhere in this book [37], and I won't repeat that discussion here. However, there's one point that I think is worth repeating, and highlighting—namely: *The relational algebra is required to be at least as powerful as the relational calculus.* (Equivalently, the relational algebra is required to be what's called *relationally complete* [7].) What this means is that, essentially, it doesn't matter which operators are included, just so long as it can be shown that every calculus expression has a semantically equivalent algebraic counterpart—that is, every relation that can be defined by means of some calculus expression can also be defined by means of some expression of the algebra. In other words, the relational completeness requirement places a lower bound on the functionality that *must* be provided. Thus, we're at liberty to include any operators we like in "our" algebra, just so long as this requirement is satisfied. In particular, we're at liberty to appeal to the principle of syntactic substitution [13] and define operators that are really nothing but shorthand for certain useful combinations of existing operators. For example, the algebra on which **Tutorial D** is based includes an attribute renaming operator, even though that operator can easily be defined in terms of the existing operators extend and project. Similarly, semijoin is just shorthand for a certain combination of join and projection; intersection is just a special case of join; and so on.

——————— ◆◆◆◆◆ ———————

Your version of the relational algebra relies heavily on attribute names. For example, the expression *A* JOIN *B* is defined to do the join on the basis of just those attributes of *A* and *B* that have the same names. Isn't this approach rather fragile? For example, what happens if we later add a new attribute to *B* (say) that has the same name as one already existing in *A?*

First let me clarify one point. It's true that the version of the algebra I advocate relies on attribute names. However, it also requires attributes of the same name to be of the same type (and hence in fact to be the same attribute, formally speaking). For example, an error would be occur (at compile time, I should add) if, in the expression *A* JOIN *B, A* and *B* both had an attribute called *X* but the two *X*'s were of different types. Note that this requirement imposes no limitation on functionality, thanks to the availability of the RENAME operator.

Now to the substance of the question. There's a popular misconception here, and I'm very glad to have this opportunity to dispel it. In current DBMSs, application program access to the database is provided either through a call level interface or else through an embedded, but conceptually distinct, data sublanguage (embedded SQL provides the standard example of the latter approach). Of course, the embedded language approach is really just a call level interface with a superficial dusting of syntactic sugar, so the two approaches really come to the same thing from the DBMS's point of view, and indeed from the host language's point of view as well. In other words, the DBMS and the host language are typically only *loosely coupled* in most systems today. As a result, much of the advantage of using a well designed, well structured programming language is lost in today's database environment. As reference [49] puts it, "most programming errors in database applications would show up as *type errors* [if the database schema were] a part of the type structure of the program."

Now, the fact that the database schema is not "part of the type structure of the program" in today's DBMSs can be traced back to a fundamental misunderstanding that existed in the database community in the early 1960s or so. The perception at that time was that, in order to achieve logical data independence, it was necessary to move the database definition out of the program so that (in principle) that definition could be changed later without changing the program. But of course that perception was incorrect. What was, and is, really needed is *two separate definitions,* one inside the program and one outside; the one inside would represent the programmer's view of the database (and would provide the necessary compile time checking on queries, etc.), the one outside would represent the database "as it really is." Then, if it subsequently becomes necessary to change the definition of the database "as it really is," logical data independence is preserved by changing the mapping between the two definitions.

Here's how the mechanism I've just briefly described might look in a real system (the following discussion is based on *The Third Manifesto,* which requires such a mechanism to be supported—see reference [41]). To be specific, the *Manifesto* prescribes support for what it calls *public relvars.* A public relvar represents the application's perception of some portion of the database. For example:

```
VAR X PUBLIC RELATION { S# S#, SNAME NAME, CITY CHAR } KEY { S# } ;

VAR Y PUBLIC RELATION { S# S#, P# P# } KEY { S#, P# } ;
```

These definitions effectively assert that "the application believes" there are relvars in the suppliers-and-parts database called X and Y, with attributes and keys as specified. Such is not the case, of course—but there are database relvars called S and SP (with attributes and keys as specified for X and

Y, respectively, but with one additional attribute in each case), and we can clearly define mappings as follows:

```
X =d S { S#, SNAME, CITY }

Y =d SP { S#, P# }
```

These mappings are defined outside the application (the symbol "=*d*" means "is defined as").

Now consider the expression X JOIN Y; clearly, the join is done on the basis of the common attribute, S#. And if, say, an attribute SNAME is added to the database relvar SP, all we have to do is change the mapping—actually no change is required at all, in this particular example!—and everything will continue to work as before; in other words, logical data independence will be preserved.

Note finally that (to spell the point out) today's SQL products don't work this way. Thus, for example, the SQL expression

```
SELECT DISTINCT * FROM S NATURAL JOIN SP
```

(which is an SQL analog of the join example discussed above) is, sadly, subject to exactly the "fragility" problem mentioned in the original question.[1] In other words, today's SQL products suffer from a very undesirable (and unfortunate, and unnecessary) loss of logical data independence.

———————— ♦ ♦ ♦ ♦ ♦ ————————

I've heard various people refer to something called "the join trap," suggesting (to me at least) that there's some flaw in the join operation that users need to know about. Can you elaborate?

Yes, I can. The first time I ever encountered this term was in a draft of a paper by an old friend of mine, Adrian Larner, titled "A New Foundation for the ER Model." (The copy I have is undated, and I don't know where if anywhere it was published or if it was ever widely distributed.) The following text is an extract from that paper (I've edited it for consistency with our usual terminology but haven't changed the sense):

Consider the following relvars, with sample values as indicated:

SP	S#	P#		PJ	P#	J#
	S1	P1			P1	J1
	S2	P1			P2	J1
	S2	P2			P1	J2
	..	..			..	..

---

1. So too is the simpler expression SELECT DISTINCT * FROM S, for that matter.

The predicates are as follows:

SP: *Supplier S# supplies part P#.*

PJ: *Part P# is used in project J#.*

Now we form the composition of SP and PJ (i.e., the join of SP and PJ on P#, projected on S# and J#). The predicate for the result is:

```
EXISTS p# EXISTS p#' ( s# supplies p# and p# = p#'
                                 and p#' is used in j# )
```

Or more simply:

```
EXISTS p# ( s# supplies p# and p# is used in j# )
```

In English, one instantiation is: There is something supplied by S1 and used in J1; or, S1 supplies something used in J1. But this does *not* follow from our base data; it could be false while the base data (shown above) is true (if none of the P1's supplied by S1 are used in J1): the classic join trap.

My response to this example is: Stuff and nonsense! Values of attribute S# are supplier numbers; they identify specific suppliers. Likewise, values of attribute J# are project numbers, and they identify specific projects. But values of attribute P#, though we do call them part numbers, do *not* identify specific parts—rather, they identify specific *kinds of* parts.[1] The interpretation as given in the sentence beginning "In English" should thus more correctly be:

There is some kind of part supplied by S1 and used in J1; or, S1 supplies some kind of part used in J1.

As far as I'm concerned, this interpretation is 100 percent correct.

What's more, it seems to me that the so called "join trap" is identical to what James Martin called (in reference [47] and possibly elsewhere) "semantic disintegrity." I wrote a short paper [15] over 20 years ago that tried, among other things, to debunk that notion. What follows is a lightly edited version of the relevant portion of that paper:

A good illustration of lack of clear thinking—arising presumably from an inadequate understanding of the relational model and its interpretation—is provided by what's sometimes

---

1. I should know!—I invented this example (though I based it on an earlier one of Codd's), and I've been using it since 1972, if not earlier. Though in fairness I should admit that my explanations of the example might not always have been as clear as they should have been.

called *semantic disintegrity*. Here's an example, taken from a book by James Martin ... Consider the relvars:

```
EMP  { EMP#, DEPT# }
DEPT { DEPT#, LOCATION }
```

Suppose a given department can have any number of locations. Now consider the relvar:

```
RESULT { EMP#, DEPT#, LOCATION }
```

(the natural join of EMP and DEPT, on DEPT#). Martin says this join is invalid, because if employee *e* works in department *d* and department *d* has locations *x* and *y*, it certainly doesn't follow that *e* is located in both *x* and *y*. The assumption seems to be that relation RESULT states otherwise. But of course it doesn't; it merely states what we already know—namely, that *e* works in *d* and *d* has locations *x* and *y*. Relation RESULT does represent the answer to a certain query, but that query is not "Get employee locations." Thus, it's definitely wrong to say the join is invalid (though it might be legitimate to warn against incorrect interpretation of that join).

I'd also like to comment on Larner's use of the term "classic join trap." First, I'm not aware of that term appearing anywhere else in the literature, so I'm not at all sure the epithet "classic" is warranted. More to the point, I think what Larner is calling "the join trap" is essentially identical to what Codd, in his 1970 paper [4], called the *connection* trap. In that paper, however, Codd was arguing *against* precisely the kind of confusion that Larner and James Martin are both guilty of! In reference [22] I commented on this issue as follows:

> [*Codd wrote:*] "A lack of understanding of [the semantics of the relational operators] has led several systems designers into what may be called the *connection trap*. [For example, suppose we have a nonrelational system in which] each supplier description is linked by pointers to the descriptions of each part supplied by that supplier, and each part description is similarly linked to the descriptions of each project which uses that part. A conclusion is now drawn which is, in general, erroneous: namely that, if all possible paths are followed from a given supplier via the [corresponding] parts ... to the projects using those parts, one will obtain a valid set of all projects supplied by that supplier."
>
> [*To the foregoing I added:*] Of course, we don't have to be following pointers in order to fall into the connection trap—the very same logical error can unfortunately be made in a purely relational system too [*as the Larner discussion demonstrates!*]. Indeed, some writers have criticized relational systems on exactly these grounds ... I hope it's obvious, however, that such criticisms are invalid, betraying as they do a sad lack of understanding of the relational model.

The point is—at least, so it seems to me—we can never stop users from falling into errors of interpretation; but in a relational context, at least, the errors rise to the surface (as it were) and can be clearly identified and perhaps avoided. So Larner is blaming the relational model for a problem that, at its worst, is more easily recognized and fixed in a relational system than in systems of other kinds. This criticism seems to me less than fair.

RELVAR PREDICATES

The predicate for relvar S (suppliers) is:

Supplier S# is under contract, is named SNAME, has status STATUS, and is located in city CITY.

If we project suppliers on all but CITY, the predicate for the result is:

Supplier S# is under contract, is named SNAME, has status STATUS, and is located in some city.

But why do we mention the city in this predicate at all, since it's not part of the result? We might as well include further arbitrary terms such as "... and is located at some address, and has some person as CEO, and employs some number of staff" (and so on). Do we mention the city only because the projection is derived from a relvar that has a CITY attribute?

Imagine we had a relvar that has the same heading as relvar S except that it has no CITY attribute. This is the same as the result of the projection of S on all but CITY, yet I believe the correct predicate is:

Supplier S# is under contract, is named SNAME, and has status STATUS.

Am I right?

These are good questions! They're important—in some ways, in fact, they get to the heart of what databases are all about—so I'll do my best to answer them as carefully as I can. For that reason, I need to approach them slowly and lay quite a bit of groundwork first ... Please bear with me.

Essentially, your questions have to do with what the symbols that happen to appear in some database mean, or represent. Now, I hope you agree that the kinds of symbols we're talking about don't, in general, have any absolute or fixed meaning. Even a familiar symbol like "3" doesn't mean much in the absence of appropriate additional information; three whats? Of course, if I'm a DBA, I might design a certain database in such a way that the appearance of that symbol "3" in a certain position is to be interpreted to mean that (for example) employee Joe has three weeks of vacation. And then, if you're a user of my database, I would have to explain that interpretation to you in order for you to be able to understand and use that piece of data correctly and effectively. Of course, I'd try to choose relvar names, attribute names, and so forth that make that explanation as intuitively obvious as possible. For example, I might use names as indicated in the following picture:

```
VACATIONS

 ┌────────┬─────────────┐
 │ NAME   │ NO_OF_WEEKS │
 ╞════════╪═════════════╡
 │ Joe    │           3 │
 │ ...    │          .. │
 └────────┴─────────────┘
```

But the fact remains that I would still have to explain the interpretation to you, even when it's "intuitively obvious" as in this example. (In any case, I'm sure we've all seen real world examples where the relvar and attribute names make the intended interpretation very far from obvious indeed.)

Now, the way to explain the interpretation of a given relvar—equivalently, the way to explain what that relvar means—is by stating the corresponding predicate. In the case at hand, the predicate looks something like this:

The employee called NAME has NO_OF_WEEKS weeks of vacation.

Next, it's important to understand that *every* relvar has a corresponding predicate; the predicate *is* the intended interpretation. It's also important to understand that users must *always* be told the predicate for every relvar they want to use. (In practice, we don't often talk in such high flown terms, of course—that is, we don't often use the terms *predicate* or *interpretation* in the sense in which I'm using them here—but we do have to say what relvars mean; and however we choose to carry out that necessary task, whatever we do is logically equivalent to stating the predicate.)

Note very carefully too that the predicate for a given relvar is not innate (if it were, we wouldn't have to spell it out). Even the VACATIONS relvar might conceivably have a very different interpretation—for example: *The dog called NAME has had NO_OF_WEEKS visits to the vet.* Of course, if this latter is the intended interpretation, the names VACATIONS and NO_OF_WEEKS aren't very well chosen from an intuitive point of view, but so what? There's nothing *logically* wrong with them. Names are arbitrary—right?

Next, given some relvar, each tuple appearing in that relvar at some given time *t* represents some proposition that's true at that time *t* (more accurately, some proposition that *we believe* is true at that time *t,* but I'm going to ignore this nicety here). The proposition in question is derived from the relvar predicate by substituting attribute values from the tuple in question for the parameters appearing in the predicate. In the case of relvar VACATIONS, for example, with its predicate *The employee called NAME has NO_OF_WEEKS weeks of vacation,* the tuple for Joe represents the proposition *The employee called Joe has 3 weeks of vacation* (and if that tuple appears in the relvar, then that proposition is supposed to be a true one).

I turn now to the suppliers relvar that your questions are based on. I'll also make use of the shipments relvar, SP, with its attributes S# and P# (I'll ignore attribute QTY for simplicity). Suppose, then, that I'm the DBA and you're the user. So I tell you—and you have no choice but to believe me!—that the predicate for relvar S (suppliers) is:

Supplier S# is under contract, is named SNAME, has status STATUS, and is located in city CITY.

And the predicate for relvar SP (shipments) is:

Supplier S# supplies part P#.

Armed with this information, you now know that, at any given time, the tuples in the relation that's the value of relvar S at that time represent propositions of a certain form that are true at that time (and likewise for relvar SP). *And you rely on that knowledge in a variety of ways—in particular, when you do queries.* As a simple example, suppose you form the join of suppliers and shipments:

```
S JOIN SP
```

Then you know that every tuple in the relation that's the output from that join represents a true proposition of the following form:

Supplier S# is under contract, is named SNAME, has status STATUS, is located in city CITY, and supplies part P#.

In other words, this latter statement is (by definition) the predicate for the output from the join, and it effectively dictates how you interpret the result of the query. In fact, it's precisely because you understand that the result of the join is to be interpreted in this way that you formulated the query the way you did. The natural language formulation of the query is "Get supplier number, name, status, city, and part number for each supplier under contract and each part supplied by the supplier in question."

By way of another example, suppose you restrict suppliers to just the ones in Paris ("Get supplier number, name, status, and city for suppliers under contract and located in Paris"):

```
S WHERE CITY = 'Paris'
```

The predicate for the output is:

Supplier S# is under contract, is named SNAME, has status STATUS, is located in city CITY, and city CITY is Paris.

Of course, there's little point in retaining the CITY attribute in the output in this example, because we know its value is Paris in every tuple. So a more reasonable form of the query is the following, which projects away the CITY attribute ("Get supplier number, name, and status, but not city, for suppliers under contract and located in Paris"):

```
( S WHERE CITY = 'Paris' ) { ALL BUT CITY }
```

And the predicate for the output is now (obviously enough):

Supplier S# is under contract, is named SNAME, has status STATUS, and there exists some city CITY such that supplier S# is in city CITY, and city CITY is Paris.

Or more simply:

Supplier S# is under contract, is named SNAME, has status STATUS, and is located in Paris.

What I'm trying to show by these examples is that for *every* relational operation (join, restrict, project, and so on), given the predicate(s) satisfied by the tuples of the input relation(s), *there's a well defined predicate that's satisfied by the tuples of the output relation*—and that "output predicate" is determined from the "input predicate(s)" by the semantics of the operation in question, as the examples illustrate.

Now, the particular case you ask about is the projection of suppliers on all but CITY ("Get supplier number, name, and status for suppliers under contract"):

```
S { ALL BUT CITY }
```

Adopting an obvious simplified notation for tuples, it's clear that the tuple $<s\#,sn,st>$ appears in the output here if and only if the tuple $<s\#,sn,st,sc>$ appears in the input for some city *sc*. So the output predicate is:

> *Supplier S# is under contract, is named SNAME, has status STATUS, and is located in some (unspecified) city sc.*

Now, you ask why we mention the city in this predicate at all, since it's not part of the result (i.e., the result has no CITY attribute). You go on to suggest that we might as well include further arbitrary terms such as "... and is located at some address, and has some person as CEO, and employs some number of staff" (and so on). However, later you say: "Do we mention the city only because the projection is derived from a relvar that has a CITY attribute?" I hope you now see that the answer to this latter question is *yes*. *The output predicate depends on the input predicate* (or input predicates, plural, but there's only one in the example). If the input predicate had mentioned the CEO (for example), the output predicate would have had to have done so too.

You also say:

> Imagine we had a relvar that has the same heading as relvar S except that it has no CITY attribute. This is the same as the result of the projection of S on all but CITY, yet I believe the correct predicate is:

> *Supplier S# is under contract, is named SNAME, and has status STATUS.*

I'm afraid you're under a serious misconception here. This latter relvar is *not* "the same as the result of the projection of relvar S on all but CITY." I agree it has the same attributes; it might even have the same tuples (at the time under discussion); but it doesn't follow that the two are the same. *It depends on the predicates;* in fact, they would be the same if and only if they had the same predicates. But we've already agreed (I hope!—see the VACATIONS example earlier) that the predicate for a given relvar is whatever the definer says it is—it's not innate. Thus, you're at liberty to say the predicate for your revised suppliers relvar is what you say it is:

> *Supplier S# is under contract, is named SNAME, and has status STATUS.*

But even if you do, there's no contradiction or inconsistency with my claim to the effect that the predicate for the projection of the original suppliers relvar on all but CITY is what I say it is:

> *Supplier S# is under contract, is named SNAME, has status STATUS, and is located somewhere.*

Of course, you're also at liberty to say the predicate for your revised suppliers relvar is something entirely different—perhaps:

> *Supplier S# is a friend of mine, has a cat called SNAME, and lives STATUS miles outside town.*

Still no contradiction—though it's probably a bad design. But this latter objection is likely to be the case no matter what the intended interpretation is for your revised suppliers relvar.[1] However, that's a topic for another day.

RELATION VALUED ATTRIBUTES

In recent writings you seem to embrace the idea of relation valued attributes (RVAs). Don't RVAs violate first normal form (1NF)?

The idea that relation valued attributes might violate 1NF is based on a confusion between RVAs and repeating groups (a confusion to which I was subject myself for many years, I hasten to add). Repeating groups certainly do violate 1NF, but RVAs don't. For a detailed elaboration of this position, see reference [29].

Let's look at an example in which a relation valued attribute might be a good idea. Suppose we need to design a relvar to represent the predicate *X and Y live together*—which I take to mean, more precisely, *X and Y are distinct, they live together, and nobody else lives with X and Y*. The obvious design involves a binary relvar R2{X,Y}, with the constraint—I'll call it *C2*—that if the tuple $<x,y>$ appears in R2, then so does the tuple $<y,x>$. (In other words, R2 is *symmetric*, as discussed earlier in this appendix.) However, I greatly prefer an alternative design involving a unary relvar R1{XY} whose sole attribute XY has values that are unary relations containing exactly two tuples each (see the next page for a sample value for this relvar). This design, it seems to me, more directly reflects the symmetric predicate *X and Y live together* (more precisely, the predicate *XY is a pair of persons who live together*). By contrast, the R2 design seems to correspond to the less obviously symmetric predicate *X lives with Y,* and it explicitly requires enforcement of constraint *C2* in order to capture the symmetry property. Of course, both designs require a constraint to ensure that each "pair" does indeed contain exactly two persons, and another to ensure that no person is included in more than one pair. Here are suitable definitions for relvar R1 (the one with the RVA):

```
CONSTRAINT R1_PAIRS_HAVE_CARDINALITY_TWO
    IS_EMPTY ( R1 WHERE COUNT ( XY ) ≠ 2 ) ;

CONSTRAINT R1_PAIRS_ARE_DISJOINT
    COUNT ( R1 UNGROUP ( XY ) ) = 2 * COUNT ( R1 ) ;
```

---

1. I'm assuming here that we're talking about a design that includes both that revised suppliers relvar and my original one. If it includes just one of the two, there's no problem.

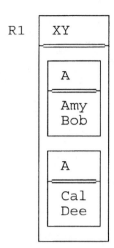

For relvar R2 (the one without the RVA), by contrast, life is a little more complicated; we need the combination of (a) constraint *C2* (the symmetry constraint), (b) a constraint to the effect that no tuple has X = Y, and (c) a constraint to the effect that either {X} or {Y} is a key. Together, these constraints do the trick—though having to decide whether to specify {X} is a key or {Y} is a key or both is slightly worrisome. (To be more specific: If we specify just one, the specifications are asymmetric and a trifle arbitrary; if we specify both, one is redundant.)

Now, you might be thinking there's still a third possible design, a binary relvar R3 with attributes PAIR and PERSON (where PAIR is a "pair identifier" of some kind). However, this design really represents a different predicate—*Person PERSON is a member of pair PAIR*. I won't discuss this possibility any further here. However, there's a little more I want to say in connection with the other two designs.

First, either of those designs can of course be derived from the other (i.e., they're information equivalent). The following expression defines R1 in terms of R2:

```
R1 =d ( EXTEND R2
            ADD ( RELATION
                  { TUPLE { A X }, TUPLE { A Y } } AS XY ) ) { XY }
```

And this one defines R2 in terms of R1:

```
R2 =d ( ( ( EXTEND R1 ADD ( XY AS TT,
                            ( XY RENAME ( A AS X ) ) AS X,
                            ( TT RENAME ( A AS Y ) ) AS Y,
                            ( X JOIN Y ) AS Z ) ) UNGROUP ( Z ) )
         WHERE X ≠ Y ) { X, Y }
```

Second, a particularly strong argument, it seems to me, in favor of the R1 design is that it extends gracefully to the case of *N* people living together for arbitrary *N* (the predicate is *X, Y, ..., Z are all distinct, they live together, and nobody else lives with X, Y, ..., Z).* The R2 design does not extend well.

Following on from the previous question, what about Codd's *Guaranteed Access Rule?* Don't relation valued attributes (RVAs) violate that?

Well, it depends on how you interpret the rule! I strongly suspect that Codd would have said that RVAs do violate it (see reference [4]), but I don't agree. Here's the exact wording of the rule from Codd's original *Computerworld* article [9]:

> Each and every datum (atomic value) in a relational database is guaranteed to be logically accessible by resorting to a combination of table name, primary key value, and column name.

The wording in Codd's book [10] is almost but not quite identical:

> Each and every datum (atomic value) stored in a relational database is guaranteed to be logically accessible by resorting to a combination of R-table name, primary key value, and column name.

The only differences are that (a) "datum ... in" has been replaced by "datum ... stored in" and (b) "table name" has been replaced by "R-table name."

Now, there are things I like about this rule as stated and things I don't (with, perhaps, the former outweighing the latter). I like the idea that all access is associative—more specifically, I like the implication that columns are referenced by name and not by ordinal position—and I like the implication that no two rows in the same table are identical, and hence that every "datum" is logically accessible by, in effect, specifying the row and column intersection that contains it. (*Note:* Although I usually prefer to use the terminology of relations, tuples, and attributes, I'll use the terminology of tables, rows, and columns here because the rule as stated does the same.) By contrast, here are some things I don't like so much:

- I reject the notion of "each and every datum" being an "atomic value"; more precisely, I reject the notion of data value atomicity, at least if that term is supposed to have any kind of absolute meaning. My reasons for rejecting this notion are discussed in detail in many places; see in particular reference [29]. That's why I don't agree that RVAs violate the rule—a "datum" that's a relation value is still a perfectly valid "datum." (As noted in my answer to the previous question, I do agree that repeating groups violate the rule, but that's not the same thing [29].)

- I reject the suggestion that "each and every datum" must be "stored." To the extent *The Guaranteed Access Rule* applies to relations at all, it must apply to *all* relations, be they "stored relations" (whatever those might be), base relations, views, snapshots, intermediate results, final results, catalog relations, or whatever. (Actually I'm quite surprised to see Codd mentioning "stored relations" at all, since the relational model very deliberately has nothing to say about physical storage matters.)

- I would prefer to see the rule being formulated in terms of *relvars* rather than relations (or tables, or "R-tables"). It's true that *at any given time* a database can be thought of as containing relations as such (those relations being the values at that time of the relvars in the database), but we surely want a rule that applies at all times, not just at some given time. (I should explain that Codd's terminology of "R-tables" wasn't an attempt to get at the distinction between relations and relvars; rather, it was intended to get at the distinction between those tables that faithfully represent relations and those—like SQL tables—that don't.)

- For reasons documented in reference [19], I reject the reference to, specifically, primary keys. I do believe every relvar has at least one candidate key (which for simplicity I usually abbreviate to just *key*). Moreover, I don't object to the idea of allowing (though not requiring) some key out of the set of keys that apply to a given relvar to be chosen as "primary." However, I don't agree with the idea that a primary key is required, and I don't agree with any approach that gives primary keys some special semantic properties that don't apply to keys in general.

As you can see, therefore, on some of these points at least I find myself in disagreement with Codd. If you find this state of affairs surprising, let me also say this: Ted Codd was my friend and mentor, and I'll always be grateful to him for inventing the relational model and thereby giving me (and so many others) the basis for such an endlessly interesting career. What's more, I worked directly with Ted for many years—first at IBM, subsequently in our joint consulting company Codd and Date, Inc. But these facts don't mean that we always saw eye to eye on technical matters, and sometimes we didn't.

———— ♦ ♦ ♦ ♦ ♦ ————

One more question on relation valued attributes (RVAs): Don't such attributes take us into the realms of second order logic?

This is a big question!—and it's one that's asked very frequently. Now, I'm not a logician, so there's no way I can answer it definitively; but I know the relational model fairly well, and I've been impressed (not positively, I should add) by the logicians I've discussed the issue with, who have universally failed to answer the question in a way that's comprehensible to me. More specifically, I've been impressed, again not positively, by the fact that none of those logicians has managed to demonstrate to me any actual problem that might be caused by the fact, if fact it is, that RVAs do mean second order logic. Nor have I seen anything close to a comprehensible account of the matter in the literature.

Given all of the foregoing, I think it's worth my attempting to provide at least a kind of layperson's response to the question. In fact, I'd like to raise a few related questions of my own. Thus, what follows can be seen as a plea for somebody who really knows both logic and the relational model to come up with a coherent, comprehensible, and definitive statement on the issue. Indeed, the very fact that no such statement exists at the time of writing (so far as I know) is, I think, telling in itself. *Note:* Speaking purely for myself here, I'd like to add that what I'd really like to see is not just some kind of abstract discussion of the matter; rather, I'd like to see a concrete proposal for a second order relational language,[1] with concrete examples of what problems (if any) might occur with such a language.

I'll start with a little historical background. The debate over first *vs.* second order logic goes all the way back to Codd's original papers. In 1969, in the very first paper on the relational model [3], Codd wrote:

> The adoption of a relational view of data ... permits the development of a universal retrieval sublanguage based on the second order predicate calculus.

(*Note:* For the purposes of the present discussion, at least, the terms *predicate calculus* and *logic* can be taken as meaning the exact same thing.) In his better known 1970 paper [4], by contrast, he wrote:

> The adoption of a relational model of data ... permits the development of a universal data sublanguage based on an applied predicate calculus. A first order predicate calculus suffices if the collection of relations is in normal form.

The term *normal form* here just means "no RVAs." (Indeed, one of the biggest differences between the 1969 and 1970 papers was precisely that the 1969 paper permitted RVAs and the 1970 paper didn't.) As you can see, therefore, Codd was effectively claiming that RVAs meant second order logic; what's more, he was also claiming, at least implicitly, that second order logic was somehow undesirable and first order logic was preferred.

So what do the terms mean? Well, here are some definitions (taken from reference [26] but slightly reworded here):

- **first order logic** A form of predicate logic in which the sets over which parameters range aren't allowed to contain predicates.

- **second order logic** A form of predicate logic in which the sets over which parameters range are allowed to contain predicates.

An example of a predicate that's definitely first order is the relvar predicate for the suppliers relvar S:

> *Supplier S# is under contract, is named SNAME, has status STATUS, and is located in city CITY.*

The parameters here are S#, SNAME, STATUS, and CITY, and they range over the set of all supplier numbers, the set of all names, the set of all integers, and the set of all character strings, respectively. Since the values in those sets certainly aren't predicates, we can say the predicate for S is first order.

An example of a second order predicate is the predicate that defines the fundamental notion of *equality:*

---

1. Unless **Tutorial D** already is such a language, I suppose I should add.

```
FORALL x FORALL y ( ( x = y ) ≡ FORALL P ( P ( x ) ≡ P ( y ) ) )
```

In somewhat stilted English: For all *x* and *y*, *x* and *y* are equal if and only if, for all predicates *P*, the effect of applying *P* to *x* and the effect of applying *P* to *y* are equivalent. So the parameter *P* ranges over the set of all monadic predicates (I assume *P* to be monadic here for reasons of simplicity), and the overall predicate is thus second order.

One question that arises immediately is thus: The relational model certainly relies on the notion of equality; so doesn't this fact mean we're already relying on second order logic anyway, regardless of whether we allow RVAs or not?

Onward. I believe one simple way to point up the difference between first and second order logic in database terms is as follows (this characterization might help if, like me, you have no training in formal logic):

- First order logic allows us to ask, for example, whether there exists a tuple for supplier S1 in [the current value of] relvar S.

- Second order logic, by contrast, would enable us to ask whether there exists a tuple for supplier S1 in [the current value of] any relvar in the database.

So my next question is: Is the foregoing characterization accurate? If it is, it certainly suggests that support for second order logic might be a nice thing to have.

Aside: I should explain that second order logic isn't the end of the road. Here's a definition: Let *P* be a predicate, and let *P* have a parameter that's a predicate of order *N* (and no parameter that's a predicate of order greater than *N*); then *P* is of order *N*+1. *Note:* For the purposes of this definition, anything that has no parameters at all is considered to be of order zero. Propositions in particular are thus of order zero. Also, with reference to the definition I gave earlier for equality, I suppose we have to assume that predicate *P* in that definition is first order; otherwise the definition might be third or even higher order. *End of aside.*

Anyway, the question now arises: What exactly is the connection between second order logic as briefly described above and RVAs? Well, every relvar *R* represents some predicate *P*, and the attributes of *R* represent the parameters of *P*; thus, if *R* has an RVA, then the corresponding parameter is relation valued. Note carefully, however, that the corresponding parameter *is* relation valued!—it isn't *relvar* valued. If it were relvar valued (if that possibility could somehow be made to make sense), then I suppose we might say that relvar *R* was "a second order relvar," since it would apparently represent a predicate one of whose parameters represented a predicate in turn. But a relvar with an RVA is not, it seems to me, a "second order relvar"; in any given tuple of such a relvar, the attributes have values that are ... well, values, not variables. At the time of writing, at least, the relational model provides no support for "second order relvars."

Aside: A relvar with a relvar valued attribute would be a variable with other variables nested inside itself. Now, I've argued elsewhere [28] that "variables containing variables" makes no logical sense. But maybe I was wrong. (This is another question for the logicians, perhaps, though I observe that logicians have no concept of variables at all, in the sense in which I'm using that term here, so I'm not even sure it's a matter of logic anyway.) Be that as it may, it does seem as if "relvar valued attributes" is what we would have to add to the relational model in order to support second order logic. *Note:* I believe some programming languages today support variables whose values are functions. Does this make those languages second order? *End of aside.*

Onward again. Those who complain that RVAs mean second order logic often go on to claim that second logic can lead to a lack of decidability or the possibility of paradoxes or both. I respond to these claims as follows:[1]

- *Undecidability:* Apparently we have this problem anyway, regardless of whether we support second order logic, and I've dealt with it in detail elsewhere in this book (see reference [39]).

- *Paradoxes:* As far as I know, the paradoxes in question all arise from some kind of self reference. I've dealt with this issue elsewhere in this book as well (see reference [38]). Though perhaps I should add that, as I understand it, there are ways, even in second (and higher) order logic, of preventing paradoxes from occurring: Basically, all we have to do is enforce a rule to the effect that no predicate of order N is allowed to have a parameter of order $M \geq N$.

One last point: RVAs might not be the only point at issue here. To be specific, *The Third Manifesto* [41] embraces at least two other constructs that might be regarded as introducing some aspects of second order logic into the relational model. The first is the transitive closure operator, TCLOSE; the second is the *N*-adic versions of certain operators (for example, union and join). All of these operators have definitions that are essentially recursive and (so far as I know) can't be expressed in first order logic. Hence my final questions: Does the availability of these operators have any negative implications for the model—with respect to second order logic in particular? And if so, what are they?

KEYS AND FURTHER NORMALIZATION

I'm confused about normal forms. In your book *An Introduction to Database Systems* (8th edition), page 369, you give an example of a relvar you say is in 3NF but not BCNF. But it seems to me it isn't even in 2NF, and hence not in 3NF either, let alone BCNF. What's going on?

I'll begin by repeating the example in question. We're given a relvar SSP as follows—

```
SSP { S#, SNAME, P#, QTY }
    KEY { S#, P# }
    KEY { SNAME, P# }
```

---

1. Though honesty compels me to admit that we—where by "we" I mean those who embrace the idea of RVAs—might be in violation of *The Principle of Cautious Design* here [17].

—satisfying the additional functional dependencies (FDs)

```
{ S#    } → { SNAME }
{ SNAME } → { S#    }
```

In reference [23], I claim, correctly, that relvar SSP is not in BCNF. But is it in 2NF? (If it isn't, then I agree that, as the question says, it's not in 3NF or BCNF either, a fortiori.) The reason it might be thought not to be in 2NF is that:

- If we choose—arbitrarily—{S#,P#} as the primary key, then {SNAME}, though necessarily functionally dependent on that primary key, isn't irreducibly so, and

- 2NF is usually thought of as requiring every attribute to be irreducibly dependent on the primary key.

I fear this misconception is a common one, and it's partly my fault. In the section of reference [23] that explains 2NF (and 1NF and 3NF), I deliberately indulged in some "creative lying," as it were; that is, I deliberately simplified some of the material for pedagogic reasons. In my own defense, however, let me note that I did call this fact out quite explicitly in the book! The very first paragraph of the section in question reads as follows (bold face and italics as in the original):

> *Caveat: Throughout this section, we assume for simplicity that each relvar has exactly one candidate key, which we further assume is the primary key. These assumptions are reflected in our definitions, which (we repeat) are not very rigorous. The case of a relvar having more than one candidate key is discussed in [a later section].*

And here is the "not very rigorous" definition of 2NF from that same section, quoted verbatim:

- **Second normal form** *(definition assuming only one candidate key, which we assume is the primary key):* A relvar is in 2NF if and only if it is in 1NF and every nonkey attribute is irreducibly dependent on the primary key.

Note the qualification in parentheses in this definition! Two points:

- First, in a relvar with a primary key and no other candidate keys, a nonkey attribute is just an attribute that's not part of the primary key. More generally, a nonkey attribute is any attribute that isn't a key attribute, where a key attribute is any attribute that participates in some candidate key; equivalently, a key attribute is any attribute that's contained in a subkey [36].

- Second, if I were to rewrite that book today, I'd frame the foregoing definition of 2NF (and all other normal form definitions) in terms of *sets* of attributes, or equivalently in terms of subsets of the heading, instead of in terms of attributes per se.

Anyway, here by contrast is a precise definition, essentially as given by Codd back in 1971 [6]:[1]

- A relvar is in 2NF if it's in 1NF and every nonkey attribute is irreducibly dependent on each candidate key.

Going back to the SSP example, then, the problem with that relvar is that attributes S# and SNAME are both key attributes. Relvar SSP is thus in 2NF (and also 3NF, in fact) by Codd's original definition, even though it looks as if it isn't in 2NF (or 3NF) according to my simplified definition.

In various writings you give as an example of a violation of fourth normal form (4NF) a relvar CTX with attributes C (course), T (teacher), and X (text). You say that relvar is all key. But a key by definition has to be the identifier of something, and there's no entity that's identified by the combination of C, T, and X. So making a relvar out of the three attributes was senseless and in my opinion wrong from the beginning ... I believe a relvar should consist of a key and at least one additional attribute, functionally dependent on that key. For practical reasons, a relvar might consist of a key only (if we're not interested in any additional attribute), but it must at least be shown that conceptually there *exists* an attribute that depends on this key. I believe that with this definition every relvar is automatically in 4NF.

First let me summarize the CTX example. As you say, the relvar has just three attributes, C, T, and X. The predicate is:

Course C can be taught by teacher T and uses text X as a textbook.

It's also the case that, for a given course, the set of teachers and the set of texts are quite independent of each other (that is, no matter which teacher actually teaches [some particular offering of] some course, the same texts are used). It follows that, as reference [23] shows, the relvar is in BCNF but not 4NF. Now I can respond to the various points in the question.

- First, and despite what the question claims, the relvar just is all key. Of course, I'm appealing here to the formal definition of the term *key*. After all, the relational model is a formal system, and all of its components have formal definitions—necessarily so. Now, we naturally hope those formal definitions have a good correspondence with certain informally defined constructs in the real world; to the extent such a correspondence can be found, the relational model will be a good basis for dealing with real world problems. Do please note, however, that the correspondence will be informal too!—we can't have a formal mapping between something formal and something informal, by definition.

---

1. Codd used the term "nonprime attribute" in place of my "nonkey attribute," but the meaning is the same.

- By contrast, you seem to think the term *key* should be used to mean something informal, not formal. Well, you're at liberty to use the term that way if you want to. But you're not then at liberty to criticize the relational model because its use of terminology is different from yours!

- Even with your informal concept of what a key is, I can't believe you really want to insist that "entities" *must* have additional attributes. For example, consider the relvar HOLIDAYS, with just one attribute, DATE, which simply lists all the national holidays for some country. For another example, consider the relvar FRIENDS with two attributes A and B, with predicate "A and B are friends." And so on.

- "Making a relvar out of attributes C, T, and X was senseless in the first place" (paraphrased). Now, that's probably true. And the discussion in reference [23] goes on to make exactly that point (see page 386)! But the point is an informal one ... The whole point of normalization theory is to come up with formal arguments to bolster up our informal intuitions. Informally, we might say CTX is a bad design. Formally, normalization theory tells us exactly why it's a bad design. What's more, if we can formalize such matters, we can go on to mechanize them, too (i.e., we can get the machine to do the work). So your objection here really misses the point. (You're not alone here, by the way—most critics of normalization make exactly the same mistake.)

- "I believe a relvar should consist of a key and at least one additional attribute, functionally dependent on that key ... I believe that with this definition every relvar is automatically in 4NF." First, given a relvar *R,* every attribute of *R* is functionally dependent on every key of *R,* so the clause "functionally dependent on that key" in the first sentence here is redundant. Second, here's a relvar (with, I trust, self-explanatory semantics) that "consists of a key and at least one additional attribute":

EMP { EMP#, DEPT#, BUDGET }

Here {EMP#} is the key, and the functional dependencies (FDs)

{ EMP# } → { DEPT# }
{ EMP# } → { BUDGET }

certainly hold. The trouble is, the FD

{ DEPT# } → { BUDGET }

holds as well; as a consequence, the relvar isn't even in 3NF, let alone BCNF or 4NF.

──────── ◆ ◆ ◆ ◆ ◆ ────────

I have difficulty understanding domain-key normal form (DK/NF). Can you help? In particular, if a relvar has an atomic key and is in 3NF, is it automatically in DK/NF?

I don't blame you for having difficulties here; there's certainly been some nonsense published on this topic in the trade press and elsewhere. Let me try to clarify matters.

First of all, DK/NF is best thought of as a kind of trial balloon. It was introduced by Ron Fagin in reference [45]. In that paper, Fagin defines a relvar R to be in DK/NF if and only if every constraint on R is a logical consequence of what he calls the *domain constraints* and *key constraints* on R, where:

- A domain constraint—better called an *attribute* constraint—is simply a constraint to the effect a given attribute A of R takes its values from some given domain D.

- A key constraint is simply a constraint to the effect that a given subset of the heading of R constitutes a key for R.

If R is in DK/NF, therefore, it's sufficient to enforce the domain and key constraints for R, and all constraints on R will be enforced automatically. And enforcing those domain and key constraints is, of course, very simple (most DBMSs do it already). To be specific, enforcing domain constraints just means checking that attribute values are always values from the applicable domain (i.e., values of the right type), and enforcing key constraints just means checking that key values are unique.

The trouble is, lots of relvars aren't in DK/NF in the first place. For example, suppose there's a constraint on R to the effect that R must contain at least ten tuples. Then that constraint is certainly not a consequence of the domain and key constraints that apply to R, and so R isn't in DK/NF. The sad fact is, not all relvars can be reduced to DK/NF; nor do we know the answer to the question "Exactly when *can* a relvar be so reduced?"

Now, it's true that Fagin proves in his paper that if relvar R is in DK/NF, then it's automatically in 5NF (and hence 4NF, BCNF, etc.) as well. However, it's wrong to think of DK/NF as another step in the progression from 1NF to 2NF to ... to 5NF, because the operation that takes us from 1NF to 2NF to ... to 5NF is projection, while the operation (if it even exists) that takes us from 5NF to DK/NF is certainly not projection. What's more, 5NF is always achievable, but (as we already know) DK/NF is not.

It's also wrong to say there are no normal forms higher than DK/NF. A recent book by Darwen, Lorentzos, and myself [43] describes a new *sixth* normal form, 6NF (see Chapter 8 of the present book for a definition and brief explanation). 6NF is higher than 5NF (meaning all 6NF relvars are in 5NF, but the converse isn't true); moreover, 6NF is always achievable, but it isn't implied by DK/NF. In other words, there are relvars in DK/NF that aren't in 6NF. A trivial example is:

```
EMP { EMP#, DEPT#, SALARY } KEY { EMP# }
```

(with the obvious semantics).

"If a relvar has an atomic key and is in 3NF, is it automatically in DK/NF?" Sadly, no.[1] If the EMP relvar just shown is subject to the constraint that there must be at least ten employees, then EMP is in 3NF, and in fact 5NF, but not DK/NF. (Incidentally, this example also answers another frequently asked question: "Can you show a relvar that's in 5NF but not in DK/NF?") *Note:* I'm assuming here that the term "atomic key" means what would more correctly be called a *simple* key; a simple key is a

---

1. Though if a relvar is such that *all* of its keys are atomic and it's in 3NF, it's at least in 5NF [44].

key that's not composite, and a composite key is a key that consists of two or more attributes.

The net of this discussion is that DK/NF is (at least at the time of writing) a concept that's of some theoretical interest but little practical interest. The reason is that, while it would be nice if all relvars in the database were in DK/NF, we know that goal is impossible to achieve in general; moreover, we don't know when it *is* possible. For practical purposes, therefore, we have to stick to 5NF (and 6NF).

────────── ♦ ♦ ♦ ♦ ♦ ──────────

Keys (meaning candidate keys specifically) are supposed to be unique and irreducible. I understand the uniqueness part, of course, but not the irreducibility part. Please explain.

Your statement is correct: Keys are indeed supposed to be both unique and irreducible. *Irreducible* here means that if K is a key for relvar R, then no proper subset of K has the uniqueness property (recall that keys are sets of attributes, so that expressions like "subset of K" do make sense).[1] In other words, we require keys not to contain any attributes that aren't needed for unique identification purposes. See, e.g., Chapter 8 in this book, where the concept of a key is formally defined.

There are at least two reasons why such irreducibility is desirable. To see what they are, consider the usual suppliers relvar S and the set of attributes {S#,CITY}. Let's call that set SC. Then SC certainly has the uniqueness property—no relation that's a possible value for relvar S has two distinct tuples with the same value for SC—but it doesn't have the irreducibility property, because we could discard the CITY attribute and what's left, the set {S#}, would still have the uniqueness property. So we wouldn't regard SC as a key, because it's "too big" (i.e., it's reducible). By contrast, {S#} is irreducible, and it's a key.

Here, then, is one reason why we want keys to be irreducible. Suppose we were to specify a "key" that was *not* irreducible; then the DBMS wouldn't be able to enforce the uniqueness constraint properly. For example, suppose we told the DBMS (lying!) that SC = {S#,CITY} was a key for relvar S. Then the DBMS couldn't enforce the constraint that supplier numbers are "globally" unique; instead, it could enforce only the weaker constraint that supplier numbers are "locally" unique, in the sense that they're unique within city.

A second reason has to do with foreign keys. Suppose again that we specified SC = {S#,CITY} as a key for relvar S. Now consider the corresponding foreign key in the shipments relvar SP. Clearly, that foreign key, in order to *be* a foreign key according to the formal definition, would also have to include the CITY attribute—and relvar SP would thus involve redundancy. To be specific, it would satisfy the functional dependency {S#} → {CITY}; as a consequence, it wouldn't be in second normal form (let alone 3NF, BCNF, or any higher normal form).

By the way, it's worth pointing out that, while the DBMS can obviously enforce the uniqueness requirement on keys, it can't enforce the irreducibility requirement. So it can't stop users from lying in

---

1. We've met the term *irreducible* before in this appendix, with a distinct (though related) meaning. To be specific, let A and B be subsets of the heading of some relvar R. Then B is *irreducibly dependent* on A if it's functionally dependent on A and not on any proper subset of A.

this regard.[1] And I've even seen situations described in the literature in which such lying is positively encouraged. Such situations usually involve two relvars, *R1* and *R2* say, such that some subset of the heading of *R2* is required to match some proper superkey for *R1* (where a proper superkey is a proper superset of some key). By way of example, suppose we're given the following relvars:

```
ED { EMP#, DEPT# }
   KEY { EMP# }

DE { DEPT#, EMP# }
   KEY { DEPT# }
```

The predicates are as follows:

- ED: *Employee EMP# works in department DEPT#.*

- DE: *Department DEPT# is managed by employee EMP#.*

Clearly, {EMP#} in DE is a foreign key matching the key {EMP#} in ED. But suppose now that there's a constraint in effect that says that the manager of a given department must be an employee working in the department in question. In other words, if relvar DE shows department *d* as being managed by employee *e,* then relvar ED must show employee *e* as working in department *e.* Thus, if we could specify {EMP#,DEPT#} as a "key" for ED, then we could formulate the constraint by simply specifying {DEPT#,EMP#} as a matching "foreign key" for DE.

Well, I don't know what you think about this example. My own feeling is that such a comparatively trivial increase in functionality isn't worth destroying the (very well established, and very familiar) semantics of the key notion for. And in any case, the increase in functionality isn't really an increase, anyway. In the case at hand, for example, we can easily specify the desired constraint as follows:

```
CONSTRAINT ... DE ‖≤‖ ED ;
```

──────── ◆ ◆ ◆ ◆ ◆ ────────

Talking of irreducibility, I've heard people talking about irreducible relations. What do they mean?

Well, indeed you probably have heard people talking about "irreducible relations," but what they probably should have been talking about is irreducible *relvars;* irreducibility in the sense in which I'm sure they meant it is a property of relvars, not relations. To be specific, a relvar is irreducible if and only if it's in sixth normal form (in other words, *irreducible* in this context is just another term for sixth

---

1. Note, therefore, that, formally speaking, declaring the key constraint KEY{*K*} for relvar *R* doesn't necessarily mean that {*K*} is a key for *R*—it only means it's at least a superkey (proper or otherwise) for *R*.

normal form). A 6NF relvar is irreducible because it can't be "reduced" or nonloss decomposed via projection into relvars of smaller degree.

However, there's a point worth making here: The "reducibility," or lack thereof, does refer to reducibility via projection specifically. It doesn't mean the relvar in question can't be "reduced" via some other operation. As a concrete example, consider the familiar shipments relvar SP:

```
SP { S#, P#, QTY }
```

This relvar is of degree three, and it's certainly irreducible in the 6NF sense; I mean, the relvar is indeed in sixth normal form. However, we could "reduce" it (in a nonloss way, moreover) to a relvar of degree two by means of the GROUP operator, thus:

```
SP GROUP ( { P#, QTY } AS PQ )
```

Given our usual sample data, this expression yields the result shown here:

S#	PQ	

S1	P#	QTY
	P1	300
	P2	200
	P3	400
	P4	200
	P5	100
	P6	100

S2	P#	QTY
	P1	300
	P2	400

S3	P#	QTY
	P2	200

S4	P#	QTY
	P2	200
	P4	300
	P5	400

This result is indeed of degree two—its type is as follows (note that attribute PQ is a relation valued attribute or RVA):

```
RELATION { S# S#, PQ RELATION { P# P#, QTY QTY } }
```

Note, moreover, that (unlike relvar SP) a relvar of this type could include tuples for suppliers who supply no parts at all. The PQ value in such a tuple would be an empty relation. Here's an example of such a tuple:

S#	PQ	
S5	P#	QTY

The foregoing discussion touches on another important matter, however. As you might know, many writers have argued over the years that binary relvars are all we need—general *N*-ary relvars are unnecessary. And the fact that a 6NF relvar of degree greater than two can always be "reduced" to a binary relvar as suggested by the foregoing example does perhaps lend some credibility to this position. Indeed, several early systems—prototypes, at any rate, if not commercial products—were based exclusively on binary instead of *N*-ary relvars. I have in mind here the following systems among others:

- The Relational Data File (see R. E. Levein and M. E. Maron, "A Computer System for Inference Execution and Data Retrieval," *CACM 10,* No. 11, November 1967)

- TRAMP (see W. Ash and E. H. Sibley, "TRAMP: An Interpretive Associative Processor with Deductive Capabilities," *Proc. ACM 23rd Nat. Conf.,* 1968)

- LEAP (see J. A. Feldman and P. D. Rovner, "An Algol-Based Associative Language," *CACM 12,* No. 8, August 1969)

Note that these systems all predate the relational model as such.

Now, I've shown that any or relvar of degree greater than two can be replaced by one or more relvars of degree exactly two; in the shipments example, I replaced a relvar of degree three by one of degree two. However, those early systems would typically use three binary relvars, not one, to represent shipment information, like this:

```
XS { X#, S# }     XP { X#, P# }     XQ { X#, QTY }
```

Here X# is a shipment surrogate, and each real world shipment is represented by exactly one tuple in each of the three relvars XS, XP, and XQ.

So there are at least three approaches to representing shipment information, which I'll refer to for present purposes as "*N*-ary relvar," "binary relvar with an RVA," and "several relvars," respectively. Now I'd like to compare those three approaches from various points of view. The first is the number of names the user has to deal with:

- *N-ary relvar:* Four names (one relvar name and three attribute names). In general, of course, an *N*-ary relvar without RVAs always involves *N*+1 names.

- *Binary relvar with an RVA:* Five names (one relvar name, two attribute names S# and PQ, and two "nested attribute" names P# and QTY). But suppose the original relvar without RVAs had four attributes instead of three; for definiteness, consider the extended shipments relvar SPJ{S#,P#,J#,QTY}, where J# is a project number. If all relations must be binary,[1] we'll have to replace this relvar by one looking like this, perhaps (I hope my improvised notation here is clear):

```
SPJ { S#, PJQ { P#, JQ { J#, QTY } } }
```

Now the user has to deal with seven names instead of five. In general, in fact, it should be clear that this approach requires $2N - 1$ names instead of $N+1$ (a factor of nearly double; if $N = 30$, for example, it means 59 names instead of 31).

- *Several relvars:* Seven names (or, more generally, $2N+1$ names instead of $N+1$—the original N attribute names, N relvar names, and the surrogate name).

Next, let's think about constraints: specifically, the constraint that every shipment has exactly one supplier number, exactly one part number, and exactly one quantity. How is this constraint formulated in the three cases?

- *N-ary relvar:* The key constraint on SP suffices:

```
KEY { S#, P# }
```

- *Binary relvar with an RVA:* First, we need the key constraint:

```
KEY { S# }
```

But we also need a constraint to the effect that part numbers are "unique within supplier":

```
CONSTRAINT ... COUNT   ( SPQ UNGROUP ( PQ ) ) =
               COUNT ( ( SPQ UNGROUP ( PQ ) ) { S#, P# } ) ;
```

Note: I'm assuming here that SPQ is the binary relvar name.[2]

- *Several relvars:* First, the key constraint KEY {X#} must be specified for each of XS, XP, and XQ. But we also need to say that each of XS, XP, and XQ contains exactly the same set of X# values. Here's one way to do that:

---

1. It's a reasonable assumption that relations as well as relvars must all be binary in the kind of system we're talking about.

2. I'm on record elsewhere [31] as suggesting that it might be nice if we could specify key constraints for general relational expressions. Such a mechanism would let us specify the constraint under consideration more simply thus: CONSTRAINT *xyz* (SPQ UNGROUP (PQ)) KEY {S#,P#}.

```
CONSTRAINT ... XS { X# } = XP { X# } AND XP { X# } = XQ { X# } ;
```

Or we might make use of the system's foreign key mechanism. Note, however, that whatever formulation we choose does seem to involve (necessarily) either some redundancy or some arbitrariness or both.

Finally, I'd like to say a little more on the topic of arbitrariness (these observations apply specifically to the design involving an RVA). The fact is, there are three possible designs for shipments that involve just one binary relvar with an RVA. I'll call them SPX, SPY, and SPZ. They look like this:

```
SPX { S#, PQ { P#, QTY } }

SPY { P#, QS { QTY, S# } }

SPZ { QTY, SP { S#, P# } }
```

More generally, an N-ary relvar without RVAs can be replaced by any of $N!$ binary relvars with an RVA (where $N! = $ factorial $N = N * (N-1) * ... * 2 * 1$).

The net of the foregoing analysis is surely obvious: Almost always, the simple N-ary relvar without RVAs is the best design. And now let me add the following further observations:

- As should be clear from discussions elsewhere in this book, we certainly need relations of degree zero (TABLE_DEE and TABLE_DUM), and possibly relvars of degree zero as well.

- It's obvious that we need relations and relvars of degree one as well.

- Relational operators (join and so on) are currently defined to work on operands of arbitrary degree and to produce results of arbitrary degree as well. If we're to limit ourselves to binary relations only, therefore, all of those operators will have to be redefined to take operands and produce results that are always binary relations specifically. (And it's very tempting to add: So what's the point?)

- Updates are much more complicated on the "binary relvar with an RVA" and "several relvars" designs than they are with the conventional relational design. I'll leave it as an exercise to think through the specifics of this point for yourself. However, some hint as to what's involved can be found in reference [29].

What I've tried to do in the foregoing discussion is outline some of the reasons why the "binary relations only" (or "binary relvars only") movement has been thoroughly discredited over the years. Despite which, I believe I'm right in saying that much of the current work on "the semantic web" is based on exclusively binary relations ... I hope I'm wrong; but if I'm not, then I leave you to draw your own conclusions.

All right, I believe you when you say we don't want binary relations only. But isn't there a good argument for saying that base relvars, at least, should always be binary?

Not quite. It's true that there's a good argument for saying that base relvars should usually be irreducible, and it's true that irreducible relvars are often binary. But there are some logical differences here!—between your suggested position, that is, and the true state of affairs. Let's investigate.

Base relvars should usually be irreducible: Irreducibility means sixth normal form, and sixth normal form is the end of the further normalization road (as further normalization is usually understood), so all of the usual normalization advantages apply. I'll skip the details here.

But not always: Sometimes there's no good reason for breaking a 5NF relvar down into 6NF projections. Consider, for example, a relvar representing scheduled flights. Every flight always has a scheduled departure time and a scheduled arrival time. Thus, there doesn't seem to be much benefit in replacing the 5NF relvar

```
FLIGHT { FLIGHT#, DEP, ARR }
```

by its 6NF projections on {FLIGHT#,DEP} and {FLIGHT#,ARR}, respectively.

Irreducible relvars are often binary: A relvar *R* with just one key *K* and at most one other attribute *A* (*A* not included in *K*) is almost certainly irreducible; and if *K* includes just one attribute, then *K* is binary. This is a common case. For example, the projections of relvar S on {S#,SNAME}, {S#,STATUS}, and {S#,CITY} are all irreducible, and they're all binary.

But not always: Relvar SP is irreducible, too, but it's ternary, not binary. And some irreducible relvars are unary, or even have no attributes at all.

And not all binary relvars are irreducible: Consider the relvar R{X,Y}, with predicate *X and Y are members of the Green Party*. This relvar can be nonloss decomposed into its projections on {X} and {Y}. (In fact, these two projections are identical! One of them could be discarded. I'll leave it as an exercise for you to find a more realistic example of a binary relvar that's not in 6NF.)

And a relvar with a key K and at most one other attribute isn't necessarily in 6NF, either: Well, the Green Party example illustrates this point, too. But here's another example (taken from reference [23]): Relvar SJT{S,J,T} has predicate *Student S is taught subject J by teacher T,* and the following constraints apply:

- For each subject, each student of that subject is taught by only one teacher.

- Each teacher teaches only one subject (but each subject is taught by several teachers).

I'll leave you to work out the specifics of this example. In particular, what normal form is the relvar in?

MISSING INFORMATION

Many of your writings attack the idea of nulls and three-valued logic (3VL) as a basis for dealing with missing information. In particular, you claim that nulls lead to wrong answers (you've referred to this state of affairs as a "showstopper"). But many people seem to be able to use nulls correctly and get answers they're perfectly happy with. So what's going on? Aren't you worrying about nothing? (Joke.) Conversely, if you're right and we do have to avoid nulls, what should we be doing instead?

Well, there are many issues all mixed together here. Let me take the last one first: If we do have to avoid nulls, what should we be doing instead? I wish I had a good answer to this question! To quote somebody or other—I forget who—I feel your pain ... In particular, I know that if you do make the, to me, very sensible decision not to use nulls, you'll have a very difficult row to hoe with today's products, because those products have all been designed on the assumption that you will use nulls. As a result, they don't just not help, they actively hinder, attempts to avoid them. And when I say hinder here, I mean two things: They make it harder to use the system from a logical point of view (perhaps harder to formulate queries, for example), *and,* just to rub salt into the wound, they probably deliver worse performance too.

All of that being said, I still think you should avoid nulls. I'm not going to repeat all of the arguments here, since I've given them before in many, many places (see, e.g., references [16], [24], and [32]); but I will at least summarize a few of the main points, in a form that's at least partly different from the way I've put them before.

- It isn't up to me to prove that nulls can give wrong answers—I've already done this, many times and in many places. Rather, it's up to the nulls advocates to prove the converse: that is, that *in their particular situation,* at least, nulls can't (or at least never do) give wrong answers.[1] Only if they can provide such a proof will it be safe for them to use nulls, and then again *only in their particular situation.* Of course, I venture to suggest that providing such a proof will be quite difficult, and very likely impossible.

- Following on from the previous point, I have it on good authority that nulls really do give wrong answers in practice. In fact it's happened to me! Luckily, I was able to tell right away that the answer was wrong, because it failed to include a particular "datum" (as Codd might have called it) that I knew should have been included; but suppose I hadn't noticed? *Note:* The cynic might say that then it wouldn't have mattered. The operational definition of an error is one that's noticed—if it isn't noticed, it isn't an error. But I digress.[2]

---

1. They obviously can't prove that nulls can't give wrong answers *in general,* since I've already proved the opposite.

2. Of course, it's true that if the error is literally never noticed, then it doesn't matter. The real problem occurs with errors that are noticed, but too late—i.e., only when the damage they've caused can't reasonably be undone.

- A related point, following on from both of the previous ones: Nulls can give right answers as well as wrong ones, of course, but in general we have no way of knowing which are right and which are wrong. Another showstopper, it seems to me.

- The question asserts that "many people seem to be able to use nulls correctly" and that they "get answers they're perfectly happy with." I'll take these points one at a time.

  1. I'm not sure what it might mean "to use nulls correctly." In particular, I've never claimed that three-valued logic can't be made to work correctly (though SQL's attempt—to make it work correctly, that is—fails, because it embodies various inconsistencies). But that's not the point. The point is that 3VL, even when "working correctly," doesn't solve the problem!—it yields answers to queries that are correct according to the logic but not correct in the real world. In other words, the nulls problem isn't just a problem with SQL (though SQL does exacerbate it).

  2. As for people being happy with the answers they're getting out of nulls, there are various possibilities: Either they're lucky, and they actually are getting right answers; or they're failing to notice the errors (see above); or, possibly for reasons that aren't technical in nature, they're keeping quiet about the errors; or they're just not thinking critically; or some combination of all of these possibilities. And, of course, even if it's true that some people are happy with the answers they're getting, it doesn't follow that other people aren't having the opposite experience ... The two aren't mutually exclusive. I believe that the defenders of nulls should be concerned with producing evidence that people never get incorrect results, not making arm waving and unsupported statements to the effect that they sometimes get correct ones.

With respect to the point about reasons possibly being nontechnical in nature, by the way, I'm often asked to give concrete examples of practical situations where nulls and 3VL have given rise to genuine (and perhaps costly) errors in the real world. But a moment's thought should show why I won't do this, even if I could. Suppose I were to go around telling stories of how Product X caused Company Y to commit some huge blunder, causing who knows what damage and costing money and possibly even lives. At best, I would surely be sued by the vendor or the customer or both. And I'm not going to do it. But the fact that I won't doesn't mean I can't, or that such situations can't occur, or that they haven't occurred.

There are a few more points I'd like to make, a little more technical than the ones I've been making so far. First of all, it seems to me that a perceived need for nulls in a given database design often arises out of what I call "mixing predicates." The following example is based on a real application. The designer wanted to represent the results of a series of earth-drilling experiments, in which some but not all of the holes drilled reached what I'll refer to here as "the green layer." So he—the designer was a he—came up with the following design (I'll use SQL here because the designer did so too):

```
CREATE TABLE H ( HOLE_ID ..., TOTAL_DEPTH ..., D_GREEN ...
/* if D_GREEN is null, the green layer wasn't reached */, ... ) ;
```

But there are really two distinct predicates here:

- *Hole HOLE_ID of depth TOTAL_DEPTH reached the green layer at depth D_GREEN.*

- *Hole HOLE_ID of depth TOTAL_DEPTH failed to reach the green layer.*

So there should be two relvars (sorry, two tables)! It's always a bad idea to mix—i.e., "OR"—two predicates in one relvar, especially (but not only) if the predicates in question have different numbers of parameters, as they do in the example. Of course, there'll also be constraints to the effect that (a) the same hole can't be represented in both relvars, and (b) if a hole has a D_GREEN value it can't be greater than the TOTAL_DEPTH value. But at least now there's no "need" for nulls.

Note: The two-relvar design does mean that some queries might now have to examine both relvars. If you think such queries are awkward, then of course you can always use views to conceal some of the awkwardness.

My second technical point is as follows. Many writers have argued that the real world isn't as black and white as two-valued logic (2VL) might suggest and that we need 3VL in order to get various kinds of "gray" answers to queries. As I've explained at length in reference [35], however, it isn't necessary to embrace nulls and three-valued logic in order to get "don't know" answers out of the database. The fact is, I can always write a query, even in SQL, and even limiting myself to 2VL, that returns the value "true" when true is the right answer, "false" when false is the right answer, and "unknown" when unknown is the right answer. The trick is to make these responses not truth values but character strings.[1] See reference [35] for further discussion.

My third point is that nulls and 3VL *completely undermine the relational model*. By definition, a null isn't a value. As a direct consequence, a "type" that contains a null isn't a type, an "attribute" that contains a null isn't an attribute, a "tuple" that contains a null isn't a tuple, a "relation" that contains a null isn't a relation, and a "relvar" that contains a null isn't a relvar ... and the overall foundation for what we're doing, whatever else it might be, is thus no longer the relational model. I don't know what it is, but it isn't the relational model.

Following on from the previous point, incidentally, I'd like to caution you not to be blinded by science in connection with this topic. Several quite formal and academic texts on relational theory include detailed discussions of nulls and 3VL, and you might therefore be forgiven for thinking that nulls and 3VL are academically respectable after all. But it's all too easy to hide a paucity of thinking behind an excess of formalism. Just because some ideas are presented with a lot of formalism, it doesn't necessarily mean those ideas are right! For example, one textbook on relational theory (specifics omitted to protect the guilty) includes an entire chapter—out of only nine altogether—titled "The Theory of Null Values." Now, there's a problem right there in the title, because a large part of the point about nulls is precisely that they aren't values; but that's not the point I want to make here. Rather, tucked away among the formalisms in that chapter (which is indeed quite formal) we find this sentence: "The term *unknown* is used both for the null value and for the third truth value, since their respective meanings are

---

1. In SQL, in fact, I'm more or less forced into using this trick, even with 2VL, precisely because SQL (at least as implemented in the mainstream products) fails to support a truth value data type. It's odd, really: You would think the very first thing a language would have to do, if it's going to claim to be founded on logic of any kind, would be to support a corresponding data type. Oh well.

identical." But they aren't; indeed, there's a serious logical difference between them [27].

As an aside, I remark that I much prefer the treatment in another formal textbook, reference [46], which, though it does include a whole chapter on "null values" [*sic*], at least has the honesty to say "It all makes sense if you squint a little and don't think too hard." Precisely.

Finally, let me come back to the last part of the question: If we do have to avoid nulls, what should we be doing instead? As I've said, I don't have a good, definitive answer to this question. But there are some things I want to say:

- Although I haven't given a good solution to the problem of "missing information," I've at least tried to convince you that nulls and 3VL are a disastrously bad one. Please don't use them.

- Elsewhere [20] I've described an approach based on "default values" (better called *special* values). I'm not particularly proud of that solution and would advocate it only in simple cases, but at least it does work sometimes, and you ought to understand it.

- I rather like Hugh Darwen's approach as described in reference [14]; given today's rather poor product architectures, however, it will probably cause performance and other problems.

- In reference [48] David McGoveran describes another approach, similar to Darwen's but not quite the same, to which similar remarks apply.

- Finally, I really think it's incumbent on users to educate themselves with respect to this matter and to lobby the vendors for better solutions ... and I offer discussions like the present one, and that in reference [35], as one small contribution to such efforts.

VARIABLES, TYPES, AND CONSTRAINTS

I've often heard you draw a distinction between what you call *variables in the programming language sense* and *variables in the sense of logic*—but I'm not clear what exactly the difference is that you're getting at here. Can you please elaborate?

Indeed yes; in fact, there's a huge logical difference between these two concepts, and it's rather unfortunate that the same term is used with two such very different meanings. Of course, I'm sure you know what a variable is in the programming language sense, but let me spell it out for the record. Basically, a programming language variable is a holder, or container, for a value (more precisely, for a representation of a value): different values at different times, in general, which is why we call it a variable—its value varies over time. For example, in the code fragment that follows, N is declared to be a variable of type INTEGER, and the two assignment statements have the effect of assigning, first, the integer value three, and then the integer value five, to that variable:

```
DECLARE N INTEGER ;

N := 3 ;
N := N + 2 ;
```

As the example suggests, the crucial thing about programming language variables is that they can be updated—that is, the current value of the variable in question can be replaced by another value. In other words, to be a variable is to be updatable (equivalently, to be a variable is to be assignable to), and to be updatable, or to be assignable to, is to be a variable. Indeed, that's more or less the *definition* of a variable in the programming language sense.

Note: You can think of a variable in the foregoing sense as an abstraction of a piece of storage, if you find that way of thinking helpful (since "pieces of storage" are what are used at the machine level to hold values). Personally, however, I prefer not to explain one level of abstraction in terms of another—I think it's better for each level to be self-contained, as it were. One important logical difference in the case at hand is that pieces of storage at the machine level are referenced by address, whereas variables are referenced by name.[1]

Perhaps I should state explicitly that elsewhere in this appendix (and indeed throughout my writings in general), the term *variable* should be understood to mean a variable in the programming language sense, barring explicit statements to the contrary.

Turning now to variables in the sense of logic: There are two kinds of such variables, called free and bound, respectively. A free variable is basically just a parameter, or placeholder, to some predicate. For example, let COPRIME(x,y) denote the predicate *Integers x and y have no common factors*. This predicate has two parameters (i.e., free variables): namely, x and y. When we invoke or "instantiate" the predicate, we substitute arguments for the parameters, and we obtain a truth value—or, rather, we obtain a proposition, and that proposition evaluates to either TRUE or FALSE by definition. Thus, for example, the proposition COPRIME(27,14) evaluates to TRUE, while the proposition COPRIME(27,12) evaluates to FALSE. In programming language terms, we can imagine COPRIME being defined as a truth valued read-only operator, or function, as follows (pseudocode):

```
OPERATOR COPRIME ( X INTEGER, Y INTEGER ) RETURNS BOOLEAN ;
    RETURN ( if X and Y have no common factors
             THEN TRUE ELSE FALSE ) ;
END OPERATOR ;
```

As for bound variables: A better term here might be quantified variables, as we'll see. Like free variables, bound variables can appear within predicates (indeed, they can't appear anywhere else). Unlike free variables, however, they don't act as parameters; in fact, they have no exact counterpart in conventional programming terms at all—instead, they serve as a mechanism for constructing one predicate out of another, as it were. Consider the following example:

- Again let COPRIME(x,y) stand for the predicate *Integers x and y have no common factors*. Note that this predicate is dyadic: It involves exactly two parameters.

---

1. Usually. In object systems, however, objects (which are the OO counterpart to conventional programming language variables) *are* typically referenced by address instead of by name. I'm on record elsewhere [21] as criticizing object systems for exactly this reason, among others.

- Suppose we substitute the argument 27 for *x* but make no substitution for *y*. Clearly, we obtain the expression COPRIME(27,*y*), which—by definition—stands for the predicate *Integers 27 and y have no common factors*. Note that this is a still a predicate (a monadic predicate, in fact); we can't meaningfully say that it returns any particular truth value until we substitute an argument for the parameter *x*.

- Now, we can obtain a proposition from the predicate COPRIME(27,*y*) by substituting an argument for *y*, as we already know. But we can also obtain a proposition from that predicate by *quantifying* over *y*. For example, the expression

```
EXISTS y ( COPRIME ( 27, y ) )
```

denotes the proposition *There exists an integer y such that integers 27 and y have no common factors* (which returns TRUE, of course). Alternatively, the expression

```
FORALL y ( COPRIME ( 27, y ) )
```

denotes the proposition *For all integer y, integers 27 and y have no common factors* (which returns FALSE).

I don't want to go into lots of details on quantification here—I assume you're already familiar with the basic idea. (In any case, a tutorial on such matters appears in Chapter 1 of this book.) I'd just like to make the following points:

- In the example, the effect of the quantification was to construct a niladic predicate, or in other words a proposition, out of a monadic predicate. More generally, given an *N*-adic predicate, if we quantify over *M* parameters ($M \leq N$), then we obtain an *R*-adic predicate, where $R = N - M$.

- As you can see (and as I've written elsewhere), bound variables behave as a kind of *dummy*—they serve only to link the predicate inside the parentheses to the quantifier outside, as it were. That's why they have no exact counterpart in conventional programming terms.

- I've said that the crucial thing about variables in the programming language sense is that can be updated. Bound variables, by contrast, can't; that is, they can't be the target of an assignment statement.

Finally, I need to say that logicians, or logic texts at any rate, tend to be a bit slapdash regarding *exactly* what a bound variable is (or a free variable, come to that). Sometimes, at least, the terms seem to refer more specifically to certain *appearances* of certain symbols within certain predicates. For example, consider the expression

```
EXISTS x ( COPRIME ( x, y ) ) AND EXISTS y ( x > y )
```

This expression contains three appearances each of the symbols *x* and *y*. Of these, the first two appearances of *x* and the last two appearances of *y* are all bound, while the last appearance of *x* and the first appearance of *y* are both free. In other words, there are really two different *x*'s and two different *y*'s in this example—that is, there are two distinct variables both called *x* and two distinct variables both called *y*. The following systematic renaming makes the point clear:

```
EXISTS a ( COPRIME ( a, y ) ) AND EXISTS b ( x > b )
```

Of course, such renaming is legitimate—i.e., it doesn't change the meaning of the overall expression—because bound variables (or bound variable appearances, perhaps I should say) are only dummies anyway.

Suppose some variable, or some attribute, is declared to be "of type CHAR(5)." I've always been a little unclear as to what this specification really signifies. Is the type really CHAR(5)? Or is CHAR the type, and the "(5)" just an integrity constraint—i.e., a constraint on the length of the pertinent character strings?

The answer to this question obviously depends to some extent on what language we're talking about, and in particular on whether the language in question supports supertypes and subtypes (and type inheritance) or not. However, I can offer some general remarks that might be useful. I'll assume until further notice that supertypes and subtypes are not supported.

First we need to agree on what the specification CHAR(5) actually means. For definiteness, let's suppose it's some variable V that's declared to be "of type CHAR(5)." If the pertinent language is SQL, then (to pick an example entirely at random, of course), the declaration would mean that legal values of V are character strings of length exactly five characters. In such a language, then, if CHAR(5) is indeed regarded as a type as such, we'll be forced to consider, e.g., CHAR(3) as a completely different type (since the set of strings of length five isn't the same as the set of strings of length three). As a consequence, a comparison of the form

```
'xyz  ' = 'xyz'
```

(note the trailing blanks in the left comparand):

- Will be illegal, because the comparands are of different types;

- Or will necessarily return FALSE, because the comparands are of different types;

- Or will have to involve some coercion (i.e., implicit conversion) of one comparand to the type of the other.

Note: With reference to the third possibility here, I remark that most writers agree that coercions are error prone and just generally a bad idea; personally, I'd prefer not to support them at all. But if we want the particular comparison under consideration to return TRUE (which SQL does want it to do, sometimes), then coercions of some kind will have to be supported, and SQL does support them.

Alternatively, the pertinent language might be such that the declaration—i.e., that variable V is "of type CHAR(5)"—means that legal values of V are character strings of length *at most* five characters. Again, then, if CHAR(5) is indeed regarded as a type as such, we'll be forced to consider, e.g., CHAR(3) as a different type, since the set of strings of length at most five isn't the same as the set of strings of length at most three. On the other hand, the set of strings of length at most five does include the set of strings of length at most three as a proper subset; under this interpretation, in other words, every value of type CHAR(3) is also a value of type CHAR(5), though the converse isn't true. But what happens to our sample comparison under this interpretation? As a moment's thought should make clear, the possibilities are exactly the same as before!

So the alternative interpretation, to the effect that, e.g., CHAR(5) is still a type but the specification "(5)" represents a maximum instead of an exact length, solves nothing. What's more, it leads to a rather strange situation in which supertypes and subtypes aren't supported (that was my assumption, remember) and yet some types are effectively subtypes of others, anyway. In fact, I think it unlikely that the alternative interpretation would be supported at all unless supertypes and subtypes were supported as well. So let's take a look at this possibility.

Again, then, let CHAR(3) and CHAR(5) denote the set of all character strings of length at most three and the set of all character strings of length at most five, respectively. Clearly, then, CHAR(3) is a proper subset of CHAR(5), as we've seen—every value in the set CHAR(3) is also a value in the set CHAR(5). So it seems eminently reasonable to say that CHAR(3) and CHAR(5) are types—after all, a type basically is just a set of values—and to say further that CHAR(3) is a proper subtype of CHAR(5) and CHAR(5) is a proper supertype of CHAR(3). Now the comparison

```
'xyz  '  =  'xyz'
```

is certainly a legitimate expression, thanks to the type inheritance mechanism called value substitutability (which says that wherever a value of type *T* is permitted, a value of type *T'*, where *T'* is a subtype of *T*, can always be substituted—because a value of type *T'* *is* a value of type *T*). In the example, the left comparand is of type CHAR(5), while the right comparand is of type CHAR(3) and therefore of type CHAR(5) as well, and so the comparison is legal. (It still returns FALSE, of course, since the values are different.)

Note: In this approach the length specifications are indeed basically integrity constraints (as the original question suggested they might be), but they're constraints that are part of the pertinent type constraints specifically. I'll have a little more to say about type constraints and other kinds of constraints in the subsection immediately following this one.

All of that being said, I'd now like to add that I think the most elegant approach to the problem is to regard the type as just CHAR, meaning character strings of arbitrary length, and to regard the length specifications as (once again) constraints, but, specifically, constraints on the use of that type in various contexts. For example, defining attribute CITY of the suppliers relvar as, say, CHAR(10) would be shorthand for a constraint—actually a *relvar* constraint—that might look like this:

```
CONSTRAINT ...
     IS_EMPTY ( P WHERE CHAR_LENGTH ( COLOR ) > 10 ) ;
```

In this approach, the comparison

```
'xyz  '  =  'xyz'
```

again involves comparands of the same type, but now we don't need to appeal to the notion of value substitutability in order to show that the comparison is legitimate. (Though it still gives FALSE!)

Incidentally, considerations very similar to those discussed above apply to types—or specifications, rather—of the form NUMERIC(p,q). I omit detailed discussion here, except to point out that, unlike the character string example already discussed, this case involves multiple inheritance. The reason is that, e.g., a number with no more than p digits before the decimal point and no more than q digits after is both (a) a special case of a number with no more than $p+1$ digits before the decimal point and no more than q digits after and (b) a special case of a number with no more than p digits before the decimal point and no more than $q+1$ digits after.

In various writings you've classified integrity constraints into type, attribute, relvar, and database constraints. It seems to me there's an obvious omission here: tuple constraints. Aren't tuple constraints a legitimate and useful concept?

Let me begin by summarizing the constraint classification scheme you're referring to (see reference [34] for further discussion):

- A *type* constraint is simply a definition of the set of values that constitute a given type.

- An *attribute* constraint is a constraint on the values a given attribute is permitted to assume.

- A *relvar* constraint (sometimes called a *single*-relvar constraint, for emphasis) is a constraint on the values a given relvar is permitted to assume.

- A *database* constraint (which I now prefer to call a *multi-relvar* constraint) is a constraint on the values two or more given relvars are permitted to assume in combination.

For the purposes of the present discussion, it's single-relvar constraints we need to focus on. Such a constraint can be arbitrarily complex, just so long as it mentions exactly one relvar.[1] Here are some examples:

```
CONSTRAINT SC1 COUNT ( S ) = COUNT ( S { S# } ) ;
```

This one just says that, within relvar S, supplier numbers are unique.

```
CONSTRAINT SC2 IS_EMPTY ( S WHERE STATUS < 1 OR STATUS > 100 ) ;
```

---

1. Or, to be absolutely accurate, at most one relvar; for example, CONSTRAINT SCX 1 > 0 and CONSTRAINT SCY TRUE are both "single-relvar constraints," technically speaking. (No such constraint can mention any variables apart from relvars, of course.)

This one says that supplier status values must be in the range 1 to 100 inclusive. Unlike the previous example, it has the property that it can be checked for a given supplier tuple by examining just that tuple in isolation—there's no need to look at any other tuples in the relvar or any other relvars in the database—and that's the definition (at least, the informal definition) of a *tuple constraint*. In other words, tuple constraints are a special case of single-relvar constraints; they can be arbitrarily complex, just so long as they can be checked for a given tuple by examining just that tuple in isolation. Here's another example:

```
CONSTRAINT SC3 IS_EMPTY
                ( S WHERE CITY = 'London' AND STATUS ≠ 20 ) ;
```

This one says that suppliers in London must have status 20. The constraint is more complicated than constraint SC2 because it involves two distinct attributes, but it's clearly still a tuple constraint.

So, as the question says, aren't tuple constraints a legitimate and useful concept? Why aren't they included in the classification scheme? The short answer is: They might be legitimate, and they could have been included; as a matter of fact, they *were* included, originally.[1] As for their being useful, I've made use of them myself on occasion. For example, my view updating proposals [40,42] are partly described in terms of them—though I hasten to add that they don't rely on such constraints in any formal sense, they merely use them in an attempt to make the proposals easier to understand (and possibly easier to implement as well).

Incidentally, it's interesting to note that the SQL standard too used to call out tuple constraints as a special case (in fact they were the only constraints it supported, apart from primary and foreign key constraints, prior to SQL:1992). It's also interesting to note that various SQL products adopted (and in some cases continue to adopt) very much the same position; in fact, I believe I'm right in saying that some of those products don't support anything much more sophisticated than simple tuple constraints, even today.

That said, I believe I'm also right in saying that the standard, and the products in question, adopted the position they did for implementation reasons, not model reasons (it's clear that tuple constraints are much easier to implement than constraints in their full generality).[2] From a logical point of view, however, I see tuple constraints as just a simple special case of relvar constraints in general. It might be pragmatically useful from the point of view of the user and/or the DBA and/or the DBMS to call out that special case and give it some special syntactic treatment, but (to say it again) I don't see such considerations as a model issue.

One last point: As I've explained elsewhere [24], a given constraint might be a relvar constraint

---

1. They don't fit very neatly into the overall classification scheme, though, at least from an intuitive point of view. A relvar constraint is a constraint on a relation variable. What's a tuple constraint a constraint on? It can't be a tuple variable, because there aren't any tuple variables in the relational model. And it certainly can't be a tuple value, because values never change, and the concept of a constraint applying to them makes no sense.

2. In particular, if a tuple presented for insertion fails to satisfy some pertinent tuple constraint, it can be rejected out of hand (i.e., there's no need to do the update at all). See reference [34] for further discussion.

with one design and a database constraint with another; that is, the distinction between relvar and database constraints (or, as I would now prefer to say, between single- and multi-relvar constraints) is more one of pragma than of logic. In exactly the same way, a given constraint might be a tuple constraint with one design and a more general relvar constraint (or even a database constraint) with another; that is, the distinction between tuple constraints and more general relvar constraints is again more one of pragma than of logic.

Could tuple constraints be useful in helping us decide when we need to introduce another type? For example, suppose I have a relvar with, among other things, attributes HIRE_YEAR, HIRE_MONTH, and HIRE_DAY, with the obvious semantics. There are clearly various tuple constraints involved here—for example, if HIRE_MONTH is April, then HIRE_DAY can't be 31. Does the existence of these constraints imply that we'd be better off introducing a HIRE_DATE type and treating HIRE_YEAR, etc., as operators that return the appropriate value from a given hire date?

If I understand you correctly, I think what you're trying to do is come up with some guidelines, if not formal principles, to help answer the question:

When I'm doing logical database design, what types do I need?

(Presumably you're talking about a system in which we're not limited to system defined types but can introduce types of our own—so called user defined types.)

I also understand you to be suggesting that if we find that a tuple constraint interrelates attributes *A1, A2, ..., An* of some relvar in some way, then we might be better off replacing that set of attributes by a single attribute *A* defined over some type *T* that has a possible representation ("possrep") whose components map one to one to those attributes *A1, A2, ..., An. Note:* See reference [24] for an informal discussion of the idea of "possreps," and reference [41] for a detailed formal treatment.

I find myself in some sympathy with this suggestion. I also have to say that, sadly, I'm not aware of any formal work that has been done on the issue. Deciding types has always seemed to me just as difficult as deciding entities! (I hasten to add, probably unnecessarily, that the two issues are certainly not the same.) As far as I'm concerned, therefore, the field is wide open for new contributions ... So I guess your question becomes: How can we precisely characterize those "tuple constraints" that mean we should be thinking about a new type instead? That looks like a research topic to me.

Note: I observe that if your hunch is right—i.e., that the existence of certain tuple constraints suggests that we might have done the design wrong and we should be thinking about a new type instead—then presumably the pragmatic usefulness of tuple constraints will be diminished somewhat, since they'll effectively become type constraints instead.

I think it should be possible to query types as well as relations. For example, suppose we're given type COLOR; how can we get a list of all valid colors?

I agree it could be useful to be able to ask queries like the one you mention. At the same time, I certainly don't want to makes types "queryable objects" like relations; as I'm sure you can see, to do that would effectively double the size of the query language at a stroke, and would lead to all kinds of problems that we don't need (or have, in the relational world). Indeed, it would be the first step on a road that could, I suspect, eventually lead to all of the complexities and redundancies of OO languages. And it would certainly would violate *The Information Principle*.

So what we have to do is find a way of getting the information we want to query—the type information, if you like—into relational form. Are you familiar with the concept of a universal relation? Here's a definition: Given a relation type RELATION {*H*}, where {*H*} is a heading, the universal relation of that type is the relation with heading {*H*} and body consisting of all possible tuples of type TUPLE {*H*}. So suppose we define a relvar as follows:

```
VAR COLORS BASE RELATION { COLOR COLOR } KEY { COLOR } ;
```

Now if we had a way of assigning to relvar COLORS the universal relation of type RELATION {COLOR COLOR}, our job would be almost done (the relational expression COLORS—or the SQL expression SELECT * FROM COLORS—would then evaluate to the desired result). So let me now extend the language **Tutorial D** by adding a new kind of relation selector, of the form

```
U_RELATION <heading>
```

This expression is defined to evaluate to the (unique) universal relation corresponding to the specified < *heading* >. (Simplifying just slightly, a < *heading* > in **Tutorial D** is a commalist of < *attribute* >s enclosed in braces, and an < *attribute* > is a pair consisting of an attribute name and a type name.) Thus, for example, the following statement has the effect of assigning the desired universal relation to relvar COLORS:

```
COLORS := U_RELATION { COLOR COLOR } ;
```

Let me now add what I'm sure you've realized already: namely, that in fact we don't need relvar COLORS at all for the purpose at hand (I introduced it purely as a prop). Rather, the query "List all valid colors" can be formulated just as:

```
U_RELATION { COLOR COLOR }
```

I hope this answers your original question. But there's one more point I want to make ... If we did indeed extend **Tutorial D** in the manner I've suggested, we'd certainly want to be very circumspect in our use of this new feature. Imagine, for example, what would happen if we asked the system to evaluate any of the following expressions:

```
U_RELATION { X INTEGER }

U_RELATION { Y RATIONAL }

U_RELATION { Z CHAR }
```

I've seen claims to the effect that *type* is the most fundamental concept of all. Can you explain this claim?

Here's a lightly edited extract from reference [41], by Hugh Darwen and myself:

For definiteness, we assume throughout [*The Third Manifesto*] that the language **D** is imperative in style. Like all such languages, therefore, it's based on the four core concepts *type, value, variable,* and *operator* ... For example, we might have a type called INTEGER; the integer 3 might be a value of that type; N might be a variable of that type, whose value at any given time is some integer value (i.e., some value of that type); and " + " might be an operator that applies to integer values (i.e., to values of that type) ... We remark that if it's true that the *Manifesto* can be regarded as defining a foundation for database technology, then the concepts of type, value, variable, and operator can be regarded as providing a foundation for that foundation. And since the value, variable, and operator concepts in turn all rely on the type concept, we might go further and say the type concept can be regarded as a foundation for the foundation for the foundation. In other words, *the type concept is the most fundamental of all*.

I think the foregoing text answers the question as stated. But there's more I want to say; in fact, I want to introduce what might be regarded as a kind of reductionist argument and use it to raise an additional question or two of my own.

Reference [41] adopts as its philosophical starting point the position that all values simply exist, a priori. In other words, values aren't—can't be—created or destroyed (or updated); instead, they're simply available for use, by anyone, anywhere, for any purpose, at any time. For example, I might use the integer value three to assert that I have three weeks of vacation owing to me, while you might use that same integer value three to assert that you have three dependents. (In effect, I'm talking here about two distinct variables, representing number of weeks vacation and number of dependents, respectively, both of which happen to have three as their current value.)

If you can accept the foregoing position (that all values do indeed exist a priori), then consider this series of logical consequences of that position:

- Names are values, so all names exist a priori.

- Sets are values, so all sets exist a priori.

- Types are < *name, set* > pairs, so all types exist a priori.

- Relation headings are sets, so all headings exist a priori.

- Relation bodies are sets, so all bodies exist a priori.

- Relations are < *heading, body* > pairs, so all relations exist a priori.

- Operators are relations, so all operators exist a priori.

- Variables are *<name, value>* pairs (though the pairs contain different value components at different times), so all variables exist a priori too, in a sense.

And so on. So all we really need is values!

Now, I have to admit that I find this conclusion, if valid, still a little troubling. One question I want to ask is: What type are those values?

Moreover—again, if the foregoing conclusion is valid—an appropriate rhetorical question to ask is this: By what pragma exactly do we decide (as we do in reference [41]) that we should construct our scheme on the basis of the four "primitive" notions *type, value, variable,* and *operator?* The answer, presumably, is that the "extra" (i.e., actually nonprimitive) notions *type, variable,* and *operator,* though perhaps logically unnecessary, are of enormous pragmatic usefulness; they represent certain highly important bundles of concepts that could otherwise be discussed only in terms of inordinately longwinded circumlocutions. But is this the only answer? Or the best? And is it even correct?

SQL CRITICISMS

You're very critical of SQL. But to me SQL's SELECT statement seems much simpler and easier to understand than relational algebra or relational calculus! How do you respond?

It's tempting to respond by just saying there's no accounting for taste and leaving it at that. But I do think there's quite a bit more that can usefully be said, so let me give it a try.

SQL was originally intended to be different from both the relational algebra and the relational calculus. Indeed, the suggestion that SQL's SELECT statement might be "simpler and easier to understand than relational algebra or relational calculus" reminds me of certain remarks in the paper [2] that first unleashed SQL on an unsuspecting world:

Consider the [query] "Find the total volume of items of type A sold by departments on the second floor" ... The calculus programmer must be concerned with:

1.   Setting up three variables ... to sequence through each table

2.   The notions of existential quantifiers and bound variables

3.   The explicit linking terms ... [to specify cross references from one table to another]

4.   The actual matching criteria for membership in the output set

[But] this query could be expressed in [SQL] simply by composing three mapping blocks. *[Note: A "mapping block" is basically what I refer to below as a SELECT expression, and "composing" such blocks means combining them in various ways—in particular, by nesting them inside each other. See further discussion later.]*

And elsewhere in the same paper, the authors say:

> We believed that the applied predicate calculus with its concepts of variables and quantifiers required too much sophistication for the ordinary user.

In other words, one of the motivations for creating SQL in the first place was a perception that the calculus was what might be called "user hostile." However, I believe quite strongly that such a perception was and is mistaken; to be more specific, I believe it displays a confusion between syntax and semantics. I've noted elsewhere in this appendix that the calculus "looks a little like natural language"—and what I mean by that remark is that the semantics of the calculus are rather close to the semantics of (precise) natural language, and hence not too difficult to teach or learn. (I speak from experience here.) As for the syntax, I believe it's easy enough to come up with a language design that hides most of the syntactic complexities, if complexities they truly are, of "applied predicate calculus." In support of this contention, I might point to Query-By-Example [51]; Query-By-Example, better known as QBE, is essentially nothing more than a specific concrete syntax for relational calculus, and most users will agree that the syntax of QBE is nothing if not user friendly.

Now, the authors of reference [2] didn't say so explicitly, but I believe it can fairly be inferred from their paper that they had misgivings with respect to relational algebra similar to those they had in connection with the calculus. (For otherwise why not just use the algebra and have done with it?) If so, however, then I have to say that, again, I think they were confusing syntax and semantics. The algebraic syntax in Codd's early papers (and indeed in most treatments of the algebra in the literature to this day) can indeed be regarded as somewhat user hostile, but again I don't believe this state of affairs reflects anything intrinsic. The language **Tutorial D** is algebraic, and experience suggests that it's quite easy to understand (and use).

To summarize so far, then:

- First, if you want to claim something is complex, you'd better be very clear as to exactly what it is you're imputing that quality of complexity to—in particular, you'd better be very clear as to whether the complexity you're talking about is intrinsic or is merely an artefact of some specific representation. In other words: Complexity, or alleged complexity, can be spurious ... and in the case at hand (relational calculus or relational algebra), I think it is.

- Second, *exactly the same is true of simplicity:* Simplicity, or alleged simplicity, can be spurious too ... and in the case of SQL in particular, I think it is. Although it's true that very simple queries can look simple when they're expressed in SQL, I really don't think SQL is simple at all; it doesn't take much in the way of "intrinsic query complexity" to get us into serious, and in my view quite unnecessary, SQL complexities. (In any case, simple queries probably look simple no matter what language they're expressed in.)

So much for generalities; now let me get a little more specific. The question talks in terms of the SQL SELECT construct specifically, so I'll concentrate on that construct too in what follows. After all, it's certainly true that most SQL queries are formulated as SELECT expressions—by which I mean expressions that involve, in order, a SELECT clause (with an optional DISTINCT specification), a FROM clause, a WHERE clause, a GROUP BY clause, and a HAVING clause (the last three of which are optional). And I'm going to assume you're familiar with the semantics of such expressions, at least

in general terms. Note, incidentally, that I do prefer to talk in terms of SELECT expressions rather than
SELECT statements, because expressions, unlike statements, can (in general) be nested inside other
expressions; i.e., the expression we're talking about might be a subexpression embedded within some
larger expression.

Note: To repeat, the DISTINCT specification is optional. If it's omitted, however, the result of
the SELECT expression might contain duplicate tuples (or duplicate rows, rather), which I'm going to
assume for the purposes of this discussion are never a good idea. Now, sometimes other factors are at
work and the DISTINCT can safely be omitted; e.g., the query is such that the result can't possibly
contain duplicate rows, or the context is such that a temporary appearance of duplicate rows in the
middle of processing the query has no effect on the overall result. In my opinion, however, it's far too
much trouble to work out when it's safe to omit the DISTINCT and when it isn't. For that reason, the
SELECT clauses in my examples will always include a DISTINCT, even when it's logically
unnecessary. And if the implementation isn't smart enough to optimize such DISTINCTs away when
they're unnecessary, then I regard that state of affairs as a deficiency of the implementation in question
(as well as a criticism of SQL per se, I suppose I should add).

To begin my analysis, let me remind you of a crucial property of the algebra (I choose the algebra
for definiteness, though I could frame my remarks in terms of the calculus instead if necessary). The
algebra consists of a set of operators, of course, and—thanks to the well known algebraic closure
property—*those operators can be combined to form expressions in arbitrary ways.* For example, we can
do a restriction, then form the join of that restriction with some other relation, then project the result
over certain attributes, then form the union of that projection with some other relation ... and so on. In
other words, the operators are *mutually orthogonal,* in the sense that any given operator can be defined
independently of all the rest, and the input(s) to any such operator can be denoted by (in turn) essentially
arbitrary algebraic expressions. It's this orthogonality property that makes the algebra easy to learn and
use—once you've learned how to write (e.g.) a join expression, you know without any need for further
study that such an expression can be used wherever the syntax requires a relation of the applicable type.
What's more, the semantics of that join expression, or whatever kind of expression it might be, are
totally independent of context—*A* JOIN *B* means *A* JOIN *B,* no matter where it happens to appear.

So does SQL display any analogous nice properties? In my opinion, it does not (not much, at any
rate), as I'll now try to show.

Consider first the following generic example, which is close to being the simplest possible
example of a SELECT expression:

```
SELECT DISTINCT X, Y
FROM    A, B
WHERE   p
```

Speaking *very* loosely, this expression is the SQL counterpart to the following algebraic
expression:

$$(\ (\ A \ \text{TIMES} \ B \ ) \ \text{WHERE} \ p \ ) \ \{ \ X, \ Y \ \}$$

In other words (and still speaking very loosely), the FROM clause corresponds to cartesian
product, the WHERE clause to restriction, and the SELECT clause with its DISTINCT specification to
projection. And the clauses are executed, or evaluated, in the order FROM, then WHERE, then

SELECT.

Observe now, however, that those clauses *must* be written in the order shown (SELECT, then FROM, then WHERE)—which is, of course, not the order in which they're executed. Thus, even if we limit ourselves to the corresponding algebraic operators (i.e., product, restriction, and projection), it's far from obvious how to write the SQL analog of an algebraic expression that uses just these operators but applies them repeatedly and/or in a different sequence—for instance (to pick an example almost at random):

```
( TIMES { A,
          B { X },
          C WHERE pc,
          TIMES { ( D { Y } ) WHERE pd,
                  ( E WHERE pe ) { Z } } } ) { X, Z, X }
```

Here for the record is a possible SQL analog (at least, I think it's such an analog, though I'm far from certain—and, of course, that lack of certainty on my part is precisely part of my point):

```
SELECT DISTINCT X, Z
FROM ( SELECT DISTINCT *
       FROM A ) AS POINTLESS1,
     ( SELECT DISTINCT X
       FROM   B ) AS POINTLESS2,
     ( SELECT DISTINCT *
       FROM   C
       WHERE  pc ) AS POINTLESS3,
     ( SELECT DISTINCT *
       FROM ( SELECT DISTINCT Y
              FROM   D
              WHERE  pd ) AS POINTLESS4,
            ( SELECT DISTINCT Z
              FROM   E
              WHERE  pe ) AS POINTLESS5 ) AS POINTLESS6
```

Observe that in order to come up with this formulation, the user must:

- Be aware of certain algebraic laws of transformation

- Be able to nest subqueries in the FROM clause (an ability that wasn't even supported in SQL for the first 20 years or so of its existence, and might not be supported in all SQL products even today)

- Be aware of the pointless rule that tables resulting from subqueries in the FROM clause must be given names, even when those names are never referenced

- Not forget to include at least some of those DISTINCTs—possibly not all, but if not, then the user must additionally be aware of when it's safe to omit them

All in all, it seems to me that these requirements taken together imply the need for quite a lot in the way of "sophistication" (to quote reference [2]) on the part of the SQL user.

Still staying with product, restriction, and projection only, let me now make a couple of additional points:

- I've said that FROM is the rough analog of product, but note that the FROM clause can't appear in isolation—there must always be an accompanying SELECT clause (even if it's only "SELECT *").[1] Thus, SQL doesn't *really* support the product operation; instead, it supports only "projection of product." *Note:* Here and elsewhere I rely on the fact that the "product" of a single relation (or table, in SQL terms) *r* is just *r*.

- I've said that WHERE is the rough analog of restriction, but of course it too can't appear in isolation—there must always be an accompanying FROM clause, and hence an accompanying SELECT clause as well. In other words, SQL doesn't really support restriction; instead, it supports only "projection of restriction of product."

Now I observe that matters are actually much more complicated than I've been pretending so far. The fact is, the SELECT clause isn't just the SQL analog of projection—it's the SQL analog of, in general, some combination of projection and/or extension and/or attribute (i.e., column) renaming. For example, the SQL expression

```
SELECT DISTINCT S# AS SUPPLIER, CITY AS LOCATION
FROM    S
```

is the SQL analog of this algebraic expression:

```
S RENAME ( S# AS SUPPLIER, CITY AS LOCATION )
```

Likewise, the SQL expression

```
SELECT DISTINCT P#, WEIGHT AS POUNDS, WEIGHT * 454 AS GRAMS
FROM    P
```

is the SQL analog of this algebraic expression:

```
( EXTEND P ADD ( WEIGHT AS POUNDS, WEIGHT * 454 AS GRAMS ) )
                                   { P#, POUNDS, GRAMS }
```

---

1. I observe too that the FROM clause isn't "just" the SQL analog of product—it also acts as the SQL mechanism for defining range variables (at least implicitly, and often explicitly). Another awkward bundling, in my opinion.

Obvious questions therefore arise in connection with the SQL analog of an algebraic expression that uses some combination of product, restriction, projection, extension, and renaming but applies them repeatedly and/or in a different sequence. As a trivial example, consider this query: "Find part numbers and gram weights for parts with weight greater than 7000 grams." Here's an algebraic formulation:

```
( ( EXTEND P ADD ( WEIGHT * 454 AS GRAMS ) )
            WHERE GRAMS > WEIGHT ( 7000 ) ) { P#, GRAMS }
```

And here's an SQL analog (note the need to repeat the subexpression WEIGHT * 454 in this SQL formulation):

```
SELECT DISTINCT P#, WEIGHT * 454 AS GRAMS
FROM    P
WHERE   WEIGHT * 454 > WEIGHT ( 7000 )
```

Alternatively, here's another SQL analog that (unlike the previous one) makes use of a subquery in the FROM clause:

```
SELECT DISTINCT P#, GRAMS
FROM ( SELECT DISTINCT P#, WEIGHT * 454 AS GRAMS
       FROM   P ) AS POINTLESS
WHERE  GRAMS > WEIGHT ( 7000 )
```

The latter formulation does avoid the need to repeat the subexpression, but it raises another point: The opening SELECT clause mentions an attribute (column) called GRAMS, *but that attribute isn't defined until we get some way down into the FROM clause.* In other words, the (desirable) ability to include subqueries in the FROM clause implies that, frequently, attributes will have to be referenced a long time before they're defined. Consider, for example, a SELECT expression of the form:

```
SELECT DISTINCT Z ...
FROM ( humongous great expression that, somewhere in its depths,
       defines Z )
   ...
```

This state of affairs means that SELECT expressions can't always be understood in a single "reading" from beginning to end. Of course, the criticism I'm making here is only a psychological one—but remember that we're supposed to be talking about "simplicity" and ease of use. In fact, I think one trivial fix that would help matters quite a bit, psychologically speaking, would be to move the SELECT clause to the very end of the overall SELECT expression; then we could at least say, loosely, that the various clauses are executed in the order in which they're written. But as I've already indicated, I also think there are much bigger problems with SELECT expressions in general than just the sequence of the clauses.

Now I turn to the GROUP BY clause. Consider the following SQL expressions (shown side by side to facilitate comparison):

```
SELECT DISTINCT QTY   |   SELECT DISTINCT QTY
FROM    SP            |   FROM    SP
                     |   GROUP   BY S#
```

The expression on the left is straightforward. By contrast, the one on the right is illegal!—loosely speaking, it's illegal because the expression QTY in the SELECT clause isn't "single valued per group." However, it's not so much the legality *vs.* illegality of the expressions that concerns me here; rather, it's the fact that *the SELECT clauses are syntactically identical but have different semantics in the two cases.* In other words, the semantics of the SELECT clause can't be defined in isolation; they vary, depending on whether a GROUP BY clause is present or not.

> *Aside:* Also, it follows from the example that omitting the GROUP BY clause is not equivalent to specifying "GROUP BY no columns at all." Why not? Because the latter would—or should—either produce no groups at all, if the table being grouped is empty, or consider the entire table as a single group otherwise, and in the example QTY is certainly not single valued with respect to the entire table. *Note:* The reason I say "or should" in the foregoing sentence has to do with another SQL flaw, this time in the HAVING clause, which I'll get to later. *End of aside.*

Here's a slightly more realistic example to illustrate the same point:

```
SELECT DISTINCT              |   SELECT DISTINCT
       SUM ( QTY ) AS TQTY   |          SUM ( QTY ) AS TQTY
FROM    SP                   |   FROM    SP
                            |   GROUP   BY S#
```

Now both expressions are legal, but of course they have different semantics: The one on the left gives the total of quantities taken over all shipments, the one on the right gives total quantities per supplier (with duplicate totals eliminated). Again, therefore, the semantics of the very same SELECT clause—in this case, SELECT DISTINCT SUM(QTY) AS TQTY—depend on whether the GROUP BY clause is present or not.

Next, I observe that the expression on the right (the one with the GROUP BY) isn't a very sensible query, anyway! Given our usual sample values, for example, here's what it returns:

TQTY
1300
900
200
700

The query isn't very sensible because (as you can see) it fails to indicate which total quantity belongs to which supplier. So another criticism of SQL's SELECT ... GROUP BY ... construct is that it permits the formulation of queries that aren't very sensible, and the user therefore has to take care to avoid them. *Note:* I should add that the same criticism doesn't apply to the relational algebra "analog"—the relation that results from the expression

```
SUMMARIZE SP BY { S# } ADD ( SUM ( QTY ) AS TQTY )
```

includes (by definition) both the "BY attribute" S# and the "added attribute" TQTY:

S#	TQTY
S1	1300
S4	900
S3	200
S2	700

The SQL analog of this "sensible" query is, of course, as follows:

```
SELECT DISTINCT S#, SUM ( QTY ) AS TQTY
FROM    SP
GROUP   BY S#
```

But now there's another problem! To be specific, the SELECT clause shown here—SELECT DISTINCT S#, SUM(QTY) AS TQTY—would be illegal if we were to delete the GROUP BY clause—right? (And I remind you in passing that the same was not the case when the specification S# was omitted from the SELECT clause.) Yet again, therefore, we see that the semantics of the SELECT clause can't be defined in isolation but depend on context.

I haven't finished with the GROUP BY clause. My next point is that it doesn't really do the job it's supposed to do, anyway. Consider again the query "For each supplier, get the supplier number and the corresponding total quantity." The desired result is:

S#	TQTY
S1	1300
S4	900
S3	200
S2	700
S5	0

As we've already seen, however, the SELECT ... GROUP BY ... expression doesn't deliver this result—it misses supplier S5, with total quantity zero. A relational algebra formulation that does give the desired result is:

```
SUMMARIZE SP PER ( S { S# } ) ADD ( SUM ( QTY ) AS TQTY )
```

(I've replaced the BY specification by a PER specification, and that does the necessary.) By contrast, an "equivalent" SQL formulation is rather more complicated:

```
SELECT DISTINCT S#, COALESCE ( TQTY, 0 ) AS TQTY
FROM    S, LATERAL ( SELECT DISTINCT SUM ( QTY ) AS TQTY
                     FROM    SP
                     WHERE   SP.S# = S.S# ) AS POINTLESS
```

Note in particular that this latter formulation doesn't involve a GROUP BY clause at all—a fact that might reasonably raise questions in your mind as to why GROUP BY is supported at all.[1] I'll come back to this point when I discuss the HAVING clause, later.

Still another point on GROUP BY: GROUP BY might be thought to be the SQL analog of the algebraic GROUP operator—and so it is, in a way. For example, GROUP BY S# applied to SP is roughly analogous to the algebraic expression SP GROUP ({P#,QTY} AS ...)—P# and QTY being the attributes of SP not mentioned in the GROUP BY clause (note that the algebraic GROUP operator specifies the attributes to be grouped, not the ones controlling the grouping).[2] However:

- Unlike GROUP, GROUP BY can't appear in isolation; there must always be, among other things, an accompanying SELECT clause. And one of the effects of that SELECT clause is precisely to undo the effects of the grouping (i.e., to perform a corresponding UNGROUP, in algebraic terms).[3] In SQL, therefore, UNGROUP can't appear in isolation either—GROUP and UNGROUP always appear together, and any given grouping operation is followed immediately (well, almost immediately) by a corresponding ungrouping operation.

- Once again, questions arise regarding SQL analogs of algebraic expressions involving arbitrary mixtures of (now) summarizing, grouping, and ungrouping, as well as all of the operations discussed previously (product, restriction, projection, extension, and renaming).

And then there's the HAVING clause ... The HAVING clause is a kind of "WHERE clause for

---

1. It also illustrates two further SQL complications—a COALESCE invocation in the SELECT clause, and a LATERAL specification in the FROM clause. I'll leave it to you to figure out what these constructs do and why they're necessary. (*Are* they necessary?)

2. The algebraic GROUP example can alternatively be specified thus: SP GROUP ({ALL BUT S#} AS ...). This form is a little closer to GROUP BY in SQL.

3. So now we see the SELECT clause isn't just the SQL analog of some combination of projection and/or extension and/or renaming—it might have to do some ungrouping too, in general.

groups";[1] in other words, if the overall expression includes a HAVING clause, it usually includes a GROUP BY clause as well. However, that clause can be omitted, in which case it's as if "GROUP BY no columns at all" had been specified, and SQL treats the entire table as a single group. Here I'd just like to point out that this treatment is logically incorrect if the table in question happens to be empty; in that case, there shouldn't be any groups at all, but SQL says there's exactly one group (necessarily empty, of course). Note that there *is* a logical difference here: It's exactly the difference between the empty set and what the empty set contains (what the empty set contains is nothing at all, but the empty set itself isn't nothing but something—if you see what I mean).

It isn't easy to say exactly what the algebraic analog of the HAVING clause is. However, it's certainly the case that any relation that can be obtained by means of an SQL expression that includes a HAVING clause can also be obtained by means of some algebraic expression. In fact, I've shown elsewhere [25] that HAVING is effectively redundant in SQL, anyway; that is, any sensible SQL expression that involves a HAVING clause is logically equivalent to one that doesn't. (The same is true of GROUP BY, incidentally, as reference [25] also shows.) Which isn't to say that HAVING and GROUP BY can easily be defined in terms of syntactic substitution [13]; if they could, they wouldn't be so difficult to teach, learn, and use. *Au contraire,* in fact: The mappings are quite complicated, and vary from case to case; I mean, they suffer from the "many special cases" syndrome. See reference [25] for further discussion.

Well, I think I've covered enough territory to show that SQL's SELECT expressions in general are very far from simple. Let me summarize the main points I've been trying to make.

- The SELECT, FROM, WHERE, GROUP BY, and HAVING clauses don't really correspond to distinct relational operations. Instead, various combinations of those clauses correspond, in no very straightforward or systematic manner, to various combinations of those operators. In other words, the precise effect of any individual clause is highly context sensitive, and the various clauses are a long way from being mutually orthogonal.

- This lack of orthogonality among the clauses contrasts strongly with the orthogonality of the relational operations. Note in particular that it's that lack of orthogonality that, quite apart from anything else, makes SQL hard to *define,* as well as hard to document, teach, learn, remember, and use. (That's one reason why the SQL standard is such an enormous document—not to mention the fact that it's also full of errors.) In effect, that lack of orthogonality means that SQL is rife with special cases. As a consequence, we might say, loosely but not entirely incorrectly, that, measuring them in terms of the number of concepts they involve, relational algebra is linear (additive), while SQL is multiplicative, in nature. Orthogonality means, among other things, that there's less for the user to learn, and in effect more functionality ("more bang for the buck") in what's learned.

---

1. Well, no, it isn't—not exactly. A WHERE clause for groups would presumably involve boolean expressions of the form < *group* > < *comparison op* > < *group* > . In fact, however, the HAVING clause typically involves boolean expressions of the form < *summary* > < *comparison op* > < *scalar* > , where < *summary* > is some expression such as SUM(QTY) that's single valued per group.

——————— ♦ ♦ ♦ ♦ ♦ ———————

With regard to that business of always specifying DISTINCT, I've heard some people refer to the debate over duplicate rows as "religious." What do they mean? Do you agree with them?

I most certainly do not agree with them! Let me explain. First, of course, you're absolutely correct when you say some people characterize the debate as religious in nature. For example, here's what Don Chamberlin has to say on the matter:

> During the early development of SQL ... some decisions were made that were ultimately to generate a great deal more controversy than anyone anticipated. Chief among these were the decisions to support null values and to permit duplicate rows to occur in tables and in query results. I will devote a small amount of space here to examining the reasons for these decisions and the context in which they were made. My purpose here is historical rather than persuasive—I recognize that nulls and duplicates are religious topics, and I do not expect anyone to have a conversion experience after reading this chapter.

Don Chamberlin is, of course, widely recognized as the inventor (along with Raymond Boyce) of the SQL language, and this is the opening paragraph of a section titled "Some Controversial Decisions" in Chapter 1 (A Brief History of SQL) of his book on DB2 [1].

> *Aside:* It's a little tangential to the main point at issue, but I do have a couple of technical quibbles with the quoted paragraph. First, note the reference (once again) to "null values." To say it one more time, a very large part of the point about nulls is precisely that they aren't values. Second, note the reference to "tables and ... query results," a phrase that suggests fairly strongly that query results and tables are different things; yet a very large part of the point about the relational model is precisely that query results are tables (or, as I would prefer to say, relations). *End of aside.*

Be that as it may, there's clearly at least one writer who thinks that duplicates are a religious topic. What does this mean? All it can possibly mean, it seems to me, is that:

- There are no *scientific* reasons in favor of either side of the argument (i.e., in favor of either permitting or prohibiting duplicates)—it's just a matter of faith: Some people believe in duplicates and some don't, and that's all there is to be said.

- As a consequence, it's just as scientifically respectable to permit duplicates as to prohibit them, and it's a waste of time trying to have a scientific discussion of the issue.

I reject this position absolutely. There are all kinds of solid scientific reasons for prohibiting duplicates (see, e.g., reference [30]). By contrast, I'm not aware of any good reasons—emphasis on good—for permitting them. Note that it's only those in the "duplicates permitted" camp who describe the issue as religious!—nobody in the opposing camp does so. In fact, I think those who describe the issue as religious do so precisely because they know they have little science to support their position. (Alternatively, I suppose, they might simply be unaware of, or might not understand, the scientific counterarguments. If so, however, then I don't think they have any right to foist their lack of knowledge or understanding on the community at large. Though I suppose there's plenty of precedent for *that,* in other disciplines as well as our own. Examples that come to mind include *<please supply your own>.)*

Incidentally, I'd like to add that one good philosophical argument against duplicates is that if you use position as the sole distinguishing feature of some object—which is effectively what you're forced to do if you "permit duplicates" [30]—then changing an object's position apparently changes its identity! But surely identity is, or should be, intrinsic to the object in question, not a mere quirk of where that object happens to be located. I'm still me, regardless of whether I happen to be in California, or Australia, or Mexico, or anywhere else. *Note:* Of course, I'm using the term *object* in its generic sense here, not its specialized OO sense. But this argument is in fact a good argument against object IDs, at least as a concept for use in "modeling reality." One of the reasons objects and databases are such a bad fit is that OO people want to write programs and chase pointers, while database people want to model reality. Two different objectives, and two different mindsets, and two different problems—and two different sets of tools are appropriate.

I've heard you complain that SQL's GROUP BY construct is "too procedural." Can you elaborate?

Well, I can try. First, though, I think I should say it seems to be quite difficult to pin down the meaning of *procedural* in any very precise manner; I think the best we can say is that some language *A* is either more or less procedural than some other language *B* ... or, perhaps better, that some formulation *A* of some given problem (e.g., some database query) is either more or less procedural than some other formulation *B* of the same problem. As a consequence, it's quite difficult to pin down the precise meaning of *declarative,* too, since *declarative* (whatever else it might mean) is usually equated with *nonprocedural.*

That said, yes, I do think GROUP BY is more procedural than certain other parts of SQL, in a sense. To my way of thinking, an expression like (say)

```
SELECT  S#, AVG ( QTY ) AS AQ
FROM    SP
GROUP   BY S#
```

seems to me to be saying to the system: First, rearrange the rows of table SP into groups such that the S# value is (a) the same in every row in a given group and (b) different from the S# value in any row in any other group; then, for each such group, extract the common S# value and the average AQ of the quantities in the rows in that group; then what results from the foregoing process is what I want. To me, this looks more like a recipe—i.e., a step by step algorithm, or procedure—for solving the problem, not just a simple declarative statement of what the problem is. A declarative statement might be just:

Get supplier numbers and corresponding average quantities.

It's not immediately obvious from this declarative statement of the problem that GROUP BY is the operator that's required, and of course it's not required: I mean, we can solve the problem (i.e., formulate the query) without it—e.g., as follows:[1]

```
SELECT DISTINCT SPX.S#,
                  LATERAL ( SELECT DISTINCT AVG ( SPY.QTY ) AS AQ
                            FROM   SP AS SPY
                            WHERE  SPY.S# = SPX.S# ) AS POINTLESS
FROM    SP AS SPX
```

Or in relational calculus:

```
( SPX.S#, AVG ( SPY WHERE SPY.S# = SPX.S#, QTY ) AS AQ )
```

Note: I've assumed in this latter formulation that SPX and SPY have both been defined somewhere to be range variables that range over the relation that's the value of relvar SP at the time the overall expression is evaluated. See reference [23] for further explanation.

REFERENCES AND BIBLIOGRAPHY

1.   Don Chamberlin: *Using the New DB2: IBM's Object-Relational Database System.* San Francisco, Calif.: Morgan Kaufmann (1996).

2.   Donald D. Chamberlin and Raymond F. Boyce: "SEQUEL: A Structured English Query Language," Proc. 1974 ACM SIGMOD Workshop on Data Description, Access, and Control, Ann Arbor, Mich. (May 1974).

3.   E. F. Codd: "Derivability, Redundancy, and Consistency of Relations Stored in Large Data Banks," IBM Research Report RJ599 (August 19th, 1969).

4.   E. F. Codd: "A Relational Model of Data for Large Shared Data Banks," *CACM 13,* No. 6 (June 1970).

5.   E. F. Codd: "A Data Base Sublanguage Founded on the Relational Calculus," Proc. 1971 ACM SIGFIDET Workshop on Data Description, Access and Control, San Diego, Calif. (November 1971).

6.   E. F. Codd: "Further Normalization of the Data Base Relational Model," in Randall J. Rustin (ed.), *Data Base Systems: Courant Computer Science Symposia Series 6.* Englewood Cliffs, N.J.: Prentice-Hall (1972).

---

1. The SELECT expression shown is not standard SQL, because the standard doesn't currently allow subqueries in the SELECT clause; however, several products do. What's more, I'm not sure whether the LATERAL specification is required in this context, nor do I know whether it's even permitted. What's more, I don't care.

7. E. F. Codd: "Relational Completeness of Data Base Sublanguages," in Randall J. Rustin (ed.), *Data Base Systems, Courant Computer Science Symposia Series 6.* Englewood Cliffs, N.J.: Prentice Hall (1972).

8. E. F. Codd: "Understanding Relations," series of columns in *FDT* (previous title of *ACM SIGMOD Record*), beginning with *FDT 5,* No. 1 (June 1973).

9. E. F. Codd: "Is Your DBMS Really Relational?" and "Does Your DBMS Run By The Rules?", *Computerworld* (October 14th, 1985; October 21st, 1985).

10. E. F. Codd: *The Relational Model for Database Management Version 2.* Reading, Mass.: Addison-Wesley (1990).

11. Hugh Darwen (writing as Andrew Warden): "TABLE_DEE and TABLE_DUM," in C. J. Date, *Relational Database Writings 1985-1989.* Reading, Mass.: Addison-Wesley (1990).

12. Hugh Darwen: "The Nullologist in Relationland," in C. J. Date and Hugh Darwen, *Relational Database Writings 1989-1991.* Reading, Mass.: Addison-Wesley (1992).

13. Hugh Darwen: "Valid Time and Transaction Time Proposals: Language Design Aspects," in Opher Etzion, Sushil Jajodia, and Suryanaryan Sripada (eds.): *Temporal Databases: Research and Practice.* New York, N.Y.: Springer Verlag (1998).

14. Hugh Darwen: "How to Handle Missing Information Without Using Nulls" (presentation slides), *www.thethirdmanifesto.com* (May 9th, 2003).

15. C. J. Date: "The Relational Model and its Interpretation," in *Relational Database: Selected Writings.* Reading, Mass.: Addison-Wesley (1986).

16. C. J. Date: "NOT Is Not "Not"! (Notes on Three-Valued Logic and Related Matters)," in *Relational Database Writings 1985-1989.* Reading, Mass.: Addison-Wesley (1990).

17. C. J. Date: "The Principle of Cautious Design," in C. J. Date and Hugh Darwen, *Relational Database Writings 1989-1991.* Reading, Mass.: Addison-Wesley (1992).

18. C. J. Date: "Tables with No Columns," in *Relational Database Writings 1991-1994.* Reading, Mass.: Addison-Wesley (1995).

19. C. J. Date: "The Primacy of Primary Keys: An Investigation," in *Relational Database Writings 1991-1994.* Reading, Mass.: Addison-Wesley (1995).

20. C. J. Date: "Faults and Defaults" (in five parts), in C. J. Date, Hugh Darwen, and David McGoveran, *Relational Database Writings 1994-1997.* Reading, Mass.: Addison-Wesley (1998).

21.   C. J. Date: "Why 'the Object Model' Is Not a Data Model," in C. J. Date, Hugh Darwen, and David McGoveran, *Relational Database Writings 1994-1997*. Reading, Mass.: Addison-Wesley (1998).

22.   C. J. Date: *The Database Relational Model: A Retrospective Review and Analysis*. Reading, Mass.: Addison-Wesley (2001).

23.   C. J. Date: *An Introduction to Database Systems* (8th edition). Boston, Mass.: Addison-Wesley (2004).

24.   C. J. Date: *Database in Depth: Relational Theory for Practitioners*. Sebastopol, Calif.: O'Reilly Media, Inc. (2005).

25.   C. J. Date: "Grievous Bodily Harm" (in two parts), in *Relational Database Writings 1998-2001*. Privately published (2006).

26.   C. J. Date: *The Relational Database Dictionary*. Sebastopol, Calif.: O'Reilly Media Inc. (2006).

27.   C. J. Date: "On the Notion of Logical Difference," in *Date on Database: Writings 2000-2006*. Berkeley, Calif.: Apress (2006).

28.   C. J. Date: "On the Logical Differences Between Types, Values, and Variables," in *Date on Database: Writings 2000-2006*. Berkeley, Calif.: Apress (2006).

29.   C. J. Date: "What First Normal Form Really Means," in *Date on Database: Writings 2000-2006*. Berkeley, Calif.: Apress (2006).

30.   C. J. Date: "Double Trouble, Double Trouble," in *Date on Database: Writings 2000-2006*. Berkeley, Calif.: Apress (2006).

31.   C. J. Date: "Data Redundancy and Database Design: Further Thoughts Number One," in *Date on Database: Writings 2000-2006*. Berkeley, Calif.: Apress (2006).

32.   C. J. Date: "Why Three- and Four-Valued Logic Don't Work," in *Date on Database: Writings 2000-2006*. Berkeley, Calif.: Apress (2006).

33.   C. J. Date: "Some Operators Are More Equal than Others" (Chapter 2 in this book).

34.   C. J. Date: "Constraints and Predicates" (Chapter 3 in this book).

35.   C. J. Date: "The Closed World Assumption" (Chapter 4 in this book).

36.   C. J. Date: "Normalization from Top to Bottom" (Chapter 8 in this book).

37.   C. J. Date: "Why Is It Called Relational Algebra?" (Chapter 10 in this book).

38.   C. J. Date: "Gödel, Russell, Codd: A Recursive Golden Crowd" (Chapter 13 in this book).

39.   C. J. Date: "And Now for Something Completely Computational" (Chapter 15 in this book).

40.   C. J. Date: "The Logic of View Updating" (Chapter 16 in this book).

41.   C. J. Date and Hugh Darwen: *Databases, Types, and the Relational Model: The Third Manifesto* (3rd edition). Boston, Mass.: Addison-Wesley (2006).

42.   C. J. Date and Hugh Darwen: Appendix E ("View Updating") of reference [41].

43.   C. J. Date, Hugh Darwen, and Nikos Lorentzos: *Temporal Data and the Relational Model.* San Francisco, Calif.: Morgan Kaufmann (2003).

44.   C. J. Date and Ronald Fagin: "Simple Conditions for Guaranteeing Higher Normal Forms in Relational Databases," *ACM Transactions on Database Systems 17,* No. 3 (September 1992). Republished in C. J. Date and Hugh Darwen, *Relational Database Writings 1989-1991.* Reading, Mass.: Addison-Wesley (1992).

45.   Ronald Fagin: "A Normal Form for Relational Databases that Is Based on Domains and Keys," *ACM TODS 6,* No. 3 (September 1981).

46.   David Maier: *The Theory of Relational Databases.* Rockville, Md.: Computer Science Press (1983).

47.   James Martin: "Semantic Disintegrity in Relational Operations," Chapter 18 of *Fourth-Generation Languages Volume I: Principles.* Englewood Cliffs, N.J.: Prentice-Hall (1985).

48.   David McGoveran: "Nothing from Nothing" (in four parts), in C. J. Date, Hugh Darwen, and David McGoveran, *Relational Database Writings 1994-1997.* Reading, Mass.: Addison-Wesley (1998).

49.   Atsushi Ohori, Peter Buneman, and Val Breazu-Tannen: "Database Programming in Machiavelli—A Polymorphic Language with Static Type Inference." Proc. ACM SIGMOD International Conference on Management of Data, Portland, Ore. (June 1989).

50.   Patrick Suppes: *Introduction to Logic.* Princeton, N.J.: Van Nostrand (1957).

51.   Moshé M. Zloof: "Query-By-Example," Proc. NCC *44,* Anaheim, Calif. (May 1975). Montvale, N.J.: AFIPS Press (1977).

Index

For alphabetization purposes, (a) differences in fonts are ignored; (b) punctuation symbols—hyphens, underscores, parentheses, quotation marks, etc.—are treated as blanks; (c) numerals precede letters; (d) lowercase precedes uppercase; (e) blanks precede everything else.

ε (contained in), 26,284
≡ (equivalent to), 9
⇒ (implies), 56
⇐⇒ (bi-implies), 57
⊢ (it is the case that), 48,56
⊨ (it is necessarily the case that), 48
→ (FD), 200
↠ (MVD), 192
⊰{ . . . } (JD), 184
‖<‖ (properly included in), 284
‖>‖ (properly includes), 284
‖≤‖ (included in), 284,380
‖≥‖ (includes), 284

1NF, *see* first normal form
2NF, *see* second normal form
2VL, 56
3NF, *see* third normal form
3VL, 58
4NF, *see* fourth normal form
5NF, *see* fifth normal form
6NF, *see* sixth normal form

A, 257-258
    ◄AND►, 258,259,261
    ◄NAND►, 257,258,259
    ◄NOR►, 257,258,259
    ◄NOT►, 258,259
    ◄OR►, 258,259,261
    ◄REMOVE►, 257,258,259,260-261
    ◄TCLOSE►, 257,258,262
Abbey, Edward, 85
Abel, Niels Henrik, 265
Abelian group, *see* group
absorption, 250
ACID properties, 80
Ackermann function, 338

Albert, Joseph, 270,298
algebra, 237,242,262
    abstract, 244
    bag, *see* bag algebra
    basic, 238-242
    boolean, 248-255
    generalized, 242-246
    matrix, 255-256
    model of, 242,243-244
    other definitions, 263-264
    relational, *see* relational algebra
    set, 252-255
    SQL, 266-269
ALGEBRA, 258
ALPHA, 316,333
antisymmetry, 250,285
appearance of a value, 317
argument, 11,127
    vs. parameter, 11,33
assignment, 311,317
    multiple, *see* multiple assignment
    relational, 309,315
    sole update operator, 310
Assignment Principle, 343
associativity, 239
    +, 240
    *, 241
Atsushi, Ohori, 437
attribute, 178
    relation valued, *see* relation valued attribute
attribute constraint, *see* constraint
axiom, 91,121

bag, 269,283
bag algebra, 268-269,294-297
    complement, 290-292
    concatenation, 268,288

difference, 268,285
intersection, 268,285
intersection star, 288
product, 286,288
restriction, 289
sum, 288
union, 268,285
union plus, 288
base relvar, 81
BCNF, *see* Boyce/Codd normal form
Bell, John L., 62
bi-implication, 44-61
bijection, 166
binary relation, 175
binary relvars inadequate, 405-408
Birkhoff, Garrett, 270,271
Biskup, Joachim, 146
Bochvar, D. A., 147
Booch, Grady, 175
boolean algebra, *see* algebra
Boolos, George, 62
bound variable, 16,32,76
Boyce, Raymond F., 183,208,434
Boyce/Codd normal form, 201-202,204
Breazu-Tannen, Val, 437
Bronowski, Jacob, 377
Buneman, O. Peter, 437
Burke, Edmund, 3
business rule, 4ff

Cage, John, 135
calculus, 272
Campbell, Thomas, 339
candidate key, 178
cardinality constraint, *see* constraint
Carnap, Rudolf, 62
Celko, Joe, 270
Chamberlin, Donald D., 434
CHAR, 415-417
Clark, John, O. E., 62,270
Clark, K. L., 96,114
Clarke, Michael, 63
class, 252
Clinton, Bill, 409
Closed World Assumption, 85,95ff,305

not for constraints, 86,305
closure, 242
+, 240
*, 241
Codd, E. F., *passim*
codomain, 164
coercion, 415
commutativity, 239
+, 240
*, 241
compensatory update, 344-346
complement, 250
bag, *see* bag algebra
complementarity, 250
complete (logical system), 52
computable function, 330-331
computational completeness, 330-332
connection trap, 384-386
connective, 9,121
dyadic, 34-35
monadic, 34
see also truth tables
consistency, 86-87
logical system, 125
constraint
attribute, 89,90,417
cardinality, 163
checking, 79ff
database, 78
is a proposition, 76
multi-relvar, 75,89,417
relvar, 78,339-340,417
single-relvar, 75,88,417
total (database), 78
total (relvar), 78
transition, 91
tuple, 418-419
type, 89-90,417
view, 88-89
constraint classification scheme, 417
contradiction, 125
correctness, 86-87
see also soundness
Crossley, J. N., 62
CWA, *see* Closed World Assumption

D, 299-300
    core concepts, 421
    vs. **Tutorial D,** 300,329
Daintith, John, 62,270
Darwen, Hugh, *passim*
data independence, 120,383-384
Data Sublanguage ALPHA, *see* ALPHA
database
    is a logical system, 91-92
    is propositions, 81
    value, 69,326
    variable, 69,326,341-343
    see also dbvar
database constraint, *see* constraint
database design, 87-88,155ff
database equivalence, 347-349
database inclusion, 347-349
database predicate, 88
database variable, *see* dbvar
Date, C. J., *passim*
dbvar, 69,326
    is a tuplevar, 341-342
de Brock, E. O., 327
De Morgan's Laws, 151,250
decidable, 126,330
decision procedure, 330
deductive completeness, 126
DEE, *see* TABLE_DEE
dependency preservation, 185-186
DELETE anomaly, 229
DELETE expansion, 311
DeLong, Howard, 62
denormalization, 215ff
    defined, 219
Derbyshire, John, 271
designator, 46,77
deviant (logic), 137-138,139-142
DeVidi, David, 62
difference
    set, 253
    symmetric, 253
disjoint union, 350
DISTINCT (SQL), 278,424,432-433
distributivity, 240,241
DK/NF, *see* domain-key normal form

domain (function), 164
domain (relational model), 378
domain-key normal form, 400-402
double underlining, 179
dual, *see Principle of Duality*
DUM, *see* TABLE_DUM
D_UNION, *see* disjoint union

element, 156,283
empty bag, 285
empty range, 21
empty set, 285
equality, 45-47
    axiom of, 239
    SQL, 63-64
equivalence, 47-55
    database, 347-349
    see also bi-implication
equivalence class, 54-55
equivalence relation, 55
error
    definition, 409
    "mild *vs.* severe," 145
existential quantification, 13ff
    iterated OR, 22,128
EXISTS, *see* existential quantification
expressive completeness, 126
    2VL, 246
extension (logic), 127,137,138-142

Fagin, Ronald, 183,203,207,208,209,437
FD, *see* functional dependency
field (mathematics), 264
fifth normal form, 188-189
Finkelstein, Richard, 225,233
first normal form, 206
first order logic, 395
Fitzgerald, Edward, 329
FORALL, *see* universal quantification
fourth normal form, 199,399-400
fragment (logic), 137,138
free variable, 11,16,32
    see also parameter
Fry, James P., 176
fully normalized, 188

function, 164
functional dependency, 199-201
    implied by superkey, 201
    trivial, 201

Gallaire, Hervé, 115
Garcia-Molina, Hector, 267,271
Geach, P. T., 62
Gilbert, W S., 303
Gödel, Kurt, 303,331,332
    incompleteness theorems, 331-332
Golden Rule, 78-79,80,343
Goodstein, R. L., 271
Gorman, Michael M., 176
Grahne, G., 146,150
Graves, Robert, 5
Gray, Jim, 93
Gray, Peter M. D., 62
Groucho Principle, 366
group (mathematics), 264
    Abelian, 265
Guaranteed Access Rule, 393
Gullberg, Jan, 271
Guttenplan, Samuel, 62

Hall, Patrick A. V., 257,271
Hamdan, Sam, 217-218,222-224,233
Heath, I. J., 183,207
Hitchcock, Peter, 257,271
Hodge, Alan, 5
Hodges, Wilfrid, 62

idempotence, 250
identity
    +, 240
    *, 241
identity (equality), 43-44
identity predicate, 43
identity projection, 184
IF, 9
    see also implication
if and only if, *see* bi-implication;
        equivalence; IFF
IFF, 9
    see also bi-implication; equivalence

image, 165
implication, 73ff
inclusion
    bag, 284
    database, 347-349
    relation, 259
    set, 252
indiscernibility *vs.* interchangeability, 45
Information Principle, 70
injection, 167
Inmon, William H., 233
INSERT anomaly, 229
INSERT expansion, 310-311
instantiation, *see* predicate
integrity constraint, *see* constraint
intended interpretation, 126
interchangeability, *see*
        Principle of Interchangeability
interpretation, 124
inverse
    +, 241
    *, 241
involution, 250
irreducibility
    FD, 402
    key, *see* key
    relvar, 209,403-407
isomorphism, 173,246-248

Jacobson, Ivar, 175
JD, *see* join dependency
Johnson, Samuel, 67
Johnston, Tom, 150
join
    associativity, 184
    commutativity, 184
join dependency, 183-191
    implied by superkeys, 187
    N-ary, 191
    trivial, 186
join trap, *see* connection trap

key, 178,179
    irreducibility, 402-403
    uniqueness, 179

key attribute, 179
al-Khwarizmi, 239
Kimball, Ralph, 68,93
Kleene, Stephen C., 147
Kneebone, G. T., 62

Lampedusa, Giuseppe di, 309
Land, Frank, 271
Larner, Adrian, 386
Laws of Algebra, 242-243
Lehrer, Tom, 177
Leibniz, Gottfried Wilhelm von, 41,45
Lincoln, Abraham, 17
Lipski, Witold, 148
literal, 42,74
Livingstone, David, 269
logical difference, 215
Loomis, Mary E. S., 176
Lorentzos, Nikos A., 115,209,257,271,437
lossless decomposition, 181
lossy decomposition, 181
Lukasiewicz, Jan, 147

Mac Lane, Saunders, 270,271
Machover, Moshé, 62
Maier, David, 437
Manna, Zohar, 62,337
map, *see* function
mapping, *see* function
Martin, James, 155,176,385-386,437
MATCHING, *see* semijoin
mathematics *vs.* relational model, 377-381
matrix algebra, *see* algebra
many-to-many correspondence, 171
many-to-one correspondence, 169
McCawley, James D., 31,32,63
McGoveran, David, 63,108,115,116,119,132,
        132,135,150,437,304
Melton, Jim, 94
Melzak, Z. A., 132
Minker, Jack, 115
Mirsky, L., 271
modal logic, 25
modus ponens, 122,151
modus tollens, 151

multiple assignment, 82-83,324-325
multiplicity, 164
        bag theory, 283
        UML, 164
multi-relvar constraint, *see* constraint
multiset, *see* bag
multivalued dependency, 192
        implied by superkey, 196
        trivial, 196
MVD, *see* multivalued dependency

NAND, 35
Nagel, Ernest, 31
Nicolas, Jean-Marie, 115
Nobody, The, 127
nonkey attribute, 398
nonloss decompostion, 181
NOR, 35
normalization, 177ff
        defined, 218
NOT MATCHING, *see* semidifference
nulls, 108,117,140-141,228,266,409-412

Odell, James J., 155,176
one-to-many correspondence, 170
one-to-one correspondence, 168
Open World Assumption, 99ff
Orwell, George, iii
outer join, 116-117
OWA, *see* Open World Assumption

Paradox of Epimenides, 303-304
parameter
        in predicates, 11,127
        vs. argument, *see* argument
Parker, Sybil P., 63,271
partial ordering, 250,285
Pascal, Fabian, 28,30,92,94
Peirce arrow, 35
Pietarinen, Lauri, 5
PJ/NF, *see* projection-join normal form
placeholder, *see* parameter
Polya, George, 362,363,369,375
Pospesel, Howard, 63
possible worlds, 48

Post, Emil, 147
power set, 252
predicate, 11,31
    compound, 12
    instantiation, 12
    simple, 12
predicate calculus, 12,127-128
predicate logic, *see* predicate calculus
prenex normal form, 23
primary key, 179
primitive recursive, *see* recursive
Principle of Cautious Design, 307
Principle of Duality, 249
Principle of Identity of Indiscernibles, 45
Principle of Incoherence, 117
Principle of Insufficient Reason, 363
Principle of Interchangeability, 81,346-347
Principle of Orthogonal Design, 229,345
    Darwen's objections, 367-369
*Principle of View and Pseudovariable
        Equivalence,* 369
projection-join normal form, 188
proposition, 8,50
    compound, 9
    simple, 9
propositional calculus, *see* propositional logic
propositional logic, 41,42,121-123
propositional variable, 43
pseudovariable, 326,341
public relvar, 383-384

quantification, 12ff,72,128
    range coupled, 26,33,72
    see also existential quantification; predicate;
        UNIQUE; universal quantification

real relvar, *see* base relvar
recursive (computable), 338
    primitive, 338
recursively defined type, 306
Reeves, Steve, 63
reflexivity, 43,250,285,380
Reiter, Raymond, 63,96,115
relation, 178
relation value, *see* relation

relation valued attribute, 112,193-194,306-308,
        391-397
relation variable, *see* relvar
relational algebra, 237,256-261,262,378,381-387
    see also **A**
relational assignment, *see* assignment
relational calculus, 272-273,381-382
relationship, 156
    vs. relation, 379-380
relvar, 178,215
relvar constraint, *see* constraint
relvar predicate, 84ff,104-105,339,387-391
    view, 88
Rescher, Nicholas, 63,150
restriction set, 295-296
Reuter, Andreas, 93
Richards, Tom, 63
ring (mathematics), 265
Rissanen, Jorma, 183,208
Robson, Peter, 114
Ross, Ronald G., 3ff,31,68,92,94
rule of inference, 91,121
Rumbaugh, James, 175
Russell, Bertrand, 305,309,374

second normal form, 205-206,397-399
second order logic, 394-397
selector, 89-90
    vs. literal, 90
semantics *vs.* syntax, 28
semidifference, 277-278,280
semijoin, 276,277,278-279
semiminus, *see* semidifference
sentence, 31
    closed, 31
    open, 31
set, 156
set algebra, *see* algebra
Sheffer stroke, 35
Simon, Alan R., 94
single-relvar constraint, *see* constraint
sixth normal form, 209,403-405
Slupecki T-function, 138
Smullyan, Raymond M., 63
Solomon, Graham, 62

sorted logic, 25-27
soundness, 52
SQL, *passim*
    criticisms, 29,266-269,296,297,384,
        422-434
    see also nulls
Stillwell, John, 271
Stoll, Robert R., 63,271
Stonebraker, Michael, 68,94
subbag, 284
subkey, 180
substitutability, 43
substitution (rule of inference), 123
superbag, 284
superkey, 179
Suppes, Patrick, 63,150,437
suppliers-and-parts database, *passim*
surjection, 166
symmetric difference, *see* difference
symmetry, 43,362,380

T-function, *see* Slupecki T-function
Tabak, John, 271
TABLE_DEE, 101,261,303-304
TABLE_DUM, 101,261,303-304
tautology, 51,52,125
    2VL, 150-152
Teller, Paul, 63
Teorey, Toby J., 176
theorem, 91,122
Third Manifesto, The, passim
third normal form, 204-205
"time-varying relation," 309,313
Todd, Stephen J. P., 257,271
total database constraint, *see* constraint
total relvar constraint, *see* constraint
transaction, 83
transform, *see* function
transformation, *see* function
transition constraint, *see* constraint
transitivity, 43,250,285,380
truth function, 51
truth functional completeness, 125
truth tables, 9
    2VL, 34

3VL, 58-60
truth_value_of, 46-47
Tutorial D, *passim*
type as most fundamental concept, 421-422
type design, 419
type queries, 419-420

Ullman, Jeffrey D., 68,94,115,271
ungroup, 113,193
UNIQUE (quantifier), 24
uniqueness (key), *see* key
universal quantification, 13
    iterated AND, 22,128
    not in SQL, 20
universal relation, 259,420
universal set, 252
universe of discourse, 26,126,296
UPDATE anomaly, 229
UPDATE expansion, 82-83,311

value_of, 45
variable
    logic, 413-415
    programming languages, 412-413
    see also bound variable; free variable
Vassiliou, Yannis, 146
view updating, 339ff
    Darwen's objections, 357ff
    Darwen's proposals, 369ff
virtual relvar, 81

Waldinger, Richard, 62,337
Weisstein, Eric, 272
well formed formula, 121
wff, *see* well formed formula
Widom, Jennifer, 68,94,271
Wittgenstein, Ludwig J. J., iii,107,115,215

XML, 269
XOR, 245

Zloof, Moshé M., 437

ISBN 142512290-6